Chemistry

by
Kathleen A. Packard,
Donald H. Jacobs,
and
Robert H. Marshall

PEARSON

AGS Globe

Shoreview, Minnesota

About the Authors

Kathleen A. Packard, B.S., taught high school honors and advanced placement chemistry for Anne Arundel County Public Schools in Maryland and at Iolani School in Honolulu.

Donald H. Jacobs, M.Ed., taught mathematics for many years in the Baltimore City Public Schools. He is currently with the Upton Home and Hospital School Program in the technology department. Other AGS textbooks that he has coauthored include *Physical Science, General Science, Basic Math Skills,* and *Life Skills Math.*

Robert H. Marshall, M.Ed., teaches high school physics and algebra for the Baltimore School for the Arts. He is coauthor of several AGS textbooks, including *Physical Science, Earth Science, General Science,* and *Matter, Motion, and Machines.*

Photo and illustration credits for this textbook can be found on page 840.

The publisher wishes to thank the following consultants and educators for their helpful comments during the review process for *Chemistry.* Their assistance has been invaluable.

Charmain Barker, Department Head of Science, St. Augustine Catholic High School, Markham, ON, Canada; **Rebecca Barnott,** Special Education Teacher, Paul Laurence Dunbar High School, Lexington, KY; **Philip Dumas,** Department of Chemistry, College of New Jersey, Ewing, NJ; **Adam Gehring,** Chemistry Teacher, Palmdale High School, Palmdale, CA; **Deborah Hartzell,** Lead Teacher for Special Education, East DeKalb Campus, Stone Mountain, GA; **Gregory B. Hendrix,** Science Department Chair, Lakeside High School, Atlanta, GA; **Debby Houston,** Associate in Research, Florida State University, Tallahassee, FL; **Jan Manchester,** Special Education Resource, St. Paul Public Schools, St. Paul, MN; **Richard McHenry,** Chemistry Teacher, Leon High School, Tallahassee, FL; **Thelma J. Page,** Special Education Teacher and Department Chair, Calumet Career Preparatory Academy, Chicago, IL; **Katherine Pasquale,** Intervention Specialist, Euclid High School, Euclid, OH; **Merrie Jean Peters,** Instructional Liaison, Ft. Bend Independent School District, Sugar Land, TX; **Diana Shelton,** Homebound Special Education Teacher, Ysleta Independent School District, El Paso, TX; **Susan Sztain,** Teacher, Desert Sands Charter High School, Lancaster, CA; **J. B. Whitten,** SLD Teacher, Durant High School, Plant City, FL

Publisher's Project Staff

Vice President of Curriculum and Publisher: Sari Follansbee, Ed.D.; Director of Curriculum Development: Teri Mathews; Managing Editor: Julie Maas; Editor: Jan Jessup; Development Assistant: Bev Johnson; Director of Creative Services: Nancy Condon; Project Coordinator/Designer: Carol Bowling; Production Artist: Mike Vineski; Senior Buyer: Mary Kaye Kuzma; Product Manager–Curriculum: Brian Holl

ISBN 0-7854-4045-3

A 0 9 8 7 6 5 4 3 2 1

1-800-328-2560
www.agsglobe.com

Contents

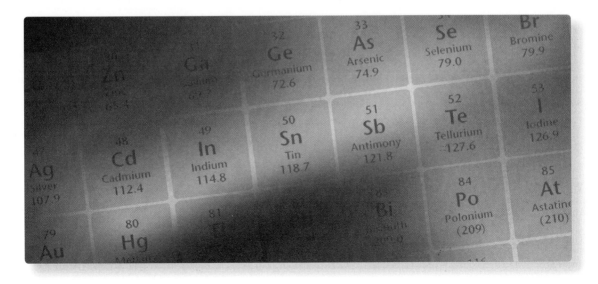

How to Use This Book: A Study Guide

Welcome to *Chemistry*. Science touches our lives every day, no matter where we are—at home, at school, or at work. This book covers the scientific field of chemistry. It also focuses on skills that scientists use. These skills include asking questions, making predictions, designing experiments, collecting and organizing information, calculating data, making decisions, drawing conclusions, and exploring more options. You probably already use these skills every day. You ask questions to find answers. You gather information and organize it. You use that information to make all sorts of decisions. In this book, you will have opportunities to use and practice all of these skills.

As you read this book, notice how each lesson is organized. Information is presented in a straightforward manner. Tables, illustrations, and photos help clarify concepts. Read the information carefully. If you have trouble with a lesson, try reading it again.

It is important that you understand how to use this book before you start to read it. It is also important to know how to be successful in this course. Information in this first section of the book can help you achieve these goals.

How to Study

These tips can help you study more effectively.

◆ Plan a regular time to study.

◆ Choose a desk or table in a quiet place where you will not be distracted. Find a spot that has good lighting.

◆ Gather all of the books, pencils, paper, and other materials you will need to complete your assignments.

◆ Decide on a goal. For example: "I will finish reading and taking notes on Chapter 1, Lesson 1, by 8:00."

◆ Take a five- to ten-minute break every hour to stay alert.

◆ If you start to feel sleepy, take a break and get some fresh air.

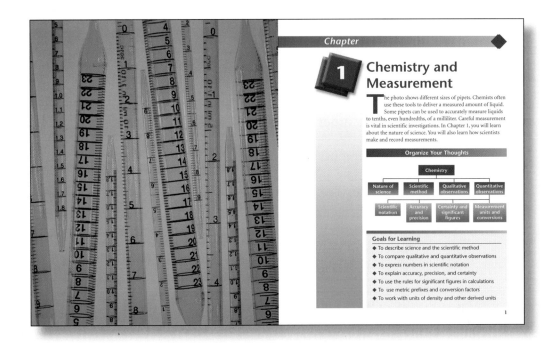

Chapter

1

Chemistry and Measurement

The photo shows different sizes of pipets. Chemists often use these tools to deliver a measured amount of liquid. Some pipets can be used to accurately measure liquids to tenths, even hundredths, of a milliliter. Careful measurement is vital in scientific investigations. In Chapter 1, you will learn about the nature of science. You will also learn how scientists make and record measurements.

Organize Your Thoughts

Chemistry

Nature of science | Scientific method | Qualitative observations | Quantitative observations

Scientific notation | Accuracy and precision | Certainty and significant figures | Measurement units and conversions

Goals for Learning

◆ To describe science and the scientific method
◆ To compare qualitative and quantitative observations
◆ To express numbers in scientific notation
◆ To explain accuracy, precision, and certainty
◆ To use the rules for significant figures in calculations
◆ To use metric prefixes and conversion factors
◆ To work with units of density and other derived units

1

Before Beginning Each Chapter

◆ Read the chapter title and study the photograph.
  What does the photo tell you about the chapter title?
◆ Read the opening paragraph.
◆ Study the Organize Your Thoughts concept map. It gives the main ideas in the chapter and shows how they are related.
◆ Read the Goals for Learning. These are the main objectives of the chapter. Tests will ask questions related to these goals.
◆ Look at the Chapter Review at the end of the chapter.
  The questions cover the most important information from the chapter.

Note These Features

Notes
Points of interest or additional information that relate to the lesson

Science Myth
Common science misconceptions followed by the correct information

Science Myth

Chemistry in Your Life

Examples of chemistry in real life with connections to the environment, technology, and consumer choices

■ ◆ ■ ◆ ■ ◆ ■ ◆ ■ ◆ ■ ◆ ■ ◆ ■ ◆ ■ ◆ ■ ◆ ■ ◆ ■

Chemistry in Your Life

Achievements in Science

Historical scientific discoveries, events, and achievements

★ ★

Achievements in Science

Science at Work

Careers in science

▼ ◄ ▲ ▼ ◄ ▲ ▼ ◄ ▲ ▼ ◄ ▲ ▼ ◄ ▲ ▼ ◄ ▲ ▼ ◄

Science at Work

Technology and Society

Examples of chemistry in real life with connections to technology and society

✲ ✲ ✲ ✲ ✲ ✲ ✲ ✲ ✲ ✲ ✲ ✲ ✲ ✲ ✲ ✲ ✲ ✲ ✲ ✲

Technology and Society

Investigation

Experiments that give practice with chapter concepts

Discovery Investigation

Experiments involving student input that give practice with chapter concepts

Chemistry in the World

Examples of real-life problems or issues and their chemistry-related solutions

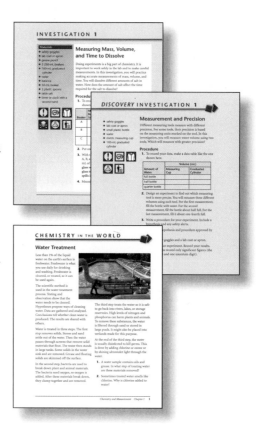

Spotlight on
Interesting facts about elements and their uses

Spotlight on

11
Na
Sodium
23.0

Example
Step-by-step solutions to example problems

Example

Math Tip
Short math reminders or tips connected to a lesson

Math Tip

Express Lab
Short experiments that give practice with chapter concepts

Express Lab

Link to
Facts that connect chemistry to another subject area, such as biology, environmental science, physics, earth science, social studies, language arts, math, health, home and career, arts, and cultures

Link to ≫ ≫ ≫

Research and Write
Opportunities to research a topic and write about it

Research and Write

Before Beginning Each Lesson

Read the lesson title and restate it in the form of a question.

For example, write:
What are derived units?

Look over the entire lesson, noting the following:
- ◆ bold words
- ◆ text organization
- ◆ notes in the margins
- ◆ photos and illustrations
- ◆ Lesson Review questions

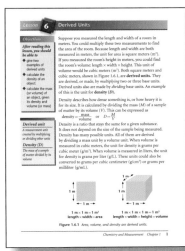

As You Read the Lesson

◆ Read the lesson title.

◆ Read the subheads and paragraphs that follow.

◆ Before moving on to the next lesson, make sure you understand the concepts you read. If you do not, reread the lesson. If you are still unsure, ask for help.

◆ Practice what you have learned by completing the Lesson Review.

Using the Bold Words

Bold type
Words used for the first time will appear in bold type
Glossary
Words listed in this column are also found in the glossary

Knowing the meaning of the boxed vocabulary words in the left column will help you understand what you read.

These words are in **bold type** the first time they appear in the text. They are also defined in the paragraph.

Chemistry is the study of matter and how it changes.

All of the boxed vocabulary words are also defined in the **glossary.**

Chemistry (kəm´ə strē) The study of matter and how it changes (p. 2)

Word Study Tips

◆ Start a vocabulary file with index cards to use for review.

◆ Write one term on the front of each card. Write the definition, chapter number, and lesson number on the back.

◆ You can use these cards as flash cards by yourself or with a study partner to test your knowledge.

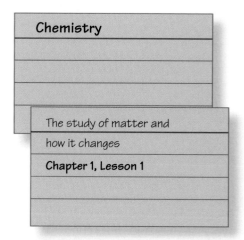

Chemistry

The study of matter and how it changes

Chapter 1, Lesson 1

Taking Notes

It is helpful to take notes during class and as you read this book.

◆ Use headings to label the main sections of your notes. This organizes your notes.

◆ Summarize the important information, such as main ideas and supporting details.

◆ Do not try to write every word your teacher says or every detail in a chapter.

◆ Do not be concerned about writing in complete sentences. Use short phrases.

◆ Use your own words to describe, explain, or define things.

◆ Sometimes the best way to summarize information is with a graphic organizer. Use simple concept maps, charts, diagrams, and graphs in your notes.

◆ Try taking notes using a three-column format. Draw two lines to divide your notebook page into three columns. Make the middle column the widest. Use the first column to write headings or vocabulary words. Use the middle column to write the main information. Use the last column to draw diagrams, write shortcuts for remembering something, write questions about something you do not understand, record homework assignments, or for other purposes. An example of three-column note-taking is shown below.

◆ Right after taking notes, review them to fill in possible gaps.

◆ Study your notes to prepare for a test. Use a highlighter to mark what you need to know.

Dot diagrams of molecules	Octet rule—most bonds result in a full valence level of 8 electrons.	
	Covalent bonds	
	Single bond—2 shared electrons	:C̈l:C̈l:
		Cl—Cl
	Double bond—4 shared electrons	:Ö::Ö:
		O=O
	Triple bond—6 shared electrons	:N:::N:
		N≡N

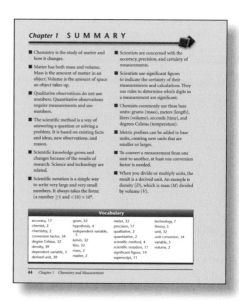

Chapter 1 SUMMARY

- Chemistry is the study of matter and how it changes.
- Matter has both mass and volume. Mass is the amount of matter in an object. Volume is the amount of space an object takes up.
- Qualitative observations do not use numbers. Quantitative observations require measurements and use numbers.
- The scientific method is a way of answering a question or solving a problem. It is based on existing facts and ideas, new observations, and reason.
- Scientific knowledge grows and changes because of the results of research. Science and technology are related.
- Scientific notation is a simple way to write very large and very small numbers. It always takes the form: (a number ≥1 and <10) × 10ⁿ.

- Scientists are concerned with the accuracy, precision, and certainty of measurements.
- Scientists use significant figures to indicate the certainty of their measurements and calculations. They use rules to determine which digits in a measurement are significant.
- Chemists commonly use these base units: grams (mass), meters (length), liters (volume), seconds (time), and degrees Celsius (temperature).
- Metric prefixes can be added to base units, creating new units that are smaller or larger.
- To convert a measurement from one unit to another, at least one conversion factor is needed.
- When you divide or multiply units, the result is a derived unit. An example is density (D), which is mass (M) divided by volume (V).

Vocabulary

accuracy, 17	gram, 32	meter, 32	technology, 7
chemist, 2	hypothesis, 4	precision, 17	theory, 5
chemistry, 2	independent variable, 5	qualitative, 2	unit, 32
conversion factor, 34	kelvin, 32	quantitative, 2	unit conversion, 34
degree Celsius, 32	liter, 32	scientific method, 4	variable, 5
density, 39	mass, 2	scientific notation, 11	volume, 2
dependent variable, 5	matter, 2	significant figure, 19	
derived unit, 39		superscript, 11	

44   Chapter 1   Chemistry and Measurement

Using the Summaries

◆ Read each Chapter Summary to be sure you understand the chapter's main ideas.

◆ Review the vocabulary words in the Vocabulary box.

Using the Reviews

◆ Answer the questions in each Lesson Review.

◆ In the Chapter Review, answer the questions about vocabulary under the Vocabulary Review. Study the words and definitions. Say them aloud to help you remember them.

◆ Answer the questions under the Concept Review, Problem Solving, and Critical Thinking sections of the Chapter Review.

◆ Read the Test-Taking Tip.

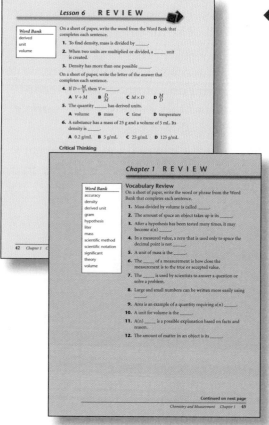

Lesson 6   REVIEW

Word Bank
derived
unit
volume

On a sheet of paper, write the word from the Word Bank that completes each sentence.

1. To find density, mass is divided by _____.

2. When two units are multiplied or divided, a _____ unit is created.

3. Density has more than one possible _____.

On a sheet of paper, write the letter of the answer that completes each sentence.

4. If $D = \frac{M}{V}$, then $V =$ _____.

   A $V + M$ B $\frac{D}{M}$ C $M \times D$ D $\frac{M}{D}$

5. The quantity _____ has derived units.

   A volume   B mass   C time   D temperature

6. A substance has a mass of 25 g and a volume of 5 mL. Its density is _____.

   A 0.2 g/mL   B 5 g/mL   C 25 g/mL   D 125 g/mL

Critical Thinking

42   Chapter 1   C

Chapter 1   REVIEW

Word Bank
accuracy
density
derived unit
gram
hypothesis
liter
mass
scientific method
scientific notation
significant
theory
volume

Vocabulary Review

On a sheet of paper, write the word or phrase from the Word Bank that completes each sentence.

1. Mass divided by volume is called _____.

2. The amount of space an object takes up is its _____.

3. After a hypothesis has been tested many times, it may become a(n) _____.

4. In a measured value, a zero that is used only to space the decimal point is not _____.

5. A unit of mass is the _____.

6. The _____ of a measurement is how close the measurement is to the true or accepted value.

7. The _____ is used by scientists to answer a question or solve a problem.

8. Large and small numbers can be written more easily using _____.

9. Area is an example of a quantity requiring a(n) _____.

10. A unit for volume is the _____.

11. A(n) _____ is a possible explanation based on facts and reason.

12. The amount of matter in an object is its _____.

Continued on next page

Chemistry and Measurement   Chapter 1   45

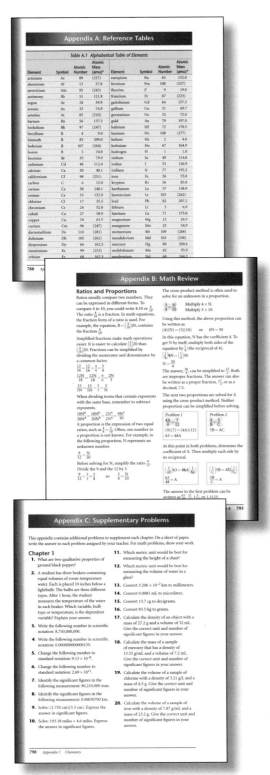

Using the Appendixes

This book contains three appendixes. Become familiar with these appendixes before starting your study of chemistry.

◆ Appendix A contains reference tables. These tables are a quick way to find information. The first table lists the elements alphabetically by name. The other tables list polyatomic ions, metric prefixes, symbols and abbreviations, and equations that are used throughout the book.

◆ Appendix B is a math review. Use this appendix to brush up on ratios and proportions, percents and decimals, algebra, and graphing.

◆ Appendix C contains extra problems for each chapter. You may use these to practice or review what you have learned. Your teacher may assign problems from this appendix.

Preparing for Tests

◆ Complete the Lesson Reviews and Chapter Review(s). Study your answers.

◆ Review the Investigations and Discovery Investigations you performed.

◆ Study the Chapter Summary.

◆ Make up a sample test. You may want to do this with a classmate and share your questions.

◆ Use graphic organizers as study tools.

◆ Review your notes and test yourself on vocabulary words and key ideas.

◆ Practice writing about some of the main ideas from the chapter(s).

Using Graphic Organizers

Graphic organizers are visual representations of information. Concept maps, flowcharts, circle diagrams, Venn diagrams, column charts, and graphs are some examples of graphic organizers. You can use graphic organizers to organize information, connect related ideas, or understand steps in a process. You can use them to classify or compare things, summarize complex topics, and communicate information. You can also use them to study for tests.

As you read this book, practice making your own graphic organizers. You will find that graphic organizers are helpful tools for learning chemistry and any other subject.

Concept Maps

A concept map consists of a main concept or idea and related concepts. Each concept—usually one or two words or a short phrase—is written in a circle or box. The organization of concepts in the map shows how they are related.

In the concept map below, the main concept is organic molecules in living things. It appears at the top of the map. Carbohydrates, lipids, proteins, and nucleic acids are kinds of organic molecules essential to life. Each one appears in a box below the main concept. Each one is connected to the main concept with a straight line to show they are related. The main concept is the most general. The other concepts are more specific. You will find a concept map at the beginning of each chapter of the book. This simple concept map identifies the main concepts discussed in the chapter and shows how they are connected.

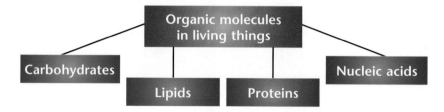

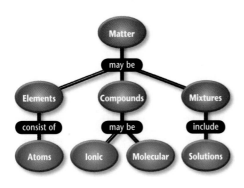

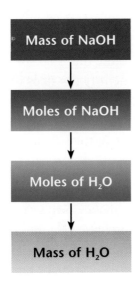

The graphic organizer at the left is another example of a concept map. To create this concept map, write the main concept. Draw a circle around it. Next, identify important ideas related to the main concept. Choose a word or a short phrase for each idea. Arrange these under or around the main concept. Draw a circle or box around each idea. Then add lines to link related ideas and concepts. The lines should not cross. You can label the lines to tell why the circles are linked.

Flowcharts

You can use a flowchart to diagram the steps in a process or procedure. The flowchart at the left is a conversion map for solving a chemistry problem. Notice it is a vertical chart. Flowcharts can be vertical or horizontal. To make a flowchart, identify the steps to include. Write each step in the correct order, either in a vertical column or in a horizontal row. Draw a box around each step. Connect the boxes with arrows to show direction. You can label the arrows to tell what must happen to get from one step to the next.

Tables

You can use a table to record information and organize it into groups or categories for easy reference. A table is data systematically arranged in rows and columns. To create a table, determine the number of items, groups, or categories you want to use. Decide on the numbers of columns and rows. Write a heading at the top of each column. Sometimes rows have headings, too. Fill in the table and add a title.

Table 8.2.1 Particles in an Atom			
Particle	Symbol	Assigned Charge	Location
electron	e^-	$1-$	outside nucleus
proton	p^+	$1+$	inside nucleus
neutron	n^0	0	inside nucleus

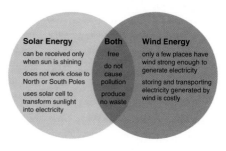

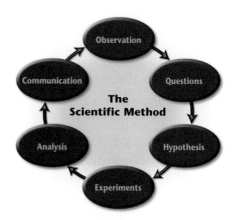

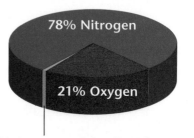

1% Argon, carbon dioxide, water vapor, neon, helium, krypton, xenon, methane, hydrogen, ozone

Venn Diagrams

A Venn diagram can help you compare and contrast two objects or processes. To create a Venn diagram, draw two circles of equal size that partially overlap. The circles represent the two things you want to compare. List the characteristics of one in the left circle. List the characteristics of the other in the right circle. List the characteristics both have in common in the area where the two circles intersect.

Circle Diagrams

A circle diagram shows a cycle that repeats. A circle diagram is similar to a flowchart except the last step is connected to the first step. To make a circle diagram, first identify the steps in the process or procedure. Then write the steps in a circle instead of a line. Use arrows to connect the steps. The circle diagram at the left shows the scientific method.

Graphs

You can use a graph to make comparisons and identify patterns among data. Graphs come in many forms, such as line graphs, bar graphs, and circle graphs. To create a line or bar graph, draw two perpendicular axes. Label each axis to represent one variable. Add data. Each point or bar indicates a set of values for the two variables. Connect the points or compare the bars to see how the two variables relate. A circle graph shows the size of parts in a whole. To make one, draw a circle. Draw pie-shaped sections of the circle in proportion to the parts. Label each section and write its percentage of the whole. For more help with graphing, see pages 796–97 in Appendix B.

Safety Rules and Symbols

In this book, you will learn about chemistry through investigations and labs. During these activities, it is important to follow safety rules, procedures, and your teacher's directions. You can avoid accidents by following directions and handling materials carefully. Read and follow the safety rules below, and learn the safety symbols. To alert you to possible dangers, safety symbols will appear with each investigation or lab. Reread the rules below often and review what the symbols mean.

General Safety

◆ Read each Express Lab, Investigation, and Discovery Investigation before doing it. Review the materials list and follow the safety symbols and safety alerts.

◆ Ask questions if you do not understand something.

◆ Never perform an experiment, mix substances, or use equipment without permission.

◆ Keep your work area clean and free of clutter.

◆ Be aware of other students working near you.

◆ Do not play or run during a lab activity. Take your lab work seriously.

◆ Know where fire extinguishers, fire alarms, first aid kits, fire blankets, and the nearest telephone are located. Be familiar with the emergency exits and evacuation route from your room.

◆ Keep your hands away from your face.

◆ Immediately report all accidents to your teacher, including injuries, broken equipment, and spills.

◆ Wash your hands when you are finished with a lab activity.

Eye Protection

◆ Wear safety goggles at all times or as directed by your teacher.

◆ If a substance gets in your eyes or on your face, use an eyewash station or flush your eyes and face with running water immediately. Tell your teacher.

Clothing Protection

◆ Wear a lab coat or apron at all times or as directed by your teacher.

◆ Tie back long hair, remove dangling jewelry, and secure loose-fitting clothing.

◆ Do not wear open-toed shoes, sandals, or canvas shoes in the lab.

Hand Safety

◆ Wear protective gloves when directed by your teacher.

◆ Do not touch an object that could be hot.

◆ Use tongs or utensils to hold a container over a heat source.

◆ Wash your hands when you are finished with a lab activity.

Flame/Heat Safety

◆ Clear your work space of materials that could burn or melt.

◆ Before using a burner, know how to operate the burner and gas outlet.

◆ Be aware of all open flames. Never reach across a flame.

◆ Never leave a flame or operating hot plate unattended.

◆ Do not heat a liquid in a closed container.

◆ When heating a substance in a test tube or flask, point the container away from yourself and others.

◆ Do not touch hot glassware or the surface of an operating hot plate or lightbulb.

◆ In the event of a fire, tell your teacher and leave the room immediately.

◆ If your clothes catch on fire, stop, drop to the floor, and roll.

Chemical Safety

◆ Check labels on containers to be sure you are using the right substance.

◆ Do not directly smell any substance. If you are instructed to smell a substance, gently fan your hand over the substance, waving its vapors toward you.

◆ When handling substances that give off gases or vapors, work in a fume hood or well-ventilated area.

◆ Do not taste any substance. Never eat, drink, or chew gum in your work area.

◆ Do not return unused substances to their original containers.

◆ Avoid skin contact with substances used in lab. Some can irritate or harm skin.

◆ If a substance spills on your clothing or skin, rinse the area immediately with plenty of water. Tell your teacher.

◆ When diluting an acid or base with water, always add the acid or base to the water. Do not add water to the acid or base.

◆ Wash your hands when you are finished with a lab activity.

Electrical Safety

◆ Never use electrical equipment near water, on wet surfaces, or with wet hands or clothing.

◆ Alert your teacher to any frayed or damaged cords or plugs.

◆ Before plugging in equipment, be sure the power control is in the "off" position.

◆ Do not place electrical cords in walkways or let cords hang over table edges.

◆ Electricity flowing in wire causes the wire to become hot. Use caution.

◆ Turn off and unplug electrical equipment when you are finished using it.

Glassware Safety

◆ Check glassware for cracks or chips before use. Give broken glassware to your teacher; do not use it.

◆ Keep glassware away from the edge of a work surface.

◆ If glassware breaks, tell your teacher. Dispose of glass according to your teacher's directions.

Sharp Object Safety

◆ Take care when using scissors, toothpicks, compasses, or pointed tools or blades.

◆ Cut objects on a suitable work surface. Cut away from yourself and others.

◆ If you cut yourself, notify your teacher.

Cleanup/Waste Disposal

◆ If a substance spills, alert your teacher and ask for cleanup instructions.

◆ Follow your teacher's directions to dispose of substances.

◆ Turn off burners, water faucets, electrical equipment, and gas outlets.

◆ Clean equipment if needed and return it to its proper location.

◆ Clean your work area and work surface.

◆ Wash your hands when you are finished.

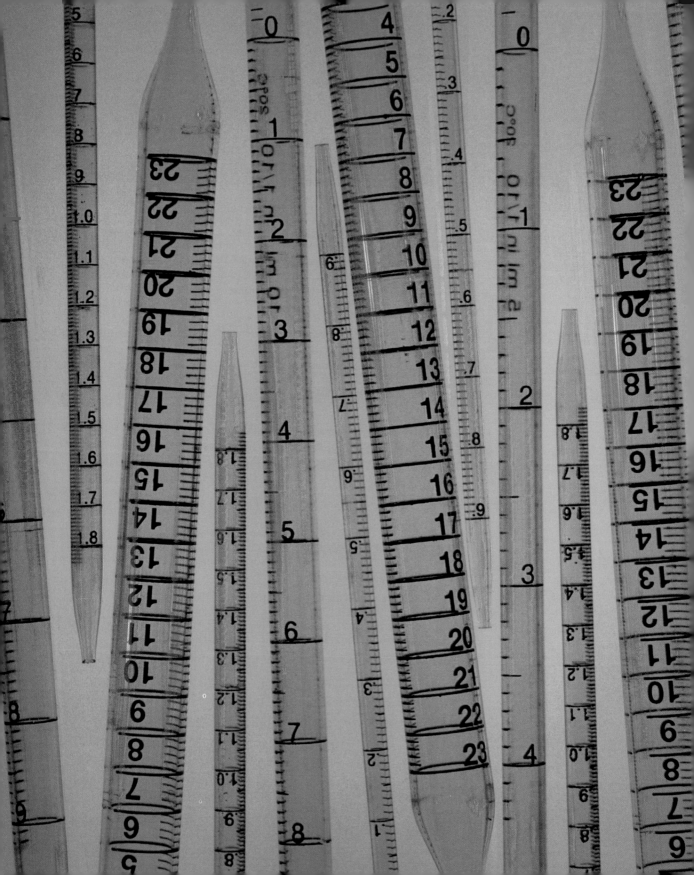

1 Chemistry and Measurement

The photo shows different sizes of pipets. Chemists often use these tools to deliver a measured amount of liquid. Some pipets can be used to accurately measure liquids to tenths, even hundredths, of a milliliter. Careful measurement is vital in scientific investigations. In Chapter 1, you will learn about the nature of science. You will also learn how scientists make and record measurements.

Organize Your Thoughts

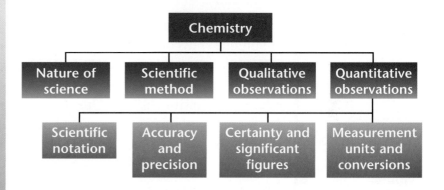

Chemistry

- Nature of science
- Scientific method
- Qualitative observations
- Quantitative observations
  - Scientific notation
  - Accuracy and precision
  - Certainty and significant figures
  - Measurement units and conversions

Goals for Learning

◆ To describe science and the scientific method

◆ To compare qualitative and quantitative observations

◆ To express numbers in scientific notation

◆ To explain accuracy, precision, and certainty

◆ To use the rules for significant figures in calculations

◆ To use metric prefixes and conversion factors

◆ To work with units of density and other derived units

After reading this lesson, you should be able to

◆ define chemistry

◆ identify qualitative and quantitative observations

◆ list some steps in the scientific method

◆ describe the nature of science

Chemistry

The study of matter and how it changes

Matter

Anything that has mass and takes up space

Mass

How much matter an object contains

Volume

The amount of space an object takes up

Chemist

A scientist who studies matter and how it changes

Qualitative

Describing something without using numbers

Science is a system of knowledge about the natural world. It is also a way of improving and increasing that knowledge. The word *science* comes from the Latin word *scientia,* which means "to have knowledge." There are many fields of science. Geology, biology, astronomy, zoology, and ecology are just a few. You may have already studied some of these fields. This book will help you explore the field of chemistry.

Chemistry is the study of **matter** and how it changes. Matter is anything that has **mass** and **volume.** Mass is a measure of how much matter an object contains. Volume is the amount of space an object occupies. Matter is all around you: the air you breathe, the juice you had for breakfast, and this book, for example.

Chemists are scientists who study matter and its changes. What do they want to know about matter? First of all, they observe, or look at, the characteristics of a substance. Characteristics are unique traits or properties. A substance is a certain kind of matter. What color is the substance? Does it have a particular shape? Does it have an odor? Is it hot? These types of questions ask for **qualitative** answers. Qualitative observations describe a substance without using numbers. You make qualitative observations all the time. "It is hot and windy" is a qualitative observation of the weather.

Chemists also measure quantities, or amounts. What is the mass of this substance? What is its volume? How hot is it? These questions need **quantitative** answers. They require measurements to be made. Quantitative observations use numbers. You use quantitative observations, too. "It is 87 degrees outside" is a quantitative observation. In this chapter, you will learn how to work with quantitative observations, or measurements.

Fields of science overlap. A discovery in one field may bring about a discovery in another field. Sometimes, a new field of science is created where two fields overlap. Biochemistry is one example. This field involves the study of both biology and chemistry.

What quantitative and qualitative observations could you make about the key in Figure 1.1.1? Chemists make both qualitative and quantitative observations about matter. After carefully observing a substance, they may classify it, or place it in a category. Matter is organized into categories based on common characteristics. After observing a substance, a chemist might classify it as a metal, for example. You will learn many ways to classify matter as you study chemistry.

Besides studying the characteristics of a substance, chemists want to know how the substance changes. Does it react, or combine with, other substances? You might know that hydrogen and oxygen combine to form water. In this reaction, oxygen and hydrogen are gases. How can two gases combine to form a liquid? What causes this reaction? How fast does it happen? To answer these types of questions, chemists begin by observing and measuring. But that is only part of what they do.

Figure 1.1.1 *This gold house key is about 5.4 centimeters long.*

The Scientific Method

Science is a system of knowledge. It is based on observations about the natural world. But it is more than that. It is also a process of learning about the natural world. Like all scientists, chemists use the **scientific method** to try to answer questions or solve problems. They try to explain why matter behaves the way it does. The scientific method is a way of improving and increasing existing knowledge. It is based on

- existing facts and ideas
- new observations
- reason, or logic

This process can vary quite a bit. It often involves the following steps, although not always in this order:

1. Observe the natural world. Scientists are curious and interested. They want to know more.

2. Ask a question or state a problem based on observations. For example, "Why do certain plastics break easily when they are cold?" Then gather all known facts about this topic.

3. Based on these facts, state a **hypothesis.** A hypothesis is a possible explanation based on facts and reason. It predicts what might happen.

4. Test the hypothesis by designing and performing experiments. The qualitative and quantitative observations made during experiments are called data, or results.

5. Analyze the results. This means organizing the data, looking for patterns, and making sense of the data. Then make conclusions. Scientists ask, Did the results support the hypothesis? What other data might be helpful? Do other experiments need to be performed? Depending on their results, scientists may change their hypothesis or suggest other experiments.

6. Share the results and conclusions with others. Scientists publish their results in journals and present them in meetings. This allows scientists around the world to repeat experiments, compare results, and check for error.

In many experiments, certain conditions or characteristics of matter are measured or controlled. These are **variables.** Variables may change during an experiment, or they may be held constant, or kept the same. For example, volume or temperature might be measured for different substances or at different times. Volume, temperature, substance, and time are variables. Some experiments are designed to see how one variable changes when another variable is changed. The variable that is changed by the experimenter is the **independent variable.** The other variable is the **dependent variable**—it responds to the independent variable.

Suppose you have three glasses of water, each with the same volume and temperature. You place glass A under a lamp for 1 hour. You place glass B there for 2 hours, and glass C there for 3 hours. After the assigned time, you measure the water volume in each glass. You hypothesize that the water volume decreases as time under the lamp increases. The independent variable is the one you controlled: time under the lamp. The water volume is the dependent variable because it depends on the time. The starting conditions of temperature and volume are the same for all samples.

One way to analyze the results of an experiment is to make a graph. The relationship between two variables can be seen on a graph. The independent variable is usually plotted on the *x* axis. The dependent variable is plotted on the *y* axis. A graph or an organized table of data is a good way to show results to others.

Experiments cannot prove that a hypothesis is correct. However, scientists perform experiments many times. Each time new results support a hypothesis, the hypothesis becomes more likely. If the results of many experiments support the same hypothesis, scientists may call the hypothesis a **theory.** A theory is a well-tested hypothesis that is widely accepted.

An example is the atomic theory of matter. It explains matter in terms of atoms and the tiny particles that make up atoms: protons, neutrons, and electrons. Many experiments have supported the idea that matter is made of these tiny particles. In Chapter 8, you will learn more about atomic theory.

The Nature of Science

The scientific method is a modern way of learning about the natural world. However, science is not a new activity. People in all cultures have been observing and studying the world for many centuries. Because of this, the body of scientific knowledge continues to grow and change. A new discovery may change an existing theory. New results may give meaning to old observations. New tools may measure or show something for the first time. As the process of science answers one question, it leads to many new questions. In this way, scientific knowledge will continue to expand.

The process of testing hypotheses and analyzing results is called research. Research takes time and is expensive to do. Funding, or money, for a research project may come from businesses, individuals, or the government. The people who provide the funding usually decide on the research topic. Because of this, research topics are often related to issues in health, transportation, agriculture, or communication.

> Research is based on reason and observations. However, opinions and beliefs affect the focus of research. People may give money to a research project because they believe it is important. Scientists may choose to study a certain topic because they feel strongly about it. In this way, science is part of society.

Express Lab 1

Materials
- safety goggles
- lab coat or apron
- plastic or glass container
- teaspoon
- baking soda
- 10-mL graduated cylinder
- vinegar

Procedure
1. Put on safety goggles and a lab coat or apron.

2. Write a hypothesis about what might happen when you add vinegar to baking soda.

3. Place 1 teaspoon of baking soda in the container. Add 5 milliliters of vinegar to the baking soda.

4. Observe what happens. Record your observations.

Analysis
1. What happened when the vinegar was added?

2. Do your results support your hypothesis? Explain your answer.

3. What parts of this lab are quantitative? What parts are qualitative?

INVESTIGATION 1

Materials

- safety goggles
- lab coat or apron
- grease pencil
- 3 250-mL beakers
- 100-mL graduated cylinder
- water
- balance
- 50-mL beaker
- 3 plastic spoons
- table salt
- timer or clock with a second hand

Measuring Mass, Volume, and Time to Dissolve

Doing experiments is a big part of chemistry. It is important to work safely in the lab and to make careful measurements. In this investigation, you will practice making accurate measurements of mass, volume, and time. You will dissolve different amounts of salt in water. How does the amount of salt affect the time required for the salt to dissolve?

Procedure

1. To record your data, make a data table like the one shown here.

Beaker	Mass of Beaker and Salt (g)	Mass of 50-mL Beaker (g)	Mass of Salt (g)	Time to Dissolve (s)
A				
B		(same as above)		
C		(same as above)		

2. Put on safety goggles and a lab coat or apron.

3. With the grease pencil, label the 250-mL beakers A, B, and C. Use the graduated cylinder to add 100 mL of water to each beaker. **Safety Alert: Handle glass with care. Report any broken or chipped glass to your teacher immediately. Wipe up all spills immediately.**

4. Measure and record the mass of the 50-mL beaker.

Continued on next page

5. Add 1 level spoonful of salt to the 50-mL beaker. Measure and record the mass of the beaker and salt. Then subtract the mass of the beaker, and record the mass of the salt.

6. Pour the salt into the water in beaker A. Immediately begin stirring the salt and water with the spoon. Measure the amount of stirring time needed for the salt to completely dissolve. Record this time in seconds.

7. Repeat steps 5 and 6 using a clean, dry spoon, 2 level spoonfuls of salt, and beaker B.

8. Repeat steps 5 and 6 using a clean, dry spoon, 3 level spoonfuls of salt, and beaker C.

Cleanup/Disposal

Pour the solutions down the drain. Wash all glassware and clean up any spills. Return the equipment and wash your hands.

Analysis

1. Are the data you recorded qualitative or quantitative?

2. What variable in the experiment did you change? If this is the independent variable, what is the dependent variable?

3. What variables were kept the same throughout the experiment?

Conclusions

1. How does the mass of salt relate to the dissolving time?

2. Why is it important to change only one variable at a time?

3. Why might your results vary from someone else's results?

Explore Further

Graph your data, plotting mass on the *x* axis and time on the *y* axis. Connect the points with a line. Use the graph to predict how long it will take for 4 spoonfuls of salt to dissolve in 100 mL of water. Then measure this dissolving time in the lab. Compare the actual time to your predicted time.

After reading this lesson, you should be able to

◆ write a number in scientific notation

◆ convert a number in scientific notation to standard notation

Scientific notation

A shortcut method for writing very large and very small numbers; for example, 9.88×10^{12} or 1.3×10^{-7}

Superscript

A number that is written just above the writing line

Math Tip

A number ≥ 1 and <10 is read "a number greater or equal to 1 and less than 10."

Scientists often have to measure very large amounts or very small amounts. To make it easier to work with these measurements, scientists write numbers in **scientific notation.** Scientific notation is a shortcut that uses powers of 10. Powers of 10 are written as 10^x, where x is a number called an exponent. The exponent is shown as a **superscript,** a number written just above the writing line. The exponent tells how many times 10 is multiplied by itself. For example, $10^3 = 10 \times 10 \times 10 = 1{,}000$.

In scientific notation, any number, no matter how large or small, is expressed as

(a number ≥ 1 and <10) $\times$ (a power of 10)

For example, in scientific notation, 1,000 is written as 1×10^3. When a number is not written in scientific notation, it is in standard notation.

1,000 is standard notation.

1×10^3 is scientific notation.

To see how scientific notation works, look at the examples in Table 1.2.1.

Table 1.2.1 Examples of Standard and Scientific Notation				
Standard Notation				Scientific Notation
996,000	=	$9.96 \times 100{,}000$	=	9.96×10^5
0.0005327	=	5.327×0.0001	=	5.327×10^{-4}
1,000,000	=	$1 \times 1{,}000{,}000$	=	1×10^6
10	=	1×10	=	1×10^1

Scientific notation comes in handy with very large and very small numbers. For example,

$602{,}000{,}000{,}000{,}000{,}000{,}000{,}000 = 6.02 \times 10^{23}$

$0.00000000000000000037 = 3.7 \times 10^{-19}$

Math

In scientific notation, the number 1 is written as 1×10^0. The number 8 is written as 8×10^0. 10^0 equals 1. Scientists rarely use powers of 0, 1, or -1 in scientific notation. Such numbers are more easily written in standard notation. For example, 0.475 is simpler to write than 4.75×10^{-1}.

If you were to guess the number of sand grains shown in Figure 1.2.1 below, you would want to write your answer in scientific notation.

There is an easy way to express a number in scientific notation. You do not have to memorize powers of 10. Just move the decimal point in the given number to create a number that is between 1 and 10. For example,

6,359,002   and   0.0003474

The decimal point should end up to the right of the first digit that is not a zero. Move the decimal point one place at a time. Count how many places you move the decimal point. The total count becomes the exponent of 10 in scientific notation. If the given number is greater than 1, the exponent of 10 is positive. If the given number is less than 1, the exponent of 10 is negative. The numbers above become

6.359002×10^6 and 3.474×10^{-4}

Look at Example 1 on page 13 and Example 2 on page 14 to see how this works.

Figure 1.2.1 *Very large numbers, like the number of sand grains on a beach, are easiest to work with when they are in scientific notation.*

Example 1	Write the number 765,000,000,000 in scientific notation.
Read	The given number is in standard notation. You are asked to write it in scientific notation.
Plan	Scientific notation has this form: (a number ≥ 1 and <10) $\times 10^x$ The given number is greater than 1, so x will be positive.
Solve	Move the decimal point to create a number that is between 1 and 10. Count how many places you move the decimal point. $765{,}000{,}000{,}000 \; = \; 7.65 \times 10^{11}$ The decimal point needs to move here, to the right of the first nonzero digit. The decimal point is currently here. The number 765,000,000,000 is the same as 7.65×10^{11}.
Reflect	The exponent of 10 is 11 because the decimal point moved 11 places.
Practice	Write the number 605,120,000 in scientific notation.

In Example 1, the exponent of 10 is positive because the given number is greater than 1. The next example shows how to handle a number that is less than 1.

❈ ❈

Technology and Society

Heating oil is a common fuel for heating homes and buildings. It is used at an alarming rate. The natural processes that produce this oil underground take millions of years. Scientists are researching ways to turn other materials into fuel. They have developed a way to change waste products into an oil similar to heating oil. However, the cost of making the oil is greater than its selling price.

Example 2   Write the number 0.000000349 in scientific notation.

Read   The given number is in standard notation. You are asked to write it in scientific notation.

Plan   Scientific notation has this form: (a number ≥ 1 and <10) $\times 10^x$. The given number is less than 1, so x will be negative.

Solve   Move the decimal point to create a number that is between 1 and 10. Count how many places you move the decimal point.

$$0.000000349 \quad = \quad 3.49 \times 10^{-7}$$

The decimal point   The decimal point needs to move here.
is currently here.

The number 0.000000349 is the same as 3.49×10^{-7}.

Reflect   The exponent of 10 is –7 because the decimal point moved 7 places and the given number is less than 1.

Practice   Write the number 0.0042 in scientific notation.

Suppose a number is given in scientific notation. You want to write it in standard notation. First look at the exponent of 10. Move the decimal point in the given number that many places (the given number is the number before " $\times 10^x$ "). If the exponent of 10 is positive, move the decimal point to the right. If the exponent is negative, move the decimal point to the left.

Technology and Society

Suppose corn is planted every year in the same field. The substances in the soil that corn plants need are soon used up. Using chemical fertilizers is one way to replace them. A natural way to replace them is to plant different crops in the field from year to year. This is called crop rotation. Corn, soybeans, and wheat, for example, remove and replace different substances in the soil.

Example 3	Write the number 3×10^{-4} in standard notation.
Read	You are given a number that is in scientific notation. You are asked to write it in standard notation.
Plan	Look at the exponent of 10. It is –4, a negative exponent. This means you will move the decimal point 4 places to the left.
Solve	In the number 3, move the decimal point 4 places to the left. Before you can do this, you will have to write some zeros to the left of 3. The extra zeros just mark places. They do not change the value of 3.

$$3 \times 10^{-4} = 00003 \times 10^{-4} = 0.0003$$

3×10^{-4} equals 0.0003 in standard notation.

Reflect	When you move a decimal point 4 places to the left, you are really multiplying by 0.0001, or 10^{-4}.
Practice	Write the number 1.1524×10^{-9} in standard notation.

Spotlight on Nitrogen

7
N
Nitrogen
14.0

Nitrogen is a gas that makes up about 78% of the air you breathe. All living things need nitrogen. However, most plants and animals cannot use nitrogen gas. Instead, bacteria in the soil change this nitrogen gas into substances that plants use. Animals take in nitrogen when they feed on plants or plant-eating animals. Nitrogen is returned to the soil when plants and animals die. Then bacteria break down these nitrogen-containing materials, releasing nitrogen gas. This is called the nitrogen cycle.

Nitrogen is important to many industries. Ammonia, a common cleaning agent, contains nitrogen. Nitrous oxide contains nitrogen. It is the anesthetic, or painkiller, known as "laughing gas." Nitrogen is part of nitric acid, which is used to make explosives, fertilizers, and other products.

Some substances that contain nitrogen are harmful. Many power plants and small engines produce nitrogen oxides. When nitrogen oxides react with water in the air, acids form. When acid rain falls, it harms plants and animals and wears away rocks.

Interesting Fact: Lightning changes nitrogen gas into substances plants use.

Word Bank

decimal point
scientific notation
standard notation

On a sheet of paper, write the phrase from the Word Bank that completes each sentence.

1. A shortcut method of writing numbers is _____.

2. To write the number 6.23×10^3 in standard notation, move the _____ in 6.23.

3. The number 10,361 is in _____.

On a sheet of paper, write the answer to each problem.

4. Write 93,000,000 in scientific notation.

5. Write 6.3×10^3 in standard notation.

6. Write 0.24983 in scientific notation.

Critical Thinking

On a sheet of paper, write the answer to each question.

7. How does scientific notation make writing certain numbers easier?

8. What does a negative exponent of 10 tell you about the number?

9. Why is the number 36.2×10^2 not written in scientific notation?

10. Which is larger: 3.23×10^3 or 3.23×10^4? How can you tell quickly?

Objectives

After reading this lesson, you should be able to

◆ give examples of accurate measurements and precise measurements

◆ know how the quality of a measuring tool affects certainty

◆ identify the significant figures in a measured value

Are some measurements better than others? Do measuring tools affect measurements? Does it matter how measurements are written down? As you will discover, the answer to all three questions is yes.

Accuracy, Precision, and Certainty

In science, it is important to make measurements that are both accurate and precise. **Accuracy** is how close a measurement is to the correct or accepted value. **Precision** is how close a measurement is to other measurements of the same thing. Let's say you decide to measure your weight at four different times during the day. You know that you weigh about 125 pounds. Here are the results using three different scales:

Time	Scale 1	Scale 2	Scale 3
8 a.m.	110 pounds	124 pounds	142 pounds
noon	119 pounds	126 pounds	103 pounds
4 p.m.	109 pounds	125 pounds	115 pounds
8 p.m.	110 pounds	126 pounds	129 pounds

Accuracy

How close a measurement is to the correct or accepted value

Precision

How close a measurement is to other measurements of the same thing

From these results, you can see that the measurements using Scale 3 are not accurate or precise. They are not close to each other, and they are not close to 125 pounds. The measurements taken from Scale 1 are close to each other. These measurements are much more precise. However, they are not accurate because they are not close to the accepted value of 125 pounds. The measurements from Scale 2 are both precise and accurate. They are close to each other *and* close to the accepted value. Figure 1.3.1 shows the difference between precision and accuracy.

Figure 1.3.1 *In the first bull's-eye, the darts are not close to the center and not close to each other. In the second, the darts are close to each other, but not to the center. In the third, they are close to the center and each other.*

Not precise or accurate

Precise, not accurate

Precise and accurate

To review place names, look at the number **3,470.591**. Here are the place names of each digit:

3—**thousands** place
4—**hundreds** place
7—**tens** place
0—**ones** place
5—**tenths** place
9—**hundredths** place
1—**thousandths** place

Scientists work carefully to obtain accurate and precise measurements. Scientists also need to know how *certain* their measurements are. After measuring something, scientists record the measurement as a number. In any number that represents a measurement, there are digits that are certain and one digit that is uncertain. The last digit on the right in the number is an estimate, or best guess. This digit is the uncertain one.

In the weight example, each measurement has three digits. The digits in the tens place and hundreds place are certain. The digit in the ones place is uncertain—it is an estimate.

125 pounds

certain digits   one uncertain digit

Using a better quality scale, you may be able to measure your weight to the tenths place. For example, such a scale may give your weight as 124.8 pounds. In that case, the uncertain digit is in the tenths place. The 8 is an estimate.

124.8 pounds

certain   uncertain

A value of 124.8 pounds has greater certainty than a value of 125 pounds. The better quality scale gave the more certain measurement. The certainty of a measurement depends on the measuring tool that is used. Look at the rulers in Figure 1.3.2. Which ruler will give a more certain measurement?

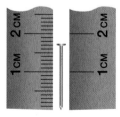

Figure 1.3.2 *The ruler on the left shows that the nail is 1.73 centimeters. The 3 is estimated and is the uncertain digit. The ruler on the right shows that the nail is 1.7 centimeters. The 7 is uncertain.*

Significant Figures

It is important that scientists correctly record the certainty of their measurements. For any measurement value, scientists only record all of the certain digits plus one uncertain, or estimated, digit. The uncertain digit is the last one on the right. Together, these are the meaningful digits, or **significant figures.**

<table>
<tr><td></td><td>124.8 pounds</td><td></td></tr>
<tr><td>3 certain digits</td><td></td><td>1 uncertain digit</td></tr>
<tr><td></td><td>4 significant figures</td><td></td></tr>
</table>

The value 124.8 pounds has 4 significant figures.

Significant figure

A meaningful digit in a measured value; the significant figures in a given value are all of the certain digits plus one estimated digit

---

Example 1	A scientist records a measurement of 6.2345 meters. All of the digits are significant. Which digits are certain?
Read	The number 6.2345 is a measured value that has 5 significant figures.
Plan	The significant figures in a measured value always include one uncertain digit at the far right.
Solve	In the number 6.2345, the 6, 2, 3, and 4 are certain. The 5 is uncertain.
Reflect	Every measured value contains one uncertain digit. The rest are certain.
Practice	A scientist records a measurement of 57 seconds. Both digits are significant. Which one is certain?

Scientists use the following set of rules for counting the significant digits in a measurement.

Rule 1. Nonzero digits—1, 2, 3, 4, 5, 6, 7, 8, and 9—are significant.

Rule 2. Final zeros to the right of the decimal point are significant.

Rule 3. Zeros between two significant digits are significant.

Rule 4. Zeros used for spacing the decimal point are not significant.

Rule 5. For numbers in scientific notation, all of the digits before " $\times 10^x$ " are significant.

Rule 2 says that if a scale gives a weight as 124.8 pounds, it is incorrect to write this number as 124.80. The added zero is counted as significant. Did the scale really measure to the hundredths place? No. Writing 124.80 indicates that the scale can give a more certain value than it actually can. However, adding a zero to the *left* of a number—such as writing .67 as 0.67—is fine. This zero is not counted as significant.

Rule 4 says that "12,000 meters" has only 2 significant figures. The zeros are just used for spacing the decimal point. If a measurement of 12,000 meters actually has 5 significant figures, a decimal point should be added to make this clear. "12,000. meters" means the measurement was made to the nearest 1 meter. It has 5 significant figures, not 2. Another way to show 5 significant figures is to write the number in scientific notation: 1.2000×10^4 meters. According to rule 5, this shows 5 significant figures.

To understand how to apply these rules, study the examples in Table 1.3.1. The significant figures in each measurement are in red.

Table 1.3.1 Using the Rules for Significant Figures		
Measurement*	Number of Significant Figures	Rules Used
135.3	4 significant figures	1
4.6025	5 significant figures	1, 3
200,035	6 significant figures	1, 3
0.0000300	3 significant figures	1, 2, 4
2.0000300	8 significant figures	1, 2, 3
0.002	1 significant figure	1, 4
4.44×10^3	3 significant figures	1, 5
2.0×10^{-2}	2 significant figures	1, 2, 5
10.00	4 significant figures	1, 2, 3
10	1 significant figure	1, 4
102,000	3 significant figures	1, 3, 4

*Red digits are significant figures.

Example 2	How many significant figures are in the measurement 209,000.10 grams?
Read	This number has a total of 8 digits. You need to find out how many of these are significant.
Plan	Apply the five rules on page 19. Rule 1 says that the 2, 9, and 1 are significant—they are nonzero digits. Rule 2 says that the last zero is significant since it is to the right of the decimal point. Rule 3 says that the other 4 zeros are also significant—they are between significant figures. Rule 4 is about zeros that space the decimal point—there are none in this number. Rule 5 does not apply.
Solve	All 8 digits in 209,000.10 are significant.
Reflect	Of the 8 significant figures, 7 are certain. The digit on the far right, a zero, is uncertain.
Practice	How many significant figures are in the measurement 30,780 grams?

What if the measurement in Example 2 was 209,000 grams? This value has only 3 significant digits. The last three zeros just space the decimal point (rule 4).

Example 3	How many significant figures are in the measurement 7,050 minutes?
Read	This measurement has a total of 4 digits. You need to find out how many of these are significant.
Plan	Apply the five rules on page 19. Rule 1 says that the 7 and 5 are significant—they are nonzero digits. Rule 2 does not apply—there are no digits to the right of the decimal point. Rule 3 says that the zero between the 7 and 5 is significant. Rule 4 says that the zero used to space the decimal point—the last zero—is not significant. Rule 5 does not apply.
Solve	There are 3 significant figures.
Reflect	The last zero is needed to hold the ones place. Without it, the measurement would be 705 minutes. In scientific notation, 7,050 is 7.05×10^3 minutes. Suppose all 4 digits in 7,050 were meant to be significant. Then the measurement should have been written as 7,050. minutes or 7.050×10^3 minutes.
Practice	How many significant figures are in the measurement 3.0501×10^3 grams?

Chemistry in Your Life

Technology:
Carbon Monoxide Detectors

Fuels like gasoline, oil, wood, and natural gas need oxygen to burn. This burning usually produces carbon dioxide gas—the same gas you breathe out. Sometimes, these fuels burn even when there is little oxygen. When this happens, carbon monoxide gas can form. Flame-fueled devices such as furnaces, stoves, grills, or water heaters might produce carbon monoxide. Usually this carbon monoxide is vented harmlessly into the outside air. Because this gas has no color or odor, people do not know when they are breathing it. Carbon monoxide replaces oxygen in the blood. People can get sick or even die from carbon monoxide poisoning.

How can you be sure you are safe? Use carbon monoxide detectors. These devices sound an alarm if dangerous levels of the gas are present. They warn you when 100 parts of carbon monoxide are present in 1×10^6 parts of air for 90 minutes. Carbon monoxide detectors should be placed on the ceiling and near sleeping areas in homes. If a detector alarm goes off, leave the home or building quickly and telephone for help.

1. Compare how fuels might burn in the presence of different amounts of oxygen.

2. Why do you think carbon monoxide detectors are not placed next to a furnace?

3. If you have a carbon monoxide detector at home, is it in a good location? If not, where could you move it?

Word Bank

accurate

certain

precise

On a sheet of paper, write the word from the Word Bank that completes each sentence. Use this example: A tree is 69 feet tall. It is measured twice using the same tool. The measurements are 64.9 feet and 65.0 feet.

1. The two measurements are not _____.

2. The two measurements are _____.

3. Each measurement has 3 significant figures, but only 2 of these are _____.

On a sheet of paper, write the answer to each question.

4. How many significant figures are in the measurement 50.04 grams?

5. How many significant figures are in the measurement 800 yards?

6. How many significant figures are in the measurement 6.1230×10^1 meters?

Critical Thinking

On a sheet of paper, write the answer to each question.

7. How do significant figures tell the certainty of a measurement?

8. Explain the difference between accuracy and precision.

9. Give the number of significant figures in each measurement: 4,200 miles and 4.200×10^3 miles.

10. How can you make it clear that a measured value of 980 inches actually has 3 significant figures?

Materials

- safety goggles
- lab coat or apron
- small plastic bottle
- water
- metric measuring cup
- 100-mL graduated cylinder

Measurement and Precision

Different measuring tools measure with different precision. For some tools, their precision is based on the measuring units marked on the tool. In this investigation, you will measure water volume using two tools. Which will measure with greater precision?

Procedure

1. To record your data, make a data table like the one shown here.

Amount of Water	Volume (mL)	
	Measuring Cup	Graduated Cylinder
full bottle		
half bottle		
quarter bottle		

2. Design an experiment to find out which measuring tool is more precise. You will measure three different volumes using each tool. For the first measurement, fill the bottle with water. For the second measurement, fill the bottle about half full. For the last measurement, fill it about one-fourth full.

3. Write a procedure for your experiment. Include a hypothesis and any safety alerts.

4. Have your hypothesis and procedure approved by your teacher.

5. Put on safety goggles and a lab coat or apron.

6. Carry out your experiment. Record your results. Make sure you record only significant figures (the certain digits and one uncertain digit).

Cleanup/Disposal

Clean your work area and return the materials.

Analysis

1. How precisely can you measure using the measuring cup?

2. How precisely can you measure using the graduated cylinder?

3. How do the two recorded values for each volume compare?

Conclusions

1. Which measuring tool was more precise?

2. How do you know which tool was more precise?

Explore Further

Design a similar investigation to measure length. Use one ruler that is marked in only centimeters and another ruler that is marked in centimeters and millimeters.

Many chemistry problems involve measurements. Measured values are often multiplied or divided. Significant figures are important when solving these problems.

Multiplying and Dividing with Significant Figures

Suppose you measure a room and find that it is 22 feet long and 9 feet wide. The length value, 22, has 2 significant figures. The width value, 9, has 1 significant figure. The area of the room is length × width:

$$\text{area} = 22 \text{ feet} \times 9 \text{ feet} = 198 \text{ square feet} \xrightarrow{\text{round}} 200 \text{ square feet}$$

Why was the answer rounded to 1 significant figure? When multiplying or dividing measurements, the answer must have the same number of significant figures as the measurement with the fewest significant figures. If the answer has more significant figures than this, it must be rounded to the correct number of significant figures. Often, an answer from a calculator includes more significant figures than allowed. If so, the answer needs to be rounded.

To understand this rule, study the examples in Table 1.4.1. The significant figures in each measurement are in red.

Table 1.4.1 Significant Figures When Multiplying and Dividing Measurements		
Calculation*	**Answer from Calculator**	**Rounded Answer with Correct Significant Figures***
2.86 feet × 1.824 feet	5.21664 square feet	5.22 square feet
21 miles ÷ 8 hours	2.625 miles/hour	3 miles/hour
98.0 inches × 1.22 inches	119.56 square inches	120. square inches
2.100 meters × 0.00030 meters	0.00063 square meters	0.00063 square meters
10.00 grams ÷ 5.000 liters	2 grams/liter	2.000 grams/liter
$(4.2546 \times 10^3 \text{ feet}) \times (4.4 \times 10^4 \text{ feet})$	1.872024×10^8 square feet	1.9×10^8 square feet

*Red digits are significant figures.

Math Tip

To round a number, look at the digit to the right of the one to be rounded. If that digit is *less than 5,* round down. If that digit is *5 or more,* round up.

To round 4.231 feet to the tenths place (the 2 is in the tenths place), look at the 3. It is less than 5, so the answer is rounded *down.*

$4.231 \xrightarrow{\text{round}} 4.2$

To round 4.269 to the tenths place, look at the 6. It tells you to round *up.*

$4.269 \xrightarrow{\text{round}} 4.3$

Example 1   Multiply 4.610 feet by 1.7 feet. Express your answer in significant figures.

Read   You are asked to multiply two measurements. The first number, 4.610, has 4 significant figures. The second number, 1.7, has 2 significant figures.

Plan   The answer can have only 2 significant figures—this is the fewest number of significant figures among the measured values. The answer will be in square feet.

Solve   Using a calculator, $4.610 \times 1.7 = 7.837$. But this answer has 4 significant figures. It has to be rounded to 2 significant figures.

4.610 feet $\times$ 1.7 feet $= 7.837$ square feet
$\xrightarrow{\text{round}}$ 7.8 square feet

The correct answer is 7.8 square feet.

Reflect   When you multiply two measurements A and B, and B has more significant figures than A, the answer always has the same number of significant figures as A.

Practice   Divide 653 miles by 3 hours. Express your answer in significant figures.

Sometimes, a number in a problem is not a measurement. It might be a defined number. A defined number is part of a definition and is not measured. For example, suppose you measure something that is 725 centimeters long. You want to change this to meters. You find out that 100 centimeters = 1 meter. You divide 725 by 100 to get 7.25 meters. Since 100 has only 1 significant figure, does this mean the answer should be rounded to 7 meters? No. The number 100 is part of a definition. Defined numbers do not limit the significant figures in an answer.

In another case, a number in a problem might be a counting number. Say you have a 28-inch submarine sandwich. You want to divide it evenly into 5 pieces. The number 28 is a measurement. The number 5 is a counting number, not a measurement. You want 5 pieces to serve 5 people. Counting numbers, like defined numbers, do not limit the significant figures in an answer. How long should you make each sandwich piece? Divide 28 by 5 to find out. The answer should have 2 significant figures (like 28), not 1 significant figure (like 5). 28 inches ÷ 5 = 5.6 inches. Only measured numbers in a problem determine the significant figures in the answer.

Example 2	How many meters long is a 1,005-centimeter driveway? Express your answer in significant figures.
Read	You are asked to change the units of a measurement. You are given a value in centimeters and are asked to change it to meters. The number you are given has 4 significant figures.
Plan	This calculation will involve the definition of meter: 1 meter = 100 centimeters. A defined number in a calculation—the 100 here—does not affect the number of significant figures in the answer. The answer will have the same number of significant figures as the measured value of 1,005—4 significant figures.
Solve	Since there are 100 centimeters in a meter, divide 1,005 by 100. The final answer should have 4 significant figures. 1,005 ÷ 100 = 10.05 meters
Reflect	The answer, 10.05 meters, does not need to be rounded because it already has 4 significant figures.
Practice	How many inches long is a piece of string that measures 37.9 feet?

Adding and Subtracting with Significant Figures

When adding or subtracting measurements, the number of significant figures in the answer is determined differently. The answer cannot have more certainty than the least certain measurement. This means the answer must have the same number of significant figures to the right of the decimal point as the measurement with the fewest significant figures to the right of the decimal point. When needed, round the answer to the correct number of significant figures.

This rule is only concerned with significant figures to the right of the decimal point. Digits to the *left* of the decimal point can be ignored when adding and subtracting. Suppose you want to add three measurements:

$$
\begin{array}{ll}
4.271 \text{ grams} & \text{(3 significant figures to right of decimal point)} \\
2 \text{ grams} & \text{(0 significant figures to right of decimal point)} \\
+\,10.0 \text{ grams} & \text{(1 significant figure to right of decimal point)} \\
\hline
16.271 \text{ grams} & \xrightarrow{\text{round}} \quad 16 \text{ grams}
\end{array}
$$

The correct sum is 16 grams—not 16.271 grams. Why? One measurement, 2 grams, has 0 significant figures to the right of the decimal point. So the answer must also have 0 significant figures to the right of the decimal point. Remember, this rule is only used when adding and subtracting measured values.

Example 3   Add these measurements: 4.35 seconds and 212.2 seconds. Express your answer using significant figures.

Read   The first number, 4.35, has 2 significant figures to the right of the decimal point. The second one, 212.2, has 1 significant figure to the right of the decimal point.

Plan   The answer can have only 1 significant figure to the right of the decimal point.

Solve   Using a calculator, the sum is 216.55 seconds. This sum has to be rounded to 216.6 seconds (1 significant figure to the right of the decimal point).

$$4.35 \text{ seconds}$$
$$+212.2 \text{ seconds}$$
$$216.55 \text{ seconds} \xrightarrow{\text{round}} 216.6 \text{ seconds}$$

Reflect   When working with measurements, a calculator answer may show too many significant figures. In this example, 216.55 had to be rounded up to 216.6 seconds.

Practice   Add these measurements: 2.423 meters + 0.001365 meters. Express your answer in significant figures.

On a sheet of paper, write the answer to each problem. Express your answers using the correct number of significant figures.

1. 8.35 meters × 3.996 meters

2. 11 feet ÷ 7 seconds

3. 7 centimeters × 1.86 centimeters × 0.002 centimeters

4. 98.0 pounds−1.22 pounds

5. 4.6215 milligrams ÷ 0.0000150 liters

6. 2.1 yards × 0.000300 yards

Critical Thinking

On a sheet of paper, write the answer to each question.

7. Give an example of a defined number.

8. Give an example of a counting number.

9. How are defined numbers and counting numbers treated in calculations that involve measurements?

10. Two measurements, 43.15 hours and 10.2 hours, are added. Explain why the correct answer is not 53.35 hours.

Unit

A standard amount used for measuring

Meter (m)

The SI unit for measuring length

Gram (g)

A unit for measuring mass

Liter (L)

A unit for measuring volume

Kelvin (K)

The SI unit for measuring temperature

Degree Celsius (°C)

A unit for measuring temperature

An important part of the scientific method is sharing results with other scientists. Results usually include measured values that have **units.** A unit is a standard amount used for measuring. There is usually more than one unit for measuring something. Meters, yards, and feet are all units for measuring distance. Each of these units represents a different standard distance.

Base Units

In 1960, scientists around the world agreed on one system of measurement. In French, this system is called the Système International d'Unités, or SI. This system uses the unit **meter** for measuring length. The symbol for meter is m. The SI unit for mass is the kilogram. However, the **gram** is much smaller and more commonly used in chemistry. The symbol for gram is g. A blueberry is about 1 g. Table 1.5.1 lists some base units used in chemistry. They are called base units because they have no prefixes.

Table 1.5.1 Common Base Units		
Quantity	Unit	Unit Symbol
distance or length	meter	m
mass	gram	g
volume	liter	L
temperature	degree Celsius	°C
time	second	s

The SI unit for volume is the cubic meter (m^3), but the **liter** (**L**) is also used. $1\ m^3 = 1,000\ L$. The liter is a more practical size for measuring liquid volumes in chemistry. The SI unit of temperature is the **kelvin (K),** but **degree Celsius (°C)** is also used. You will learn more about the Kelvin temperature scale in Chapter 7. The SI unit for time is the second (s). Time may also be expressed in minutes or hours.

Scientists use unit symbols when they record measurements. It is faster to record *17 L* than *17 liters*. In this book, unit symbols are used to express measurements.

Math Tip

It is a good idea to memorize metric prefixes and their meanings. For example, the prefix *milli-* means "0.001 times." A milligram is 0.001 times a gram. There are 1,000 mL in a liter.

Metric Prefixes

The base units in Table 1.5.1 are sometimes too big or too small, depending on what is being measured. Suppose you want to measure the length and width of this book. The meter is too big for this task. To solve this problem, metric prefixes are added to base units to create new units that are the right size. Metric prefixes are used frequently in chemistry. Common prefixes are listed in Table 1.5.2. As the table shows, a base unit and its prefixed units are related by powers of 10.

Table 1.5.2 Common Metric Prefixes			
Prefix	Multiplying Factor	Symbol	Example
micro-	0.000001 (or 1×10^{-6})	μ (Greek letter *mu*)	micrometer (1 μm = 0.000001 m)
milli-	0.001 (or 1×10^{-3})	m	milligram (1 mg = 0.001 g)
centi-	0.01 (or 1×10^{-2})	c	centimeter (1 cm = 0.01 m)
deci-	0.1 (or 1×10^{-1})	d	deciliter (1 dL = 0.1 L)
kilo-	1,000 (or 1×10^{3})	k	kilogram (1 kg = 1,000 g)

Each prefix is written to the left of a base unit, as the table shows. A prefixed unit is either a larger or smaller unit than the base unit. By adding the prefix *centi-* to meter, a new unit, the centimeter (cm), is created. A centimeter is 0.01 (or 10^{-2}) times a meter. It is smaller than a meter. There are 100 cm in a meter, as shown in Figure 1.5.1. This smaller unit is a good size for measuring a book. Measure the width and length of this book in centimeters. It is about 19.1 cm by 23.9 cm.

Figure 1.5.2 *The metric unit for length is the meter. By adding prefixes, smaller units are created. 1 meter = 10 decimeters = 100 centimeters = 1,000 millimeters.*

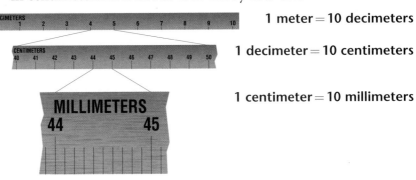

1 meter = 10 decimeters

1 decimeter = 10 centimeters

1 centimeter = 10 millimeters

Unit Conversions

Have you ever calculated your height in inches or your age in minutes? If so, you have made a **unit conversion.** A unit conversion is a method of changing a measurement from one unit to another unit. For example, a person measuring 6 feet in height is also 72 inches tall. How is that conversion made? The 6 is multiplied by 12 to get 72. Why pick 12? There are 12 inches in 1 foot. In the study of chemistry, you will need to make similar conversions.

No matter what unit or prefix is used, all conversions in the metric system are based on powers of 10. This makes metric conversions easier than conversions with feet, pounds, or gallons. In the customary system, 6 feet = 72 inches and 2 pounds = 32 ounces. In the metric system, 6 m = 600 cm and 2 kg = 2,000 g. Most metric conversions just move the decimal point!

The important part of any unit conversion is using the correct **conversion factor.** A conversion factor is a ratio or fraction that shows how two units are related. Table 1.5.3 gives some examples of metric conversion factors.

All measurements consist of a number and a unit. Using the correct unit is important. Without a unit, a measurement has no meaning. Using a wrong unit can also cause trouble. There is a big difference between 8 *seconds* and 8 *hours.*

Math Tip

A pound is about 450 g. A gallon is about 3.5 L. A kilometer is about 0.62 mile. A meter is a little more than a yard. Pounds, gallons, miles, and yards are customary units.

Table 1.5.3 Examples of Metric Conversion Factors		
Conversion Factor	**Meaning**	**Use**
$\dfrac{1\ cm}{0.01\ m}$	1 cm = 0.01 m	for converting meters to centimeters
$\dfrac{0.01\ m}{1\ cm}$	0.01 m = 1 cm	for converting centimeters to meters
$\dfrac{1\ mL}{0.001\ L}$	1 mL = 0.001 L	for converting liters to milliliters
$\dfrac{1\ kg}{1,000\ g}$	1 kg = 1,000 g	for converting grams to kilograms

Mass is not the same as weight. Weight is a force caused by the pull of gravity on an object's mass. Mass does not depend on gravity. You have the same mass whether you are standing on the earth or on the moon. But your moon weight is very different from your earth weight.

To make a unit conversion, you need a conversion factor that relates the *given unit* to the *unit you want.* Say you want a conversion factor to change 784 mm to meters. To create this factor,

1. Place the given unit in the denominator (the bottom of the fraction): $\frac{}{mm}$.

2. Place the desired unit in the numerator (the top of the fraction): $\frac{m}{mm}$.

3. For conversions that involve a base unit, put a *1* in front of the prefixed unit: $\frac{m}{1\ mm}$.

4. Then put the multiplying factor for that prefix (from Table 1.5.2) in front of the base unit: $\frac{0.001\ m}{1\ mm}$.

Once you have the correct conversion factor, the actual conversion is easy.

1. Write the given number and unit: 784 mm.

2. Multiply it by the conversion factor: $784\ mm \times \frac{0.001\ m}{1\ mm}$.

3. Cancel the given units: $784\ \cancel{mm} \times \frac{0.001\ m}{1\ \cancel{mm}}$.

4. Use a calculator to multiply. The answer is in the unit you want: $784 \times 0.001\ m = 0.784\ m$.

Conversion factors are made up of defined numbers, not measurements. After multiplying a measurement by a conversion factor, the answer should have the same number of significant figures as the starting measurement.

Link to ➤➤➤

Language Arts

The metric system is simple and easy to use. The English, or customary, system is much harder to use. For example, there are many English units of length, and none are related by simple powers of 10. You probably know that there are 12 inches in a foot, 3 feet in a yard, and 5,280 feet in a mile. You may not know that there are 16½ feet in a *rod*, 220 yards in a *furlong*, and 3 miles in a *league*.

Example 1	Convert 8.96 L to milliliters.
Read	You are given 8.96 L. You are asked to convert this to milliliters.
Plan	To do this, you need a conversion factor that relates liters and milliliters. This factor will have the desired unit (milliliters) on the top and the given unit (liters) on the bottom. The multiplying factor for *milli-* is 0.001—this goes in front of the base unit. The factor is $\frac{1 \text{ mL}}{0.001 \text{ L}}$.
Solve	Multiply the given number by the conversion factor. The given units cancel out. $$8.96 \text{ L} \times \frac{1 \text{ mL}}{0.001 \text{ L}} = 8{,}960 \text{ mL} = 8.96 \times 10^3 \text{ mL}$$
Reflect	The answer has the correct unit. It may be written in standard or scientific notation.
Practice	Convert 1,975 g to kilograms.

▼◄▲▼◄▲▼◄▲▼◄▲▼◄▲▼◄▲▼◄▲▼◄▲▼◄▲▼◄▲▼◄▲▼◄▲▼

Science at Work

Research Technician

Research technicians conduct experiments. They work as part of a research team that is led by a chemist or chemical engineer. The team leader designs the research, and the research technician conducts the experiments and records the results. The technician needs to understand the research hypothesis in order to interpret the results and make conclusions. Research technicians work with a variety of lab equipment, including computerized equipment.

A two-year degree is typically required to become a research technician. Some positions require a bachelor's degree. Research technicians should have a background in science and math. They must be able to focus on details and work well with others.

Link to ➤➤➤

Health

Humans need certain vitamins and minerals for good health. The amount needed varies, depending on the vitamin or mineral. For an adult, the suggested amount of calcium is 1 g per day. The amount of vitamin C is 60 mg per day. The daily amount of vitamin B12 is only 6 μg.

So far, you have looked at metric conversions between a base unit and a prefixed unit. What if you want to convert between two prefixed units, such as from centimeters to millimeters? *Two* conversion factors are needed to convert from a unit with a prefix to another unit with a prefix.

1. Multiply the given number by a conversion factor that converts from the given unit to the base unit.

2. Then multiply by a second conversion factor that converts from the base unit to the desired unit.

Example 2	Convert 14.25 dg to kilograms.
Read	The given number is in decigrams. You are asked to convert this to kilograms. Both the given unit and the desired unit have prefixes.
Plan	You will need two conversion factors. First convert from decigrams to grams, then convert from grams to kilograms. Here is a "map" of this conversion: decigrams → grams → kilograms
Solve	Write the given number and unit. After it, set up the two conversion factors. Make sure you use the correct multiplying factor in each. Cancel units. Then use a calculator to multiply. $14.25 \text{ dg} \times \dfrac{0.1 \text{ g}}{1 \text{ dg}} \times \dfrac{1 \text{ kg}}{1{,}000 \text{ g}} = 0.001425 \text{ kg}$ $= 1.425 \times 10^{-3} \text{ kg}$
Reflect	All units cancel out except for the desired unit, kilograms. Since a decigram is a small amount and a kilogram is a much larger amount, the answer makes sense.
Practice	Convert 105,400 μm to millimeters. There are only 4 significant figures in this measurement.

Lesson 5   R E V I E W

Word Bank

base unit

conversion factor

prefix

On a sheet of paper, write the word or phrase from the Word Bank that completes each sentence.

1. For all scientists, the _____ for measuring distance is the meter.

2. A _____ is used to change a measurement from one unit to another.

3. In the metric system, a _____ is added to a base unit to make it smaller or bigger.

On a sheet of paper, write the letter of the answer that completes each sentence.

4. To convert from centimeters to kilometers, you need two conversion factors. The first factor converts centimeters into _____.

A centimeters   **C** kilometers

B meters   **D** millimeters

5. The prefix *kilo-* means _____.

A 1,000 times   **C** 0.01 times

B 100 times   **D** 0.001 times

6. To convert 23 cm to meters, the correct conversion factor is _____.

A $\dfrac{0.01 \text{ cm}}{1 \text{ m}}$ **B** $\dfrac{1 \text{ cm}}{0.01 \text{ m}}$ **C** $\dfrac{1 \text{ m}}{0.01 \text{ cm}}$ **D** $\dfrac{0.01 \text{ m}}{1 \text{ cm}}$

Critical Thinking

On a sheet of paper, write the answer to each problem.

7. Convert 500 mg to grams.

8. Convert 15.3 L to milliliters.

9. 1,500 mL is equal to how many liters?

10. A 2.5-km road is how many centimeters long?

Derived unit

A measurement unit created by multiplying or dividing other units

Density (D)

The mass of a sample of matter divided by its volume

Suppose you measured the length and width of a room in meters. You could multiply these two measurements to find the area of the room. Because length and width are both measured in meters, the unit for area is square meters (m^2). If you measured the room's height in meters, you could find the room's volume: length × width × height. This unit of volume would be cubic meters (m^3). Both square meters and cubic meters, shown in Figure 1.6.1, are **derived units.** They are derived, or made, by *multiplying* two or three base units. Derived units also are made by *dividing* base units. An example of this is the unit for **density (*D*).**

Density describes how dense something is, or how heavy it is for its size. It is calculated by dividing the mass (*M*) of a sample of matter by its volume (*V*). This can be expressed as

$$\text{density} = \frac{\text{mass}}{\text{volume}} \quad \text{or} \quad D = \frac{M}{V}$$

Density is a ratio that stays the same for a given substance. It does not depend on the size of the sample being measured. Density has many possible units. All of them are derived by dividing a mass unit by a volume unit. When volume is measured in cubic meters, the unit for density is grams per cubic meter (g/m^3). When volume is measured in liters, the unit for density is grams per liter (g/L). These units could also be converted to grams per cubic centimeter (g/cm^3) or grams per milliliter (g/mL).

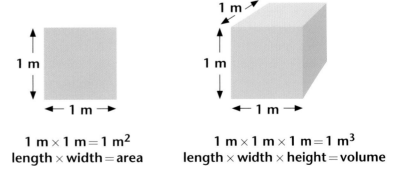

1 m × 1 m = 1 m²   1 m × 1 m × 1 m = 1 m³
length × width = area   length × width × height = volume

Figure 1.6.1 *Area, volume, and density are derived units.*

Example 1   Calculate the density of a substance with a mass of 24.3 g and a volume of 32.9 mL. Use the correct unit and the correct number of significant figures in your answer.

Read   You are asked to find the density of something. You are given a mass and a volume. Both numbers have 3 significant figures.

Plan   Density is mass divided by volume. Two measurements are divided. The answer can have only 3 significant figures.

Solve   Use the given values in the equation for density. Include the unit with each number. No units can be canceled this time. Use a calculator to find the answer. Round the answer.

$$D = \frac{M}{V} = \frac{24.3 \text{ g}}{32.9 \text{ mL}} = \frac{0.7386018 \text{ g}}{\text{mL}} \xrightarrow{\text{round}} 0.739 \text{ g/mL}$$

The calculator answer, 0.7386018 g/mL, is rounded to 0.739 g/mL because there are only 3 significant figures in each of the given measurements. The correct unit is included in the answer.

Practice   Find the density of a 39-g object that has a volume of 0.0421 L. Express your answer using the correct unit and number of significant figures.

★ ✦ ★

Achievements in Science

The Length of a Meter

To measure length, you might use a meterstick. The precision of this tool is limited. If it is made of wood, its length might swell or shrink. The printed lines that mark centimeters and millimeters might be thick or thin, depending on the meterstick. Thick lines can cause a measurement to be less precise. Exactly how long is a meter? Its length has not changed, but its definition has.

In the 1700s, the meter was defined as 10^{-7} times the distance from the North Pole to the equator. However, this length was found to be short by 0.2 mm. In the late 1800s, the meter was defined as the distance between two marks on a certain bar of metal kept at 0°C.

In 1983, the current definition of a meter was given. It is based on the speed of light. A meter is the distance light travels in a vacuum in $\frac{1}{299,792,458}$ of a second. This time is about 3×10^{-9} s.

The density of pure water is 1 g/mL. This is the same as 1 g/cm³. Any amount of water has this density.

If you know the mass and density of a substance, you can find its volume. (Check that the units for mass are the same.) If you know volume and density, you can find mass. (Check that the units for volume are the same). Use the known values in the density equation. Then solve for the unknown.

Example 2 What is the volume of an object with a density of 1.25 g/mL and a mass of 281 g?

Read You are given a density and a mass. Both measurements have 3 significant figures and use the same unit for mass. You are asked to find volume.

Plan Use the given values, with their units, in the density equation. The unknown is volume, *V*. The answer can have only 3 significant figures.

Solve Set up the density formula. Replace the *D* and the *M* with the given values. A density of 1.25 g/mL means the same as $\frac{1.25\ g}{1\ mL}$.

$$D = \frac{M}{V} \qquad \frac{1.25\ g}{1\ mL} = \frac{281\ g}{V}$$

To solve for *V*, multiply each side of the equation by *V*. With a little algebra, you get

$$V = \frac{(281\ g)(1\ mL)}{1.25\ g}$$

Using a calculator, $281 \div 1.25 = 224.8$ mL. However, only 3 significant figures are allowed, so the volume is rounded to 225 mL.

Reflect Rounding an answer because of significant figures is only necessary when working with measurements. The answer, 225 mL, has the correct unit and number of significant figures.

Practice What is the mass of an object with a density of 1.2 g/mL and a volume of 3 L? (Hint: First convert 3 L to milliliters so it matches the volume unit in the density value.)

Lesson 6   R E V I E W

Word Bank

derived

unit

volume

On a sheet of paper, write the word from the Word Bank that completes each sentence.

1. To find density, mass is divided by _____.

2. When two units are multiplied or divided, a _____ unit is created.

3. Density has more than one possible _____.

On a sheet of paper, write the letter of the answer that completes each sentence.

4. If $D = \dfrac{M}{V}$, then $V =$ _____.

   A $V + M$ **B** $\dfrac{D}{M}$ **C** $M \times D$ **D** $\dfrac{M}{D}$

5. The quantity _____ has derived units.

   A volume   **B** mass   **C** time   **D** temperature

6. A substance has a mass of 25 g and a volume of 5 mL. Its density is _____.

   A 0.2 g/mL   **B** 5 g/mL   **C** 25 g/mL   **D** 125 g/mL

Critical Thinking

On a sheet of paper, write the answer to each question.

7. How would you find the volume of a substance when you are given its mass and density?

8. Which has the greater density, substance A or substance B?

Substance A with a mass of 12.3 g and a volume of 3.4 mL
Substance B with a mass of 22.6 g and a volume of 6.1 mL

9. Why is a cubic meter considered a derived unit?

10. Rewrite the density equation, $D = \dfrac{M}{V}$, solving for mass (M).

CHEMISTRY IN THE WORLD

Water Treatment

Less than 1% of the liquid water on the earth's surface is freshwater. Freshwater is what you use daily for drinking and washing. Freshwater is cleaned, or treated, so it can be used again.

The scientific method is used in the water treatment process. Testing and observation show that the water needs to be cleaned. Hypotheses propose ways of cleaning water. Data are gathered and analyzed. Conclusions tell whether clean water is produced. The results are shared with others.

Water is treated in three steps. The first step removes solids. Stones and sand settle out of the water. Then the water passes through screens that remove solid materials that float. The water then stands in large tanks. Some solids in the water sink and are removed. Grease and floating solids are skimmed off the surface.

In the second step, bacteria are used to break down plant and animal materials. The bacteria need oxygen, so oxygen is added. After these materials break down, they clump together and are removed.

The third step treats the water so it is safe to go back into rivers, lakes, or storage reservoirs. High levels of nitrogen and phosphorus can harm plants and animals. To remove these substances, the water is filtered through sand or stored in large pools. It might also be placed into wetlands made for this purpose.

At the end of the third step, the water is usually disinfected to kill germs. This is done by adding chlorine or ozone or by shining ultraviolet light through the water.

1. A water sample contains oils and grease. In what step of treating water are these materials removed?

2. Sometimes treated water smells like chlorine. Why is chlorine added to water?

Chapter 1   S U M M A R Y

- Chemistry is the study of matter and how it changes.

- Matter has both mass and volume. Mass is the amount of matter in an object. Volume is the amount of space an object takes up.

- Qualitative observations do not use numbers. Quantitative observations require measurements and use numbers.

- The scientific method is a way of answering a question or solving a problem. It is based on existing facts and ideas, new observations, and reason.

- Scientific knowledge grows and changes because of the results of research. Science and technology are related.

- Scientific notation is a simple way to write very large and very small numbers. It always takes the form: (a number ≥ 1 and <10) $\times 10^x$.

- Scientists are concerned with the accuracy, precision, and certainty of measurements.

- Scientists use significant figures to indicate the certainty of their measurements and calculations. They use rules to determine which digits in a measurement are significant.

- Chemists commonly use these base units: grams (mass), meters (length), liters (volume), seconds (time), and degrees Celsius (temperature).

- Metric prefixes can be added to base units, creating new units that are smaller or larger.

- To convert a measurement from one unit to another, at least one conversion factor is needed.

- When you divide or multiply units, the result is a derived unit. An example is density (D), which is mass (M) divided by volume (V).

Vocabulary

accuracy, 17	gram, 32	meter, 32	technology, 7
chemist, 2	hypothesis, 4	precision, 17	theory, 5
chemistry, 2	independent variable, 5	qualitative, 2	unit, 32
conversion factor, 34		quantitative, 2	unit conversion, 34
degree Celsius, 32	kelvin, 32	scientific method, 4	variable, 5
density, 39	liter, 32	scientific notation, 11	volume, 2
dependent variable, 5	mass, 2	significant figure, 19	
derived unit, 39	matter, 2	superscript, 11	

Chapter 1 REVIEW

<table>
<tr><td>**Word Bank**</td></tr>
<tr><td>accuracy</td></tr>
<tr><td>density</td></tr>
<tr><td>derived unit</td></tr>
<tr><td>gram</td></tr>
<tr><td>hypothesis</td></tr>
<tr><td>liter</td></tr>
<tr><td>mass</td></tr>
<tr><td>scientific method</td></tr>
<tr><td>scientific notation</td></tr>
<tr><td>significant</td></tr>
<tr><td>theory</td></tr>
<tr><td>volume</td></tr>
</table>

Vocabulary Review

On a sheet of paper, write the word or phrase from the Word Bank that completes each sentence.

1. Mass divided by volume is called _____.

2. The amount of space an object takes up is its _____.

3. After a hypothesis has been tested many times, it may become a(n) _____.

4. In a measured value, a zero that is used only to space the decimal point is not _____.

5. A unit of mass is the _____.

6. The _____ of a measurement is how close the measurement is to the true or accepted value.

7. The _____ is used by scientists to answer a question or solve a problem.

8. Large and small numbers can be written more easily using _____.

9. Area is an example of a quantity requiring a(n) _____.

10. A unit for volume is the _____.

11. A(n) _____ is a possible explanation based on facts and reason.

12. The amount of matter in an object is its _____.

Continued on next page

Chemistry and Measurement Chapter 1 **45**

Concept Review

On a sheet of paper, write the letter of the answer that completes each sentence.

13. An example of a qualitative description is _____.

    A "She ran 1.45 km in 15 minutes."
    B "The hydrogen gas had a volume of 5 L."
    C "The substance began to dissolve."
    D "The mass was 131.265 g."

14. The number _____ has 3 significant figures.

    A 3,337   **B** 340.0   **C** 123   **D** 0.003

15. The number 0.00529 is written as _____ in scientific notation.

    A 5.29×10^3 **B** 52.9×10^{-2} **C** 52.9×10^4 **D** 5.29×10^{-3}

16. A beaker is 152 g. A student measures the mass of this beaker three times and gets these results: 137 g, 136 g, and 137 g. These measurements are _____.

    A accurate, but not precise   **C** accurate and precise
    B precise, but not accurate   **D** not accurate or precise

Problem Solving

On a sheet of paper, write the answer to each problem. You may use a calculator. Include the correct unit and give the correct number of significant figures. Show your work.

17. Multiply these measurements: 0.4330 cm × 209,000 cm.

18. Convert 75.3 cm to millimeters.

19. Convert 0.186 kg to decigrams.

20. A substance has a mass of 257 g and a volume of 352 mL. Find its density in grams per milliliter.

21. A substance has a density of 0.876 g/mL and a volume of 25.6 mL. Find its mass in grams.

Critical Thinking

On a sheet of paper, write the answer to each question.

22. Why is communication an important part of the scientific method?

23. Give an example of a number that has one zero that is significant and one zero that is not.

24. Show the steps involved in converting 10 L into milliliters.

25. A substance has a density of 1.52 g/mL and a mass of 220 g. What is its volume in milliliters? (Hint: Watch the significant figures.)

Test-Taking Tip When your teacher announces a test, listen carefully. Write down the topics that will be included. Write down the specific chapters or reading material you should review.

2

Matter

These colorful bumper boats are ready for riders—and action. What are the boats made of? What are they filled with? Why do they float on water? Why do they bounce off each other when they bump? To answer these questions, you must know something about the nature of matter. In Chapter 2, you will study physical and chemical properties of matter. You will learn about different types of matter and how these types combine.

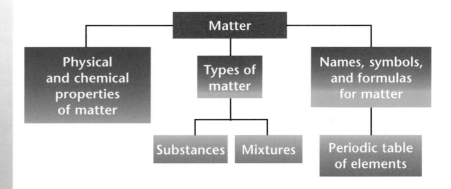

Organize Your Thoughts

Matter
- Physical and chemical properties of matter
- Types of matter
  - Substances
  - Mixtures
- Names, symbols, and formulas for matter
  - Periodic table of elements

Goals for Learning

◆ To identify physical and chemical properties and changes

◆ To compare substances and mixtures

◆ To compare heterogeneous and homogeneous mixtures

◆ To become familiar with the periodic table and chemical symbols

◆ To compare elements and compounds

◆ To tell the kind and number of atoms in a chemical formula

Physical property

A characteristic of a substance that can be observed without changing the substance

State

The physical form of a substance; solid, liquid, or gas

Solid

A state of matter that has a definite shape and volume

Liquid

A state of matter that has a definite volume, but takes the shape of its container

Matter comes in all shapes and forms. The substances around you have many different characteristics. In chemistry, the characteristics of a substance are called properties. Matter is organized, or classified, into categories based on properties. Matter can also change. When a substance changes, one or more of its properties change.

Properties of Matter

All properties of matter are either physical or chemical. **Physical properties** are characteristics of a substance that can be observed without changing the substance. Physical properties include *qualitative* observations, such as color and smell. Physical properties also can be *quantitative* observations that are measured, such as size, density, and boiling point.

One physical property is the **state**, or physical form, of a substance. There are three states of matter: solid, liquid, and gas. **Solids** have a definite shape and volume. The bike frame in Figure 2.1.1 is a solid. The particles that make up a solid are tightly packed. The particles in the metal bike frame can move, but not very far.

Liquids have a definite volume, but their shape depends on their container. Water is a liquid. It splashes around in the biker's water bottle, but keeps the same volume until the biker takes a drink. The particles in a liquid are also tightly packed, but they can easily slide around each other. Because of this, liquids can flow and be poured.

Figure 2.1.1 *The state of matter— solid, liquid, or gas—is a physical property.*

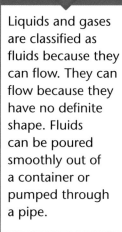

Liquids and gases are classified as fluids because they can flow. They can flow because they have no definite shape. Fluids can be poured smoothly out of a container or pumped through a pipe.

Gases can also flow, but they take the shape and volume of their container. The air in the bike tires is under pressure. The particles are squeezed closer together than they are in the atmosphere. When a tire leaks, the air that is released changes shape. It occupies a larger volume because the particles move apart. The particles that make up gases are spaced widely apart.

Besides states of matter, what other physical properties could be observed or measured in the bike scene?

- The color of the bike
- The body temperature of the biker
- The width of the bike tires
- The density of the plastic bottle
- The mass of the helmet

When a physical property is observed, the substance stays the same substance. This is not true for chemical properties.

Every substance has both physical and chemical properties. **Chemical properties** describe how a substance changes into one or more different substances. This often happens when the substance reacts with another substance. Wood can burn by reacting with oxygen. The wood turns to ashes, a different substance. The ability to burn is a chemical property of wood. Iron rusts by reacting with oxygen. It changes into an orange-colored substance that is not iron. The ability to rust is a chemical property of iron. Some substances rarely react with other substances. Until recently, scientists have not been able to make helium react with anything. Being unable to react is also a chemical property.

Link to ➤➤➤

Earth Science

Plasma is a fourth state of matter. A plasma contains particles with electric charges, so it can conduct electricity. A lightning bolt is an example of a plasma. Plasmas also produce the lights in neon signs.

Table 2.1.1 gives a few physical and chemical properties of copper. Suppose you have a piece of copper. You could observe or measure any of its physical properties and still have copper. If you tested a chemical property, however, you might not end up with copper.

Table 2.1.1 Some Properties of Copper	
Physical Properties	**Chemical Properties**
is a shiny solid at room temperature	reacts with oxygen to form a black substance
has a density of 8.96 g/mL	does not react when placed in saltwater
has a melting point of 1,084°C	reacts with silver nitrate (a clear solution) to form solid silver and a blue solution

Changes in Matter

All changes in matter are either physical or chemical. A **physical change** is a change in a substance that affects only its physical properties. A physical change does not result in a different substance. There are many examples of physical changes. A copper pipe being cut in half is a change in size. An ice cube melting is a change in state. Even salt dissolving in water is just a change in form. In each case, physical properties change, but the substance itself does not change. Water—as a solid or a liquid—is still water. Salt—as tiny grains or dissolved in water—is still salt.

A **chemical change** is a change in a substance that results in one or more new substances being formed. The new substances have different chemical properties. A **chemical reaction** is the set of chemical changes involved when one or more substances react, forming one or more different substances. You have already learned about two chemical reactions: When you burn a piece of wood in oxygen, carbon dioxide gas, water vapor, and ashes are created. When a piece of iron rusts in the presence of oxygen, some of the iron changes to "rust," or iron oxide. In all chemical reactions, substances react, producing new substances. Figure 2.1.2 shows a physical change and a chemical change.

Sidebar

Physical change

A change in a substance that affects its physical properties, but not its chemical properties

Chemical change

A change in a substance that results in one or more different substances being formed

Chemical reaction

The chemical changes involved when one or more substances react, forming one or more different substances

The state of matter is a qualitative observation. It does not involve numbers. Density is a quantitative observation. It involves numbers. Both are physical properties.

Figure 2.1.2 *Burning wood is a chemical change. Boiling water is a physical change of state.*

All physical and chemical changes involve a change in **energy.** Energy is the ability to do work or produce heat. For example, work occurs when an object is pushed, a sound is created, or a new substance forms. You are familiar with many forms of energy: light, heat, sound, and electricity. Chemical energy and nuclear energy are also forms of energy.

Some chemical reactions give off energy in the form of heat. Burning a piece of wood gives off heat. It also gives off light. Other chemical reactions require energy in order to occur. These reactions take in energy. Physical changes involve changes in energy, too. When an ice cube melts, it takes in heat. Whenever matter changes, energy is either taken in or given off.

Besides an energy change, a chemical reaction might also involve a color change, the release of a gas, or the formation of a solid. These are some of the signs of a chemical reaction.

Express Lab 2

Materials

- safety goggles
- lab coat or apron
- chalk dusk
- 4 cm of magnesium ribbon
- 4 test tubes and rack
- 10-mL graduated cylinder
- water
- 20 mL of 5% vinegar solution

Procedure

1. Put on safety goggles and a lab coat or apron.

2. Examine the chalk and the magnesium. Record their physical properties.

3. Place the magnesium ribbon in a test tube. Place half of the chalk dust in a second test tube.

4. Add 10 mL of water to each tube.

5. Record your observations. Include any evidence of chemical or physical changes.

6. Pour the contents of each tube down the drain, but save the magnesium ribbon.

7. Repeat step 3 with the other two test tubes, using the same piece of magnesium. Add 10 mL of vinegar to each tube.

8. Record your observations, including any evidence of chemical or physical changes. Feel the bottom of each tube after any change.

Analysis

1. What happened when water was added to the magnesium and the chalk?

2. What evidence did you see that chemical reactions occurred?

Link to ➤➤➤

Home and Career

Cooking involves both physical and chemical changes. Cutting, slicing, chopping, and grinding produce physical changes in food. Baking, grilling, frying, boiling, and broiling usually produce chemical changes. During cooking processes, substances and mixtures are rearranged into different substances and mixtures. This creates the flavors, textures, and aromas of cooked food.

Match each term in the first column with an example in the second column. On a sheet of paper, write the letter of the answer.

1. physical property

2. chemical property

3. solid

4. liquid

5. physical change

6. chemical change

A ability to burn

B rust appears on a nail

C a puddle freezes

D substance that has a definite shape and volume

E temperature or density

F substance that has a definite volume, but no definite shape

Critical Thinking

On a sheet of paper, write the answer to each question.

7. What is the difference between a gas and a liquid?

8. How are physical changes related to physical properties?

9. What is a chemical reaction?

10. How is energy related to changes in matter?

Physical and chemical properties are used to classify matter into categories. As you read the rest of this chapter, refer to Figure 2.2.1 to help you understand how matter is classified.

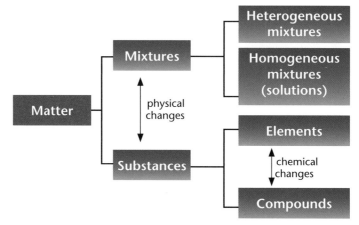

Figure 2.2.1 *Matter is classified into mixtures and substances.*

Substances and Mixtures

As the figure shows, every sample of matter is either a mixture or a substance. A **substance** has a definite makeup, or composition. It also has definite chemical and physical properties. Carbon dioxide, table sugar, and aluminum are examples of substances. Any sample of carbon dioxide will have *exactly* the same makeup and properties as another sample of carbon dioxide. Substances are either elements or compounds. These terms will be discussed in Lessons 3 and 4.

Most of the matter you see is a **mixture.** A mixture is two or more substances mixed together. The properties of the individual substances are not affected. This is because the substances in a mixture are not chemically combined. Air, garden soil, and saltwater are mixtures. The makeup and properties of mixtures can vary. Air may contain more oxygen in one sample than another. Garden soil may be more sandy in one place than another. Saltwater may be made with varying amounts of salt and water.

Substance

A kind of matter with a definite makeup and definite chemical and physical properties; an element or a compound

Mixture

Two or more substances mixed together; the properties of each substance are not affected by mixing

Heterogeneous Mixtures

Mixtures can be described as either heterogeneous or homogeneous. The substances in a **heterogeneous mixture** are not evenly mixed. In one part of the mixture, there may be more of one substance than in another part. Often, the different substances in such a mixture can be seen. You can "pick out" the substances in a heterogeneous mixture, even if you have to use a microscope.

Three examples of heterogeneous mixtures are beach sand, a taco salad, and oil and water. Up close, beach sand consists of different kinds of particles. These particles are not evenly mixed along the beach. If you had the time and patience, you could separate these particles in a sample. You can easily see the ingredients that make up a taco salad. One serving of the salad will likely have different ingredient amounts than another serving. You can see how oil and water separate after they are shaken in a jar. In this mixture, the oil and water are hardly mixed at all—they are certainly not evenly mixed.

Homogeneous Mixtures: Solutions

The substances in a **homogeneous mixture** cannot be seen by looking at the mixture. This is because the substances are evenly mixed throughout. All parts of a homogeneous mixture have the same makeup. An example of such a mixture is a teaspoon of sugar stirred into a cup of hot water. Even with a microscope, the sugar could not be seen in the mixture. You could not pick out or filter out the sugar. Other examples of homogeneous mixtures are maple syrup and stainless steel. Compare the mixtures shown in Figure 2.2.2.

Figure 2.2.2 *Orange juice is a heterogeneous mixture. The pulp in the juice settles to the bottom of the glass. Brass and maple syrup are homogeneous mixtures.*

Homogeneous mixtures are also called **solutions.** A solution contains a **solvent** and one or more **solutes.** The solvent is the substance that the solute is dissolved in. The solvent is usually the substance present in the greatest amount. A solute is a substance that dissolves in a solvent to make the solution. In the sugar-and-water example, the water is the solvent. The sugar is the solute. The process of dissolving is not a chemical change, but a physical change. This is because a solvent and solute do not chemically combine. Their individual properties are not affected, even though they are evenly mixed. **Aqueous solutions** are solutions in which the solvent is water. There are other solvents besides water. Solutes and solvents can be solids, liquids, or gases. You are familiar with many kinds of solutions. Table 2.2.1 lists some examples. In some solutions, one state of matter is dissolved in another state of matter.

Table 2.2.1 Examples of Solutions		
Solution	Solute	Solvent
air	oxygen, carbon dioxide, other gases	nitrogen (gas)
rubbing alcohol	isopropyl alcohol (liquid)	water (liquid)
saltwater	salt (solid)	water (liquid)
brass	zinc (solid)	copper (solid)
stainless steel	chromium, nickel (solids)	iron (solid)

As the table shows, brass is a solution of zinc dissolved in copper. Brass is an example of an **alloy.** An alloy is a solid solution containing metals. Steel is a term that describes a variety of iron alloys. The iron in steel might be mixed with chromium, nickel, carbon, manganese, or molybdenum. Sterling silver is an alloy of silver and copper. The gold used in jewelry is mixed with copper and silver. Pure gold is soft and can be bent easily. An alloy of copper, silver, and gold is much stronger.

Separating Mixtures

As shown in Figure 2.2.1 on page 56, mixing substances to create a mixture involves only physical changes. No chemical changes occur when a mixture is made. Likewise, separating a mixture into its substances involves only physical changes. In other words, without any chemical changes, a mixture can be separated.

Suppose you want to separate a heterogeneous mixture of iron filings and salt. Iron is magnetic. Iron filings can be collected on a magnet, but salt cannot. You could use these physical properties to separate the mixture. Another way to separate this mixture uses water. The ability to dissolve in water is a physical property of salt, but not iron filings. If the mixture were stirred in warm water, only the salt would dissolve. The iron could then be filtered out—or the salt solution could be poured off. The substances in a mixture do not change chemically during separation.

✽ ✽

Technology and Society

The properties of an alloy are different from the properties of the individual metals. For example, aluminum is lightweight, but weak. Aluminum alloys contain small amounts of other metals. They can be as strong as steel, but three times as light. Because of these properties, aluminum alloys are used to build aircraft. Gold is a very soft metal. Gold alloys are harder and stronger. These alloys may contain copper, silver, nickel, palladium, or zinc. Gold alloys are used in jewelry. The amount of gold in jewelry is described in terms of karats. 18-karat gold is an alloy containing 75% gold. 14-karat gold contains 58% gold.

Consumer Choices: Which Water to Drink?

The water you drink is a mixture. It may contain tiny amounts of solid material, dissolved minerals, and dissolved gases. Dissolved oxygen gas makes water taste better. Some dissolved minerals make water taste worse. Tap water is the water out of a faucet. It usually comes from a city water system or a well. City water systems treat water to make it safe and improve its taste. Still, some people prefer bottled water.

There are many types of bottled water. Filtered water is tap water that has been passed through a filter to remove solids. Spring water is usually bottled directly from a natural water source. Water containing enough carbon dioxide gas to fizz slightly is called sparkling water. Water containing large amounts of dissolved minerals is called mineral water. Many people consider mineral water to be a healthy drink. Deionized, demineralized,

and distilled waters have been treated to remove dissolved substances. The processing, bottling, and shipping of water is expensive. A bottle of water might cost a thousand times more than a glass of tap water!

1. How is filtered water different from tap water?

2. What produces sparkling water?

3. What type of water do you drink? Why?

Technology and Society

Chemists use chromatography to separate and identify parts of a mixture. Inks, dyes, paints, blood, and DNA are mixtures. When a colored mixture is separated, areas of different colors are produced. This colored pattern is unique for that mixture. Patterns of different mixtures can be compared. Crime investigators use chromatography to identify evidence such as blood and DNA. DNA chromatography can determine if two people belong to the same family.

Word Bank

aqueous

heterogeneous

homogeneous

solute

solvent

substance

On a sheet of paper, write the word from the Word Bank that completes each sentence.

1. One sample of a(n) _____ has the same makeup and properties as another sample.

2. A solution is a mixture of a solute and a(n) _____.

3. In a(n) _____ solution, the solvent is water.

4. In a(n) _____ mixture, the substances are not evenly mixed.

5. If you dissolve some salt in a glass of water, the salt would be called the _____.

6. In a(n) _____ mixture, the substances are evenly mixed.

Critical Thinking

On a sheet of paper, write the answer to each question.

7. What is the difference between a mixture and a substance?

8. What is the difference between a heterogeneous mixture and a solution?

9. A chemist mixes two substances and later separates them. Did the substances change chemically? Explain.

10. Ten samples of ocean water are taken from different places. Each sample contains a different amount of salt and tiny living things. Because of this, the samples have slightly different properties. Is ocean water a substance, a heterogeneous mixture, or a solution? Explain.

Research and Write

People often use the word *chemical* to refer to harmful materials. Do research to find out what a chemical really is. Give some examples of chemicals. What materials are not chemicals? What vocabulary word from this lesson has the same meaning as *chemical*?

INVESTIGATION 2

Materials

- safety goggles
- lab coat or apron
- pencil
- ruler
- 10 cm × 10 cm piece of filter paper
- pen or marker with black water-soluble ink
- pen or marker with another color of water-soluble ink
- clear pint jar
- ethanol-water mixture
- watch glass or glass plate

One Substance or a Mixture?

Using a process called paper chromatography, a mixture on a piece of paper can be separated. A solvent moves from one end of the paper to the other, causing different substances in the mixture to travel different distances. Does the ink in a pen or marker consist of one substance or a mixture? In this investigation, you will use paper chromatography to find out.

Procedure

1. Put on safety goggles and a lab coat or apron.

2. Make a very light pencil line about 3 cm from one edge of the filter paper. Fold the paper and the pencil line in half, as shown. Unfold the paper.

3. Place a very small dot of black ink on the left side of the pencil line, as shown. Use the other pen or marker to place a small ink dot on the right side of the line.

4. Pour about 1 cm of the ethanol-water mixture into the jar. Fold the paper along the fold line. Carefully lower it into the jar so it stands upright.

5. Gently place the watch glass or glass plate over the jar to seal it. **Safety Alert: Handle glass with care. Report any broken or chipped glass to your teacher immediately.**

6. Observe what happens as the solvent soaks upward through the paper.

7. When the solvent reaches 1 cm from the top, remove the paper. Let it dry.

8. Record your observations. Describe what happened in step 6. Describe the appearance of the dried filter paper.

Cleanup/Disposal

Pour the solvent down the drain with plenty of running water. Rinse the jar with clean water, and return all materials. Wash your hands. Keep the filter paper with your written observations.

Analysis

1. Compare the chromatography results of the two inks on your filter paper.

2. How does your filter paper compare with the results of your classmates?

Conclusions

1. Was the black ink a single substance or a mixture? Explain.

2. Was the other ink a single substance or a mixture? Explain.

3. What can you conclude about the composition of these water-soluble inks?

Explore Further

Use paper chromatography to analyze the colored shells of chocolate candies. Find out if they are mixtures. Use a 0.1% salt solution as a solvent. Use toothpicks dipped in water to dissolve and remove a tiny piece of colored shell from several candies of different colors.

Objectives

After reading this lesson, you should be able to

◆ identify the particles in an atom

◆ recognize elements and their symbols

◆ locate metals and nonmetals on the periodic table

◆ explain what a subscript means when it follows a chemical symbol

As you learned in Lesson 2, a substance is not a mixture. A substance has a definite composition and definite properties. A substance can be either an element or a compound, as shown in Figure 2.2.1 on page 56. All of the matter around you consists of elements, compounds, or mixtures of these. In this lesson, you will learn about elements. In Lesson 4, you will learn about compounds.

Atoms

All matter is made of tiny particles called atoms. Atoms are made of even smaller particles: **protons, neutrons,** and **electrons,** as shown in Figure 2.3.1. Protons have a positive **charge,** and electrons have a negative charge. A charge is a certain amount of electricity. Neutrons have no charge, which means they are neutral. Protons and neutrons are packed together in a very tiny **nucleus,** which is the atom's center. Electrons move around the nucleus in a much bigger space.

Proton

A particle with a positive charge in the nucleus of an atom

Neutron

A particle with no charge in the nucleus of an atom

Electron

A particle with a negative charge in an atom

Charge

A certain amount of electricity

Nucleus

The center of an atom; consists of neutrons and protons

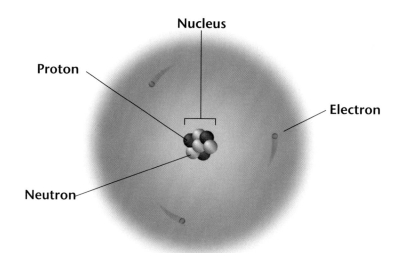

Figure 2.3.1 *A lithium atom has 4 neutrons and 3 protons in its nucleus. Outside the nucleus are 3 electrons.*

Link to ➤➤➤

Math

A positive number and a negative number with the same absolute value add up to zero: $(+8) + (-8) = 0$. In a similar way, an equal number of electrons and protons in an atom create a neutral atom—an atom with a charge of zero.

When atoms bond, or combine chemically, electrons are always involved. Sometimes two atoms share electrons. Sometimes an atom gives one or more electrons to another atom. A **chemical bond** forms when two atoms share or transfer electrons.

When a neutral atom is not bonded with other atoms, it has the same number of electrons as protons. For example, a lithium atom has 3 electrons, 3 protons, and 4 neutrons. The electrons each have a negative charge. The protons each have a positive charge. The atom, however, is neutral. This is because the positive and negative charges cancel each other out. In later chapters, you will learn more about the structure of atoms and how they bond.

Elements

Elements are substances made of only one kind of atom. They are the simplest forms of matter. Oxygen and calcium are two elements. What makes an oxygen atom different from a calcium atom? It is the number of protons in the atom. Any atom with 8 protons is an oxygen atom. Any atom with 20 protons is a calcium atom. The number of protons in an atom is called the **atomic number.** Every element has a unique atomic number. The atomic number for oxygen is 8. The atomic number for calcium is 20.

In a sample of calcium, each atom has 20 protons. A calcium atom is the smallest particle that has the unique properties of calcium. In general, an **atom** is the smallest particle of an element that has the properties of that element.

There are at least 111 officially named elements. About 90 of these exist naturally on the earth. You know the names of many of them: iron, tin, helium, and sodium, just to name a few. Almost all of the matter in the universe is made of just 90 kinds of atoms. This is like a language: all of the words you use are made from just 26 letters. Each element has a **chemical symbol,** such as S for sulfur, Ca for calcium, and C for carbon. These symbols consist of one or two letters. The first letter is always capitalized.

The Periodic Table of Elements

Perhaps you have seen a chart hanging in your classroom called the **periodic table** of elements. This table is shown on pages 68 and 69 (Figure 2.3.2). It is also printed on the inside back cover of this book. The periodic table gives the names and symbols of every element. The elements are placed in order by atomic number. The table also organizes the elements by their electron arrangement. You will use the periodic table more than any other tool in chemistry. It contains a great deal of information. Chapter 11 will explain how the periodic table is organized and used.

The periodic table has two main sections: **metals** and **nonmetals.** These sections are separated by a "staircase." The staircase begins on the left side of boron (B) and ends on the left side of astatine (At). Elements on the left side of the staircase are metals. They are shown in green. Metals are usually shiny solids that can conduct, or transfer, heat and electricity. Elements on the right side of the staircase are nonmetals. They are shown in blue. Nonmetals are usually gases or dull solids that do not conduct heat or electricity well. By looking at the periodic table, you can see that oxygen (O), helium (He), and carbon (C) are nonmetals. Hydrogen (H) is also a nonmetal, even though it is in the left corner of the table. Most of the elements that touch the staircase on either side are **semimetals.** Semimetals, also called metalloids, are shown in red. They have some properties of both metals and nonmetals. The exception is aluminum (Al)—it is definitely a metal. Are most elements metals, nonmetals, or semimetals?

You may have noticed some strange chemical symbols in the periodic table. Most symbols match the name of the element, such as I for iodine and Si for silicon. However, some symbols seem to make no sense at all, at least in English. The symbols for mercury (Hg) and sodium (Na) do not use any letters from the element's name. That is because these symbols are based on Latin names. Mercury is *hydrargyrum* in Latin, and sodium is *natrium.* What other chemical symbols are not based on English names?

He

O_2

P_4

Figure 2.3.3
Helium is monatomic, oxygen is diatomic, and phosphorus is polyatomic.

You may have also noticed that some elements at the bottom of the table are named after famous people or places. Where do you think the names *einsteinium* and *californium* came from? These and other elements with symbols shown in white type do not occur naturally.

If you have trouble locating an element on the table, consult the Alphabetical Table of Elements found in Appendix A. For example, if you can't find osmium on the periodic table, look for it in the alphabetical table. This list gives its atomic number: 76. Use this number to locate osmium on the periodic table.

Forms of Elements

Elements can be classified as metals, semimetals, or nonmetals. They can be classified by other properties, too. You know that all of the atoms in a piece of tin are tin atoms. Tin atoms exist individually, or as single atoms. All of the atoms in oxygen gas are oxygen atoms. However, oxygen atoms exist in pairs, or groups of two. The two oxygen atoms of each pair are bonded together. The natural form of an element—as single atoms or as groups of bonded atoms—is a physical property.

Elemental form is used to classify elements into three categories. Most elements are **monatomic,** like tin. When atoms of these elements are not bonded with other kinds of atoms, they exist as single atoms. Seven elements are **diatomic.** They are hydrogen, nitrogen, oxygen, fluorine, chlorine, bromine, and iodine. When atoms of these elements are not bonded with other kinds of atoms, they exist as bonded pairs. A few elements are **polyatomic.** They can exist as groups of 3 or more identical atoms that are bonded together.

The symbol of an element indicates when atoms are in pairs or groups. For example, the symbol Br_2 shows that bromine is diatomic. The small 2 written below the line and to the right of Br is a **subscript.** It tells the number of atoms of that element. Br_2 means 2 bonded Br atoms. Sulfur is polyatomic. It can exist in groups of 8 atoms. This form of sulfur has the symbol S_8. To show monatomic atoms, no subscript is used. Figure 2.3.3 shows models of some atoms in their elemental form.

The Periodic Table of Elements

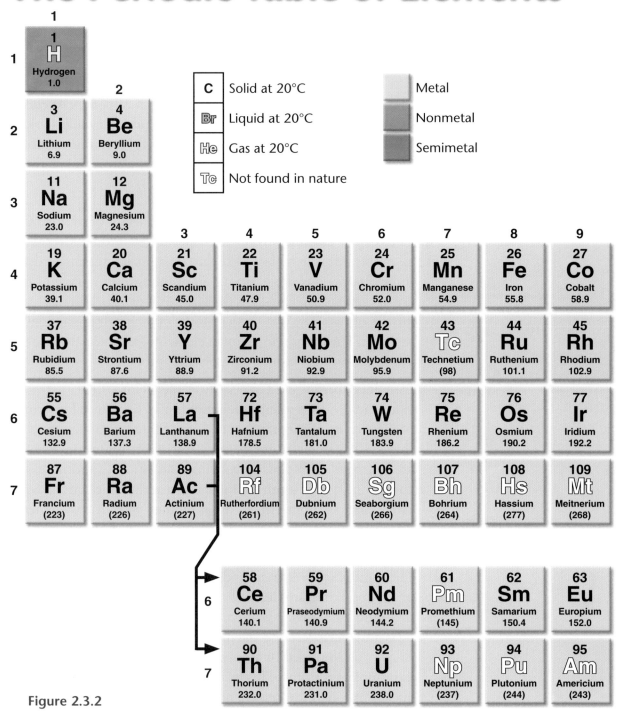

	Solid at 20°C
C	Solid at 20°C
Br	Liquid at 20°C
He	Gas at 20°C
Tc	Not found in nature

Metal
Nonmetal
Semimetal

Figure 2.3.2

Periodic table (partial)

Labels pointing to Boron cell:
- Atomic number
- Element symbol
- Element name
- Atomic mass

18
2 **He** Helium 4.0

13	14	15	16	17	
5 **B** Boron 10.8	6 **C** Carbon 12.0	7 **N** Nitrogen 14.0	8 **O** Oxygen 16.0	9 **F** Fluorine 19.0	10 **Ne** Neon 20.2
13 **Al** Aluminum 27.0	14 **Si** Silicon 28.1	15 **P** Phosphorus 31.0	16 **S** Sulfur 32.1	17 **Cl** Chlorine 35.5	18 **Ar** Argon 39.9

10	11	12					
28 **Ni** Nickel 58.7	29 **Cu** Copper 63.5	30 **Zn** Zinc 65.4	31 **Ga** Gallium 69.7	32 **Ge** Germanium 72.6	33 **As** Arsenic 74.9	34 **Se** Selenium 79.0	35 **Br** Bromine 79.9	36 **Kr** Krypton 83.8
46 **Pd** Palladium 106.4	47 **Ag** Silver 107.9	48 **Cd** Cadmium 112.4	49 **In** Indium 114.8	50 **Sn** Tin 118.7	51 **Sb** Antimony 121.8	52 **Te** Tellurium 127.6	53 **I** Iodine 126.9	54 **Xe** Xenon 131.3
78 **Pt** Platinum 195.1	79 **Au** Gold 197.0	80 **Hg** Mercury 200.6	81 **Tl** Thallium 204.4	82 **Pb** Lead 207.2	83 **Bi** Bismuth 209.0	84 **Po** Polonium (209)	85 **At** Astatine (210)	86 **Rn** Radon (222)
110 **Ds** Darmstadtium (281)	111 **Rg** Roentgenium (272)	112 **Uub*** Ununbium (285)	113 **Uut*** Ununtrium (284)	114 **Uuq*** Ununquadium (289)	115 **Uup*** Ununpentium (288)	116 **Uuh*** Ununhexium		

*Official name and symbol have not been assigned.

64 **Gd** Gadolinium 157.3	65 **Tb** Terbium 158.9	66 **Dy** Dysprosium 162.5	67 **Ho** Holmium 164.9	68 **Er** Erbium 167.3	69 **Tm** Thulium 168.9	70 **Yb** Ytterbium 173.0	71 **Lu** Lutetium 175.0
96 **Cm** Curium (247)	97 **Bk** Berkelium (247)	98 **Cf** Californium (251)	99 **Es** Einsteinium (252)	100 **Fm** Fermium (257)	101 **Md** Mendelevium (258)	102 **No** Nobelium (259)	103 **Lr** Lawrencium (262)

Note: Atomic mass values are in atomic mass units (amu). Most atomic masses are averages based on the element's isotopes. They are rounded to the tenths place. An atomic mass in parentheses is the mass of the element's most stable isotope.

Science at Work

Forensic Examiner

Forensic examiners use science to identify evidence. They often examine tiny pieces of evidence called trace evidence. At a crime scene, trace evidence might include a drop of blood, a strand of hair, or a piece of glass. The forensic examiner applies a variety of tests to this evidence. Tests may involve matching colors, testing DNA, using chromatography to separate a mixture, or finding the density of a material. Some tests may destroy the trace evidence, while others may not.

Forensic examiners usually have a four-year degree in physics, biology, or chemistry. They do not always work with crime evidence. Some work to improve the reliability of consumer products.

Others analyze failed equipment or technology to determine what went wrong.

2
He
Helium
4.0

Spotlight on Helium

Helium is a nonmetal that is present in all stars. It is the second most abundant element in the universe after hydrogen. It is also the second lightest element after hydrogen. The chemical properties of helium made its discovery difficult. Helium is a monatomic gas that does not form any chemical compounds. Helium was first discovered as a substance in the sun. Later, small amounts of helium were found trapped in rocks. Most of the helium in the earth is mixed with natural gas.

A helium environment is created for certain types of welding and for producing electronic circuits. Deep-sea divers breathe a mixture of helium and oxygen. The mixture used depends on the depth of the dive. In hospitals, liquid helium is used to cool the magnets in machines that create images called MRIs.

Interesting Fact: Helium is used in balloons and blimps.

Lesson 3   R E V I E W

Word Bank

atom
electrons
elements
metal
nonmetal
protons

On a sheet of paper, write the word from the Word Bank that completes each sentence.

1. An element is made of only one kind of _____.

2. An element is a gas at 20°C. It is probably a(n) _____.

3. An element on the left side of the periodic table is probably a(n) _____.

4. Particles in an atom that are involved in bonding are _____.

5. Atomic number is the number of _____ in an atom.

6. The periodic table lists all of the _____ and their symbols.

Critical Thinking

On a sheet of paper, write the answer to each question.

7. What does the 2 in the symbol Cl_2 mean?

8. How is an atom different from an element?

9. From the periodic table, what do you know about chromium?

10. What identifies an atom as an iron atom?

Research and Write

Some elements on the periodic table have three-letter symbols. They appear at the right end of row 7. These are the most recently discovered elements. Find out more about these elements, their names, and their symbols. Write a paragraph about these elements.

The last category of matter to study is compounds. Both elements and compounds are substances with a definite makeup and definite properties. Elements consist of only one kind of atom. The atoms of elements can be bonded or physically mixed in endless ways. **Compounds** consist of two or more kinds of atoms that are bonded. Mixtures also consist of two or more kinds of atoms, but not all atoms in a mixture are bonded. Figure 2.4.1 compares elements, compounds, and mixtures. Compounds are substances, like elements. Compounds contain two or more kinds of atoms, like mixtures.

The atoms of the 90 natural elements bond to form many compounds. Water, table salt, and baking soda are examples of compounds.

Chemical Formulas

A **chemical formula** is used to represent a compound. A chemical formula is a group of symbols that shows the number and kinds of atoms in a compound. For example, table salt is NaCl, water is H_2O, and baking soda is $NaHCO_3$. A formula shows the definite makeup of the compound. Because mixtures do not have a definite makeup, they do not have formulas.

Compound

A substance that consists of two or more kinds of atoms that are bonded

Chemical formula

A group of symbols that shows the number and kinds of atoms in a compound

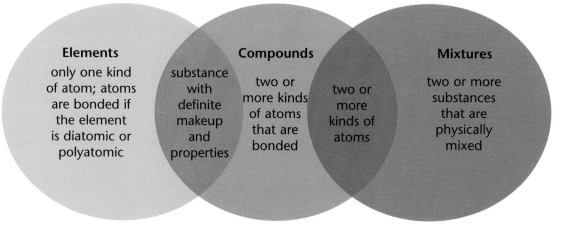

Elements	Compounds	Mixtures
only one kind of atom; atoms are bonded if the element is diatomic or polyatomic	substance with definite makeup and properties / two or more kinds of atoms that are bonded / two or more kinds of atoms	two or more substances that are physically mixed

Figure 2.4.1 *Both elements and compounds have a definite makeup and definite properties.*

Chemical formulas are an easy, short way to refer to compounds. It is much faster to write CO_2 than *carbon dioxide.*

In the formula for a compound, each element is indicated by its symbol. NaCl is made of only sodium (Na) and chlorine (Cl) atoms. A subscript to the right of a symbol tells how many atoms of that element are in the smallest unit of the compound. The formula for water, H_2O, has a subscript in it. The number 2 means there are 2 atoms of hydrogen (H) in the smallest unit of water. If there is no subscript to the right of an element's symbol, it means there is 1 atom of that element. A subscript of 1 is assumed and not written. The smallest unit of H_2O has 2 H atoms and 1 O atom. The smallest unit of NaCl has 1 Na atom and 1 Cl atom. Now look at the formula for baking soda.

$NaHCO_3$ 1 Na atom + 1 H atom + 1 C atom + 3 O atoms

The smallest unit of baking soda, $NaHCO_3$, contains 6 atoms.

Example 1	Give the name and number of each kind of atom in the formula for sucrose, $C_{12}H_{22}O_{11}$. Sucrose is table sugar.
Read	You are given the chemical formula for a compound named sucrose. The formula contains three chemical symbols: C, H, and O. Each symbol has a subscript to the right of it.
Plan	Each symbol represents an element, as shown in the periodic table. A subscript in a formula tells the number of atoms in the smallest unit of the compound.
Solve	According to its formula, $C_{12}H_{22}O_{11}$, the smallest unit of sucrose has 12 C atoms + 22 H atoms + 11 O atoms.
Reflect	The smallest unit of table sugar has 45 atoms.
Practice	Give the name and number of each kind of atom in the chemical formula for aluminum chloride, $AlCl_3$.

Some formulas contain parentheses, as in $Mg(NO_3)_2$ for magnesium nitrate. A subscript after a set of parentheses applies to everything in the parentheses. The subscript 2 means there are two (NO_3) groups. To find out how many atoms of nitrogen (N) and oxygen (O) are present, you multiply the subscript outside the parentheses by each subscript inside, like this:

$$Mg(NO_3)_2 = 1 \text{ Mg atom} + 2(1 \text{ N atom}) + 2(3 \text{ O atoms})$$
$$= 1 \text{ Mg atom} + 2 \text{ N atoms} + 6 \text{ O atoms}$$

Example 2	Give the name and number of each kind of atom in the chemical formula for ammonium carbonate, $(NH_4)_2CO_3$.
Read	This formula contains four chemical symbols: N, H, C, and O. There is one set of parentheses with a subscript outside it: $(NH_4)_2$. This means that there are two groups of (NH_4).
Plan	The subscript 4 is related only to the H. The subscript 3 is related only to the O. There is no subscript after the N and the C, so a 1 is assumed in each case. However, the subscript 2 affects everything in the parentheses.
Solve	The smallest unit of ammonium carbonate has these atoms: $$(NH_4)_2CO_3 = 2(N) + 2(H_4) + C + O_3$$ $$= 2(1 \text{ N atom}) + 2(4 \text{ H atoms}) + 1 \text{ C atom} + 3 \text{ O atoms}$$ $$= 2 \text{ N atoms} + 8 \text{ H atoms} + 1 \text{ C atom} + 3 \text{ O atoms}$$
Reflect	The formula for ammonium carbonate has 14 atoms.
Practice	Give the name and number of each kind of atom in the chemical formula, $Ca_5(PO_4)_3F$.

Science Myth

Myth: Formulas for compounds are all fairly simple.

Fact: Some compounds consist of several elements and a large number of atoms. Many large compounds are found in living things. For example, the chemical formula for one form of hemoglobin has 9,512 atoms! Its formula is $C_{3,032}H_{4,816}O_{872}N_{780}S_8Fe_4$
Hemoglobin is a protein that carries oxygen in the bloodstream.

Separating Compounds

Recall that making mixtures and separating mixtures are physical changes. This is not true for compounds. As Figure 2.2.1 on page 56 shows, a chemical change occurs when two or more elements combine to form a compound. To separate a compound into its elements, the compound must be *chemically* changed. Forming and separating compounds require chemical reactions to occur.

From Lesson 1, you know that chemical reactions occur when one or more substances react, forming one or more new substances. The properties of the new substances are different. Because of this, the properties of a compound are different from the properties of the elements it contains. Salt, NaCl, is quite different from sodium metal or chlorine gas. Sodium metal explodes in water, and chlorine gas is poisonous and green! You will learn more about chemical reactions in Chapter 5.

★ ★

Achievements in Science

Chemical Formulas

By 1800, chemists needed a way to describe newly discovered elements and compounds. The first scientist to come up with a method to do this was John Dalton. Unlike many chemists of the time, Dalton thought matter was made of atoms. He believed atoms were extremely small, hard spheres, or balls, that did not have any parts. Dalton used circles to represent atoms in his drawings. He showed hydrogen as a circle with a dot in the center. Carbon was a filled-in circle. Oxygen was an empty circle. Dalton drew combinations of these circles to represent compounds.

Dalton's symbols were not very practical. A more useful system of symbols was developed by Jöns Jakob Berzelius. Berzelius used letters to represent elements. He used combinations of these letters to represent compounds. Numbers showed how many of an element's atoms were in a compound. This system is basically still used today. However, the numbers in Berzelius's formulas were superscripts. He would have written CO_2 as CO^2.

Word Bank

compound

element

mixture

On a sheet of paper, write the word from the Word Bank that completes each sentence.

1. A substance that contains two or more kinds of atoms is a(n) _____.

2. A(n) _____ contains two or more substances that are physically mixed.

3. A compound is different from a(n) _____ because a compound contains two or more kinds of atoms.

On a sheet of paper, write the letter of the answer that completes each sentence.

4. The formula H_2SO_4 shows _____ oxygen atoms.

A 1 **B** 2 **C** 4 **D** 7

5. The formula $(NH_4)_3PO_4$ shows _____ nitrogen atoms.

A 1 **B** 3 **C** 4 **D** 12

6. The formula $Zn(CN)_2$ shows _____ *kinds* of atoms.

A 2 **B** 3 **C** 4 **D** 5

Critical Thinking

On a sheet of paper, write the answer to each question.

7. In the formula $N(CH_3)_3$, the first 3 means 3 hydrogen atoms. What does the second 3 mean?

8. When a compound is formed or separated, what kinds of changes occur?

9. "The compound Ni_3S_2 should have properties similar to nickel (Ni)." Why is this statement false?

10. $CaBr_2$ is a compound, but Br_2 is not. Why?

Materials

- safety goggles
- lab coat or apron
- gloves
- bar magnet
- conductivity tester
- iron strip
- piece of solid sulfur
- small paper plate
- 4 self-sealing plastic bags, each containing one of the following:
  iron filings
  sulfur powder
  chunks of iron(II) sulfide
  mixture of powdered sulfur and iron filings

Comparing Elements and Compounds

Iron and sulfur can be stirred together to make a simple mixture. These two elements also can combine chemically to form the compound, iron(II) sulfide. How do the properties of a compound differ from the properties of its elements?

Procedure

1. Create a data table like the one shown at the bottom of the page.
2. Write a procedure to test the four kinds of matter for the properties listed in the table. Include safety alerts and at least one hypothesis. Use only the materials listed. Do not remove the iron filings, sulfur powder, or the mixture from their bags. The figure on the next page shows how to set up the conductivity test.
3. Have your procedure approved by your teacher.
4. Put on safety goggles, gloves, and a lab coat or apron.
5. Carry out your experiment. Record your observations and results in the table.

Sample of Matter	Bendable or Brittle?	Color and Appearance	Magnetic?	Conducts Electricity?	Metal or Nonmetal?
iron					
sulfur					
iron(II) sulfide					
mixture					

Continued on next page

Cleanup/Disposal

Return all materials. Clean your work area, and wash your hands.

Analysis

1. Compare the appearance and color of iron, sulfur, and iron(II) sulfide.

2. What evidence tells you if the elements are metals or nonmetals?

3. Are the properties of the mixture most like those of the elements or iron(II) sulfide? Explain.

4. What properties of iron(II) sulfide differ from the properties of either iron or sulfur?

Conclusions

1. Can iron and sulfur be broken down into simpler substances? Explain.

2. How could you show someone that a mixture of iron and sulfur is not the same as a compound of iron and sulfur?

3. What observations show that iron and sulfur atoms bond to form a new substance?

Explore Further

Suppose you have a solvent that will dissolve sulfur, but not iron. How could you use this solvent to separate an iron-sulfur mixture? How could you reclaim the solid sulfur after separating the mixture?

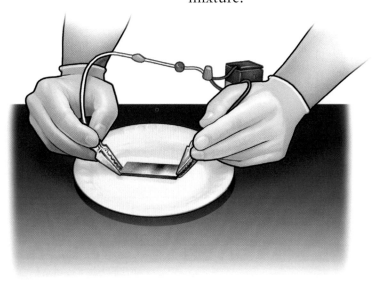

Safety Air Bags

Air bags are important safety devices in cars and other vehicles. They help protect passengers during high-speed collisions. Did you know that air bags rely on an explosion to work properly? Sensors in the car detect a collision and send a signal to the air bag. The air bag inflates, or fills, fast enough to cushion the passenger.

An air bag really should be called a nitrogen bag, since it is inflated with nitrogen gas, not air. The nitrogen gas is produced when a compound is exploded. This compound varies, but is often sodium azide, NaN_3. It is not the only substance in the airbag. Sodium azide is part of a mixture with two other substances.

When sodium azide explodes, it produces nitrogen gas, sodium metal, and heat. The heat helps to expand the nitrogen gas and inflate the air bag faster. Sodium metal can easily react with other substances, and this property makes it dangerous. That is why potassium nitrate, KNO_3, is also in the air bag mixture. The sodium metal and potassium nitrate react, forming more nitrogen gas and two compounds that are less dangerous. The third substance in the mixture is silicon dioxide, SiO_2. It is a type of sand.

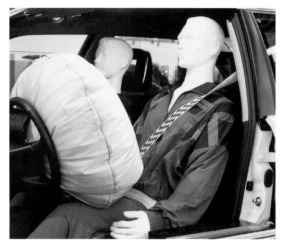

High temperatures melt the silicon dioxide into glass. The glass traps any remaining dangerous materials. All of these chemical reactions happen in a few hundredths of a second! The reactions depend on exact quantities of each substance in the air bag mixture. Scientists and engineers continue to improve the design and contents of air bags. These devices have already saved many lives.

1. Two elements are produced by the first explosive reaction. Which one is diatomic? Which is monatomic?

2. What is the purpose of the silicon dioxide? What might happen if not enough of this was in the mixture?

3. What might happen if too much sodium azide was in the mixture?

Chapter 2 S U M M A R Y

- Matter can be described by physical and chemical properties.

- Matter can change physically and chemically. Chemical changes produce a new substance with new properties. Both chemical and physical changes involve a change in energy.

- All matter can be classified as either mixtures or substances. Substances are either elements or compounds.

- Mixtures contain two or more substances that are physically combined.

- Heterogeneous mixtures are not mixed evenly. Homogeneous mixtures, also called solutions, are mixed evenly. A solution is made of one or more solutes dissolved in a solvent.

- All matter is made of atoms. Atoms are made of electrons, protons, and neutrons.

- Elements are made of only one kind of atom. Each element has a unique chemical symbol and a unique atomic number.

- The periodic table lists all elements. Most elements are metals. Most elements are monatomic.

- Compounds are made of two or more kinds of atoms. The atoms in a compound are bonded.

- A compound is represented by a chemical formula. The formula shows the number and kind of atoms in the smallest unit of the compound.

Vocabulary

alloy, 58	chemical symbol, 65	liquid, 50	polyatomic, 67
aqueous solution, 58	compound, 72	metal, 66	proton, 64
atom, 65	diatomic, 67	mixture, 56	semimetal, 66
atomic number, 65	electron, 64	monatomic, 67	solid, 50
charge, 64	element, 65	neutron, 64	solute, 58
chemical bond, 65	energy, 53	nonmetal, 66	solution, 58
chemical change, 52	gas, 51	nucleus, 64	solvent, 58
chemical formula, 72	heterogeneous mixture, 57	periodic table, 66	state, 50
chemical property, 51		physical change, 52	subscript, 67
chemical reaction, 52	homogeneous mixture, 57	physical property, 50	substance, 56

Chapter 2 R E V I E W

Vocabulary Review

For each set, match a term in the first column with an example in the second column. On a sheet of paper, write the letter of the answer.

Set A

1. heterogeneous mixture
2. solution
3. physical property
4. chemical property
5. physical change

A density
B ability to burn
C saltwater
D vegetable soup
E ice melting

Set B

6. polyatomic element
7. state
8. chemical formula
9. diatomic element
10. chemical change

A Cl_2
B magnesium reacting with water
C $CaCl_2$
D solid, liquid, or gas
E S_8

Set C

11. metal
12. nonmetal
13. mixture
14. solvent
15. solute

A the water in a bleach solution
B soil or a solution
C aluminum
D the sugar in hot tea
E helium

Continued on next page

Concept Review

On a sheet of paper, write the letter of the answer that completes each sentence.

16. A substance that contains two or more kinds of atoms is _____.

    A an element **B** a solution **C** a mixture **D** a compound

17. An element's atomic number tells the number of _____ in its atoms.

    A electron   **B** neutrons **C** protons   **D** subscripts

18. Changes in energy occur _____.

    A only during chemical reactions
    B when physical or chemical changes occur
    C only during changes of state
    D when mass is created or destroyed

19. The solvent in an aqueous solution containing dissolved KCl is _____.

    A KCl   **B** water   **C** potassium **D** Cl_2

Problem Solving

20. What is the chemical symbol for gold?

21. Give the number and kind of each atom in the formula, $FeCl_2$.

22. How many atoms of oxygen are in the formula, $Pb(C_2H_3O_2)_4$?

Critical Thinking

Read the following paragraph. On a sheet of paper, write the answer to each question.

Mercury is a metal. It is a shiny, silvery liquid at room temperature. Its atomic number is 80. It forms tiny balls of liquid when spilled. Mercury reacts with oxygen. It is poisonous to humans. Mercury is very dense for a liquid—its density is 13.2 g/mL. Mercury forms a heterogeneous mixture with water.

23. What is one chemical property of mercury?

24. What are two physical properties of mercury?

25. What does *heterogeneous mixture* mean in the last sentence?

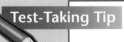

Test-Taking Tip Be sure you understand what a test question is asking. Read it twice if necessary.

3

Formulas and Names of Compounds

Deep underground, chemical and physical processes formed these cave decorations in Carlsbad Caverns, New Mexico. When groundwater seeps through limestone rock, the compound calcium carbonate dissolves in the water. Inside a cave, the water gives up the dissolved calcium carbonate through various processes. The compound is deposited as a solid, creating these unusual and eerie structures. In Chapter 3, you will learn about compounds and their names and formulas.

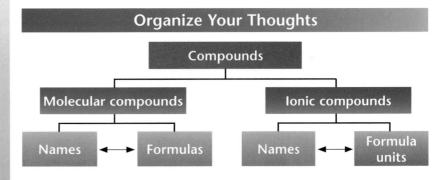

Goals for Learning

◆ To write a formula for a binary molecular compound

◆ To identify the anion and cation of an ionic compound

◆ To identify the charge and symbol of an ion

◆ To write the formula unit of a ionic compound

◆ To understand and recognize polyatomic ions

◆ To name a compound, given its formula or formula unit

Objectives

After reading this lesson, you should be able to

◆ define a molecular compound

◆ give the meaning of prefixes in molecular compound names

◆ write the formula for a binary molecular compound, given its name

In Chapter 2, you learned about two types of substances: elements and compounds. All compounds contain atoms of two or more elements that are bonded. There are two types of compounds: molecular compounds and ionic compounds. Their properties are different because their atoms are bonded in different ways. In this lesson, you will learn about molecular compounds and their formulas. **Molecular compounds** contain atoms of two or more elements that are bonded together by sharing electrons. Examples are CO_2, H_2O, and CCl_4. These are chemical formulas of molecular compounds.

Chemists use certain rules for naming compounds and writing formulas. Because of this, the name of a compound gives clues about its formula. For example, compound names that end in *-ide* are usually **binary.** Binary compounds contain only two elements (only two kinds of atoms). Silicon diox*ide* (SiO_2) is a binary compound shown in Figure 3.1.1. Compound names that end in *-ate* or *-ite* usually contain three or more elements. This lesson focuses on binary molecular compounds.

Molecular compound

A compound containing atoms of two or more elements that are bonded together by sharing electrons

Binary

Containing two elements

Figure 3.1.1 *Silicon dioxide, SiO_2, is a molecular compound. It is also a mineral called quartz (left). Quartz is found in nearly every type of rock. Most sand grains (center) are bits of quartz. Glass is made from sand.*

In chemistry, each prefix below means a certain number of atoms.

mono-	1
di-	2
tri-	3
tetra-	4
penta-	5
hexa-	6
hepta-	7
octa-	8
nona-	9
deca-	10

Binary molecular compounds consist of two elements.

silicon dioxide: silicon + oxygen
dihydrogen sulfide: hydrogen + sulfur

Each name is made of two words. The words are based on the names of the two elements. The second element's name is changed so it ends in -ide. Both names also contain the prefix di-. Prefixes in names of molecular compounds do the same job as subscripts in formulas. They tell the number of atoms of each element. The prefix di- means "two." In the smallest unit of silicon dioxide, SiO_2, there are 2 O atoms. In dihydrogen sulfide, H_2S, there are 2 H atoms. Besides di-, other prefixes are used in naming molecular compounds.

The prefix mono- is not written with the first element's name, but it is understood to be there. If an element is named with no prefix, you can assume there is only 1 atom of that element in the formula. Carbon monoxide is CO, while carbon dioxide is CO_2. The prefixes mono- and di- tell you how many atoms of oxygen are in each formula. There is no prefix in front of carbon in either name, so you can assume 1 carbon atom.

▼◄▲▼◄▲▼◄▲▼◄▲▼◄▲▼◄▲▼◄▲▼◄▲▼◄▲▼◄▲▼◄▲▼◄▲▼◄▲▼◄▲▼◄▲▼

Science at Work

Chemical Indexer

Chemical Abstracts Service (CAS) is a major distributor of scientific information. Every compound known to exist is named by CAS and given an index number. Indexers who work for CAS are chemists. Their job is to study the results of research and accurately name any new chemical compound. A chemical name must describe the composition and structure of the compound precisely. For example, the chemical name of vitamin A is 3,7-dimethyl-9-(2,6,6-trimethyl-1-cyclohexen-1-yl)-2,4,6,8-nonatetraen-1-ol. An experienced chemist can draw the exact structure of vitamin A by looking at this name.

Indexers at CAS have a bachelor's degree in chemistry. They also receive special training at CAS. They must be able to understand research papers and analyze complex chemical structures. Many jobs at CAS require a doctoral degree in chemistry.

If you know the name of a binary molecular compound, you can often write its formula. Suppose you are given the name *carbon tetrachloride.*

1. Write the chemical symbol for each element mentioned— in the order given in the name. Look at the periodic table for element names and symbols. For carbon tetrachloride, the chemical symbols are C and Cl.

2. Add subscripts according to prefixes in the name. A subscript goes on the right side of its symbol. When there is no prefix or the prefix is *mono-*, do not write any subscript. Carbon tetrachloride contains the prefix *tetra-*, meaning 4 atoms. Add a 4 subscript to the right of Cl. The formula becomes CCl_4.

Example 1	Write the chemical formula for each molecular compound. sulfur hexafluoride tetraphosphorus decoxide dinitrogen monoxide
Read	Each name is based on two element names and contains one or two prefixes.
Plan	Look up the chemical symbol of each element in the periodic table. Look up the meaning of each prefix on page 87.
Solve	Write the symbol for each element in the order given in the name. Then add subscripts to the formula based on the prefixes. Place each subscript to the right of the symbol. A subscript of 1 is not written. sulfur hexafluoride $\qquad$ SF_6 tetraphosphorus decoxide $\quad$ P_4O_{10} dinitrogen monoxide $\qquad$ N_2O
Reflect	In sulfur hexafluoride, there is no prefix on sulfur. This is because *mono-* is not written when there is 1 atom of the first element.
Practice	Write the formula for the molecular compound, phosphorus pentachloride.

Molecule

A neutral group of two or more atoms that are bonded together by sharing electrons; the smallest unit of a molecular compound

Research and Write

The elements in a molecular compound are written in a certain order. For example, you write *dinitrogen monoxide* (N_2O), not *oxygen dinitride* (ON_2). Why is nitrogen given first? Find out what rule is used to decide the order of elements in molecular compounds. Write a summary of this rule. Include a few examples and any exceptions.

The formula of a compound shows the atoms in the smallest unit of the compound. The smallest unit of a molecular compound is a **molecule.** For example, one molecule of carbon tetrachloride, CCl_4, is a group of 5 atoms: 1 carbon atom and 4 chlorine atoms. In general, a molecule is a neutral group of atoms that are bonded together by sharing electrons. The atoms in a molecule may be of the same element (such as Cl_2) or different elements (such as CCl_4). In a molecule of Cl_2, there are 2 chlorine atoms. A sample of Cl_2 is not a molecular compound, however. Why? A compound contains two or more elements. There is only one element in Cl_2.

Express Lab 3

Materials
- safety goggles
- lab coat or apron
- stoppered test tube of dihydrogen monoxide
- sucrose (table sugar)
- spatula

Procedure

1. Put on safety goggles and a lab coat or apron.

2. Observe the appearance of dihydrogen monoxide. It is a molecular compound.

3. Remove the stopper from the test tube. Use your hand to sweep, or waft, the vapors from the compound toward your nose. Describe its odor. **Safety Alert: Do not directly smell any substance.**

4. Using the spatula, add a small amount of sucrose to the test tube. Replace the stopper, shake, and record what happens to the sugar.

Analysis

1. In the name *dihydrogen monoxide,* the prefix *di-* means "two." The prefix *mono-* means "one." Use the prefixes and element names to write the formula for this compound.

2. What is the common name for dihydrogen monoxide?

On a sheet of paper, write the letter of the answer that completes each sentence.

1. A compound name that ends in *-ide* usually contains _____ elements.

    A metal   **B** diatomic   **C** more than two **D** two

2. CH_3Br is a molecular compound. The subscript 3 means there are 3 _____ atoms in one molecule.

    A carbon   **B** hydrogen **C** boron   **D** bromine

3. The prefix _____ is not always written in a molecular compound's name.

    A *mono-*   **B** *di-*   **D** *tri-*   **D** *tetra-*

4. A(n) _____ is a neutral group of atoms bonded together by shared electrons.

    A atom   **B** element   **C** molecule **D** compound

5. The chemical formula for tetraphosphorus trisulfide is _____.

    A PS_3 **B** S_4P_3 **C** P_3S_4 **D** P_4S_3

6. The chemical formula for nitrogen monoxide is _____.

    A NO   **B** ON   **C** N_2O_2 **D** N_2O_4

Critical Thinking

On a sheet of paper, write the answer to each question.

7. A substance has the formula H_2. Is it a molecular compound? Explain your answer.

8. How are prefixes in names of compounds like subscripts in formulas?

9. What is the formula for iodine heptafluoride?

10. What is the formula for diphosphorus pentoxide?

Objectives

After reading this lesson, you should be able to

◆ explain how molecular compounds and ionic compounds are different

◆ identify the cation and anion in a binary ionic compound

◆ write the symbol for an ion

◆ explain what a roman numeral means in a compound name

Ion

An atom or group of atoms with a charge

Cation

An atom or group of atoms with a positive charge; a positive ion

Anion

An atom or group of atoms with a negative charge; a negative ion

Ionic compound

A compound consisting of one kind of cation and one kind of anion

In Lesson 1, you learned that molecular compounds are formed when atoms share electrons. Sometimes one atom has enough power to take one or more electrons from another atom. When this happens, the atoms are no longer neutral. Electrons are negatively charged particles, so the atom that gained electrons has a negative charge. The atom that gave up electrons has a positive charge. The atoms are now **ions.** An ion is an atom or a group of atoms that has a charge. There are two kinds of ions: **cations** and **anions.** A cation has a positive charge because it gave up one or more electrons. An anion has a negative charge because it has one or more extra electrons. The word *cation,* when pronounced, sounds like CAT-eye-on. The word *anion,* when pronounced, sounds like AN-eye-on.

An **ionic compound** consists of one kind of cation and one kind of anion. These ions are held together by the attraction of opposite charges. This attraction creates a bond between the ions. Common table salt, NaCl, is an ionic compound. It is made of sodium cations and chloride anions.

ionic compound = cation + anion
sodium chloride = cation of sodium + anion of chlorine

In names and formulas of ionic compounds, the cation is always first. In NaCl, sodium is listed first, so it is the cation. Chlorine is listed second, so it is the anion. Calcium oxide, CaO, is another ionic compound. You can tell that calcium is the cation and oxygen is the anion.

Link to ➤➤➤

Physics

Like charges (a + and a +) repel. Opposite charges (a + and a −) attract. Objects with opposite electric charges attract each other with a force called electrostatic attraction. The cations and anions in solid ionic compounds are held together by this attraction. Electrostatic attraction is much stronger than the force of gravity.

NaCl and CaO, shown in Figure 3.2.1, are *binary* ionic compounds. They are made from only two elements. The cations and anions are single atoms that have a charge. Besides being positive or negative, the charge on an ion has a number value. For example, a sodium (Na) ion has a charge of 1+. This is because it gave up 1 electron. An electron is assigned a charge of 1−. A chloride (Cl) ion has a charge of 1− because it gained an electron. A calcium (Ca) ion has a charge of 2+. This ion gave up 2 electrons. An oxygen (O) ion has a 2− charge because it has 2 extra electrons. Ionic charges are written with the number first, followed by a + or − sign. No ionic charge is greater than 7±.

Ionic charges are based on the number of electrons that an atom loses or gains. Chapter 10 will explain why certain atoms lose electrons while others gain electrons. For now, you need to know that the elements within one column of the periodic table often form ions with the same charge. These charges are shown in red at the top of some columns in the periodic table shown in Figure 3.2.2 on the next page. Column 18 is not assigned a charge. The elements in this column rarely form ionic or molecular compounds.

Figure 3.2.1 *Crystals of sodium chloride, NaCl (left), can form from saltwater. Calcium oxide, CaO (right), is called lime or quicklime. It is used to treat water and make paper.*

The columns in the table below are numbered from 1 to 18 (in black). Columns 1, 2, and 13–17 are labeled with an ionic charge (in red). When elements in these columns form ions, they have the charge shown. For example, lithium (Li) is in column 1. Elements in this column form ions with a charge of 1+. Now find column 15. An atom of nitrogen (N) becomes an anion with a charge of 3−. A phosphorus (P) ion has a 3− charge also.

An ion is represented by its chemical symbol followed by its charge. The charge is written as a superscript on the right side of the symbol. The superscript includes the + or − sign. The symbol for a lithium cation is Li^{1+}. The symbol for a phosphorus anion is P^{3-}.

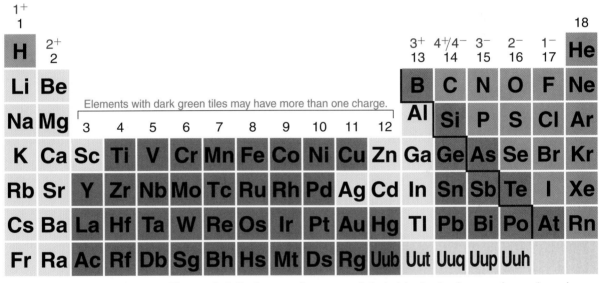

Figure 3.2.2 *Some columns are labeled by ionic charge, shown in red. Most elements in columns 3–12 can have more than one charge.*

Example 1	What is the symbol for the magnesium ion? Is it a cation or anion?
Read	You are asked to give a symbol for an ion.
Plan	The symbol for an ion includes a chemical symbol and a charge. The charge is shown as a superscript. The symbol for magnesium is Mg. Magnesium is in column 2 of the periodic table. Elements in column 2 form ions with the charge 2+.
Solve	Magnesium ions have a charge of 2+. So the magnesium ion's symbol is Mg^{2+}. It is a cation since it has a positive charge.
Reflect	Ions of metals usually have a positive charge—they are usually cations. The ions of nonmetals are usually anions.
Practice	What is the symbol for the nitrogen ion? Is it a cation or anion?

Math Tip

Review these roman numerals and their meanings: I (1), II (2), III (3), IV (4), V (5), VI (6), VII (7).

Look at Figure 3.2.2 on page 93 again. Columns 3–12 are not labeled with an ionic charge. The dark green tiles are metals that can have more than one charge as ions. These metals always have a positive charge as ions. However, this charge can vary. For example, in one ionic compound, iron (Fe) has a charge of 2+. In another compound, it has a charge of 3+. In cases like this, the cation's charge is shown by a roman numeral after its name. For example,

• In iron(II) sulfide, the cation is iron(II) or Fe^{2+}.
• In iron(III) sulfide, the cation is iron(III) or Fe^{3+}.

Figure 3.2.3 *The soil on Mars contains iron oxides such as FeO and Fe_2O_3. Fe_2O_3, commonly known as rust, gives the planet its red color.*

The iron compounds on the surface of Mars, shown in Figure 3.2.3, include both Fe^{2+} and Fe^{3+} ions. Many metals have two possible charges like iron. Copper ions have either a 1+ or 2+ charge. Lead ions have either a 2+ or 4+ charge. Some metals have several possible charges. Manganese ions have one of five charges: 2+, 3+, 4+, 6+, or 7+. There are a few metals in columns 3–12 that only have one charge. They include zinc (Zn^{2+}), silver (Ag^{1+}), cadmium (Cd^{2+}), and scandium (Sc^{3+}).

It is important to know how to find the charge on an ion. In the next lesson, you will use ionic charges to determine the formulas of ionic compounds.

Spotlight on Iron

26
Fe
Iron
55.8

Iron is a metal that has been known and used for at least 5,000 years. Iron is the fourth most abundant element by weight in the earth's crust. The earth's core is thought to be mostly molten, or melted, iron, along with some hydrogen. Iron is also found in most stars. The amount of iron in a star shows the star's age. Old stars contain more iron than young ones. Steel is an alloy of iron and other metals. Steel is much stronger than iron and does not rust as easily. It is widely used in construction and manufacturing.

Iron is a cation in a variety of ionic compounds. In most of them, iron's charge is 2+ or 3+. In a few compounds, iron has a charge of 4+ or 6+. An iron compound that is essential to warm-blooded animals is hemoglobin, a protein in red blood cells. Iron carries a charge of 2+ in hemoglobin.

Interesting Fact: Very small amounts of this metal are added to some dry cereals.

Technology and Society

Table salt is sodium chloride. Two sources of table salt are mines and seawater. Mined salt is mixed with rocks and dirt and is called rock salt. Seawater contains dirt, dissolved salt, and other ionic compounds.

Lesson 2   R E V I E W

Match each word in the first column with a definition in the second column. On a sheet of paper, write the letter of the correct definition.

1. ionic compound

2. molecular compound

3. ion

4. cation

5. anion

6. charge

A an ion with a positive charge

B atoms of two or more elements sharing electrons

C cations and anions held together by their opposite charges

D an atom, or a group of atoms, that carries a charge

E an ion with a negative charge

F a positive or negative value shown as a superscript in an ion's symbol

Critical Thinking

On a sheet of paper, write the answer to each question.

7. What is the symbol for the oxygen ion? Is it an anion or a cation?

8. What is the symbol for the potassium ion? Is it an anion or a cation?

9. A certain compound name begins with *copper(I)*. What does the roman numeral mean?

10. An element is in column 12 of the periodic table. A second element is in column 2. Can these two form an ionic compound? Explain your answer.

Math Tip

If a symbol in a formula has no subscript after it, assume a subscript of 1. This is true for formulas of both molecular and ionic compounds.

You have just learned how to find the charges of ions from Figure 3.2.2 on page 93. An ionic compound contains positive and negative ions. However, all ionic compounds are electrically neutral. In an ionic compound, the total positive charge equals the total negative charge. This is the main idea to remember when writing formulas for ionic compounds. The next example shows you how to find the neutral formula for calcium chloride.

Example 1 Calcium chloride is an ionic compound. What is its formula?

Read You are given an ionic compound containing calcium and chloride ions.

Plan Find calcium and chlorine in Figure 3.2.2 on page 93. Calcium is in column 2. A calcium ion has a charge of 2+. Chlorine is in column 17. Its ion has a charge of 1−.

Solve The compound is made of Ca^{2+} cations and Cl^{1-} anions. Its formula has the form Ca_xCl_y, where x and y are possible subscripts. Find the simplest formula that has a total charge of 0. Possible formulas are

CaCl	1 Ca^{2+} + 1 Cl^{1-}	$(2+)+(1-)=1+$
Ca_2Cl	2 Ca^{2+} + 1 Cl^{1-}	$(2+)+(2+)+(1-)=4+$
$CaCl_2$	1 Ca^{2+} + 2 Cl^{1-}	$(2+)+(1-)+(1-)=0$

The only formula that is neutral is $CaCl_2$. Its total charge is 0. $CaCl_2$ is the correct formula for calcium chloride. For every 1 Ca^{2+} cation in this compound, there are exactly 2 Cl^{1-} anions.

Reflect The simplest unit of calcium chloride has these three ions: Ca^{2+}, Cl^{1-}, Cl^{1-}. The calcium ion gave up 2 electrons to the chloride ions. Each chloride ion gained 1 electron.

Practice What is the formula for the ionic compound, potassium sulfide?

Formula unit

A chemical formula for an ionic compound

For ionic compounds, the correct formula is the simplest one. Consider the example of calcium chloride. Ca_2Cl_4 and Ca_4Cl_8 are also neutral formulas. But they are not the simplest. $CaCl_2$ is the simplest. To find the simplest ionic formula, reduce the subscripts to the smallest whole-number ratio. This rule is only true for ionic compounds. It is not true for molecular compounds. Because an ionic formula is always reduced to its simplest form, it is called a **formula unit** instead of a formula. It represents the simplest unit of an ionic compound.

- Ionic compounds have formula units.
- Molecular compounds have formulas.

How do you find the smallest whole-number ratio? Consider Ca_4Cl_8. The subscript ratio is 4:8. Both numbers can be divided by a common factor of 4. Dividing both by 4 gives the smallest possible ratio: 1:2. Ca_1Cl_2 is the simplest formula unit, but the 1 is dropped to give $CaCl_2$. What is the simplest formula unit for Li_6N_2? It is Li_3N—the correct formula unit.

In Example 1, three formula units were tested before the correct one was found. There is an easier way to find the formula unit of an ionic compound. Use the crisscross method below.

1. Write the cation and anion in symbols with ionic charges. For calcium chloride,
$$Ca^{2+} \qquad Cl^{1-}$$

2. Make the number in the positive charge into a subscript for the anion. Make the number in the negative charge into a subscript for the cation. Ignore the $-$ and $+$ signs.
$$Ca^{2+} \quad Cl^{1-}$$
$$Ca_1 \underset{\curvearrowright}{\diagdown\diagup} Cl_2 = CaCl_2$$

3. If necessary, reduce the resulting formula to its smallest whole-number ratio. To do this, divide all subscripts by the largest common factor.

The crisscross method will always create a formula unit that is neutral, but it may not be in simplest form. That is why step 3 is important. For example, consider the ionic compound, tin(IV) oxide. The roman numeral IV means that this particular cation of tin carries a 4+ charge. The ions are Sn^{4+} and O^{2-}. Crisscrossing the superscripts gives

$$Sn^{4+} \quad O^{2-}$$
$$Sn_2 \quad O_4 \quad = \quad Sn_2O_4$$

The result is Sn_2O_4. This formula unit is neutral, but it is *not in simplest form.* The subscripts can be divided by 2.

$$Sn_2O_4 \xrightarrow{reduced} Sn_1O_2 = SnO_2$$

SnO_2 is the correct formula unit for tin(IV) oxide. It shows three ions: Sn^{4+}, O^{2-}, and O^{2-}. The ionic charges add up to 0: $(4+)+(2-)+(2-)=0$. The subscripts have the smallest whole-number ratio: 1:2.

Example 2   Aluminum sulfide is an ionic compound. What is its formula unit?

Read   This compound is made of aluminum and sulfur.

Plan   Based on the charges shown in Figure 3.2.2 on page 93, the ions are Al^{3+} and S^{2-}.

Solve   Write the symbols for the cation and anion. Then use the crisscross method. The 3 becomes the subscript of S, and the 2 becomes the subscript of Al.

$$Al^{3+} \quad S^{2-}$$
$$Al_2 \quad S_3 \quad = \quad Al_2S_3$$

Al_2S_3 is neutral because the ionic charges add up to 0: $(3+)+(3+)+(2-)+(2-)+(2-)=0$. The subscript ratio 2:3 is the smallest whole-number ratio. Al_2S_3 is the correct formula unit.

Reflect   In terms of electrons, the two Al atoms gave up 3 electrons each, for a total of 6. The three S atoms gained 2 electrons each, for a total of 6. The smallest unit of this compound contains five ions, and their positive and negative charges add up to 0.

Practice   What is the formula unit of the ionic compound, iron(II) fluoride?

On a sheet of paper, write the letter of the answer that completes each sentence.

1. The ions Ag^{1+} and O^{2-} form an ionic compound. Its formula unit is _____.

   A AgO **B** AgO_2 **C** Ag_2O_2 **D** Ag_2O

2. Formulas of ionic compounds are always reduced to the smallest whole-number ratio. They are referred to as _____.

   A formula units   **C** binary compounds
   B molecular compounds   **D** polyatomic ions

3. The formula unit _____ is neutral.

   A CsO **B** AlS **C** RbI **D** $BeCl$

4. The formula unit of sodium sulfide is _____.

   A NaS_2 **B** Na_2S **C** NaS **D** Na_2S_2

5. The formula unit for chromium(III) oxide is _____.

   A Cr_2O_3 **B** Cr_4O_6 **C** Cr_4O_{12} **D** Cr_3O_9

6. The formula unit of iron(III) bromide is _____.

   A Fe_3Br_3 **B** Fe_3Br **C** $FeBr$ **D** $FeBr_3$

Critical Thinking

On a sheet of paper, write the formula unit for each compound. As part of your answer, show the crisscross method.

7. calcium phosphide

8. titanium(III) oxide

9. iron(III) iodide

10. barium oxide

Objectives

After reading this lesson, you should be able to

◆ recognize common polyatomic ions

◆ write a formula unit containing a polyatomic ion

Polyatomic ion

A group of two or more atoms that acts as one ion and has one charge

---

All ionic compounds consist of one kind of cation and one kind of anion. So far, you have studied *binary* ionic compounds, such as CaI_2. In these compounds, the cations and anions are single, charged atoms (Ca^{2+} and I^{1-}, for example).

Some ionic compounds, such as $NaNO_3$, contain more than two elements. These compounds are still made of one kind of cation and one kind of anion. They contain a **polyatomic ion** as the cation, anion, or both. A polyatomic ion is a group of two or more atoms that acts as one ion and has one charge. For example, in $NaNO_3$, the cation is Na^{1+} and the anion is NO_3^{1-}. NO_3^{1-} is called the nitrate ion. This polyatomic ion consists of 1 nitrogen atom and 3 oxygen atoms. The group of 4 atoms, NO_3, acts as one anion and has one charge, $1-$.

A polyatomic ion is not the same as a polyatomic molecule of an element. Polyatomic ions, such as NO_3^{1-}, contain two or more different atoms and have a charge. Polyatomic molecules, such as P_4, contain two or more identical atoms and have no charge.

❋ ❋

Technology and Society

Some sunglasses are clear indoors, but darken in sunlight. The lenses contain a small amount of the ionic compound, silver chloride. Direct sunlight provides the energy to move an electron from a chloride anion to a silver cation. This produces a silver atom and a chlorine atom. Large numbers of silver atoms make the lenses appear dark. The process reverses in indoor lighting, and the lenses look clear.

Some common polyatomic ions are listed in Table 3.4.1. You will work with these ions frequently in chemistry. It is a good idea to memorize their names, symbols, and charges.

To write the formula unit of an ionic compound containing a polyatomic ion, follow the same steps you used for binary ionic compounds (see page 98). However, first add parentheses around the symbol of a polyatomic ion, putting the charge outside, like this: $(NO_3)^{1-}$. Then use the crisscross method to create a neutral formula unit.

Table 3.4.1 Some Common Polyatomic Ions	
Name	Symbol
ammonium	NH_4^{1+}
acetate	$C_2H_3O_2^{1-}$
carbonate	CO_3^{2-}
chlorate	ClO_3^{1-}
chlorite	ClO_2^{1-}
chromate	CrO_4^{2-}
dichromate	$Cr_2O_7^{2-}$
hydrogen carbonate (also called bicarbonate)	HCO_3^{1-}
hydrogen sulfate (also called bisulfate)	HSO_4^{1-}
hydroxide	OH^{1-}
hypochlorite	ClO^{1-}
nitrate	NO_3^{1-}
nitrite	NO_2^{1-}
perchlorate	ClO_4^{1-}
permanganate	MnO_4^{1-}
phosphate	PO_4^{3-}
sulfate	SO_4^{2-}
sulfite	SO_3^{2-}

For example, the ions Ba^{2+} and NO_3^{1-} form the ionic compound, barium nitrate. To find the formula unit, first place NO_3 in parentheses with the charge outside. Then use the crisscross method:

$$\begin{array}{l} Ba^{2+}\ \ (NO_3)^{1-} \\ Ba_1\ \diagdown\!\!\!\diagup\ (NO_3)_2 \quad = \quad Ba(NO_3)_2 \end{array}$$

When working with a polyatomic ion, treat it like an ion of a single atom. When crisscrossing superscripts to subscripts, do not move or change any subscripts *inside* the parentheses. Only the charge *outside* the parentheses is moved to become a subscript. After crisscrossing, remember to reduce the subscripts *outside* the parentheses to simplest form if needed. Subscripts must be in the smallest whole-number ratio.

Example 1	Sodium carbonate is an ionic compound. What is its formula unit?
Read	Sodium carbonate consists of a sodium cation and a polyatomic anion, carbonate.
Plan	From Table 3.4.1 (page 102), the carbonate anion is CO_3^{2-}. From Figure 3.2.2 (page 93), the sodium cation is Na^{1+}.
Solve	Add parentheses to the carbonate symbol, keeping the charge outside. Then use the crisscross method. The 1+ charge on Na becomes the subscript outside the parentheses of CO_3. The 2− charge on CO_3 becomes the subscript of Na.

$$\begin{array}{l} Na^{1+}\ \ (CO_3)^{2-} \\ Na_2\ \diagdown\!\!\!\diagup\ (CO_3)_1 \quad = \quad Na_2CO_3 \end{array}$$

The formula unit for sodium carbonate is $Na_2(CO_3)_1$, or simply Na_2CO_3. Because the subscript of (CO_3) is 1, the parentheses and the 1 may be dropped.

Reflect	Notice that the 3 in $(CO_3)^{2-}$ is not involved at all. $(CO_3)^{2-}$ acts like one charged atom of the form $(X)^{2-}$.
Practice	Magnesium sulfate is an ionic compound. What is its formula unit?

If a polyatomic ion has a subscript of 1 in a formula unit, both the 1 and the parentheses may be dropped. If a polyatomic ion has a subscript other than 1, the parentheses must stay. You will see why in the next example.

Example 2	Lead(II) phosphate is an ionic compound. What is its formula unit?
Read	Lead is the cation. The roman numeral means the charge on this particular lead cation is 2+. Phosphate is the name of a polyatomic anion.
Plan	The cation's symbol is Pb^{2+}. As shown in Table 3.4.1, the phosphate symbol is $PO_4{}^{3-}$.
Solve	Add parentheses to the phosphate symbol, keeping the charge outside. Then use the crisscross method. The 2+ charge on Pb becomes the subscript outside the parentheses of PO_4. The 3− charge on PO_4 becomes the subscript of Pb.

$$Pb^{2+} \quad (PO_4)^{3-}$$

$$Pb_3 \bigtimes (PO_4)_2 \ = \ Pb_3(PO_4)_2$$

	Remember that everything inside the parentheses is not involved in crisscrossing. The formula unit for lead(II) phosphate is $Pb_3(PO_4)_2$. The subscript ratio is 3:2, so it is in simplest form.
Reflect	The parentheses must remain in the formula unit to separate the 4 and the 2. Without the parentheses, the formula unit would be Pb_3PO_{42}!
Practice	Magnesium perchlorate is an ionic compound. What is its formula unit?

Link to ➤➤➤

Earth Science

The formula units of some ionic compounds are very complex. Many minerals are complex ionic compounds. For example, a mineral found in clay has the formula $Al_2(OH)_4Si_2O_5$.

Most polyatomic ions have names that end in *-ite* or *-ate*. This can help you tell the difference between a binary compound and one that contains a polyatomic ion. Compound names that end in *-ide* are usually binary compounds. However, there are two main exceptions.

- *All* compounds containing the hydroxide anion have names ending in *-ide*.
- *Some* compounds containing the ammonium cation have names ending in *-ide*.

Examples are sodium hydroxide and ammonium sulfide. Both contain three elements, but end in *-ide*.

Example 3	Ammonium nitrate is an ionic compound. What is its formula unit?
Read	This compound has a polyatomic ion for both the cation and anion.
Plan	From Table 3.4.1, the two ion symbols are NH_4^{1+} and NO_3^{1-}.
Solve	Add parentheses to both ions and use the crisscross method. Remember to leave everything inside the parentheses as written. $$(NH_4)^{1+} \ (NO_3)^{1-}$$ $$(NH_4)_1 \ (NO_3)_1 \ = NH_4NO_3$$ The formula unit may be given as NH_4NO_3 or $(NH_4)(NO_3)$ or $(NH_4)_1(NO_3)_1$. All are correct.
Reflect	The two nitrogen atoms in NH_4NO_3 cannot be combined. $N_2H_4O_3$ is not correct! To avoid doing this, you may choose to keep the parentheses.
Practice	Ammonium sulfide is an ionic compound. What is its formula unit?

Example 4

Example 4	Iron(II) sulfate is an ionic compound. What is its formula unit?
Read	Iron is the cation. It has a charge of 2+. Sulfate is a polyatomic anion.
Plan	The ion symbols are Fe^{2+} and SO_4^{2-}.
Solve	Add parentheses and use the crisscross method.

$$Fe^{2+} \quad (SO_4)^{2-}$$
$$Fe_2 \diagdown (SO_4)_2 \xrightarrow{\text{reduced}} Fe_1(SO_4)_1 \text{ or } FeSO_4$$

After crisscrossing, the subscript ratio is 2:2. This is reduced to the smallest whole-number ratio of 1:1. The subscripts of 1 may be dropped along with the parentheses. The formula unit for iron(II) sulfate is $FeSO_4$.

Reflect	When $Fe_2(SO_4)_2$ is reduced to $FeSO_4$, the 4 in the sulfate symbol is *not* reduced. Only subscripts outside parentheses are reduced.
Practice	Write the formula unit of the ionic compound, lead(IV) acetate.

★ ✦ ★

Achievements in Science

Ionic Theory

Before the 1880s, chemists thought all substances were made of molecules. However, they noticed that the properties of certain substances are very different than the properties of others. For example, the boiling point of a sugar solution increases when more sugar is added. When salt is added to a salt solution, the rise in boiling point is twice as great.

Svante Arrhenius, a Swedish chemist, proposed that some substances are made of charged particles. These substances "fall apart" in water solutions. Salt produces two kinds of charged particles in a solution. Sugar, a molecular compound, does not produce these particles. This explains why the rise in boiling point with more solute is twice as great for a salt solution as for a sugar solution.

Arrhenius's ideas were not accepted at first. Before the end of the 1890s, however, the electron and radioactivity were discovered. These discoveries showed that atoms are made of charged particles. Chemists began to understand that atoms can gain an electric charge to form ions. They realized that ionic compounds are held together by electric charges. In 1903, Arrhenius won the Nobel Prize in Chemistry for his work on ionic theory.

Lesson 4   R E V I E W

On a sheet of paper, write the letter of the answer to each question.

1. Which statement is true of a polyatomic ion?

A It contains one atom.   **C** It has two or more charges.
B It is one ion.   **D** It is two or more ions.

2. Which compound contains a polyatomic ion?

A NaCl   **B** $FeBr_3$ **C** NaOH   **D** Li_2O

3. Which compound contains a polyatomic ion?

A iron(II) chloride   **C** potassium chloride
B ammonium chloride   **D** zinc chloride

4. Which compound contains two different polyatomic ions?

A Cr_2O_3 **B** $K_2Cr_2O_7$ **C** $Mg(NO_3)_2$ **D** NH_4OH

5. What is the formula unit of potassium hydrogen carbonate?

A $KHCO_3$ **B** $K(HCO_3)_2$ **C** K_2CO_3 **D** $K(CO_3)_2$

6. What is the formula unit of cobalt(II) perchlorate?

A Co_2ClO_4 **B** $Co_4(ClO)_2$ **C** $Co(ClO_4)_2$ **D** $CoClO_4$

Critical Thinking

On a sheet of paper, write the answer to each question.

7. Are parentheses required in formula units of binary compounds? Explain your answer.

8. Show how you find the simplest formula unit of calcium dichromate. Use arrows to show the crisscross method.

9. What are the formula units for sodium sulfide, sodium sulfite, and sodium sulfate?

10. What are the formula units for cobalt(II) hydroxide and cobalt(III) hydroxide?

Writing Formulas of Ionic Compounds

Cations and anions are charged particles. One kind of cation and one kind of anion combine to form an ionic compound. They combine in a certain ratio so the positive charges cancel the negative charges. How do you determine this ratio? In this investigation, you will practice combining ions to make neutral compounds.

Procedure

1. For each cation below, use the blue pen to make three cards. For example, write K^{1+} on three cards. Do the same for the anions using the red pen.

Cations	Anions
K^{1+}	S^{2-}
NH_4^{1+}	F^{1-}
Mg^{2+}	NO_3^{1-}
Cu^{1+}	ClO_4^{1-}
Cu^{2+}	CO_3^{2-}
Fe^{2+}	SO_4^{2-}
Fe^{3+}	PO_4^{3-}
Sn^{2+}	
Sn^{4+}	

2. Select one cation and one anion. Combine their cards to find the simplest neutral compound with a total ionic charge of zero. For example, combining two K^{1+} cards with one S^{2-} card gives a total charge of $(1+)+(1+)+(2-)=0$.

3. Make a data table like the one below. In the first two columns, record the two ions you selected. In the last two columns, write the formula unit and name of the ionic compound.

Cation	Anion	Formula Unit	Compound Name
K^{1+}	S^{2-}	K_2S	potassium sulfide

4. Repeat steps 2 and 3 until you have recorded at least 25 different ionic compounds. Use every ion at least once. If you need more than three cards for any of the ions, use the extra blank cards to make them.

Cleanup/Disposal
Return all materials.

Analysis
1. Why do cations and anions combine to form compounds that have no electric charge?

2. Give the formula and name of a compound for which you had to make extra cards.

3. Which cations required roman numerals in compound names?

Conclusions
1. Suppose cation X has a 2+ charge and anion Z has a 1− charge. Write the formula of the ionic compound of X and Z.

2. Suppose cation X has a 2+ charge and anion Z has a 3− charge. Write the formula of the ionic compound of X and Z.

3. Suppose cation X has a 3+ charge and anion Z has a 2− charge. Write the formula of the ionic compound of X and Z.

Explore Further
Write formulas for the following ionic compounds.

1. antimony(V) oxide

2. arsenic(V) sulfide

3. chromium(VI) oxide

4. manganese(VII) oxide

Prefixes are used for naming molecular compounds, not ionic compounds. Prefixes tell the number of atoms of an element. Their meanings are given below.

mono-	1
di-	2
tri-	3
tetra-	4
penta-	5
hexa-	6
hepta-	7
octa-	8
nona-	9
deca-	10

In this chapter, you have learned how to write the formula or formula unit of a compound if you know its name. In this lesson, you will learn how to name a compound if you know its formula or formula unit.

Naming Molecular Compounds

To name a binary molecular compound if you know its formula, follow these steps:

1. Write the name of the first element in the formula. For SO_3, it is *sulfur.*

2. Then write the name of the second element, but change its ending to *-ide.* For SO_3, oxygen is changed to *oxide.*

3. Add prefixes to indicate the number of atoms of each element. Prefixes and their meanings are shown to the left. The prefix *mono-* is dropped for the first element only. For SO_3, *sulfur* does not need the prefix *mono-*, but *oxide* requires the prefix *tri-*. The name for SO_3 is sulfur trioxide.

Here are some examples of names of binary molecular compounds:

SiC	silicone monocarbide
SiO_2	silicone dioxide
N_2O_4	dinitrogen tetroxide
SF_6	sulfur hexafluoride
P_4O_{10}	tetraphosphorus decoxide

Binary molecular compounds have two-word names: one name from each element. However, some molecular compounds are known by common names. Water (H_2O) is dihydrogen monoxide, and ammonia (NH_3) is nitrogen trihydride. Imagine asking for a glass of dihydrogen monoxide at a restaurant!

There are many molecular compounds that contain three or more elements. Some of their names are given in Chapter 19.

Example 1	Name the molecular compound, IF_7.
Read	This compound contains 1 iodine atom and 7 fluorine atoms.
Plan	Start with the names iodine and fluorine, in that order.
Solve	Change the second name so it ends in *-ide.* Then add prefixes to show the number of atoms. *Hepta-* means 7, so IF_7 is iodine heptafluoride.
Reflect	OF_2 is another molecular compound. Its name is oxygen difluoride.
Practice	Name the molecular compound, N_4S_4.

■◆■

Chemistry in Your Life

The Environment: Nitrogen Oxides

Nitrogen is a very stable gas. Under the right conditions, however, nitrogen can combine with oxygen to form molecular compounds called nitrogen oxides. Burning something at a high temperature can produce nitrogen oxides. Extreme temperatures in a bolt of lightning can also produce them. The main producers of nitrogen oxides are small engines, such as car engines. They produce NO and NO_2. In the atmosphere, both compounds contribute to smog and acid rain. Smog is a hazy fog that occurs when smoke and other substances pollute the air. Acid rain occurs when nitrogen oxides react with water in the atmosphere. The acids that form fall with rain. Smog and acid rain are harmful to people, plants, and animals.

Nitrogen oxide, NO, is produced in the human body. The immune system uses NO to fight infection. Nerves use it for

communication. NO also regulates blood pressure. Another nitrogen oxide, N_2O, is known as "laughing gas." N_2O is also used in race cars to increase engine power.

1. Name these molecular compounds: NO, NO_2, and N_2O.

2. How are nitrogen oxides used in the body?

3. Are emissions tests for cars required where you live? If so, which nitrogen compounds are tested?

Naming Ionic Compounds

The cations and anions in ionic compounds may be single, charged atoms or polyatomic ions. Ionic compounds are named in a similar way as molecular compounds, *except prefixes are not used.* If you know the formula unit of an ionic compound, you can name it by following these steps:

1. Write the name of the cation. In a formula unit, the cation is given first. If the cation is an element, write its name. If the cation is a polyatomic ion, write its name.

2. Write the name of the anion. If the anion is an element, change the ending to *-ide.* If the anion is a polyatomic ion, do not change its name. *There are no prefixes to add to ionic compound names.*

3. Many metals in the center of the periodic table have more than one possible charge (see Figure 3.2.2 on page 93). These metals include iron, chromium, manganese, nickel, copper, tin, lead, and gold. If the cation in a formula unit is one of these, the correct charge needs to be shown in the name. The correct charge is the one that makes the compound neutral. It is shown by adding a roman numeral in parentheses after the cation's name. For example, SnI_2 is tin(II) iodide, and SnI_4 is tin(IV) iodide.

Compare these steps with the steps for molecular compound names on page 110. You can see these similarities and differences:

- Binary compounds—both molecular and ionic—have names ending in *-ide.*
- If an ionic compound contains a polyatomic ion, its name usually does not end in *-ide.*
- Binary molecular compounds have two-word names: one word from each element.
- Ionic compounds also have two-word names: the name of the cation followed by the name of the anion.
- Molecular compound names may include prefixes (but never roman numerals).
- Ionic compound names may include roman numerals (but never prefixes).

Several ionic compound names are listed in Table 3.5.1. The spelling of names is important. Look at the first three names in the table. *Sulfide, sulfate,* and *sulfite* differ by only a letter or two. The formula units of these three compounds also look similar. However, each compound is very different! Look at the last name listed, potassium dichromate. This contains a polyatomic ion named *dichromate.* The *di-* is just part of the name. It is not an added prefix. (Prefixes are only added when naming molecular compounds.)

Table 3.5.1 Some Ionic Compounds	
Formula Unit	Name
Na_2S	sodium sulfide
Na_2SO_4	sodium sulfate
Na_2SO_3	sodium sulfite
$AlBr_3$	aluminum bromide
Al_2O_3	aluminum oxide
$Al(NO_3)_3$	aluminum nitrate
$Cu(ClO_3)_2$	copper(II) chlorate
NH_4F	ammonium fluoride
$NaHCO_3$	sodium bicarbonate (or sodium hydrogen carbonate)
$K_2Cr_2O_3$	potassium dichromate

In Table 3.5.1, notice the use of parentheses. A polyatomic ion is present whenever an ionic compound contains three or more elements. Parentheses around a polyatomic ion are not needed if that ion has an unwritten subscript of 1.

Research and Write

Carbon dioxide, CO_2, is produced naturally by living things. You exhale carbon dioxide in every breath. Carbon monoxide, CO, is poisonous. Inhaling CO can cause death. Do research to find out why CO is poisonous. Then learn how carbon monoxide can be produced and detected in a home. Write two paragraphs describing what you learned.

Example 2   Name the ionic compound, $FeBr_3$.

Read   This compound is made of two elements.

Plan   Start with the names iron and bromine, in that order. Iron is in column 8 of the periodic table and has more than one possible charge. Bromine is in column 17. It has a 1− charge.

Solve   Put the cation and anion names together: iron bromine. Change the second name so it ends in –*ide:* iron bromide. Now find the charge on iron that will make the compound neutral. This charge will be shown by a roman numeral in the compound's name.

$FeBr_3 = 1\ Fe^{?+}$ cation $+ 3\ Br^{1-}$ anions

iron(?) bromide

The compound contains $3\ Br^{1-}$ anions, so the total negative charge is 3−. To form a neutral compound, the total positive charge must be 3+. This charge is carried by 1 Fe ion.

Fe^{3+} Br^{1-} Br^{1-} Br^{1-}

$(Fe^{3+})(Br^{1-})_3$

The charge on iron is 3+. Show this charge with the roman numeral III. The name of $FeBr_3$ is iron(III) bromide.

Reflect   Why is this compound not called iron tribromide? Names of ionic compounds do not contain prefixes. Prefixes are only used to name molecular compounds.

Practice   Name the ionic compound, Bi_2O_3.

Example 3   Name the ionic compound, $Pb(C_2H_3O_2)_2$.

Read   This compound contains more than two elements. The parentheses indicate a polyatomic anion. The subscript 2 outside the parentheses means there are two of these anions.

Plan   Start with the cation's name, lead. The anion $C_2H_3O_2{}^{1-}$ is listed in Table 3.4.1 on page 102. It is the acetate ion. The base name is lead acetate. Because lead can carry more than one positive charge, a roman numeral is needed in the name.

Solve	Determine the charge on the cation, Pb. The anion, $C_2H_3O_2$, has a charge of $1-$.

$Pb(C_2H_3O_2)_2 = 1\ Pb^{?+}$ cation $+ 2\ (C_2H_3O_2)^{1-}$ anions

lead(?) acetate

The compound contains $2\ C_2H_3O_2{}^{1-}$ anions, so the total negative charge is $2-$. To form a neutral compound, the total positive charge must be $2+$. This charge is carried by 1 Pb ion, so the charge on that ion must be $2+$.

$Pb^{2+}\quad C_2H_3O_2{}^{1-}\quad C_2H_3O_2{}^{1-}$
$(Pb^{2+})(C_2H_3O_2{}^{1-})_2$

The name of this compound is lead(II) acetate. |
| *Reflect* | In this name, the word *acetate* is not changed so it ends in *-ide*. This is only done when the second word comes from an element name. Polyatomic ion names are not changed. |
| *Practice* | Name the ionic compound, $Cr_2(SO_4)_3$. |

Acid

A compound that produces H^{1+} ions when dissolved in water

Naming Acids

Acids are compounds that produce H^{1+} ions when dissolved in water. Acids are molecular compounds that can act like ionic compounds in water. Acids are not named the same way as other compounds. Table 3.5.2 lists common acids that you should know. It is easier to learn this list than follow the rules for naming acids. Notice that the formula of each acid begins with hydrogen.

Table 3.5.2 Common Acids	
Formula	**Name**
HCl	hydrochloric acid
HBr	hydrobromic acid
HNO_3	nitric acid
$HClO_3$	chloric acid
$HClO_4$	perchloric acid
H_2SO_4	sulfuric acid
H_3PO_4	phosphoric acid
$HC_2H_3O_2$	acetic acid

Lesson 5 REVIEW

Word Bank

ionic

molecular

molecule

On a sheet of paper, write the word from the Word Bank that completes each sentence.

1. The formula of a molecular compound shows the atoms in one _____.

2. When naming any _____ compound, check to see if a roman numeral is needed.

3. When naming a(n) _____ compound, the prefix *mono-* may be dropped from the first word.

On a sheet of paper, write the answer to each question.

4. What is the name of the molecular compound, SO_2?

5. What is the name of the ionic compound, CaF_2?

6. What is the name of the ionic compound, NaOH?

Critical Thinking

On a sheet of paper, write the answer to each question.

7. How can you recognize an acid by its chemical formula?

8. An ionic compound contains a cation that has more than one possible charge. How do you indicate the correct charge in the compound's name?

9. A compound contains a polyatomic ion. Are parentheses needed in its formula unit? Explain your answer.

10. Two ionic compounds are labeled CrF_2 and CrF_3. From these labels, a chemist knows 1) the compounds do not contain polyatomic ions, and 2) their names contain roman numerals. Explain how the chemist knows each fact.

DISCOVERY INVESTIGATION 3

Materials

- safety goggles
- lab coat or apron
- conductivity tester
- 5-g samples of sodium chloride, copper(II) sulfate, sucrose, and ethanol
- hand lens
- 4 100-mL beakers
- distilled water
- 50-mL graduated cylinder
- spatula
- stirring rod
- 3 small crucibles
- tongs
- hot plate

Comparing Ionic and Molecular Compounds

Sodium chloride (table salt) and copper(II) sulfate are ionic compounds. Sucrose (table sugar) and ethanol are molecular compounds. How do the properties of ionic compounds differ from the properties of molecular compounds? You will find out in this investigation.

Procedure

1. Make a data table like the one shown here.

Property	Sodium Chloride, NaCl	Copper(II) Sulfate, $CuSO_4$	Sucrose, $C_{12}H_{22}O_{11}$	Ethanol, C_2H_5OH
state of matter				
appearance				
compound melts when heated?				
compound conducts electricity?				
solution conducts electricity?				

2. Put on safety goggles and a lab coat or apron.

3. Examine each sample. Use the hand lens if needed. Write your observations in the first two rows of the table.

Continued on next page

4. Write a procedure to test each compound for the properties described in the last three rows of the table. Use only the materials listed. (Ethanol is a liquid so it does not require a melting test.) Include hypotheses and safety alerts.

5. Have your procedure approved by your teacher.

6. Carry out your procedure, recording your results in the data table.

Cleanup/Disposal

Pour all solutions down the drain with plenty of running water. Wash the glassware and return all equipment. Clean your work area and wash your hands.

Analysis

1. Compare the appearances of the three solids. Can you use these observations to separate them into ionic and molecular compounds?

2. Which compounds conduct electricity? Which ones conduct electricity when dissolved in water?

3. Which solid melts at a warm temperature?

Conclusions

1. Compare the melting points of ionic compounds and molecular compounds.

2. Did the conductivity testing of the compounds identify them as molecular or ionic? Explain your answer.

3. A solution conducts electricity only if it has charged particles that are free to move. What can you conclude about the particles in each of the four solutions?

Explore Further

You also observed the properties of a third molecular compound in this investigation. What is it, and what are its properties? How do you know if it conducts electricity?

High-Sulfur Coal

Coal is a fossil fuel. It forms naturally from the remains of plants and animals deep underground. Coal is burned in power plants to produce electricity. Coal is a mixture of mostly carbon compounds. When carbon compounds are burned, they supply useful energy. Coal also contains sulfur and sulfur compounds. When these substances are burned, they produce sulfur dioxide, SO_2. SO_2 is a toxic gas with a very sharp odor. It reacts with water and oxygen in the air to form sulfuric acid, H_2SO_4. SO_2 contributes to air pollution and acid rain.

These problems could be reduced by removing the sulfur from coal before burning it. However, the energy and cost to do this is great. Another solution is to burn coal that has a low sulfur content. However, a large part of the world's coal supply is high in sulfur.

A more practical solution is to remove the SO_2 after burning the coal. This is done by "scrubbing" the gases produced when coal is burned. Scrubbing involves a series of chemical reactions. Calcium carbonate,

$CaCO_3$, is added to the furnace. When heated, it breaks down into calcium oxide, CaO, and carbon dioxide, CO_2. The CaO reacts with some of the SO_2 to produce calcium sulfite, $CaSO_3$, an ionic compound. The remaining SO_2 reacts with a mixture of CaO and water. This forms additional $CaSO_3$.

The $CaSO_3$ slowly reacts with oxygen, changing into calcium sulfate, $CaSO_4$. $CaSO_4$ does not dissolve well in water. It is not very acidic. Because of these properties, it can be safely buried without causing pollution. However, $CaSO_4$ is useful as a building material. It is part of gypsum, the major component of drywall.

1. Compare the formula units of calcium carbonate, calcium oxide, calcium sulfite, and calcium sulfate. How are they alike and different?

2. Why is low-sulfur coal better than high-sulfur coal?

3. Find out the source of electricity for your neighborhood. Is it a coal-burning plant? If not, where does your electricity come from?

Chapter 3   S U M M A R Y

- The atoms of a molecular compound are bonded together by sharing electrons. The formula of a molecular compound shows the atoms in one molecule of that compound. Binary compounds contain two elements.

- To name a binary molecular compound, write the name of the first element in the formula. Then write the name of the second element, but change its ending to *-ide*. Give each name a prefix to indicate the number of atoms of that element. For the first name, the prefix *mono-* is dropped.

- To write the formula of a binary molecular compound, write the symbol of each element. Then write subscripts after each symbol based on prefixes in the name.

- Ionic compounds contain cations and anions. The cation is always given first in a name or formula unit.

- The symbol for an ion is its element symbol(s) followed by the charge as a superscript.

- When ionic compounds contain more than two elements, the cation, anion, or both are polyatomic ions.

- To name an ionic compound, write the name of the cation and then the name of the anion. If the anion is a single, charged atom, change its name ending to *-ide*. If the cation has more than one charge, write a roman numeral after the cation name to indicate its charge.

- To write the formula unit of an ionic compound, write the cation symbol followed by the anion symbol. Use subscripts to create the simplest neutral compound. Use the crisscross method.

- The names of acids do not follow the naming rules in this chapter.

Vocabulary

acid, 115	cation, 91	ionic compound, 91	molecule, 89
anion, 91	formula unit, 98	molecular compound, 86	polyatomic ion, 101
binary, 86	ion, 91		

Chapter 3 REVIEW

Vocabulary Review

For each set, match a term in the first column with one set of examples in the second column. On a sheet of paper, write the letter of the answer.

Set A

1. anions
2. cations
3. binary compounds
4. formula units
5. polyatomic ions
6. acids

A $C_2H_3O_2^{1-}$ and NH_4^{1+}

B Ba^{2+} and NH_4^{1+}

C $CrCl_3$ and Li_2CO_3

D $PbBr_2$ and carbon dioxide

E Cl^{1-} and NO_3^{1-}

F acetic acid and H_2SO_4

Set B

7. superscripts
8. molecular compounds
9. ionic compounds
10. charges
11. ions
12. molecules

A phosphorus trifluoride and H_2O

B ClO_3^{1-} and Mg^{2+}

C the 2 in Ba^{2+} and in 10^2

D $KMnO_4$ and chromium(III) fluoride

E 3+ and 1−

F I_2, P_4, and CO_2

Continued on next page

Concept Review

On a sheet of paper, write the letter of the answer to each question.

13. Which statement is correct?

    A Potassium nitrate is KNO_3.
    B Calcium carbonate is $Ca(CO_3)_2$.
    C Iron(III) oxide is Fe_3O_2.
    D Dinitrogen monoxide is NO_2.

14. Given the formula unit CuO, which roman numeral needs to be added to the name *copper oxide*?

    A I   **B** II   **C** III   **D** IV

15. Which statement is *not* true?

    A CO is carbon monoxide.
    B Rb_2SO_4 is dirubidium sulfate.
    C CCl_4 is carbon tetrachloride.
    D $Mg(HCO_3)_2$ is magnesium bicarbonate.

16. What is the formula unit of iron(II) hydroxide?

    A Fe_2H **B** $FeOH_2$ **C** $Fe(OH)_2$ **D** FeOH

17. What is the formula of silicon disulfide?

    A SiS_2 **B** Si_2SO_4 **C** Si_2S **D** $Si(SO_4)_2$

Problem Solving

On a sheet of paper, write the answer to each question.

18. What is the name of the ionic compound, NH_4F?

19. What is the name of the molecular compound, P_4S_3?

20. What is the formula unit of nickel(II) acetate?

21. What is the formula of tetraphosphorus decoxide?

Critical Thinking

On a sheet of paper, write the answer to each question.

22. Suppose you discover a new metal called elementium (El). It combines with chromate to form $El_2(CrO_4)_3$. As an ion, it has only one possible charge. What is the formula unit for elementium phosphate?

23. Copper and zinc are next to each other on the periodic table. When copper and bromine are combined, two different ionic compounds form. When zinc and bromine are combined, only one ionic compound forms. How can you explain this?

24. When is it necessary to add prefixes to a compound name?

25. You are shown two bottles from a chemistry lab. Each is labeled, but part if each label is missing. The name on the first bottle ends in ". . . acetate." The name on the second bottle ends in ". . . disulfide." What can you tell from this information?

Test-Taking Tip Look over a test before you begin answering questions. Read the directions for each section. Try to set aside enough time to complete each section.

4

Chemical Quantities

Dozens of long rows of giant sunflowers make up this field. Each sunflower head is actually hundreds of individual flowers. So the number of flowers in this field is much bigger than meets the eye. In Chapter 4, you will learn how chemists describe very large quantities of atoms and molecules. You will also learn about different kinds of chemical formulas for compounds.

Organize Your Thoughts

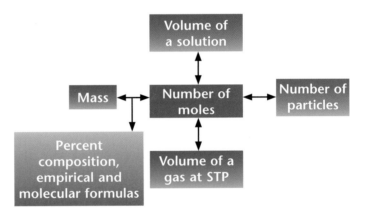

Goals for Learning

◆ To convert between moles and number of particles

◆ To convert between mass and moles

◆ To convert between moles and gas volume at STP

◆ To use molarity in conversions involving solutions

◆ To calculate the percent composition of a compound

◆ To find an empirical formula from percent composition

◆ To use an empirical formula to find a molecular formula

Objectives

After reading this lesson, you should be able to

◆ explain what a mole is

◆ convert between moles and number of particles

All matter is made of different kinds of particles. These particles can be atoms, molecules, or ions. Elements such as helium and iron exist as single atoms. Other elements, like hydrogen, oxygen, and nitrogen, are diatomic molecules. Molecular compounds, like carbon dioxide and water, also exist as molecules. Ionic compounds, like ammonium carbonate, consist of cations and anions in formula units. Depending on the substance, different names for the particles are used. In this chapter, all atoms, molecules, and formula units are referred to as particles.

The Mole

Mole (mol)

A unit for measuring the amount of a substance; 1 mol contains 6.02×10^{23} atoms, molecules, or formula units

The particles in matter are very, very small—too small to see, even with a microscope. Counting the number of particles in a sample is not possible. Instead of counting them, chemists measure the number of particles with a unit called a **mole.** The abbreviation for mole is *mol.* The mole is a unit for measuring the amount of a substance (an element or compound). The word *mole* means a number, similar to the word *dozen.*

   1 dozen eggs $= 12$ eggs

   1 mole of particles $= 6.02 \times 10^{23}$ particles

One mole of any substance contains 6.02×10^{23} particles. These particles can be atoms, molecules, or formula units.

Link to ➤➤➤

Language Arts

While the word *atom* is about 2,400 years old, the words *molecule* and *mole* are fairly new. Both words come from the Latin word *mole,* meaning "mass." *Mole* suggests a large mass (6.02×10^{23} particles). *Molecule* means "little mass" (one particle). *Molecule* was first used in the early 1800s by Joseph Gay-Lussac and Amadeo Avogadro. The current definition of a chemical *mole* first appeared around 1896.

Avogadro's number

6.02×10^{23}; the number of particles in 1 mol

The official definition of a mole is based on this standard: 1 mol of the most common form of carbon atoms is exactly 12.000 g.

The number, 6.02×10^{23}, is called **Avogadro's number.** It is a very, very large number. A mole of eggs is more eggs than have ever been eaten in the history of the world. To give you an idea of the size of this number, if you stacked 6.02×10^{23} sheets of paper, the pile would reach to the sun and back more than a million times! However, when dealing with very tiny particles, a mole is a small amount, as shown in Figure 4.1.1.

Mole-Particle Conversions

Chemists use Avogadro's number to calculate the number of particles in a sample of matter. Suppose you are told that a balloon contains 2.00 mol of the gas argon (Ar)—and nothing else. You want to know how many particles are in the balloon. In other words, you want to change measurement units from moles to number of particles.

moles of argon → particles of argon

You will need a conversion factor that relates these two units. It will be one of these factors:

$$\frac{6.02 \times 10^{23} \text{ particles}}{1 \text{ mol}} \quad \text{or} \quad \frac{1 \text{ mol}}{6.02 \times 10^{23} \text{ particles}}$$

Figure 4.1.1 *The balloon contains 1 mol of helium gas. Also shown are 1 mol of water and 1 mol of salt.*

To solve a problem involving scientific notation, use a calculator with an exponent button. Calculators vary in the way scientific notation is entered and displayed. Many have a button labeled EE or EXP for entering an exponent (a power of 10). Sometimes a second function of a button is used. To enter (2.00)(6.02 $\times 10^{23}$) with an EE button, press 2.00 $\times$ 6.02 EE 23 $=$. Depending on the calculator, the answer might be shown as 1.204 E 24, 1.204　24, or 1.204^24. If your calculator has a ^ button in addition to an EE or EXP button, use the EE or EXP button for scientific notation.

Since number of particles is your desired unit, you will use the first conversion factor. Follow the same steps you use for other unit conversions.

1. Write the given number and unit. Include the chemical symbol or formula of the substance.

2. Multiply this by a conversion factor. This factor must have the new unit on top and the given unit on the bottom. The given units will cancel out.

3. Give the answer with the correct unit. Use the correct number of significant figures.

Now look at Example 1 to find out how many particles of argon are in the balloon.

Example 1   How many atoms are in 2.00 mol of argon?

Read   You are given the number of moles of argon, an element. You are asked to find the number of atoms in this amount.

Plan   You need a conversion factor that changes moles into number of atoms. The factor will use Avogadro's number. The new unit, atoms of Ar, should be on top.

Solve   Multiply the given amount by the conversion factor. Use a calculator with an exponent button (often labeled EE or EXP). The given unit, moles of Ar, cancels out.

$$2.00 \; \cancel{\text{mol Ar}} \left(\frac{6.02 \times 10^{23} \text{ atoms Ar}}{1 \; \cancel{\text{mol Ar}}} \right) = 1.204 \times 10^{24}$$

$\xrightarrow{\text{round}} 1.20 \times 10^{24}$ atoms of argon

The answer can have only 3 significant figures. The rounded answer is 1.20×10^{24} atoms of argon.

Reflect   If you do not have a calculator with an exponent button, you could multiply (2.00)(6.02) to get 12.04. Then multiply this by 10^{23} to get 12.04×10^{23}. Putting this in scientific notation and rounding to 3 significant figures gives 1.20×10^{24}.

Practice   How many atoms are in 4.5 mol of zinc?

Example 2	How many moles are in 4.35×10^{24} molecules of carbon dioxide?
Read	You are given the number of molecules of CO_2. You are asked to find the number of moles.
Plan	You need a conversion factor to change number of molecules to moles. The new unit, moles, should be on the top.
Solve	Multiply the given number by the correct conversion factor. Cancel identical units.

$$4.35 \times 10^{24} \text{ molecules CO}_2 \left(\frac{1 \text{ mol CO}_2}{6.02 \times 10^{23} \text{ molecules CO}_2} \right) = 7.23 \text{ mol CO}_2$$

The answer has been rounded to 3 significant figures. It includes the unit (moles) and identifies the substance (CO_2).

Reflect	A mole can be 6.02×10^{23} atoms, molecules, or formula units. To enter Avogadro's number on a calculator, remember to use the EE or EXP button.
Practice	How many moles are in 1.62×10^{23} atoms of argon?

In Example 1, the substance was argon, so the particles were atoms. In Example 2, the particles were molecules. In the next example, the substance is an ionic compound, so the particles are formula units.

Example 3	How many formula units are in 3.15 mol of sodium oxide?
Read	You are given the number of moles. You are asked to find the number of formula units.
Plan	You need a conversion factor with the number of formula units on top.
Solve	Multiply 3.15 mol of Na_2O by the correct conversion factor. Cancel identical units. Round the answer to 3 significant figures and include the unit and substance.

$$3.15 \text{ mol Na}_2\text{O} \left(\frac{6.02 \times 10^{23} \text{ formula units Na}_2\text{O}}{1 \text{ mol Na}_2\text{O}} \right) = 1.90 \times 10^{24} \text{ formula units Na}_2\text{O}$$

Reflect	This answer makes sense. By estimating, you might have guessed the answer to be close to $(3)(6 \times 10^{23}) = 18 \times 10^{23} = 1.8 \times 10^{24}$.
Practice	How many formula units are in 25 mol of lithium iodide?

On a sheet of paper, write the word or phrase from the Word Bank that completes each sentence.

Word Bank
Avogadro's
mole
number of particles

1. A(n) _____ is a unit that means 6.02×10^{23} atoms, molecules, or formula units.

2. The number 6.02×10^{23} is also called _____ number.

3. To convert moles to number of particles, the correct conversion factor has _____ on the top.

On a sheet of paper, write the letter of the answer that completes each sentence.

4. There are _____ molecules in 1.52 mol of dinitrogen monoxide.

   A 9.15   **B** 3.96   **C** 9.15×10^{23} **D** 2.52×10^{-24}

5. There are _____ mol in 8.23×10^{24} formula units of calcium carbonate.

   A 13.7   **B** 4.95×10^{24} **C** 1.37×10^{24} **D** 1.37

6. There are _____ atoms in 5.31 mol of iron.

   A 32.0   **B** 3.20×10^{24} **C** 0.882   **D** 8.82×10^{22}

Critical Thinking

On a sheet of paper, write the answer to each problem. Use the correct unit and the correct number of significant figures.

7. How many moles are in 3.3×10^{22} molecules of chlorine?

8. How many formula units are in 4.89 mol of sodium oxide?

9. How many moles are in 4.89×10^{23} formula units of sodium oxide?

10. How many molecules are in 0.357 mol of water?

Objectives

After reading this lesson, you should be able to

◆ define molar mass

◆ find the molar mass of an element using the periodic table

◆ calculate the molar mass of a compound

◆ use molar mass to convert between mass and moles

Atomic mass

The average mass of an atom of an element

Molar mass

The mass in grams of 1 mol of a substance; molar mass has the unit grams per mole (g/mol)

In Lesson 1, you learned that 1 mol of a substance is a certain number of particles. In this lesson, you will learn that 1 mol of a substance has a certain mass. It is impossible to count the particles in a sample of matter. However, it is easy to find the sample's mass. If you know the mass of a substance, you can determine the number of moles in it.

To make a mass-to-mole conversion, you need to know about another piece of information on the periodic table. Look at the periodic table printed on the inside back cover of this book. In each element tile, two numbers are shown. The first number is the atomic number. This is the number of protons in an atom of the element. The second number is the **atomic mass.** The atomic mass is the average mass of an atom of the element. It has units called atomic mass units (amu). These units are usually not shown in periodic tables. You will learn more about atomic mass units in Chapter 8.

The Molar Mass of Elements

The atomic mass of an element is related to its **molar mass.** The molar mass of any substance is the mass in grams of 1 mol of that substance.

molar mass = mass of 1 mol of substance

The unit for molar mass is grams per mole (g/mol). Unlike Avogadro's number, molar mass is not the same for all substances. It depends on the substance. For elements, molar mass is numerically equal to atomic mass. The units are different, but the numbers are exactly the same. Find potassium in column 1 of the periodic table.

atomic mass of potassium = 39.1 amu

This means

molar mass of potassium = 39.1 g/mol

atomic number

atomic mass
39.1 amu

molar mass
39.1 g/mol

Now find oxygen in column 16. What is its molar mass? It is 16.0 g/mol, since its atomic mass is 16.0 amu. In other words, 1 mol of oxygen atoms is 16.0 g. However, this is not the molar mass of O_2. The molar mass of diatomic molecules is twice the molar mass of single atoms.

molar mass of $O = 16$ g/mol
molar mass of $O_2 = 2(16$ g/mol$) = 32.0$ g/mol

Remember, the seven elements that naturally occur as diatomic molecules are I_2, Br_2, N_2, Cl_2, H_2, O_2, and F_2. What about polyatomic molecules like S_8? The molar mass for the element sulfur is 32.1 g/mol, so

molar mass of $S_8 = 8(32.1$ g/mol$) = 256$ g/mol

The Molar Mass of Compounds

To find the molar mass of a compound of two or more elements, add the masses of 1 mol of each atom in the compound's formula or formula unit. For example, to find the molar mass of CO_2, count the number of C and O atoms in the formula. Then locate the molar mass of carbon and oxygen on the periodic table (see the tiles at the left). Add the molar masses of the atoms.

molar mass of $CO_2 = 12.0$ g/mol $+ 16.0$ g/mol $+ 16.0$ g/mol
                 1 C atom   1 O atom   1 O atom

              $= 44.0$ g/mol

Here is another way to calculate this:

molar mass of $CO_2 = 12.0$ g/mol $+ 2(16.0$ g/mol$) = 44.0$ g/mol

Watch the subscripts in a compound's formula when counting the number of each kind of atom.

Example 1   Calculate the molar mass of the ionic compound, $Ba(C_2H_3O_2)_2$.

Read   This formula unit contains 1 Ba atom, 4 C atoms, 6 H atoms, and 4 O atoms.

Plan   The compound's molar mass is the sum of the molar masses for each atom in the formula unit. Find the molar mass of Ba, C, H, and O. Use the atomic mass numbers on the periodic table.

Solve   Add the molar masses.

molar mass of $Ba(C_2H_3O_2)_2$
$$= 137.3 \text{ g/mol} + 4(12.0 \text{ g/mol}) + 6(1.0 \text{ g/mol}) + 4(16.0 \text{ g/mol})$$
$$= 255.3 \text{ g/mol}$$

Reflect   In this calculation, the numbers 4, 6, and 4 are counting numbers. They do not affect the significant figures in the answer. Remember that *adding* significant figures involves different rules than *multiplying* them.

Practice   Calculate the molar mass of the compound, Cu_2O.

Example 2   Calculate the molar mass of ammonium sulfate.

Read   Ammonium and sulfate are names of polyatomic ions. This is an ionic compound made of ammonium cations and sulfate anions.

Plan   Find the symbol and charge of each ion in Table 3.4.1 on page 102: NH_4^{1+} and SO_4^{2-}. Then find the neutral formula unit: $(NH_4)_2SO_4$. There are 2 N atoms, 8 H atoms, 1 S atom, and 4 O atoms.

Solve   Add the molar masses of the atoms in the formula unit.

molar mass of $(NH_4)_2SO_4$
$$= 2(14.0 \text{ g/mol}) + 8(1.0 \text{ g/mol}) + 32.1 \text{ g/mol} + 4(16.0 \text{ g/mol})$$
$$= 132.1 \text{ g/mol}$$

Reflect   As you can see, knowing the names and formulas of substances is an important part of chemistry.

Practice   Calculate the molar mass of nickel(II) nitrate.

Mole-Mass Conversions

Molar mass can be used to convert between the mass of a sample and the number of moles in that sample. If you know a sample's mass, you can find the number of moles in the sample. If you know how many moles are in a sample, you can find its mass. To do this, follow the basic steps for any unit conversion.

1. Write the given number and unit as well as the formula for the substance.

2. Create the right conversion factor. If the substance is not an element, you will need to calculate its molar mass. The conversion factor will have one of these two forms:

$$\frac{\text{molar mass of substance (in grams)}}{1 \text{ mol of substance}}$$

or

$$\frac{1 \text{ mol of substance}}{\text{molar mass of substance (in grams)}}$$

3. Multiply the given information by the conversion factor. Cancel identical units.

4. Write the answer using the correct number of significant figures. Add the unit and identify the substance.

Example 3	How many moles are in 12.5 g of CO_2?
Read	You are asked to convert a mass in grams to moles.
Plan	Find the molar mass of CO_2. It is 44.0 g/mol, as shown on page 132. Use this to create a conversion factor with the new unit (moles) on top.
Solve	Multiply 12.5 g by this factor. Cancel the given units. $12.5 \text{ g } CO_2 \left(\dfrac{1 \text{ mol } CO_2}{44.0 \text{ g } CO_2} \right) = 0.2840909 \xrightarrow{\text{round}} 0.284 \text{ mol } CO_2$
Reflect	Using a calculator, 12.5/44.0 = 0.2840909. This is rounded to 3 significant figures. Adding the unit and formula, the answer becomes 0.284 mol of CO_2.
Practice	How many moles are in 83.2 g of H_2SO_4?

Now convert in the other direction. You are given moles, and you want to find mass.

Example 4   What is the mass in grams of 1.5 mol of NaCl?

Read   You are given moles of NaCl. You want to convert this to grams of NaCl.

Plan   Find the molar mass of NaCl. It is $23.0 + 35.5 = 58.5$ g/mol. Use this sum to create a conversion factor with the desired unit (grams) on top.

Solve   Multiply 1.5 mol by this factor. Cancel given units.

$$1.5 \ \cancel{\text{mol NaCl}} \left(\frac{58.5 \ \text{g NaCl}}{1 \ \cancel{\text{mol NaCl}}} \right) = 87.75$$

$$\xrightarrow{\text{round}} 88 \ \text{g NaCl}$$

Reflect   The answer is rounded to 2 significant figures because 1.5 mol is a measurement with only 2 significant figures.

Practice   What is the mass in grams of 0.774 mol of water?

Express Lab 4

Materials
- safety goggles
- 20 identical marbles
- plastic bowl
- balance

Procedure

1. Put on safety goggles. Measure and record the mass of the empty bowl.

2. Measure the mass of the bowl with 5 marbles. Calculate the total mass of the 5 marbles.

3. Repeat step 2 with 10 marbles and then with 20 marbles.

4. Draw a graph of marble mass versus marble number.

Analysis

1. Use your graph to estimate the mass of 5,000 marbles.

2. Suppose you had 6.02×10^{23} marbles. What would their total mass be?

3. How are the atoms in 1 mol of an element like the marbles in this lab?

On a sheet of paper, write the letter of the answer to each question.

1. Which statement about molar mass is *not* true?

    A It depends on the number of atoms in a formula.
    B Its unit is grams per mole.
    C It is the same for all monatomic elements.
    D It has a different unit than atomic mass.

2. What is the molar mass of $CuCl$?

    A 35.5 g/mol   **B** 71.0 g/mol   **C** 99.0 g/mol   **D** 135 g/mol

3. What is the molar mass of Cl_2?

    A 35.5 g/mol   **B** 71.0 g/mol   **C** 99.0 g/mol   **D** 135 g/mol

4. You want to convert grams of H_2 gas to moles. What conversion factor would you use?

    A $\dfrac{1.0\ g}{1\ mol}$ **B** $\dfrac{2.0\ g}{1\ mol}$ **C** $\dfrac{1\ mol}{1.0\ g}$ **D** $\dfrac{1\ mol}{2.0\ g}$

5. What is the mass of 2.30 mol of $CuCl$? (Hint: Use your answer from question 2.)

    A 228 g   **B** 99.0 g   **C** 43.0 g   **D** 2.30 g

6. How many moles are in 8.0 g of H_2 gas? (Hint: Use your answer from question 4.)

    A 2.0 mol   **B** 4.0 mol   **C** 8.0 mol   **D** 16 mol

Critical Thinking

On a sheet of paper, write the answer to each question.

7. How do you find the mass of 1 mol of diatomic molecules?

8. What conversion factor would you use to change moles of calcium carbonate to grams?

9. How many moles are in 82.5 g of $Ca(C_2H_3O_2)_2$?

10. You have 6.02×10^{23} molecules of H_2O. What is the mass of this sample?

Objectives

After reading this lesson, you should be able to

◆ define STP and standard molar volume

◆ convert between gas volume, moles, mass, and number of particles

---

Atmosphere (atm)

A unit for measuring pressure

Standard temperature and pressure (STP)

A temperature of 0°C and a pressure of 1 atm

Standard molar volume

22.4 L/mol; the volume of 1 mol of any gas at STP

Remember that the liter is a unit that measures volume. Its abbreviation is L.

Gases have a property that liquids and solids do not have. Under certain conditions, 1 mol of any gas has a volume of 22.4 L. The two conditions that make this true are

- A temperature of 0°C
- A pressure of 1 **atmosphere (atm)**

Atmosphere (atm) is a unit for measuring pressure. The air pressure at sea level is about 1 atm. You will learn more about pressure and gases in Chapter 7. The two conditions above are called **standard temperature and pressure (STP).** For now, it is important to know that 1 mol of any gas at STP has a volume of 22.4 L. The value 22.4 L/mol is called **standard molar volume.**

For gases at STP, standard molar volume, 22.4 L/mol, is used to convert between gas volume and moles. It is written as a fraction so it can be used as a conversion factor.

- To convert the volume of a gas into moles, use $\frac{1 \text{ mol}}{22.4 \text{ L}}$.

- To convert the moles of a gas into volume, use $\frac{22.4 \text{ L}}{1 \text{ mol}}$.

These conversion factors only work for gases at STP. At other temperatures or pressures, 1 mol of a gas would not be 22.4 L.

Example 1	What is the volume of 1.50 mol of CO_2 at STP?
Read	You are given the moles of a gas. You are asked to find the volume in liters.
Plan	The gas is at STP, so you can use standard molar volume. The conversion factor has liters on top.
Solve	Multiply 1.50 mol by the conversion factor. Cancel the given units.
	$$1.50 \text{ mol } CO_2 \left(\frac{22.4 \text{ L } CO_2}{1 \text{ mol } CO_2} \right) = 33.6 \text{ L } CO_2$$
Reflect	The values of STP (0°C and 1 atm) are not part of mole-volume conversions.
Practice	What is the volume of 3.75 mol of He gas at STP?

Pressure is a measure of force acting on a unit of area. In this case, it is the force of a gas pushing on an area. Pressure can be measured with units other than the atmosphere.

The next example uses standard molar volume to find the moles in a certain volume of gas. This conversion is from liters to moles.

Example 2	How many moles are in 75.3 L of O_2 gas at STP?
Read	You are given a volume of a gas. You are asked to convert liters into moles.
Plan	Because the gas is at STP, you can use standard molar volume. Find the right conversion factor.
Solve	Multiply 75.3 L by the conversion factor. Cancel the given units.

$$75.3 \text{ L } O_2 \left(\frac{1 \text{ mol } O_2}{22.4 \text{ L } O_2} \right) = 3.36 \text{ mol } O_2$$

This rounded answer has 3 significant figures.

Reflect	In conversions involving standard molar volume, the identity of the gas does not affect the answer. If this example asked about a sample of H_2 or He gas at STP, your answer would be the same.
Practice	How many moles are in 2,500 L of Cl_2 gas at STP?

Link to ➤➤➤

Earth Science

Even in a gas, atoms are rather close together. The volume of a helium atom is 4.9×10^{-25} cm^3. The average amount of space surrounding a helium atom is 7.4×10^{-23} cm^3. This space is about 150 times as large as the atom. By comparison, the space between the sun and the nearest star is about 10^{23} times larger than the sun's volume.

★ ★

Achievements in Science

Avogadro's Number

In 1811, Amadeo Avogadro proposed that equal volumes of all gases at the same temperature and pressure contain the same number of particles. However, no one knew what that number might be. In 1860, Stanislao Cannizarro showed that Avogadro's idea could be used to determine molar masses. But the number of particles in a mole was still unknown. No one knew how large molecules were.

In 1865, Josef Loschmidt was the first to determine molecular size. He assumed that the volume of a liquefied gas nearly equaled the volume of the molecules themselves. From this, he calculated the number of molecules per cubic centimeter in a gas at STP. Loschmidt's assumptions produced incorrect results. However, his method was the basis for finding the quantity now known as Avogadro's number: 6.02×10^{23}.

Lesson 3 REVIEW

On a sheet of paper, write the answer to each question.

1. What does STP mean?

2. What is the volume of 1 mol of any gas at STP?

3. To convert gas volume into moles, what conversion factor do you need? Assume the gas is at STP.

Critical Thinking

On a sheet of paper, write the answer to each problem.

4. How many moles are in 43.7 L of oxygen gas, O_2, at STP?

5. What is the volume in milliliters of 0.0100 mol of CH_4 gas at STP?

Spotlight on Hydrogen

Hydrogen is the simplest element in nature. Most hydrogen atoms consist of a proton and an electron. Less common forms of hydrogen contain one or two neutrons in the nucleus.

Hydrogen is the most common element in the universe. It makes up about 90% of all matter. On the earth, hydrogen is a gas that is lighter than air. In the universe, however, its most common state is as a plasma. Hydrogen is chemically unique: it can easily accept or give up an electron. Because it reacts easily and is abundant, it is in most compounds. In particular, hydrogen is found in most carbon compounds. Hydrogen also bonds with oxygen to form water. Without hydrogen, life as we know it would not exist.

Interesting Fact: Under extreme pressure, hydrogen has the properties of a liquid metal.

Objectives

After reading this lesson, you should be able to

◆ calculate the molarity of a solution

◆ calculate the mass of solute

◆ calculate the volume of a solution

Concentrated

Having a large amount of solute compared to another solution; strong

Dilute

Having a small amount of solute compared to another solution; weak

Concentration

The amount of solute in a certain volume of solution

Molarity (M)

The number of moles of solute per liter of solution

You read about solutions in Chapter 2. Solutions are homogeneous mixtures. They consist of one or more solutes dissolved in a solvent.

Concentration and Molarity

Solutions can be **concentrated** or **dilute,** depending on the amount of solute and solvent. A concentrated solution has more solute compared to another solution with the same volume. A dilute solution has less solute compared to another solution.

Think of making orange juice from a can of frozen concentrate. The directions say to add three cans of water to the contents of the can. If you add only one can of water, your juice will be very concentrated, or strong. If you add six cans of water, your juice will be very dilute, or weak. Chemists use different units to measure the **concentration** of a solution. Concentration is the amount of solute in a certain volume of solution. One unit for concentration is **molarity *(M)*.** Molarity is the number of moles of solute per liter of solution. It has this equation form:

$$M = \frac{\text{moles of solute}}{\text{liters of solution}}$$

To calculate a solution's molarity, divide the number of moles of solute by the volume of the solution in liters. The more moles of solute in a given volume, the higher the concentration and the higher the molarity, as shown in Figure 4.4.1.

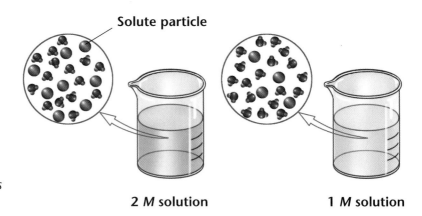

Solute particle

2 *M* solution   **1 *M* solution**

Figure 4.4.1 *The two aqueous solutions have the same volume. The 2 M solution has twice as many solute particles as the 1 M solution.*

Molarity is a derived unit. It is made by dividing moles by liters. The abbreviation for molarity is a capital *M.* The abbreviation for meters is a lowercase m. The abbreviation for mass can be *M* or *m.*

Example 1	The volume of an aqueous solution is 1.50 L. It contains 12.5 g of NaCl. What is the molarity of the solution?
Read	You are asked to give the molarity of a solution. You know the mass of the solute in grams. You know the volume of the solution in liters.
Plan	Molarity is moles of solute divided by liters of solution. You are given the liters of solution, 1.50 L. You need the moles of solute. To get this, convert grams of solute to moles using molar mass.

$$12.5 \text{ g NaCl} \left(\frac{1 \text{ mol NaCl}}{58.5 \text{ g NaCl}} \right) = 0.214 \text{ mol NaCl}$$

Solve	To find molarity, divide moles by liters.

$$\frac{0.214 \text{ mol NaCl}}{1.50 \text{ L}} = 0.142 \ M \text{ NaCl solution}$$

The concentration of this NaCl solution is 0.142 *M.*

Reflect	The concentration of an aqueous solution is often written with the solute at the end, like this: 0.142 *M* NaCl.
Practice	The volume of a solution is 1.67 L. It contains 39.0 g of diatomic bromine. What is the molarity of the solution?

If you were given a volume of 1,500 mL in Example 1, you would have to convert this to liters first. Molarity is always moles divided by liters.

❀ ❀

Technology and Society

Tap water is drinking water from a tap, or faucet. This water is really a very dilute solution. Most tap water is first treated by adding small amounts of substances. One of these substances is chlorine dioxide. This common disinfectant destroys harmful bacteria that might live in untreated water.

Link to >>>

Health

For a person to remain healthy, solutions in the body must be kept at certain concentrations. For example, diabetes is a disease that causes high concentrations of glucose in the blood. This happens when the body does not produce enough insulin. People who have diabetes must check the amount of glucose in their blood. They may need to inject insulin to keep a healthy glucose concentration.

The definition of molarity involves three values: molarity in moles per liter, moles, and liters:

$$M = \frac{\text{moles of solute}}{\text{liters of solution}}$$

If you know two of the values in this equation, you can solve for the missing one.

- If you know moles of solute and solution volume, you can find molarity.
- If you know the molarity and solution volume, you can find moles of solute.
- If you know molarity and moles of solute, you can find volume.

Example 1 showed the first problem type. The next two examples show the other types.

Example 2	A 1.35 M solution of KF has a volume of 1.33 L. How many moles of solute does it contain?
Read	You are given molarity and solution volume. You need to find the moles of solute.
Plan	Use the two given values in the definition of molarity. Solve for the moles of solute.
Solve	To solve for x below, multiply both sides of the equation by 1.33 L. Round your answer to 3 significant figures. $$1.35\ M = \frac{x\ \text{mol KF}}{1.33\ \text{L}}$$ $x = 1.80$ mol KF When 1.80 mol of KF is dissolved in water to make 1.33 L, the result is a 1.35 M solution of KF.
Reflect	Another way to solve this is to use molarity as a conversion factor: $\frac{1.35\ \text{mol KF}}{1\ \text{L solution}}$. Multiply the given volume by this fraction. $$1.33\ \text{L solution} \left(\frac{1.35\ \text{mol KF}}{1\ \text{L solution}}\right) = 1.80\ \text{mol KF}$$
Practice	A 2.85 M solution of KCl has a volume of 0.425 L. How many moles of solute are in this solution?

Example 3 An NH_4Cl solution has a concentration of 0.573 M. It contains 0.323 mol of solute. What is the volume of the solution?

Read You are given molarity and moles of solute. You are asked to find solution volume.

Plan Use the definition of molarity to find the solution volume.

Solve Use the given values in the equation.

$$0.573\ M = \frac{0.323\ \text{mol}\ NH_4Cl}{x\ \text{L solution}}$$

Solve for the missing value x. This involves some algebra. Then round your answer to significant figures.

$$x\ \text{L solution} = \frac{0.323\ \text{mol}\ NH_4Cl}{0.573\ M} = 0.564\ \text{L}$$

The volume of the solution is 0.564 L or 564 mL.

Reflect Another way to solve this problem is to use molarity as a conversion factor, with liters on top.

$$0.323\ \cancel{\text{mol}\ NH_4Cl} \left(\frac{1\ \text{L}\ NH_4Cl}{0.573\ \cancel{\text{mol}\ NH_4Cl}} \right) = 0.564\ \text{L}\ NH_4Cl$$

Practice A $BaBr_2$ solution has a concentration of 1.95 M. It contains 1.25 mol of solute. What is the volume of the solution?

Science Myth

Myth: A dilute solution always contains less solute than a concentrated solution.

Fact: The concentration of a solution depends on the amount of solute *and the volume of solution.* One liter of a dilute solution may contain more solute than 100 mL of a concentrated solution. For example, 1 L of a 0.20 M sugar solution contains more sugar than 100 mL of a 1.0 M sugar solution.

To do conversions involving gas volume, the gas must be at STP.

Conversion Review

For a given element or compound, you have learned how to convert between:

- moles and the number of particles (Lesson 1)
- moles and mass (Lesson 2)
- moles and gas volume at STP (Lesson 3)
- moles and solution volume (this lesson)

Figure 4.4.2 summarizes the relationships between these units. The arrows show the direction of conversion from one unit to another. Conversion factors are in green and red to match the arrows.

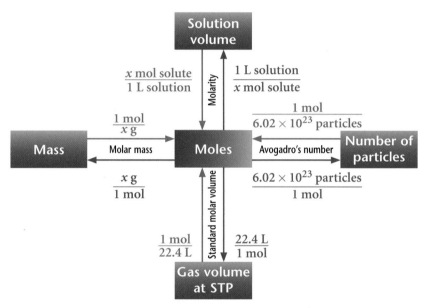

Figure 4.4.2 *Conversions are represented by arrows. Conversion factors are next to arrows.*

Suppose you want to convert between moles (in the center) and one of the four outside units (particles, mass, or volume). Find the arrow that shows this conversion, and use the conversion factor next to it. For example, to convert mass to moles, find the arrow pointing from mass to moles. Find the conversion factor that goes with this arrow: $\frac{1\,\text{mol}}{x\,\text{g}}$. Replace the x with the molar mass of the substance. Multiply the given mass by this factor.

If you want to convert an outside unit in Figure 4.4.2 to another outside unit, *you must go through moles.* Suppose you know the mass of substance X. You want the number of molecules in this substance. It may help to make a conversion "map" of this:

mass of X → moles of X → number of molecules of X

This requires two conversion factors, one for each arrow.
- The first factor is used to convert the given unit to moles.
- The second factor is used to convert moles to the desired unit.

Example 5	How many atoms are in a 44.3-g piece of iron?
Read	You know the mass of the iron piece. You are asked to find the number of atoms.
Plan	Mass and number of particles are outside units in Figure 4.4.2. First convert mass to moles, then convert moles to number of atoms. mass of Fe → moles of Fe → number of atoms of Fe This requires two conversion factors. The first factor goes with the first arrow in the map. It should have moles—the desired unit—on top. The second factor goes with the second arrow. It should have number of atoms—the desired unit—on top.
Solve	Multiply the given value by the two conversion factors. Cancel the two sets of identical units. $$44.3 \text{ g Fe} \left(\frac{1 \text{ mol}}{55.8 \text{ g Fe}} \right) \left(\frac{6.02 \times 10^{23} \text{ atoms Fe}}{1 \text{ mol}} \right) = 4.78 \times 10^{23} \text{ atoms Fe}$$
Reflect	A mass-mole conversion always involves the molar mass of the substance. A mole-particle conversion always involves Avogadro's number.
Practice	What is the mass of 5.24×10^{22} molecules of iodine, I_2?

Each example on the next page requires two conversion factors. As you read these examples, trace the conversions on Figure 4.4.2. Why are these conversions important? In Chapter 5, you will use conversion skills to understand the amounts in chemical reactions. Reactions take place between whole numbers of particles. Substances in reactions combine and form according to moles.

Example 6	What is the volume of 68.4 g of fluorine gas, F_2, at STP?
Read	You are asked to convert mass to volume. The substance is a gas at STP.
Plan	First convert to moles, then convert to volume. Here is the conversion map:
	mass of $F_2 \rightarrow$ moles of $F_2 \rightarrow$ volume of F_2
	Each arrow represents a conversion factor. Since fluorine is a diatomic molecule, its molar mass is 2(molar mass of F) = 2(19.0 g/mol) = 38.0 g/mol. This will be part of the first conversion factor. The second conversion factor involves standard molar volume. In each factor, put the desired unit on top.
Solve	Multiply the given amount by the two conversion factors. Cancel identical units.
	$$68.4 \text{ g } F_2 \left(\frac{1 \text{ mol}}{38.0 \text{ g } F_2} \right) \left(\frac{22.4 \text{ L}}{1 \text{ mol}} \right) = 40.32 \xrightarrow{\text{round}} 40.3 \text{ L } F_2$$
Reflect	In conversions like this, you are multiplying and dividing measurements. Remember to watch significant figures.
Practice	How many molecules are in 0.75 L of nitrogen gas, N_2, at STP?

Example 7	You have 0.75 L of a 1.9 M solution of NaCl. What is the mass of the solute?
Read	You are asked to convert the volume of a solution to grams of solute. The molarity of the solution is 1.9 M.
Plan	First convert the solution volume to moles using molarity. Then convert moles to mass using molar mass. Here is the conversion map:
	volume of NaCl solution $\rightarrow$ moles of NaCl $\rightarrow$ mass of NaCl
	The first conversion involves molarity. 1.9 M NaCl can be written as $\frac{1.9 \text{ mol NaCl}}{1 \text{ L solution}}$. The second conversion involves the molar mass of NaCl.
Solve	Multiply the given solution volume by the two conversion factors.
	$$0.75 \text{ L solution} \left(\frac{1.9 \text{ mol NaCl}}{1 \text{ L solution}} \right) \left(\frac{58.5 \text{ g NaCl}}{1 \text{ mol NaCl}} \right) = 83 \text{ g NaCl}$$
	The answer, 83 g of NaCl, has been rounded to 2 significant figures because of the values 0.75 and 1.9.
Reflect	When you use the correct conversion factors, all units cancel except the unit you want.
Practice	A 0.47 M KNO_3 solution contains 4.56×10^{23} particles of KNO_3. What is the volume of the solution?

Lesson 4   R E V I E W

On a sheet of paper, write the word from the Word Bank that completes each sentence.

Word Bank

solute

solution

solvent

1. Molarity is moles of solute divided by liters of _____.

2. Solutions are diluted by adding _____.

3. A concentrated solution has a larger amount of _____ than a dilute solution of the same volume.

On a sheet of paper, write the letter of the answer to each question.

4. 0.541 mol of $C_{12}H_{22}O_{11}$ is dissolved in water to make 0.223 L of solution. What is the molarity of this solution?

A 0.00153 M **B** 0.00243 M **C** 1.53 M **D** 2.43 M

5. 16.3 g of NaCl is dissolved in water to make 1.75 L of solution. What is the molarity of this solution?

A 0.159 M **B** 0.278 M **C** 9.31 M **D** 33.4 M

6. Solid $CaCl_2$ was added to water to make a 1.70 M $CaCl_2$ solution. Its volume is 0.450 L. What mass of $CaCl_2$ was added? (Hint: The molar mass of $CaCl_2$ is 111.1 g/mol.)

A 50.0 g   **B** 85.0 g   **C** 189 g   **D** 420. g

Critical Thinking

On a sheet of paper, write the answer to each problem.

7. What conversion factor would you need to convert the volume of a solution to the moles of solute?

8. How many moles of solute are needed to make 2.66 L of a 1.99 M $C_{12}H_{22}O_{11}$ solution?

9. You need to make a 1.50 M solution using 48.0 g of NaCl. Draw a conversion map and solve the problem.

10. 1.63 mol of NaOH in 1.63 L of solution has the same molarity as 17 mol of HCl in 17 L of solution. Explain.

INVESTIGATION 4

Concentrations of Copper(II) Sulfate Solutions

Can you tell the concentration of a solution just by looking at it? In this investigation, you will observe how solution color varies with solute concentration. You will use this information to estimate the concentration of an unknown solution.

Procedure

1. Put on safety goggles and a lab coat or apron.

2. Place a clean, empty beaker on the balance. Measure and record its mass. Keep the beaker on the balance.

3. Using the spatula, begin to add very small amounts of copper(II) sulfate to the beaker. Stop when the mass is 1.0 g more than the mass of the beaker alone. Record the mass of the beaker and copper(II) sulfate.

4. Carefully measure 100 mL of distilled water using the graduated cylinder.

5. Add the water to the beaker. Stir the solution with the stirring rod until the copper(II) sulfate is completely dissolved. Set the solution aside. **Safety Alert: Be careful with glassware, especially the stirring rod. Report any chipped or broken glass to your teacher.**

6. Repeat steps 2 through 5 three more times, except use 5.0 g, 10.0 g, and 20.0 g of copper(II) sulfate. Label the four beakers. **Safety Alert: Do not taste any of the solutions.**

7. Prepare a fifth solution with the same concentration as one of the other solutions. Record the mass of copper(II) sulfate in this solution. Do not label the beaker. Give this solution to another student or group to analyze.

8. Analyze the unknown solution you are given. Compare its color to the four solutions you prepared. Estimate how much copper(II) sulfate is in the unknown solution. Record your estimate.

Cleanup/Disposal

Pour the copper(II) sulfate solutions into a proper waste container. Wash and dry the glassware. Return all equipment, then wash your hands.

Analysis

1. What is the molar mass of copper(II) sulfate pentahydrate? Use the formula $CuSO_4 \cdot 5H_2O$.

(This substance contains 1 $CuSO_4$ formula unit and 5 water molecules.)

2. How many moles are in 1 g of the solute?

3. How many moles of solute are in each of the solutions you prepared?

4. What is the molarity of each of these four solutions?

Conclusions

1. How does the solution's appearance vary with concentration?

2. What was your estimate of the unknown concentration?

3. How did you determine your estimate?

Explore Further

Do a similar investigation by preparing 0.4 M, 0.2 M, 0.1 M, and 0.05 M solutions in 500-mL volumetric flasks.

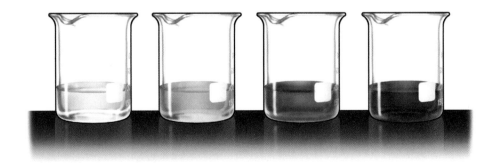

After reading this lesson, you should be able to
◆ find the total molar mass for each element in a compound
◆ find the percent composition of a compound

Compounds have a definite composition, given by their formula or formula unit. Look at water, H_2O, as an example. Each molecule of water contains 2 atoms of hydrogen and 1 atom of oxygen. Each mole of water contains 2 mol of hydrogen and 1 mol of oxygen. If we had exactly 1 mol of water, we would know that it contains

$$2(1.0 \text{ g/mol}) = 2.0 \text{ g/mol of hydrogen}$$
$$\underline{1(16.0 \text{ g/mol}) = 16.0 \text{ g/mol of oxygen}}$$
$$18.0 \text{ g/mol} = \text{molar mass of } H_2O$$

The molar mass of any compound can be broken down into the molar masses of each element.

total molar mass of hydrogen in $H_2O = 2.0$ g/mol

total molar mass of oxygen in $H_2O = 16.0$ g/mol

Percent composition

A set of values that tells the percentage by mass of each element in a compound

This breakdown can be expressed as a set of percentages called **percent composition.** Percent composition tells the percentage by mass of each element in a compound. In 1 mol of water, hydrogen is 2.0 g of the 18.0 g total. As a percentage, this is

$$\left(\frac{2.0 \text{ g/mol}}{18.0 \text{ g/mol}} \right) 100\% = 11.111111 \xrightarrow{\text{round}} 11\% \text{ hydrogen}$$

Oxygen is 16.0 g of the 18.0-g total. As a percentage, this is

$$\left(\frac{16.0 \text{ g/mol}}{18.0 \text{ g/mol}} \right) 100\% = 88.888888 \xrightarrow{\text{round}} 88.9\% \text{ oxygen}$$

Math Tip

In the formula for percent composition, the same unit (g/mol) is on both the top and the bottom. These units are canceled, and the desired unit, percent (%), remains.

The two percentages add to 100%, or close to it. By mass, water is 11% hydrogen and 88.9% oxygen. This is the percent composition of H_2O, as shown in Figure 4.5.1.

H_2O	Oxygen	Hydrogen
18.0 g/mol	2.0 g/mol	16.0 g/mol
100%	88.9%	11%

Figure 4.5.1 *The percent composition of water is 88.9% oxygen and 11% hydrogen.*

To calculate percent composition for a compound, follow the steps below.

1. Find the total molar mass *of each element* in the compound. For the compound C_3F_6,
   total molar mass of $C = 3(12.0 \text{ g/mol}) = 36.0 \text{ g/mol}$
   total molar mass of $F = 6(19.0 \text{ g/mol}) = 114 \text{ g/mol}$

2. Find the molar mass *of the entire compound*. To do this, add the molar masses from step 1. The molar mass of C_3F_6 is $36.0 \text{ g/mol} + 114 \text{ g/mol} = 150. \text{ g/mol}$.

3. Divide the total molar mass *of each element* by the molar mass of the compound. Then multiply by 100%. The percent composition for one element has this formula:

$$\left(\frac{\text{total molar mass of element}}{\text{molar mass of compound}}\right)100\%$$

For carbon in C_3F_6: $\left(\dfrac{36.0 \text{ g/mol}}{150. \text{ g/mol}}\right)100\% = 24.0\% \text{ carbon}$

For fluorine in C_3F_6: $\left(\dfrac{114 \text{ g/mol}}{150. \text{ g/mol}}\right)100\% = 76.0\% \text{ fluorine}$

Multiplying by 100% does not affect the number of significant figures in the answer.

4. Check that you have a percentage for each element in the compound. Check that the percentages add up to 100%, or close to it. Check that the percentages have the correct number of significant figures.

Science Myth

Myth: A large percent composition for a certain element means more atoms of that element are in the compound.

Fact: Percent composition depends on element mass and compound mass. An atom with a large atomic mass can have a large percent composition. For example, the percent composition of lead in lead dioxide (PbO_2) is 86.6%. The percent composition of carbon in carbon dioxide (CO_2) is 27.3%.

Example 1	Calculate the percent composition of $Ca(C_2H_3O_2)_2$.
Read	You are asked to find percentages for four elements.
Plan	Find the total molar mass for each element. The molar masses are Ca: $1(40.1 \text{ g/mol}) = 40.1 \text{ g/mol}$ C: $4(12.0 \text{ g/mol}) = 48.0 \text{ g/mol}$ H: $6(1.0 \text{ g/mol}) = 6.0 \text{ g/mol}$ O: $4(16.0 \text{ g/mol}) = 64.0 \text{ g/mol}$ The molar mass of the compound is the sum: 158.1 g/mol.
Solve	Use these numbers in the formula for percent composition. The units cancel. Ca: $\left(\dfrac{40.1 \text{ g/mol}}{158.1 \text{ g/mol}}\right)100\% = 25.4\%$ calcium C: $\left(\dfrac{48.0 \text{ g/mol}}{158.1 \text{ g/mol}}\right)100\% = 30.4\%$ carbon H: $\left(\dfrac{6.0 \text{ g/mol}}{158.1 \text{ g/mol}}\right)100\% = 3.8\%$ hydrogen O: $\left(\dfrac{64.0 \text{ g/mol}}{158.1 \text{ g/mol}}\right)100\% = 40.5\%$ oxygen
Reflect	The percentages add to 100.1%. The extra 0.1% is due to rounding.
Practice	Calculate the percent composition of $PbSO_4$.

▼◄▲▼◄▲▼◄▲▼◄▲▼◄▲▼◄▲▼◄▲▼◄▲▼◄▲▼◄▲▼◄▲▼◄▲▼◄▲▼◄▲▼◄▲▼

Science at Work

Analytical Chemist

Analytical chemists study the chemical composition of substances. They find out what is in a substance and how much there is. They use a variety of chemical and physical techniques.

The work of analytical chemists varies. They analyze the quality of water and air. They examine crime evidence. Analytical chemists make sure that foods and drugs are safe. They determine the structures of complex molecules. They also develop techniques to improve the accuracy of their work.

Analytical chemists work for governments, universities, and businesses. They work with computers and lab equipment. They need a four-year degree in chemistry.

On a sheet of paper, write the letter of the answer that completes each sentence.

1. The percent composition of $NaClO_4$ is a set of _____ percentages.

   A 1   **B** 2   **C** 3   **D** 4

2. The percent composition of NH_3 is a set of _____ percentages.

   A 1   **B** 2   **C** 3   **D** 4

3. The percentage of sulfur, by mass, in SF_6, is _____.

   A 22.0%   **B** 39.0%   **C** 61.0%   **D** 78.0%

4. The percentage of fluorine, by mass, in SF_6, is _____.

   A 22.0%   **B** 39.0%   **C** 61.0%   **D** 78.0%

5. The percent composition of NH_3 is closest to _____.

   A 82% N and 18% H   **C** 75% N and 25% H
   B 79% N and 21% H   **D** 67% N and 33% H

6. Lead(II) carbonate, $PbCO_3$, has a molar mass of 267.2 g/mol. The percentage of oxygen in $PbCO_3$ is _____.

   A 5.99%   **B** 13.5%   **C** 18.0%   **D** 35.9%

Critical Thinking

On a sheet of paper, write the answer to each question.

7. What is the percent composition of potassium nitrate?

8. Can you find the percent composition of a mixture? Explain your answer.

9. "The percent composition of a compound is 22.6% sulfur and 15.0% oxygen." What is wrong with this statement?

10. A compound has a molar mass is 42.4 g/mol. It contains elements X and Y. The total molar mass of element X is 6.9 g/mol. What is the percent composition of this compound?

Empirical formula

A formula that shows the smallest whole-number ratio of atoms in a compound

Molecular formula

A formula that gives the actual number of each kind of atom in a molecule

A chemist is given a molecular compound. She does not know what it is. How can she identify it? By doing experiments, she can find its percent composition. From this, she can find the **empirical formula** of the compound. An empirical formula shows the smallest whole-number ratio of atoms in a compound. Sometimes an empirical formula is also the compound's chemical formula. If it is not, the subscripts in the empirical formula are important clues to the chemical formula.

Types of Formulas

A good example is dextrose. Its chemical formula is $C_6H_{12}O_6$. But this is not the empirical formula of dextrose. Look at the subscripts. The smallest whole-number ratio of the atoms in dextrose is shown by these subscripts: $C_1H_2O_1$, or 1:2:1. CH_2O is the empirical formula of dextrose. The empirical formula gives the simplest ratio of atoms in the compound. On a larger scale, it gives the simplest ratio of moles of atoms. In any sample of dextrose, there are twice as many hydrogen atoms as carbon or oxygen atoms. For every 1 mol of carbon, there are 2 mol of hydrogen and 1 mol of oxygen. A *molecule* of dextrose, however, always has 6 carbon atoms, 12 hydrogen atoms, and 6 oxygen atoms. $C_6H_{12}O_6$ is the **molecular formula** of dextrose. A molecular formula gives the actual number of atoms in a molecule. The term *molecular formula* means the same as *chemical formula*. Figure 4.6.1 compares the molecular formula and the empirical formula of dextrose.

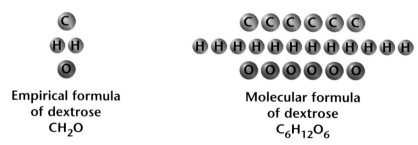

Empirical formula
of dextrose
CH_2O

Molecular formula
of dextrose
$C_6H_{12}O_6$

Figure 4.6.1 *The empirical formula of dextrose shows that there is a 1:2:1 ratio of C, H, and O atoms. The molecular formula shows the number of atoms in one molecule.*

Suppose you have a small sample of dextrose. It contains

0.01 mol of carbon atoms

0.02 mol of hydrogen atoms

0.01 mol of oxygen atoms

This is a 1:2:1 ratio, like the empirical formula, CH_2O, shows. But each molecule in your sample is a $C_6H_{12}O_6$ molecule, as given by the molecular formula.

Both ionic and molecular compounds have empirical formulas. But only molecular compounds have molecular formulas. Ionic compounds have formula units.

- An empirical formula shows the simplest ratio of atoms in a compound.
- A molecular formula, or chemical formula, shows the actual number of atoms in one molecule.
- A formula unit shows the simplest ratio of cations to anions in an ionic compound.

The subscripts in all three show the ratio of moles of each element in a compound. Consider the ionic compound, NH_4NO_2. It has an empirical formula of NH_2O. However, NH_4NO_2 is the actual formula unit, consisting of one cation (NH_4^{1+}) and one anion (NO_2^{1-}). NH_4NO_2 does not represent a molecule.

Determining Empirical Formulas

Recall that the atoms of elements combine in certain ratios to form compounds. For example, 1 mol of H_2O contains 2 mol of H atoms and 1 mol of O atoms. Hydrogen and oxygen always combine in a 2:1 ratio in water. To express this relationship, chemists use a **mole ratio.** A mole ratio is a ratio or fraction that compares the moles of one substance to the moles of another substance. Look at the mole ratios for water and dextrose on the next page.

Mole ratios for water: $\dfrac{2\ \text{mol H}}{1\ \text{mol O}}$ $\dfrac{1\ \text{mol O}}{2\ \text{mol H}}$

Mole ratios for dextrose: $\dfrac{6\ \text{mol C}}{12\ \text{mol H}}$ $\dfrac{12\ \text{mol H}}{6\ \text{mol C}}$ $\dfrac{6\ \text{mol O}}{6\ \text{mol C}}$

$\dfrac{6\ \text{mol O}}{12\ \text{mol H}}$ $\dfrac{12\ \text{mol H}}{6\ \text{mol O}}$ $\dfrac{6\ \text{mol C}}{6\ \text{mol O}}$

If you know the percent composition of a compound or the mass of each element, you can find the compound's empirical formula. To do this, you use a mole ratio.

1. Assume you have a 100-g sample of a compound. If you know its percent composition, you can change each percent symbol to grams. Keep the number the same. For example, 30% becomes 30 g.

   30% of element 1: assume 30 g of element 1 in sample
   70% of element 2: assume 70 g of element 2 in sample

   (If you are given a mass for each element, skip this step.)

2. For each element, convert grams to moles using molar mass.

   grams of element 1 → moles of element 1
   grams of element 2 → moles of element 2

   Treat all elements as monatomic. Remember significant figures.

3. Create a mole ratio using the mole amounts from step 2.

   moles of element 1 : moles of element 2

   (For compounds with more than two elements, this ratio will compare more than two amounts.) Change this ratio into the simplest ratio of *whole numbers.* To do this, divide each mole amount by a common factor. Usually, the common factor is the smallest mole amount.

4. The numbers in the simplest ratio become the subscripts in the empirical formula. Write the empirical formula using these numbers.

The next example shows how to find the empirical formula of a sample containing nitrogen and oxygen.

Example 1 What is the empirical formula of an unknown compound that contains 30.4% nitrogen and 69.6% oxygen by mass?

Read   You are given the percent composition for a molecular compound. You are asked to find its empirical formula.

Plan   Assume you have a 100-g sample. Change the percent symbols to grams. For example, 30.4% becomes 30.4 g. Then convert grams to moles using a conversion factor. Round each answer to significant figures.

30.4% N: $30.4 \text{ g N} \left(\dfrac{1 \text{ mol N}}{14.0 \text{ g N}} \right) = 2.17 \text{ mol N}$

69.6% O: $69.6 \text{ g O} \left(\dfrac{1 \text{ mol O}}{16.0 \text{ g O}} \right) = 4.35 \text{ mol O}$

Solve   Now create a mole ratio of nitrogen to oxygen.

2.17 mol N : 4.35 mol O

This is not a ratio of whole numbers. Divide each number by the smallest mole amount, which is 2.17 mol. The units cancel out. Express the ratio in whole numbers.

$\dfrac{2.17 \text{ mol}}{2.17 \text{ mol}} : \dfrac{4.35 \text{ mol}}{2.17 \text{ mol}}$ or   1:2

The smallest whole-number ratio of nitrogen to oxygen is 1:2. (Because the final mole ratio must be in whole numbers, you may ignore significant figures.) The empirical formula of the unknown compound is $N_{(1)}O_2$, or NO_2.

Reflect   The empirical formula NO_2 shows that there is 1 mol of nitrogen for every 2 mol of oxygen. NO_2 may or may not be the molecular formula.

Practice   What is the empirical formula of a compound that contains 80.0% carbon and 20.0% hydrogen by mass?

Because 1 mol $= 6.02 \times 10^{23}$ particles, an empirical formula tells you both a particle ratio and a mole ratio—the ratios are the same. In the compound in Example 1, there is 1 N atom for every 2 O atoms. There is 1 mol of N for every 2 mol of O.

Example 2   What is the empirical formula of a molecular compound that contains 4.37 g of phosphorus and 5.63 g of oxygen?

Read   You are given the mass of two elements in a molecular compound.

Plan   You can skip step 1 in the process, since you already have the number of grams of each element. Convert grams to moles. Round.

$$4.37 \text{ g P} \left(\frac{1 \text{ mol P}}{31.0 \text{ g P}} \right) = 0.141 \text{ mol P}$$

$$5.63 \text{ g O} \left(\frac{1 \text{ mol O}}{16.0 \text{ g O}} \right) = 0.352 \text{ mol O}$$

Solve   Now create a mole ratio of phosphorus to oxygen.

0.141 mol P : 0.352 mol O

This is not a ratio of whole numbers. Divide each number by 0.141 mol.

$$\frac{0.141 \text{ mol}}{0.141 \text{ mol}} : \frac{0.352 \text{ mol}}{0.352 \text{ mol}} \quad \text{or} \quad 1:2.5$$

The new ratio, 1:2.5, is still not in whole numbers. Multiply each number in the ratio by 2. This gives 2:5. The empirical formula of the compound is P_2O_5.

Reflect   The ratio 2:5 equals the ratio 1:2.5. Both show that there are 2.5 times more oxygen atoms than phosphorus atoms. They also show that 2.5(moles of oxygen) = moles of phosphorus.

Practice   A sample contains 3.70 g of iron and 1.59 g of oxygen. What is the empirical formula of this compound?

❋ ❋

Technology and Society

An important method for determining an empirical formula is mass spectroscopy. A mass spectrograph is a device that removes an electron from atoms in a sample. These ions then move through a magnetic field. This separates ions of different masses. The amounts of each element separated by the spectrograph are compared. This provides information for finding the empirical formula.

On a sheet of paper, write the word from the Word Bank that completes each sentence.

Word Bank

empirical

mole

molecular

1. A(n) _____ formula shows the smallest whole-number ratio of atoms or moles in a compound.

2. A(n) _____ formula represents an actual molecule.

3. A(n) _____ ratio compares the mole amounts of two or more substances.

On a sheet of paper, write the letter of the answer to each question.

4. What is the empirical formula of the compound, $C_5H_{15}O_{10}$?

   A $C_5H_{15}O_{10}$ **B** $C_3H_5O_3$ **C** CH_3O_2 **D** $C_2H_3O_2$

5. A compound has a mole ratio of 1 mol of lead to 2 mol of chlorine, or 1:2. What is its empirical formula?

   A $PbCl$ **B** Pb_2Cl **C** $PbCl_2$ **D** $PbCl_4$

6. A compound contains 63.5% iron and 36.5% sulfur. What is its empirical formula?

   A FeS **B** Fe_2S **C** Fe_2S_2 **D** FeS_2

Critical Thinking

On a sheet of paper, write the answer to each question.

7. What is the difference between molecular formulas, empirical formulas, and formula units?

8. "An ionic compound has an empirical formula of Mn_2O_3. This is also its molecular formula." What is wrong with this statement?

9. How is a mole ratio related to a formula?

10. A compound contains 4.20 g of carbon, 4.21×10^{23} atoms of hydrogen, and 16.8 g of oxygen. What is the empirical formula of this compound?

Objectives

After reading this lesson, you should be able to

◆ find the molecular formula of a compound

◆ find the empirical formula of a hydrate

Ionic compounds do not have molecular formulas. They have formula units.

As you learned in Lesson 6, a molecular formula gives the actual number of atoms in a molecule. An empirical formula gives the smallest whole-number ratio of atoms in a compound. A molecular formula is either the empirical formula or a multiple of the empirical formula.

$$\text{molecular formula} = n(\text{empirical formula})$$

n must be a whole number. For the compound dextrose, $n = 6$.

empirical formula of dextrose: CH_2O

molecular formula of dextrose: $C_6H_{12}O_6 = 6(CH_2O)$

When the subscripts in the empirical formula are multiplied by 6, you get the molecular formula. The ratios 1:2:1 and 6:12:6 are equal.

For many molecular compounds, the empirical formula and the molecular formula are the same. In these cases, $n = 1$. Common examples are H_2O and CO_2. Can you think of others?

Determining Molecular Formulas

To find the molecular formula of a compound, you must know

- the empirical formula
- the molar mass of the compound

Think of dextrose as an example again. Suppose you don't know its molecular formula. However, you do know its empirical formula, CH_2O. You also know that the mass of 1 mol of dextrose is 180.0 g/mol. To find the molecular formula, follow these steps:

1. Calculate the mass of the empirical formula. This is not necessarily the molar mass of the compound. For dextrose,

$$\text{mass of } CH_2O = 12.0 \text{ g/mol} + 2(1.0 \text{ g/mol}) + 16.0 \text{ g/mol}$$
$$= 30.0 \text{ g/mol}$$

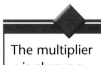

The multiplier *n* is always a whole number. However, because of rounding, a calculator might give a decimal value of *n* that is very close to a whole number.

2. Compare the mass from step 1 with the given molar mass. Find a whole number *n* so that:

molar mass of compound $= n$(mass of empirical formula)

For dextrose, $180.0 \text{ g/mol} = n(30.0 \text{ g/mol})$, so $n = 6$.

3. Multiply each subscript in the empirical formula by *n*. The result is the molecular formula. For dextrose, this is

$$6(CH_2O) = C_{6 \times 1}H_{6 \times 2}O_{6 \times 1} = C_6H_{12}O_6$$

Check that the molecular formula has the molar mass you were given. If not, recheck your answer.

molar mass of $C_6H_{12}O_6$
$$= 6(12.0 \text{ g/mol}) + 12(1.0 \text{ g mol}) + 6(16.0 \text{ g/mol})$$
$$= 180.0 \text{ g/mol}$$

Example 1	The empirical formula of a compound is NO_2. The molar mass of the compound is 92.0 g/mol. What is its molecular formula?
Read	You are given an empirical formula and a molar mass. These are the two facts you need to find the molecular formula.
Plan	First find the mass of the empirical formula. mass of $NO_2 = 14.0 \text{ g/mol} + 2(16.0 \text{ g/mol}) = 46.0 \text{ g/mol}$
Solve	Use this mass and the given molar mass to find *n*. *n* must be a whole number. molar mass of compound $= n$(mass of empirical formula) $92.0 \text{ g/mol} = n(46.0 \text{ g/mol})$ $n = 2$ Multiply the subscripts in NO_2 by 2. This gives N_2O_4. Check that this formula has the given molar mass. molar mass of $N_2O_4 = 2(14.0 \text{ g/mol}) + 4(16.0 \text{ g/mol}) = 92.0 \text{ g/mol}$
Reflect	The calculated molar mass is the same as the given molar mass, so the molecular formula N_2O_4 is correct.
Practice	The empirical formula of a compound is CH. The molar mass of the compound is 78.0 g/mol. What is its molecular formula?

Example 2   An unknown compound contains 2.17 g of carbon, 0.362 g of hydrogen, and 0.966 g of oxygen. Its molar mass is 116.0 g/mol. What are its empirical and molecular formulas?

Read

You are given the masses of three elements in a compound. You are also given the molar mass of the compound.

Plan

From the element masses, find a mole ratio. From this, find the empirical formula. From this and the molar mass, find the molecular formula.

element masses → mole ratio → empirical formula → molecular formula

First convert grams to moles using a conversion factor for each element.

$$2.17 \text{ g C} \left(\frac{1 \text{ mol C}}{12.0 \text{ g C}} \right) = 0.181 \text{ mol C}$$

$$0.362 \text{ g H} \left(\frac{1 \text{ mol H}}{1.0 \text{ g H}} \right) = 0.36 \text{ mol H}$$

$$0.966 \text{ g O} \left(\frac{1 \text{ mol O}}{16.0 \text{ g O}} \right) = 0.0604 \text{ mol O}$$

Solve

Use these mole amounts to make a ratio of C:H:O.

0.181 mol:0.36 mol:0.0604 mol

Divide each number by 0.0604 mol to find a ratio of whole numbers.

$$\frac{0.181 \text{ mol}}{0.0604 \text{ mol}} : \frac{0.36 \text{ mol}}{0.0604 \text{ mol}} : \frac{0.0604 \text{ mol}}{0.0604 \text{ mol}} \quad \text{or} \quad 3 : 6 : 1$$

This ratio gives the subscripts in the empirical formula, which is C_3H_6O. The mass of this formula is

mass of $C_3H_6O = 3(12.0 \text{ g/mol}) + 6(1.0 \text{ g/mol}) + 16.0 \text{ g/mol} = 58.0 \text{ g/mol}$

To find the molecular formula, use the given molar mass and solve for n.

molar mass of compound $= n$(mass of empirical formula)
116.0 g/mol $= n$(58.0 g/mol)
$n = 2$

Multiply the empirical formula's subscripts by 2.

$2(C_3H_6O) = C_6H_{12}O_2$

This is the molecular formula.

Reflect

Check the molar mass using the molecular formula.

molar mass of $C_6H_{12}O_2 = 6(12.0 \text{ g/mol}) + 12(1.0 \text{ g/mol}) + 2(16.0 \text{ g/mol})$
$= 116.0 \text{ g/mol}$

Practice

An unknown compound contains 21.8 g of phosphorus and 28.2 g of oxygen. Its molar mass is 284 g/mol. What are its empirical and molecular formulas?

Ionic compounds that easily form hydrates are stored in air-tight containers. When exposed to water in the air, these solid compounds begin to form hydrates.

Hydrates

Some compounds have molecules of water trapped as part of the compound. **Hydrates** are compounds that are chemically combined with water in a specific ratio. The compound in a hydrate is usually an ionic compound. In a hydrate's empirical formula, the water molecules are written at the end. For example, $Ni(NO_3)_2 \cdot 6H_2O$ shows that there are 6 molecules of water with each formula unit of nickel nitrate. On a larger scale, this means there are 6 mol of H_2O for every 1 mol of $Ni(NO_3)_2$. The dot in the formula is *not* a multiplication sign.

When a hydrate is heated, the water molecules leave and mix with the surrounding air. What remains after heating is the ionic compound without the water. Its formula unit shows no water molecules. For example,

$$CuSO_4 \cdot 5H_2O \xrightarrow{\text{heat}} CuSO_4$$

Figure 4.7.1 shows this hydrate before heating and the compound without water after heating. This change can be used to calculate the empirical formula of the hydrate.

Figure 4.7.1 *The hydrate, $CuSO_4 \cdot 5H_2O$, is a blue solid. After heating, only $CuSO_4$ remains. It is a white solid.*

Suppose you measure the mass of a sample of hydrate. Then you heat it until the water is gone. You measure the mass of the compound that is left. You know the following information.

- mass of hydrate
- mass of compound without water
- mass of water in sample (hydrate mass − compound mass)

From this information, you can find the empirical formula of the hydrate. It is based on the ratio of moles of the compound to moles of water. A hydrate's empirical formula is not based on moles of elements, like other empirical formulas. Example 3 shows how to determine the empirical formula of a hydrate of $MgSO_4$.

Chemistry in Your Life

Consumer Choices: Dehydrated Products

You may have heard the expression "just add water." Many food products have had water removed from them, like the dry soup mix on the plate. You need to add water when you are ready to use them.

For example, you can buy orange juice in the form of a frozen concentrate. Some beverages come in a dehydrated, or powdered, form. Soups can be purchased in a condensed or concentrated form in cans. Soups are also available as dry mixes or bouillon cubes. You can even buy milk as a dehydrated powder. Then you "just add water."

You can usually store dehydrated products for a long time. In a dried, condensed, or concentrated form, food products take up less space. However, they are not always convenient to use because you have to add

water. Also, they often do not taste quite the same, or quite as good, as the original or fresh food.

1. What are two advantages of dehydrated products?

2. What are two examples of dehydrated products in your household?

3. Do your own taste test. Compare a dehydrated product to a similar fresh food. Do they taste different? Describe how each product tastes.

Example 3	A hydrate of magnesium sulfate, $MgSO_4$, is heated, with the following results. What is the empirical formula of the hydrate?
	mass of hydrate before heating $= 5.65$ g
	mass of compound after heating $= 2.76$ g
Read	You are given the mass of the hydrate and the mass of the compound with no water.
Plan	To find the empirical formula, you need the mass of the water. Subtract the given masses: $5.65g - 2.76$ g $= 2.89$ g of water.
Solve	Calculate the moles of the compound and the moles of water. To do this, convert grams to moles.

$$2.76 \text{ g } MgSO_4 \left(\frac{1 \text{ mol } MgSO_4}{120.3 \text{ g } MgSO_4} \right) = 0.0229 \text{ mol } MgSO_4$$

$$2.89 \text{ g } H_2O \left(\frac{1 \text{ mol } H_2O}{18.0 \text{ g } H_2O} \right) = 0.160 \text{ mol } H_2O$$

To find the hydrate's empirical formula, create a mole ratio using the above numbers. The $MgSO_4$:H_2O ratio is

0.0229 mol : 0.160 mol

Create a whole-number ratio from this. Divide both mole amounts by 0.0229 mol. This yields a 1:7 ratio of $MgSO_4$ to H_2O.

There are 7 H_2O molecules for every 1 formula unit of $MgSO_4$. The empirical formula of the hydrate is $MgSO_4 \cdot 7H_2O$.

Reflect	The mole ratio in this example compares the moles of two compounds, $MgSO_4$ and H_2O. Earlier in the chapter, you created mole ratios comparing the moles of elements within one compound.
Practice	A hydrate of sodium sulfide, Na_2S, is heated, with the following results. What is the empirical formula of the hydrate?
	mass of hydrate before heating $= 154$ g
	mass of compound after heating $= 50.$ g

Word Bank

empirical formula

hydrate

molecular formula

On a sheet of paper, write the word or phrase from the Word Bank that completes each sentence.

1. If you know the molar mass of a compound and its empirical formula, you can find its _____.

2. A(n) _____ is an ionic compound that contains water.

3. A molecular formula is a whole-number multiple of the _____.

On a sheet of paper, write the letter of the answer to each question.

4. A compound has the empirical formula, C_2H_3O. Its molar mass is 172.0 g/mol. What is the molecular formula?

A C_2H_3O **B** $C_4H_6O_2$ **C** $C_8H_{12}O_4$ **D** $C_{16}H_{24}O_8$

5. A compound has the empirical formula, CH_2. Its molar mass is 140.0 g/mol. What is the molecular formula?

A C_2H_4 **B** C_4H_8 **C** C_7H_{14} **D** $C_{10}H_{20}$

6. A hydrate of $CuSO_4$ has a mass of 56.59 g. After it is heated, the compound has a mass of 38.99 g. What is the mass of the water that evaporated?

A 17.60 g   **B** 38.99 g   **C** 56.59 g   **D** 95.58 g

Critical Thinking

On a sheet of paper, write the answer to each problem.

7. A compound contains 14.4 g of carbon and 1.8 g of hydrogen. It has a molar mass of 54.0 g/mol. What is its empirical formula?

8. What is the molecular formula of the compound in question 7?

9. A hydrate of $ZnSO_4$ has a mass of 2.875 g. After it is heated, the mass is 1.615 g. What is the hydrate's empirical formula?

10. Do you think hydrates have molecular formulas? Explain.

DISCOVERY INVESTIGATION 4

Materials

- safety goggles
- lab coat or apron
- ring stand
- ring clamp
- clay triangle
- Bunsen burner
- crucible and lid
- sample of unknown hydrate
- balance
- tongs

The Formula of a Hydrate

Water molecules combine with certain ionic compounds to form hydrates. Heating a hydrate removes the water, leaving the compound. How can you find the number of water molecules combined with one formula unit in an unknown hydrate?

Procedure

1. Put on safety goggles and a lab coat or apron.

2. Set up the ring stand, clamp, clay triangle, and burner as shown below. Adjust the ring height so the burner flame will just touch the crucible. Do not turn on the burner yet.

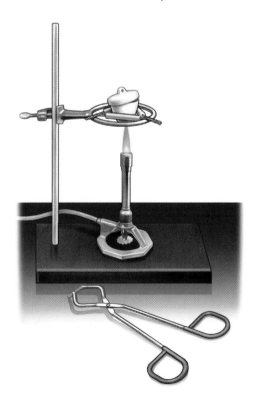

Continued on next page

3. Be sure the crucible and lid are clean and dry. Place them on the balance and record their mass. Place the sample in the crucible. Record the mass of the sample, crucible, and lid. Find the mass of the sample. **Safety Alert: Do not touch or taste any substances.**

4. Use the tongs to place the crucible containing the hydrate on the clay triangle. Place the cover on the crucible so that the crucible is slightly off-center. Light the burner.

5. Heat the crucible gently over the burner for 15 minutes. Turn off the burner. Use the tongs to place the crucible cover completely over the crucible. Let the crucible cool for 7 to 10 minutes. **Safety Alert: Do not touch the heated crucible with your hands.**

6. Use the tongs to place the crucible, lid, and contents on the balance. Record this mass. Find the mass of the contents.

Cleanup/Disposal

Put the contents of the crucible in the proper waste container. Wash and dry the crucible. Return all equipment. Then wash your hands.

Analysis

1. What is the mass difference between the hydrate and the ionic compound? What does this mass represent?

2. To determine the formula of the hydrate, what piece of information do you need? Ask your teacher for this information.

3. What is the empirical formula of the hydrate? Show your work.

Conclusions

1. Suppose the heating did not remove all of the water from the hydrate. How would this affect your results?

2. List at least two other possible sources of error in this investigation.

Explore Further

A desiccant is a compound used to absorb moisture from the air. How could the formula of a hydrate indicate its effectiveness as a desiccant?

Desiccants

Water is a common and important compound. It is needed for life. However, there are some situations when water should not be present. For instance, some medicines break down if exposed to water in the air for too long. Lenses and mirrors in some equipment need to be kept dry at all times. Water in the air can cause mold to grow on these glass surfaces.

To keep air dry, desiccants are used. Desiccants are often ionic compounds. They easily form hydrates. When water molecules are present, desiccants trap them. Several water molecules can combine with one formula unit of a desiccant. This makes desiccants effective drying agents for the surrounding air.

A common desiccant is silica gel. This is a form of silicon dioxide—the molecular compound in sand and glass. Silica gel is placed in packets or plastic containers. These are then placed with products that are affected by moisture, like medicines or electronics components. Silica gel packets are placed in boxes of new shoes to remove moisture. They are used around certain foods to prevent mold and spoilage.

Desiccants are used on a large scale in some industries. For example, natural gas consists mostly of methane (CH_4) and can combine with water vapor.

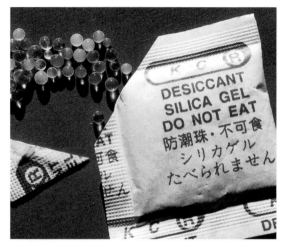

Desiccants, such as calcium chloride or lithium chloride, are used near natural gas to remove water vapor. These desiccants are replacing older drying methods that wasted large amounts of methane. Using desiccants saves fuel, reduces operation costs, and is better for the environment.

1. How are desiccants related to hydrates?

2. How can silica gel prevent mold growth on lenses or foods?

3. What are some advantages of using desiccants for drying methane?

- A mole is a unit that measures the amount of a substance. 1 mol is 6.02×10^{23} particles. These particles can be atoms, formula units, or molecules.

- Molar mass is the mass in grams of 1 mol of a substance. The molar mass of an element is its atomic mass expressed in grams per mole. The molar mass of a compound is the sum of the molar masses of the atoms in its formula.

- Standard molar volume is 22.4 L/mol. This is the volume of 1 mol of any gas at STP.

- A dilute solution has less solute than another solution of the same volume.

- Solution concentration is measured by molarity. Molarity is moles of solute divided by liters of solution. This definition can be used to solve for moles of solute or volume of solution.

- Conversion factors are needed to convert between number of particles, moles, mass, and volume. Figure 4.4.2 summarizes these conversions.

- Percent composition tells the percentage by mass of each element in a compound. The percentage for element X in compound XYZ is

$$\left(\frac{\text{total molar mass of X}}{\text{molar mass of XYZ}} \right) 100\%$$

- A mole ratio compares the mole amounts of two or more substances.

- An empirical formula shows the smallest whole-number ratio of atoms in a compound. A molecular formula shows the actual atoms in a molecule.

- The empirical formula of a compound can be determined from its percent composition.

- The molecular formula of a compound can be determined from the empirical formula and the compound's molar mass.

- Hydrates are compounds that contain water molecules. The empirical formula of a hydrate can be calculated from the mass of the compound and the mass of the water.

Vocabulary

atmosphere, 137	dilute, 140	mole, 126	standard molar volume, 137
atomic mass, 131	empirical formula, 154	molecular formula, 154	
Avogadro's number, 127	hydrate, 163	mole ratio, 155	standard temperature and pressure (STP), 137
concentrated, 140	molar mass, 131	percent composition, 150	
concentration, 140	molarity, 140		

Word Bank

concentrated

dilute

empirical

hydrate

molar mass

molarity

mole

molecular

mole ratio

percent composition

standard molar volume

standard temperature and pressure (STP)

Vocabulary Review

On a sheet of paper, write the word or phrase from the Word Bank that completes each sentence.

1. One _____ of any substance contains 6.02×10^{23} particles.

2. The _____ of CO_2 tells how much carbon and oxygen, by mass, are in the compound.

3. A gas at 0°C and under 1 atm of pressure is at _____.

4. The mass in grams of 1 mol of a substance is its _____.

5. A(n) _____ is a compound that contains water molecules.

6. A(n) _____ formula gives the actual number of atoms in a molecule.

7. A(n) _____ formula shows the smallest whole-number ratio of atoms in a compound.

8. The concentration unit, _____, is defined as moles of solute divided by liters of solution.

9. A 0.8 *M* solution is more _____ than a 0.9 *M* solution.

10. The _____ of any gas is 22.4 L/mol.

11. A(n) _____ solution has more solute per liter than another solution of the same volume.

12. A(n) _____ compares two or more mole amounts.

Continued on next page

Concept Review

On a sheet of paper, write the letter of the answer to each question.

13. What is the percentage by mass of carbon in CO_2?

    A 1.0%   **C** 18.4%

    B 12.0%   **D** 27.3%

14. What is the molar mass of aluminum hydroxide, $Al(OH)_3$?

    A 44.0 g/mol   **C** 78.0 g/mol

    B 46.0 g/mol   **D** 138.0 g/mol

15. How many moles are in 6.34×10^{24} molecules of CO_2?

    A 1.05 mol   **C** 463 mol

    B 10.5 mol   **D** 3.82×10^{48} mol

16. 389 g of $CaCl_2$ is dissolved in water to make 1 L. What is the concentration of the solution?

    A 0.285 *M*   **C** 3.89 *M*

    B 3.50 *M*   **D** 5.15 *M*

17. What is the empirical formula of ethane, C_2H_6?

    A C_2H_3 **C** CH_3

    B CH_2 **D** CH

Problem Solving

18. What is the mass in grams of 2.301 mol of Na_3PO_4?

19. What is the volume of 17.3 g of NH_3 gas at STP?

20. What is the empirical formula of a compound that contains 0.529 g of aluminum and 0.471 g of oxygen?

21. 15.7 g of KF is dissolved in water to make 475 mL of solution. What is the molarity of this solution?

Critical Thinking

22. A compound contains 17.89 g of carbon, 4.473 g of hydrogen, and 23.824 g of oxygen. What is its percent composition?

23. A chemist has a 1 mol sample of a solid ionic compound. Its mass is 44.5 g. The sample is left uncovered for many days. It becomes a hydrate with a mass of 98.5 g. How many molecules of water are trapped with each formula unit? (Hint: Find the moles of water that are trapped.)

24. How many moles of hydrogen are in 17.3 mL of a 2.96 M solution of $C_{12}H_{22}O_{11}$?

25. The empirical formula of ascorbic acid (vitamin C) is CH_2O_3. Its molar mass is 372 g/mol. How many atoms of hydrogen are in the molecular formula of ascorbic acid?

Test-Taking Tip Remember to include units with answers that need them. At the end of a test, check that the unit with each answer is correct.

Chemical Reactions

This bronze statue of a lion stands in front of the Art Institute of Chicago. The bronze in this statue is mostly copper mixed with some tin and zinc. When the statue was made in 1893, it was as shiny as a new penny. Over the years, a chemical reaction occurred between oxygen in the air and copper in the bronze. As a result, a blue-green compound now coats the lion. In Chapter 5, you will learn about chemical reactions and how to represent them as equations.

Organize Your Thoughts

Chemical reactions

Chemical equations

- Balancing equations
- Predicting products from reactants

Types of reactions

- Combination
- Decomposition
- Combustion
- Single replacement
- Double replacement

◆ To identify the reactants and products in a chemical equation

◆ To balance a chemical equation with coefficients

◆ To identify combination, decomposition, and combustion reactions

◆ To identify single-replacement reactions

◆ To identify double-replacement reactions

◆ To predict the products of a reaction

After reading this lesson, you should be able to

◆ identify the reactants and products in a chemical equation

◆ understand the symbols used in a chemical equation

Chemical equation

An equation that uses symbols to represent a chemical reaction

Reactant

A substance that is used up in a chemical reaction

Product

A substance that is produced by a chemical reaction

In Chapter 2, you learned that chemical reactions occur when one or more substances change chemically. The result is one or more different substances. You are familiar with many chemical reactions, although you may not realize it. The yeast in bread dough produces carbon dioxide gas, causing the dough to rise. When food spoils, its odor and color change. Soap reacts with the minerals in hard water, producing soap scum. All of these are chemical reactions.

Consider this simple chemical reaction:

Hydrogen and oxygen react to produce water.

This reaction can be written as a **chemical equation.**

$$H_2 + O_2 \rightarrow H_2O$$

A chemical equation uses symbols to represent a chemical reaction. The elements H_2 and O_2 are **reactants.** Reactants are substances that are used up in a chemical reaction. Reactants are written on the left side of a chemical equation. Because hydrogen and oxygen are both diatomic, they are written as H_2 and O_2, not H and O. Water, H_2O, is the only **product.** Products are substances that are produced by a chemical reaction. Products are written on the right side of the equation.

$$\text{reactants} \rightarrow \text{products}$$

If there are two or more reactants or products, they are separated by + signs. In a chemical equation, reactants and products are separated by an arrow. The arrow means "react to produce" or "produces." The arrow shows the direction of the reaction.

The state of each reactant and product is often indicated in an equation by a symbol. The symbols are

$s =$ solid
$l =$ liquid
$g =$ gas
$aq =$ aqueous solution

The last symbol, *aq*, means that the substance is dissolved in water. State symbols are always placed in parentheses, as shown.

$$H_2(g) + O_2(g) \rightarrow H_2O(g)$$

In this reaction, the reactants and products are gases. This chemical equation is the same as this word equation:

Gaseous hydrogen and gaseous oxygen react to produce gaseous water.

You can write a chemical equation from a word equation. You can also write a word equation from a chemical equation.

Example 1	Write the following word equation as a chemical equation.
	Solid aluminum and liquid bromine react to produce solid aluminum bromide.
Read	This word equation gives two reactants, aluminum and bromine. The "react to produce" phrase will become the arrow. There is one product, aluminum bromide.
Plan	The element bromine is diatomic, so its symbol is Br_2. Aluminum's symbol is Al. To write the correct formula unit for aluminum bromide, refer to the ionic charges listed on page 93. The ions in this compound are Al^{3+} and Br^{1-}, so the neutral formula unit is $AlBr_3$.
Solve	Write the chemical symbols of the reactants. Add a + sign between them. Add an arrow after the reactants. Write the formula unit of the product. For all three substances, add the state symbol in parentheses. $$Al(s) + Br_2(l) \rightarrow AlBr_3(s)$$
Reflect	In this reaction, a solid metal and a liquid nonmetal form a solid ionic compound.
Practice	Write the following word equation as a chemical equation. The charge on zinc is $2+$.
	Solid zinc oxide and aqueous hydrochloric acid react to produce aqueous zinc chloride and liquid water.

Example 2	Write the following chemical equation as a word equation.
	$CaCO_3(s) + HCl(aq) \rightarrow CaCl_2(aq) + H_2O(l) + CO_2(g)$

Read	Two reactants combine to form three products. All of the substances are compounds. One of the products is water.
Plan	To write a word equation, you need to know the name of each substance in the chemical equation. If needed, review naming and formula writing in Chapter 3.
Solve	Name each substance in the equation. Then add the state—solid, liquid, aqueous, or gaseous—in front of each name. In place of the arrow, use the phrase "react to produce."
	Solid calcium carbonate and aqueous hydrochloric acid react to produce aqueous calcium chloride, liquid water, and gaseous carbon dioxide.
Reflect	In this equation, a solid and a solution are mixed. A different solution is formed, and a gas is released.
Practice	Write the following chemical equation as a word equation.
	$Zn(s) + HCl(aq) \rightarrow ZnCl_2(aq) + H_2(g)$

Express Lab 5

Materials
- safety goggles
- lab coat or apron
- gloves
- 25 mL of 0.1 *M* copper(II) chloride
- aluminum strip
- 100-mL beaker

Procedure
1. Put on safety goggles, a lab coat or apron, and gloves.

2. Put the aluminum strip in the beaker. **Safety Alert: Be careful when working with glassware.**

3. Add the copper(II) chloride solution. **Safety Alert: Handle with care.**

4. Record your observations.

5. Put the solid waste in a proper waste container. Pour the solution down the drain with running water. Wash and return the beaker. Wash your hands.

Analysis
1. What did you observe during the reaction?

2. What were the reactants?

3. What product was formed?

Lesson 1   R E V I E W

On a sheet of paper, write the answer to each question.

1. In the following equation, what are the reactants and their states?

$$Cl_2(g) + KI(s) \rightarrow I_2(s) + KCl(s)$$

2. In the following equation, what are the products and their states?

$$K_2SO_4(aq) + Ba(NO_3)_2(aq) \rightarrow BaSO_4(s) + KNO_3(aq)$$

3. What separates reactants from products in a chemical equation?

4. What separates two reactants in a chemical equation?

5. Write the following equation in words.

$$Ba(s) + H_2O(l) \rightarrow Ba(OH)_2(s) + H_2(g)$$

6. Solid aluminum and solid iodine react to produce solid aluminum iodide. What is the chemical equation for this reaction?

Critical Thinking

On a sheet of paper, write the answer to each question.

7. What are the parts of a chemical equation?

8. What is the difference between $Br_2(l)$ and $Br_2(aq)$?

9. Write the following equation in words.

$$Li(s) + H_2O(l) \rightarrow LiOH(aq) + H_2(g)$$

10. Write the following as a chemical equation: Aqueous sodium hydroxide and aqueous hydrochloric acid react to produce liquid water and aqueous sodium chloride.

When a chemical reaction takes place, reactants react to form products. It may seem like the reactants are destroyed and the products are created. This is not true! The same atoms in the reactants have just rearranged into products.

Laws of Conservation

New atoms are not created or destroyed in a chemical reaction. There are the same number and kind of atoms *after* a reaction as *before* it. This shows the **law of conservation of matter**. This law says that matter cannot be created or destroyed. The atoms in the reactants have combined in new ways to form the products. The number and kind of atoms on each side of a chemical equation must be the same.

From Chapter 2, you know that chemical reactions involve a change in energy. There are two general forms of energy represented in Figure 5.2.1. **Kinetic energy** is the energy of motion. Objects in motion have high kinetic energy. **Potential energy** is the energy of position or composition. A bowling ball at the top of a hill has potential energy because of its position. If it rolled down the hill, its potential energy would be transformed, or changed, into kinetic energy.

Law of conservation of matter

A law that says matter cannot be created or destroyed

Kinetic energy

The energy of motion

Potential energy

The energy of position or composition

All energy is one of these three forms: kinetic energy, potential energy, or energy contained by a field, such as an electric, magnetic, or gravitational field.

Figure 5.2.1 *At the top of a roller coaster track, the riders have a great deal of potential energy. As they begin to speed downward, this is converted to kinetic energy.*

In chemistry, the word *conserve* means "to save or keep an amount of something." The conservation of matter is the saving of the number and kinds of atoms in a reaction. No atoms are destroyed. No atoms are created. This law is also called the law of conservation of mass. The total mass of matter before and after a reaction is the same. Mass is conserved.

A sandwich has potential energy because of its composition. When you eat a sandwich, its chemical composition produces energy for your body. The **law of conservation of energy** says that energy cannot be created or destroyed during any process. When a bowling ball rolls down a hill, its potential energy decreases as its kinetic energy increases. However, the total amount of energy does not change; it just changes form. When a chemical reaction occurs, the same is true. Energy changes form or moves from one place to another, but no energy is lost or created. Both matter and energy are conserved during chemical reactions.

Balancing Equations

In Lesson 1, you may have noticed that the number of atoms on each side of an equation was *not* the same. Look at this equation:

$$H_2(g) + O_2(g) \rightarrow H_2O(g)$$

There are 2 oxygen (O) atoms in the reactants. There is only 1 oxygen atom in the product. Is 1 oxygen atom destroyed? No. The problem is that this equation is *not balanced.* Chemists balance the numbers of atoms on each side of an equation by using **coefficients**. A coefficient is a whole number to the left of the symbol or formula for a substance. It is similar to a coefficient in algebra.

- In algebra, $3y$ means "3 times y" or $y + y + y$.
- In chemistry, $3H_2O$ means "3 water molecules" or $H_2O + H_2O + H_2O$.

In each case, the coefficient is 3. "$3H_2O$" means there are a total of 6 H atoms and 3 O atoms.

Chemical equations must be balanced because of the law of conservation of matter. To balance a chemical equation, coefficients are used according to this rule:

The number of atoms of each element in the reactants	equals	The number of atoms of each element in the products

There must be the same number and type of atoms on both sides of the arrow. Now go back to this *unbalanced* equation:

$$H_2(g) + O_2(g) \rightarrow H_2O(g)$$

You can ignore state symbols when balancing equations. Count the number of atoms on each side of the arrow.

H_2 + O_2	$\rightarrow$	H_2O	
2 H atoms		2 H atoms	*balanced*
2 O atoms		1 O atom	*not balanced*

For the O atoms to balance, you need 2 O atoms on the right side. To do this, place a coefficient of 2 to the left of H_2O. This is the same as multiplying H_2O by 2.

$$2H_2O = H_2O + H_2O = 4 \text{ H atoms and 2 O atoms}$$

To count the atoms in $2H_2O$, you may also think of it this way:

$$2H_2O = 2(H_2) + 2(O) = 4 \text{ H atoms and 2 O atoms}$$

This coefficient changes the number of atoms of H and O in the equation.

H_2 + O_2	$\rightarrow$	$2H_2O$	
2 H atoms		4 H atoms	*not balanced*
2 O atoms		2 O atoms	*balanced*

Now the H atoms are not balanced. Place a coefficient of 2 to the left of the reactant H_2. $2H_2$ means $H_2 + H_2$—this is 4 H atoms.

$2H_2$ + O_2	$\rightarrow$	$2H_2O$	
4 H atoms		4 H atoms	*balanced*
2 O atoms		2 O atoms	*balanced*

The equation is now balanced. It shows the law of conservation of matter. Notice two things:

- The coefficient to the left of the H_2 *only* multiplies the H_2 by 2, not the O_2.
- There is no coefficient shown to the left of the O_2. However, it is understood that the coefficient is 1.

The state symbols can be added back into the equation now.

$$2H_2(g) + O_2(g) \rightarrow 2H_2O(g)$$

This balanced equation shows that 2 H_2 molecules and 1 O_2 molecule react to form 2 H_2O molecules. On a larger scale, 2 mol of H_2 gas reacts with 1 mol of O_2 gas to produce 2 mol of gaseous water.

Achievements in Science

Conservation of Mass

Conservation of mass is one of the most important laws in chemistry. Before the late 1700s, chemists believed in a substance called phlogiston. They thought phlogiston was involved in many chemical reactions. They thought it moved through the air and had mass like any other substance. When a substance was heated, chemists believed the substance took on phlogiston from the air. For example, when an ore was heated to get its metal, the ore supposedly gained phlogiston and mass. When a metal rusted, it supposedly lost phlogiston and mass.

The French chemist Antoine Lavoisier did not believe in phlogiston. He performed experiments to show that the phlogiston theory was false. He carefully measured the masses of reactants before a chemical reaction. Then he measured the masses of the products. His results showed that the total mass before and after the reaction is the same. Lavoisier concluded that matter is not created or lost in a chemical reaction. This idea has been proved many times. It is now known as the law of conservation of mass.

Example 1   Balance the following equation.
$$N_2(g) + H_2(g) \rightarrow NH_3(g)$$

Read

You are asked to balance an equation. A balanced equation has the same number and kind of atoms on each side of the arrow. State symbols are given, but are not needed for balancing.

Plan

Count the atoms on each side of the equation. Coefficients may be needed.

N_2 + H_2 $\rightarrow$	NH_3	
2 N atoms	1 N atom	*not balanced*
2 H atoms	3 H atoms	*not balanced*

Solve

This may look hard to balance. However, you will find that it just works out. To balance the N atoms on each side, give NH_3 a coefficient of 2. The coefficient multiplies both the N and the H_3 by 2.

N_2 + H_2 $\rightarrow$	$2NH_3$	
2 N atoms	2 N atoms	*balanced*
2 H atoms	6 H atoms	*not balanced*

Now give H_2 a coefficient of 3. This balances the H atoms on each side.

N_2 + $3H_2$ $\rightarrow$	$2NH_3$	
2 N atoms	2 N atoms	*balanced*
6 H atoms	6 H atoms	*balanced*

Reflect

Using two coefficients, the equation is balanced. It says that 1 mol of nitrogen gas reacts with 3 mol of hydrogen gas to produce 2 mol of ammonia gas.

Practice

Balance the following equation.
$$Zn(s) + HCl(aq) \rightarrow ZnCl_2(aq) + H_2(g)$$

Example 2	Balance the following equation.

$$NH_4NO_3(aq) + NaOH(aq) \rightarrow NaNO_3(aq) + H_2O(l) + NH_3(g)$$

Read   You are asked to balance an equation. This may involve coefficients.

Plan   Remove the state symbols for now. Carefully count the atoms. There are N, O, and H atoms in many places.

NH_4NO_3 +	NaOH →	$NaNO_3$ +	H_2O +	NH_3
2 N atoms	1 Na atom	1 Na atom	2 H atoms	1 N atom
4 H atoms	1 O atom	1 N atom	1 O atom	3 H atoms
3 O atoms	1 H atom	3 O atoms		

Solve   For each side, the total number of atoms of each element is listed below.

NH_4NO_3 + NaOH →	$NaNO_3$ + H_2O + NH_3	
2 N atoms	2 N atoms	*balanced*
5 H atoms	5 H atoms	*balanced*
4 O atoms	4 O atoms	*balanced*
1 Na atom	1 Na atom	*balanced*

Reflect   This equation is already balanced! No coefficients are needed.

Practice   Balance the following equation.

$$Ca(NO_3)_2(aq) + K_2SO_4(aq) \rightarrow CaSO_4(s) + KNO_3(aq)$$

As you can see, it is important to be careful when counting atoms. Elements like oxygen and hydrogen are often found in more than two places in an equation. When an element is present in more than two places in an equation, balance that element last. Example 3 on the next page shows why it is helpful to balance oxygen and hydrogen last.

Sometimes the last element to be balanced cannot be balanced with a whole-number coefficient. In this case, balance this element with a coefficient such as $\frac{1}{2}, \frac{3}{2}, \frac{5}{2}, \frac{7}{2}$, etc. Then double (multiply by 2) all of the coefficients in the equation. Remember to double unwritten coefficients of 1. The coefficient containing the fraction will become a whole number. This is shown in Example 4 on page 187.

Example 3 Balance the following equation.

$$H_2SO_4(aq) + Al(OH)_3(s) \rightarrow H_2O(l) + Al_2(SO_4)_3(aq)$$

Read　You are asked to balance an equation. Each substance in the equation contains oxygen. Three of the four substances contain hydrogen.

Plan　Count the atoms on each side. Remember to distribute the subscript 3 in $Al(OH)_3$: 1 Al atom, 3 O atoms, and 3 H atoms. Also distribute the subscript 3 in $Al_2(SO_4)_3$: 2 Al atoms, 3 S atoms, and 12 O atoms.

H_2SO_4 + $Al(OH)_3$ →	H_2O + $Al_2(SO_4)_3$	
1 S atom	3 S atoms	not balanced
1 Al atom	2 Al atoms	not balanced
5 H atoms	2 H atoms	not balanced
7 O atoms	13 O atoms	not balanced

Solve　Wow, this could be really ugly. Since hydrogen and oxygen are present in more than two substances, save them for last. To balance sulfur, give H_2SO_4 a coefficient of 3. To balance aluminum, give $Al(OH)_3$ a coefficient of 2. Count again.

3H_2SO_4 + 2$Al(OH)_3$ →	H_2O + $Al_2(SO_4)_3$	
3 S atoms	3 S atoms	balanced
2 Al atoms	2 Al atoms	balanced
12 H atoms	2 H atoms	not balanced
18 O atoms	13 O atoms	not balanced

Hydrogen atoms are found in three places, but oxygen atoms are found in four. So balance hydrogen next. To get 12 H atoms on the right, give H_2O a coefficient of 6. Recount.

3H_2SO_4 + 2$Al(OH)_3$ →	6H_2O + $Al_2(SO_4)_3$	
3 atoms S	3 atoms S	balanced
2 atoms Al	2 atoms Al	balanced
12 atoms H	12 atoms H	balanced
18 atoms O	18 atoms O	balanced

Reflect　Look at that! By saving O for last, the O atoms ended up balancing without doing anything. Quite often, that will happen.

Practice　Balance the following equation.

$$H_3PO_4(aq) + Ca(OH)_2(aq) \rightarrow Ca_3(PO_4)_2(s) + H_2O(l)$$

Example 4 Balance the following equation.

$$C_6H_{14}(l) + O_2(g) \rightarrow CO_2(g) + H_2O(g)$$

Read

In this equation, carbon and hydrogen are each found in two places. Oxygen is found in three places.

Plan

Count the atoms on each side.

C_6H_{14} + O_2 $\rightarrow$	CO_2 + H_2O	
6 C atoms	1 C atom	*not balanced*
14 H atoms	2 H atoms	*not balanced*
2 O atoms	3 O atoms	*not balanced*

Solve

Balance carbon and then hydrogen. Save oxygen for last. Multiply CO_2 by 6 and H_2O by 7. Then count again.

C_6H_{14} + O_2 $\rightarrow$	$6CO_2$ + $7H_2O$	
6 C atoms	6 C atoms	*balanced*
14 H atoms	14 H atoms	*balanced*
2 O atoms	19 O atoms	*not balanced*

Oxygen is the only element left to balance. However, 19 is not a whole-number multiple of 2. Try giving O_2 a coefficient of $\frac{19}{2}$. Count the atoms.

C_6H_{14} + $\frac{19}{2}O_2$ $\rightarrow$	$6CO_2$ + $7H_2O$	
6 C atoms	6 C atoms	*balanced*
14 H atoms	14 H atoms	*balanced*
19 O atoms	19 O atoms	*balanced*

Now double each coefficient so they all are whole numbers. Remember to double the unwritten coefficient of 1 in front of C_6H_{14}. The coefficient for O_2 becomes 19, a whole number. The atom count is still balanced.

$2C_6H_{14}$ + $19O_2$ $\rightarrow$	$12CO_2$ + $14H_2O$	
6 C atoms	6 C atoms	*balanced*
14 H atoms	14 H atoms	*balanced*
19 O atoms	19 O atoms	*balanced*

Reflect

The equation is balanced with the simplest set of whole-number coefficients: 2, 19, 12, 14.

Practice

Balance the following equation.

$$C_4H_{10}(l) + O_2(g) \rightarrow CO_2(g) + H_2O(g)$$

Lesson 2 R E V I E W

On a sheet of paper, write the letter of the answer to each question.

1. During a chemical reaction, energy _____.

   A is lost

   B increases

   C may change form

   D stays in the same place

2. Which number is *not* a coefficient in the equation, $2C_6H_{14} + 19O_2 \rightarrow 12CO_2 + 14H_2O$?

   A 6   **B** 12   **C** 14   **D** 19

3. What coefficient is needed to balance the equation, $Zn + HCl \rightarrow ZnCl_2 + H_2$?

   A a 2 before Zn

   B a 2 before HCl

   C a 2 before $ZnCl_2$

   D a 2 before H_2

4. Placing a coefficient of 3 to the left of H_2CO_3 gives a total of _____ oxygen atoms.

   A 3   **B** 6   **C** 9   **D** 12

5. Placing a coefficient of 3 to the left of $Pb_3(PO_4)_2$ gives a total of _____ phosphorus atoms.

   A 3   **B** 6   **C** 9   **D** 12

6. Which set of coefficients balances the equation, $NH_4Cl + Ca(OH)_2 \rightarrow NH_3 + H_2O + CaCl_2$?

   A 1:2:2:1:2   **B** 2:2:2:2:1   **C** 2:1:2:2:1   **D** 3:2:2:1:2

Critical Thinking

On a sheet of paper, write the answer to each question.

7. How do the conservation laws apply to chemical reactions?

8. In the following equation, which element would you balance last? Why?
   $BaCl_2 + (NH_4)_2CO_3 \rightarrow BaO + CO_2 + NH_4Cl$

9. Balance the equation, $NH_3 + O_2 \rightarrow NO_2 + H_2O$.

10. Balance the equation, $Na + N_2 \rightarrow Na_2N$.

Combination reaction

A chemical reaction in which two or more small reactants form one larger product

Combination reactions are also called synthesis reactions. The word *synthesis* means "production" or "creation."

Chemical reactions are classified by the kinds of reactants and products. Five types of reactions are described in this chapter. The first three types are described in this lesson.

Combination

When aluminum reacts with oxygen in the air, it produces aluminum oxide.

$$4Al(s) + 3O_2(g) \rightarrow 2Al_2O_3(s)$$

Airplanes are made of aluminum for many reasons. One reason is this: A coating of aluminum oxide on an aluminum surface does not flake off. Aluminum oxide is tough and hard. The body of the airplane remains strong. Other metals, like iron, react with oxygen to form oxides that do flake off. Iron(III) oxide, or rust, weakens a piece of iron.

The formation of Al_2O_3 is a **combination reaction**. Combination reactions are chemical reactions in which two or more small reactants form one larger product. The reactants are often elements. These reactions have this basic model:

$$X + Y \rightarrow XY$$

two or more reactants $\rightarrow$ only one product

The reaction that produces water, $2H_2 + O_2 \rightarrow 2H_2O$, is a combination reaction. Here are other combination reactions:

$$N_2 + 3H_2 \rightarrow 2NH_3$$
$$2Al + 3S \rightarrow Al_2S_3$$
$$MgO + CO_2 \rightarrow MgCO_3$$
$$P_2O_5 + 3H_2O \rightarrow 2H_3PO_4$$

In each reaction, two or more reactants combine to form only one product.

Decomposition

In carbonated water, a substance breaks down into water and carbon dioxide gas. This reaction causes CO_2 bubbles to form.

$$H_2CO_3(aq) \rightarrow H_2O(l) + CO_2(g)$$

This is a **decomposition reaction.** In decomposition reactions, one large reactant breaks down into two or more smaller products. The word *decompose* means "to break down or break apart." Decomposition is the opposite of combination. These reactions have this basic model:

$$XY \rightarrow X+Y$$

only one reactant $\rightarrow$ two or more products

In some decomposition reactions, a compound breaks down into its elements. For example,

$$2Al_2O_3(s) \rightarrow 4Al(s) + 3O_2(g)$$

The reactant Al_2O_3 breaks down into its elements, aluminum and oxygen. Other compounds decompose to produce smaller compounds. One kind of reaction like this is the breaking down of a **carbonate.** A carbonate is a compound that contains the CO_3^{2-} ion. Carbonates decompose to produce carbon dioxide and another product containing the O^{2-} anion.

$$XCO_3 \rightarrow CO_2 + XO$$

carbonate $\rightarrow$ carbon dioxide + compound with O^{2-} anion

Other decomposition examples are given below. Which one is the decomposition of a carbonate?

$$2NH_3 \rightarrow N_2 + 3H_2$$
$$2H_2O \rightarrow 2H_2 + O_2$$
$$Na_2CO_3 \rightarrow CO_2 + Na_2O$$
$$2KClO_3 \rightarrow 2KCl + 3O_2$$

Each decomposition reaction has only one reactant, but two or more products.

Combustion

In **combustion reactions**, a compound or element burns in the presence of oxygen. The word *combust* means "to burn." These reactions always have oxygen as a reactant. At least one product contains oxygen.

Hydrocarbon

A compound that contains only carbon and hydrogen; when burned, it produces carbon dioxide and water

Link to ➤➤➤

Social Studies

In the past, calcium oxide, CaO, was a main ingredient in plaster, whitewash, and mortar for buildings. It is made when the calcium carbonate in limestone and marble is heated to 900°C. At this temperature, calcium carbonate decomposes, forming calcium oxide and carbon dioxide. During the Middle Ages, Romans used broken marble from ancient buildings to make calcium oxide, also called quicklime.

Combustion reactions look like this:

$$X + O_2 \rightarrow YO$$

main reactant + oxygen → one or more products

One kind of compound that combusts is a **hydrocarbon**. A hydrocarbon is a compound made of carbon and hydrogen. It has the formula C_xH_y. When it burns, the products are carbon dioxide and water.

$$C_xH_y + O_2 \rightarrow CO_2 + H_2O$$

hydrocarbon + oxygen → carbon dioxide + water

Some hydrocarbons are used as fuel. Fuels are substances that produce heat when burned. One hydrocarbon that burns well is propane, C_3H_8. Propane is a common fuel for outdoor gas grills, electric generators, and some farm equipment.

$$C_3H_8 + 5O_2 \rightarrow 3CO_2 + 4H_2O$$

The combustion of methane, CH_4, also called natural gas, is

$$CH_4 + 2O_2 \rightarrow CO_2 + 2H_2O$$

C_8H_{18} is the formula for octane and related 8-carbon fuels. C_8H_{18} is part of gasoline. The combustion of C_8H_{18} provides the energy for the cars in the race in Figure 5.3.1.

$$2C_8H_{18} + 20O_2 \rightarrow 16CO_2 + 18H_2O$$

Every combustion reaction needs oxygen and one other reactant. Combustion reactions that have only one product can also be classified as combination reactions. This is true for the reactions below.

$$2Mg + O_2 \rightarrow 2MgO$$
$$2H_2 + O_2 \rightarrow 2H_2O$$

Figure 5.3.1 *The power of a car engine comes from the combustion of fuel.*

The Environment: Recycling Plastics

How many plastic objects do you see around you? If you look around your home, school, and neighborhood, you may notice more than you thought. Plastic products include containers, packing materials, and housing for electronics. Plastics are inexpensive to make and very durable. Unfortunately, many plastics take hundreds of years to decompose in landfills. Landfills are areas where garbage is collected and stored.

Since the 1960s, efforts have been made to recycle plastic products. Recycling reduces the amount of plastic products in landfills. Recycling also reduces the amount of oil and coal needed to make new plastic products. These natural resources are conserved.

Some plastics cannot be recycled. Scientists are studying ways to change these plastics into useful materials. One technology, called thermal conversion, uses high temperatures and pressures to convert carbon-based materials like plastics into short molecules of crude oil.

1. What are two advantages of recycling plastics?

2. What is the purpose of thermal conversion?

3. Does your community recycle plastics? If so, which ones?

Word Bank

combination

combustion

decomposition

On a sheet of paper, write the word from the Word Bank that completes each sentence. Use each word in the Bank twice.

1. $MgCO_3 \rightarrow MgO + CO_2$ is an example of a _____ reaction.

2. $C_5H_{12} + 8O_2 \rightarrow 5CO_2 + 6H_2O$ is an example of a _____ reaction.

3. $4K + O_2 \rightarrow 2K_2O$ is an example of a _____ reaction.

4. $3Ca + N_2 \rightarrow Ca_3N_2$ is an example of a _____ reaction.

5. $Ba(ClO_3)_2 \rightarrow BaCl_2 + 3O_2$ is an example of a _____ reaction.

6. $4CuS + 5O_2 \rightarrow 2Cu_2O + 4SO_2$ is an example of a _____ reaction.

Critical Thinking

On a sheet of paper, carefully copy each equation. Write the type of reaction it is. Then balance the equation.

7. $ZnCO_3 \rightarrow ZnO + CO_2$

8. $C_9H_{20} + O_2 \rightarrow CO_2 + H_2O$

9. $H_2O + N_2O_5 \rightarrow HNO_3$

10. $KClO_3 \rightarrow KCl + O_2$

Materials

- safety goggles
- lab coat or apron
- porcelain evaporating dish
- balance
- spatula
- 5.0 g of basic copper(II) carbonate ($CuCO_3 \cdot Cu(OH)_2$)
- ring stand
- ring clamp
- Bunsen burner
- tongs
- glass stirring rod

The Decomposition of Basic Copper(II) Carbonate

In a decomposition reaction, a compound is broken down into smaller products. How can you tell when a decomposition reaction takes place? In this investigation, you will observe the decomposition of basic copper(II) carbonate.

Procedure

1. Put on safety goggles and a lab coat or apron.

2. Measure and record the mass of a clean, dry evaporating dish.

3. Use the spatula to add between 1.0 g and 5.0 g of basic copper(II) carbonate to the dish.

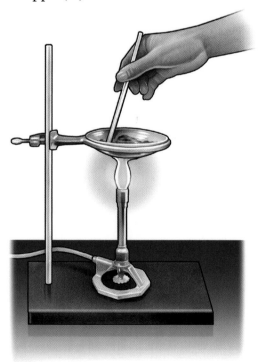

4. Measure and record the mass of the dish and reactant. Find the mass of the reactant. Write a description of this solid.

5. Set up the ring stand and clamp as shown. Place the burner below the ring so its flame will just touch the dish.

6. Place the dish on the ring. Light the burner. **Safety Alert: Do not touch heated objects with your hands. Keep clothing and hair away from open flames.**

7. Heat the dish over a medium flame. Stir the reactant gently with the glass rod. Turn off the burner when the reactant has entirely changed color from green to black.

8. Let the dish cool for 7 to 10 minutes. Write a description of the product.

9. Use the tongs to place the dish and product on the balance. Measure and record the mass. Find the mass of the product.

Cleanup/Disposal
Put the cooled product in the proper waste container. Wash and dry the dish and stirring rod. Return all equipment. Then wash your hands.

Analysis
1. Use the reactant's mass and formula to find the number of moles of reactant.

2. The product is copper(II) oxide, CuO. Use its mass and formula to find the number of moles of product.

3. What is the mole ratio of CuO to $CuCO_3 \cdot Cu(OH)_2$?

Conclusions
1. How do your descriptions of the reactant and product tell you that a reaction has occurred?

2. How do the reactant and product masses tell you that a decomposition reaction has occurred?

3. What do you think is the unbalanced equation for the decomposition reaction?

4. From the mole ratio you calculated, what is the balanced equation? (Hint: The coefficients in a balanced equation represent moles.)

Explore Further
Use your results and the balanced equation for the reaction to calculate the mass of carbon dioxide produced.

Objectives

After reading this lesson, you should be able to

◆ describe single-replacement reactions

◆ use an activity series to determine if a single-replacement reaction will occur

◆ identify a single-replacement reaction by looking at reactants

Single-replacement reaction

A reaction in which an element and a compound react to form a different element and a different compound

Activity series

A list of elements that is organized from the most reactive element to the least reactive element

There are two more types of reactions to study: single replacement and double replacement. In this lesson, you will learn about single replacement.

Recent U.S. pennies are almost all zinc. They have a plating, or thin outside coating, of copper. One way to copper-plate a piece of zinc is by this reaction:

$$Zn(s) + Cu(NO_3)_2(aq) \rightarrow Zn(NO_3)_2(aq) + Cu(s)$$

The zinc atoms on the surface react and are replaced by copper atoms. This is an example of single replacement. In a **single-replacement reaction**, an element reacts with a compound to form a different element and a different compound. The reactant compound is usually an ionic compound.

$$E + XY \rightarrow EY + X \quad \text{or} \quad E + XY \rightarrow XE + Y$$

element + ionic compound → ionic compound + element

The starting element E is like a single dancer who "cuts in" on a dancing pair XY. The single dancer E takes the place of one dancer in the pair. The other dancer in the pair becomes a single dancer. In the first model above, E takes the place of cation X. In the second model, E takes the place of anion Y. The ion that is kicked out becomes an uncharged element. E becomes an ion in the new compound. However,

• E will only replace an ion in a compound if E is more "active" than the ion.

• If E is not more "active," the reaction will not occur.

You can tell if an element is more active than another by looking at an **activity series**. An activity series is a list of elements. It is organized from the most active element to the least active element. An element at the top of the list is very active—it reacts easily. An element at the bottom of the list is inactive—it does not react easily. An element will replace any element that is below it in an activity series. Table 5.4.1 is the activity series for metals. Table 5.4.2 is the activity series for nonmetals.

Table 5.4.1 Activity Series for Metals	
	More active
lithium	Li
potassium	K
barium	Ba
calcium	Ca
sodium	Na
magnesium	Mg
aluminum	Al
zinc	Zn
iron	Fe
nickel	Ni
tin	Sn
lead	Pb
hydrogen*	H*
copper	Cu
mercury	Hg
silver	Ag
gold	Au
	Less active

*Hydrogen (H) is not a metal, but can act like one. Metals from Li to Na can replace H in any compound. Metals from Mg to Pb usually replace H in acids only.

Table 5.4.2 Activity Series for Nonmetals	
	More active
fluorine	F
chlorine	Cl
bromine	Br
iodine	I
	Less active

For example, sodium is above aluminum in the activity series for metals. This means that sodium is more active than aluminum. If sodium metal is mixed with aluminum chloride, $AlCl_3$, the sodium will replace the aluminum in the compound.

$$3Na + AlCl_3 \rightarrow Al + 3NaCl$$

uncharged   charged   uncharged   charged
Na atoms   ions   Al atoms   ions

The aluminum cations (Al^{3+}) are kicked out of the compound and become uncharged atoms (Al). The sodium atoms become charged (Na^{1+}) and react with the chloride ions (Cl^{1-}) to form NaCl.

What would happen if NaCl were mixed with aluminum? Aluminum is below sodium in the activity series for metals. Because aluminum is less active than sodium, it cannot replace sodium. There is no single-replacement reaction. This is shown by the equation,

$$Al + NaCl \rightarrow \text{no reaction}$$

Below are three more sets of reactants that do not react. Check each one against an activity series to see why there is no reaction.

$$Cu(s) + ZnCl_2(aq) \rightarrow \text{no reaction}$$
$$Fe(s) + Al_2O_3(s) \rightarrow \text{no reaction}$$
$$Br_2(aq) + KCl(aq) \rightarrow \text{no reaction}$$

❋ ❋

Technology and Society

In deserts and polar regions, heating food and water over a campfire is not practical. One solution is to use a flameless ration heater. This heater consists of cardboard pads filled with magnesium dust. Water reacts with the magnesium, producing magnesium oxide and hydrogen gas. The reaction produces a large amount of heat. This heat is used to warm pouches of food and water.

Here are three single-replacement reactions that do occur:

$$Zn(s) + CuCl_2(aq) \rightarrow Cu(s) + ZnCl_2(aq)$$
$$Cu(s) + AgNO_3(aq) \rightarrow Ag(s) + Cu(NO_3)_2(aq)$$
$$2Al(s) + Fe_2O_3(s) \rightarrow 2Fe(s) + Al_2O_3(s)$$

The first reaction takes place in a common battery. The second reaction is shown in Figure 5.4.1. The third one releases so much heat that the solid iron product actually melts!

The two activity series on page 197 are only used for determining if a single-replacement reaction will occur. When working with single replacements, always check an activity series.

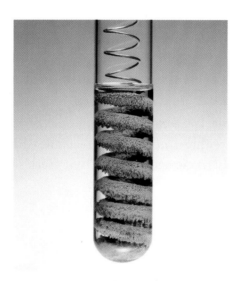

Figure 5.4.1 *When copper is placed in a solution of AgNO₃, a single replacement occurs. Solid silver forms.*

Link to ≫≫≫

Physics

The most reactive elements in the activity series are not found naturally in elemental form. Instead, they exist in compounds. Metals such as potassium, calcium, and sodium can be removed from compounds by electrolysis. This process uses electricity to separate metal cations from aqueous compounds. The English chemist Humphry Davy isolated several elements by electrolysis in the early 1800s. You will read about electrolysis in Chapter 18.

On a sheet of paper, write the letter of the answer that completes each sentence.

1. In an activity series, the elements near the top are _____.

   A charged   **B** active   **C** neutral   **D** inactive

2. A reaction will occur when $CaCl_2$ is combined with _____.

   A F_2 **B** Cl_2 **C** Br_2 **D** I_2

3. The reactants in a typical single-replacement reaction are an element and a(n) _____.

   A metal   **C** ionic compound
   B nonmetal   **D** molecular compound

4. A reaction will occur when $CaCl_2$ is combined with _____.

   A Ba   **B** Na   **C** Mg   **D** Al

5. A single replacement will occur when _____ are mixed.

   A Cu and H_2O **C** Al and H_2SO_4
   B K_2CO_3 and Mg   **D** I_2 and KCl

6. A single replacement will occur when _____ are mixed.

   A Cu and $FeSO_4$ **C** Sn and $CaCl_2$
   B Br_2 and NaF   **D** Li and H_2O

Critical Thinking

On a sheet of paper, write the answer to each question.

7. In an activity series, aluminum is below magnesium and above zinc. What does this tell you about the activity of these three metals?

8. When would you use the activity series for nonmetals?

9. Calcium and silver nitrate are mixed. Does a reaction occur? Explain your answer.

10. Iodine and zinc chloride are mixed. Does a reaction occur? Explain your answer.

DISCOVERY INVESTIGATION 5

Materials
- safety goggles
- lab coat or apron
- 16 reaction wells
- 4 eyedroppers
- 10 mL of 0.1 M aluminum nitrate ($Al(NO_3)_3$)
- 10 mL of 0.1 M copper(II) sulfate ($CuSO_4$)
- 10 mL of 0.1 M iron(II) sulfate ($FeSO_4$)
- 10 mL of 0.1 M zinc nitrate ($Zn(NO_3)_2$)
- small strips of aluminum, copper, iron, and zinc

Using the Activity Series

When an element is placed in an ionic solution, a single-replacement reaction may or may not occur. In this investigation, you will make several predictions and then design an experiment to test them. How can you predict which elements will react with which solutions?

Procedure

1. Create a data table like the one shown.

Element	$Al(NO_3)_3$ Solution	$CuSO_4$ Solution	$FeSO_4$ Solution	$Zn(NO_3)_2$ Solution
Al				
Cu				
Fe				
Zn				

2. Predict which of the 16 combinations in the table will produce a chemical reaction. Indicate your predictions with small checkmarks.

3. Write a procedure to test each combination to determine if a reaction occurs. Use only the listed materials. Include safety alerts.

4. Have your procedure approved by your teacher.

5. Put on safety goggles and a lab coat or apron.

6. Carry out your experiment. Record your observations in the table.

Cleanup/Disposal

Put used and unused substances in the proper waste containers. Wash and return the equipment. Then wash your hands.

Analysis

1. Which of the four metals is the most reactive? Which is the least reactive?

2. Describe what happened when a metal was placed in a solution containing a compound of that metal (for example, zinc in zinc nitrate solution). Explain your observations.

Conclusions

1. What did you base your predictions on?

2. Which of your predictions were supported by your results?

3. If any predictions did not match your results, can you determine why? Explain.

Explore Further

Choose five other metals. Predict which of the four solutions will react with each metal.

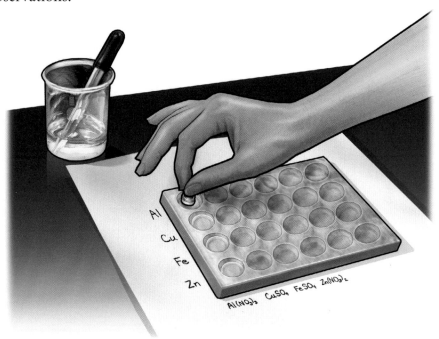

Objectives

After reading this lesson, you should be able to

◆ describe double-replacement reactions

◆ identify a double-replacement reaction by looking at reactants

◆ identify an acid-base reaction by looking at reactants

Double-replacement reaction

A reaction in which the ions in two compounds trade places, forming two new compounds

An aqueous solution of lead(II) nitrate is clear. An aqueous solution of potassium iodide is also clear. When these two solutions are mixed, however, they form a bright yellow solid and a new solution. The yellow solid is lead iodide, shown in Figure 5.5.1. It does not dissolve, but settles to the bottom of the container.

$$Pb(NO_3)_2(aq) + 2KI(aq) \rightarrow PbI_2(s) + 2KNO_3(aq)$$

This is a **double-replacement reaction**. In such a reaction, the ions of two ionic compounds trade places, like two dancing pairs might trade partners. The result is two new compounds. Most double-replacement reactions occur in solution. In other words, the reactants are aqueous.

$$AB(aq) + XY(aq) \rightarrow AY + XB$$

two ionic compounds $\rightarrow$ two new compounds

Double-replacement reactions only occur if one of the products is a solid, a gas, or a molecular compound such as water. You will learn more about this in Chapter 15. For now, assume that the double-replacement reactions in this lesson occur.

Figure 5.5.1 *Solutions of Pb(NO$_3$)$_2$ and KI react to form the yellow solid, PbI$_2$, in a KNO$_3$ solution.*

Acid-base reaction

A reaction in which an acid reacts with a base to produce water and a salt

Base

A compound that produces OH^{1-} ions when dissolved in water

Salt

An ionic compound consisting of a cation from a base and an anion from an acid

The word *salt* is commonly used to mean table salt, or sodium chloride. However, chemists use the word salt to refer to thousands of ionic compounds. Sodium chloride, potassium chloride, and calcium iodide are just a few of them.

The reactants of another double-replacement reaction are

$$BaCl_2(aq) + Na_2SO_4(aq) \rightarrow$$

The cations in the reactants switch places. (Switching the anions gives the same result.)

(Ba^{2+} goes with SO_4^{2-}) and (Na^{1+} goes with Cl^{1-})

The products are

$$BaSO_4(s) + NaCl(aq)$$

The balanced equation is

$$BaCl_2(aq) + Na_2SO_4(aq) \rightarrow BaSO_4(s) + 2NaCl(aq)$$

An **acid-base reaction** is similar to a double-replacement reaction. In an acid-base reaction, an acid reacts with a **base** to produce water and a **salt**. An acid is a compound that produces H^{1+} ions when dissolved in water. A base is a compound that produces OH^{1-} ions when dissolved in water. When an acid and a base react, water is produced from the H^{1+} and OH^{1-} ions. A salt is also produced. A salt is an ionic compound consisting of a cation from a base and an anion from an acid. An acid-base reaction usually has this model:

$$HY(aq) + XOH(aq) \rightarrow H_2O(l) + XY$$
$$\text{acid} \quad + \quad \text{base} \quad \rightarrow \text{water} + \text{salt}$$

The acid and base reactants are aqueous. The ions produced by the acid and base switch. For example, an acid, H_2SO_4, and a base, $Ca(OH)_2$, are mixed. The products are

(H^{1+} goes with OH^{1-}) and (Ca^{2+} goes with SO_4^{2-})

HOH (which is the same as H_2O) and $CaSO_4$

The balanced equation is

$$H_2SO_4(aq) + Ca(OH)_2(aq) \rightarrow 2H_2O(l) + CaSO_4(s)$$
$$\text{acid} \qquad \text{base} \qquad \text{water} \qquad \text{salt}$$

You will learn more about acid-base reactions in Chapter 17.

Lesson 5 **REVIEW**

On a sheet of paper, write the word or phrase from the Word Bank that completes each sentence.

Word Bank

acid

base

ions

molecular compounds

products

reactants

1. In a double-replacement reaction, the _____ of two compounds trade places.

2. In an acid-base reaction, the _____ are a salt and water.

3. A(n) _____ produces H^{1+} ions when dissolved in water.

4. A(n) _____ produces OH^{1-} ions when dissolved in water.

5. In double-replacement reactions, the products may be gases, solids, or _____.

6. The _____ in most double-replacement reactions are in an aqueous state.

Critical Thinking

On a sheet of paper, write the answer to each question.

7. How is a double-replacement reaction different from a single-replacement reaction?

8. Will any two ionic compounds always react? Explain your answer.

9. Describe the reactants and products in an acid-base reaction.

10. Why is the following not a double-replacement reaction? $Cl_2(g) + 2NaBr(aq) \rightarrow 2NaCl(aq) + Br_2(l)$

For many reactions, if you know the reactants, you can name the reaction type. Based on reaction type, you can then predict the products. Once you know the products, you can balance the equation.

reactants → reaction type → products → balanced equation

To find the reaction type, use what you learned in earlier lessons. Recall that each reaction type has a basic model. Follow this model to predict the products of the reaction. Predicting a product involves writing its correct formula or formula unit. From Chapter 3, you know that the formula unit of an ionic product must be neutral. It is based on the charges of ions. To balance an equation, you must start with the correct formula or formula unit of each reactant and product. If one formula is wrong, it is impossible to balance the equation. If you are having trouble balancing an equation, check your formulas.

The five types of reactions are reviewed in this lesson. An example of how to predict products is given for each type.

Spotlight on Lithium

3
Li
Lithium
6.9

Lithium is the third element in the periodic table. A lithium atom contains 3 protons and 3 electrons. Lithium has the lowest density of all of metals. It is about half as dense as water. Unlike hydrogen and helium, lithium is not found in large amounts.

Lithium is highly reactive. Lithium will replace any other element in a single-replacement reaction. Lithium reacts with water, although not as strongly as sodium or potassium. Lithium is combined with other light metals, such as aluminum and magnesium, to form low-mass alloys. Lithium carbonate is used to treat bipolar disorder, which can cause severe mood swings. Lithium hydroxide has been used to remove carbon dioxide from the air inside space shuttles.

Interesting Fact: Lithium is used in certain types of batteries.

Why can't the reactants Li and Cl_2 start a decomposition reaction? Decomposition reactions have only one reactant. Why can't these reactants start a combustion or replacement reaction? Combustion reactions require O_2, and replacement reactions require one or two ionic compounds.

Combination

Combination reactions have one product. They have two or more simple reactants. If the reactants are a metal and a nonmetal, the product is often an ionic compound. Its formula unit is based on the charges of the reactants as ions.

Example 1	Write a balanced equation given the reactants Li and Cl_2.
Read	The reactants are two elements—a metal and a nonmetal.
Plan	This looks like the model for a combination reaction. The other four reaction types do not fit. A combination reaction has one product. In this case, since a metal and a nonmetal are reacting, the product is an ionic compound.
Solve	The product is based on the ions Li^{1+} and Cl^{1-}. The neutral formula unit is LiCl. The balanced equation is $$2Li + Cl_2 \rightarrow 2LiCl$$
Reflect	Combination reactions are the only type of reaction that has one product. The reactants are often, but not always, elements.
Practice	Write a balanced equation given the reactants Ca and F_2.

Science Myth

Myth: All chemical reactions are one of five reaction types.

Fact: Most chemical reactions fit one of the five reaction models described in this chapter. However, some reactions cannot be classified as any of these five. Other reactions follow one of the five models, but break some rules in doing so. For example, the formation of a very large product called a polymer is considered a combination reaction—even though small molecules like water are sometimes produced as well. Single replacements can occur between an element and a molecular compound, although most occur between an element and an ionic compound.

Research and Write

Learn about certain combination reactions and their products. Choose one of these chemists: William Perkin, Roy Plunkett, Patsy Sherman, Ralph Wiley, Stephanie Kwolek, or Waldo Semon. Find out what compound they discovered. Find out what they were trying to do when they made their discovery. Summarize your research. Make sure to mention the useful properties of the compound.

Decomposition

Decomposition reactions begin with just one reactant. All other reaction types begin with two or more reactants. A common reaction is the decomposition of an ionic compound containing the anion CO_3^{2-}. This produces CO_2 and an ionic compound that contains the anion O^{2-}. If the reactant is not a carbonate, but is a binary compound, the products are the two elements in the compound.

Example 2	Write a balanced equation given the reactant $CaCO_3$.
Read	There is only one reactant. It is a carbonate—calcium carbonate—because it contains the carbonate ion, CO_3^{2-}.
Plan	This must be a decomposition reaction of a carbonate. One product is CO_2. The other product is the ionic compound made by Ca^{2+} and O^{2-}, or CaO.
Solve	The balanced equation is $$CaCO_3 \rightarrow CO_2 + CaO$$
Reflect	This equation was balanced without needing coefficients.
Practice	Write a balanced equation given the reactant mercury(II) oxide.

Technology and Society

Plastics and foods are made of carbon-based molecules. In landfills, decomposition reactions break these molecules into smaller molecules, such as methane and carbon dioxide. These gases can build up in landfills, causing environmental problems. In some landfills, bacteria are used to speed up decomposition reactions. The methane that is produced is used as fuel.

Link to ➤➤➤

Biology

Many reactions take place in the human body. The formation of proteins from amino acids is a combination reaction. Inhaled oxygen aids the combustion of certain molecules, producing water and carbon dioxide. Acid-base reactions occur in the stomach and bloodstream.

Combustion

Combustion reactions have two reactants, and O_2 is one of them. The oxygen reactant must be the diatomic element, O_2. It cannot be part of a compound. When a hydrocarbon (C_xH_y) is the other reactant, the products are CO_2 and H_2O.

Example 3 Write a balanced equation given the reactants C_2H_6 and O_2.

Read The reactants are a hydrocarbon and oxygen.

Plan The oxygen tells you that this is a combustion reaction. The hydrocarbon tells you that the products must be CO_2 and H_2O.

Solve The unbalanced equation is

$$C_2H_6 + O_2 \rightarrow CO_2 + H_2O$$

Balance the C atoms and then the H atoms. This gives

$$C_2H_6 + O_2 \rightarrow 2CO_2 + 3H_2O$$

The O atoms are still unbalanced. No whole-number coefficient for O_2 will work. Try a coefficient of $\frac{7}{2}$. This balances the O atoms so there are 7 on each side.

$$C_2H_6 + \frac{7}{2}O_2 \rightarrow 2CO_2 + 3H_2O$$

Now double all four coefficients so they are whole numbers.

$$2C_2H_6 + 7O_2 \rightarrow 4CO_2 + 6H_2O$$

This equation is balanced.

Reflect If the O atoms were balanced first, this would have been a very tough problem!

Practice Write a balanced equation given the reactants C_5H_{10} and O_2.

Single Replacement

These reactions typically start with an element and an ionic compound. They produce a new element and a new ionic compound. The formula unit of this new compound is based on ionic charges. The key to working with these reactions is to check the activity series first (page 197). Make sure the reactions actually occur.

Example 4	Will a reaction occur when K and CaO are mixed? If so, write a balanced equation. If not, write *no reaction.*
Read	The reactant CaO is an ionic compound. The other reactant is the element potassium.
Plan	This is a single replacement. Check Table 5.4.1 to see if it actually occurs. K is more active (higher in the series) than Ca. The reaction will occur.
Solve	K^{1+} will form a new compound with O^{2-}. To be neutral, this compound must be K_2O. The Ca^{2+} ions will become uncharged Ca atoms. $K + CaO \rightarrow K_2O + Ca$ After balancing, the equation is $2K + CaO \rightarrow K_2O + Ca$
Reflect	Remember that the two activity series are used for single replacements only.
Practice	Will a single-replacement reaction occur when Mg and H_2SO_4 are mixed? If so, write a balanced equation. If not, write *no reaction.*

To review ionic charges and polyatomic ions, see Figure 3.2.2 on page 93 and Table 3.4.1 on page 102. Common polyatomic ions are also listed in Appendix A.

Double Replacement

Double-replacement reactions start with two ionic compounds. The ions of these compounds trade places to create different compounds. First identify the four ions in the reactants, including their charges. Then create the new compounds by switching the cations (or anions). Write the formula unit of each product. Make sure the positive and negative charges in formula units add up to 0. If H^{1+} and OH^{1-} ions are paired up in an acid-base reaction, the new products are water and a salt.

Example 5	Write a balanced equation given the reactants $NaOH$ and $Ba(NO_3)_2$.
Read	The reactants are two ionic compounds.
Plan	This is a double replacement. An activity series *does not* need to be checked. Find the charges on all four ions in the reactants. They are Na^{1+}, OH^{1-}, Ba^{2+}, and NO_3^{1-}.
Solve	Switch the cations to find the products.
	(Na^{1+} goes with NO_3^{1-}) and (Ba^{2+} goes with OH^{1-})
	The switching may be easier to see if the equation is written like this:
	$(Na^{1+})(OH^{1-}) + (Ba^{2+})(NO_3^{1-})_2$
	$\rightarrow (Na^{1+})(NO_3^{1-}) + (Ba^{2+})(OH^{1-})$
	Check that each new product has a neutral formula unit. In this case, $NaNO_3$ has an overall charge of 0. It is neutral. But $BaOH$ is not neutral. A subscript is needed: $Ba(OH)_2$. One coefficient is needed to balance the equation.
	$NaOH + Ba(NO_3)_2 \rightarrow 2NaNO_3 + Ba(OH)_2$
Reflect	A subscript in a polyatomic ion moves with the ion. In the formula unit $Ba(NO_3)_2$, the 3 in NO_3^{1-} stays with the ion. It is part of the ion's formula. However, the subscript 2 is there only to balance the charges. It is not part of the ion and does not move with it.
Practice	Write a balanced equation given the reactants $Pb(NO_3)_2$ and KI.

Example 6	Write a balanced equation given the reactants HNO_3 and $Ba(OH)_2$.
Read	The reactants are an acid and a base.
Plan	An acid-base reaction is similar to a double replacement. When an acid and a base are dissolved in water, they produce ions. The products are predicted just like in Example 5. Find the charges on all four ions: H^{1+}, NO_3^{1-}, Ba^{2+}, and OH^{1-}.
Solve	Switch the cations to determine the products. One product is water. Create a neutral formula unit for the salt. (H^{1+} goes with OH^{1-}) and (Ba^{2+} goes with NO_3^{1-}) The balanced equation is $2HNO_3 + Ba(OH)_2 \rightarrow 2H_2O + Ba(NO_3)_2$
Reflect	Like all acid-base reactions, the products are water and a salt.
Practice	Write a balanced equation given the reactants $HC_2H_3O_2$ and KOH.

▼◀▲▼◀▲▼◀▲▼◀▲▼◀▲▼◀▲▼◀▲▼◀▲▼◀▲▼◀▲▼◀▲▼◀▲▼◀▲▼◀▲▼

Science at Work

Chemical Engineer

Chemical engineers apply chemistry concepts to industry. They design, operate, and improve many kinds of chemical processes. Chemical engineers are involved in many manufacturing processes. They work in industries such as petroleum refining, plastics, and pharmaceuticals (medicines). Chemical engineers are not limited to manufacturing, however. Some apply chemistry to pollution control and waste management. Others study body chemistry and design artificial organs, such as hearts and lungs. Some chemical engineers are also lawyers. They apply their knowledge to issues such as patent rights

and environmental responsibility.

Most chemical engineers work for businesses. Some work for governments and universities. They need at least a bachelor's degree in chemical engineering.

Lesson 6   R E V I E W

On a sheet of paper, write the letter of the answer that completes each sentence.

1. C_8H_{16} and O_2 react. The products are _____.

   A CO_2 and CH_4 **C** CO_2 and H_2O

   B C, O_2, and H_2O **D** CO_2 and H_2

2. Ga and S react. The products are _____.

   A Ga_2S_3 **B** GaS_3 **C** Ga_2S **D** Ga_3S_2

3. The reactant $SrCO_3$ is a carbonate that breaks down. The products are _____.

   A SrO and CO   **C** SrO_2 and CO_2

   B Sr and CO_3 **D** SrO and CO_2

4. $Al(OH)_3$ and HCl react. The products are _____.

   A $AlCl_3$ and H_2O **C** AlH and $Cl(OH)_3$

   B AlCl and $H(OH)_3$ **D** $AlCl_2$ and H_2O

5. Na and H_3PO_4 are mixed. The result is _____.

   A NaH_3 and PO_4 **C** Na_3PO_4 and H_2

   B $NaPO_4$ and H_2 **D** no reaction

6. Na reacts with $MgCl_2$, but Al does not. This is because _____.

   A Al is above Mg on the activity series

   B Na is above Mg on the activity series

   C Mg is more reactive than Na

   D Al is more reactive than Na

Critical Thinking

On a sheet of paper, write the reaction type for each set of reactants. Then write a balanced equation.

7. Na_2CO_3

8. C_3H_8 and O_2

9. magnesium and copper sulfate

10. $(NH_4)_2SO_3$ and $Al(C_2H_3O_2)_3$

Combinatorial Chemistry

Combination reactions are among the most important reactions in applied chemistry. During most of the 1900s, chemists combined molecules to create compounds called synthetics. Some synthetics are new molecules, while others are identical to molecules that occur in nature. Many pharmaceutical drugs and medicines are synthetics. Plastics are also synthetics. Plastics are long chains of molecules.

Creating new synthetics is a major part of industry today. Improving ways to make known synthetics is also important. Chemical engineers look for more efficient and cheaper ways to make synthetics.

Combinatorial chemistry is a technique that is changing how compounds are produced in industry. This technique was developed in the 1980s. It was first used for producing proteins. Before this, large molecules were formed by adding one small molecule at a time. These single combination reactions are reliable, but not very efficient. In combinatorial chemistry, mixtures of compounds are combined with mixtures of other compounds. Many combination reactions occur at once, producing many products instead of just one. The products are then carefully separated. Some have uses, while others are waste products.

Combinatorial chemistry is a new technique in the pharmaceutical industry. Many drugs with similar structures can be produced at once. However, the large variety of products requires more analysis than single-product reactions. Also, better ways to separate the products are needed.

1. What are synthetic compounds?

2. How does combinatorial chemistry differ from a traditional combination reaction?

3. Why are separation techniques especially important in combinatorial chemistry?

Chapter 5 S U M M A R Y

- In a chemical equation, the reactants are written on the left side of the arrow. The products are written on the right side. State symbols may be included.

- Laws of conservation say that matter and energy are not created or destroyed in chemical reactions.

- A balanced equation has the same number and kinds of atoms on both sides of the arrow.

- If an equation is not balanced, coefficients are needed.

- If an element is present in three or more places in an equation, balance it last.

- A combination reaction begins with two or more reactants. It results in only one product.

- A combustion reaction has two reactants. One reactant is O_2. A hydrocarbon and O_2 react to produce CO_2 and H_2O.

- A decomposition reaction begins with only one reactant. This reactant breaks down into two or more smaller products. The decomposition of a carbonate produces CO_2 and an ionic compound with the O^{2-} anion.

- A single-replacement reaction begins with one element and one ionic compound. The element replaces an ion in the compound. This results in a new element and a new ionic compound. An activity series is used.

- A double-replacement reaction begins with two ionic compounds. The cations in these reactants switch, producing two new compounds.

- In an acid-base reaction, an acid and a base react in solution, producing H_2O and a salt.

- To predict the products of a reaction, first identify the reaction type. Then determine the products. Once product formulas are in place, the equation can be balanced.

Vocabulary

acid-base reaction, 203
activity series, 196
base, 203
carbonate, 190
chemical equation, 176
coefficient, 181
combination reaction, 189

combustion reaction, 190
decomposition reaction, 190
double-replacement reaction, 202
hydrocarbon, 191
kinetic energy, 180
law of conservation of energy, 181

law of conservation of matter, 180
potential energy, 180
product, 176
reactant, 176
salt, 203
single-replacement reaction, 196

Vocabulary Review

Match a reaction type in the first column with an example in the second column. On a sheet of paper, write the letter of the answer.

1. decomposition   **A** $LiI + AgNO_3 \rightarrow AgI + LiNO_3$

2. single replacement   **B** $Ti + 2Cl_2 \rightarrow TiCl_4$

3. double replacement   **C** $2C_2H_2 + 5O_2 \rightarrow 4CO_2 + 2H_2O$

4. combustion   **D** $H_2CO_3 \rightarrow H_2O + CO_2$

5. combination   **E** $3K + FeCl_2 \rightarrow 3KCl + Fe$

Match a substance in the first column with a description in the second column. On a sheet of paper, write the letter of the answer.

6. acid   **A** Its anion is $CO_3{}^{2-}$.

7. carbonate   **B** It produces OH^{1-} ions in water.

8. hydrocarbon   **C** It produces H^{1+} ions in water.

9. base   **D** It is a product in an acid-base reaction.

10. salt   **E** It contains only carbon and hydrogen.

Concept Review

On a sheet of paper, write the letter of the answer that completes each sentence.

11. A number to the left of a formula that is added to balance an equation is a _____.

   A coefficient   **B** subscript   **C** charge   **D** superscript

Continued on next page

12. Which statement is true?

    A Kinetic energy becomes potential energy in chemical reactions.

    B Matter can be created or destroyed, but energy cannot.

    C Matter and energy are conserved in chemical reactions.

    D Energy can be created or destroyed, but matter cannot.

13. A(n) _____ is used to determine if a single-replacement reaction will occur.

    A acid   **B** activity series   **C** coefficient   **D** reactant

14. The law of conservation of matter says that atoms in a chemical reaction are not _____.

    A balanced   **C** chemically combined

    B rearranged   **D** created or destroyed

15. Hydrogen and nitrogen are the reactants in a combination reaction. This produces _____.

    A $H_2 + N_2$ **B** N_2H_2 **C** NH_3 **D** H_2N

16. In a single-replacement reaction, the sodium ion in NaCl can be replaced by _____.

    A calcium   **B** magnesium   **C** aluminum   **D** zinc

17. $CaCO_3$ decomposes. This produces _____.

    A $Ca + CO_3$ **C** $Ca + C + O_3$

    B $CaO + CO_2$ **D** $CO_2 + H_2O$

18. NaOH and HCl are mixed together. This produces _____.

    A $NaCl + HCl$ **C** $H_2O + NaCl$

    B $H_2O + CO_2$ **D** $H_2Cl + NaO$

Problem Solving

On a sheet of paper, carefully copy each equation. Name the type of reaction. Then balance the equation.

19. $C_{18}H_{20} + O_2 \rightarrow CO_2 + H_2O$

20. $N_2O_5 + H_2O \rightarrow HNO_3$

On a sheet of paper, carefully copy each set of reactants. Predict and write the product(s). Then balance the equation.

21. $Cu + CaF_2 \rightarrow$

22. $Na_3PO_4 + Ca(ClO_2)_2 \rightarrow$

Critical Thinking

For each reaction, determine the formula or formula unit of each reactant and product. On a sheet of paper, write the balanced chemical equation.

23. aluminum hydroxide + hydrochloric acid → water + aluminum chloride

24. lithium + nitrogen → lithium nitride

25. chromium(III) carbonate → carbon dioxide + chromium(III) oxide

Test-Taking Tip If you are having trouble answering a question on a test, go to the next question. Later, come back to any skipped questions.

Stoichiometry

Suppose you want to make a fruit smoothie for you and three friends. To make four servings, you need:

1 cup of strawberries   2 cups of orange juice
2 bananas   1/2 cup of vanilla yogurt

What if you have only one banana? You are limited by that ingredient. You cannot make four servings and still follow the recipe correctly. A chemical reaction is similar to a recipe. Specific amounts of reactants are needed to make a specific amount of product. In this chapter, you will find out why specific amounts of substances react.

Organize Your Thoughts

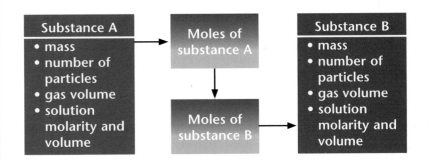

Substance A
- mass
- number of particles
- gas volume
- solution molarity and volume

Moles of substance A

Moles of substance B

Substance B
- mass
- number of particles
- gas volume
- solution molarity and volume

◆ To solve mole-mole problems using a mole ratio

◆ To solve mass-mole and mass-mass problems

◆ To solve problems that involve number of particles

◆ To solve problems that involve a gas at STP

◆ To solve problems that involve a solution

◆ To find a percent yield for a product

◆ To find the limiting reactant in a reaction

Objectives

After reading this lesson, you should be able to

◆ explain how coefficients in a balanced equation are used to create mole ratios

◆ solve a mole-mole conversion problem

Stoichiometry

The study of amounts in chemical reactions

The chapter opener discussed amounts of ingredients in a smoothie recipe. You may have guessed that **stoichiometry** has something to do with amounts. Stoichiometry is the study of amounts in chemical reactions. In the kitchen, the amount of food you make depends on the amount of ingredients you have. In the chemistry lab, the amount of a product that can form depends on the amounts of reactants available.

Using stoichiometry, you can predict how much of a product will form in a chemical reaction. You can also predict how much of a reactant will be needed. This involves three skills you have already learned:

- balancing chemical equations
- determining chemical formulas
- converting between moles and other quantities

Stoichiometry problems begin by providing a chemical reaction or equation. They also provide the amount of one substance in the reaction. They ask you to find the amount of another substance in the reaction. Amounts might be in grams, moles, or number of particles. No matter how they are measured, amounts in chemical reactions depend on moles. Numbers of moles are indicated by the coefficients in a balanced chemical equation.

Link to ➣ ➣ ➣

Language Arts

Stoichiometry comes from two Greek words. *Stoicheion* means "element." *Metron* means "measure." Stoichiometry involves measuring elements in chemical reactions. *Stoichiometry*, when pronounced, sounds like *stoy-key-AH-meh-tree.*

Math Tip

The two numbers in a mole ratio are the coefficients of two substances in a balanced equation. If there is no coefficient shown for a substance, its coefficient is 1.

Link to ➤➤➤

Home and Career

Baking powder is an ingredient in many cake recipes. Most baking powders contain acidic compounds as well as baking soda, $NaHCO_3$. When mixed with water, the acid and baking soda react to form bubbles of carbon dioxide gas, CO_2. These bubbles cause the cake batter to rise.

Balanced Equations and Mole Ratios

A balanced chemical equation is the key to solving stoichiometry problems. Look at the formation of water by burning hydrogen. The balanced equation is

$$2H_2 + O_2 \rightarrow 2H_2O$$

In Chapter 5, you learned that coefficients indicate the number of moles in a balanced equation. The coefficients are in red:

$$2H_2 \quad + \quad 1O_2 \quad \rightarrow \quad 2H_2O$$
$$2 \text{ mol} \qquad 1 \text{ mol} \qquad \qquad 2 \text{ mol}$$

The coefficients indicate that 2 molecules of H_2 and 1 molecule of O_2 react to produce 2 molecules of H_2O. Because the molecules react in this ratio, you also know that 2 mol of H_2 and 1 mol of O_2 react to produce 2 mol of H_2O. Amounts of reactants and products are always related by mole ratios. This is why specific amounts of substances react and specific amounts of substances form.

From a balanced equation, you can create several mole ratios. In Chapter 4, you saw that a mole ratio can compare the mole amounts of two substances. When a mole ratio is written as a fraction, the unit in both the numerator and denominator is moles. A mole ratio can be created from any two coefficients in a balanced chemical equation. For the above equation, some mole ratios are

$$\frac{2 \text{ mol } H_2}{1 \text{ mol } O_2} \quad \text{and} \quad \frac{2 \text{ mol } H_2}{2 \text{ mol } H_2O} \quad \text{and} \quad \frac{2 \text{ mol } H_2O}{2 \text{ mol } H_2} \quad \text{and} \quad \frac{1 \text{ mol } O_2}{2 \text{ mol } H_2O}$$

2 mol of H_2 reacts with 1 mol of O_2. | 2 mol of H_2 produces 2 mol of H_2O. Both forms of this ratio are shown. | 1 mol of O_2 produces 2 mol of H_2O.

What other mole ratios can you make for this equation? All stoichiometry calculations involve a mole ratio. It is used as a conversion factor. It converts from moles of one substance in the equation to moles of another substance.

Stoichiometry depends on a balanced chemical equation. If the coefficients in an equation are incorrect, any calculations based on the equation will be wrong.

For any two substances A and B in an equation, there are two possible mole ratios: $\frac{\text{moles of A}}{\text{moles of B}}$ and $\frac{\text{moles of B}}{\text{moles of A}}$. If you want to find moles of A, use the first one. If you want to find moles of B, use the second one.

Mole-Mole Calculations

Suppose you have 8.0 mol of oxygen and an excess of hydrogen. An *excess* means an extra, or unlimited, amount. You want to know how many moles of water you can make from these reactants. Again, the balanced equation is

$$2H_2 \quad + \quad O_2 \quad \rightarrow \quad 2H_2O$$

excess   8.0 mol   ? mol

The given amount is *moles of O_2*, and the desired amount is *moles of H_2O*. This requires a mole-mole calculation. It is the simplest type of stoichiometry calculation. In this problem, there is extra hydrogen. The amount of water produced will *not* be limited by the amount of hydrogen. Rather, the amount of water will be determined by the 8.0 mol of O_2. When there is an excess of a reactant, that reactant can be ignored. It will not determine the product amount.

To solve the problem, multiply the given amount by a conversion factor (a mole ratio). The conversion map looks like this:

moles of $O_2 \rightarrow$ moles of H_2O

Like other conversion factors, the correct mole ratio is the one that will convert the given amount to the desired amount. The given unit is always on the bottom. The answer is

$$8.0 \text{ mol } O_2 \left(\frac{2 \text{ mol } H_2O}{1 \text{ mol } O_2} \right) = 16 \text{ mol } H_2O$$

Notice these facts about this calculation:
- The calculation begins with the given amount, including its unit and substance.
- The unit that is canceled is the given unit (moles of O_2).
- The unit that remains is the desired unit (moles of H_2O).
- The numbers in the mole ratio are coefficients from the balanced equation.
- The answer has the same number of significant figures as the given amount. Coefficients are counting numbers. A mole ratio does not limit the significant figures in an answer.
- The answer makes sense. The balanced equation shows that 1 mol of O_2 is needed to produce 2 mol of water.

Now look at another mole-mole calculation using the same balanced equation.

Example 1	24 mol of water is produced by burning hydrogen. How many moles of oxygen reacted with excess hydrogen?
Read	You are given the amount of a product: 24 mol of water. You are asked to find the moles of oxygen that reacted to form this much water.
Plan	You need a balanced equation: $2H_2 + O_2 \rightarrow 2H_2O$. Hydrogen is in excess, so the answer will not depend on this reactant. Find the mole ratio that compares moles of H_2O and moles of O_2, with moles of O_2 on top.
Solve	Multiply the given amount by this ratio. $$24 \ \overline{\text{mol } H_2O} \left(\frac{1 \ \text{mol } O_2}{2 \ \overline{\text{mol } H_2O}} \right) = 12 \ \text{mol } O_2$$ If 24 mol of H_2O is produced, then 12 mol of O_2 must have reacted.
Reflect	In a stoichiometry problem, you may be given a reactant amount or a product amount.
Practice	0.86 mol of water is produced by burning hydrogen. How many moles of hydrogen reacted with excess oxygen?

Spotlight on Fluorine

9
F
Fluorine
19.0

Fluorine is a nonmetal. It is a member of the halogen family of elements. The word *halogen* means "salt former." Like chlorine, bromine, and iodine, fluorine reacts with metals to form salts.

Fluorine is the most active nonmetal. Therefore, it is always found in nature in compounds. Fluorine gas can be produced by passing an electric current through a mixture of potassium fluoride (KF) and hydrofluoric acid (HF).

Fluoride compounds have many uses. Hydrofluoric acid is extremely reactive. This acid is used to etch or frost glass and clean metals. Nonstick coatings on pots and pans contain fluorine. Fluoride compounds are commonly added to water and toothpaste to prevent tooth decay.

Interesting Fact: Some artificial blood contains fluoride compounds.

Stoichiometry is not only used to convert between a reactant a product. It is also used to convert between two reactants or two products.

Example 2	14 mol of hydrogen reacts in the formation of water. How many moles of oxygen must react?
Read	You are given the amount of H_2 and are asked for the amount of O_2.
Plan	The balanced equation is $2H_2 + O_2 \rightarrow 2H_2O$. Use this equation to create a mole ratio that relates H_2 and O_2.
Solve	Multiply the given amount by the mole ratio.$$14 \text{ mol } H_2 \left(\frac{1 \text{ mol } O_2}{2 \text{ mol } H_2} \right) = 7.0 \text{ mol } O_2$$7.0 mol of O_2 reacts with 14 mol of H_2.
Reflect	The mole ratio of O_2 to H_2 can also be written as 1:2. 1 mol of O_2 reacts with 2 mol of H_2. This also means that 1 molecule of O_2 reacts with 2 molecules of H_2.
Practice	1.2 mol of oxygen reacts in the formation of water. How many moles of hydrogen must react?

Express Lab 6

Materials
◆ 6 pennies
◆ 2 nickels

Procedure
1. Examine the balanced equation for making ammonia from nitrogen and hydrogen:

$$N_2 + 3H_2 \rightarrow 2NH_3$$

2. Use coins to model the left side of this equation. Use nickels to represent nitrogen atoms and pennies to represent hydrogen atoms.

3. Rearrange the coins to model the two ammonia molecules on the right side of the equation.

Analysis
1. The coin models show the number of molecules of each substance in the reaction. They also show the number of moles of each substance. Why?

2. Write six mole ratios for this equation.

On a sheet of paper, write the answer to each question. Use this balanced equation:

$$2Al(OH)_3 + 3H_2SO_4 \rightarrow Al_2(SO_4)_3 + 6H_2O$$

1. You want to convert moles of $Al(OH)_3$ to moles of H_2SO_4. What mole ratio would you use?

2. If 4.21 mol of $Al(OH)_3$ reacts, how many moles of H_2SO_4 react?

3. You want to convert moles of H_2SO_4 to moles of H_2O. What mole ratio would you use?

4. If 1.6 mol of H_2SO_4 reacts with excess $Al(OH)_3$, how many moles of H_2O are produced?

5. You want to convert moles of H_2O to moles of $Al_2(SO_4)_3$. What mole ratio would you use?

6. If 3.0 mol of H_2O forms, how many moles of $Al_2(SO_4)_3$ form?

Critical Thinking

On a sheet of paper, write the answer to each question.

7. Aluminum and oxygen react to form 1 mol of Al_2O_3. Before you can find out how many moles of oxygen reacted, what do you need to do?

8. How are coefficients in a balanced equation related to mole ratios?

9. The *unbalanced* equation for a reaction is $Na_2O + H_2O \rightarrow NaOH$. Write two mole ratios comparing moles of NaOH and moles of Na_2O.

10. Circle one of the ratios you wrote for question 9. Then write a stoichiometry problem that would use it.

After reading this lesson, you should be able to

◆ create a conversion map for any mass-mole or mass-mass problem

◆ convert the mass of one substance into the moles of another substance

◆ convert the mass of one substance into the mass of another substance

Lesson 1 explained mole-mole calculations. These are one-step conversions that use a mole ratio. Moles of one substance are converted to moles of another substance. However, in the chemistry lab, moles cannot be measured. Instead, mass is measured using balances like the one in Figure 6.2.1. This lesson will show you how to convert between the mass of one substance and the moles of another substance. As always, a balanced equation is very important.

Mass-Mole Calculations

Suppose R and S are two substances in a chemical reaction. You are given the mass of R. You want to find the moles of S. Here is a map of this conversion:

mass of R → moles of R → moles of S

Each arrow in the map represents a conversion factor. This stoichiometry problem requires two conversion steps.

1. Convert the mass of R to moles of R. The conversion factor uses R's molar mass.

2. Convert moles of R to moles of S. The conversion factor is a mole ratio.

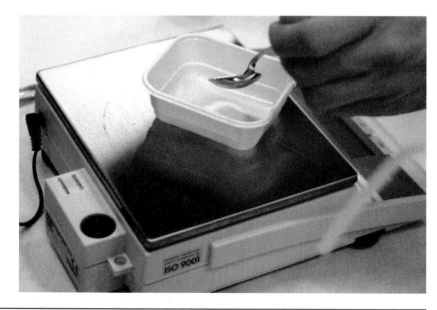

Figure 6.2.1 *There are many types of balances used in chemistry labs. This is an electronic balance.*

| _Example 1_ | 14.0 g of nitrogen reacts with hydrogen to produce ammonia. The equation is $N_2 + 3H_2 \rightarrow 2NH_3$. There is excess H_2. How many moles of NH_3 are made? |

Read   You are given the mass of one reactant, and there is extra of the other reactant. You are asked to find the moles of the product.

Plan   Here is the conversion map:

mass of $N_2 \rightarrow$ moles of $N_2 \rightarrow$ moles of NH_3

You will need two conversion factors. For the first one, find the molar mass of N_2. It is $2(14.0 \text{ g/mol}) = 28.0 \text{ g/mol}$. Since you want to end up with moles of N_2, the first conversion factor is written as

$$\frac{1 \text{ mol } N_2}{28.0 \text{ g } N_2}$$

The second factor is a mole ratio comparing NH_3 and N_2. From the coefficients in the balanced equation, the mole ratio is

$$\frac{2 \text{ mol } NH_3}{1 \text{ mol } N_2}$$

Solve   Multiply the given amount, 14.0 g of N_2, by the two factors.

$$14.0 \text{ g } N_2 \left(\frac{1 \text{ mol } N_2}{28.0 \text{ g } N_2} \right)\left(\frac{2 \text{ mol } NH_3}{1 \text{ mol } N_2} \right) = 1.00 \text{ mol } NH_3$$
mass to moles   moles to moles

Reflect   The answer, 1.00 mol of NH_3, has 3 significant figures. This is because the other two measured values in the calculation (14.0 and 28.0) have 3 significant figures.

Practice   Excess pentane, C_5H_{12}, burns in 185 g of O_2. The equation is $C_5H_{12} + 8O_2 \rightarrow 5CO_2 + 6H_2O$. How many moles of CO_2 form?

Notice the difference between the two conversion factors in Example 1.

• To convert between mass and moles, you are working with _one_ substance (call it R). The conversion factor shows "1 mol R" and the molar mass of R in grams.

• To convert between moles and moles, you are working with _two_ substances (R and S). The conversion factor shows "x mol R" and "y mol S." The x and y are coefficients taken from the balanced equation.

Always check that the given equation is balanced. In all stoichiometry problems, the link between two substances is a mole-mole link. This link is found in the balanced equation.

Example 2 51.0 g of NH_3 is produced by this reaction: $N_2 + 3H_2 \rightarrow 2NH_3$. How many moles of H_2 reacted?

Read You are given a product mass. You need to find the moles of the reactant H_2.

Plan Here is the conversion map:

mass of $NH_3 \rightarrow$ moles of $NH_3 \rightarrow$ moles of H_2

For the first conversion, you need the molar mass of NH_3: 14.0 g/mol + 3(1 g/mol) = 17.0 g/mol. For the second conversion, you need the coefficients of NH_3 and H_2 from the balanced equation: 2:3.

Solve Multiply 51.0 g of NH_3 by two conversion factors.

$$51.0 \; \cancel{g \, NH_3} \left(\frac{1 \; \cancel{mol \, NH_3}}{17.0 \; \cancel{g \, NH_3}} \right) \left(\frac{3 \; mol \, H_2}{2 \; \cancel{mol \, NH_3}} \right) = 4.50 \; mol \; H_2$$

mass to moles   moles to moles

Reflect If you multiplied by just the first factor, you would find that 51.0 g of NH_3 is 3 mol. 3 mol of NH_3 is produced from 4.5 mol of H_2. This is a 2:3 mole ratio.

Practice 61 g of water is produced by this reaction: $C_5H_{12} + 8O_2 \rightarrow 5CO_2 + 6H_2O$. How many moles of pentane, C_5H_{12}, reacted?

Mass-Mass Calculations

So far, you have converted moles into moles, and mass into moles. In both cases, the answer was in moles. Many stoichiometry problems ask for an answer in grams, not moles. In these problems, an extra step is needed to convert the answer into grams. For any two substances R and S in a chemical reaction, here are two possible conversion maps:

moles of R $\rightarrow$ moles of S $\rightarrow$ mass of S

mass of R $\rightarrow$ moles of R $\rightarrow$ moles of S $\rightarrow$ mass of S

Each arrow represents one conversion and one conversion factor. The next two examples are mass-mass problems. They have a conversion map like the second one above.

Example 3

Example 3	83.2 g of NH_3 reacts with excess oxygen according to this equation: $4NH_3 + 7O_2 \rightarrow 4NO_2 + 6H_2O$. What mass of water is produced?

Read   You are given the mass of a reactant. You need to find the mass of a product.

Plan   First check that the equation is balanced. Then map out the set of conversions:

mass of $NH_3 \rightarrow$ moles of $NH_3 \rightarrow$ moles of $H_2O \rightarrow$ mass of H_2O

For each arrow, create one conversion factor. The first factor involves the molar mass of NH_3. The middle factor is a mole ratio based on coefficients. The third factor involves the molar mass of H_2O.

Solve   Multiply the given mass by the three factors.

$$83.2 \text{ g } NH_3 \left(\frac{1 \text{ mol } NH_3}{17.0 \text{ g } NH_3} \right) \left(\frac{6 \text{ mol } H_2O}{4 \text{ mol } NH_3} \right) \left(\frac{18.0 \text{ g } H_2O}{1 \text{ mol } H_2O} \right) = 132 \text{ g } H_2O$$

mass to moles   moles to moles   moles to mass

With excess oxygen, 83.2 g of NH_3 will produce 132 g of H_2O. The answer has 3 significant figures, just like the other measured values in the calculation.

Reflect   When making each conversion factor, remember that the desired unit for that conversion goes on the top. The given unit for that conversion goes on the bottom. Then all units, except the final desired unit, will cancel.

Practice   29 g of H_2O_2 decomposes according to this equation: $2H_2O_2 \rightarrow 2H_2O + O_2$. What mass of oxygen is produced?

Research and Write

Sulfuric acid, H_2SO_4, is the most commonly produced chemical in the United States. Use the Internet to prepare a report on one product made from sulfuric acid. Write a balanced equation for the reaction. Use stoichiometry to calculate the mass of product made from 1,000 kg of sulfuric acid.

Example 4	91.3 g of oxygen reacts with ammonia. The balanced equation is $4NH_3 + 7O_2 \rightarrow 4NO_2 + 6H_2O$. What mass of NH_3 also reacts?

Read   This problem asks you to convert from grams of one reactant to grams of another reactant.

Plan   To convert from mass to mass, you have to go through moles, just like Example 3. The conversion map is

mass of $O_2 \rightarrow$ moles of $O_2 \rightarrow$ moles of $NH_3 \rightarrow$ mass of NH_3

For each arrow, create one conversion factor. The first and third factors involve molar masses. The middle factor is a mole ratio.

Solve   Multiply the given mass by the three conversion factors.

$$91.3 \text{ g } O_2 \left(\frac{1 \text{ mol } O_2}{32.0 \text{ g } O_2} \right) \left(\frac{4 \text{ mol } NH_3}{7 \text{ mol } O_2} \right) \left(\frac{17.0 \text{ g } NH_3}{1 \text{ mol } NH_3} \right) = 27.7 \text{ g } NH_3$$

mass to moles   moles to moles   moles to mass

Reflect   Why isn't the first factor $\left(\frac{1 \text{ mol } O_2}{16 \text{ g } O_2} \right)$? Remember that diatomic elements like H_2 and O_2 have a molar mass of 2(atomic mass).

Practice   37.0 g of water is produced by this reaction: $2H_2O_2 \rightarrow 2H_2O + O_2$. What mass of H_2O_2 reacted?

❀ ❀

Technology and Society

Many products you use contain metals. Some metals occur naturally only in compounds called ores. A chemical reaction is needed to obtain the pure metal. An example is aluminum. It is produced from aluminum oxide, Al_2O_3. This decomposition reaction requires a large amount of electricity. About 530 g of aluminum can be produced from 1 kg of Al_2O_3.

On a sheet of paper, write the answer to each question. Use this balanced equation:

$$2Al(OH)_3 + 3H_2SO_4 \rightarrow Al_2(SO_4)_3 + 6H_2O$$

1. You need to convert the mass of $Al_2(SO_4)_3$ to the mass of water. How many conversion factors will you need?

2. You need to convert the mass of $Al(OH)_3$ to moles of water. How many conversion factors will you need?

3. To convert from grams of H_2SO_4 to moles of H_2SO_4, what conversion factor would you use?

4. If 216 g of water forms, how many moles of $Al_2(SO_4)_3$ form?

5. If 736 g of H_2SO_4 reacts with excess $Al(OH)_3$, how many moles of $Al_2(SO_4)_3$ form?

6. You have 132 g of $Al(OH)_3$. This reacts with excess H_2SO_4. How many grams of water are produced?

Critical Thinking

On a sheet of paper, write the answer to each question.

7. A chemist burns 175 g of solid magnesium in excess O_2 gas. All of the metal reacts. He wants to know how many grams of the oxygen reacted. Write a conversion map for this problem. (Hint: This is a combination reaction. Write a balanced equation first.)

8. Solve the problem in question 7. What mass of oxygen reacted?

9. A chemist has a small amount of diatomic bromine. She uses all of it in a single-replacement reaction with excess KI. 28.2 g of KBr is produced. She wants to know the mass of the bromine. Write a conversion map for this problem. (Hint: The other product is diatomic. Write a balanced equation first.)

10. Solve the problem in question 9. How many grams of bromine did the chemist have?

Stoichiometry problems are based on balanced chemical equations. They involve converting amounts of one substance into amounts of another substance. The amounts you have used so far have been in moles or grams. In this lesson, you will work with two new quantities:

• number of particles of a substance

• volume of a gas at STP

For stoichiometry calculations, use these rules:

Rule 1. If the given unit is not moles, convert it into moles first.

Rule 2. Use a mole ratio to convert moles of one substance into moles of a different substance.

Rule 3. If the desired unit is not moles, convert moles into the desired unit.

▼◄▲▼◄▲▼◄▲▼◄▲▼◄▲▼◄▲▼◄▲▼◄▲▼◄▲▼◄▲▼◄▲▼◄▲▼◄▲▼◄▲▼◄▲▼◄▲▼

Science at Work

Quality Control Inspector

The manufacturing industry is all of the businesses that make products to be sold. Manufacturers want to make high-quality products using efficient processes. An efficient process has little waste and requires the least cost and time. Almost all products are made from other materials. The stoichiometry of an industrial process—the amounts of these materials—determines how many products are made.

Quality control inspectors study manufacturing processes. They look for ways to improve them. They examine the quality of a product and collect sample products to test. They also examine equipment to make sure it is working properly.

Quality control inspectors must be very precise in their work. They usually work by themselves, but they advise other workers. A high school diploma is a minimum requirement for a quality control inspector. Sometimes a college degree is needed.

Calculations with Number of Particles

Before you start a stoichiometry problem, make a conversion map to help you see each conversion step.

Some stoichiometry problems ask you to convert between moles and the number of particles. Avogadro's number, 6.02×10^{23}, is the number of particles in 1 mol of any substance. The conversion factor you will need is one of these:

$$\frac{1 \text{ mol of a substance}}{6.02 \times 10^{23} \text{ particles}} \quad \text{or} \quad \frac{6.02 \times 10^{23} \text{ particles}}{1 \text{ mol of a substance}}$$

Example 1 4.53×10^{23} formula units of $KClO_3$ decompose according to this equation: $2KClO_3 \rightarrow 2KCl + 3O_2$. How many oxygen molecules form?

Read   You are asked to convert particles of $KClO_3$ to particles of O_2.

Plan   Here is the conversion map for this problem:

particles of $KClO_3 \rightarrow$ moles of $KClO_3 \rightarrow$ moles of $O_2 \rightarrow$ particles of O_2

There are three arrows, so you need three conversion factors. The middle one is a mole ratio comparing the two substances. The balanced equation shows that 2 mol of $KClO_3$ decomposes to produce 3 mol of O_2. The first and third factors involve Avogadro's number.

Solve   Multiply the given amount by the three factors.

$$4.53 \times 10^{23} \text{ particles} \left(\frac{1 \text{ mol } KClO_3}{6.02 \times 10^{23} \text{ particles}} \right) \left(\frac{3 \text{ mol } O_2}{2 \text{ mol } KClO_3} \right) \left(\frac{6.02 \times 10^{23} \text{ particles}}{1 \text{ mol } O_2} \right)$$

particles to moles   moles to moles   moles to particles

$$= 6.80 \times 10^{23} \text{ particles } O_2$$

6.80×10^{23} particles of O_2 form. In this case, the particles are molecules.

Reflect   To convert between any two units that are not moles, you have to go through moles. The mole ratio is the important link between one substance and another.

Practice 4.61×10^{23} molecules of O_2 are produced according to this equation: $2KClO_3 \rightarrow 2KCl + 3O_2$. How many formula units of KCl are produced?

In Example 1, the first and third conversion factors can be completely canceled out. One factor has Avogadro's number on the top, and the other factor has Avogadro's number on the bottom. You can cancel two identical numbers or units when one appears in a denominator and one in a numerator on the same side of an equation.

Example 2 8.42×10^{23} particles of NaOH react with excess H_3PO_4 according to this equation: $3NaOH + H_3PO_4 \rightarrow Na_3PO_4 + 3H_2O$. What mass of Na_3PO_4 is produced?

Read   You are given the number of particles of a reactant. You need the mass of a product.

Plan   The equation is balanced. The conversion map looks like this:

particles of NaOH → moles of NaOH → moles of Na_3PO_4 → mass of Na_3PO_4

Three conversion factors are needed. The first one converts particles to moles for NaOH. The middle factor is a mole ratio. The third one converts moles to mass for Na_3PO_4. You will need the molar mass of Na_3PO_4. It is $3(23.0 \text{ g/mol}) + 31.0 \text{ g/mol} + 4(16.0 \text{ g/mol}) = 164 \text{ g/mol}$.

Solve   Multiply the given amount by the three conversion factors.

$$8.42 \times 10^{23} \text{ particles} \left(\frac{1 \text{ mol NaOH}}{6.02 \times 10^{23} \text{ particles}} \right) \left(\frac{1 \text{ mol Na}_3\text{PO}_4}{3 \text{ mol NaOH}} \right) \left(\frac{164.0 \text{ g Na}_3\text{PO}_4}{1 \text{ mol Na}_3\text{PO}_4} \right)$$

particles to moles   moles to moles   moles to mass

$= 76.5 \text{ g Na}_3\text{PO}_4$
76.5 g of Na_3PO_4 is produced.

Reflect   Particles of a substance may be atoms, molecules, or formula units. NaOH particles are formula units because NaOH is an ionic compound.

Practice   50.0 g of water is produced by this reaction: $3NaOH + H_3PO_4 \rightarrow Na_3PO_4 + 3H_2O$. How many formula units of Na_3PO_4 are produced?

Before moving on to stoichiometry with gas volume, here's a quick review:

- A mole-mole conversion requires a balanced equation and a mole ratio.
- A mole-mass (or mass-mole) conversion requires the molar mass of the substance.
- A mole-particle (or particle-mole) conversion requires Avogadro's number.

Calculations with Gas Volume

Stoichiometry can solve problems involving gas volumes at STP. The conversion factors that relate gas volume to moles are

$$\frac{1 \text{ mol}}{22.4 \text{ L}} \quad \text{and} \quad \frac{22.4 \text{ L}}{1 \text{ mol}}$$

These factors can be used only for gases at STP.

Example 3	Excess ethane burns in 87.3 L of oxygen. The balanced equation is $2C_2H_6(g) + 7O_2(g) \rightarrow 4CO_2(g) + 6H_2O(g)$. All gases are at STP. What volume of carbon dioxide is produced?

Read

The given amount is liters of a reactant. The desired amount is liters of a product. Both are gases at STP.

Plan

This can be solved because the gases are at STP. Check that the equation is balanced. Then map out the conversion factors.

volume of $O_2 \rightarrow$ moles of $O_2 \rightarrow$ moles of $CO_2 \rightarrow$ volume of CO_2

The first and third factors involve standard molar volume (22.4 L). The second factor is a mole ratio.

Solve

Multiply the 87.3 L of O_2 by the three conversion factors.

$$87.3 \text{ L } O_2 \left(\frac{1 \text{ mol } O_2}{22.4 \text{ L } O_2}\right)\left(\frac{4 \text{ mol } CO_2}{7 \text{ mol } O_2}\right)\left(\frac{22.4 \text{ L } CO_2}{1 \text{ mol } CO_2}\right) = 49.9 \text{ L } CO_2$$

volume to moles moles to moles moles to volume

Reflect

If the gases were not at STP, the first and third factors would not be true.

Practice

44.8 L of chlorine gas reacts according to the equation, $TiO_2(s) + C(s) + 2Cl_2(g) \rightarrow TiCl_4(l) + CO_2(g)$. There is an excess of the other reactants. All gases are at STP. What volume of carbon dioxide is produced?

Math Tip
1 mol of any gas at STP has a volume of 22.4 L. This is standard molar volume. STP is standard temperature and pressure: 0°C and 1 atm.

In Example 3, the first and third conversion factors can be canceled out. With the first factor, you divided by 22.4 L. With the third factor, you multiplied by 22.4 L. A similar thing happened in Example 1. When converting from *particles to particles* or from *volume to volume*, the first and last factors can be canceled. This is because Avogadro's number and standard molar volume do not vary with the substance. However, when converting from *mass to mass*, these factors do not cancel out. This is because molar mass depends on the substance, and so the numbers are different.

Example 4	12.6 g of magnesium reacts with excess hydrochloric acid. The equation is $Mg(s) + 2HCl(aq) \rightarrow MgCl_2(aq) + H_2(g)$. What volume of H_2 gas is produced at STP?

Read   You are given the mass of a reactant. You are asked for the volume of a gaseous product at STP.

Plan   This can be solved because the H_2 gas is at STP. Check that the equation is balanced. Map out the conversions:

mass of Mg → moles of Mg → moles of H_2 → volume of H_2

Solve   Multiply the given mass by the three conversion factors.

$$12.6 \text{ g Mg} \left(\frac{1 \text{ mol Mg}}{24.3 \text{ g Mg}} \right) \left(\frac{1 \text{ mol } H_2}{1 \text{ mol Mg}} \right) \left(\frac{22.4 \text{ L } H_2}{1 \text{ mol } H_2} \right) = 11.6 \text{ L } H_2$$

mass to moles   moles to moles   moles to volume

Reflect   To use standard molar volume, not all of the reactants and products need to be gases. Only the substance that is involved in the conversion factor needs to be a gas at STP.

Practice   0.75 L of H_2 gas reacts with excess nitrogen monoxide gas. The equation is $2NO(g) + 5H_2(g) \rightarrow 2NH_3(g) + 2H_2O(g)$. All gases are at STP. How many grams of water form?

★ ✦ ★

Achievements in Science

The Haber Process

Plants and animals need nitrogen. Even though air is mostly nitrogen gas, most living things cannot use this form of nitrogen. However, nitrogen in the form of compounds such as nitrates and ammonia are useful.

Soil often lacks the nitrogen compounds needed to raise good crops. Farmers may use fertilizers containing nitrogen compounds. These compounds are made from nitrogen gas. How is this done? The most common way is to mix nitrogen and hydrogen gases under high pressure.

They react to form ammonia, NH_3. For every 1 mol of N_2 and 3 mol of H_2 that reacts, 2 mol of NH_3 is formed.

This process was developed in the early 1900s. Fritz Haber and Carl Bosch designed equipment that can withstand the high pressures needed in this process. The Haber process is used to produce billions of kilograms of ammonia each year. Without it, food production would be limited to crops that can be grown using natural fertilizers. Natural fertilizers are effective, but are not available in the large amounts needed for crops.

Example 5	44 L of Cl_2 gas at STP reacts with excess sodium according to the equation, $2Na(s) + Cl_2(g) \rightarrow 2NaCl(s)$. How many formula units of NaCl are produced?

Read   You are given the volume of a reactant. It is a gas at STP. You are asked to find the number of particles in the product.

Plan   Check that the equation is balanced. Here is the conversion map:

volume of $Cl_2 \rightarrow$ moles of $Cl_2 \rightarrow$ moles of NaCl $\rightarrow$ particles of NaCl

The volume-mole conversion will use standard molar volume. The mole-particle conversion will use Avogadro's number.

Solve   Multiply the given volume by the three conversion factors.

$$44 \text{ L } Cl_2 \left(\underbrace{\frac{1 \text{ mol } Cl_2}{22.4 \text{ L } Cl_2}}_{\text{volume to moles}} \right) \left(\underbrace{\frac{2 \text{ mol NaCl}}{1 \text{ mol } Cl_2}}_{\text{moles to moles}} \right) \left(\underbrace{\frac{6.02 \times 10^{23} \text{ particles NaCl}}{1 \text{ mol NaCl}}}_{\text{moles to particles}} \right)$$

$= 2.4 \times 10^{24}$ particles NaCl

2.4×10^{24} formula units of NaCl are produced.

Reflect   Watch significant figures in calculations. In this example, there are three measured values: 44, 22.4, and 6.02×10^{23}. The other numbers are not measurements.

Practice 5.95×10^{23} fluorine molecules react with excess arsenic according to this equation: $2As(s) + 5F_2(g) \rightarrow 2AsF_5(g)$. How many liters of arsenic(V) fluoride are produced?

Research and Write

Carbon dioxide gas is produced by burning fuels such as coal, oil, and natural gas. Some people believe that the increased amount of CO_2 in the earth's atmosphere is contributing to global warming. Do research to estimate how much CO_2 is produced each year by burning fuels. Report your findings in kilograms, moles, and liters of CO_2 at STP.

On a sheet of paper, write the answer to each question. Use this balanced equation: $C(s) + CO_2(g) \rightarrow 2CO(g)$.

1. To convert liters of CO_2 to moles of CO_2, what conversion factor would you use?

2. 10.0 L of CO_2 at STP reacts with excess carbon. How many grams of carbon monoxide form?

3. 7.50×10^{23} atoms of carbon react with excess CO_2. If the product is at STP, what is its volume?

4. To convert grams of carbon to moles of carbon, what conversion factor would you use?

5. If 5.0 g of carbon reacts, how many molecules of CO_2 also react?

6. 35.3 L of carbon monoxide gas forms. How many molecules of carbon dioxide gas reacted? Both gases are at STP.

Critical Thinking

On a sheet of paper, write the answer to each question. Use this balanced equation: $NiO(s) + 2HCl(g) \rightarrow NiCl_2(s) + H_2O(g)$.

7. 0.25 L of HCl gas at STP reacts with excess NiO. From this, can you find the volume of $NiCl_2$ that forms? Explain your answer.

8. 1.83×10^{23} molecules of H_2O form. How many molecules of HCl reacted?

9. If 34.7 g of NiO reacts, how many liters of HCl also react?

10. To solve the problem in question 8, two conversion factors—the first and the third—cancel out. To solve the problem in question 9, this does not happen. Why?

Objectives

After reading this lesson, you should be able to

◆ write molarity as a conversion factor that converts from volume to moles

◆ solve a stoichiometry problem that involves the volume and molarity of a solution

Math Tip

To make molarity into a conversion factor, remember that it is a derived unit: moles per liter. For example, 1.25 M is $\frac{1.25 \text{ mol}}{1 \text{ L}}$.

There is one more type of stoichiometry problem. It uses the volume and molarity of a solution. Remember from Chapter 4 that molarity is a measure of solution concentration.

Suppose a chemical equation involves substances R and S. R is in a water solution, so it is written as R(aq). The difference between R and R(aq) is this:

• R is a substance.

• R(aq) is an aqueous solution containing the solute R.

If you know the volume and molarity of R(aq), you can find the moles of R. From this, you can find a quantity of S. The conversion map would look like this:

volume of R(aq) → moles of R → moles of S → quantity of S

You know that the second conversion involves a mole ratio. You know how to convert moles of S to another quantity. What about the first conversion? From Chapter 4, the definition of molarity, M, is

$$M = \frac{\text{moles of solute}}{\text{liters of solution}}$$

By doing some algebra, this equation can be rearranged to

moles of solute = (liters of solution)(M)

Suppose the molarity of R(aq) is 3 M and its volume is 2 L. The molarity 3 M is the same as $\frac{3 \text{ mol}}{1 \text{ L}}$. To find the moles of R in R(aq), multiply the liters of R(aq) by its molarity.

$$\text{moles of solute R} = 2\,\cancel{\text{L}} \left(\frac{3 \text{ mol}}{1\,\cancel{\text{L}}} \right) = 6 \text{ mol of R}$$

This is a conversion from volume of R(aq) to moles of R. What is the conversion factor? It is molarity, written as a fraction.

Example 1	250. mL of 0.350 M $Fe(NO_3)_2$ reacts with excess NaOH. The equation is $Fe(NO_3)_2(aq) + 2NaOH(aq) \rightarrow 2NaNO_3(aq) + Fe(OH)_2(s)$. How many grams of $NaNO_3$ are produced?
Read	You are given the volume and molarity of $Fe(NO_3)_2$. You are asked to find the mass of $NaNO_3$.
Plan	Check that the equation is balanced. Create a conversion map: volume of $Fe(NO_3)_2(aq) \rightarrow$ moles of $Fe(NO_3)_2 \rightarrow$ moles of $NaNO_3 \rightarrow$ mass of $NaNO_3$ The first conversion involves the molarity of $Fe(NO_3)_2$. Molarity is defined in terms of liters, not milliliters. First change the solution volume into liters. Recall from Chapter 1 that the prefix *milli-* means 0.001. $250. \text{ mL} \left(\dfrac{0.001 \text{ L}}{1 \text{ mL}} \right) = 0.250 \text{ L}$
Solve	Now start with this volume and set up the conversion factors. $0.250 \text{ L Fe(NO}_3)_2 \left(\dfrac{0.350 \text{ mol Fe(NO}_3)_2}{1 \text{ L Fe(NO}_3)_2} \right) \left(\dfrac{2 \text{ mol NaNO}_3}{1 \text{ mol Fe(NO}_3)_2} \right) \left(\dfrac{85.0 \text{ g NaNO}_3}{1 \text{ mol NaNO}_3} \right) = 14.9 \text{ g NaNO}_3$
Reflect	The molarity of the aqueous reactant is expressed as a fraction. In this form, it serves as a conversion factor.
Practice	0.152 L of 0.725 M KI reacts with excess $Pb(NO_3)_2$. The equation is $2KI(aq) + Pb(NO_3)_2(aq) \rightarrow PbI_2(s) + 2KNO_3(aq)$. How many particles of PbI_2 are produced?

In this chapter, you have seen how stoichiometry is used to find different quantities in chemical reactions. Figure 6.4.1 summarizes the conversion "routes" you have studied. Each possible route maps substance A to substance B. Each route depends on a balanced equation and correct conversion factors. A and B are always part of the same chemical equation.

Link to ➤➤➤

Biology

The energy that drives human body processes is created by chemical reactions. Food in the form of glucose reacts with oxygen to produce carbon dioxide, water, and energy. This reaction takes place in the solution inside cells. The concentrations of glucose and oxygen in this solution determine how much energy is produced.

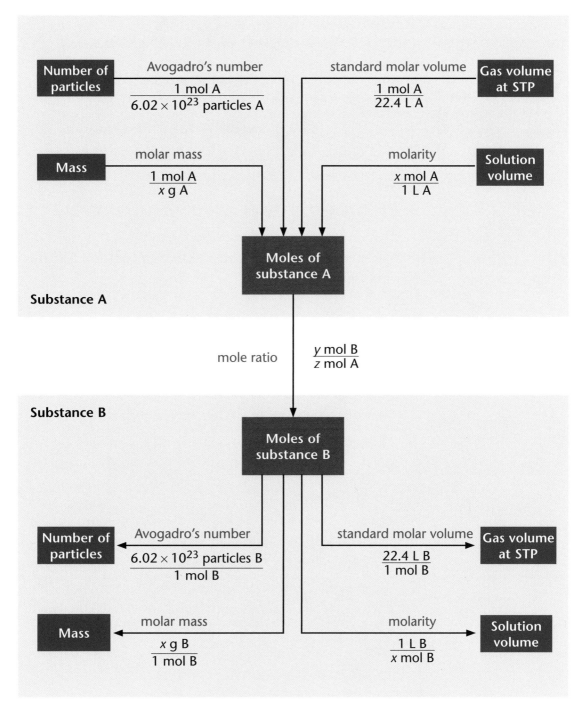

Figure 6.4.1 *Substances A and B are any two substances in a balanced chemical equation. To convert a quantity of substance A to a quantity of substance B, follow the arrows. Each arrow is labeled with its conversion factor.*

Lesson 4   R E V I E W

Word Bank

molarity

moles

volume

On a sheet of paper, write the word from the Word Bank that completes each sentence.

1. The _____ of a solution can be written as a fraction.

2. You can find the moles of solute in a solution if you know molarity and _____.

3. The factor $\dfrac{0.75 \text{ mol}}{1 \text{ L}}$ can convert liters of 0.75 M NaCl to _____.

On a sheet of paper, write the answer to each question. Use this balanced equation:
$$Ca(NO_3)_2(aq) + Na_2CO_3(aq) \rightarrow CaCO_3(s) + 2NaNO_3(aq).$$

4. You are given the molarity and volume (in liters) of $Na_2CO_3(aq)$. Draw a map for converting volume of $Na_2CO_3(aq)$ to particles of $CaCO_3$.

5. 0.095 L of 0.45 M Na_2CO_3 reacts with excess $Ca(NO_3)_2$. How many particles of $CaCO_3$ are produced?

6. 275 L of 2.00 M $Ca(NO_3)_2$ reacts with excess Na_2CO_3. What mass of $NaNO_3$ forms?

Critical Thinking

On a sheet of paper, write the answer to each question.
For questions 8–10, use this balanced equation:
$$HCl(aq) + NaOH(aq) \rightarrow H_2O(l) + NaCl(aq).$$

7. You are asked how many moles are in 1 L of reactant Z. If Z is a gas at STP, what conversion factor would you use? If Z is a 2 M solution, what factor would you use?

8. If 1.75 L of 1.00 M HCl reacts with excess NaOH, what mass of water is produced?

9. If 0.10 L of 2.5 M NaOH reacts, how many particles of HCl also react?

10. If 565 mL of 1.7 M HCl reacts, what mass of NaOH also reacts?

Objectives

After reading this lesson, you should be able to

◆ give the formula for percent yield

◆ explain the difference between actual yield and theoretical yield

◆ find a percent yield for a product, given its actual yield

Before you drive to an unfamiliar place, you might get directions from an Internet map program. The map program also gives the driving time. Suppose a route should take 23 minutes. But since you haven't been there before, it actually takes you 28 minutes. The actual amount of time is different than the predicted amount. The same is often true for amounts in chemical reactions.

For example, suppose you carefully measure amounts of certain reactants. Using these amounts and a balanced equation, you predict the amount of a product. Then you mix the reactants, causing the reaction to occur. You collect and measure the amount of product. Most likely, this amount is less than the predicted amount. Why? It could be one of these reasons:

- Perhaps not all of the reactants reacted.
- Perhaps some product stuck to glassware and was not measured.
- Some reactions simply do not go to completion. They may stop at a point when both reactants and products are present together.
- Some reactions can produce odd side products as well as the predicted products.

These situations lead to less actual product than predicted. Occasionally, the amount of measured product is more than predicted. This can happen when the product is contaminated with another substance (often water).

Science Myth

Myth: All reactions continue until at least one reactant is used up.

Fact: Some reactions occur in both the forward and backward direction. The reactants form products. These products can react to form the original reactants. A point is reached in which both reactants and products are present. You will study these reactions in Chapter 16.

Percent yield

A percentage that compares the actual product yield with the theoretical product yield; percent yield =
$$\left(\frac{actual\ yield}{theoretical\ yield}\right)100\%$$

Actual yield

The amount of product measured in a lab

Theoretical yield

The ideal amount of product predicted by stoichiometry

Percent yield is calculated only for a product, never for a reactant. If there are two or more products in a reaction, each can have a different percent yield.

To describe how much product is actually produced in a reaction, chemists calculate a **percent yield**. Percent yield compares the amount of actual product to the amount predicted by stoichiometry. It is similar to a percent score on a test. Suppose you correctly answered 18 questions out of 20. To find a percent score, you divide your points by the total points. Then you multiply by 100%.

$$percent\ score = \left(\frac{student's\ score}{total\ points\ possible}\right)100\% = \left(\frac{18}{20}\right)100\% = 90\%$$

Your percent score would be 90%. You answered 90% of the questions correctly.

Percent yield is calculated the same as a percent score. To find the percent yield for a certain product, you need to know

- the **actual yield**—the amount of product measured in a lab
- the **theoretical yield**—the ideal amount of product predicted by stoichiometry

These two amounts must have the same unit, usually grams. The formula for percent yield is

$$percent\ yield = \left(\frac{actual\ yield}{theoretical\ yield}\right)100\%$$

Calculations based on a balanced equation always give theoretical, or ideal, amounts. If a reaction worked perfectly, it would produce the theoretical yield. Percent yield tells how efficient, or productive, a real reaction is. A high percent yield, such as 95%, means the reaction is very productive. It produces close to the maximum possible amount of product.

Link to ≫ ≫ ≫

Language Arts

As a noun, the word *yield* means "the amount produced." As a verb, the word *yield* means "produce." Study these sentences: "Mixing NaOH and HCl *yields* NaCl and water. The theoretical *yield* of NaCl is calculated. The actual *yield* of NaCl is measured."

Example 1   87.3 g of NaOH reacts according to the equation, $H_2SO_4 + 2NaOH \rightarrow$
$Na_2SO_4 + 2H_2O$. There is an excess of H_2SO_4. If 32.5 g of water is actually
produced, what is the percent yield for water?

Read   You are given the mass of a reactant. You are also given the mass of water
that is produced. You are asked to find the percent yield for water.

Plan   To find percent yield, you need the actual yield and the theoretical yield.
You already know the actual yield: 32.5 g. You need to find the theoretical
yield of water in grams. This is just a stoichiometry problem like ones you
have already done. Check that the chemical equation is balanced. Then set
up the conversion factors you will need.

mass of NaOH → moles of NaOH → moles of H_2O → mass of H_2O

Solve   Multiply the mass of NaOH by three conversion factors.

$$87.3 \text{ g NaOH} \left(\frac{1 \text{ mol NaOH}}{40.0 \text{ g NaOH}} \right) \left(\frac{2 \text{ mol } H_2O}{2 \text{ mol NaOH}} \right) \left(\frac{18.0 \text{ g } H_2O}{1 \text{ mol } H_2O} \right) = 39.3 \text{ g } H_2O$$

The answer, 39.3 g, is how much water is produced if the reaction happens
perfectly. However, in this example, only 32.5 g of water is actually
produced. Use these two values to calculate the percent yield of water.

$$\text{percent yield of } H_2O = \left(\frac{32.5 \text{ g}}{39.3 \text{ g}} \right) 100\% = 82.7\%$$

The units cancel out, and the percent yield for water is 82.7%.

Reflect   82.7% of the ideal amount of water is actually produced.

Practice   14.7 g of Al reacts with excess oxygen. The equation is
$4Al(s) + 3O_2(g) \rightarrow 2Al_2O_3(s)$.
If 22.5 g of Al_2O_3 is actually produced, what is the percent yield?

❋ ❋

Technology and Society

A chemical reaction that produces a useful product might have
a low percent yield. This yield can sometimes be increased by
changing the conditions of the reaction. For example, ammonia
gas can be produced from H_2 and N_2 gases. The percent yield
of this reaction is much greater at very high pressure and a
temperature of about 450°C. These conditions allow large
amounts of ammonia to be produced at a low cost.

Lesson 5   R E V I E W

On a sheet of paper, write the word from the Word Bank that completes each sentence.

Word Bank
actual
percent
theoretical

1. The _____ yield is an amount of product calculated from a balanced equation.

2. The _____ yield is an amount of product measured in a lab.

3. The _____ yield compares two amounts and tells how efficient a reaction is.

On a sheet of paper, write the letter of the answer to each question. Use this equation: $4NH_3 + 7O_2 \rightarrow 4NO_2 + 6H_2O$. Assume 17.5 g of NH_3 reacts with excess oxygen.

4. What mass of water should be produced according to stoichiometry?

   A 18.5 g   **B** 27.8 g   **C** 175 g   **D** 315 g

5. The answer to question 4 is the _____ yield.

   A percent   **B** actual   **C** theoretical **D** measured

6. This reaction is performed in a lab, and 17.1 g of H_2O is measured. What is the percent yield of water?

   A 61.5%   **B** 74.1%   **C** 83.1%   **D** 92.4%

Critical Thinking

On a sheet of paper, write the answer to each question.

7. What does percent yield tell you about a reaction?

8. Why is the percent yield for real reactions usually less than 100%?

9. 114 mL of 0.150 M HCl reacts according to the balanced equation, $Ca(OH)_2 + 2HCl \rightarrow CaCl_2 + 2H_2O$. The actual yield of $CaCl_2$ is 1.35 g. What is the percent yield?

10. 24.2 g of $Ca(OH)_2$ reacts according to the equation in question 9. The percent yield of $CaCl_2$ is 91.3%. What is the actual yield of $CaCl_2$ in grams?

INVESTIGATION 6

Materials

- safety goggles
- lab coat or apron
- 75 cm of magnesium ribbon
- crucible
- tongs
- balance
- Bunsen burner
- clay triangle
- ring stand
- ring clamp
- eyedropper
- glass stirring rod
- distilled water

Percent Yield

Magnesium burns to form magnesium oxide. You can predict how much MgO should form. Then you can measure how much actually forms. What is the percent yield?

Procedure

1. To record your data, make a table like the one below.

Item	Mass (g)
empty crucible	
crucible and Mg ribbon	
Mg ribbon	
crucible and MgO	
MgO	

2. Put on safety goggles and a lab coat or apron.

3. Roll the magnesium into a ball that will fit in the crucible.

4. Find and record the masses of the first two items in the table. Calculate and record the mass of the ribbon.

5. Set up the ring stand, ring clamp, and burner as shown on the next page. Place the clay triangle on the ring. Place the crucible containing the metal ball on the triangle.

6. Light the burner. Heat the crucible until the magnesium starts to burn. **Safety Alert: Tie back long hair. Keep loose clothing away from the flame. Do not look directly at the burning magnesium.**

Continued on next page

7. After all the magnesium burns, turn off the burner. Allow the crucible to cool. Use the tongs to place the crucible on the counter. With the eyedropper, slowly add about 1 mL of distilled water to the crucible. Use the stirring rod to break up the product and mix it with the water. Scrape any product off the stirring rod so that it remains in the crucible.

8. Light the burner. Heat the crucible and its contents for at least 5 minutes until the mixture is dry. Turn off the burner. Allow the crucible to cool.

9. Use the tongs to place the crucible with contents on the balance. Record the mass of the crucible and MgO. Calculate and record the mass of the MgO.

Cleanup/Disposal

Discard the solid in a waste container. Wash and dry the crucible and stirring rod. Return all equipment. Then wash your hands.

Analysis

1. Write a balanced equation for this reaction.

2. What is the theoretical yield of MgO?

3. What is the actual yield of MgO?

Conclusions

1. What is the percent yield of MgO?

2. What might cause the percent yield to be less than 100%?

3. How do you think you might improve the percent yield?

Explore Further

Zinc metal burns in air with a blue-green flame to form zinc oxide, ZnO. If 2.00 g of zinc burns, what is the theoretical yield of ZnO? What is the actual yield of ZnO if the percent yield is 86%?

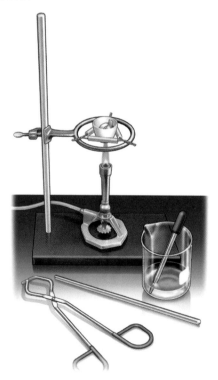

After reading this lesson, you should be able to

◆ find the limiting reactant in a reaction, given the moles of reactants

◆ find the limiting reactant in a reaction, given the masses of reactants

Limiting reactant

The reactant in a chemical reaction that is used up first; it limits the amount of product

Look back at the smoothie recipe on page 219. If you combine the amounts given in the recipe, you make 4 servings. What if you wanted to make 12 servings? You would need to make three batches of the recipe (or one triple recipe). To do this, you need three times the amount of each ingredient. In your kitchen, suppose you have the amounts given in the first column below:

Ingredients in Kitchen	Original Recipe	Triple Recipe
3 cups of strawberries	1 cup	3 cups
4 bananas	2 bananas	6 bananas
8 cups of orange juice	2 cups	6 cups
2 cups of vanilla yogurt	1/2 cup	1.5 cups

Will you be able to make a triple recipe? No. You have enough strawberries, juice, and yogurt. But you do not have enough bananas. The number of smoothie servings is limited by this ingredient. The bananas will be used up before any other ingredients are used up. This idea is seen in chemistry. In the recipe, the bananas are like the **limiting reactant**. In a chemical reaction, the limiting reactant is the reactant that is used up first. It limits the amount of product that can be produced.

Finding the Limiting Reactant Based on Moles

Reactants always combine according to the number of moles given in a balanced equation. In a chemistry lab, the actual reactant amounts usually do not match these mole amounts. There is usually one limiting reactant. Look at this familiar reaction:

$$2H_2 + O_2 \rightarrow 2H_2O$$

It shows that 2 mol of hydrogen will react with exactly 1 mol of oxygen. Suppose you combine 4 mol of hydrogen and 3 mol of oxygen. Which of these reactants will limit the amount of water produced? The limiting reactant is found by comparing the given moles (the available reactants) to the moles in the balanced equation (the "original recipe").

Available Reactants	"Original Recipe"	"Double Recipe"	"Triple Recipe"
4 mol of H_2	2 mol of H_2	4 mol of H_2	6 mol of H_2
3 mol of O_2	1 mol of O_2	2 mol of O_2	3 mol of O_2

If all of the given hydrogen (4 mol) reacts, 2 mol of O_2 is needed. You have 3 mol of O_2, so 1 mol is left over.

If all of the given oxygen (3 mol) reacts, 6 mol of H_2 is needed—you do not have this much.

Hydrogen is the limiting reactant. A simpler way to determine this is to multiply the available moles by a mole ratio:

$$4 \; \text{mol } H_2 \left(\frac{1 \text{ mol } O_2}{2 \text{ mol } H_2} \right) = 2 \text{ mol } O_2 \text{ needed to react with 4 mol } H_2$$

$$3 \; \text{mol } O_2 \left(\frac{2 \text{ mol } H_2}{1 \text{ mol } O_2} \right) = 6 \text{ mol } H_2 \text{ needed to react with 3 mol } O_2$$

You do not have enough H_2 for the second option—you do not have 6 mol. The first option, 4 mol of H_2 and 2 mol of O_2, will work. These amounts are available. When 4 mol of H_2 is combined with 3 mol of O_2, 1 mol of O_2 is left over. In this case, oxygen is the **excess reactant**. In a chemical reaction, the excess reactant is the reactant that is not completely used up. There is extra of this reactant. For reactions with only two reactants, if you know the limiting reactant, the other reactant is often in excess.

Science Myth

Myth: If you add more of a reactant during a reaction, more products are produced.

Fact: If you add more of the limiting reactant, this statement is true. If you add more of an excess reactant, the amount of product is not affected.

Example 1	If you combine 4 mol of N_2 with 6 mol of H_2, what is the limiting reactant? What is the excess reactant? Use this balanced equation: $N_2 + 3H_2 \rightarrow 2NH_3$.
Read	The reaction has two reactants. You are given a mole amount for each one.
Plan	For each reactant, use a mole ratio to find the needed moles of the other reactant.
Solve	Multiply each given amount by a mole ratio that relates the two reactants. This will tell you how much of the other reactant will combine with the given amount.

$$4 \text{ mol N}_2 \left(\frac{3 \text{ mol H}_2}{1 \text{ mol N}_2} \right) = 12 \text{ mol H}_2 \text{ needed to react with 4 mol N}_2$$

$$6 \text{ mol H}_2 \left(\frac{1 \text{ mol N}_2}{3 \text{ mol H}_2} \right) = 2 \text{ mol N}_2 \text{ needed to react with 6 mol H}_2$$

The first option is not possible—you do not have 12 mol of H_2. The second option is possible: 6 mol of H_2 will react with 2 mol of N_2 (with 2 mol left over). Hydrogen is the limiting reactant. It is completely used up. Nitrogen is the excess reactant. There is extra of it.

Reflect	Notice that the limiting reactant is not necessarily the reactant with the smaller amount. Even though you have more moles of H_2 than N_2, H_2 is the limiting reactant.
Practice	If 2.53 mol of propane, C_3H_8, reacts with 10.3 mol of O_2, which reactant is limiting? Which reactant is in excess? Use this balanced equation: $C_3H_8 + 5O_2 \rightarrow 3CO_2 + 4H_2O$.

Link to ➤➤➤

Environmental Science

In a car engine, fuel burns in excess oxygen. Carbon dioxide, water, and energy are produced. Sometimes, not enough oxygen is present, and carbon monoxide is produced instead of carbon dioxide. Carbon monoxide is an air pollutant. One purpose of a catalytic converter in a car is to cause carbon monoxide to react with more oxygen, forming carbon dioxide.

Finding the Limiting Reactant Based on Masses

Sometimes, reactant amounts are given in grams, not moles. In this case, it is easier to determine the product mass that can form from each reactant mass. Then the two product masses can be compared. The reactant that produces less product is the limiting reactant. The reactant that produces more product is the excess reactant.

Example 2	You combine 75.0 g of NH_3 with 120. g of O_2. What is the limiting reactant? What is the excess reactant? Use this balanced equation: $4NH_3(g) + 7O_2(g) \rightarrow 4NO_2(g) + 6H_2O(g)$.
Read	You are given the masses of both reactants in the reaction.
Plan	Convert each mass into grams of a product, say H_2O. You will need molar masses and mole ratios.
Solve	First convert grams of NH_3 to grams of H_2O.

mass of $NH_3 \rightarrow$ moles of $NH_3 \rightarrow$ moles of $H_2O \rightarrow$ mass of H_2O

$$75.0 \text{ g } NH_3 \left(\frac{1 \text{ mol } NH_3}{17.0 \text{ g } NH_3} \right) \left(\frac{6 \text{ mol } H_2O}{4 \text{ mol } NH_3} \right) \left(\frac{18.0 \text{ g } H_2O}{1 \text{ mol } H_2O} \right) = 119 \text{ g } H_2O$$

Now convert grams of O_2 to grams of H_2O.

mass of $O_2 \rightarrow$ moles of $O_2 \rightarrow$ moles of $H_2O \rightarrow$ mass of H_2O

$$120. \text{ g } O_2 \left(\frac{1 \text{ mol } O_2}{32.0 \text{ g } O_2} \right) \left(\frac{6 \text{ mol } H_2O}{7 \text{ mol } O_2} \right) \left(\frac{18.0 \text{ g } H_2O}{1 \text{ mol } H_2O} \right) = 57.9 \text{ g } H_2O$$

Compare the two results. The given amount of O_2 can produce only 57.9 g of water at the most. The given amount of NH_3 can produce more water (119 g), but you know that only 57.9 g is possible. The limiting reactant is the one that produces the smaller amount of product. Oxygen limits the amount of water that can form. Oxygen is the limiting reactant, and NH_3 is the excess reactant.

Reflect	The two masses of water are theoretical yields because they are based on stoichiometry.
Practice	You measure 170. g of solid $AgNO_3$ and dissolve this in 1 L of water. Then you combine this solution with 50.0 g of copper. What is the limiting reactant? What is the excess reactant? Use this balanced equation: $2AgNO_3(aq) + Cu(s) \rightarrow Cu(NO_3)_2(aq) + 2Ag(s)$.

If a stoichiometry problem asks for a product amount and gives only one reactant amount, then that reactant is the limiting one. You can assume that any other reactant is in excess.

Chemistry in Your Life

Consumer Choices: Rust-Proofing

When you buy a car, you should find out if the car has been rust-proofed. Rust, Fe_2O_3, is the product of a chemical reaction between iron and oxygen. Rust corrodes, or weakens, a piece of iron. The body of a car is mostly iron. Iron car parts will rust if they are not protected. Usually, rust-proofing involves coating the iron so oxygen cannot reach it. This process makes oxygen the limiting reactant in the formation of rust.

Car paint does the same thing as rust-proofing. Besides giving the car a sharp look, a layer of paint keeps oxygen from contacting iron car parts. However, not all iron on a car is painted. A rust-proofed car usually has an undercoat. An undercoat is a substance that is sprayed on the bottom of the car, where paint is not applied. Buying a car that is rust-proofed, or deciding to have your car undercoated, can add years of use to the car.

1. Oil lubricates the metal parts of a machine so they don't wear out so quickly. What other purpose might the oil serve?

2. Why is it important to fix a scratch on your car as soon as possible?

On a sheet of paper, write the phrase from the Word Bank that completes each sentence.

Word Bank
excess reactant
limiting reactant
product yield

1. The _____ determines the amount of product produced.

2. There is some _____ left over in a chemical reaction.

3. The reactant in excess predicts the bigger _____.

On a sheet of paper, write the answer to each question. Use the balanced equation, $2Al + 3CuCl_2 \rightarrow 2AlCl_3 + 3Cu$.

4. You combine 4 mol of Al with 8 mol of $CuCl_2$. What is the limiting reactant?

5. You combine 17.0 mol of $CuCl_2$ with excess Al. What is the limiting reactant?

6. You combine 81 g of Al with 3.0 mol of $CuCl_2$. What is the limiting reactant?

Critical Thinking

On a sheet of paper, write the answer to each question. Use this equation: $2HCl(aq) + Ba(OH)_2(s) \rightarrow 2H_2O(l) + BaCl_2(aq)$.

7. A chemist combines 1 L of 2 *M* HCl and 1 L of 2 *M* $Ba(OH)_2$. What is the limiting reactant? Show your work.

8. A chemist combines 0.73 L of 1.8 *M* HCl and 55 mL of 2.8 *M* $Ba(OH)_2$. What is the limiting reactant? Show your work.

9. For a certain amount of HCl, the theoretical yield of water is 42 g. For a certain amount of $Ba(OH)_2$, the theoretical yield of water is 2 mol. If these reactant amounts are used, which one is limiting? Show your work.

10. For certain amounts of HCl and $Ba(OH)_2$, neither reactant is in excess. Give an example.

Materials

- safety goggles
- lab coat or apron
- 3 500-mL Erlenmeyer flasks
- grease pencil
- 100-mL graduated cylinder
- 240 mL of 1.0 M HCl
- 3.5 g of Mg ribbon
- balance
- 3 large round balloons

Limiting Reactants

Magnesium and hydrochloric acid react to form magnesium chloride and hydrogen. Given certain amounts of the reactants, how can you identify the limiting reactant? In this investigation, you will combine different amounts of magnesium with a fixed amount of acid.

Procedure

1. Read the following steps of the procedure. Write a paragraph describing what you expect to happen in this investigation. Predict differences among the three flasks.

2. Design and draw a table to record your observations and any important data.

3. Put on safety goggles and a lab coat or apron.

4. Use the grease pencil to label the flasks 1, 2, and 3.

5. Add 80 mL of hydrochloric acid to each flask. **Safety Alert: Do not let the acid contact your skin or clothing. Alert your teacher immediately if any acid spills.**

6. Cut pieces of magnesium ribbon so that you have a 0.5-g sample, a 1.0-g sample, and a 2.0-g sample.

Continued on next page

7. Place 0.5 g of magnesium in a balloon. Stretch the neck of the balloon over the top of flask 1, keeping the metal in the balloon. Do the same for the 1.0-g sample and 2.0-g sample, as shown.

8. Lift up each balloon so the magnesium drops into the acid. Keep the balloons on the flasks. Observe what happens. Record your observations.

Cleanup/Disposal

Pour liquids down the drain with plenty of running water. Any remaining solids should be rinsed thoroughly with water in the flask and then put in the proper waste container. Wash and dry the glassware. Return all equipment. Wash your hands.

Analysis

1. Compare the volumes of gas produced in each reaction.

2. What did you observe in flask 3 that you did not see in the other flasks?

3. How did your observations compare with your predictions?

Conclusions

1. What is the limiting reactant in flask 1? In flask 3?

2. What is in excess in flask 1? In flask 3?

3. Why can't you easily identify the limiting and excess reactants in flask 2?

Explore Further

Find the number of moles of magnesium in each sample. Find the number of moles in 80 mL of 1.0 M HCl. Use this information and a balanced equation to explain your results.

Luminol

Forensic science uses scientific concepts to solve crimes. Technology is an important part of forensic science. Computers are used to see a small part of a picture or hear a certain noise in a recording. Chemistry is also an important part of forensic science. Chemical tests are used to identify evidence found at a crime scene. One substance used at many crime scenes is luminol.

Luminol is a compound that contains nitrogen, hydrogen, oxygen, and carbon. Before using luminol, a forensic scientist mixes it with certain amounts of hydrogen peroxide and other substances. The substances in this mixture do not react with each other unless a catalyst is present. A catalyst is a substance that speeds up a reaction. The catalyst that is needed to cause a reaction is hemoglobin. Hemoglobin is a compound found in human blood.

Suppose that during a crime, a person is injured. The criminal cleans the area so that no blood is seen. Later, forensic scientists spray the luminol mixture around the crime scene. If any blood is present, even in very small amounts, the hemoglobin will cause the luminol and hydrogen peroxide to react. The product that forms will glow enough to see at night or in a dark room. The glowing product shows where blood is present.

A few other substances, such as chlorine bleach, also cause the mixture to react. Trained forensic scientists can usually tell if blood caused the reaction by how quickly the glowing appears. Other chemical tests can prove that the glowing was caused by blood.

1. Do you think luminol could be used to identify the person whose blood it is? Explain your answer.

2. How might luminol help in studying an object used during a crime?

Chapter 6   S U M M A R Y

- Stoichiometry involves conversions between amounts of substances in a chemical equation. Most stoichiometry problems give the amount of one substance and ask for the amount of another substance. Amounts may be in moles, grams, number of particles, or liters.

- To convert the moles of substance A to the moles of substance B, refer to a balanced equation and use a mole ratio.

- To convert between mass and moles for one substance, use molar mass in the form of a fraction.

- To convert the mass of substance A to the mass of substance B, go through moles. Two of the three conversion factors involve molar mass.

- To convert from particles of A to particles of B, go through moles. Two of the three conversion factors involve Avogadro's number.

- To convert the volume of gas A at STP to the volume of gas B at STP, go through moles. Two of the three conversion factors involve standard molar volume.

- For reactions that involve solutions, use molarity to convert between liters and moles.

- For substances A and B in a balanced chemical equation, there are many possible stoichiometry problems. Refer to Figure 6.4.1 for a summary.

- Percent yield compares a measured amount to the predicted amount.

$$\text{percent yield} = \left(\frac{\text{actual yield}}{\text{theoretical yield}} \right) 100\%$$

- A limiting reactant limits the amount of product. The reactant amount that gives the smallest yield for a certain product indicates the limiting reactant. The other reactant is usually in excess.

Vocabulary

Vocabulary Review

On a sheet of paper, write the word or phrase from the Word Bank that completes each sentence.

1. The _____ is the amount of product measured in a lab.

2. The _____ is the amount of product calculated by stoichiometry.

3. The _____ tells how efficient, or productive, a reaction is.

4. A(n) _____ is a fraction used to convert moles of one substance to moles of another substance.

5. The study of amounts in chemical reactions is called _____.

6. The reactant that is used up in a chemical reaction is the _____.

7. The reactant that is not used up in a chemical reaction is the _____.

8. To create a mole ratio between two reactants, a(n) _____ is needed.

Concept Review

On a sheet of paper, write the letter of the answer that completes each sentence.

9. According to the balanced equation, $N_2 + 2O_2 \rightarrow N_2O_4$, _____ of nitrogen will react with 6 mol of oxygen.

    A 2 mol   **B** 3 mol   **C** 6 mol   **D** 9 mol

10. One mole ratio based on the equation, $N_2 + 2O_2 \rightarrow N_2O_4$, is _____.

    A $\dfrac{2 \text{ mol } N_2}{2 \text{ mol } O_2}$ **B** $\dfrac{2 \text{ mol } N_2}{1 \text{ mol } O_2}$ **C** $\dfrac{1 \text{ mol } N_2}{1 \text{ mol } O_2}$ **D** $\dfrac{1 \text{ mol } N_2}{2 \text{ mol } O_2}$

Continued on next page

11. You know the moles of reactant R. You want to find the mass of product P. The conversion map is _____.

A moles of R → mass of P

B moles of R → moles of P → mass of P

C mass of R → mass of P

D mass of R → moles of R → mass of P

12. 123.2 L of O_2 at STP is combined with excess heptane, C_7H_{16}. This reaction occurs: $C_7H_{16}(l) + 11O_2(g) \rightarrow 7CO_2(g) + 8H_2O(g)$. The greatest amount of water that can be made is _____.

A 4 mol   **B** 5 mol   **C** 7 mol   **D** 8 mol

13. 4.21×10^{23} molecules of CO_2 are formed by the reaction, $C_7H_{16}(l) + 11O_2(g) \rightarrow 7CO_2(g) + 8H_2O(g)$. This means that _____ of oxygen reacted.

A 11 g   **B** 15.2 g   **C** 67.4 g   **D** 35.2 g

14. A chemist wants to make 1 L of a 2 M solution of NaCl. She needs _____ of NaCl.

A 23.0 g   **B** 35.5 g   **C** 58.5 g   **D** 117 g

15. A reaction in a lab produces 1.53 g of product. According to stoichiometry, 1.96 g of product should have been made. The percent yield is _____.

A 56.2%   **B** 67.0%   **C** 78.1%   **D** 128%

16. 5 mol of N_2 is combined with 8 mol of O_2. This reaction occurs: $N_2 + 2O_2 \rightarrow N_2O_4$. The limiting reactant is _____.

A N_2 **B** N_2O_4 **C** O_2 **D** H_2O

Problem Solving

On a sheet of paper, write the answer to each question. Use this balanced equation:

$$3Mg(NO_3)_2(aq) + 2Na_3PO_4(aq) \rightarrow 6NaNO_3(aq) + Mg_3(PO_4)_2(s)$$

17. 0.150 L of 2.44 M Na_3PO_4 reacts with excess $Mg(NO_3)_2$. What mass of $Mg_3(PO_4)_2$ can be made?

18. If the actual yield of $Mg_3(PO_4)_2$ is 45.3 g, what is the percent yield? (Hint: Use your answer from question 17.)

On a sheet of paper, write the answer to each question. Use this balanced equation:

$$N_2(g) + 3H_2(g) \rightarrow 2NH_3(g)$$

19. 37.5 g of nitrogen reacts with 15.5 g of hydrogen. What mass of ammonia can be made? What is the limiting reactant?

20. 25.2 L of N_2 at STP reacts with 55.3 L of H_2 at STP. What volume of ammonia can be made? What is the excess reactant?

Critical Thinking

On a sheet of paper, write the answer to each question. Use this *unbalanced* equation:

$$K_2CO_3(aq) + Ca(NO_3)_2(aq) \rightarrow CaCO_3(s) + KNO_3(aq)$$

21. What is the balanced equation?

22. You are given a certain number of liters of 3.00 M K_2CO_3. You are asked to find the grams of $Ca(NO_3)_2$. Based on stoichiometry, write a conversion map for this problem.

23. What conversion factors do you need for question 22? Write them in order.

24. How many grams of $Ca(NO_3)_2$ will react with 0.100 L of 3.00 M K_2CO_3? Use your answers from questions 22 and 23.

25. Why is a balanced equation needed to answer the above questions?

Test-Taking Tip As you read a stoichiometry problem, make a conversion map. Decide how many conversion factors you will need.

7

Gases

The scuba tank in the photo contains a compressed mixture of gases. The ability to be compressed is one of the unique properties of gases. Unlike the particles of solids and liquids, gas particles move almost independently of one another. In Chapter 7, you will find out more about the properties of gases. You will also study laws that describe the behavior of gases.

Organize Your Thoughts

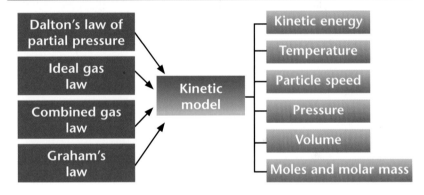

Goals for Learning

◆ To describe an ideal gas in terms of the kinetic model

◆ To understand pressure units, temperature scales, and conversions

◆ To explain how partial pressures contribute to the pressure of a gas mixture

◆ To use the combined gas law to solve temperature, pressure, and volume problems

◆ To use the ideal gas law to solve for an unknown

◆ To explain how the molar mass and particle speed of a gas are related

Objectives

After reading this lesson, you should be able to

◆ compare the behavior of particles in solids, liquids, and gases

◆ state how temperature and kinetic energy are related

◆ explain how temperature and pressure affect gas volume

◆ describe an ideal gas using the kinetic model

Open a bottle of perfume or cologne and you will soon smell it. This is because some particles in the bottle move into the air. This simple example shows how easily gas particles move around. Not all particles move this freely. From Chapter 2, you know that the particles of a solid are closely packed and cannot move far. As a result, a solid has a definite shape. The particles in a liquid can easily slide past each other. Thus, a liquid takes on the shape of its container. The volume of solids and liquids do not change much, even with changes in temperature. Gas particles have much more freedom of movement. They are relatively far apart. Unlike solids and liquids, the volume of a gas depends greatly on both temperature and pressure.

To understand gases, you need to know how energy, temperature, pressure, and volume are related. All of these are physical properties of matter.

Kinetic Energy, Particle Speed, and Temperature

From Chapter 5, you know that kinetic energy is the energy of motion. Anything that is moving has kinetic energy. The particles in matter have kinetic energy. The temperature of a sample of matter is related to the kinetic energy of its particles. Temperature is a measure of average kinetic energy (particle speed). This is true for solids, liquids, and gases. As the temperature of a sample increases, so does the kinetic energy of its particles. This is because the average speed of the particles increases. Figure 7.1.1 shows this relationship.

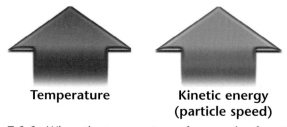

Temperature   Kinetic energy
(particle speed)

Figure 7.1.1 *When the temperature of a sample of matter increases, particle speed increases. Thus, kinetic energy increases.*

Pressure

The force acting on a certain area

Atmospheric pressure

The pressure exerted by the weight of the atmosphere

Link to ➤➤➤

Social Studies

The Dead Sea, which borders Israel and Jordan in the Middle East, has been a famous health resort for centuries. The waters of the Dead Sea are rich in minerals. Because the surface of the Dead Sea is more than 400 m below sea level, the atmospheric pressure is about 5% higher than at sea level. The increased pressure is helpful for people with breathing difficulties.

Pressure and Volume

Pressure is the force acting on a certain area. Compare two people walking on a wood floor. Both are the same weight. One is wearing tennis shoes, and the other is wearing high heels. Each person's weight is a force acting on the floor. The area of this force is the bottom of their shoes. The amount of force is the same for both, but the surface area of the high heels is much smaller. As a result, the person with high heels applies a greater pressure on the floor than the person with tennis shoes.

Pressure is a physical property of a gas. It is the force of billions of gas particles colliding with the walls of their container. The more collisions there are, the higher the gas pressure.

You live at the bottom of a "sea" of air called the atmosphere. Because of gravity, the weight of the atmosphere exerts a force on you and everything else on the earth's surface. **Atmospheric pressure** is the pressure exerted by the weight of the atmosphere. It is also called air pressure. Atmospheric pressure is exerted by the collisions of air molecules with other objects. There is less atmospheric pressure on top of a mountain than at sea level, as shown in Figure 7.1.2. When you are high in the atmosphere, there is less atmospheric weight pressing on you.

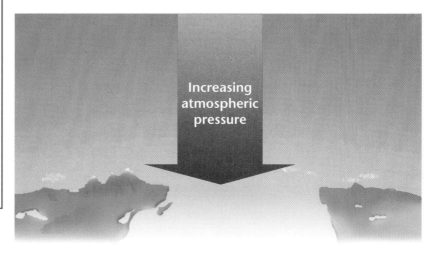

Figure 7.1.2 *Air pressure is greater in lower regions of the atmosphere.*

Gases expand to fill their container completely. The volume of a gas is the volume of its container. If the gas is in a sealed container, it expands to fill it. When a perfume bottle is opened, the gas in it quickly expands to fill the room. Because there is so much empty space between gas particles, a gas can be easily compressed, or packed into a smaller volume. Solids and liquids cannot be compressed very much. When a gas is compressed, the gas particles move closer together and collide more often with the walls of the container. As a result, the pressure of the gas increases, as shown in Figure 7.1.3.

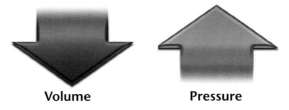

Volume   Pressure

Figure 7.1.3 *When the volume of a gas decreases, its pressure increases.*

If there are no particles to collide with the walls of a container, there is no pressure. A vacuum is created.

The Kinetic Model

To understand how gas particles act, chemists use the concept of an **ideal gas.** Most gases are considered "ideal" at normal temperatures and pressures. The particles in an ideal gas are described by the **kinetic model.** This model is a set of assumptions about how particles act. It states that the particles in matter are in constant motion. The kinetic model is used to explain the physical properties of gases. The kinetic model, also called kinetic-molecular theory, assumes the following:

- Gases are made of atoms (like He) or molecules (like CO_2). These particles are in constant motion. They act like tiny balls that are far apart from each other, bouncing around inside a container. Between the particles is empty space—nothing. The volume of the particles themselves is very small compared to the volume of empty space. Because of this, ideal gas particles are considered to have a volume of zero.

In a real gas, forces such as friction and gravity affect the motion of particles.

• Gas particles move randomly and travel in straight lines. Once in a while they collide with, or hit, each other or some object. After a collision, a gas particle bounces off in another straight line. This is similar to billiard balls moving around on a pool table. Gas particles do not combine when they collide.

• Collisions between two gas particles or between a gas particle and another object conserve energy. In such a collision, the total kinetic energy of the colliding particles stays the same. No energy is lost. The energy is completely transferred. If energy was not conserved, gas particles would lose energy with each collision. The particles would slow down and eventually fall to the bottom of the container.

Express Lab 7

Materials
◆ household ammonia in a small plastic bottle with cap
◆ perfume in a small plastic bottle with cap
◆ timer or watch with second hand

Procedure
1. Have two classmates stand side-by-side about 2 m away from the bottle of ammonia. Remove the cap from the bottle and start the timer.

2. When both classmates can smell the ammonia, stop the timer and place the cap back on the bottle. Record the elapsed time.

3. When the ammonia smell has lessened, repeat steps 1 and 2 with the bottle of perfume.

Analysis
1. Compare the times for the observers to smell the ammonia and the perfume.

2. Which moves faster, gas particles of ammonia or gas particles of perfume?

On a sheet of paper, write the word or phrase from the Word Bank that completes each sentence.

Word Bank

collision

force

kinetic energy

movement

pressure

temperature

1. The volume of a gas greatly depends on its _____ and pressure.

2. When gas temperature increases, so does the _____ of the particles.

3. Gas pressure is created by the _____ of gas particles.

4. Pressure is the _____ acting on a certain area.

5. When the volume of a gas sample decreases, its _____ increases.

6. Unlike particles in liquids and solids, gas particles have great freedom of _____.

Critical Thinking

On a sheet of paper, write the answer to each question.

7. Contrast particles in solids and liquids with particles in gases.

8. Why is atmospheric pressure higher at sea level than on mountaintops?

9. Based on the kinetic model, describe how ideal gas particles act.

10. A small container of perfume is opened in a classroom. Soon every student in the room smells the perfume. Explain this in terms of molecules.

Barometer

An instrument that measures atmospheric pressure

Pascal (Pa)

The SI unit for measuring pressure

Pressure is force per unit of area. One pascal equals about the force of a stick of butter spread over 1 m². Because the pascal is such a small unit, the kilopascal is often used instead.

Suppose you want to calculate the volume of 100 g of a substance. If the substance is a solid or liquid, you would use its density to find the volume. If the substance is a solution, you would use its molarity. If the substance is a gas, you need to know its temperature and pressure. In this lesson, you will learn how these two properties are measured.

Pressure

Gas pressure can be measured in different ways and with different units. One tool that measures atmospheric pressure is a **barometer.** There are many types of barometers. The one in Figure 7.2.1 consists of a glass tube that is filled with liquid mercury and placed upside-down in a dish of mercury. The atmospheric pressure presses on the mercury in the dish. This pressure supports the mercury in the tube. When atmospheric pressure increases, the height of mercury in the tube rises. This height—in millimeters of mercury (mm Hg)—is one unit of pressure. Gas pressure is also measured in units of atmospheres (atm) and **pascals (Pa).** The pascal is the official SI unit for pressure, although the kilopascal (kPa) is commonly used. Standard atmospheric pressure, 1.00 atm, is the same as 760. mm Hg or 101.3 kPa.

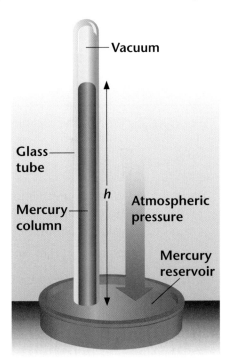

Figure 7.2.1 *A simple mercury barometer measures atmospheric pressure in millimeters of mercury (mm Hg). This is the height, h, of the mercury in the tube.*

To convert from one pressure unit to another, use these equations in the form of conversion factors:

1.00 atm = 760. mm Hg

1.00 atm = 101.3 kPa

Follow the basic conversion steps, remembering to put the desired unit on the top of the conversion factor.

Example 1	What is the pressure in atmospheres of a gas at 153 kPa?
Read	You are given a gas pressure in units of kilopascals. You are asked to convert this to atmospheres.
Plan	Create a conversion factor that relates the two units. The desired unit, atmospheres, should be on top.
Solve	Multiply the given value by the conversion factor. $153 \text{ kPa} \left(\dfrac{1.00 \text{ atm}}{101.3 \text{ kPa}} \right) = 1.51 \text{ atm}$
Reflect	153 kPa is the same as 1.51 atm.
Practice	What is the pressure in millimeters of mercury of a gas at 0. 90 atm?

Example 2	What is the pressure in kilopascals of a gas at 811 mm Hg?
Read	You are given a gas pressure of 811 mm Hg. You are asked to convert this pressure to kilopascals.
Plan	With the given information, you cannot convert directly from millimeters of Hg to kilopascals. Two conversion steps are required. First convert the given value to atmospheres. Then convert this to the desired unit, as shown. pressure in mm Hg → pressure in atm → pressure in kPa
Solve	Multiply the given value by two conversion factors. $811 \text{ mm Hg} \left(\dfrac{1.00 \text{ atm}}{760. \text{ mm Hg}} \right) \left(\dfrac{101.3 \text{ kPa}}{1.00 \text{ atm}} \right) = 108 \text{ kPa}$
Reflect	Remember to watch significant figures in your calculations.
Practice	What is the pressure in pascals of a gas at 1.25 atm?

Temperature

There are three different scales for measuring temperature. You are probably familiar with the Fahrenheit and Celsius scales. Both measure temperature in degrees (°F or °C). When working with gases, it is important to use **absolute temperature,** which is measured on the Kelvin scale. Absolute temperature has no negative values. Its unit is the kelvin (K), the SI unit of temperature. The symbol K does not use a degree symbol. The lowest possible temperature is 0 K, called **absolute zero.** At absolute zero, the particles in matter stop moving. They have zero kinetic energy. Absolute zero, 0 K, is the same as $-273°C$. This is an extremely cold temperature that has never been achieved in a laboratory. To convert from degrees Celsius to kelvins, use this equation:

$$T_C + 273 = T_K$$

T_C is a temperature in degrees Celsius, and T_K is a temperature in kelvins. Remember from Chapter 4 that standard temperature and pressure, STP, is 0°C and 1.00 atm. Under these conditions, 1 mol of a gas is 22.4 L. The temperature 0°C is the same as 273 K. This is the temperature at which water freezes. Figure 7.2.2 compares the three temperature scales.

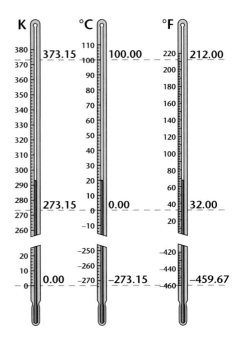

Figure 7.2.2 *Water freezes at 0°C or 32°F. This is the same as 273.15 K. Water boils at 100°C or 212°F. This is the same as 373.15 K.*

Link to ➤➤➤

Home and Career

Drinking straws are useful because of atmospheric pressure. When you draw the air from the straw into your mouth, the number of air particles in the straw decreases. This reduces the air pressure inside the straw. The atmospheric pressure on the surface of the liquid is now greater than the pressure inside the straw, so liquid is pushed up the straw to equalize the pressure.

Example 3   Convert 25°C to kelvins.

Read   You are given a temperature in degrees Celsius. You are asked to convert this to kelvins.

Plan   Use the equation, $T_C + 273 = T_K$, where T_C is 25°C.

Solve   This is a simple addition problem.
$25°C + 273 = 298$ K

Reflect   Remember that temperatures in kelvins do not use a degree symbol. Also, remember the rules for adding significant figures (see page 29).

Practice   Convert 73 K to degrees Celsius.

▼◄▲▼◄▲▼◄▲▼◄▲▼◄▲▼◄▲▼◄▲▼◄▲▼◄▲▼◄▲▼◄▲▼

Science at Work

Meteorologist

A meteorologist studies and predicts weather. Weather is the result of the unequal heating of gases in the earth's atmosphere. Unequal heating causes unequal air pressure. And unequal pressure causes winds and changes in weather.

There are several types of meteorologists. Some meteorologists, such as those on radio or television, present weather information. Other meteorologists provide weather information to businesses, such as insurance companies. Forecasters analyze weather patterns and predict expected changes in weather. Climatologists study and predict long-term weather patterns.

Meteorologists need a college degree in meteorology. Many meteorology courses involve mathematics and physics. Some meteorologists must have advanced degrees. Meteorologists need to be able to work with computer programs that help them predict the weather.

On a sheet of paper, write the word or number that completes each sentence.

1. The SI unit for pressure is the _____.

2. When doing calculations involving gases, use the _____ temperature scale.

3. To convert a Celsius temperature to an absolute temperature, add _____ to the value.

On a sheet of paper, write the letter of the answer to each question.

4. A gas has a pressure of 735 mm Hg. What is this pressure in atmospheres?

    A 0.967 atm **B** 1.03 atm **C** 7.26 atm **D** 98.0 atm

5. A gas has a pressure of 121 kPa. What is this in millimeters of mercury?

    A 1.19 mm Hg   **C** 16.1 mm Hg
    B 908 mm Hg   **D** 101.3 mm Hg

6. A substance is at −95°C. What is this temperature in kelvins?

    A − 95 K   **B** 273 K   **C** 368 K   **D** 178 K

Critical Thinking

On a sheet of paper, write the answer to each question.

7. What is the approximate atmospheric pressure at sea level in millimeters of mercury?

8. What happens to all particles at absolute zero?

9. What is STP in kelvins and kilopascals?

10. What is absolute zero in degrees Celsius?

The air around you is a mixture of gases. Air is about 78% nitrogen and 21% oxygen. It also contains very small amounts of argon, carbon dioxide, and other gases, as Figure 7.3.1 shows. Each of these gases contributes to the total atmospheric pressure, or the pressure of the air around the earth. The pressure that each gas contributes is its **partial pressure.** A partial pressure is the pressure of one particular gas in a mixture of gases. If the partial pressures of the gases in a mixture are added, the sum is the total pressure of the mixture. This idea, called **Dalton's law of partial pressure,** can be expressed as an equation.

$$P_{total} = P_A + P_B + P_C + \cdots$$

P_{total} is the total pressure of the mixture. P_A is the partial pressure of gas A, P_B is the partial pressure of gas B, P_C is the partial pressure of gas C, etc. To use this equation, all values must have the same unit.

Partial pressure

The pressure of one particular gas in a mixture of gases

Dalton's law of partial pressure

The law that states that the total pressure of a gas mixture is the sum of the pressures of each gas in the mixture;
$P_{total} = P_A + P_B + P_C + \cdots$

Figure 7.3.1 *Air is a mixture of gases.*

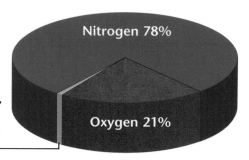

Argon, carbon dioxide, water vapor, neon, helium, krypton, xenon, methane, hydrogen, ozone 1%

Nitrogen 78%

Oxygen 21%

Link to ≫≫≫

Biology

Scuba divers breathe a mixture of oxygen and helium, not air. Air is mostly nitrogen and oxygen. Breathing air can produce a painful condition known as "the bends." Extra pressure under water causes inhaled nitrogen gas to dissolve in the diver's blood. When the diver returns to the surface, this dissolved nitrogen forms bubbles. Almost no helium dissolves in blood, so it does not cause "the bends."

Example 1   A gas mixture of neon and krypton has a total pressure of 1.75 atm. If the partial pressure of neon is 0.35 atm, what is the partial pressure of krypton?

Read   You are given a partial pressure and a total pressure. Both values are in atmospheres.

Plan   Use Dalton's law of partial pressure.

Solve   Solve for the partial pressure of krypton.

$P_{total} = P_{Ar} + P_{Kr}$

$1.75 \text{ atm} = 0.35 \text{ atm} + P_{Kr}$

$P_{Kr} = 1.40 \text{ atm}$

Reflect   The answer has 2 significant figures to the right of the decimal point, just like the given values.

Practice   Two gases are mixed, and the total pressure is 855 mm Hg. If the partial pressure of one gas is 563 mm Hg, what is the partial pressure of the other gas?

Water vapor

Gaseous water

Dalton's law of partial pressure can be used to find the pressure of a gas that is mixed with **water vapor,** or gaseous water. When a gas is bubbled through water and collected in an upside-down container full of water, no air is mixed with the gas. However, because the gas bubbled through water, it is mixed with water vapor. The pressure of this mixture is

$$P_{total} = P_{water} + P_{gas}$$

The pressure of the collected mixture, P_{total}, can be measured. The pressure of water vapor, P_{water}, depends only on the temperature of the water. Table 7.3.1 on the next page lists some water vapor pressures at different temperatures. The partial pressure of the gas collected over water is

$$P_{gas} = P_{total} - P_{water}$$

❖ ❖

Technology and Society

The regulator on a scuba tank allows a diver to adjust the pressure of the gas entering the lungs. This pressure must match the water pressure surrounding the diver. The composition of the gas mixture in the tank depends on the depth and length of the dive.

Myth: All gases in
a mixture of gases
have the same
pressure.

Fact: Pressure
is the result of
the number
of collisions of
particles with their
container. If one
gas is present in
a greater amount
than the others,
this gas will have
more particles.
More particles
means more
collisions. This
gas will have a
higher partial
pressure than the
other gases in the
mixture.

Table 7.3.1 Water Vapor Pressures		
Temperature (°C)	Pressure (mm Hg)	Pressure (kPa)
0	4.6	0.61
5.0	6.5	0.87
10.0	9.2	1.23
15.0	12.8	1.71
20.0	17.5	2.34
25.0	23.8	3.17
30.0	31.8	4.25
40.0	55.3	7.38
60.0	149.4	19.93
80.0	355.1	47.37
100.0	760.0	101.32

Example 2   A sample of oxygen gas is collected over water at 25°C. The total pressure of the mixture is 771 mm Hg. What is the partial pressure of the oxygen?

Read   A mixture of oxygen gas and water vapor is made. The total pressure is given. You are asked to find the partial pressure of the oxygen.

Plan   At 25°C, the vapor pressure of water is 23.8 mm Hg (see Table 7.3.1). Use Dalton's law to solve for P_{oxygen}.

Solve   Using the known values, the equation is

$$P_{oxygen} = P_{total} - P_{water}$$
$$= 771 \text{ mm Hg} - 23.8 \text{ mm Hg}$$
$$= 747 \text{ mm Hg}$$

Reflect   The water temperature is not used in the calculation, except to look up the vapor pressure of water. The answer has no significant figures to the right of the decimal point.

Practice CO_2 gas is collected over water at 60°C. The total pressure of the mixture is 86 kPa. What is the partial pressure of the CO_2?

On a sheet of paper, write the letter of the answer to each question.

1. In a mixture of dry air, the partial pressures of N_2, O_2, and CO_2 are 593.4 mm Hg, 159.2 mm Hg, and 7.4 mm Hg, respectively. What is the total pressure of this mixture?

   A 426.8 mm Hg   **C** 759.7 mm Hg

   B 593.4 mm Hg   **D** 760.0 mm Hg

2. In a gas mixture of He, Ne, and Kr, the total pressure is 125 kPa. The partial pressure of Ne is 73 kPa, and the partial pressure of Kr is 21 kPa. What is the partial pressure of He?

   A 31 kPa   **B** 73 kPa   **C** 125 kPa   **D** 219 kPa

3. A sample of H_2 is collected over water at 20°C. The total pressure of the H_2 and H_2O mixture is 743.2 mm Hg. What is the partial pressure of the H_2 gas? (Hint: Use Table 7.3.1.)

   A 21.2 mm Hg   **C** 743.2 mm Hg

   B 725.7 mm Hg   **D** 764.4 mm Hg

Critical Thinking

On a sheet of paper, write the answer to each question. Show all calculations. You may have to convert between units.

4. A gas mixture has these partial pressures: helium at 1.52 atm, neon at 455 mm Hg, and argon at 25.2 kPa. What is the total pressure of the mixture in atmospheres?

5. A sample of oxygen is collected over water at 40°C. The total pressure of the mixture is 102.0 kPa. What is the partial pressure of the oxygen in kilopascals? (Hint: Use Table 7.3.1.)

Objectives

After reading this lesson, you should be able to

◆ explain how a change in gas volume, pressure, or temperature affects the other two

◆ write the equation for the combined gas law

◆ use this law to calculate the pressure, volume, or temperature of a gas

Boyle's law

The law that says that gas pressure and gas volume are inversely proportional at constant temperature; $P_1V_1 = P_2V_2$

Inverse proportion

A relationship between two quantities in which one increases as the other decreases

The volume of a gas depends greatly on its temperature and pressure. Because of this, it is possible to predict how gas volume will change when temperature or pressure changes. In the 1600s and 1700s, several scientists studied the relationships between the volume, temperature, and pressure of gases.

Boyle's Law: Pressure and Volume

In the 1600s, an English scientist named Robert Boyle studied how gas pressure and volume change when temperature is constant. He found that when pressure increases, volume decreases. This relationship between the volume and pressure of a gas is **Boyle's law.** It is an **inverse proportion.** When one quantity increases, the other decreases. This makes sense. If you compress, or squeeze, a sample of gas, its volume will shrink. If you release gas that is under pressure, it will expand. The two quantities also change proportionately. This means that when the pressure of a gas triples at constant temperature, its volume shrinks to one-third the original size, as shown in Figure 7.4.1. Boyle's law can be expressed as

$$P_1V_1 = P_2V_2$$

For a certain gas, P_1 and P_2 are two pressures and V_1 and V_2 are two volumes. When the gas has a pressure of P_1, its volume is V_1. When the gas has a pressure of P_2, its volume is V_2. You can use this equation to solve for an unknown pressure or volume. Label one pressure-volume pair with 1's and the other pressure-volume pair with 2's. The units for P_1 and P_2 must be the same, and the units for V_1 and V_2 must be the same.

$\frac{1}{3}$ **the volume**

3 times the pressure

Figure 7.4.1 *For a gas at constant temperature, its pressure increases as its volume decreases.*

Example 1 A sample of a gas has a volume of 1.40 L and a pressure of 225 mm Hg. What will the new volume be when the pressure increases to 510. mm Hg? The temperature of the gas stays the same.

Read You are given the initial and final pressure of a gas sample. You are given its initial volume. You need to find its final volume.

Plan Since this problem involves volume and pressure at a constant temperature, use Boyle's law. Identify the known variables in $P_1 V_1 = P_2 V_2$. Label the first pressure-volume pair with 1's. Label the second pair with 2's.

$P_1 = 225$ mm Hg $\qquad$ $P_2 = 510.$ mm Hg

$V_1 = 1.40$ L $\qquad\qquad$ $V_2 = ?$

Solve The pressure values have the same unit. Use the given values to solve for V_2.

$P_1 V_1 = P_2 V_2$

$(225 \text{ mm Hg})(1.40 \text{ L}) = (510. \text{ mm Hg})(V_2)$

$V_2 = 0.618$ L

Reflect Because the initial volume is in liters, the final volume is in liters. The answer makes sense. Since the pressure increased, you would expect the volume to decrease.

Practice A sample of gas has a volume of 3.52 L and a pressure of 98.2 kPa. If it is compressed to a new volume of 1.15 L, what is its pressure? The temperature does not change.

Math Tip

Write the equations for Boyle's law and Charles's law. Write "inverse proportion" under the equation for Boyle's law. Write "direct proportion" under the equation for Charles's law. Use these labeled equations to help you remember the two types of proportions.

To summarize, Boyle's law says that

Increasing the pressure of a gas at constant temperature will decrease its volume.

Charles's Law: Volume and Temperature

Jacques Charles was a French scientist and hot-air balloonist. In the late 1700s, he studied the relationship between gas temperature and volume at constant pressure. Temperature is a measure of average kinetic energy. As gas temperature increases, the average kinetic energy of the particles increases. Think of a container of gas that is being warmed. As the gas particles move faster, they begin to collide more often with the walls of the container. If the container is free to expand, the pressure stays the same and the volume increases. For example, when the air inside a tied balloon is heated or cooled, the balloon's size changes.

Charles's law

The law that says that gas volume and gas temperature are directly proportional at constant pressure; $\dfrac{V_1}{T_1} = \dfrac{V_2}{T_2}$

Direct proportion

A relationship between two quantities in which one increases as the other increases

This relationship between volume and temperature, called **Charles's law,** is a **direct proportion.** An increase in volume means an increase in temperature, and vice versa. The two quantities increase and decrease together. They also increase and decrease in a proportional way. This means that if the absolute temperature doubles, the volume doubles. If the absolute temperature drops by half, the volume is halved. Charles law is expressed by this equation:

$$\frac{V_1}{T_1} = \frac{V_2}{T_2}$$

V_1 is the volume at temperature T_1, and V_2 is the volume at T_2. The unit for volume can vary as long as both V_1 and V_2 have the same unit. However, the unit for temperature *must* be kelvins. When using this equation, convert all temperatures to kelvins before setting up the calculation. Charles's law says that

> Increasing the temperature of a gas at constant pressure will increase its volume.

Example 2	A gas has a volume of 5.30 L at 25°C. What is its new volume when its temperature rises to 100°C? The pressure does not change.
Read	You are given the initial and final temperature of a gas. You are given its initial volume. You need to find its final volume.
Plan	This problem involves changes in gas volume and temperature, not pressure. Use Charles's law to find the unknown. Identify the known variables and convert temperature to kelvins.

$$V_1 = 5.30 \text{ L} \qquad\qquad V_2 = ?$$
$$T_1 = 25°C + 273 = 298 \text{ K} \quad T_2 = 100°C + 273 = 373 \text{ K}$$

Solve	Use these values in the equation and solve for V_2.

$$\frac{V_1}{T_1} = \frac{V_2}{T_2} \qquad \frac{5.30 \text{ L}}{298 \text{ K}} = \frac{V_2}{373 \text{ K}}$$
$$V_2 = 6.63 \text{ L}$$

The answer has the same unit (liters) as the given volume.

Reflect	The volume of a gas increases with temperature at constant pressure.
Practice	A sample of gas at 90°C is cooled to 44°C under a constant pressure. Its new volume is 737 mL. What was its initial volume at 90°C?

Gay-Lussac's Law: Pressure and Temperature

Gay-Lussac's law	

The law that states that gas pressure and gas temperature are directly proportional at constant volume; $\frac{P_1}{T_1} = \frac{P_2}{T_2}$

Another French scientist, Joseph Gay-Lussac, studied the relationship between gas pressure and temperature at constant volume. He found that pressure increases as absolute temperature increases—a direct proportion. As temperature increases, gas particles move faster and collide more often with the walls of their container. More collisions cause more pressure. **Gay-Lussac's law** shows how absolute temperature and pressure are related. It is expressed as

$$\frac{P_1}{T_1} = \frac{P_2}{T_2}$$

Pressure units must match, and temperatures must be in kelvins.

Example 3	A gas at 25°C has a pressure of 1.5 atm. It is heated to 323°C. If its volume does not change, what is its new pressure?
Read	You are given the initial and final temperature of a gas. You are given its initial pressure. You are asked to find its final pressure.
Plan	This problem involves changes in temperature and pressure at constant volume. Use Gay-Lussac's law. Identify the known variables and convert both Celsius temperatures into kelvins. $P_1 = 1.5$ atm $\qquad\qquad P_2 = ?$ $T_1 = 25°C + 273 = 298$ K $\quad T_2 = 323°C + 273 = 596$ K
Solve	Use these values in the equation and solve for P_2. $\frac{P_1}{T_1} = \frac{P_2}{T_2} \qquad \frac{1.5 \text{ atm}}{298 \text{ K}} = \frac{P_2}{596 \text{ K}}$ $P_2 = 3.0$ atm The answer has the same unit as the known pressure.
Reflect	When absolute temperature doubles, the pressure doubles—at constant volume. This direct proportion is only true for temperatures in kelvins (the initial Celsius temperature is not doubled).
Practice	A gas sample has a pressure of 687 mm Hg. This pressure is increased to 755 mm Hg, but the volume does not change. If the final temperature is 15°C, what was the sample's initial temperature?

Gay-Lussac's law says that

> Increasing the temperature of a gas at constant volume will increase its pressure.

As water in popcorn kernels is heated, it forms water vapor. As this water vapor heats, its pressure increases. This causes the popcorn hull to burst open and the popcorn to pop.

The Combined Gas Law

The laws of Boyle, Charles, and Gay-Lussac can be combined into one equation. This is called the **combined gas law:**

$$\frac{P_1 V_1}{T_1} = \frac{P_2 V_2}{T_2}$$

To use this equation to find an unknown value, follow the rules for the previous laws. The units for P_1 and P_2 must match. The units for V_1 and V_2 must match. T_1 and T_2 must be in kelvins. If you remember just this equation, you can always remove one pair of quantities to get Boyle's, Charles's, or Gay-Lussac's equations. For example, suppose a problem involves changes in pressure and volume, but temperature is constant. Just drop T_1 and T_2 from the combined gas law. You end up with $P_1 V_1 = P_2 V_2$.

★✦★✦★✦★✦★✦★✦★✦★✦★✦★✦★✦★✦★✦★✦★

Achievements in Science

Hot-Air Balloons

The idea of flying by balloon was proposed for centuries before a flight actually occurred. The first hot-air balloon flight took place in France in 1783. A sheep, a duck, and a chicken were the passengers. Early hot-air balloons used materials such as wood or straw for fuel. Burning these fuels provided the hot air to fill the balloon. Today, propane is the usual fuel for hot-air balloons. Over the years, balloons have also changed in shape, size, and material of construction. But the basic principles of a hot-air balloon are the same.

Hot-air balloons rise because the hot air inside the balloon is less dense than the air outside the balloon. There are fewer particles per volume inside the balloon. This difference in density creates lift. The balloon and its load rise through the air. The air inside and outside the balloon differ in density, but not pressure. If the pressure in the balloon were less than atmospheric pressure, the balloon would collapse. Particles in hot air move faster than particles in cool air. Thus, the air pressure (the force of collisions) is the same inside and outside the balloon.

Research and Write

Research Boyle, Charles, or Gay-Lussac. Find out how he studied gases. Find out if other scientists studied gases at the same time. Write a summary of what you learn.

Example 4 A gas has a volume of 15.3 L at 25°C and 1.11 atm. What is its volume at STP?

Read You are given a gas volume at a certain temperature and pressure. Then the conditions change to STP (0°C and 1.00 atm). You need to find the new volume.

Plan In this problem, all three conditions—volume, temperature, and pressure—change. The combined gas law relates these three. Identify the known variables. Convert the temperatures to kelvins. Make sure the pressure units match.

$P_1 = 1.11$ atm $P_2 = 1.00$ atm

$V_1 = 15.3$ L $V_2 = ?$

$T_1 = 25°C + 273 = 298$ K $T_2 = 0°C + 273 = 273$ K

Solve Use these values in the ideal gas equation. Solve for V_2.

$$\frac{P_1 V_1}{T_1} = \frac{P_2 V_2}{T_2}$$

$$\frac{(1.11 \text{ atm})(15.3 \text{ L})}{298 \text{ K}} = \frac{(1.00 \text{ atm})(V_2)}{273 \text{ K}}$$

$$V_2 = 15.6 \text{ L}$$

Reflect When all three conditions change, it is harder to predict if the answer will show an increase or decrease. In this case, the volume increased slightly.

Practice A gas has a volume of 3.00 L and a pressure of 75.4 kPa. When the volume expands to 4.00 L and the pressure drops to 72.7 kPa, the gas temperature is 0°C. What was the initial temperature of the gas?

Link to ➤➤➤

Earth Science

Scientists use weather balloons attached to transmitters to measure temperature, pressure, humidity, and wind velocity in the upper atmosphere. A weather balloon contains helium gas. The balloon is only partially inflated when released from the ground. As it rises, the surrounding air pressure drops and the balloon expands until it eventually bursts.

Lesson 4   R E V I E W

On a sheet of paper, write *decreases* or *increases* to complete each sentence.

1. When the pressure of a gas is increased at constant temperature, the volume _____.

2. When the temperature of a gas is increased at constant pressure, the volume _____.

3. When the temperature of a gas is increased at constant volume, the pressure _____.

On a sheet of paper, write the answer to each question.

4. A gas sample has a volume of 2.33 L at −25°C. What is the volume at a temperature of 25°C? Pressure is constant.

5. A gas has a volume of 1.50 L at 1.11 atm. What is its volume at 2.22 atm? Temperature is constant.

6. A gas has a pressure of 120. kPa at 100°C. What is the pressure at 50°C if the volume is the same?

Critical Thinking

On a sheet of paper, write the answer to each question. Show all calculations.

7. A gas has a volume of 12.3 L at 150°C and 700. mm Hg. Its volume is decreased to 9.15 L at a pressure of 770. mm Hg. What is the new temperature in degrees Celsius?

8. If fully inflated tires are driven on a hot day, there is a risk of the tires bursting. Explain why.

9. What happens to an inflated balloon that is taken from a heated room to a cold outdoor location? Explain your answer.

10. The gas volume in an aerosol can is constant because the can is made of metal. Why is it so dangerous to heat an aerosol can? Explain in terms of temperature and pressure.

Materials

- safety goggles
- lab coat or apron
- 2 pairs of rubber gloves
- round balloon
- black permanent marker
- string
- meterstick
- 2 buckets
- ice water
- warm water

The Volume and Temperature of a Gas

How can you see the effect of a change in temperature on the volume of a gas? In this investigation, you will examine what happens to the volume of a sample of gas when its temperature changes.

Procedure

1. Make a data table like the one below.

Temperature	Circumference (cm)
room temperature	
cold	
warm	

Continued on next page

2. Put on safety goggles and a lab coat or apron.

3. Partially inflate the balloon, making sure it is not completely inflated. Tie it closed. Use the marker to make three dots equally spaced around the middle of the balloon. **Safety Alert: Be sure to wear safety goggles in case a balloon breaks.**

4. Use a piece of string to measure the circumference of the balloon. Place the string around the balloon so that it goes over all three dots. Mark this string length with your fingers. Measure this length on the meterstick and record it.

5. Place the ice water in one bucket. Put on rubber gloves and hold the balloon in the ice water for 10 minutes. With a partner, take turns holding the balloon in the water.

6. Remove the balloon. Quickly measure and record its circumference as in step 4.

7. Repeat steps 5 and 6 using warm water.

Cleanup/Disposal

Return or dispose of your materials. Wash your hands.

Analysis

1. What happened to the circumference of the balloon as it was cooled?

2. What happened to the circumference of the balloon as it was warmed?

3. Why doesn't the pressure of the gas in the balloon affect the results?

Conclusions

1. When the circumference of the balloon increases, what happens to gas volume? Explain.

2. Based on your results, how is the volume of a gas affected by a change in temperature?

Explore Further

Design a similar investigation using different methods to cool and warm the balloon. Have your teacher approve your procedure first. Do your new results confirm your original results? Explain.

Objectives

After reading this lesson, you should be able to

◆ write the equation for the ideal gas law and identify each quantity in it

◆ use this law to solve for an unknown

Ideal gas law

The law that shows the relationship between the pressure, volume, number of moles, and temperature of a gas; $PV = nRT$

Constant

A fixed number in an equation, often represented by a letter or symbol.

Gas constant

The fixed value of R in the ideal gas law; $R = 0.0821$ *L·atm/mol·K or 8.31 L·kPa/mol·K*

So far, you have seen how the pressure, volume, and temperature of a gas are related. These three are also related to the moles of gas. If more gas is pumped into a container of gas, the number of moles increases. If some gas is let out of the container, the number of moles decreases. The party balloon in Figure 7.5.1 is being filled with helium gas. As the number of moles of helium in the balloon increases, the pressure, volume, and even temperature of the gas can be affected. The **ideal gas law** shows how the number of moles in a sample of gas is related to its pressure, volume, and temperature:

$$PV = nRT$$

This equation contains four variables: P, V, n, and T. These are quantities that can change.

- P is the gas pressure in atm or kPa.
- V is the gas volume in liters.
- n is the number of moles of gas (not grams).
- T is the gas temperature in kelvins.

The equation also contains one **constant,** R. A constant is a fixed number in an equation. R is called the **gas constant.** It is true for all gases. Its value, however, depends on the pressure unit used.

If pressure is in atmospheres,

$$R = \frac{0.0821 \text{ L·atm}}{\text{mol·K}}$$

If pressure is in kilopascals,

$$R = \frac{8.31 \text{ L·kPa}}{\text{mol·K}}$$

Figure 7.5.1
The number of moles of helium gas in this balloon are related to the pressure, volume, and temperature of the gas.

Math Tip

The equation in the Solve step of Example 1 contains two *atm* units, two *mol* units, two *K* units, and one *L* unit. The two *atm* units can be canceled because both are in the numerator on opposite sides of the = sign. The two *mol* units can be canceled because both are on the same side of the = sign, one in the numerator and one in the denominator. The two *K* units can be canceled for the same reason. The *L* unit is left.

The ideal gas law is used whenever a problem involves the mass or moles of a gas. If you are given the mass of a gas, use its molar mass to change the mass to moles first. The ideal gas law only works when *n* is in moles, not grams. Remember that you already know the value of *R*. For a certain gas sample, if you know three of the four variables, you can use $PV = nRT$ to find the fourth one.

Example 1 What is the volume of 1.00 mol of O_2 at STP?

Read You are given the following conditions for an O_2 sample: number of moles (1.00 mol), temperature (0°C), and pressure (1.00 atm). You are asked to find its volume.

Plan Because moles are involved, use the ideal gas law. The earlier laws do not account for moles. First identify the known values in the equation, $PV = nRT$. Remember that *R* is a constant. Choose the *R* value that has atmospheres in its unit. *T* must be in kelvins.

$P = 1.00$ atm

$V = ?$

$n = 1.00$ mol

$R = \dfrac{0.0821 \text{ L} \cdot \text{atm}}{\text{mol} \cdot \text{K}}$

$T = 0°C = 273$ K

Solve Use these values in $PV = nRT$ and solve for *V*. The answer will be in liters.

$PV = nRT$

$(1.00 \text{ atm})(V) = (1.00 \text{ mol})\left(\dfrac{0.0821 \text{ L} \cdot \text{atm}}{\text{mol} \cdot \text{K}}\right)(273 \text{ K})$

$V = 22.4$ L

Reflect You might recognize the answer as standard molar volume. This is the volume of 1 mol of any gas at STP.

Practice A sample of gas at STP has a volume of 934 mL. How many moles are in the sample?

The next two examples involve the mass of a gas sample, not the number of moles.

Example 2	What is the mass of NH_3 gas in a volume of 15.3 L at STP?
Read	You are given the volume, temperature, and pressure of ammonia gas. STP is 0°C and 1.00 atm. You need to find the mass of the gas.
Plan	Identify the known values in $PV=nRT$. In this problem, the unknown is n, the number of moles. Once you solve for n, you can convert it to mass. $P=1.00$ atm $V=15.3$ L $n=?$ $R=\dfrac{0.0821\ \text{L·atm}}{\text{mol·K}}$ $T=0°C=273$ K
Solve	Use these values in the ideal gas law and solve for n. $PV=nRT$ $(1.00\ \text{atm})(15.3\ \text{L})=(n)\left(\dfrac{0.0821\ \text{L·atm}}{\text{mol·K}}\right)(273\ \text{K})$ $n=0.683$ mol NH_3 Your answer must be a mass, not the number of moles. Use the molar mass of NH_3 to find your answer. $0.683\ \text{mol }NH_3\left(\dfrac{17.0\ \text{g }NH_3}{1\ \text{mol }NH_3}\right)=11.6\ \text{g }NH_3$
Reflect	Since the gas is at STP, you could also solve this problem using standard molar volume as a conversion factor: $15.3\ \text{L }NH_3\left(\dfrac{1\ \text{mol }NH_3}{22.4\ \text{L }NH_3}\right)\left(\dfrac{17.0\ \text{g }NH_3}{1\ \text{mol }NH_3}\right)=11.6\ \text{g }NH_3$ This method will only work if the gas is at STP.
Practice	A sample of carbon dioxide gas at STP has a mass of 0.169 g. What is its volume in milliliters?

Example 3	What is the volume of 83.2 g of NO gas at 25°C and 135 kPa?
Read	You are given the mass, temperature, and pressure of a sample of gas.
Plan	First convert mass to moles. The molar mass of NO is 30.0 g/mol.

$$83.2 \text{ g NO} \left(\frac{1 \text{ mol NO}}{30.0 \text{ g NO}} \right) = 2.77 \text{ mol NO}$$

Now identify the values to use in $PV = nRT$. Convert 25°C to kelvins.

$P = 135$ kPa

$V = ?$

$n = 2.77$ mol

$R = \dfrac{8.31 \text{ L} \cdot \text{kPa}}{\text{mol} \cdot \text{K}}$

$T = 25°C + 273 = 298$ K

Solve	Use these values in $PV = nRT$ to solve for V.

$$(135 \text{ kPa})(V) = (2.77 \text{ mol}) \left(\frac{8.31 \text{ L} \cdot \text{kPa}}{\text{mol} \cdot \text{K}} \right) (298 \text{ K})$$

$$V = 50.9 \text{ L}$$

Reflect	All units in the equation cancel except for the desired unit, liters.
Practice	16.0 g of argon gas has a pressure of 37.1 kPa and a volume of 1.50 L. What is its temperature in degrees Celsius?

Chemistry in Your Life

Technology: Tire-Pressure Gauges

When placed on a tire valve inlet, a tire-pressure gauge measures the pressure in the tire. The head of the gauge contains a moveable pin. When the head is placed on the inlet, the pin is pushed down. Air from the tire enters the gauge. This air pushes a piston out the other end of the gauge. When the pressure in the gauge equals the tire pressure, the piston stops. You can then read the scale on the piston, which gives the tire pressure. Proper tire pressure is given in an owner's manual or is indicated on the tire.

1. A certain tire should be inflated to 34 pounds per square inch (psi).

A tire gauge reads 28 psi. What should you do to the tire?

2. Tires heat up as they move on a road. On a long trip, how does the starting tire pressure compare to the final pressure? Explain.

3. Have you used a tire-pressure gauge?

On a sheet of paper, write the word or phrase that completes each sentence.

1. In the ideal gas law, *R* is a fixed value called the _____.

2. In the ideal gas law, *n* stands for the number of _____.

3. If you are given the mass of a gas sample, you must convert this to _____ before using the ideal gas law.

On a sheet of paper, write the letter of the answer to each question.

4. What is the volume of 82.0 g of NH_3 gas at STP?

   A 0.215 L   **B** 17.0 g   **C** 62.2 L   **D** 108 L

5. What mass of krypton gas has a volume of 2.33 L at 53°C and 311 kPa?

   A 22.4 g   **B** 44.8 g   **C** 342 g   **D** 2,080 g

6. 17.0 g of Cl_2 gas has a volume of 9.22 L at 17°C. What is its pressure?

   A 0.618 atm   **B** 1.24 atm   **C** 43.8 atm   **D** 62.6 atm

Critical Thinking

On a sheet of paper, write the answer to each question. Show all calculations.

7. Solve the equation $PV = nRT$ for *R*. What is the unit of *R* if *P* is in atmospheres, *V* is in liters, *n* is in moles, and *T* is in kelvins?

8. 25.7 L of O_2 gas is at 35°C and 121 kPa. What is its mass?

9. 83.2 g of N_2O gas is at 75°C and 0.352 atm. What is its volume?

10. 75.2 g of SO_3 gas has a volume of 42.1 L and a pressure of 69.6 kPa. What is its temperature in kelvins?

Materials

- safety goggles
- lab coat or apron
- empty soft drink can
- hot plate
- beaker tongs
- large plastic bowl
- 10-mL graduated cylinder
- ice
- water

Temperature, Pressure, and Number of Gas Particles

Gases have pressure because gas particles collide with their container. If gas volume stays constant, a change in temperature or the number of particles affects the pressure of a gas. How are temperature, pressure, and number of particles related? In this investigation, you will examine these properties for a sample of gas.

Procedure

1. Read all of the steps of the procedure. Then proceed to step 2.

2. Predict what will happen when the top of the can is lowered into the ice water. Record your prediction.

3. Put on safety goggles and a lab coat or apron.

4. Pour 10 to 15 mL of water into the soft drink can. Place the can on the hot plate. Turn on the hot plate. Heat the can until steam comes out of the opening. **Safety Alert: Do not touch any hot objects. Keep the electrical cord of the hot plate away from water.**

5. While the water in the can is heating, fill the plastic bowl halfway with ice and water.

6. Using the tongs, quickly move the can over the ice water, then turn the can over and plunge the top of the can into the ice water. Record your observations.

Cleanup/Disposal
Return or dispose of your materials. Wash your hands.

Analysis
1. What happened to the gases in the can when they were cooled?

2. What happened to the can?

3. Describe the contents of the can after it cooled.

Conclusions
1. Explain what happened to the can. Include the importance of temperature and number of gas particles.

2. Compare your results with your predictions. Explain any differences.

Explore Further
At home, twist the cap onto an empty 1-L or 2-L plastic bottle at room temperature. Place the bottle in the freezer. Wait 10 minutes. Then remove the bottle and observe its appearance. Leave the cap on the bottle and allow it to warm up to room temperature. Observe what happens. Record your observations. Explain the changes that occurred in the bottle.

The last gas law you will study does not deal with pressure or volume. It involves the speed at which gas particles travel. Recall that temperature is a measure of the average kinetic energy of gas particles. As the temperature of a gas increases, so does its kinetic energy. Increased kinetic energy means increased particle speed.

Particle Speed

In a sample of gas, particle speed varies. Some particles travel faster and some travel slower. Compare this to cars on a highway. Most cars travel near the speed limit, but some go slower or faster. Figure 7.6.1 shows the speed of O_2 molecules at 25°C (blue curve) and at 1,000°C (red curve). The peak of each curve represents the most common speed of molecules at that temperature. For each curve, you can see that most molecules have a speed near the most common speed. Some molecules are going faster or slower than this speed. Now compare the two curves. At 25°C, the most common speed is lower. Molecular speed increases when a gas is heated. So at the higher temperature, the most common speed is higher.

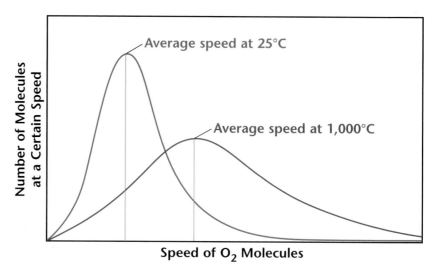

Figure 7.6.1 *At a higher temperature, more gas molecules are moving at high speeds.*

Diffusion Rates

Diffusion is the movement of particles from an area of high concentration to an area of low concentration. When the smell of perfume travels throughout a room, this is diffusion. When two gases or liquids flow into each other and mix, this is also diffusion. If two gases are at the same temperature, they have the same average kinetic energy. However, if their mass differs, their average particle speed—and their diffusion rate—also differs.

Thomas Graham was a Scottish scientist who studied the speed at which gases spread out to fill their container. He discovered that the average speed of gas particles is related to the molar mass of the gas. The greater the molar mass of a gas, the slower its particles move. This idea, called **Graham's law,** is used to compare the particle speeds of two gases.

Suppose you have a container of CO_2 gas and another of Cl_2 gas. Both are at the same temperature. Which gas particles are moving faster? Compare their molar masses: 44.0 g/mol for CO_2 and 71.0 g/mol for Cl_2. At the same temperature, CO_2 molecules move faster than Cl_2 molecules.

For two gases, A and B, at the same temperature, Graham's law is expressed as an equation with a square root.

$$\frac{\nu_A}{\nu_B} = \sqrt{\frac{M_B}{M_A}}$$

The variable ν stands for **velocity**. Velocity is the speed of an object in a certain direction. ν_A is the velocity of gas A, and ν_B is the velocity of gas B. M_A is the molar mass of gas A, and M_B is the molar mass of gas B. Gas A is always chosen as the gas with the smaller molar mass (and the higher speed). This equation does not allow you to find actual velocities. Instead, it gives a number that represents a ratio, $\frac{\nu_A}{\nu_B}$, comparing the two velocities. Notice that, in the ratio, gas A's velocity is on top. However, inside the square root, gas B's molar mass is on top. $\frac{\nu_A}{\nu_B}$ should have a value greater than 1. If not, check to see that the molar masses of A and B are in the right place.

Diffusion

The movement of particles from an area of high concentration to an area of low concentration

Graham's law

A law that states that the greater the molar mass of a gas, the slower its particles move at constant temperature;

Velocity

The speed of an object in a certain direction

Effusion is similar to diffusion. Effusion is the passage of gas particles through a tiny hole. Graham's law describes both effusion and diffusion rates.

Example 1 Which gas is faster at the same temperature, PCl_3 or N_2? How much faster?

Read You are asked to compare the molecular speed of two gases at the same temperature.

Plan First find the molar mass of each gas. The gas with the smaller molar mass has faster molecules. Then use the equation that describes Graham's law. The ratio $\frac{v_A}{v_B}$ compares the velocity of two gases, A and B. To calculate this ratio, use the two molar masses (call them M_A and M_B). The gas with the smaller molar mass is always gas A.

Solve The molar mass of N_2 is 28.0 g/mol. The molar mass of PCl_3 is 137.5 g/mol. So N_2 molecules are faster than PCl_3 molecules at the same temperature. Now determine how much faster using Graham's law. Gas A is N_2 and gas B is PCl_3.

$$\frac{v_A}{v_A}=\sqrt{\frac{M_B}{M_A}}$$

$$\frac{v_{N_2}}{v_{PCl_3}}=\sqrt{\frac{137.5 \text{ g/mol}}{28.0 \text{ g/mol}}}=2.22$$

The answer, 2.22, has no unit. It means that gas A (N_2) is 2.22 times faster than gas B (PCl_3).

Reflect The ratio $\frac{v_A}{v_B}$ does not give the actual particle speed of either gas; it just compares them.

Practice Which gas is faster at the same temperature, UF_6 or NCl_3? How much faster?

Math Tip

When solving for $\frac{v_A}{v_B}$ in Graham's law, be sure that you divide M_B by M_A and take the square root of that answer.

To summarize Graham's law:

For two different gases at the same temperature, the gas with the lower molar mass has the higher particle speed.

✦ ✦

Technology and Society

Most materials contain small holes, or pores. Gases can often pass through these pores. The number and size of pores are important when choosing packaging materials. Some food products must be packaged in material having few, small pores. This reduces the amount of gas moving through the packaging and helps to keep the food fresh.

Summary of Gas Laws

Table 7.6.1 summarizes the gas laws you have studied.

Table 7.6.1 A Summary of Gas Laws		
Gas Law	**Rules**	**Use This to**
Dalton's law $P_{total} = P_A + P_B + \cdots$	Pressure units match.	Find the pressure of a gas mixture (P_{total}) or the partial pressure of one gas.
combined gas law $\dfrac{P_1 V_1}{T_1} = \dfrac{P_2 V_2}{T_2}$	Volume units match. Pressure units match. Temperatures in kelvins.	Find the pressure, temperature, or volume of a gas when moles or grams are not involved.
ideal gas law $PV = nRT$	Pressure in atm or kPa (this determines R). Volume in liters. Temperature in kelvins.	Find the pressure, temperature, volume, or mole amount of a gas when moles or grams are involved.
Graham's law $\dfrac{\nu_A}{\nu_B} = \sqrt{\dfrac{M_B}{M_A}}$	Gas A has the smaller molar mass.	Compare the particle speeds of gases A and B.

Spotlight on Oxygen

8
O
Oxygen
16.0

Oxygen is the most common element in the earth's crust. Here, oxygen is found in the form of compounds. Oxygen's most common elemental form is O_2, which is a colorless, odorless gas. This gas makes up about 21% of the earth's atmosphere. Green plants produce oxygen through photosynthesis. Almost all animals use oxygen, which reacts with food to create energy.

Oxygen also occurs as ozone, O_3. Ozone is an air pollutant that is harmful to humans. However, a layer of ozone high in the earth's atmosphere helps to protect the earth from ultraviolet rays.

Because oxygen is very reactive, it is found in many compounds, including water, sand, and carbon dioxide. Many minerals contain metals combined with oxygen. The only elements that do not react with oxygen are helium, neon, and argon. Some elements form more than one compound with oxygen. For example, hydrogen and oxygen form water, H_2O, and hydrogen peroxide, H_2O_2.

Interesting Fact: Lightning converts oxygen gas into ozone.

Word Bank

diffusion

molar mass

temperature

On a sheet of paper, write the word or phrase from the Word Bank that completes each sentence.

1. At constant temperature, gas particles with a lower _____ move faster.

2. The movement of a gas from an area of high concentration to an area of low concentration is _____.

3. The particles in a sample of gas move faster when the _____ increases.

On a sheet of paper, write the answer to each question.

4. The gases H_2O, SF_6, CCl_4, and Ne are at the same temperature. Which gas has the highest average speed?

5. The gases SO_2, CH_4, PCl_5, and Cl_2 are at the same temperature. Which gas particles are moving fastest?

6. The gases SO_3, CO_2, H_2, and O_2 are at the same temperature. Which has the lowest particle speed?

Critical Thinking

On a sheet of paper, write the answer to each question.

7. One balloon is filled with He gas at 25°C. Another balloon is filled with CO_2 gas at 25°C. The rate at which each gas moves through tiny holes in the balloons is the same rate at which the gas diffuses. Which balloon deflates first? Explain your answer.

8. At a given temperature, neon gas atoms move faster than radon gas atoms. How much faster?

9. Two gas samples, HCN and CCl_4, are at the same temperature. In which sample are the molecules moving faster? How much faster?

10. The particles of an unknown gas are 2.76 times faster than particles of CCl_4 at the same temperature. Is the unknown gas Ne or O_2?

Gases and Fires

A fire needs fuel, oxygen, and high temperature. If any one of these things is missing, the fire does not burn. Some fuels are gases. Hydrogen gas, for example, burns. Common fuels such as methane and propane are gases. Oxygen is a gas that combines with a fuel to produce two other gases: water vapor and carbon dioxide.

Gases are often used to extinguish, or put out, fires. These gases are nonflammable, which means they do not burn. Instead, they remove at least one of the three requirements for a fire. Some fire extinguishers contain a liquid under pressure. This liquid changes to a gas and expands as it leaves the extinguisher. This change of state cools the gas. The cooled gas lowers the temperature of the fire. The gas coming out of a fire extinguisher is also denser than air. It acts like a blanket over the fire, keeping oxygen away from the fuel.

Some extinguishers spray dry chemicals or water to put out a fire. Even these extinguishers use a dense, nonflammable gas to push the chemicals or water out of the tank.

Carbon dioxide is commonly used in fire extinguishers. This gas does not burn, is denser than air, and is

inexpensive to make. Halon was used in fire extinguishers for many years. This gas extinguishes fires without leaving materials behind. However, halon harms the environment. It can no longer be used in fire extinguishers.

1. Why do you think halon extinguishers were used in places like libraries?

2. Name two gases that would never be used in a fire extinguisher.

■ The kinetic model of gases describes an ideal gas.

■ Ideal gas particles have no volume. They travel in straight lines until they collide with an object or another particle and bounce off. Energy is conserved during these collisions.

■ Pressure is created when gas particles collide with container walls. Pressure is measured in atmospheres, millimeters of mercury, or kilopascals.

■ The temperature of a gas is a measure of average kinetic energy.

■ Temperature is often measured in degrees Celsius, but it must be in kelvins for gas law calculations. To convert degrees Celsius to kelvins, use $T_K = T_C + 273$.

■ The pressure of a mixture of gases can be expressed as $P_{total} = P_A + P_B + P_C + \cdots$ Dalton's law of partial pressure can be used to find the pressure of a gas that is mixed with water vapor.

■ The pressure, temperature, and volume of a gas are related. Pressure and volume are inversely proportional. Temperature and volume are directly proportional. Temperature and pressure are directly proportional.

■ The laws of Boyle, Charles, and Gay-Lussac are summed up by the combined gas law:
$$\frac{P_1V_1}{T_1} = \frac{P_2V_2}{T_2}.$$

■ The ideal gas law is $PV = nRT$. This equation includes n, the number of moles of gas, and R, the gas constant. It is used to solve problems that involve the mass or mole amount of a gas.

■ Graham's law says that the average particle speed of a gas is related to its molar mass. The lower the molar mass of a gas, the faster its particles move. The particle velocities of two gases can be compared using this ratio:
$$\frac{\nu_A}{\nu_B} = \sqrt{\frac{M_B}{M_A}}.$$

Vocabulary

absolute temperature, 271

absolute zero, 271

atmospheric pressure, 265

barometer, 269

Boyle's law, 278

Charles's law, 280

combined gas law, 282

constant, 287

Dalton's law of partial pressure, 274

diffusion, 295

direct proportion, 280

gas constant, 287

Graham's law, 295

Gay-Lussac's law, 281

ideal gas, 266

ideal gas law, 287

inverse proportion, 278

kinetic model, 266

partial pressure, 274

pascal, 269

pressure, 265

velocity, 295

water vapor, 275

Vocabulary Review

On a sheet of paper, write the word or phrase from the Word Bank that completes each sentence.

1. The _____ is the SI unit for pressure.

2. The _____ describes the characteristics of an ideal gas.

3. In a(n) _____, as one quantity increases, the other quantity increases.

4. For a gas, _____ is caused by collisions of gas particles with container walls.

5. The temperature at which all motion stops is _____.

6. The behavior of a(n) _____ is described by the kinetic model.

7. 273 K and 1.00 atm are the conditions of _____.

8. When two gases flow into each other and mix, this is _____.

9. A(n) _____ is a common unit of pressure.

10. In a(n) _____, as one quantity increases, the other quantity decreases.

11. Energy of motion is called _____.

12. The _____ at sea level is 1.00 atm.

13. The _____ temperature scale shows absolute temperature.

14. For gas laws involving temperature, use _____ values.

15. The pressure of one gas in a mixture is a(n) _____.

Continued on next page

Concept Review

On a sheet of paper, write the letter of the answer to each question.

16. In a gas mixture of H_2, He, and Ar, the total pressure is 101.3 kPa. The partial pressure of Ar is 50.7 kPa, and the partial pressure of He is 10.1 kPa. What is the partial pressure of H_2?

    A 40.5 kPa   **B** 50.7 kPa   **C** 60.8 kPa   **D** 162.1 kPa

17. A sample of H_2 gas is collected over water at 25°C. The total pressure is 760.0 mm Hg. What is the partial pressure of the H_2 gas? (Hint: Use Table 7.3.1.)

    A 23.8 mm Hg   **C** 760.0 mm Hg

    B 736.2 mm Hg   **D** 782.8 mm Hg

18. A gas has a volume of 10.0 L at 100°C and 400. mm Hg. What is its new volume at 50°C and 600. mm Hg?

    A 3.33 L   **B** 5.77 L   **C** 13.3 L   **D** 77.7 L

Problem Solving

On a sheet of paper, write the answer to each question. Show all calculations.

19. A gas mixture of N_2, H_2, O_2, and F_2 has a total pressure of 13.53 atm. The partial pressure of N_2 is 1.75 atm. The partial pressure of H_2 is 789 mm Hg. The partial pressure of O_2 is 345 kPa. What is the partial pressure of F_2 in atmospheres?

20. An 87.3-g sample of SO_2 gas is at 45°C and 89.6 kPa. What is its volume?

21. A 43.0-g sample of helium gas is at 12.0 atm and 50°C. What is its volume?

22. What mass of krypton is present in a 2.33-L container at 53°C and 311 kPa?

Critical Thinking

On a sheet of paper, write the answer to each question. Show all calculations.

23. A gas has a pressure of 80.5 kPa and a temperature of 265°C. Its volume decreases from 651 mL to 355 mL when its pressure increases to 888 mm Hg. What is the final gas temperature in degrees Celsius?

24. Two gas samples, helium and radon, are at the same temperature. In which gas are the atoms moving faster? How much faster?

25. Compare the molecular speeds of these gases: UF_6, N_2O, SO_2, SO_3, and O_2. In which gas do the molecules move fastest? In which gas do the molecules move slowest? (Assume temperature is the same.)

Test-Taking Tip When you study for a test, review key equations and example problems. Then practice the steps for solving problems.

8

Atomic Theory

The cucumber slices in the photo could be used as models for atoms. Models help us understand what is too large or too small to observe. Each cucumber slice has a core made of small particles—the seeds. The area around the core contains no seeds. The structure of an atom is similar. It has a nucleus of protons and neutrons. The area around the nucleus contains electrons. In Chapter 8, you will learn how scientists have used models to understand atoms.

Organize Your Thoughts

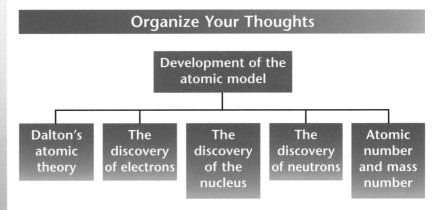

Development of the atomic model

| Dalton's atomic theory | The discovery of electrons | The discovery of the nucleus | The discovery of neutrons | Atomic number and mass number |

Goals for Learning

◆ To describe Dalton's atomic theory

◆ To explain how Thomson discovered electrons

◆ To explain what Rutherford discovered about atomic structure

◆ To compare electrons, protons, and neutrons

◆ To describe isotopes and ions in terms of atomic number, mass number, and number of electrons

◆ To understand how the average atomic mass of an element is determined

Objectives

After reading this lesson, you should be able to

◆ describe Dalton's atomic theory

◆ contrast Dalton's model of the atom with Thomson's model

◆ describe a cathode-ray tube and what Thomson discovered about cathode rays

Imagine helium atoms bouncing around inside a container. Now imagine just one of those atoms. What does it look like? What is it made of? From Chapter 2, you know that an atom is the smallest unit of an element that still has the properties of that element. You also know that an atom consists of smaller particles: protons, neutrons, and electrons. About 200 years ago, scientists were just beginning to understand the atom and its structure.

Dalton's Atomic Theory

At one time, scientists thought that atoms were the smallest particles in matter. Based on this idea, John Dalton proposed an atomic theory in 1808. His theory is summed up as follows:

- All elements are composed of tiny particles called atoms. Atoms cannot be divided into smaller parts.

- All atoms of the same element have identical properties. Atoms of different elements have different properties.

- Atoms combine in whole-number ratios to form compounds.

- Chemical reactions take place when atoms rearrange. Atoms of one element are *not* changed into atoms of another element.

Dalton's model of an atom is similar to a solid rubber ball. It is not made of smaller parts, and it is exactly the same throughout. At the time, this was a very exciting idea. It inspired other scientists to conduct further experiments. As better technology became available, new discoveries were made. In the late 1800s, scientists made some astonishing discoveries while studying electricity. As a result, Dalton's model of the atom was improved. Some of Dalton's ideas were proved wrong.

The Discovery of Electrons

Cathode-ray tube

A glass tube with an electrode at each end

Electrode

A metal piece that conducts electricity

Anode

The positively charged electrode in a cathode-ray tube; the electrode toward which electrons move

Cathode

The negatively charged electrode in a cathode-ray tube; the electrode from which electrons move

One of these scientists, J. J. Thomson, was working with a device called a **cathode-ray tube.** A cathode-ray tube, shown in Figure 8.1.1, is a sealed glass tube with a metal plate, called an **electrode,** at each end. To study the flow of electricity, Thomson added a long fluorescent plate between the two electrodes. He pumped most of the air out of the tube. When he connected the electrodes to an electrical source, the tube glowed. One of the electrodes, called the **anode,** became positively charged. The other electrode, called the **cathode,** became negatively charged. A glowing beam appeared on the fluorescent plate between the cathode and anode. Thomson called the glowing beam a cathode ray.

Thomson found that the cathode ray could be deflected by a nearby magnet. To deflect means to cause a turn in a straight path. If the cathode ray was made of only light energy, it would not be deflected by a magnet. Thomson reasoned that the cathode ray was made of matter, not energy.

J. J. Thomson did not give the electron its name. George J. Stoney, an Irish physicist, called the smallest quantity of negative electrical charge an electron. Later, Thomson applied the name to the negative subatomic particle.

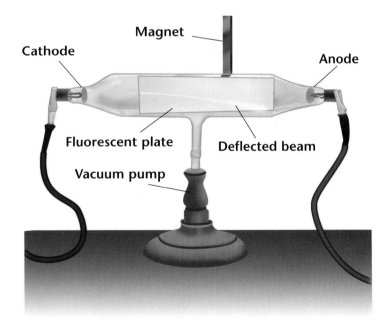

Figure 8.1.1 *The cathode ray inside the tube is deflected by a magnet. Thomson concluded that the cathode ray is made of negatively charged particles of matter.*

Link to ≻≻≻

Physics

Around 1875, the cathode-ray tube was invented by the English physicist, William Crookes. Later, both J. J. Thomson in England and Wilhelm Roentgen in Germany experimented with the cathode-ray tube. Roentgen discovered that invisible rays, which he called X-rays, are given off when cathode rays strike a metal plate. Within two months of this discovery, an American doctor used X-rays to help set a broken bone.

Link to ≻≻≻

Earth Science

Robert Millikan gave the name "cosmic rays" to the high-energy radiation from outer space.

Thomson also found that the cathode ray was attracted by a positively charged anode and repelled by a negatively charged cathode. This was true even when the tube contained different gases or the electrodes were made of different metals. Thomson proposed that cathode rays are made of negatively charged particles. He believed that all elements contain these particles. Later, these particles were named electrons. In a cathode-ray tube, electrons move from the cathode to the anode. This flow of electrons is electricity.

Further research by Robert Millikan determined the charge of an electron and its mass. An electron is about $\frac{1}{2,000}$ times the mass of a hydrogen atom. This meant an electron is smaller than an atom. This also showed that atoms are made of smaller particles, disproving one of Dalton's ideas.

Because atoms are neutral, negatively charged electrons must be balanced by some positive charge in the atom. Thomson proposed an atomic model that is very different from Dalton's, as Figure 8.1.2 shows. Thomson's model was originally called the plum pudding model, but a more modern description might be a blueberry muffin model. His model was a ball of positively charged matter with electrons scattered throughout, much like blueberries in a muffin.

After Thomson's work, other scientists identified the positively charged matter in atoms: particles called protons. A proton has a mass about 2,000 times that of an electron. Protons are much, much larger than electrons. Both electrons and protons are subatomic particles, meaning they are smaller than an atom.

Dalton's model   **Thomson's model**

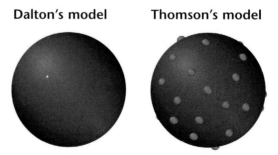

Figure 8.1.2 *Dalton's atomic model has no subatomic particles. Thomson's model has negatively charged particles in a ball of positively charged matter.*

Materials
◆ safety goggles
◆ balloon
◆ wool cloth
◆ strip of newspaper, about 3 cm wide
◆ small bits of paper

Procedure
1. Put on safety goggles.
2. Rub the balloon with the wool cloth.

3. Hold the strip of paper near the balloon. What happens?
4. Hold the strip just above the bits of paper. What happens?

Analysis
1. The balloon becomes electrically charged when rubbed. It attracts paper because opposite charges attract. The balloon and paper are matter, and matter is made of atoms. What do these observations tell you about atoms?
2. If the balloon is negatively charged, what kind of charge does it attract?

★ ✦ ★

Achievements in Science

Evidence for Dalton's Atomic Theory

John Dalton is credited with proposing the first atomic theory. Like most great ideas in science, however, his ideas were based on the work of others. For example, Antoine Lavoisier had already shown that matter is conserved in a chemical reaction. He proved that a combination of reactants do not create new matter. Likewise, no matter is lost in a reaction. Dalton reasoned that a chemical reaction altered only the arrangement of matter. This was evidence that atoms are indestructible—they cannot be destroyed.

Joseph Proust, a French chemist, first suggested that substances combine in definite proportions. This means that different samples of the same compound contain exactly the same ratio of elements by mass. This supported the idea that substances are made of small individual particles. Dalton used the law of definite proportions and his own experiments to propose the law of multiple proportions. According to this law, when two elements combine to form more than one compound, the mass ratio for one element is small whole numbers. For example, 1.00 g of N will combine with 1.14 g of O to form NO. Also, 1.00 g of N will combine with 2.28 g of O to form NO_2. The ratio of the O masses, 1.14 to 2.28, is a 1:2 ratio. This was additional support for the existence of indestructible atoms.

Lesson 1 REVIEW

On a sheet of paper, write the word from the Word Bank that completes each sentence.

Word Bank

atom

electrons

mass

neutral

protons

subatomic

1. The smallest part of any element that still has all the properties of that element is called a(n) _____.

2. Thomson found that a cathode ray contains negatively charged subatomic particles, later called _____.

3. The atom also contains positively charged subatomic particles called _____.

4. Millikan determined the electron's _____.

5. Dalton's atomic model had no _____ particles.

6. Thomson proposed a(n) _____ atomic model in which negative and positive charges are balanced.

Critical Thinking

On a sheet of paper, write the answer to each question.

7. What are the four parts of Dalton's atomic theory?

8. Why did Thomson conclude that a cathode ray is composed of negatively charged particles of matter, not energy?

9. Describe Dalton's model of the atom.

10. When Thomson did his experiment with the cathode-ray tube, he discovered something that changed Dalton's model. What was his discovery, and how did Thomson's model differ from Dalton's?

❋ ❋

Technology and Society

Some television picture tubes and computer monitors are complex cathode-ray tubes, or CRTs. Both use high voltages to produce a beam of electrons. The electrons hit gas molecules in the cathode-ray tube and produce light.

Alpha particle

A helium nucleus, which consists of 2 protons and 2 neutrons, but no electrons

In the early 1900s, new discoveries changed the model of the atom yet again.

The Discovery of the Nucleus

Ernest Rutherford agreed with Thomson's model of electrons scattered throughout a positively charged atom. He and a team of other scientists began research. In 1909, they aimed a beam of **alpha particles** at a piece of thin gold foil, as shown in Figure 8.2.1. An alpha particle is a helium nucleus. It consists of 2 protons and 2 neutrons, but no electrons. An alpha particle has a 2+ charge and four times the mass of a proton. Rutherford expected the alpha particles to pass through the foil and hit a fluorescent screen on the opposite side.

Most of the alpha particles passed through the foil in a straight path. However, some particles bounced off to the sides, and a few even went backwards. This surprised the researchers. Rutherford said, "It was as if you fired a 15-inch shell into a piece of tissue paper and it came back and hit you." He concluded that each deflected alpha particle had hit a dense region of positive charge inside a gold atom. This region has more mass than the alpha particles it deflects. Since protons are positive subatomic particles, Rutherford believed this region must consist of several protons clustered together in a nucleus.

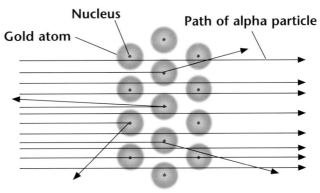

Figure 8.2.1 *Rutherford's gold foil experiments showed that gold atoms are mostly empty space.*

Rutherford's explanation gave way to a new atomic model, sometimes called the nuclear model. As shown in Figure 8.2.2, the model has a nucleus of protons. It is a small, dense region at the atom's center. Electrons travel in a big empty space around the nucleus. To understand how small the nucleus is, imagine an atom the size of a football stadium. The nucleus would be the size of a golf ball on the 50-yard line. Almost all of an atom's volume is the space where electrons move about. In the gold foil experiments, most of the alpha particles did not hit a gold nucleus—they passed through this empty space.

Niels Bohr worked with Rutherford. He proposed that electrons move around the nucleus like planets orbiting the sun. Bohr's model is called the planetary model. However, the movement of electrons is even more complicated than this. Electrons do not follow an orbital path. In fact, you cannot know the exact location of an electron at any given time. You will learn more about Bohr's model and the movement of electrons in Chapter 10.

Rutherford's model   **Bohr's model**

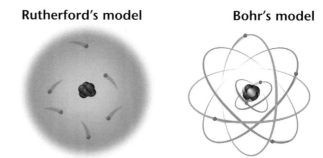

Figure 8.2.2 *In Rutherford's atomic model, the nucleus is tiny, but very dense. It contains only protons. In Bohr's planetary model, the electrons have orbital paths.*

Link to ➤➤➤

Health

Alpha particles—helium nuclei—do not penetrate the skin from the outside. Because of this, they are sometimes mistakenly thought to be safe. However, if alpha particles are emitted inside the lungs, they can cause injury. Radon is a gas that can accumulate in the basements of homes. It is harmful when inhaled because it emits alpha particles.

The attractive force between a positively charged object and a negatively charged object is called electromagnetic force. In an atom, this force occurs between the nucleus and the electrons. It is what holds the atom together.

The Discovery of the Neutron

Scientists continued to study atomic structure. They determined that electrons and protons have equal but opposite charges. A neutral atom has the same number of protons as electrons. They also calculated the masses of these charged particles. A major problem arose. Except for hydrogen, the mass of an atom is more than the combined mass of its protons and electrons. What is causing this extra mass?

$$\text{mass of atom} > \text{mass of protons} + \text{mass of electrons}$$

In 1932, James Chadwick discovered another subatomic particle. It has no electrical charge, so he called it a neutron. It has a mass similar to a proton. The neutron solved the mystery of the atom's mass. When the masses of all three particles in an atom are added, the sum equals the atom's mass. Both protons and neutrons are located in the nucleus of atoms. Hydrogen is the only atom that contains no neutrons in its nucleus. Table 8.2.1 compares the three subatomic particles. Notice that each particle has a symbol: e^-, p^+, or n^0. Compared to protons and neutrons, electrons have almost no mass at all.

Table 8.2.1 Particles in an Atom				
Particle	Symbol	Charge	Mass	Location
electron	e^-	$1-$	9.110×10^{-28} g	outside nucleus
proton	p^+	$1+$	1.673×10^{-24} g	inside nucleus
neutron	n^0	0	1.675×10^{-24} g	inside nucleus

❈ ❈

Technology and Society

Plasmas are ionized, or charged, matter, usually gases. They are a mixture of positive ions and electrons. Plasmas conduct electricity, but are electrically neutral. On the earth, most plasmas are produced by electricity. Plasmas are responsible for the light produced by fluorescent lights and neon signs. A more recent plasma application is in video displays. Plasmas produce areas of color that make the picture.

Spotlight on Gold

79
Au
Gold
197.0

Gold has been known from the time of the earliest humans. The chemical properties of gold allow it to exist in nature as an elemental metal. Gold also occurs as a chemical compound in certain ores.

Gold is relatively unreactive. Unlike most other metals, gold does not tarnish when exposed to air. It does not react with common acids. It forms only a small number of compounds. Gold is a good conductor of heat and electricity. It is an excellent reflector of light, especially infrared light. Some satellites are coated with gold because it is unreactive and reflects heat.

Gold can be drawn into extremely fine wires. Some are only a few micrometers in diameter. Such wires are used to connect the chip in an integrated circuit to the pins on the package. Gold can also be beaten into very thin sheets, often called gold foil. A sheet of paper is hundreds of times thicker than gold foil. 1 cm^3 of gold can produce a foil sheet with an area of about 40 m^2.

Interesting Fact: Arthritis is sometimes treated with a gold compound.

▼◄ ▲ ▼◄ ▲ ▼◄ ▲ ▼◄ ▲ ▼◄ ▲ ▼◄ ▲ ▼◄ ▲ ▼◄ ▲ ▼◄ ▲ ▼◄ ▲ ▼◄ ▲ ▼◄ ▲ ▼◄ ▲ ▼◄ ▲ ▼◄ ▲ ▼◄ ▲ ▼◄ ▲ ▼

Science at Work

Electron Microscopist

An electron microscope is a special kind of microscope. To produce an image, it uses the properties of electrons rather than light. An electron microscope can magnify objects up to several million times. A person who operates this instrument is an electron microscopist.

Electron microscopists usually work in research, metallurgy (the study of metals), biology, and medicine. They prepare the samples to be studied under the microscope as well as produce the final images. Samples have to be very thin so electrons can pass through them. They may be treated with certain substances to improve image quality. For example,

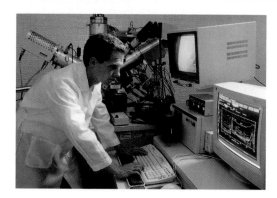

samples are sometimes coated with metal.

An electron microscopist needs a college degree in a field of science. In addition, a good background in math and computer science is very helpful.

Lesson 2   R E V I E W

Word Bank

electrons

neutrons

nucleus

Research and Write

Many of the scientists who worked out the details of atomic structure studied with J. J. Thomson or Ernest Rutherford. Do research to learn about the connections among Thomson, Rutherford, Henry Moseley, Niels Bohr, Hans Geiger, James Chadwick, and Frederick Soddy. Report on the most significant discovery of each scientist.

On a sheet of paper, write the word from the Word Bank that completes each sentence.

1. All of the protons and neutrons of an atom are located in the _____.

2. The nucleus contains subatomic particles called _____ that have no charge.

3. The _____ of an atom occupy the space around the nucleus.

On a sheet of paper, write the letter of the answer that completes each sentence.

4. The scientist who discovered a neutral subatomic particle was _____.

   A Dalton   **B** Thomson   **C** Rutherford   **D** Chadwick

5. The nucleus contains _____.

   A electrons
   B protons and electrons
   C neutrons and electrons
   D neutrons and protons

6. Rutherford showed that most of the volume of an atom is _____.

   A empty space
   B the nucleus
   C negatively charged
   D positively charged

Critical Thinking

On a sheet of paper, write the answer to each question.

7. What was Rutherford's gold foil experiment?

8. What happened in the gold foil experiment that was unexpected? Why was it unexpected?

9. Describe Rutherford's model of the atom. How is it different from Thomson's?

10. Compare the three subatomic particles.

Two centuries ago, John Dalton suggested that an atom cannot be divided into smaller parts. This idea changed when protons, electrons, and neutrons were discovered. Dalton also thought that atoms of the same element are the same, while atoms of different elements are different. In this lesson, you will find out that this idea also changed.

Atomic Number

What makes atoms of different elements different? In Chapter 2, you learned that the number of protons in an atom identifies the atom as a particular element. This number is called the atomic number. All atoms of helium contain 2 protons, or $2\,p^+$. All atoms of sodium contain 11 protons, or $11\,p^+$. Each element has a unique atomic number. It is found on the periodic table at the top of each element's tile. The atomic number is often written as a subscript to the left of the element's symbol, like this: $_{35}Br$. In a neutral atom, the number of protons equals the number of electrons.

Example 1	A neutral atom has 23 protons. Identify the element and write its symbol with the atomic number. How many electrons are in the atom?
Read	You are asked to identify an element based on the number of protons. You are asked to write its symbol and determine the number of electrons.
Plan	An atom with 23 protons has the atomic number 23. On the periodic table, find this tile.
Solve	The element is vanadium. Its symbol can be written as $_{23}V$. A neutral V atom has $23\,p^+$ and $23\,e^-$.
Reflect	Each element has a unique atomic number.
Practice	A neutral atom has 54 protons. Identify the element and write its symbol with the atomic number. How many electrons are in the atom?

The elements in the periodic table are arranged by atomic number from 1 to 116. Atomic numbers are always whole numbers.

Link to >>>

Social Studies

The British physicist Henry Moseley determined the number of protons in atoms and named this the atomic number. This resulted in a more accurate placement of elements in the periodic table. Moseley's life had a tragic end. He enlisted in the army in World War I and was killed in the battle of Gallipoli in Turkey in 1915.

Example 2 An atom has the symbol $_{80}Hg$. What is this element? How many protons and electrons are in the atom?

Read You are asked to identify the element and give the numbers of protons and electrons.

Plan Find the symbol Hg on the periodic table. It has atomic number 80. Hg is the symbol for mercury.

Solve A mercury atom has 80 p^+ and 80 e^-.

Reflect A neutral atom has the same number of protons and electrons.

Practice An atom has the symbol $_{74}W$. What is this element? How many protons and electrons are in the atom?

Neutral Atoms and Ions

In a neutral atom, the atomic number is also the number of electrons. Bromine's atomic number is 35. A neutral atom of bromine has 35 protons and 35 electrons. However, not all bromine atoms are neutral. Recall that an ion is an atom with a positive or negative charge. Ions can be understood in terms of subatomic particles.

Electrons moving outside the nucleus of an atom can be transferred to another atom. When this happens, a cation and an anion form. The atom that gave up one or more electrons becomes a cation. The atom that received these electrons becomes an anion. The number of electrons in each atom has now changed, but the number of protons in each nucleus stayed the same. Compare a bromine atom and a bromide ion:

neutral atom	$_{35}Br$	35 e^- and 35 p^+	no charge
anion	$_{35}Br^{1-}$	36 e^- and 35 p^+	1− charge

As you can see, the number of electrons in an anion is *more* than the atomic number. For a cation, such as K^{1+}, the opposite is true: the number of electrons is *less* than the atomic number:

neutral atom	$_{19}K$	19 e^- and 19 p^+	no charge
cation	$_{19}K^{1+}$	18 e^- and 19 p^+	1+ charge

In both cases, the number of protons does not change.

In a cation, the number of protons is greater than the number of electrons. In an anion, the number of protons is less than the number of electrons.

Example 3 How many protons and electrons are in each of these ions: $_9F^{1-}$ and $_{26}Fe^{3+}$?

Read You are asked to find the number of protons and electrons in an anion and a cation.

Plan The atomic number of fluorine is 9. The atomic number of iron is 26.

Solve The atomic number is the number of protons. $_9F^{1-}$ has 9 p^+ and $_{26}Fe^{3+}$ has 26 p^+.

The anion has a charge of $1-$, which means it has 1 extra e^-. In other words, it has 1 more electron than the number of protons, so $_9F^{1-}$ has 10 e^-.

The cation has a $3+$ charge, so it does not have 26 e^-. It has 3 fewer than this, so it has 23 e^-.

$_9F^{1-}$	9 p^+ and 10 e^-	$1-$ charge
$_{26}Fe^{3+}$	26 p^+ and 23 e^-	$3+$ charge

Reflect When an atom becomes an ion, the number of electrons changes, but the number of protons does not. (If the number of protons changed, the atom would become a different element.)

Practice How many protons and electrons are in each of these ions: $_{16}S^{2-}$ and $_{12}Mg^{2+}$?

Isotopes and Mass Number

All atoms of the same element have the same number of protons. As you have seen with ions, the number of electrons can vary. The number of neutrons can also vary. Atoms of the same element with different numbers of neutrons are called **isotopes.** Isotopes show that all atoms of the same element are *not* identical. Most elements have two or more isotopes. If you could examine every atom in a sample of any element, you would probably find a mixture of isotopes. Usually, one isotope is more common than the others.

Mass number

The total number of particles in the nucleus of an atom

For example, there are three isotopes of oxygen. In a sample of oxygen gas, you would likely find all three. Almost all of the oxygen atoms would have 8 p^+ and 8 n^0. That is the most common isotope. A very small percentage of the atoms would have 8 p^+ and 9 n^0, and another very small percentage would have 8 p^+ and 10 n^0. All have the same number of protons, but different numbers of neutrons.

To distinguish between different isotopes of the same element, chemists refer to their **mass numbers.** The mass number of an atom is the total number of particles in its nucleus.

mass number = number of protons + number of neutrons

Each isotope of oxygen has a different mass number. For the most common isotope with 8 p^+ and 8 n^0, its mass number is $8 + 8 = 16$. This number can be written as a superscript to the left of the element's symbol, directly above the atomic number:

mass number $\longrightarrow$ $^{16}_{8}$O
atomic number $\longrightarrow$

When writing out an isotope's name, add its mass number, like this: oxygen-16. The symbols and names of the three oxygen isotopes are given below:

$^{16}_{8}$O	oxygen-16	8 p^+ and 8 n^0
$^{17}_{8}$O	oxygen-17	8 p^+ and 9 n^0
$^{18}_{8}$O	oxygen-18	8 p^+ and 10 n^0

By the early 1900s, scientists understood much of the detailed structure of the atom. They knew

- An atom of an element has a specific number of protons in its nucleus.
- No other element has this same number of protons.
- A neutral atom has the same number of electrons as protons.
- The mass of an atom is concentrated in the nucleus, which consists of neutrons and protons.
- Atoms of the same element can have differing numbers of neutrons. These atoms, called isotopes, have slightly different masses.

Example 4	A neutral atom has 13 p^+, 13 e^-, and 14 n^0. What is the name and symbol of this isotope? Show the atomic number and mass number in the symbol.
Read	You are asked to identify an isotope based on the number of protons, electrons, and neutrons. You are asked to write its symbol.
Plan	13 p^+ means the atomic number is 13. Use this to find the element on the periodic table.
Solve	The isotope is aluminum, Al. Its mass number is 13 $p^+ + 14\ n^0 = 27$. Its symbol is $^{27}_{13}\text{Al}$, and its name is aluminum-27.

Name	Symbol	Atomic Number	Mass Number	p^+	n^0	e^-	Charge
aluminum-27	$^{27}_{13}\text{Al}$	13	27	13	14	13	0

Reflect	Because the number of protons equals the number of electrons, the atom has no charge.
Practice	An neutral atom has 24 p^+, 24 e^-, and 28 n^0. What is the name and symbol of this isotope? Show the atomic number and mass number in the symbol.

Example 5	How many electrons, protons, and neutrons are in a neutral atom of chlorine-37?
Read	You are asked to give the number of protons, electrons, and neutrons in a particular isotope, given its name.
Plan	The periodic table shows that chlorine's atomic number is 17. The name chlorine-37 indicates a mass number of 37.
Solve	A chlorine atom always has 17 p^+. In a neutral atom, the number of electrons equals the number of protons, so there are 17 e^-. The mass number is the number of particles in the nucleus: $37 = 17\ p^+ + ?\ n^0$. There are $(37 - 17) = 20\ n^0$.

Name	Symbol	Atomic Number	Mass Number	p^+	n^0	e^-	Charge
chlorine-37	$^{37}_{17}\text{Cl}$	17	37	17	20	17	0

Reflect	The number of neutrons is calculated by subtracting the atomic number from the mass number.
Practice	How many electrons, protons, and neutrons are in a neutral atom of barium-137?

Technology: Smoke Detectors

Smoke detectors use the charges on atoms to save lives. A smoke detector contains a small boxlike structure called an ion chamber. This chamber is made of metal walls with many small holes. Inside the chamber is another piece of metal. The walls and the piece of metal are connected to electronic circuits.

The ion chamber also contains a small amount of the synthetic element, americium-241. This element produces alpha particles. Alpha particles have a positive charge, which attracts electrons from the gases in the air inside the chamber. This causes some gas particles to become ionized, or charged. Ionized air is a good conductor of electricity. The electronic circuits apply a voltage between the chamber walls and the metal piece. These circuits constantly measure the current flowing through the air. Smoke particles entering the chamber interact with some of the alpha particles. This interaction reduces the number of ions inside the chamber. With fewer ions, the electric current is reduced. The electronic circuits detect this change in current and sound the alarm.

1. Alpha particles do not last a long time. Why? (Think about what happens when alpha particles attract electrons.)

2. Some elements produce beta particles instead of alpha particles. A beta particle is a high-speed electron. Would a smoke detector work if beta particles replaced alpha particles? Explain.

3. Why is it important to periodically replace smoke detectors?

Lesson 3   R E V I E W

Word Bank

isotopes

mass number

protons

On a sheet of paper, write the word or phrase from the Word Bank that completes each sentence.

1. Atoms of the same element with different numbers of neutrons are _____.

2. Atomic number indicates the number of _____ in the nucleus.

3. The total number of protons and neutrons in the nucleus of an atom is indicated by the _____ of the element.

On a sheet of paper, write the letter of the answer that completes each sentence.

4. Every atom of aluminum has the same _____.

A mass number   **C** number of neutrons
B atomic number   **D** number of subatomic
                            particles in the nucleus

5. Most boron atoms have 5 p^+ and 6 n^0. Which of the following sets could represent an isotope of boron?

A $5\,p^+, 7\,n^0$ **B** $6\,p^+, 5\,n^0$ **C** $4\,p^+, 6\,n^0$ **D** $6\,p^+, 6\,n^0$

6. Of the isotopes below, _____ contains the most neutrons.

A $^{60}_{28}\text{Ni}$ **B** $^{60}_{27}\text{Co}$ **C** $^{60}_{29}\text{Cu}$ **D** $^{60}_{30}\text{Zn}$

Critical Thinking

Copy the following table on a sheet of paper. Fill in the missing information in each row.

	Isotope Name	Symbol	Atomic Number	Mass Number	p^+	n^0	e^-	Charge
7.				76	33		36	
8.		$^{108}_{47}\text{Ag}^{1+}$						1+
9.	nitrogen-17				7			0
10.						70	54	3−

INVESTIGATION 8

Materials

- safety goggles
- 10 white foam balls
- 10 foam balls of another color
- toothpicks

Atoms and Isotopes

How does the nucleus of one atom differ from another? In this investigation, you will explore the makeup of the nucleus of different elements and different isotopes.

Procedure

1. Copy the data table below. Each column represents an atom.

Symbol	Number of Protons	Number of Neutrons	Atomic Number	Mass Number
$^4_2$He				
$^9_4$Be				
			5	11
	6			12
	7	7		
		8		15
		9	8	

2. Put on safety goggles.

3. Let the colored balls represent protons and the white balls represent neutrons. Assemble the helium nucleus represented by the symbol $^4_2$He. Then assemble the beryllium nucleus $^9_4$Be. Based on your models, fill in the missing data in the first two rows of your table.

Continued on next page

4. Assemble a nucleus model for each of the five remaining rows in the table. To do this, first determine the missing numbers in each row. Then build the model. Use the periodic table to determine the identity of the element. Write the symbol using isotope notation.

Cleanup/Disposal

Return all materials and clean your work area. Wash your hands.

Analysis

1. How did you determine the numbers of protons and neutrons for the atom in the third row?

2. How did you determine the number of neutrons in the fourth row?

3. How did you determine the mass number in the fifth row?

4. How did you determine the atomic number in the sixth row?

5. How did you determine the mass number in the last row?

Conclusions

1. Which two rows represent isotopes of the same element? What is the element?

2. What does the bottom number in an isotope symbol mean?

3. What does the mass number of an atom tell you?

Explore Further

Construct nucleus models of other atoms, such as $^{3}_{2}$He, $^{6}_{3}$Li, $^{7}_{3}$Li, $^{13}_{6}$C, $^{16}_{8}$O, $^{19}_{9}$F, and $^{19}_{10}$Ne. Use the models to quiz your classmates about atomic number, mass number, and the identity of an atom.

Lesson 4 — Atomic Mass

Objectives

After reading this lesson, you should be able to

◆ explain how the average atomic mass of an element is determined

◆ calculate the average atomic mass of an element

Atomic mass unit (amu)

A unit of mass that equals $\frac{1}{12}$ the mass of a carbon atom with 6 protons and 6 neutrons; 1 amu is approximately the mass of a proton or neutron

The actual mass of a proton is 1.0073 amu. The actual mass of a neutron is 1.0087 amu. An electron's actual mass is 0.000549 amu.

As you might have guessed, the mass number of an isotope is related to its mass. Almost all of an atom's mass is due to its protons and neutrons. Instead of measuring the mass of atoms or subatomic particles in grams, chemists use a simpler unit called an **atomic mass unit (amu).** An atomic mass unit is exactly $\frac{1}{12}$ the mass of a carbon atom with 6 protons and 6 neutrons. For most purposes, chemists use these whole-number values:

mass of 1 proton = 1 amu

mass of 1 neutron = 1 amu

mass of 1 electron = 0 amu

Mass number—the number of particles in the nucleus—is also the approximate mass of the atom in atomic mass units. An oxygen-16 atom has a mass of about 16 amu. An oxygen-17 atom has a mass of about 17 amu. Because electrons have such a tiny mass compared to protons and neutrons, their mass is generally ignored.

Atomic mass is the mass of an atom in atomic mass units (amu). This mass is the second number in each tile of the periodic table. In Chapter 4, you learned that an element's molar mass is numerically equal to its atomic mass. The units are different, but the numbers are exactly the same. For example,

The atomic mass of chlorine is 35.5 amu.

The molar mass of chlorine is 35.5 g/mol.

The household bleach shown in Figure 8.4.1 contains sodium hypochlorite, NaClO. Each chlorine atom in bleach is one of two isotopes. Both isotopes have 17 p^+. The most common isotope has 18 n^0. The other isotope has 20 n^0. Compare the atomic mass of chlorine to the mass numbers of these isotopes.

The atomic mass of chlorine is 35.5 amu.

The mass number of $^{35}_{17}Cl$ is 35.

The mass number of $^{37}_{17}Cl$ is 37.

What do you notice? Mass numbers are whole numbers. They are fairly close to the decimal number of atomic mass. Why? Atomic mass is actually an average of all isotope masses based on their abundance in nature. An element's atomic mass is sometimes called average atomic mass, although it is not calculated like other averages.

For chlorine, the atomic mass of 35.5 amu is calculated from the masses of its two isotopes. In a natural sample of chlorine, 75.8% of the atoms are chlorine-35, and 24.2% are chlorine-37 atoms. This is the percent abundance of these isotopes in nature. Scientists have determined that the mass of a chlorine-35 atom is 34.9609 amu. The mass of a chlorine-37 atom is 36.9789 amu. Using these values, chlorine's atomic mass is

$$(34.9609 \text{ amu})\left(\frac{75.8\%}{100\%}\right) + (36.9789 \text{ amu})\left(\frac{24.2\%}{100\%}\right) = 35.5 \text{ amu}$$

The value 35.5 amu is the atomic mass on the periodic table.

Figure 8.4.1
Household bleach is a weak solution of NaClO. It is the oxygen in the hypochlorite ion, ClO^{1-}, that whitens clothes.

Math Tip

When calculating the average atomic mass of an element, be certain that the abundances of the isotopes total 100%.

The atomic mass for each element can be calculated in a similar way. In general, if you know the mass and abundance of each isotope, you can find an element's atomic mass.

$$\text{atomic mass} = (\text{mass of isotope A})\left(\frac{\text{percent abundance}}{100\%}\right)$$
$$+ (\text{mass of isotope B})\left(\frac{\text{percent abundance}}{100\%}\right)$$
$$+ (\text{mass of isotope C})\left(\frac{\text{percent abundance}}{100\%}\right) + \cdots$$

A, B, C, etc. are the natural isotopes of the element. Masses are in atomic mass units (amu). The atomic masses given in the periodic table are in atomic mass units, even though the unit is not given.

Example 1	An unknown element has two natural isotopes. One has a mass of 10.01 amu and has a percent abundance of 19.8%. The second has a mass of 10.99 amu. What is the percent abundance of the second isotope? What is this element's average atomic mass? What is the element?
Read	You are asked to find the missing percent abundance, the average atomic mass, and the name of the element.
Plan	First calculate the missing percentage. Both percentages should add to 100%. Then calculate the average atomic mass, making sure each percentage is matched to the correct mass.
Solve	The missing percentage is $(100\% - 19.8\%) = 80.2\%$. The average atomic mass is $$(10.01 \text{ amu})\left(\frac{19.8\%}{100\%}\right) + (10.99 \text{ amu})\left(\frac{80.2\%}{100\%}\right) = 10.8 \text{ amu}$$ According to the periodic table, boron has an average atomic mass of 10.8 amu.
Reflect	A calculated average atomic mass should be very close to the mass given on a periodic table.
Practice	Naturally occurring magnesium is a mixture of three isotopes. 78.99% is magnesium-24 with a mass of 23.99 amu; 10.00% is magnesium-25 with a mass of 24.98 amu, and 11.01% is magnesium-26 with a mass of 25.98 amu. What is the average atomic mass of magnesium?

Lesson 4 REVIEW

Word Bank

percent
 abundances

average atomic
 mass

atomic mass

On a sheet of paper, write the phrase from the Word Bank that completes each sentence.

1. The average atomic mass of an element is based on the _____ of each isotope and its percent abundance in nature.

2. The sum of the _____ of all isotopes should equal 100%.

3. A calculated _____ should be very close to the one listed in a periodic table.

Critical Thinking

An unknown element has three natural isotopes. Using the information below, write the answer to each question on a sheet of paper.

Isotope	Atomic Mass (amu)	Percent Abundance
A	19.992	90.48%
B	20.994	?
C	21.991	9.25%

4. What is the percent abundance of isotope B?

5. What is the average atomic mass of this element? What is the identity of the element? Show your work.

Research and Write

During the first half of the 1800s, chemists tried to determine the atomic masses of the elements. John Dalton assigned hydrogen a weight of 1 and oxygen a weight of 8. Find out why Dalton gave oxygen a weight of 8 instead of 16, oxygen's true atomic mass. Write a paragraph that summarizes what you learn.

Isotopes of Centium

Most elements occur in nature as a mixture of two or more isotopes. Chlorine, for example, occurs as a mixture of 75.8% $^{35}_{17}Cl$ and 24.2% $^{37}_{17}Cl$. As a result, chlorine has an average atomic mass of 35.5 amu. How can you determine average atomic mass? In this investigation, you will find out by using pennies to model two isotopes of an atom.

Procedure

1. Put on safety goggles. Obtain a mixture of "centium isotopes." Centium is an imaginary element with the symbol Cn. The pre-1982 pennies represent the isotope ^{A}Cn. The post-1982 pennies represent the isotope ^{B}Cn.

Continued on next page

2. Determine the atomic mass of ^{A}Cn and the atomic mass of ^{B}Cn in grams. Then determine the average atomic mass of centium in grams. You can separate the two isotopes by date. Measuring the mass of one penny is not a good idea, however. Pennies may be worn in different ways, and any balance error will be significant.

Cleanup/Disposal

Return all materials and clean your work area. Wash your hands.

Analysis

1. What is the atomic mass of isotope ^{A}Cn in grams?

2. What is the atomic mass of isotope ^{B}Cn in grams?

3. How did you determine these atomic masses?

4. Based only on the mixture's total mass and the number of atoms in the mixture, what is the average mass of one atom?

Conclusions

1. What is the percentage of each isotope in your mixture of centium?

2. Based on these percentages, calculate the average atomic mass of centium. Use the atomic masses you already determined for each isotope.

3. How does the average atomic mass you determined above compare with the average mass you determined in Analysis question 4? Explain any differences.

Explore Further

Copper consists of a mixture of 69.2% $^{63}_{29}$Cu (atomic mass = 62.93 amu) and 30.8% $^{65}_{29}$Cu (atomic mass = 64.93 amu). Calculate the average atomic mass of copper.

MRI

Since their discovery in the late 1800s, X-rays have been used to diagnose medical conditions such as broken bones and gum disease. However, X-rays have limited use. They expose the patient to harmful radiation. They cannot produce images of soft tissues such as muscle and nerves. X-ray images are often cloudy.

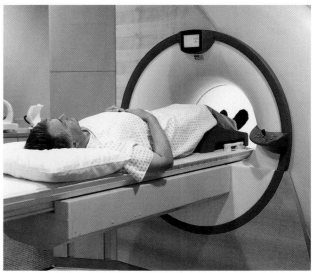

These drawbacks have been overcome by a more recent diagnostic tool called magnetic resonance imaging (MRI). MRI works because protons in a magnetic field produce radio waves. How does this happen? Water and most tissues in the human body contain hydrogen atoms. The nuclei of these hydrogen atoms are protons. A proton behaves like a magnet. The magnetic fields of protons usually cancel each other. However, when protons are placed in a strong magnetic field, they align with it. The alignment is not perfect, and the protons wobble. This wobbling produces radio waves at a specific frequency. Frequency is the number of waves produced each second.

An MRI machine applies a magnetic field in a specific part of the patient's body. The protons in this part of the body wobble and emit radio waves. Then the machine applies a short pulse of radio

waves at a matching frequency. This temporarily knocks the protons out of alignment. When the applied radio waves are gone, the protons realign and produce more radio waves. The MRI machine records the frequency and intensity of these waves. The strength of the magnetic field is changed, and new data are recorded. Then the direction of the magnetic field is changed, and the whole process is repeated. An MRI scan records data along three directions. A computer assembles these sets of data into three-dimensional images.

1. What causes protons in the human body to produce radio waves?

2. Why does an MRI machine apply magnetic fields along three different directions?

Chapter 8   S U M M A R Y

- Dalton's atomic theory states that elements are composed of atoms that cannot be divided into smaller particles. Dalton thought that all atoms of a given element are identical. These ideas were later disproved.

- Dalton's theory also states that atoms combine in whole-number ratios. Chemical reactions take place when atoms rearrange.

- Thomson discovered electrons, which are negatively charged particles smaller than an atom.

- Thomson's atomic model shows electrons scattered throughout a positively charged ball of matter.

- Rutherford discovered that protons are located in a very small center of the atom called the nucleus.

- Rutherford's atomic model shows protons in a central nucleus with electrons in a large space outside the nucleus.

- Chadwick discovered the neutron, which is a subatomic particle with no charge. It is located in the nucleus.

- An element's atomic number is the number of protons in an atom of that element.

- An element's mass number is the sum of the number of protons and number of neutrons in an atom.

- Neutral atoms have the same number of electrons as protons.

- A negatively charged atom (an anion) has more electrons than protons.

- A positively charged atom (a cation) has fewer electrons than protons.

- The average atomic mass of an element is calculated using the atomic mass and the percent abundance of each isotope.

Vocabulary

alpha particle, 311	cathode, 307	isotope, 318
anode, 307	cathode-ray tube, 307	mass number, 319
atomic mass unit, 325	electrode, 307	

Chapter 8 REVIEW

Word Bank

alpha particle

anode

average atomic mass

cathode

cathode-ray tube

electrode

isotope

mass number

proton

Vocabulary Review

On a sheet of paper, write the word or phrase from the Word Bank that completes each sentence.

1. The _____ of an element is based on the percent abundance and mass of each isotope.

2. An atom of an element with a different number of neutrons is a(n) _____.

3. The sum of the protons and neutrons in an atom is called the _____.

4. A metal plate that conducts electricity is a(n) _____.

5. A negatively charged particle will move toward the _____ in a cathode-ray tube.

6. A(n) _____ has a positive charge and a mass of about 4 amu.

7. The mass of a neutron is about the same as a(n) _____.

8. The fluorescent plate in a(n) _____ glows when electrons move between the electrodes.

9. In a cathode-ray tube, the _____ is the electrode that electrons move away from.

Concept Review

On a sheet of paper, write the letter of the answer to each question.

10. Which part of Dalton's atomic theory was proved wrong?

A Atoms cannot change into other elements in a chemical reaction.

B Atoms form compounds by combining in whole-number ratios.

C Elements are composed of atoms.

D Atoms cannot be divided into smaller parts.

Continued on next page

11. How did Thomson's model of the atom change Dalton's model?

   A It added a nucleus filled with electrons.
   B It added a nucleus filled with protons.
   C It added particles smaller than an atom that have a negative charge.
   D It added particles smaller than an atom that have no electrical charge.

12. Which fact about gold could *not* have been discovered in Rutherford's experiment?

   A Most of the mass of an atom is concentrated in a very small, central area.
   B The nucleus has a positive charge.
   C Gold has more than forty isotopes.
   D Most of the volume of an atom is empty space.

13. How did Rutherford's model of the atom change Thomson's model?

   A It added a nucleus filled with electrons.
   B It added a nucleus filled with protons.
   C It added particles smaller than an atom that have a negative charge.
   D It added particles smaller than an atom that have no electrical charge.

14. Which of the following atoms has 36 neutrons?

   A $^{63}_{29}Cu$ B $^{65}_{29}Cu$ C $^{67}_{30}Zn$ D $^{69}_{31}Ga$

15. An ion of chlorine-37 has the symbol $^{37}_{17}Cl^{1-}$. How many electrons does it have?

   A 17   B 20   C 37   D 18

16. Which of the following is an isotope of $^{108}_{47}Ag$?

   A $^{108}_{46}Pd$ B $^{110}_{48}Cd$ C $^{110}_{46}Pd$ D $^{110}_{47}Ag$

Problem Solving

Copy the following table on a sheet of paper. Fill in the missing information in each row.

	Isotope Name	Symbol	Atomic Number	Mass Number	p^+	n^0	e^-	Charge
17.	sodium-22						10	
18.		$^{40}_{20}\text{Ca}^{2+}$						
19.					9	9	10	
20.						17	18	2−
21.		$^{2}_{1}\text{H}^{1+}$						
22.	carbon-12							0

Critical Thinking

On a sheet of paper, write the answer to each question.

23. How did the atomic model change from the time of Dalton to Thomson to Rutherford? Make sure you describe the three models and the changes made from one to the next.

24. An ion has a charge of 1+, 10 electrons, and a mass number of 23. What is the symbol of this ion? (Include mass number and atomic number.)

25. Based on the information in the table below, what is the missing percent abundance? What is the average atomic mass of zinc? Show your work.

Isotope	Zinc-64	Zinc-66	Zinc-67	Zinc-68	Zinc-70
Atomic Mass (amu)	63.929	65.926	66.927	67.925	69.925
Percent Abundance	48.89%	27.81%	4.11%	?	0.62%

Test-Taking Tip To prepare for a test, study in short sessions rather than in one long session. During the week before the test, spend time each day reviewing your notes.

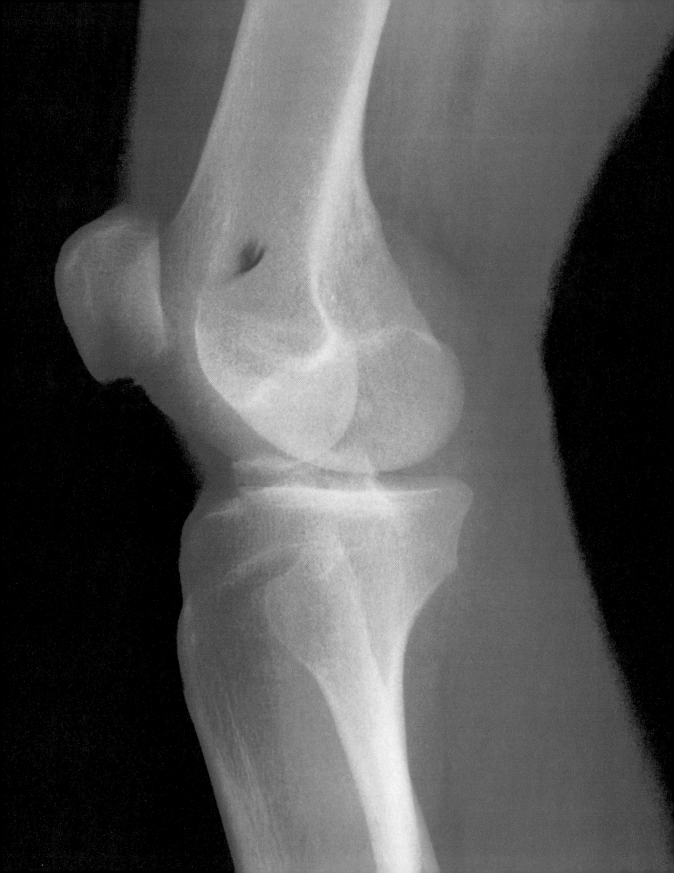

Nuclear Chemistry

The photo shows an X-ray of a human knee joint. An X-ray camera uses a beam of X-rays, instead of light, to take a picture. High-energy X-rays can penetrate materials such as body tissues. The X-rays form images of some of the structures inside. In Chapter 9, you will learn about different types of radiation, including X-rays. You will find out why radiation is related to the nuclei of atoms.

Organize Your Thoughts

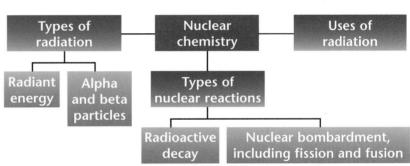

Goals for Learning

◆ To describe the nature of radiation and list some common sources

◆ To define a nuclear reaction and describe three types of radioactive decay

◆ To explain how transmutations occur naturally

◆ To explain how nuclear bombardment can create larger atoms

◆ To explain half-life and its use in dating objects

◆ To state the difference between fission and fusion

◆ To compare fission and fusion as sources of power

Objectives

After reading this lesson, you should be able to

◆ describe a wave in terms of its wavelength, frequency, and energy

◆ explain a nuclear reaction and relate it to radiation

◆ compare ionizing and nonionizing radiation

◆ list common sources of radiation

Nuclear reaction

A change within the nucleus of an atom

Radiation

Energy or particles that can travel through space

Radiant energy

Energy that can travel through space; also called electromagnetic radiation

Electromagnetic radiation

Energy that can travel through space; also called radiant energy

Chemical reactions occur when atoms in reactants rearrange, forming one or more new products. When atoms rearrange, chemical bonds are made or broken. These bonds involve only the electrons of atoms. The nuclei of the atoms are not changed. In Chapter 5, you studied many types of chemical reactions. In this chapter, you will learn about a different kind of reaction: a **nuclear reaction.** A nuclear reaction is a change within the nucleus of an atom. A nuclear reaction is not affected by temperature or pressure changes. It cannot be stopped once it has started. Both chemical reactions and nuclear reactions can produce radiation.

Radiation

What do you think of when you hear the word *radiation?* Do you think of sunlight? Or a radio playing music? **Radiation** is energy or particles that can travel through space. Radiation in the form of energy is also called **radiant energy.** Visible light is the most familiar example of radiant energy. There are many other examples of radiant energy. All radiant energy travels through space in the form of waves. Sunlight reaches the earth as waves. Radio waves carry your favorite music and TV programs. You cook food with microwaves. You see the world around you because your eyes sense visible light waves. These waves have electrical and magnetic properties. Because of this, radiant energy is also called **electromagnetic radiation.**

The Electromagnetic Spectrum

The movement of energy waves is similar to ocean waves, but much faster. All electromagnetic waves travel at the speed of light. While their speed is constant, electromagnetic waves vary greatly in **frequency** and **wavelength**. Frequency is the number of wave peaks that pass a given a point in a certain amount of time. Frequency is usually measured in a unit called **hertz** (Hz). 1 Hz is 1 cycle (wave peak) per second. Wavelength is the distance from one wave peak to the next.

Frequency

The number of wave peaks that pass a given point in a certain amount of time

Wavelength

The distance from one wave peak to the next

Hertz (Hz)

A unit for measuring wave frequency that equals 1 cycle per second

Electromagnetic spectrum

The whole range of electromagnetic radiation

Low-frequency waves are long, while high-frequency waves are short. Frequency and wavelength are inversely related. Figure 9.1.1 compares red visible light and violet visible light. Red light has a longer wavelength but a lower frequency. Fewer long waves can pass a given point per second than short waves.

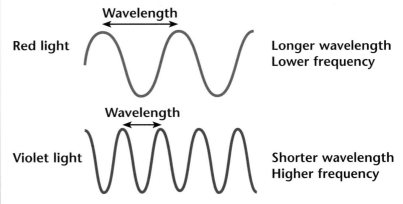

Figure 9.1.1 *As wave frequency increases, wavelength decreases.*

Every form of radiant energy is found in a range called the **electromagnetic spectrum,** shown in Figure 9.1.2. In this spectrum, wave frequency varies from less than 1 Hz to more than 10^{20} Hz. Wavelength varies from picometers to kilometers. Wavelength increases as you move to the right along the spectrum. Frequency increases as you move to the left.

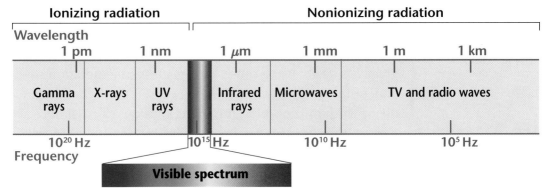

Figure 9.1.2 *The electromagnetic spectrum shows every form of radiant energy. The visible spectrum—the light you see—is just a small part of it. Visible light ranges from 400 nm (violet light) to 700 nm (red light).*

Nonionizing and Ionizing Radiation

Energy increases with wave frequency. The higher the frequency, the higher the energy of the wave. As Figure 9.1.2 shows, radiation at the low-frequency end of the spectrum is **nonionizing radiation.** *Nonionizing* means it does not have enough energy to remove an electron from another substance. The lower the frequency, the less ionizing the radiation. Visible light, **infrared rays,** microwaves, and television and radio waves are nonionizing. Infrared rays have longer wavelengths than visible light. Nuclear reactions in the sun emit infrared rays that warm the earth. The sun also emits visible light. When you open a hot oven or sit by a campfire, you can feel the effect of infrared rays. When electromagnetic radiation is absorbed by matter, the energy of the matter increases. This is why microwaves are used to heat foods.

Nuclear reactions give off **ionizing radiation.** This radiation has enough energy to remove an electron from another substance. The higher the wave frequency, the more ionizing the radiation. **Ultraviolet rays** are next to visible light on the electromagnetic spectrum. The sun emits ultraviolet rays, which can cause sunburn. **X-rays** can pass through soft body tissue, but not bone. X-rays are used to create images of bones. **Gamma rays** have the highest energy of all electromagnetic radiation. These waves can pass through most objects. Gamma rays can cause severe damage to living things.

As these examples show, some forms of radiation are more dangerous than others. The greater the energy of a wave, the greater is its ability to cause damage. Ionizing radiation can penetrate, or move through, living cells. It can cause them to die or work improperly. Ultraviolet rays can cause skin cells to darken. Gamma rays can break chemical bonds within cells. These changes can lead to **cancer.** Cancer is a disease in which cells grow without control and divide rapidly. Nonionizing radiation is less likely to cause damage. However, all forms of radiation are dangerous at high levels. Even the radiation from a hot oven can cause burns.

Nonionizing radiation

Low-energy radiation that cannot remove an electron from a substance

Infrared rays

Nonionizing radiation with wavelengths longer than visible light

Ionizing radiation

High-energy radiation that can remove an electron from a substance

Ultraviolet rays

Ionizing radiation with wavelengths shorter than visible light

X-rays

Ionizing radiation that can pass through soft body tissue, but not bone

Gamma rays

Ionizing radiation with a very high energy

Cancer

A disease in which cells grow without control and divide rapidly

---

Rem (rem)

A unit used to measure radiation that affects organisms

Although you may not realize it, you are exposed to radiation every day. Table 9.1.1 lists some common sources of radiation. It also lists typical amounts of radiation exposure per year for someone living in the United States. Some radiation is naturally present in the environment. Other types of radiation exposure depend on your technology choices, your medical needs, or where you live. Radiation can be measured using many units. The **Rem (rem)** or millirem (mrem) is used to measure radiation that affects organisms. A single dose of 100 rem can cause radiation sickness.

Table 9.1.1 Typical Radiation Exposure per Person per Year in the United States

Source	Radiation	Source	Radiation
atmosphere at sea level*	26 mrem	dental X-ray	1 mrem
ground	30 mrem	chest X-ray	6 mrem
foods	20 mrem	X-ray of hip	65 mrem
air travel above 1,800 m	4 mrem	CAT scan	110 mrem
construction site	7 mrem	nuclear power plant nearby	0.02 mrem
X-ray of arm or leg	1 mrem	TV and computer use	2 mrem

Add 3 mrem for every 300 m of elevation.

Express Lab 9

Procedure

Most of the radiation you encounter daily is electromagnetic radiation. You can see visible light, but not other types of electromagnetic radiation. The table below lists the maximum energy of some types of electromagnetic radiation. Energy is given in units of joules. Use the table to answer the Analysis questions.

Analysis

1. Which electromagnetic radiation has the highest energy? Which has the lowest?

2. Some matter can be ionized by radiation energies as low as 6.63×10^{-19} joules. Which electromagnetic radiation can be ionizing? Which is always nonionizing? Explain your answers.

Electromagnetic Radiation	Maximum Energy (joules)
radio waves	1.99×10^{-22}
visible light	4.97×10^{-19}
ultraviolet rays	3.32×10^{-18}
gamma rays	1.99×10^{-11}

Lesson 1 REVIEW

Word Bank

electromagnetic
spectrum

frequency

ionizing radiation

nuclear reaction

radiation

visible light

On a sheet of paper, write the word or phrase from the Word Bank that completes each sentence.

1. Energy or particles that can travel through space are called _____.

2. High-energy radiation is _____.

3. A change in the nucleus of an atom is a(n) _____.

4. An example of nonionizing radiation is _____.

5. As wavelength increases, _____ decreases.

6. The range of radiant energy is called the _____.

Critical Thinking

On a sheet of paper, write the answer to each question.

7. Name two forms of electromagnetic radiation that you are exposed to or use. Where are they located on the electromagnetic spectrum?

8. What are two physical properties of an electromagnetic wave? Define them.

9. All radiation is not electromagnetic radiation. Why?

10. Compare ionizing and nonionizing radiation.

Objectives

After reading this lesson, you should be able to

◆ describe and compare three types of radioactive decay

◆ define transmutation and tell how it occurs

◆ predict the product of a radioactive decay

Radioactive

Giving off radiation due to a nuclear change

Radioisotope

An isotope that has an unstable nucleus and is therefore radioactive

Radioactivity

The release of radiation caused by radioactive decay

Radioactive decay

The breakdown of an unstable nucleus, resulting in radioactivity

Nuclear reactions often produce high-energy electromagnetic radiation. Some nuclear reactions also produce radiation in the form of particles. Particle radiation is not part of the electromagnetic spectrum. In this lesson, you will learn what happens in a nucleus to cause particle radiation and electromagnetic radiation.

Elements exist as isotopes with differing numbers of neutrons. Many elements have unstable isotopes. The stability of an isotope depends on the number of neutrons and protons in the nucleus. Too many or too few neutrons create an unstable nucleus. Isotopes with an unstable nucleus are **radioactive,** which means they give off radiation when the nucleus changes. Radioactive isotopes are called **radioisotopes,** for short. As the nucleus of a radioisotope changes to become more stable, it releases radiation. This release of radiation is called **radioactivity.** It is caused by **radioactive decay,** or the breakdown of an unstable nucleus. Radioactive decay can emit radiation in the form of high-energy waves or high-energy particles. The decay of radioisotopes occurs naturally all the time.

Alpha Particles

By the early 1900s, scientists had identified three types of radioactive decay. They are named after the first three letters in the Greek alphabet: alpha (α), beta (β), and gamma (γ). The first one is the alpha particle, used by Rutherford in his gold foil experiment (see page 311). This particle is a helium nucleus of 2 protons and 2 neutrons ($2\ p^+$ and $2\ n^0$). It has a charge of $2+$. The symbol for an alpha particle is $_2^4\text{He}^{2+}$, $_2^4\text{He}$, or simply α. Even though alpha particles are highly ionizing, they do not pass through skin.

Only wavelike radiation is shown on the electromagnetic spectrum. Particles emitted from radioisotopes, such as alpha particles, are not part of this spectrum.

An element is identified by the number of protons in its atoms. When an alpha particle is released from an atom's nucleus, the numbers of protons and neutrons in the atom change. Because the proton number is different after alpha decay, the atom becomes a different element. When an isotope of one element changes into an isotope of a different element, this is called **transmutation.** For example, the uranium isotope $^{238}_{92}U$ has an unstable nucleus.

mass number $(n^0 + p^+)$ ⟶ $^{238}_{92}U$ ⟵ element symbol

atomic number (p^+) ⟶

All isotopes of uranium have 92 p^+. This particular isotope has $(238 - 92) = 146\ n^0$. Here is what happens when the nucleus of this isotope decays:

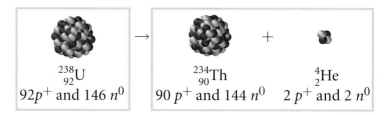

$^{238}_{92}U$ $^{234}_{90}Th$ $^{4}_{2}He$

$92p^+$ and $146\ n^0$ $90\ p^+$ and $144\ n^0$ $2\ p^+$ and $2\ n^0$

The unstable uranium atom releases an alpha particle. It becomes an atom with 90 protons: a thorium atom. A transmutation has occurred. This nuclear reaction is represented by this nuclear equation:

$$^{238}_{92}U \rightarrow\ ^{234}_{90}Th +\ ^{4}_{2}He$$

Both sides of this equation have the same total mass number: $238 = (234 + 4)$. Both sides also have the same total atomic number: $92 = (90 + 2)$. The nuclear equation is balanced. For all nuclear equations, follow these rules:

Rule 1. The sum of the mass numbers on each side of the arrow must be equal.

Rule 2. The sum of the atomic numbers on each side of the arrow must be equal.

An alpha particle is a form of radiation. It is a product of radioactive decay. An alpha particle is not, by itself, a radioisotope. An alpha particle does not decay.

Many elements have more than one radioisotope. The following example involves different radioisotopes of uranium and thorium.

Example 1	An atom of uranium-234 decays by emitting an alpha particle. What is the other product?
Read	Uranium-234 is a radioisotope. It has a mass number of 234. Alpha decay is the release of an alpha particle from the nucleus of an atom. You are asked to identify the new nucleus after an atom of uranium-234 releases an alpha particle.
Plan	You will need to write this nuclear reaction as an equation. Use the periodic table to find the atomic number of uranium. It is 92, so uranium-234 has the symbol $^{234}_{92}U$. An alpha particle has the symbol $^{4}_{2}He$.
Solve	Write the equation. Look at the mass numbers and atomic numbers on each side of the arrow.

$$^{234}_{92}U \rightarrow {}^{4}_{2}He + ?$$

234	4 + ?	*mass number*
92	2 + ?	*atomic number*

The total mass number on each side of the equation must be the same. $234 = 4 + 230$, so the product must have a mass number of 230. The total atomic number on each side must also be the same. $92 = 2 + 90$, so the product must have an atomic number of 90. On the periodic table, the atomic number 90 belongs to thorium. The new nucleus must be $^{230}_{90}Th$. The complete nuclear equation is

$$^{234}_{92}U \rightarrow {}^{4}_{2}He + {}^{230}_{90}Th$$

| **Reflect** | When the sums of the atomic numbers on each side are equal, and when the sums of the mass numbers on each side are equal, a nuclear equation is balanced. |
| **Practice** | An atom of polonium-210 decays by emitting an alpha particle. What is the other product? |

Beta Particles

Beta particle

A high-energy electron that is emitted when a neutron in the nucleus of an atom breaks down

When subatomic particles are part of nuclear equations, these symbols are used:

neutron $\,_0^1 n$

proton $\,_1^1 H$

electron $\,_{-1}^0 e$

A positron is a particle with the same mass as an electron, but with a positive charge. Some radioisotopes emit positrons. The symbol for a positron is β^+ or $\,_{+1}^0 e.$

A second type of radiation is the **beta particle.** This is a high-energy electron. Beta radiation occurs when a neutron in the nucleus of an unstable atom breaks down. The breakdown of one neutron results in one beta particle and one proton. In the equation below, the symbol used for a proton is $\,_1^1 H$, a hydrogen nucleus.

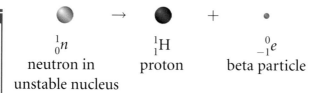

$\,_0^1 n$ $\,_1^1 H$ $\,_{-1}^0 e$

neutron in   proton   beta particle
unstable nucleus

The released electron is *not* one of the electrons outside the atom's nucleus. A beta particle has the symbol β^- or $\,_{-1}^0 e.$ It is given a mass number of 0 because an electron's mass is so small. Beta particles have less mass and move faster than alpha particles. Because of this, they also have more energy. Beta particles are also a form of ionizing radiation, although they are less ionizing than alpha particles. Beta particles can go through about 1 cm of human flesh.

When a radioisotope decays by releasing a beta particle, a transmutation also occurs. The nucleus has one more proton, but one less neutron. The transmutation of carbon-14 to nitrogen-14 looks like this:

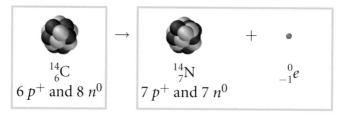

$\,_6^{14} C$ $\,_7^{14} N$ $\,_{-1}^0 e$

$6\,p^+$ and $8\,n^0$ $7\,p^+$ and $7\,n^0$

The carbon-14 isotope decays by releasing a beta particle. The result is a stable nitrogen atom.

Even though a neutron has changed into a proton and an electron, the total mass number on both sides of the equation is the same: $14 = 14 + 0$. When a beta particle is considered to have an atomic number of -1, the total atomic number also stays the same: $6 = (7 + -1)$.

Example 2 Iodine-131 undergoes beta decay. What is the product?

Read You are given a radioisotope of iodine with a mass number of 131. You are asked to identify the new nucleus after an atom of iodine-131 emits a beta particle.

Plan Write this nuclear reaction as an equation. Use the periodic table to find the atomic number of iodine. It is 53, so the isotope has the symbol $^{131}_{53}I$. A beta particle has the symbol $^{0}_{-1}e$.

Solve Write the equation. Look at the mass numbers and atomic numbers on each side of the arrow.

$$^{131}_{53}I \rightarrow\ ^{0}_{-1}e + ?$$

131	0 + ?	*mass number*
53	−1 + ?	*atomic number*

The total mass number on the left side must equal the total mass number on the right. This means that the mass number of the unknown product is 131. For the total atomic numbers on each side to be equal, the unknown must have an atomic number of 54. This identifies the unknown as xenon. The product is $^{131}_{54}Xe$.

Reflect To find the chemical symbol of a missing isotope, look up its atomic number on the periodic table.

Practice Potassium-40 undergoes beta decay. What is the product?

Technology and Society

Several devices are used to detect ionizing radiation. A common one is the Geiger counter, sometimes called the Geiger-Mueller counter. This portable device detects alpha, beta, and low-energy gamma radiation. Other devices, like ion chambers, can detect high-energy gamma radiation. Proportional counters are best for detecting alpha particles and neutrons. The choice of detector depends on the type and energy of the radiation.

The nuclear reaction in Example 2 results in a stable isotope that does not decay. Some nuclear reactions do not result in a stable product. In fact, they may be part of a series of unstable products. For example, $^{238}_{92}U$ emits an alpha particle to produce $^{234}_{90}Th$. This product is unstable, so it emits a beta particle to produce $^{234}_{91}Pa$. This product and many others after it decay in a series, like this:

$$^{238}_{92}U \xrightarrow{\alpha} {}^{234}_{90}Th \xrightarrow{\beta^-} {}^{234}_{91}Pa \xrightarrow{\beta^-} {}^{234}_{92}U \xrightarrow{\alpha} {}^{230}_{90}Th \xrightarrow{\alpha} {}^{226}_{88}Ra \xrightarrow{\alpha} {}^{222}_{86}Rn \; {}^{218}_{84}Po \xrightarrow{\alpha}$$

$$^{214}_{82}Pb \xrightarrow{\beta^-} {}^{214}_{83}Bi \xrightarrow{\beta^-} {}^{214}_{84}Po \xrightarrow{\alpha} {}^{210}_{82}Pb \xrightarrow{\beta^-} {}^{210}_{83}Bi \xrightarrow{\beta^-} {}^{210}_{84}Po \xrightarrow{\alpha} {}^{206}_{82}Pb$$

The symbol $\xrightarrow{\alpha}$ means alpha decay, and $\xrightarrow{\beta^-}$ means beta decay. The last isotope in the decay series, $^{206}_{82}Pb$, is stable and does not decay. The whole decay process, from uranium-238 to lead-206, takes millions of years.

■◆■

Chemistry in Your Life

Technology: Radon Detection

Radon, like other noble gases, is stable and does not easily react. Radon, however, is radioactive. It is dangerous to inhale even small amounts of it. Radon is produced by the decay of uranium in the earth's crust. The radon seeps upward through porous rock and soil until it reaches the earth's surface. In open air, radon gas spreads out, so it is never in large concentrations. However, it can accumulate in basements that have little ventilation.

Radon detection devices interact with the radioactivity from radon. These interactions are later measured at a laboratory. Some devices use charcoal to collect the decay products from the radon. The collection takes a few days. In other devices, alpha particles from radon leave indentations

in a plastic film. After several months of exposure, these indentations are counted. Both types of devices indicate how much radon is present.

1. What causes radon to accumulate in houses?

2. Why is good ventilation important in a home?

Gamma Rays

Some radioisotopes transmit high-energy electromagnetic waves, not particles. A third type of radioactive decay discovered in the early 1900s is the gamma ray. The gamma ray has the symbol γ or $^0_0\gamma$. Gamma rays are highly ionizing radiation. But they are energy, not particles of matter. They have no mass or charge. When a nucleus gives off gamma rays, no transmutation occurs. However, gamma radiation is often emitted during alpha and beta decay. Gamma radiation does not affect mass number or atomic number, so it is not always written in a nuclear equation. Figure 9.2.1 compares the different forms of radioactive decay.

Figure 9.2.1 *Alpha particles have less energy than beta particles and cannot pass through cardboard. Gamma rays have high energy and are only stopped by a thick piece of cement or lead.*

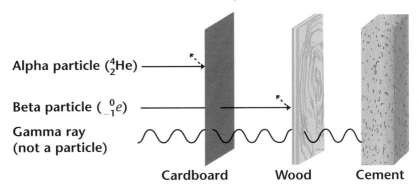

Alpha particle ($^4_2$He)

Beta particle ($^{\ 0}_{-1}e$)

Gamma ray (not a particle)

Cardboard   Wood   Cement

* *

Achievements in Science

The Discovery of Radioactivity

The elements uranium and thorium were discovered before 1800. However, their radioactivity was not detected until 1896. In that year, Henri Becquerel accidentally detected radioactivity in uranium. He believed that uranium absorbed sunlight and converted it to X-rays. He tested this hypothesis by exposing a uranium compound to sunlight. He put the compound on top of photographic plates wrapped in light-proof paper and placed it in sunlight. The plates were exposed. Becquerel thought this supported his hypothesis. On a cloudy day, he performed his experiment again. The plates were exposed as always. How could that happen on a cloudy day? Becquerel realized that his hypothesis was wrong—sunlight played no part in the process.

Becquerel ran other experiments and discovered that uranium's radiation consists of charged and uncharged particles. Later, Marie and Pierre Curie called these emissions *radioactivity*. In 1898, the Curies discovered that thorium was radioactive. They also discovered the radioactive elements polonium and radium.

Word Bank

beta particle

radioisotope

transmutation

On a sheet of paper, write the word or phrase from the Word Bank that completes each sentence.

1. An unstable atom called a _____ goes through a process called radioactive decay to become more stable.

2. When an isotope of one element is changed into an isotope of a different element, a _____ has occurred.

3. A high-energy electron emitted when a neutron in a nucleus breaks down is called a _____ .

On a sheet of paper, write the letter of the answer that completes each sentence.

4. When polonium-210 undergoes alpha decay, the product is _____ .

   A $^{210}_{84}$Po   **B** $^{4}_{2}$He   **C** $^{206}_{82}$Pb   **D** $^{214}_{86}$Rn

5. When cesium-134 undergoes beta decay, the product is _____ .

   A $^{134}_{54}$Xe   **B** $^{134}_{56}$Ba   **C** $^{0}_{-1}e$ **D** $^{134}_{55}$Cs

6. When molybdenum-99 undergoes beta decay, the product is _____ .

   A $^{99}_{43}$Tc   **B** $^{99}_{42}$Mo   **C** $^{100}_{42}$Mo   **D** $^{95}_{40}$Zr

Critical Thinking

On a sheet of paper, write the answer to each question.

7. What is the missing product in the following reaction?
$^{243}_{94}$Pu $\rightarrow$ $^{0}_{-1}e +$?

8. What is the missing product in the following reaction?
$^{28}_{13}$Al $\rightarrow$ $^{28}_{14}$Si $+$?

9. What is the missing product in the following reaction?
$^{225}_{89}$Ac $\rightarrow$ $^{4}_{2}$He $+$?

10. When balancing a nuclear equation, what must be balanced?

After reading this lesson, you should be able to
◆ tell how scientists create nuclear bombardment
◆ identify elements that have been created by bombardment
◆ predict the product of a nuclear bombardment

Transuranium element

Any of the elements with atomic numbers greater than 92

When an unstable nucleus decays, it emits one or more types of radiation. In the process, it becomes more stable. Often, it becomes a completely different element by transmutation. Transmutation occurs naturally by radioactive decay. Transmutation can also occur when a high-speed particle bombards, or hits, the nucleus of an atom. This does not happen in nature. Scientists use a device called a particle accelerator to give particles very high speeds. Figure 9.3.1 shows such a device. The high-speed particles can be neutrons ($_0^1n$), protons ($_1^1H$), alpha particles ($_2^4He$), or other small atoms. When a high-speed particle bombards a nucleus, it may join the nucleus, forming a new, heavier element. The new element is usually unstable and radioactively decays. All of the elements on the periodic table beyond uranium—those with atomic numbers greater than 92—are made in laboratories by bombardment. These elements, called **transuranium elements,** do not occur in nature. Some exist for only a few seconds before decaying.

Figure 9.3.1 *Scientists use a particle accelerator like this one to create elements that are not found in nature. The heaviest element created by bombardment so far is roentgenium, atomic number 111.*

Link to >>>

Language Arts

The discovery of radioactive elements influenced some writers of fiction. Radium is notable in stories written in the 1920s. One example is Jack Williamson's story, "The Metal Man." Another example is F. Scott Fitzgerald's "Diamond as Big as the Ritz." In that story, a man buys vast amounts of radium, which at the time cost $120,000 per gram.

Many transuranium elements are named after places or famous scientists. For example, neptunium, named after the planet Neptune, has atomic number 93. It was first produced in 1940 by bombarding uranium-238 with neutrons. This reaction has two steps:

$$^{238}_{92}U + ^{1}_{0}n \rightarrow ^{239}_{92}U + ^{0}_{0}\gamma \qquad ^{239}_{92}U \rightarrow ^{0}_{-1}e + ^{239}_{93}Np$$

Because uranium-239 is extremely unstable, it immediately decays by beta emission, forming neptunium-239. The $^{239}_{93}Np$ isotope was the first transuranium element made.

Nuclear reactions caused by bombardment can be written as equations. To find a missing product or reactant, follow the same balancing rules used for radioactive decay.

Rule 1. The sum of the mass numbers on each side of the arrow must be equal.

Rule 2. The sum of the atomic numbers on each side of the arrow must be equal.

Spotlight on Technetium

43
Tc
Technetium
(98)

Technetium was the first element to be artificially created. Technetium and promethium are the only elements lighter than polonium that have no stable isotopes. Little if any natural technetium exists on the earth. Technetium was discovered in 1937. It was found in molybdenum that had been bombarded with neutrons and deuterons (a heavy hydrogen nucleus).

Technetium has the remarkable property of preventing steel from corroding. As little as five parts of technetium to one million parts of steel will prevent corrosion. However, this application is very limited because technetium is radioactive.

The isotope technetium-99m is used in many nuclear medicine procedures. The m means metastable, because this isotope decays to technetium-99 by gamma ray emission. Technetium-99m decays quickly. This keeps the isotope from being a long-term danger to patients.

Interesting Fact: Technetium has been found in certain types of stars.

The first transmutation was performed by Ernest Rutherford. He bombarded nitrogen atoms with alpha particles. The alpha particles combined with nitrogen nuclei and ejected a proton in the process. The final result was the formation of an oxygen isotope.

Example 1 A nitrogen atom, $^{14}_{7}N$, is bombarded by an alpha particle. One product is a proton, or the hydrogen nucleus, $^{1}_{1}H$. What is the other product?

Read You are given two reactants, a nitrogen atom and an alpha particle. You are given one product, a hydrogen atom. You are asked to find a second product.

Plan Write the symbol for each known nucleus or particle. Include the mass number and atomic number. An alpha particle is $^{4}_{2}He$.

Solve Write the nuclear equation using the given information. Add the mass numbers and atomic numbers on each side.

$$^{14}_{7}N + {}^{4}_{2}He \quad \rightarrow \quad ^{1}_{1}H + ?$$

$14 + 4 = 18$	$1 + ?$	*mass number*
$7 + 2 = 9$	$1 + ?$	*atomic number*

The mass number sum on the left, 18, must equal the mass number sum on the right. The missing mass number must be 17. The atomic number sum on the left, 9, must equal the atomic number sum on the right. The missing atomic number must be 8. Oxygen has the atomic number 8, so the product of this transmutation is $^{17}_{8}O$.

$$^{14}_{7}N + {}^{4}_{2}He \rightarrow {}^{1}_{1}H + {}^{17}_{8}O$$

Reflect In the nuclear equation above, check that the numbers balance. For mass numbers: $14 + 4 = 1 + 17$. For atomic numbers: $7 + 2 = 1 + 8$.

Practice A beryllium atom, $^{9}_{4}Be$, is bombarded by an alpha particle. One product is a neutron, $^{1}_{0}n$. What is the other product?

Research and Write

Use the Internet to find out how newly discovered elements are named. Research the naming rules made by the International Union of Pure and Applied Chemistry (IUPAC). Learn about the disputes over the naming of elements 104 through 109. Present your findings in a written report.

Example 2 A californium-249 atom is bombarded by a carbon-12 atom. The two nuclei combine, but 4 neutrons are emitted. What heavy isotope is produced?

Read You are given two reactant isotopes. A new isotope is produced along with 4 individual neutrons. You are asked to identify the new isotope.

Plan Find the atomic number for californium and carbon. Then write their symbols: $^{249}_{98}$Cf and $^{12}_{6}$C. A neutron has the symbol $^{1}_{0}n$.

Solve Write the nuclear equation using the given information. Add the mass numbers and atomic numbers on each side.

$$^{249}_{98}\text{Cf} + ^{12}_{6}\text{C} \rightarrow ^{1}_{0}n + ^{1}_{0}n + ^{1}_{0}n + ^{1}_{0}n + ?$$

$^{249}_{98}\text{Cf} + ^{12}_{6}\text{C}$	$\rightarrow ^{1}_{0}n + ^{1}_{0}n + ^{1}_{0}n + ^{1}_{0}n + ?$	
$249 + 12 = 261$	$1 + 1 + 1 + 1 + ?$	*mass number*
$98 + 6 = 104$	$0 + 0 + 0 + 0 + ?$	*atomic number*

The missing mass number is $261 - 4 = 257$. The missing atomic number is 104. This atomic number identifies the nucleus as rutherfordium, Rf. The new isotope is $^{257}_{104}$Rf.

Reflect In this case, the bombarding particle is an atom, not a subatomic particle. The balanced equation can be simplified to
$$^{249}_{98}\text{Cf} + ^{12}_{6}\text{C} \rightarrow 4(^{1}_{0}n) + ^{257}_{104}\text{Rf}$$

Practice A plutonium-239 isotope is bombarded by 2 neutrons. One product is americium-241. What is the other product? (Hint: It is a subatomic particle.)

Link to ➤➤➤

Social Studies

When the first radioactive elements were discovered, no rules existed for naming elements. Uranium was named in 1789 after the planet Uranus. In 1940, the elements neptunium and plutonium were named after Neptune and Pluto. Marie Curie named polonium after her native Poland. The Latin word for ray, *radius,* was used to name radium.

Lesson 3 REVIEW

Word Bank

atomic numbers

reactants

transuranium
 elements

On a sheet of paper, write the word or phrase from the Word Bank that completes each sentence.

1. The _____ do not occur in nature.

2. In nuclear bombardment, high-speed protons, neutrons, or small atoms are used as _____.

3. The sum of the mass numbers and the sum of the _____ on each side of a nuclear equation must be equal.

On a sheet of paper, write the letter of the answer that completes each sentence.

4. A nucleus is bombarded by a small particle. The product has 2 more protons and 2 more neutrons than the original nucleus. The small particle is a(n) _____.

  A proton   **C** alpha particle

  B neutron   **D** beta particle

5. A nucleus with atomic number x is bombarded by a small particle. The product's atomic number equals $(x + 1)$. The small particle is a(n) _____.

  A proton   **C** alpha particle

  B neutron   **D** beta particle

6. A nucleus is bombarded by a small particle. The product has the same atomic number as the original nucleus. The small particle is a(n) _____.

  A proton   **C** alpha particle

  B neutron   **D** beta particle

Critical Thinking

On a sheet of paper, copy each nuclear reaction. Fill in the missing reactant or product.

7. $^{254}_{99}\text{Es} + ? \rightarrow {}^{258}_{101}\text{Md}$

8. $^{12}_{6}\text{C} + ? \rightarrow {}^{254}_{102}\text{No} + 2({}^{1}_{0}n)$

9. $^{96}_{42}\text{Mo} + {}^{2}_{1}\text{H} \rightarrow ?$

10. $^{249}_{98}\text{Cf} + {}^{18}_{8}\text{O} \rightarrow ? + 4({}^{1}_{0}n)$

Half-life

The time it takes for half of a radioactive sample to decay

A radioisotope does not always remain radioactive. After a period of time, it decays into a stable, nonradioactive isotope. This decay time is an important property in many practical uses of radioisotopes.

Half-Life

Scientists use the **half-life** of a radioisotope to describe its rate of decay. Half-life is the time it takes for half of a radioactive sample to decay. Half-life is a quantity of time that does not change for a given radioisotope. It does not depend on the size of the sample. Half-lives can range from a few milliseconds to billions of years. Usually, the less stable a nucleus is, the shorter its half-life and the faster it decays. Each radioisotope has a unique half-life. Table 9.4.1 lists the half-lives of some radioisotopes.

Table 9.4.1 Half-Lives of Some Radioisotopes	
Isotope	**Half-Life**
C-14	5,730 years
U-238	4.51×10^9 years
Th-234	24.1 days
Pa-234	6.75 hours
Ra-226	1620 years
Po-214	0.00016 seconds
Bi-210	5.0 days
H-3	12.3 years

Link to ➤➤➤

Physics

The elements produced in particle accelerators typically have extremely short half-lives. These elements are usually not around long enough for their chemical properties to be confirmed. However, some artificially created elements do not decay as quickly. The longer lives of these elements help to confirm theories about the nucleus.

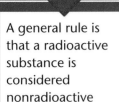

A general rule is that a radioactive substance is considered nonradioactive after 10 half-lives.

It is easiest to understand half-life by using a diagram like the one in Figure 9.4.1. Suppose you have a sample of some radioisotope. Every atom of the sample is radioactive, but no atoms have decayed yet. After 1 half-life, half of the sample has decayed. The other half is still radioactive. After 2 half-lives, half of the radioactive half has decayed. Now only a quarter of the original sample is still radioactive. Figure 9.4.1 shows this process for iodine-131, which has a half-life of 8.02 days.

Figure 9.4.1 *A 1.00-g sample of radioactive iodine-131 undergoes beta decay to become the stable isotope, xenon-131. After 1 half-life, or 8.02 days, $\frac{1}{2}$ of the original sample is still iodine-131. After 2 half-lives, $\frac{1}{4}$ of the original sample is iodine-131. After 3 half-lives, $\frac{1}{8}$ of the original sample is iodine-131.*

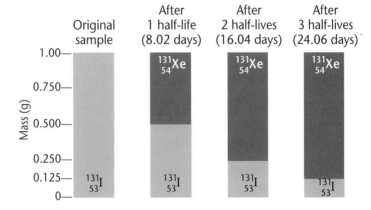

This decay process is like dividing a number by 2 again and again. The number keeps getting smaller, but never reaches zero. Even after several half-lives, there is still a small amount of radioactive substance left in a sample.

Because half-life is constant, you can predict how much of a sample will still be radioactive after a certain time. The fraction of the original radioisotope remaining after n half-lives is $(\frac{1}{2})^n$, as shown in Table 9.4.2. The term $(\frac{1}{2})^n$ means $\frac{1}{2}$ to the power of n. For $n = 4$, $(\frac{1}{2})^4 = (\frac{1}{2})(\frac{1}{2})(\frac{1}{2})(\frac{1}{2}) = \frac{1}{16}$.

Table 9.4.2 Fraction of a Radioisotope Remaining after n Half-Lives	
Number of Half-Lives (n)	**Fraction of Radioisotope Remaining**
1	$(\frac{1}{2})^1 = \frac{1}{2}$ or 0.50
2	$(\frac{1}{2})^2 = \frac{1}{4}$ or 0.25
3	$(\frac{1}{2})^3 = \frac{1}{8}$ or 0.125
4	$(\frac{1}{2})^4 = \frac{1}{16}$ or 0.0625
5	$(\frac{1}{2})^5 = \frac{1}{32}$ or 0.03125
n	$(\frac{1}{2})^n = \frac{1}{2^n}$

After each half-life, the amount of radioisotope left is half the previous amount. Each time, the amount left (as a fraction or decimal) is divided by 2. If you know the original mass of a radioisotope sample, you can predict its mass after n half-lives. Just divide the original mass by 2^n. (This is the same as dividing the original mass by 2 a total of n times.)

Example 1   A sample of bismuth-210 has a mass of 132 g. Its half-life is 5.0 days. What is the mass of bismuth-210 remaining after 20 days?

Read   An original sample of radioactive bismuth is 132 g. None of it has decayed yet. You are asked to give the mass of radioactive bismuth after 20 days.

Plan   As the sample decays, less and less of the sample's mass is bismuth-210. One way to find the remaining bismuth-210 after 20 days is to set up a simple table. At time 0, the mass is 132 g. Find the mass after 1 half-life (5.0 days) by dividing 132 g by 2. Divide this result by 2 to find the mass after 2 half-lives. Continue dividing each new mass by 2 until you have your answer.

Solve   The completed table is shown below.

Time	Number of Half-Lives	Mass Remaining
0	0	132 g
5.0 days	1	66.0 g
10.0 days	2	33.0 g
15.0 days	3	16.5 g
20.0 days	4	8.25 g

After 20.0 days, or 4 half-lives, 8.25 g of the sample is still radioactive bismuth-210. The rest of the sample has decayed. The answer, 8.25 g, can be calculated without making a table. Divide the original mass by 2^n. In this case, $n=4$ since 20 days is 4 half-lives.

$$132 \text{ g} \div 2^4 = 132 \text{ g} \div 16 = 8.25 \text{ g}$$

Reflect   Bismuth-210 decays by emitting a beta particle. The result is an unstable polonium-210 isotope. This radioisotope also decays, but at a slower rate than the bismuth.

Practice   A sample of thorium-234 has a mass of 20.0 g. Its half-life is 24.1 days. What is the mass of thorium-234 remaining after 144.6 days?

Link to ➤➤➤

Earth Science

All natural radioactive elements form in stars much larger than the sun. During the lifetime of a large star, most of the light elements form in the star's core. When the core becomes iron, the star collapses, causing a sudden release of energy. This event is called a supernova. During a supernova, elements heavier than iron are formed.

Radioactive Dating

Half-life is used to estimate the age of very old objects, such as the bone in Figure 9.4.2. Carbon-14 is usually used for this purpose, although other radioisotopes are also used. Carbon-14 has a long half-life of 5,730 years. All living things contain carbon atoms. Most of these are stable carbon-12 atoms. However, a tiny percentage is radioactive carbon-14. When an organism dies, it stops taking in carbon-containing substances. The carbon-14 in its body is no longer replaced. Scientists can measure the amount of carbon-14 in a fossil or in an object that was made from bone or wood. By comparing this to the amount of carbon-14 in living things today, they can estimate when the organism died. In other words, they can estimate how old the object is.

Figure 9.4.2 *A sample is being removed from this bone for carbon dating.*

Example 1	A scientist discovers a fossil that contains $\frac{1}{4}$ the amount of carbon-14 found in living things. About how old is the fossil?
Read	The fraction of carbon-14 remaining in the fossil is $\frac{1}{4}$. You are asked to estimate the age of the fossil, which is how long ago the organism died.
Plan	When an organism dies, it contains the same amount of carbon-14 as living things. According to Table 9.4.2, after 1 half-life, $\frac{1}{2}$ of this carbon-14 remains. After 2 half-lives, $\frac{1}{4}$ of the carbon-14 remains.
Solve	This tells you that the carbon-14 in the fossil has been decaying for 2 half-lives. This length of time is 2(5,730 years)=11,460 years.
Reflect	This age is an estimate; it is not exact.
Practice	An ancient tool made from bone contains $\frac{1}{8}$ the carbon-14 found in living things. About how old is it?

The dating of objects is just one application of radioisotopes. Radioisotopes and their radiation are used in many other ways in society. The rest of this lesson discusses applications in medicine and food preservation. Lesson 5 describes how radioisotopes are used to create nuclear power.

Nuclear Medicine

Radiation has characteristics that are useful in identifying and treating health problems. X-ray technology is one example. X-ray images can show where and how a bone is broken. They are used to identify many other types of health problems. A CAT scan is a special kind of X-ray technology. It takes many X-ray images from different angles. These images are combined to create a cross section of a particular part of the body. CAT scans are used to identify injuries or diseases, especially ones related to the head or brain.

Radiotracer

A tiny amount of a radioactive compound that is swallowed or injected so its path through the body can be traced

Radiotherapy

The treatment of cancer by directing a beam of radiation at a specific area in the body or by placing a radioactive substance inside the body

Radioisotopes are also used as **radiotracers.** These are tiny amounts of compounds containing a radioisotope. When a radiotracer is swallowed or injected, its path through the body can be traced. This process can identify some health problems without surgery. Most of the radioisotopes used, such as iodine-131, have a short half-life and quickly become nonradioactive.

Although high levels of radiation exposure can cause cancer, radiation is also used to treat some forms of cancer. Radiation therapy, or **radiotherapy,** treats cancer by directing a beam of radiation at a specific area in the body. Sometimes a radioactive substance is placed inside the body. Radiotherapy can cause fast-growing cancer cells to die, while not harming healthy cells. The kind of radiotherapy, and the choice and quantity of the radioisotope, varies from patient to patient.

Food Preservation

Fresh foods, such as meat and fruit, can spoil quickly because of the presence of mold or bacteria. Radiation can be used to keep these foods from spoiling. As foods are packaged, they are irradiated, or exposed to radiation. This kills mold and bacteria. Once packaged, the food will stay fresh in the store longer. For example, gamma rays from cobalt-60 are used to keep strawberries from getting moldy. Irradiated foods are not radioactive—they have just been exposed to radiation. The radiation passes through them like sunlight through a glass window.

Technology and Society

Radioactive dating is used to estimate the ages of rocks. Potassium-argon dating is one of the most important techniques used by geologists. Radioactive potassium-40 decays to stable argon-40. Potassium-40 has a half-life of 1.25 billion years, so it is useful for dating rocks up to a few billion years old.

Lesson 4   R E V I E W

Word Bank

carbon-14

half-life

radiotracers

On a sheet of paper, write the word from the Word Bank that completes each sentence.

1. The time it takes for half of a radioactive substance to decay is called _____.

2. To estimate the age of fossils that were once living, scientists use _____.

3. Doctors use _____ to detect some medical problems.

On a sheet of paper, write the letter of the answer to each question.

4. About how old is a fossil that contains $\frac{1}{16}$ the amount of carbon-14 in living things?

A 91,680 years   **C** 5,730 years
B 22,920 years   **D** 16 years

5. A radioactive sample has a half-life of 10 days. After 50 days, what fraction of the sample is still radioactive?

A $\frac{1}{50}$ **B** $\frac{1}{32}$ **C** $\frac{1}{16}$ **D** $\frac{1}{10}$

6. A radioactive substance has an original mass of 80.0 g. After 4 half-lives, what mass is radioactive?

A 5.00 g   **B** 10.0 g   **C** 20.0 g   **D** 40.0 g

Critical Thinking

On a sheet of paper, write the answer to each question.

7. Why is radioactive decay so predictable?

8. A sample of radioactive silver-106 has a starting mass of 200. g. After 72 minutes, 25.0 g is still radioactive. What is the half-life of this isotope?

9. Why are some radioisotopes useful for dating old objects, while others are not?

10. How is radiation used to benefit people?

INVESTIGATION 9

Materials

- safety goggles
- 64 pennies
- shoe box with lid

Modeling Radioactive Decay

It is impossible to know when a particular radioactive nucleus will decay. However, it is possible to tell how many nuclei in a large sample will decay over time. How do radioactive nuclei decay over a certain number of half-lives? In this investigation, you will model radioactive decay.

Procedure

1. Make a data table like the one below.

Number of Shakes	Pennies Removed	Pennies Remaining
0	0	64
1		
2		
3		

2. Put on safety goggles. Place the pennies in the shoe box and put the lid on the box. Shake the box for 5 seconds. **Safety Alert: Hold the lid firmly in place to keep the pennies inside the box.**

3. Remove the lid. Observe the pennies that are heads-up. Remove these pennies from the box. Count them and record this number. Then calculate and record the number of pennies remaining in the box.

4. Replace the lid on the box. Shake the box again for 5 seconds. Repeat step 3.

Continued on next page

5. Continue shaking the box, removing heads-up pennies, and recording data until all pennies are removed from the box. Add rows to your data table as necessary.

Cleanup/Disposal

Return the materials. Then wash your hands.

Analysis

1. Graph your results. On the *x* axis, show the number of times the shoe box is shaken. On the *y* axis, show the number of pennies remaining after each shake. Connect your data points, making a smooth line.

2. How does the number of remaining pennies change with the number of shakes?

3. What change in a radioactive substance does each shaking of the box represent? Explain your answer.

Conclusions

1. Based on your graph, how many shakes were required before 32 (or fewer) pennies remained? Before 16 (or fewer) remained? Before 4 (or fewer) remained?

2. Based on the definition of half-life, how many shakes should be required for just 1 penny to remain?

3. How many shakes were actually required before you were left with 1 penny in your box?

4. Do your answers for questions 2 and 3 differ? If so, what might have caused the difference?

Explore Further

Repeat the procedure with a larger number of coins or other objects. Compare the new graph with the original one. Observe any change in your results.

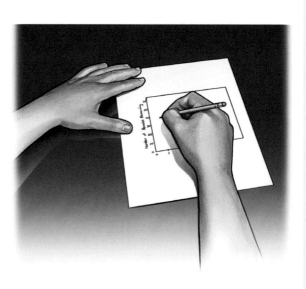

Mass defect

The difference between the mass of a nucleus and the sum of the masses of its particles

Fission reaction

The splitting of a large nucleus into two or more smaller pieces

Nuclear reactions release a large amount of energy—much more per gram of reactant than chemical reactions. For isotopes with short half-lives, this energy output does not last long. For isotopes with long half-lives, the rate of energy output is slow and gets slower. In the 1930s, scientists discovered a way to capture a large amount of nuclear energy over a long time. They split a large atom by bombardment and created a chain reaction.

Fission

Scientists discovered that the mass of a nucleus is slightly less than the sum of the masses of its protons and neutrons. For example, the mass of 8 protons and 8 neutrons is 2.67804×10^{-23} g. The mass of an oxygen-16 nucleus is slightly less: 2.65535×10^{-23} g. The difference in mass between a nucleus and the sum of its individual particles is called the **mass defect**. In this case, the mass defect is 2.269×10^{-25} g—a very small mass. An atom's mass defect is responsible for holding the nucleus together. When a nucleus is formed from individual particles, this mass amount is converted to energy and released. The energy released can be calculated using Albert Einstein's equation:

$$E = mc^2$$

energy released = (mass lost)(speed of light)^2

The speed of light, c, is 3.00×10^8 m/s, so c^2 is a very large number. Even a tiny mass of matter, m, multiplied by c^2, equals a huge amount of energy.

A **fission reaction** is the splitting of a large nucleus into two or more smaller pieces. For example, a heavy atom like uranium-235 can be split into two nuclei. When this happens, some of the mass of the original nucleus is changed into energy. The amount of this energy is $E = mc^2$. Because a portion of mass becomes energy during fission, the law of conservation of mass does not hold true. Some matter is destroyed, and a great deal of energy is created from it.

A uranium-235 nucleus is typically split by bombarding it with a neutron, $_{0}^{1}n$. Here is one possible fission equation:

$$_{92}^{235}U + _{0}^{1}n \rightarrow _{56}^{141}Ba + _{36}^{92}Kr + 3(_{0}^{1}n) + energy$$

The bombarding neutron is absorbed by the uranium atom. This makes the atom very unstable, and it breaks apart. Two smaller atoms, barium-141 and krypton-92, are formed. Three neutrons are formed as well. Energy in the form of heat and gamma rays is produced. Although the mass numbers and atomic numbers balance, the mass defect is converted to energy. Whenever an unstable isotope becomes more stable, some of the mass involved in this change is converted to energy.

This bombardment reaction is different than the ones in Lesson 3, where the product was a larger atom. In the case of fission, the products of bombardment are smaller atoms. For a given reactant, such as uranium-235, there can be more than one possible fission reaction.

Nuclear Power

As more atoms undergo fission, more energy is created. Nuclear power plants, like the one in Figure 9.5.1, are based on this idea.

Figure 9.5.1 *More than 100 nuclear power plants in the United States today are producing about 20% of the country's electricity. Many other countries have nuclear power plants.*

Nuclear power plants produce electrical energy that is sent to nearby communities. In most of these plants, this energy comes from the continuous fission of uranium-235. Figure 9.5.2 shows this nuclear reaction. A uranium atom is first bombarded by a neutron. It splits according to the reaction on page 366. Each neutron that is produced starts a fission reaction with another uranium atom. The neutrons that are produced start more fission reactions. As long as there is available uranium-235, the fission process continues in a chain reaction. Each time fission occurs, energy is given off.

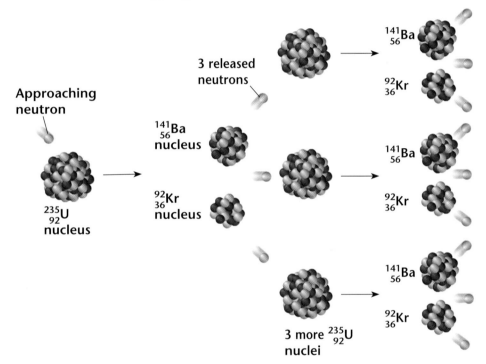

Figure 9.5.2 *During a fission chain reaction, each daughter neutron bombards another uranium atom. This causes the atom to split, releasing more energy and more neutrons.*

Inside the power plant, this nuclear energy is converted to electricity in a series of steps. Fission chain reactions occur inside a **nuclear reactor,** shown in Figure 9.5.3. A reactor has a fuel chamber that is surrounded by steel and concrete. The chamber contains fuel rods made of uranium-235. These rods are surrounded by water. As the uranium-235 undergoes fission, neutrons and energy are produced. The water around the rods heats up. This heat is transferred out of the chamber to a steam generator. Here, the heat causes water to boil, creating steam. The steam turns a turbine, which causes an electric generator to produce electricity. The steam then condenses and returns to the steam generator to be boiled again.

The speed of the chain reaction in the fuel chamber is carefully controlled. Each fuel rod has a nearby control rod that can slide up and down. When the control rods are down, they absorb extra neutrons. This slows the reaction rate. When the control rods are up, the reaction goes faster. Keeping the nuclear reaction at a safe rate is important. An uncontrolled chain reaction can produce so much heat that the steel and concrete around the fuel chamber melts. When this happens, ionizing radiation escapes into the environment. This is called a **meltdown.**

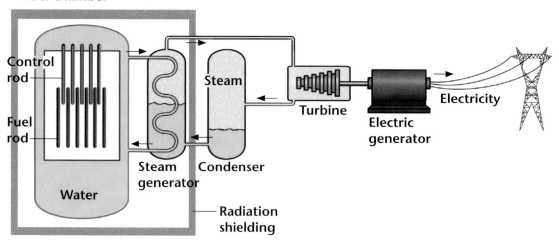

Figure 9.5.3 *In a nuclear power plant, energy from fission is converted to heat. The heat is used to boil water. The resulting steam turns a turbine, which runs an electric generator.*

Besides the danger of a meltdown, nuclear power plants produce radioactive waste. Control rods and fuel rods are made of radioisotopes with long half-lives. When these rods are replaced, the old rods must be stored for hundreds of years before they are considered safe. However, nuclear power plants produce little or no air pollution. Compare nuclear power to coal-burning power plants. Both produce electricity from heat. The difference is the energy source. Nuclear power plants use uranium or plutonium fission to heat water. Coal-burning plants burn coal to heat water. Burning coal causes air pollution, but does not produce radioactive waste. Coal-burning plants use great amounts of coal for fuel, while nuclear power plants use less natural resources. Besides fission reactions and fossil fuels like coal, there are many other sources of energy. Electricity can also be generated by using solar panels, wind turbines, hydroelectric dams, crop waste, underground heat, and hydrogen fuel.

Fusion

You have learned about three types of nuclear reactions so far:

- radioactive decay, or the natural process of radioisotopes emitting energy or particles
- nuclear bombardment reactions that create large atoms
- fission reactions that split large atoms by bombardment

There is a fourth type of nuclear reaction:

- **fusion reactions** that join two small atoms by bombardment

A fusion reaction is the joining of two small atoms to form a larger one. Fusion only occurs under high temperatures and pressures. A common fusion reaction is the creation of a helium atom from two hydrogen atoms. The equation is shown below with nuclei models.

$$^2_1\text{H} \quad + \quad ^3_1\text{H} \quad \rightarrow \quad ^4_2\text{He} \quad + \quad ^1_0n \quad + \quad \text{energy}$$

The energy produced by fission and fusion reactions is greater than the energy produced by chemical reactions. This is because chemical reactions involve electrons and electrical force. This force is weaker than the force that binds protons and neutrons together in the nucleus.

In fusion, a very small fraction of mass is converted into heat and other radiation. Again, the law of conservation of mass is not true in nuclear reactions. Instead, scientists have combined the laws of conservation of mass and conservation of energy. The law of conservation of mass-energy says that the total amount of mass and energy in the universe is constant. The mass lost in a nuclear reaction is not destroyed, but converted to energy. The combined amount of mass and energy does not change when one changes into the other.

Fusion releases a large quantity of energy. Fusion reactions occur naturally in stars. Stars are mostly hydrogen and helium. Because these nuclei are at extremely high temperatures and pressures, they collide at high speeds and fuse. As a result, stars emit tremendous quantities of light and other forms of radiation. Fusion in the sun produces a constant supply of electromagnetic radiation, supporting life on the earth. The amount of energy produced by the fusion of hydrogen is much more than that produced by an equal mass of uranium in fission.

Because of the energy produced by fusion, the idea of a fusion-based power supply is very attractive. Scientists around the world are working to design this technology to replace fission-based power plants. There are many advantages to using fusion as a source of power:

- A large quantity of energy can be produced by fusion without using a chain reaction. To increase the energy produced, simply add more hydrogen atoms. To decrease the energy produced, turn off the hydrogen supply. There is no chance of an uncontrolled reaction causing a meltdown, as with fission reactors.
- The reactants of fusion—hydrogen isotopes—are easily found. Hydrogen makes up 99% of the matter in the universe. It is present in the earth's abundant water supply. In contrast, the uranium used in fission reactors is a rare element in the earth.

- The products of fusion—stable helium atoms and neutrons—are not radioactive. Although radiation in the form of energy is also produced, it would not need to be stored. This energy would be converted to electricity.

The major disadvantage of fusion is that it requires very high temperatures and pressures. These conditions are needed to force the hydrogen nuclei to fuse. Scientists are researching ways to safely create fusion conditions. Perhaps fusion will be a major energy source in this century.

▼◂▲▼◂▲▼◂▲▼◂▲▼◂▲▼◂▲▼◂▲▼◂▲▼◂▲▼◂▲▼◂▲▼◂▲▼◂▲▼

Science at Work

Radiation Protection Technician

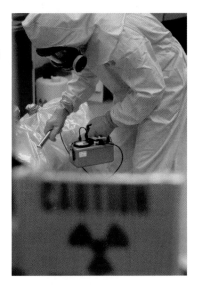

Radiation protection technicians control and monitor the use of radioactive materials and radiation. They work in hospitals and research institutes where nuclear medicine is performed. They keep records of the ordering and delivery of radioactive materials. They check labs and wards for contamination—for radioactive materials that have leaked or been spilled. They also collect and temporarily store radioactive waste. Radiation protection technicians watch for unsafe practices. They help clean up contaminated areas.

Radiation protection technicians need a strong background in physics. Knowledge of chemistry and biology is also valuable. Radiation detectors such as Geiger counters are standard equipment, so an understanding of electronics is helpful. Most technicians have a bachelor's degree in physics or chemistry.

Lesson 5   R E V I E W

On a sheet of paper, write either *fission* or *fusion* to complete each sentence.

1. The splitting of a large atom into two or more smaller atoms is a _____ reaction.

2. The joining of two atoms to produce a larger atom is a _____ reaction.

3. Nuclear power plants use _____ chain reactions to produce electricity.

On a sheet of paper, write the letter of the answer that completes each sentence.

4. The mass of a nucleus is _____ the sum of the masses of its protons and neutrons.

    A the same as   **C** slightly more than
    B slightly less than   **D** defined as

5. When a nucleus is formed or split, _____ is converted to energy and released.

    A the speed of light   **C** an electron
    B each proton and neutron   **D** the mass defect

6. The law of conservation of mass is true for _____ .

    A chemical and nuclear reactions
    B fusion and fission reactions
    C fusion reactions, but not fission reactions
    D chemical reactions, but not nuclear reactions

Critical Thinking

On a sheet of paper, write the answer to each question.

7. Compare the reactants and products of fission and fusion.

8. Explain a fission chain reaction.

9. How does the law of conservation of mass-energy apply to nuclear reactions?

10. Give one advantage and one disadvantage of each of these energy sources: fission, coal burning, and fusion.

Materials

◆ 70 dominoes

Modeling Fission Chain Reactions

When uranium-235 absorbs a neutron, 20 different fission reactions are possible. One such reaction is

$$^{235}U + {}_0^1 n \rightarrow {}^{134}Xe + {}^{100}Sr + 2({}_0^1 n)$$

Uranium fission reactions usually produce two or three neutrons, which go on to start other reactions. As more neutrons are produced, more reactions occur, producing even more neutrons. Too many reactions happening at once create an uncontrolled chain reaction. By removing some neutrons, the chain reaction can be controlled. How does removing neutrons affect a chain reaction? In this investigation, you will model a two-neutron reaction producing uncontrolled and controlled chain reactions.

Procedure

1. Write a procedure for modeling a fission chain reaction in which each splitting nucleus produces two neutrons. Use dominoes for modeling the reaction.

2. Think of a way to model an uncontrolled reaction and then a controlled reaction. (Hint: An uncontrolled reaction might show many dominoes falling. A controlled reaction might show a limited number of dominoes falling.)

3. Have your procedure approved by your teacher. Then set up and try your model.

Cleanup/Disposal

Return the dominoes. Then wash your hands.

Continued on next page

Analysis

1. How many dominoes fell over in the model of the uncontrolled reaction? How is this like an uncontrolled fission reaction?

2. How many dominoes fell over in the model of the controlled reaction? How is this like a controlled fission reaction?

Conclusions

1. Did your models accurately represent fission? Explain your answer.

2. How did your models of a controlled and uncontrolled reaction differ?

Explore Further

Think of another way to model fission reactions. Create your models. How do they compare to the domino models?

Radioimmunoassay

Radiotracers have made it possible to diagnose many medical disorders. For example, holmium-166 is used to examine liver tumors. Iron-59 is used to study the spleen. Iodine-131 has long been used to diagnose diseases of the thyroid gland. These radioisotopes have short half-lives, and small amounts are given to patients.

Another tracer technique does not involve placing radioisotopes inside the patient. Instead, it requires only a sample of blood or other fluid from the patient. This technique is called radioimmunoassay, or RIA. It was developed by Rosalyn Yalow and Solomon Berson in the late 1950s. RIA uses tiny quantities of radioactive material. This reduces the problem of tracking and disposing of large amounts of radioisotopes.

RIA uses reactions that take place in the human immune system. The immune system makes antibodies, which are proteins that react with and fight antigens. Antigens are foreign molecules that activate the immune system. In RIA, radioisotopes are attached to antigens and used as "tags." A known amount of tagged antigens is mixed with known amounts of antibodies. The mixture of antigens and antibodies is separated into several samples. Varying amounts of untagged antigens are added to the samples. The tagged and untagged antigens compete

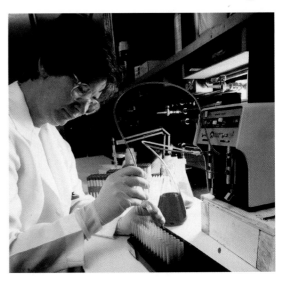

to react with the antibodies. Fewer tagged antigens react with antibodies as the amount of untagged antigens increases. For each sample, the radiation from the tagged antigens is measured. This indicates the amount of untagged antigens in the sample. This information is used to find an unknown antigen concentration in a patient sample.

RIA is so sensitive that antigen amounts equal to a trillionth of a mole can be detected. RIA is used to diagnose allergies and detect viruses in donated blood. RIA is also used to determine if certain hormone levels in the blood are normal.

1. How does RIA differ from other radiotracer techniques?

2. What type of reaction does RIA use?

3. What does measuring radioactivity in RIA show?

- Radiation is energy or particles that can travel through space.

- All forms of radiant energy are found in the electromagnetic spectrum. The frequency of electromagnetic waves increases as wavelength decreases.

- Ionizing radiation, such as ultraviolet rays, X-rays, gamma rays, alpha particles, and beta particles, can cause damage to living cells.

- Nonionizing radiation, such as microwaves, sound waves, infrared rays, and radio waves, do not ionize atoms.

- Transmutations occur when unstable atoms of one element change into a different element by releasing or absorbing radiation.

- For all nuclear equations, the sums of the atomic numbers on both sides of the equation are equal. Also, the sums of the mass numbers on both sides of the equation are equal.

- Radioactive decay is used to estimate the age of ancient artifacts. This dating is possible because an isotope's half-life is unique and its decay is predictable.

- Radiation is used to diagnose and treat many diseases. It is also used to kill mold and bacteria on foods.

- Half-life is the amount of time it takes for one-half of a radioactive sample to decay.

- Fission is the splitting of a large nucleus into smaller ones.

- Fusion is the joining of two small nuclei into a larger one.

- Fission chain reactions are used to produce electricity in nuclear power plants. Fusion is not currently used to produce electricity because of the high temperatures and pressures required.

Vocabulary

beta particle, 346
cancer, 340
electromagnetic radiation, 338
electromagnetic
  spectrum, 339
fission reaction, 365
frequency, 338
fusion reaction, 369
gamma rays, 340
half-life, 356
hertz, 338

infrared rays, 340
ionizing radiation, 340
mass defect, 365
meltdown, 368
nonionizing radiation, 340
nuclear reaction, 338
nuclear reactor, 368
radiant energy, 338
radiation, 338
radioactive, 343
radioactive decay, 343

radioactivity, 343
radioisotope, 343
radiotherapy, 361
radiotracer, 361
Rem, 341
transmutation, 344
transuranium element, 351
ultraviolet rays, 340
wavelength, 338
X-rays, 340

Vocabulary Review

Word Bank

alpha particle

beta particle

electromagnetic spectrum

fission reaction

fusion reaction

half-life

ionizing radiation

mass defect

radioactive decay

radiotracers

transmutation

transuranium element

waves

On a sheet of paper, write the word or phrase from the Word Bank that completes each sentence.

1. A(n) _____ occurs when two small atoms join together, producing a large amount of energy.

2. The amount of time required for one-half of a radioactive sample to decay is called _____.

3. A(n) _____ has the symbol $_{-1}^{0}e$.

4. Radiation that is capable of causing damage to living organisms is _____.

5. Radiant energy travels through space in the form of _____.

6. A(n) _____ occurs when one large atom splits, forming small atoms and energy.

7. To diagnose some illnesses, X-rays, CAT scans, and _____ are used.

8. The difference between the mass of a nucleus and the sum of the masses of its particles is the _____.

9. A(n) _____ is any element with an atomic number greater than 92.

10. A(n) _____ occurs when one element is changed into another, producing radiation.

11. The breakdown of an unstable nucleus is _____.

12. A(n) _____ has the symbol $_{2}^{4}\text{He}$.

13. Gamma rays, visible light, and microwaves are part of the _____.

Continued on next page

Concept Review

On a sheet of paper, write the letter of the answer to each question.

14. Why can food exposed to radiation be safely stored for a longer time?

    A Radiation kills mold and bacteria.
    B Radiation reduces contact with air.
    C Radiation lowers food temperature.
    D Radiation improves food appearance.

15. In the following nuclear reaction, what is the missing product?
    $$^{235}_{92}U + ^{1}_{0}n \rightarrow 3(^{1}_{0}n) + ^{142}_{56}Ba + ?$$

    A $^{88}_{36}Kr$ **B** $^{91}_{36}Kr$ **C** $^{89}_{34}Se$ **D** $^{238}_{92}U$

16. Chlorine-39 decays by beta emission. What is the product?

    A $^{39}_{16}S$ **B** $^{40}_{17}Cl$ **C** $^{39}_{18}Ar$ **D** $^{38}_{17}Cl$

17. The half-life of gallium is 13 seconds. What fraction of a gallium-77 sample will remain after 39 seconds?

    A $\frac{1}{2}$ **B** $\frac{1}{3}$ **C** $\frac{1}{6}$ **D** $\frac{1}{8}$

18. A scientist discovers an ancient artifact that has $\frac{1}{32}$ of the original amount of carbon-14. If the half-life of carbon-14 is 5,730 years, about how old is the artifact?

    A 5 years   **B** 32 years   **C** 5,730 years   **D** 28,650 years

Problem Solving

On a sheet of paper, write the missing product in each nuclear reaction.

19. $^{234}_{90}Th \rightarrow$ beta particle $+ ?$

20. $^{12}_{6}C + ^{244}_{96}Cm \rightarrow ^{254}_{102}No + ?$

On a sheet of paper, copy each table. Then fill in the missing information for the given radioisotope and half-life.

21. Bromine-76 has a half-life of 16 hours.

Time	Number of Half-Lives	Mass of Remaining Bromine-76
0 hours	0	512 g
32 hours		
64 hours		
80 hours		

22. Technetium-99m has a half-life of 6.0 hours.

Time	Number of Half-Lives	Mass of Remaining Technetium-99m
0 hours	0	25.6 g
6 hours		
18 hours		
24 hours		

Critical Thinking

On a sheet of paper, write the answer to each question.

23. Explain the spectrum of radiant energy in terms of wavelength, frequency, and the ability to ionize other substances.

24. How is the energy released by a nuclear fission reaction converted to electricity?

25. If you have a sample of a radioactive isotope with a half-life of 10 days, will it completely decay in 20 days? Explain.

Test-Taking Tip Read test directions carefully. Do not assume that you know what you are supposed to do.

10

Electrons

Neon lights create some of the colorful patterns in this photo. The lights are gas-filled tubes. An electric current at one end of a tube causes electrons in the gas to gain energy. When these electrons lose some of the extra energy, light is given off. Different gases produce different colors. In Chapter 10, you will learn about the electrons in atoms and how they are arranged.

Organize Your Thoughts

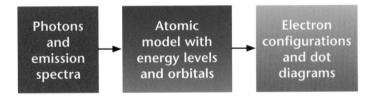

Photons and emission spectra → Atomic model with energy levels and orbitals → Electron configurations and dot diagrams

Goals for Learning

◆ To describe electron movement using Bohr's atomic model

◆ To explain energy levels and orbitals in atoms

◆ To understand electron configurations and the order of filling orbitals

◆ To write electron configurations for large atoms

◆ To write abbreviated electron configurations based on noble gases

◆ To draw dot diagrams showing the valence electrons of atoms and ions

After reading this lesson, you should be able to

◆ describe the contributions of Planck and Einstein

◆ tell what Bohr studied and how he changed the model of the atom

◆ explain how electrons are able to move from one energy level to another

◆ list the four types of orbitals and describe some of their shapes

◆ explain how orbitals are named by energy level and shape

Photoelectric effect

An effect that occurs when electrons are emitted from the surface of a metal as light strikes the metal

Photon

A bundle or package of energy

The model of the atom has changed many times, as Chapter 8 described. Niels Bohr's planetary model placed the nucleus at the center of the atom, with electrons orbiting in a relatively big space around it. By the 1920s, however, scientists knew there was more to this model. The movement and location of electrons are more complex than simple circular paths.

The Photoelectric Effect

To understand the nature of electrons in the atomic model, you need to start with energy and how it relates to matter. In 1900, a physicist named Max Planck was studying the radiation produced by a very hot piece of metal. From Chapter 9, you know that electromagnetic radiation is energy that travels through space in the form of waves. Planck explained that every form of electromagnetic radiation has a unique quantity of energy that depends on its wave frequency. The energy of a wave is related to its frequency by this equation:

$$E = h\nu$$

E is energy, ν is frequency, and h is a constant called Planck's constant. The higher the frequency of the radiation, the higher its energy.

In 1905, Albert Einstein added to Planck's work. Einstein published a paper about the **photoelectric effect.** This effect occurs when electrons are emitted from the surface of a metal as light strikes the metal. Einstein proposed that light is not a continuous form of energy, but comes in bundles or packages called **photons.** When light photons strike metal atoms, some electrons come free. Not all light can do this. Recall that electromagnetic waves of higher frequency have higher energy. Light must have a certain frequency to cause the photoelectric effect. Einstein received a Nobel Prize for this explanation.

Einstein also proved that energy has some characteristics of matter, and matter has some characteristics of energy. This is called the dual nature of light/matter. *Dual* means "double."

Energy Levels

Niels Bohr expanded on these ideas by studying the **emission spectra** of different substances. When a gaseous substance is placed in a glass tube and energized, or charged, with electricity, the gas glows brightly. When this light is viewed through a prism, the colors in the light are separated. Each line of color corresponds to a specific frequency and a specific amount of energy. The arrangement of separate colors is called an emission spectrum. Hydrogen's spectrum is shown in Figure 10.1.1. Every element and compound produces a unique spectrum. It identifies the substance like a fingerprint.

In 1913, Bohr studied the emission spectrum of hydrogen. Hydrogen is the simplest atom, having only one proton and one electron. In its spectrum, there are four separate colors, not a continuous blend of all colors, like a rainbow. Why only four colors? Bohr proposed that the electron of the hydrogen atom moves from one level of the atom to another. Each level is a certain distance from the nucleus. Each move of the electron to a different level involves a specific change in energy. The electron has to gain this amount of energy (from the electricity in the tube) to jump to a higher level. When the electron drops down to the original level, it releases the same amount of energy in the form of light. The amount of energy released when the electron moves to a lower level is represented by a unique color line in the emission spectrum. If any amount of light energy could be released, the emission spectrum would be a rainbow of many colors. But only certain colors are emitted. This shows that electrons can have only certain values of energy.

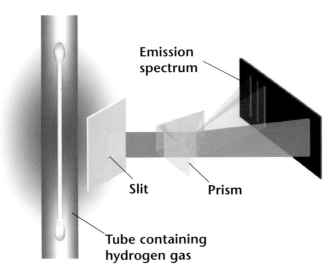

Emission spectrum

Slit

Prism

Tube containing hydrogen gas

Figure 10.1.1 *When atoms in hydrogen gas absorb energy, they release it in the form of light. Hydrogen's emission spectrum is seen as four separate lines of color.*

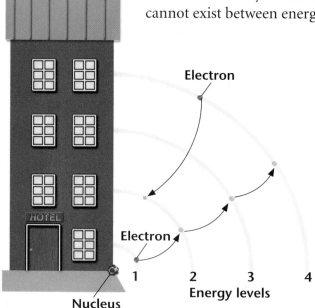

Bohr believed that these certain values of energy correspond to specific levels in an atom. He called these levels **energy levels.** He believed an atom has energy levels, or areas of space where electrons can move. Bohr believed that electrons orbit the nucleus at certain distances that correspond to these levels. The level with the lowest energy is closest to the nucleus. As levels increase in energy, they are farther from the nucleus.

In Bohr's planetary model, electrons orbit the nucleus at these certain distances. Energy levels are like the floors in a hotel, as shown in Figure 10.1.2. An elevator can take you from one floor to any other floor, higher or lower, but you cannot stop between floors. Electrons occupy energy levels. They can move from one level to another by absorbing or releasing energy. However, they cannot exist between energy levels.

Energy level

An area of space where electrons can move

Figure 10.1.2 *Electrons move between energy levels of an atom like an elevator moves between floors of a hotel. To move to a higher level, an electron must absorb a certain amount of energy. To move to a lower level, it must release a certain amount of energy.*

❋ ❋

Technology and Society

Fireworks have been around for hundreds of years, beginning with their development in China. Fireworks contain materials that emit certain colors of light when the electrons in the atoms move to lower energy levels. Sodium produces a yellow color. Compounds of calcium produce an orange color. Barium produces green, and copper produces blue.

Other scientists began to work with Bohr's model of energy levels. They realized that electrons do not travel in circular paths. In fact, it is impossible to predict where an electron is at a given time. Instead, scientists began describing electrons in terms of their *probable* location around the nucleus. The probable location of electrons is a region of space around the nucleus. Because electrons can be in any part of this region, it is usually drawn as a fuzzy **electron cloud.** Imagine taking pictures of hydrogen's one electron as it travels about the nucleus. If you took a million pictures, you would find that the electron is all over the place. It is usually near the nucleus, but occasionally, it is far away. If you plotted all of the electron's positions, it might look like Figure 10.1.3.

Figure 10.1.3 *The probable location of electrons can be represented as a fuzzy cloud around the nucleus. Each dot represents a possible location. There are no definite boundaries to this cloud.*

Sublevels and Orbitals

The emission spectra of atoms with many electrons are more complex. In these emission spectra, some color lines are very close together, as shown in Figure 10.1.4. They indicate small changes in energy corresponding to smaller levels, or **sublevels,** within each energy level. Sublevels within a level are close in energy. Electrons can travel from sublevel to sublevel or from energy level to energy—or any combination.

Figure 10.1.4 *The emission spectrum of neon shows clusters of color lines. Each cluster represents one energy level. Each line within a cluster represents a change from one sublevel to another.*

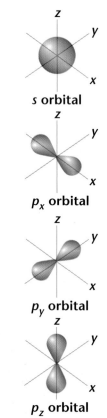

Figure 10.1.5
_Electrons travel
outside the nucleus
in orbitals that are
defined by their
energy and shape.
The nucleus is
located where the
x, y, and z axes
meet._

Energy levels have the symbol n. They are numbered 1 to infinity, although most atomic models only show levels $n = 1$ to $n = 7$. The energy level closest to the nucleus is $n = 1$. Each energy level has a certain number of sublevels. The first four sublevels have letter names: s, p, d, or f. Each sublevel is made up of a certain number of **orbitals.** An orbital is a region of space that is described by a certain shape. The shape shows the likely location of an electron within that sublevel.

- There is only one orbital in the s sublevel. This s orbital has a sphere, or ball shape, as shown in Figure 10.1.5.
- There are three orbitals in the p sublevel: p_x, p_y, and p_z. A p orbital is shaped like a peanut shell. Each one is centered on a different axis in an xyz graph, as shown in Figure 10.1.5. Together, these are called the p orbitals.
- There are five orbitals in the d sublevel. They have varying shapes and are usually grouped together.
- There are seven orbitals in the f sublevel. They have complex shapes and are usually grouped together.

Energy level 1 is closest to the nucleus. Energy levels that have higher values of n are higher in energy and contain more sublevels. Electrons in an orbital have a specific energy that corresponds closely with its sublevel (and energy level). Each orbital has a name that tells you its energy level ($n = 1, 2, 3$, etc.) and its sublevel (s, p, d, or f).

- Energy level 1 has only one sublevel, s. This sublevel has only one orbital. This orbital has the name $1s$, which tells you it is a ball-shaped s orbital in energy level 1.
- Energy level 2 has two sublevels, s and p. It has a total of four orbitals. One is an s orbital named $2s$. The others are p orbitals named $2p_x$, $2p_y$, and $2p_z$. Figure 10.1.6 on the next page shows how the orbitals in this level might look.
- Energy level 3 has three sublevels: s, p, and d. It has a total of nine orbitals. One is $3s$. Three are $3p_x$, $3p_y$, and $3p_z$. The other five are $3d$ orbitals.
- Energy level 4 has all four sublevels: s, p, d, and f. It has 16 orbitals: $4s$, $4p_x$, $4p_y$, $4p_z$, plus five $4d$ orbitals and seven $4f$ orbitals.

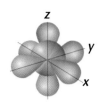

Figure 10.1.6
Energy level 2 has one s orbital and three p orbitals.

Table 10.1.1 summarizes the orbitals in the first four energy levels. Energy levels 5, 6, and 7 are not shown, but each has all four sublevels.

Table 10.1.1 Some Energy Levels and Their Orbitals			
Energy Level, n	Sublevels	Orbital Names	Number of Orbitals
1	s	1s	1
2	s, p	2s, 2p (three of these)	4
3	s, p, d	3s, 3p (three), 3d (five)	9
4	s, p, d, f	4s, 4p (three), 4d (five), 4f (seven)	16

Compare energy levels again to floors in a hotel. The orbitals in an energy level are like rooms. The first floor, energy level 1, has only one room: the 1s room. The second floor has four rooms: a 2s room and three 2p rooms. The third floor has nine rooms: a 3s room, three 3p rooms, and five 3d rooms. This pattern continues for each floor. Electrons can move from a room on one floor to any other room on any other floor. To go to a room with a lower energy, electrons must release energy. To go to a room with a higher energy, electrons must gain energy. Electrons could even gain enough energy to leave the atom altogether.

Express Lab 10

Materials
- safety goggles
- different brands of wintergreen mints, broken in half
- pliers
- transparent tape

Procedure
1. Put on safety goggles.

2. Wrap each jaw of the pliers with tape.

3. Make the room as dark as possible.

4. Place a mint between the jaws of the pliers. Closely watch the broken edge of the mint as you crush it. Record your observations.

5. Repeat step 4 with the other mints.

Analysis

1. What did you observe when you crushed the mints?

2. How do you explain this observation?

The Environment: Solar Cells

Most calculators these days do not need batteries. So how do they work? Do you plug them into an outlet? No. Most calculators contain solar cells. Solar cells use the photoelectric effect to change light into electricity. Most solar cells contain elements such as silicon. These elements are called semiconductors because they conduct electricity better than a nonmetal does but not as well as a metal. Conductivity can be controlled in a semiconductor by adding impurities, such as phosphorus. A phosphorus atom contains one more electron than a silicon atom does. When sunlight shines on an impure semiconductor, many of these extra electrons are released, forming an electric current.

Solar cells can be used to operate items that are expensive or impractical to operate with another source of electricity. Another important advantage is that using solar cells does not pollute the environment. They do not use electricity that is produced

by burning fossil fuels. However, solar cells require either constant sunlight or some way to store the electricity.

1. In what geographical areas might you have difficulty using a solar cell to produce electricity for use in homes and businesses?

2. Why might a solar cell be used to light a road sign in a desert?

3. How is using solar cells better for the environment than using electricity from a wall outlet?

Technology and Society

Have you walked through an automatic door anytime recently? These doors work because of photoelectric cells. Because these cells use an electric current to "see," they are commonly called *electric eyes*. In addition to automatic doors, electric eyes act as switches and are used in burglar alarms. They can measure amounts of light and can adjust light meters and cameras.

Word Bank

emission spectrum
orbital
photoelectric effect

On a sheet of paper, write the word or phrase from the Word Bank that completes each sentence.

1. A(n)_____ is an electron region described by its shape and energy.

2. When electrons move from a higher to a lower energy level, energy is released and a(n) _____ can be produced.

3. When certain light strikes a metal, electrons are emitted from the surface because of the _____.

On a sheet of paper, write the letter of the answer to each question.

4. Which of the following is *not* a possible orbital?

   A 4*f*   **B** 5*s*   **C** 1*p*   **D** 6*p*

5. Which of the following is not an orbital in energy level 3?

   A 3*s*   **B** 3*p*   **C** 3*d*   **D** 3*f*

6. How many total orbitals are in energy levels 1 through 3?

   A 9   **B** 14   **C** 4   **D** 30

Critical Thinking

On a sheet of paper, write the answer to each question.

7. What makes the three 3*p* orbitals different from each other? What do they have in common?

8. Describe Bohr's planetary model.

9. How did scientists improve Bohr's model?

10. What is the lowest energy level that has a *d* orbital? An *f* orbital?

Materials

- safety goggles
- lab coat or apron
- 7 index cards
- 7 wood splints or wood-handled swabs
- small sample of each compound listed in the data table
- beaker
- distilled water
- Bunsen burner

Colored Flames and Electrons

Sometimes laboratory instruments are required to identify an element by its emission spectrum. However, some elements produce colors you can see when their compounds are placed in a flame. Are the results of such tests clear enough to identify substances? In this investigation, you will use flame tests to identify an unknown compound.

Procedure

1. Make a data table like the one shown here. Then label each index card with the name of a compound from the table.

Compound	Flame Color
lithium chloride	
potassium chloride	
sodium chloride	
strontium chloride	
calcium chloride	
barium chloride	
unknown	

2. Put on safety goggles and a lab coat or apron.

3. Obtain a small sample of each compound. Use the labeled cards to carefully carry the samples to your work area.

4. Pour some distilled water into the beaker. Place the 7 splints in the water. Light the burner. **Safety Alert: Be careful around an open flame. Tie back long hair and loose clothing. Never reach across a flame. Do not leave the flame unattended.**

5. Remove one splint from the water. Dip the tip of the soaked end into the sample of lithium chloride crystals.

6. Place the crystals into the burner flame. Observe and record the color of the flame. **Safety Alert: Do not hold the splint in the flame after observing the compound's flame color. Do not allow the wood to begin burning.**

7. Repeat steps 5 and 6 for each compound in the table, including the unknown.

Cleanup/Disposal

Return all equipment. Place the splints and unused samples in the proper waste containers. Clean your work area. Wash your hands.

Analysis

1. Why doesn't the chloride ion affect the color of the flame?

2. How does the emission spectrum of an element relate to the colors produced?

Conclusions

1. What is the identity of your unknown compound?

2. Explain how you identified your unknown compound.

Explore Further

Repeat the investigation using crystals of copper(II) chloride. What color is the copper flame?

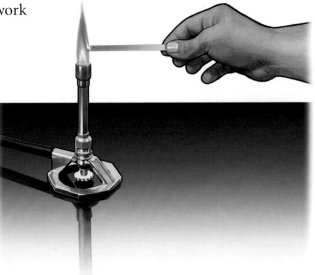

What makes some substances react violently with water, while others do not react at all? In all chemical reactions, atoms share, give, or take electrons. How electrons are arranged in an atom is the key to understanding how the atom reacts. The arrangement of electrons in an atom's energy levels is its **electron configuration.** An atom's electron configuration gives a specific "address" for each of its electrons. There are two main rules for determining the electron configuration of an atom.

Rule 1. Each orbital can hold a maximum of 2 electrons.

Rule 2. Electrons fill orbitals that have the lowest energy first. This is called the **Aufbau principle.**

To return to the hotel analogy, each room (orbital) can hold only two people (electrons). The rooms are filled starting with the first floor (energy level 1) and moving up. On each floor, *s* rooms are filled before *p* rooms, and *p* rooms are filled before *d* rooms, etc.

Row 1 Elements

Row 1 of the periodic table contains hydrogen and helium. The electrons of these elements are in the orbital in energy level 1. This energy level is closest to the nucleus and is lowest in energy. It is also the smallest level, with only a 1*s* orbital. To determine the electron configuration of hydrogen or helium, find the number of electrons each has and follow the rules above. Remember that an element's atomic number is the number of protons. In neutral atoms, the number of electrons equals the number of protons. Hydrogen's 1 electron occupies the 1*s* orbital. Its electron configuration is written as $1s^1$.

$$1s^1 \leftarrow \text{number of electrons in orbital} = 1$$
$$\leftarrow \text{orbital} = 1s$$

The 1 to the left of the letter *s* is the energy level. The superscript gives the number of electrons in that particular orbital.

Electron configuration

The arrangement of electrons in an atom's orbitals and energy levels

Aufbau principle

A rule stating that electrons fill orbitals that have the lowest energy first

Use the Internet
or other resources
to research
Hund's rule. Write
a paragraph
explaining how
this rule is related
to electron
configurations.

Helium's 2 electrons completely fill orbital $1s$ and energy level 1. The configuration for helium is $1s^2$. Like an address, it shows where helium's electrons are located. Table 10.2.1 gives the electron addresses for the row 1 elements.

Table 10.2.1 Electron Configurations of Row 1 Elements			
Element	Number of Electrons	Orbital with Electrons	Electron Configuration
hydrogen	1	$1s$	$1s^1$
helium	2	$1s$	$1s^2$

The next element on the periodic table, lithium, is in row 2.

Row 2 Elements

The electrons of row 2 elements are in energy levels 1 and 2. There are eight elements in row 2 of the periodic table. Energy level 2 is bigger than the first. It has four orbitals: one $2s$ orbital and the set of three $2p$ orbitals. Since each orbital can hold only 2 electrons, energy level 2 can hold a total of 8 electrons. However, before electrons can fill these four orbitals, they must fill the $1s$ orbital down on level 1 first.

Lithium is the first element in this row, with 3 electrons. Two of them are in the $1s$ orbital. The third electron goes into the next lowest orbital: $2s$. The result is $1s^2 2s^1$. The next element, beryllium, has 4 electrons. They completely fill the $1s$ and $2s$ orbitals: $1s^2 2s^2$. Boron has 5 electrons. Four of them are in the $1s$ and $2s$ orbitals. The fifth one goes into one of the $2p$ orbitals. The result is $1s^2 2s^2 2p^1$. Notice that the p_x, p_y, and p_z orbitals are not written individually. All three are represented by $2p$ in the configuration.

Since there are three $2p$ orbitals, as a set they can hold up to 6 electrons. The configurations for carbon, nitrogen, oxygen, and fluorine are similar to boron's, except they show more electrons in the $2p$ orbitals. Neon is the last element in row 2. It has 10 electrons: $1s^2 2s^2 2p^6$. With neon, the four orbitals of energy level 2 are full. Some row 2 elements and their electron configurations are given in Table 10.2.2 on the next page.

Table 10.2.2 Electron Configurations of Some Row 2 Elements

Table 10.2.2 Electron Configurations of Some Row 2 Elements

Element	Number of Electrons	Orbitals with Electrons	Electron Configuration
beryllium	4	$1s$, $2s$	$1s^2 2s^2$
carbon	6	$1s$, $2s$, $2p_x$, $2p_y$, $2p_z$	$1s^2 2s^2 2p^2$
fluorine	9	$1s$, $2s$, $2p_x$, $2p_y$, $2p_z$	$1s^2 2s^2 2p^5$

Valence electron

An electron in an s or p orbital in the highest energy level of an atom

---

Math Tip

When writing an electron configuration, remember to check the superscripts by adding them. The sum of the superscripts is the total number of electrons in the atom. Compare this sum to the atomic number of the element. The numbers should be the same for neutral atoms.

Row 3 Elements

The elements in row 3 have enough electrons to begin filling energy level 3. This level has nine orbitals: one $3s$, three $3p$, and five $3d$ orbitals. This means energy level 3 can hold a total of 18 electrons. Some electron configurations for row 3 elements are given in Table 10.2.3. You may notice that the configurations in the table do not show $3d$ orbitals. You will see how these orbitals are filled in Lesson 3.

Element	Number of Electrons	Electron Configuration
sodium	11	$1s^2 2s^2 2p^6 3s^1$
aluminum	13	$1s^2 2s^2 2p^6 3s^2 3p^1$
argon	18	$1s^2 2s^2 2p^6 3s^2 3p^6$

Table 10.2.3 Electron Configurations of Some Row 3 Elements

You may have noticed that the rows of the periodic table are arranged by electron configuration. A new row is the start of filling a new energy level. The columns of the periodic table are also meaningful. There is a pattern in the electron configurations within a column. The configurations of elements in column 1, such as H, Li, and Na, all end in ns^1 (n = energy level). Elements in column 13, such as B and Al, have configurations ending in $ns^2 np^1$. The electrons in the s and p orbitals of the highest energy level of an atom are called **valence electrons.** They are highlighted in red on the next page. Valence electrons are always in the outermost energy level of an atom. In general, the valence electrons of an element in row X are in level X orbitals.

Link to >>>

Health

Chlorine and bromine are often added to spas and hot tubs to prevent the growth of disease-causing microorganisms. These elements are in the same column in the periodic table. Their electron configurations, and thus their chemical properties, are similar. Both react in ways that prevent water contamination.

H: $1s^1$

Li: $1s^2 2s^1$

Na: $1s^2 2s^2 2p^6 3s^1$

]   Column 1 elements have 1 valence electron.

B: $1s^2 2s^2 2p^1$

Al: $1s^2 2s^2 2p^6 3s^2 3p^1$

]   Column 13 elements have 3 valence electrons.

The elements in the same column have the same number of valence electrons. The only difference is the energy level of these electrons and the number of electrons in lower levels. This trend is true for each column of the periodic table. Elements in the same column have the same outer orbitals (with different n values) and the same number of electrons in them. Because of this, they share similar chemical properties. Elements in the same column react in similar ways. In Chapter 11, you will learn about other trends in the periodic table.

★ ★

Achievements in Science

Electron Microscopes

Electron microscopes use the properties of electrons to produce clear images of small objects. A common light microscope might be able to magnify something 1,000 times. Some electron microscopes can magnify an object several million times. The object can be as small as a molecule or atom. Using this microscope, DNA molecules can be studied and single atoms can be rearranged.

There are several types of electron microscopes. All of them use electron beams and magnetic or electric fields that act as lenses. In some of these microscopes, the electron beam stays on the surface of the object. In others, the beam goes through the object. Some microscopes are designed so the electron beam can scan the object.

Word Bank

Aufbau principle

electron
 configuration

valence electrons

On a sheet of paper, write the phrase from the Word Bank that completes each sentence.

1. The _____ are in the s and p orbitals of the highest energy level of an atom.

2. The _____ states that electrons fill the lowest energy levels first.

3. A(n) _____ shows how the electrons of an atom are arranged into energy levels and orbitals.

On a sheet of paper, write the letter of the answer to each question.

4. Which element has the electron configuration $1s^2 2s^2 2p^6 3s^2 3p^3$?

A Al   **B** Mg   **C** P   **D** Cl

5. Which electron configuration is *not* correct?

A carbon: $1s^2 2s^2 2p^2$
B oxygen: $1s^2 2s^2 2p^2 3s^2$
C silicon: $1s^2 2s^2 2p^6 3s^2 3p^2$
D magnesium: $1s^2 2s^2 2p^6 3s^2$

6. Which electron configuration is impossible?

A $1s^2 2s^3 2p^6 3s^2$ **C** $1s^2 2s^2 2p^6 3s^2 3p^3$
B $1s^2 2s^2 2p^6$ **D** $1s^2 2s^2 2p^6 3s^1$

Critical Thinking

On a sheet of paper, write the answer to each question.

7. How many electrons can be in any one orbital? How many electrons can fill the p orbitals in an energy level? The d orbitals? The f orbitals?

8. What is the electron configuration of nitrogen?

9. What is the electron configuration of sulfur?

10. What is the electron configuration of chlorine?

Materials

- safety goggles
- lab coat or apron
- 0.10 g of magnesium ribbon
- 0.11 g of aluminum foil
- balance
- 2 Erlenmeyer flasks
- 2 1-hole stoppers that fit the flasks
- 2 pieces of glass or hard plastic tubing
- 2 pieces of flexible plastic or rubber tubing, each about 0.5 m
- 2 250-mL beakers
- 2 water troughs or plastic basins
- 20 mL of 3 *M* hydrochloric acid
- 10-mL graduated cylinder

Valence Electrons of Metals

The number of valence electrons in an atom helps determine how the atom reacts with other atoms. In this investigation, you will use an acid and a metal to produce hydrogen gas. How do the volumes of hydrogen gas compare for two different metals? How does each volume relate to the number of valence electrons in the metal?

Procedure

1. Write a procedure describing how you will react excess hydrochloric acid (10 mL) with metal in a flask and collect the hydrogen gas produced. (Hint: You can collect gas by bubbling it into an upside-down beaker filled with water. The gas will displace the same volume of water.) You will follow the procedure twice, once for each metal. Include a hypothesis and the following safety alerts in your procedure. **Safety Alerts: Take care with glassware. Hydrogen gas burns; do not have open flames in the lab. Report any acid spills to your teacher immediately.**

2. Have your teacher approve your procedure.

3. Put on safety goggles and a lab coat or apron. Follow your procedure using magnesium, then aluminum.

4. For each metal, estimate the volume of hydrogen gas produced. Find a simple, whole-number ratio that relates the two volumes.

Continued on next page

Cleanup/Disposal

Dispose of the reaction products properly. Clean and dry the glassware. Return all equipment. Clean your work area, and wash your hands.

Analysis

1. Write a balanced chemical equation for each reaction that took place.

2. From these equations, how many moles of hydrogen can be produced from 1 mol of each metal?

3. Use your answer to question 2 to predict the smallest whole-number ratio of the two volumes of hydrogen produced.

Conclusions

1. How did your experimental ratio (from Procedure step 4) compare to your predicted ratio (from Analysis question 3)?

2. Locate magnesium and aluminum on the periodic table. How many valence electrons does each atom have? Compare the ratio of hydrogen volumes to the ratio of valence electrons.

Explore Further

Use the periodic table to find the number of valence electrons in a sodium atom. Predict the ratio of volumes of hydrogen produced if sodium and magnesium were the metals used in this investigation.

The electron configurations for the elements in row 4 are more complicated. There are 18 elements in this row. They will require more than just the *s* and *p* orbitals used so far.

Orbitals of Higher Energy Levels

In higher energy levels of the atom, the hotel analogy breaks down. On upper floors (energy levels) of the hotel, some rooms are filled before rooms on the floor below are filled. This is because energy levels 3 and up overlap, as shown in Figure 10.3.1. Some orbitals are at a lower energy than others, even though they are on a higher level. For example, the 4*s* orbital is at a lower energy than the 3*d* orbitals. The 4*s* orbital must be filled with 2 electrons before starting to fill the 3*d* orbitals. The orbitals in levels 5, 6, and 7 are not shown, but they overlap in an even more complicated way.

The overlapping that occurs in energy levels 3 and up determines the order that electrons fill orbitals. This order is followed when writing electron configurations.

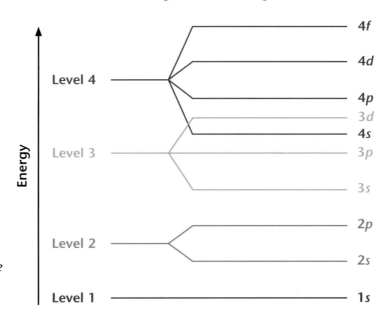

Figure 10.3.1 *Energy levels 3 and higher overlap. This affects the order of filling orbitals with electrons.*

Link to ➤➤➤

Earth Science

The northern lights, or aurora borealis, are colorful lights in the sky. They are caused by charged particles such as electrons. These particles are released by the sun and travel to the earth. The earth's magnetic field traps the particles. The colors come from the interaction between these particles and gases in the atmosphere.

Electron Configurations

In Lesson 2, you learned two rules about electron configurations:

Rule 1. Each orbital can hold a maximum of 2 electrons.

Rule 2. Electrons fill orbitals that have the lowest energy first.

To write the electron configurations of elements in rows 4 through 7, a third rule is needed:

Rule 3. The order in which orbitals are filled is not always based on energy level.

The 1s orbital in energy level 1 is always filled first. After that, the four orbitals in level 2 are filled. However, all nine orbitals in level 3 are *not* filled before going on to fill some level 4 orbitals. Likewise, all 16 orbitals in level 4 are *not* filled before starting to fill level 5. An easy way to remember the order of filling orbitals is to use the diagonal chart in Figure 10.3.2. It can be used to determine the electron configuration of any element. A *p* entry means filling three orbitals. A *d* entry means filling five orbitals, and an *f* entry means filling seven orbitals.

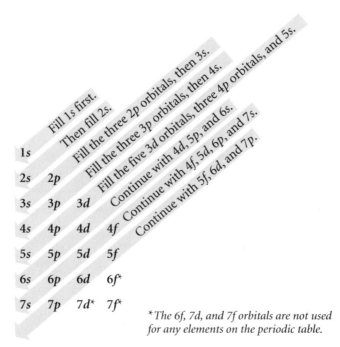

Figure 10.3.2 *The arrows in the chart show the order of placing electrons in orbitals. Start with the top arrow on the left (the lowest energy) and work downward. Fill the orbitals as the arrows cross through them.*

Fill 1s first.
Then fill 2s.
Fill the three 2p orbitals, then 3s.
Fill the three 3p orbitals, then 4s.
Fill the five 3d orbitals, three 4p orbitals, and 5s.
Continue with 4d, 5p, and 6s.
Continue with 4f, 5d, 6p, and 7s.
Continue with 5f, 6d, and 7p.

1s			
2s	2p		
3s	3p	3d	
4s	4p	4d	4f
5s	5p	5d	5f
6s	6p	6d	6f*
7s	7p	7d*	7f*

*The 6f, 7d, and 7f orbitals are not used for any elements on the periodic table.

Using the diagonal chart in Figure 10.3.2, you can write the electron configuration of any element. The order shown in the diagonal chart is sometimes called the diagonal rule.

Example 1	Determine the electron configurations of cobalt and krypton.
Read	You are asked to write the electron configurations for two elements in row 4 of the periodic table.
Plan	First find out how many electrons each atom has. For a neutral atom, this number equals the atomic number given in the periodic table. Then start placing these electrons in orbitals according to Figure 10.3.2. Remember that *s* orbitals hold up to 2 electrons, *p* orbitals hold up to 6, *d* orbitals hold up to 10, and *f* orbitals hold up to 14.
Solve	The configurations are given below. The valence electrons are shown in red.

Element	Row	Number of Electrons	Electron Configuration
Co	4	27	$1s^2 2s^2 2p^6 3s^2 3p^6 4s^2 3d^7$
Kr	4	36	$1s^2 2s^2 2p^6 3s^2 3p^6 4s^2 3d^{10} 4p^6$

With this many electrons to place in orbitals, it is a good idea to add the superscripts in each electron configuration. Make sure they add up to the number of electrons. For example, for cobalt: $2+2+6+2+6+2+7=27$. Cobalt has atomic number 27.

Reflect	By looking at these electron configurations, you can see that the diagonal chart is very helpful. The filling order for larger elements is not by energy level.
Practice	Determine the electron configurations of scandium and zinc.

The elements in Example 1 are in different columns of row 4. Their valence electrons are in energy level 4, the highest level for these elements. There is a similar pattern for all rows: the valence electrons of row 5 elements are in level 5 orbitals. The valence electrons of row 6 elements are in level 6 orbitals. You will see this in the next example.

Example 2   Determine the electron configurations of technetium and xenon.

Read   You are asked to write the electron configurations for two elements.

Plan   First find out how many electrons each atom has by looking up the atomic number. Notice that both elements are in row 5—this tells you that their valence electrons are in energy level 5. Using Figure 10.3.2, start placing electrons in orbitals (place all of them, not just the valence electrons).

Solve   Valence electrons are in red below.

Element	Row	Number of Electrons	Electron Configuration
Tc	5	43	$1s^2 2s^2 2p^6 3s^2 3p^6 4s^2 3d^{10} 4p^6 5s^2 4d^5$
Xe	5	54	$1s^2 2s^2 2p^6 3s^2 3p^6 4s^2 3d^{10} 4p^6 5s^2 4d^{10} 5p^6$

Reflect   Find the valence electrons in each configuration. Remember that valence electrons are the ones in the highest energy level in the configuration. The number of this level is also the element's row number. Tc and Xe, both in row 5, have valence electrons in level 5.

Practice   Determine the electron configurations of tin and mercury.

In these examples, you can see that d orbitals are in levels below the highest level (the valence level). Valence electrons are always in s and p orbitals. The d and f orbitals are not part of the valence level and do not contain valence electrons.

Research and Write

Full outer energy levels make atoms stable. Atoms are slightly less stable when they have a full sublevel or a half-full sublevel. Research the electron configurations for copper and chromium. Write one or two paragraphs explaining why the electron configurations for these elements are not what is expected from the Aufbau principle.

On a sheet of paper, write the word or phrase from the Word Bank that completes each sentence.

Word Bank

atomic number

diagonal

overlap

1. Orbital 4*s* is filled before orbital 3*d* because energy levels _____.

2. A(n) _____ chart can be used to determine the order of filling orbitals when writing electron configurations.

3. The number of electrons in a neutral atom equals the _____ of the element.

On a sheet of paper, write the letter of the answer to each question.

4. Of the following orbitals, which one will fill first?

A 3*d*   **B** 4*s*   **C** 4*p*   **D** 4*d*

5. Of the following orbitals, which has the highest energy?

A 3*s*   **B** 3*p*   **C** 3*d*   **D** 4*s*

6. Look at the following electron configuration. In which energy level are the valence electrons?
$1s^2 2s^2 2p^6 3s^2 3p^6 4s^2 3d^{10} 4p^6 5s^2 4d^{10} 5p^6 6s^2 4f^{14} 5d^7$

A 3   **B** 4   **C** 5   **D** 6

Critical Thinking

On a sheet of paper, write the answer to each question.

7. What is the electron configuration for selenium? Use the diagonal chart in Figure 10.3.2.

8. An electron configuration shows that the highest-energy electrons completely fill the 4*d* orbitals. What is the element?

9. How many electrons are in the atom represented by this configuration: $1s^2 2s^2 2p^6 3s^2 3p^6 4s^2 3d^{10} 4p^6 5s^2 4d^{10} 5p^6 6s^1$?

10. An atom contains 5 electrons in an *f* sublevel. How many more electrons can this sublevel hold?

Objectives

After reading this lesson, you should be able to

◆ describe a noble gas in terms of its valence electrons

◆ write an abbreviated electron configuration

◆ use a labeled periodic table to write an electron configuration

◆ determine the electron configuration of an ion

You may have noticed that electron configurations all start out the same, and some are quite long. There is an easy way to abbreviate long configurations. To do this, you need to know about the unusual elements in the last column of the periodic table.

Noble Gases

The elements in column 18 are called **noble gases.** Look at their electron configurations in Table 10.4.1. Their valence electrons are in red. Remember that electrons in d and f orbitals are not in the highest level, so they are not valence electrons.

Table 10.4.1 Noble Gas Electron Configurations		
Noble Gas	**Electron Configuration**	**Highest Energy Level, n**
He	$1s^2$	1
Ne	$1s^2 2s^2 2p^6$	2
Ar	$1s^2 2s^2 2p^6 3s^2 3p^6$	3
Kr	$1s^2 2s^2 2p^6 3s^2 3p^6 4s^2 3d^{10} 4p^6$	4
Xe	$1s^2 2s^2 2p^6 3s^2 3p^6 4s^2 3d^{10} 4p^6 5s^2 4d^{10} 5p^6$	5
Rn	$1s^2 2s^2 2p^6 3s^2 3p^6 4s^2 3d^{10} 4p^6 5s^2 4d^{10} 5p^6 6s^2 4f^{14} 5d^{10} 6p^6$	6

Noble gas

An element in column 18 of the periodic table

Except for helium, noble gases have electron configurations that end in np^6. Each has 8 valence electrons, 2 in an s orbital and 6 in p orbitals. These elements are extremely stable and unreactive. This is because the s and p orbitals in their outermost energy level are completely filled.

Abbreviated Electron Configurations

To abbreviate long electron configurations, chemists use noble gas configurations as bases. Then the entire configuration does not need to be written. For example, calcium's configuration can be written using the noble gas, argon, as a base.

argon (18 electrons): $\quad 1s^2 2s^2 2p^6 3s^2 3p^6$

calcium (20 electrons): $\quad 1s^2 2s^2 2p^6 3s^2 3p^6 4s^2$ or $[\text{Ar}]4s^2$

The abbreviation $[\text{Ar}]4s^2$ tells you that this atom has the same core of electrons as argon, plus 2 more. The electrons added after the base are the atom's valence electrons. Valence electrons are usually the ones that interact in chemical reactions. Thus, abbreviated configurations show the important electrons.

▼◄▲▼◄▲▼◄▲▼◄▲▼◄▲▼◄▲▼◄▲▼◄▲▼◄▲▼◄▲▼◄▲▼

Science at Work

Neon Sign Maker

Neon signs have become a form of art. But there is a lot of science involved, too. The light in neon signs comes from passing an electric current through a gas in a glass tube. The electrons in the atoms of gas absorb energy from the electric current. As a result, the electrons move to a higher energy level. When they drop down to their original energy level, they give off light of a certain color. Tubes that glow red contain neon. Tubes of most other colors contain argon and other gases. About 150 colors are possible. No matter what gases are used, these signs are usually called neon signs.

A person who makes neon signs learns most of the skills on the job. To make a certain color, the sign maker must know what gases to place in the tube. Before a sign is made, a graphic designer often plans what the sign will look like. Another craftsperson may bend the glass tubing to the desired shape.

Using a Labeled Periodic Table to Write Electron Configurations

You can always use the diagonal chart (Figure 10.3.2) to determine any electron configuration. However, by using Figure 10.4.1, you can write electron configurations more quickly. In this special periodic table, sections of rows are labeled with orbital names. Each element tile in a section represents space for 1 electron. Follow these steps to write an abbreviated configuration for a given element:

1. Find the noble gas in the row *above* the given element. Write its symbol in brackets. The lower-level electrons in the given element have the same configuration as this noble gas.

2. Using Figure 10.4.1, start at the first tile in the given element's row (the tile in column 1). Move across the row until you reach the element. Write the orbital name of each section you pass through. Count the tiles in each of these sections. Write the tile counts as superscripts for the orbital names. For the section that contains the given element, count this element's tile and the tiles to the left of it.

Figure 10.4.1 *This labeled periodic table is used to write electron configurations. Rows are divided into sections that have orbital names. Each tile represents an electron space.*

	1	2		3	4	5	6	7	8	9	10	11	12		13	14	15	16	17	18
1	1s H																			1s He
2	2s Li	Be													2p B	C	N	O	F	Ne
3	3s Na	Mg													3p Al	Si	P	S	Cl	Ar
4	4s K	Ca	3d Sc	Ti	V	Cr	Mn	Fe	Co	Ni	Cu	Zn			4p Ga	Ge	As	Se	Br	Kr
5	5s Rb	Sr	4d Y	Zr	Nb	Mo	Tc	Ru	Rh	Pd	Ag	Cd			5p In	Sn	Sb	Te	I	Xe
6	6s Cs	Ba	5d* La	Hf	Ta	W	Re	Os	Ir	Pt	Au	Hg			6p Tl	Pb	Bi	Po	At	Rn
7	7s Fr	Ra	6d** Ac	Rf	Db	Sg	Bh	Hs	Mt						7p					

4f* Ce	Pr	Nd	Pm	Sm	Eu	Gd	Tb	Dy	Ho	Er	Tm	Yb	Lu
5f** Th	Pa	U	Np	Pu	Am	Cm	Bk	Cf	Es	Fm	Md	No	Lr

*Fill the 4f section before the 5d section.
**Fill the 5f section before the 6d section.

Example 1 Use the labeled periodic table in Figure 10.4.1 to find the abbreviated electron configuration of phosphorus.

Read You are asked to write the electron configuration of phosphorus using a noble gas base.

Plan This element's atomic number is 15. It is in row 3. The noble gas in the row above it is neon, with atomic number 10. In Figure 10.4.1, start at sodium, the first element in row 3. Move through the section named 3s. Continue into the section named 3p. Stop at phosphorus's tile. You passed 2 tiles in section 3s and 3 tiles in section 3p.

Solve Write the neon base in brackets. Write the two section names you passed. Use the tile counts as superscripts. The abbreviated electron configuration is $[\text{Ne}]3s^2 3p^3$.

Reflect Make sure that the electron configuration matches the atomic number of the element. Neon has 10 electrons, and 5 more are added, for a total of 15.

Practice Use Figure 10.4.1 to find the abbreviated electron configuration of bromine.

Using Figure 10.4.1 becomes easier with practice. It is a handy method for writing electron configurations of elements with many electrons. You can use it to write an abbreviated configuration or a complete one. To write a complete configuration, start with hydrogen's tile and move through the rows from left to right. Write each orbital name you pass. Stop when you reach the element you want. Write the tile count from each section as a superscript for the orbital name.

The metals in columns 3–12 of the periodic table are called **transition metals.** Several transition metals have configurations that cannot be predicted. For example, copper, chromium, and palladium have configurations that are different from the ones predicted by the diagonal chart or the labeled periodic table. The elements in columns 1, 2, and 13–18 are called **representative elements.** Their electrons have predictable configurations.

Having the same number of electrons (the same electron configuration); an ion of one element is isoelectronic with a neutral atom of another element

Math Tip

Use a number line to help you find the number of electrons in an ion. Start with the atomic number of the element. If the charge on the ion is positive, go to the left on the number line. If the charge is negative, go to the right. Move the number of units shown by the charge.

Electron Configurations of Ions

You can also write electron configurations for ions. Recall that ions are atoms with a charge. A positive charge means the ion has fewer electrons than protons. A negative charge means the ion has more electrons than protons. For example,

neutral calcium atom: 20 electrons (atomic number 20)

calcium cation, Ca^{2+}: 18 electrons (2+ charge)

neutral argon atom: 18 electrons

The electron configuration of Ca^{2+} is the same as argon's. An ion of one element will have the same number of electrons as a neutral atom of another element. The neutral atom is often a noble gas. When an ion and an atom have the same number of electrons (same electron configuration), they are **isoelectronic.** It is easy to determine an ion's electron configuration when it is isoelectronic with a noble gas.

Example 2	Find the electron configuration of the ion, Se^{2-}. Use either the diagonal chart or the labeled periodic table. This ion is isoelectronic with what atom?
Read	You are asked to write the electron configuration of an ion with a 2− charge. You may use either method.
Plan	Selenium has atomic number 34. However, the 2− charge means it has 2 extra electrons, for a total of 36.
Solve	Using the diagonal chart (Figure 10.3.2), 36 electrons are arranged like this: $1s^2 2s^2 2p^6 3s^2 3p^6 4s^2 3d^{10} 4p^6$. Looking at Figure 10.4.1, you can see that krypton has 36 electrons, just like this ion. The electron configurations of Kr and Se^{2-} are the same. Se^{2-} is isoelectronic with Kr.
Reflect	It is easier to use the labeled periodic table to find abbreviated configurations of ions.
Practice	Find the electron configuration of P^{3-}. Use either method. This ion is isoelectronic with what atom?

When using the labeled periodic table to write ion configurations, remember to adjust the electron count first. Then count tiles to the isoelectronic atom. Not all ions are isoelectronic with a noble gas.

For the representative elements (columns 1, 2, and 13–18), their valence electrons are the electrons involved in bonding. However, when some transition metals (columns 3–12) form ions in bonds, they can lose different numbers of electrons to form cations with different charges. For these metals, the bonding electrons are not always the valence electrons.

18
Ar
Argon
39.9

Spotlight on Argon

Argon was the first noble gas to be discovered. In the late 1800s, English physicists Lord Rayleigh and Sir William Ramsey removed N_2, O_2, CO_2, and H_2O gases from a sample of air. What remained was a gas that did not react with other elements. They named the gas *argon*, meaning "inert" or "idle." Some of the heavier noble gases can form compounds with active elements, but no known compounds of argon exist.

Argon has many uses. All are based on its property of not reacting with other elements. Argon is used at low pressure in light bulbs. This prevents the filament from burning up. Argon is used in places where chemical reactions should not occur. An example is the production of the active element, titanium. In the welding and cutting of metals, argon is used as a shield. The argon prevents the metals from reacting with the air.

Interesting Fact: The atmosphere of Mars contains almost twice as much argon as Earth's atmosphere.

Word Bank

isoelectric

krypton

noble gases

On a sheet of paper, write the word or phrase from the Word Bank that completes each sentence.

1. An atom and an ion with the same electron configuration are _____.

2. Elements in the last column of the periodic table are extremely stable and are called _____.

3. The element that is isoelectronic with Br^{1-} is _____.

On a sheet of paper, write the letter of the answer to each question.

4. Which electron configuration is *not* correct?

A gallium: $1s^2 2s^2 2p^6 3s^2 3p^6 4s^2 3d^{10} 4p^1$
B sulfur: $1s^2 2s^2 2p^6 3s^2 3p^4$
C tellurium: $[Kr]5s^2 4d^{10} 5p^4$
D magnesium: $[Ne]4s^2$

5. What is the abbreviated electron configuration for Zr?

A $[Ar]4s^2 3d^{10} 4p^6 5s^2 4d^2$ **C** $[Kr]5s^2 5p^2$
B $[Kr]5s^2 4d^2$ **D** $[Y]4d^1$

6. Which ion has the electron configuration $1s^2 2s^2 2p^6 3s^2 3p^6 4s^2 3d^{10} 4p^6 5s^2 4d^{10} 5p^6$?

A Ag^{1+} **B** Te^{2-} **C** Se^{2-} **D** Sn^{2+}

Critical Thinking

On a sheet of paper, write the electron configuration of each atom or ion. Give either the full configuration or the abbreviated one.

7. Mn

8. Sn^{2+}

9. As^{3-}

10. I

Dot diagram

A simple diagram that uses dots to represent the valence electrons of an atom or ion

Dot diagrams are usually not written for transition metals.

Valence electrons are very important in understanding why atoms react. When atoms rearrange in chemical reactions, valence electrons are shared, gained, or given away. These electrons are in the *s* and *p* orbitals of the highest energy level. Altogether, there are four orbitals in this outermost level: one *s* orbital and three *p* orbitals. Because of this, atoms can have up to 8 valence electrons. Chemists use a simple diagram to show the valence electrons of an atom or ion. It is called a **dot diagram** because it uses dots to represent electrons. It is also called a Lewis dot diagram or an electron dot diagram.

Before you can draw a dot diagram for an atom or ion, you need to know its electron configuration. This will tell you how many valence electrons it has. Start a dot diagram by writing the element symbol. The four sides of the symbol—top, bottom, left, and right—represent the four valence orbitals. Add dots around the symbol, one for each valence electron. Since each orbital can hold only 2 electrons, each side can have a maximum of 2 dots. Begin by putting 1 dot on a side, then pair them up as needed. It does not matter which side is filled first.

Here are the dot diagrams for the row 2 elements:

Li·   Be·   ·B·   ·C·   ·N: ·O: :F: :Ne:

Elements in the same column have the same number of valence electrons. Their dot diagrams have the same number of dots. For example, all column 1 elements have 1 valence electron, just like lithium.

H·   Li·   Na·   K·   Rb·   Cs·   Fr·

The noble gases, except helium, have dot diagrams like neon's. Their 8 valence electrons completely fill the four outer orbitals.

To draw a dot diagram, first determine its electron configuration and count the valence electrons. The following examples show you how.

Link to ➤➤➤

Biology

The accidental release of radioactive strontium isotopes into the atmosphere is one risk of a nuclear power plant. Strontium is a waste product of producing nuclear energy. Strontium has an electron configuration similar to calcium, so these elements have similar chemical properties. Radioactive strontium can replace calcium in bones and teeth, exposing people to harmful radiation.

Example 1   Draw the dot diagram of phosphorus.

Read   You are asked to draw a diagram showing the valence electrons of a phosphorus atom.

Plan   Phosphorus, atomic number 15, has an electron configuration of $1s^2 2s^2 2p^6 3s^2 3p^3$. It has $2 + 3 = 5$ valence electrons.

Solve   Its dot diagram is $\cdot \overset{\cdot}{P} \colon$

Reflect   It is not important where the dots are located around the symbol. It is easiest to start with 1 dot on a side, then add a second dot to a side as needed.

Practice Draw the dot diagram of magnesium.

You may use an abbreviated electron configuration to determine a dot diagram.

Example 2   Draw the dot diagram of bromine.

Read   You are asked to draw a diagram showing the valence electrons of a bromine atom.

Plan   Bromine has an electron configuration of $[Ar]4s^2 3d^{10} 4p^5$. In its highest level, it has $2 + 5 = 7$ valence electrons.

Solve   The dot diagram for bromine is $\cdot \overset{\cdot \cdot}{Br} \colon$

Reflect   Remember that valence electrons are in the s and p orbitals of the highest level only.

Practice Draw the dot diagram for Ar.

Dot diagrams can also be drawn for ions. To do this,

1. Adjust the electron count to reflect the ion's charge. The atomic number is *not* the number of electrons in the ion. Cations have fewer electrons; anions have more.

2. Based on this count, write the ion's electron configuration.

3. Count the valence electrons, and draw the dot diagram.

4. Place the dot diagram in brackets with the charge outside.

Example 3	Draw the dot diagram of the ion, O^{2-}.
Read	You are asked to draw the dot diagram for an oxygen atom with a 2− charge.
Plan	A neutral oxygen atom has 8 electrons, so an O^{2-} ion must have 10. Neon's atomic number is 10, so O^{2-} is isoelectronic with Ne. In other words, their electron configurations are the same. Neon is a noble gas with 8 valence electrons, so O^{2-} has 8 valence electrons as well.
Solve	Its dot diagram is $\left[:\ddot{O}:\right]^{2-}$
Reflect	If you used the diagonal chart (Table 10.3.2) for placing 10 electrons in orbitals, you would get the configuration $1s^2 2s^2 2p^6$, which shows 8 valence electrons.
Practice	Draw the dot diagram for Ca^{2+}.

Dot diagrams only show valence electrons. If you know the dot diagram for one element in a column, you can easily draw the diagram for any other element in the same column.

Example 4	Using the dot diagram of phosphorus (Example 1), draw the dot diagrams of arsenic, antimony, and bismuth.
Read	You are asked to use the dot diagram of one element to draw the diagrams of other elements in the same column.
Plan	Example 1 shows phosphorus as $\cdot\dot{P}:$ Because P, As, Sb, and Bi are all in column 15, their dot diagrams have the same number of dots. Only the element symbols differ.
Solve	The dot diagrams are $\cdot\dot{As}:$ $\cdot\dot{Sb}:$ $\cdot\dot{Bi}:$
Reflect	Check these diagrams by looking at the electron configuration of each element. Each has 5 valence electrons, in red below. P: $1s^2 2s^2 2p^6 3s^2 3p^3$ As: $1s^2 2s^2 2p^6 3s^2 3p^6 4s^2 3d^{10} 4p^3$ Sb: $1s^2 2s^2 2p^6 3s^2 3p^6 4s^2 3d^{10} 4p^6 5s^2 4d^{10} 5p^3$ Bi: $1s^2 2s^2 2p^6 3s^2 3p^6 4s^2 3d^{10} 4p^6 5s^2 4d^{10} 5p^6 6s^2 4f^{14} 5d^{10} 6p^3$
Practice	Using the dot diagram of bromine (Example 2), draw the dot diagrams of chlorine and iodine.

Word Bank

column

dot

dot diagram

On a sheet of paper, write the word or phrase from the Word Bank that completes each sentence.

1. A _____ is used to show the valence electrons of an atom or ion.

2. Elements in the same _____ of the periodic table have the same number of valence electrons.

3. A _____ is used to symbolize a valence electron in a dot diagram.

On a sheet of paper, write the letter of the answer to each question.

4. The dot diagram of a neutral atom shows 6 dots. Which element could it be?

   A oxygen   **B** silicon   **C** argon   **D** fluorine

5. How many dots are in the dot diagram of boron?

   A 1   **B** 2   **C** 3   **D** 13

6. How many dots are in the dot diagram of As^{3-}?

   A 2   **B** 3   **C** 6   **D** 8

Critical Thinking

On a sheet of paper, draw the dot diagram of each atom or ion.

7. C

8. Mg

9. Cl^{1-}

10. Al^{3+}

Spectroscopy and Pollution

Emission spectroscopes are instruments that can identify almost any substance by the pattern of light it emits. Every substance produces a unique pattern. The location of bands of light identifies the substance. The size of the bands tells how much of the substance is present.

These instruments have many uses. They are used to identify traces of substances left at a crime scene. They are used to identify the substances that make up a consumer product. They are also used to analyze air and water samples for pollutants.

By analyzing water samples taken at different locations, scientists can locate the source of the pollution as well as identify the pollutant. Air samples can be analyzed in the same way. Air near a landfill can be analyzed for pollutants. Emissions produced by factories can be checked. Animal feed lots can be monitored to be sure they do not pollute air and water.

Many spectroscopes require a sample to be tested in a vacuum. This can affect the results for samples that contain water. When a vacuum is used, water evaporates from aqueous samples. This evaporation changes the concentration of any solutes dissolved in the sample. Scientists and

engineers have now developed emission spectroscopes that do not require a vacuum.

1. A water sample was taken from point A along a stream. Another sample was taken from point B. Point B is 100 m upstream from point A. Much more of a pollutant was found at point A. What conclusion can be drawn about the location of the source of pollution? (Hint: Draw a diagram to help you.)

2. What advantage might there be for using emission spectroscopy to check car exhaust?

Chapter 10 SUMMARY

■ The development of atomic theory, including the location of electrons in the atom, is the result of contributions of many scientists.

■ Electrons move about the nucleus in energy levels that are at different distances from the nucleus.

■ Each energy level contains a certain number of sublevels. Electrons can travel between sublevels or energy levels by absorbing or releasing energy.

■ Each type of sublevel contains a certain number of orbitals. An *s* sublevel has one orbital, and a *p* sublevel has three orbitals. A *d* sublevel has five orbitals, and an *f* sublevel has seven orbitals.

■ Each orbital can contain a maximum of 2 electrons.

■ Electron configurations describe how electrons are arranged within the energy levels and orbitals of atoms. Electrons fill orbitals with the lowest energy first.

■ As the number of sublevels in an energy level increases, energy levels overlap. This overlap affects the order in which electrons fill orbitals.

■ To determine the electron configuration of an atom or an ion, you can use the diagonal chart or the labeled periodic table. Configurations can be abbreviated by using noble gas bases.

■ Valence electrons are the electrons in the *s* and *p* orbitals of the highest energy level of an atom or ion. They are usually the electrons involved in bonding.

■ Dot diagrams show the number of valence electrons in an atom or ion.

Vocabulary

Aufbau principle, 392	energy level, 384	photon, 382
dot diagram, 411	isoelectronic, 408	representative element, 407
electron cloud, 385	noble gas, 404	sublevel, 385
electron configuration, 392	orbital, 386	transition metal, 407
emission spectrum, 383	photoelectric effect, 382	valence electron, 394

Chapter 10 R E V I E W

Word Bank

Aufbau principle

dot diagram

electron cloud

electron configuration

emission spectrum

energy level

isoelectric

noble gas

orbital

photoelectric effect

photon

sublevel

valence electron

Vocabulary Review

On a sheet of paper, write the word or phrase from the Word Bank that completes each sentence.

1. A(n) _____ is a region of space described by shape that shows the probable location of an electron.

2. Electrons are emitted when certain light strikes metal because of the _____.

3. The _____ states that electrons fill orbitals with the lowest energy first.

4. A(n) _____ is an extremely stable, nonreactive element with a set of 8 valence electrons.

5. A(n) _____ is located in an *s* or *p* orbital in the outermost energy level of an atom.

6. Atoms or ions with the same electron configuration are said to be _____.

7. A(n) _____ describes the arrangement of electrons in an atom.

8. A(n) _____ shows the number of valence electrons in an atom.

9. The region of space around the nucleus where electrons are probably located is best described as a(n) _____.

10. Bohr called an area of space in which electrons can move a(n) _____.

11. A bundle or package of energy is called a(n) _____.

12. A(n)_____ is the pattern of light resulting from electrons releasing light as they drop back to their normal energy level.

13. A small level within an energy level is called a(n) _____.

Continued on next page

Concept Review

On a sheet of paper, write the letter of the answer to each question.

14. How many valence electrons are in an atom of germanium?

    A 2   **B** 3   **C** 4   **D** 14

15. Which electron configuration is *not* possible?

    A $1s^2 2s^2 2p^6 3s^2 3p^6 4s^2 4p^{10}$
    B $1s^2 2s^2 2p^6 3s^2 3p^6 4s^2 3d^{10} 4p^6 5s^2 4d^{10} 5p^6 6s^2 4f^{14}$
    C $1s^2 2s^2 2p^6 3s^2 3p^5$
    D $1s^2 2s^2 2p^6 3s^2 3p^6 4s^2 3d^{10} 4p^6 5s^2 4d^{10} 5p^6 6s^2 4f^{11}$

16. Which element has the electron configuration $[Xe]6s^2 4f^{14} 5d^6$?

    A Ti   **B** Os   **C** W   **D** Pt

17. Which ion is isoelectronic with argon?

    A Ca^{2+} **B** S^{2+} **C** Cl^{1+} **D** Si^{4+}

Problem Solving

On a sheet of paper, write the electron configuration of each atom or ion. Give either the full configuration or the abbreviated one.

18. Ga

19. P^{3-}

On a sheet of paper, draw the dot diagram of each atom.

20. Al

21. Te

22. Sr

Critical Thinking

On a sheet of paper, write the answer to each question.

23. Describe the electron cloud model of the atom. Where are the protons, neutrons, and electrons? How do the electrons move about the nucleus?

24. How are the $2p_x$, $2p_y$, and $2p_z$ orbitals similar and different?

25. Explain how the periodic table can be used to find the electron configuration of nickel.

Test-Taking Tip When you write an electron configuration, check the superscripts. When you draw a dot diagram, check the dots. Make sure you represent the correct number of electrons.

Patterns in the Periodic Table

What patterns do you see in the photo? Rows and columns of rooms form this apartment building in London, England. Each column has windows or balconies of the same size and shape. Each row, or floor, has both windows and balconies. The periodic table of elements has patterns, too. In Chapter 11, you will learn about this table and several patterns among the elements.

Organize Your Thoughts

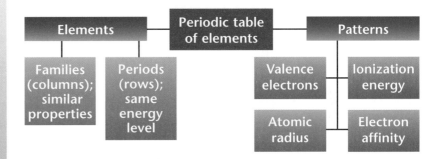

Elements — Periodic table of elements — Patterns

Families (columns); similar properties

Periods (rows); same energy level

Valence electrons

Ionization energy

Atomic radius

Electron affinity

Goals for Learning

◆ To tell how the periodic table developed and is arranged

◆ To explain the pattern of valence electrons

◆ To describe the pattern of atomic size

◆ To compare the sizes of atoms and ions

◆ To explain the patterns of ionization energy and electron affinity

◆ To describe some properties of each family of elements

◆ To predict the properties of an element

You may have noticed that the periodic table is arranged to provide a lot of information about the elements. It was not always so. In this lesson, you will learn how the modern periodic table developed.

Early Periodic Tables

By 1800, chemists knew of about 28 elements. They began to see patterns in the properties of these elements. The first periodic table was created to try to make sense of these patterns. In 1829, Johann Dobereiner, a German chemist, put elements with similar properties into groups of three. He called them triads. One triad contained the elements chlorine, bromine, and iodine. However, as he tried to expand the triad idea to the rest of the elements, it did not work well.

In 1864, another chemist, John Newlands, suggested that elements could be arranged in groups of eight, called octaves. Each element in an octave had different properties. This was a bit more successful, but it still did not explain the properties of all 62 elements known at the time.

In 1869, Dmitri Mendeleev, a Russian chemist, created the first version of the modern periodic table. He listed the elements by atomic mass because the concept of atomic number had not been developed yet. He placed elements with similar properties in the same column. He arranged the rows of the table so that the same pattern of properties was repeated in each one. For this reason, Mendeleev used the word *periodic* to describe his table. The same set of physical and chemical properties periodically appears—once in each row. Although this useful arrangement was quite a contribution, Mendeleev's work went even further. Mendeleev left blanks in his periodic table for elements that seemed to be missing. Using this table and his knowledge of chemistry, he predicted the properties of some missing elements—gallium, for example. His predictions turned out to be very accurate. Figure 11.1.1 shows one of Mendeleev's periodic tables.

Tabelle II.

Reihen	Gruppe I. — R²O	Gruppe II. — RO	Gruppe III. — R²O³	Gruppe IV. RH⁴ RO²	Gruppe V. RH³ R²O⁵	Gruppe VI. RH² RO³	Gruppe VII. RH R²O⁷	Gruppe VIII. — RO⁴
1	H=1							
2	Li=7	Be=9,4	B=11	C=12	N=14	O=16	F=19	
3	Na=23	Mg=24	Al=27,3	Si=28	P=31	S=32	Cl=35,5	
4	K=39	Ca=40	—=44	Ti=48	V=51	Cr=52	Mn=55	Fe=56, Co=59, Ni=59, Cu=63.
5	(Cu=63)	Zn=65	—=68	—=72	As=75	Se=78	Br=80	
6	Rb=85	Sr=87	?Yt=88	Zr=90	Nb=94	Mo=96	—=100	Ru=104, Rh=104, Pd=106, Ag=108.
7	(Ag=108)	Cd=112	In=113	Sn=118	Sb=122	Te=125	J=127	
8	Cs=133	Ba=137	?Di=138	?Ce=140	—	—	—	— — — —
9	(—)	—	—	—	—	—	—	
10	—	—	?Er=178	?La=180	Ta=182	W=184	—	Os=195, Ir=197, Pt=198, Au=199.
11	(Au=199)	Hg=200	Tl=204	Pb=207	Bi=208	—	—	
12	—	—	—	Th=231	—	U=240	—	— — — —

der chemischen Elemente.

Figure 11.1.1 *This is Mendeleev's second periodic table, created in 1871.*

The Modern Periodic Table

A modern periodic table is shown on the inside back cover of this book. The elements are organized by atomic number, from lowest to highest. Both atomic number and atomic mass are given for each element. From Chapter 2, you already know that the periodic table can be divided into metals, semimetals, and nonmetals. The colors of the element tiles indicate these three categories. The table also indicates the state of each element at 20°C. Most elements are solids at room temperature.

Link to ≻≻≻

Language Arts

Mendeleev named missing elements in his periodic table after known elements in similar families. He then added a prefix to show how far each missing element was from the known element. The prefixes he used were in Sanskrit, an ancient language of India. For example, eka in Sanskrit means "one." So the element one tile away from aluminum (gallium) was called ekaaluminum.

Family

A column of elements in the periodic table; also called a group

Alkali metal

An element other than hydrogen in column 1 of the periodic table

Alkaline earth metal

An element in column 2 of the periodic table

Halogen

An element in column 17 of the periodic table

Lanthanide

Any of the elements with atomic numbers 58 to 71; the lanthanides follow lanthanum (57) in the periodic table

Actinide

Any of the elements with atomic numbers 90 to 103; the actinides follow actinium (89) in the periodic table

Inner transition metal

Any of the elements in the lanthanide or actinide series

In Chapter 10, you learned that elements in the same column have the same number of valence electrons. As a result, elements in the same column have similar chemical and physical properties. Each column is called a **family**. There are 18 families, and some have special names. You already know that elements in columns 1, 2, and 13–18, as a group, are the representative elements. Elements in columns 3–12, as a group, are the transition metals.

- Column 1 elements are the **alkali metals**. The exception is hydrogen. It is a nonmetal, and its properties are not like the rest of its family.
- Column 2 elements are the **alkaline earth metals**.
- Column 17 elements are the **halogens**.
- Column 18 elements are the noble gases. You learned about these stable, unreactive elements in Chapter 10.

You may have wondered about the elements in the two rows at the bottom of the periodic table. They really belong in rows 6 and 7 of the table. They are placed below so the table is not so wide.

- The 14 elements with atomic numbers 58 to 71 are called **lanthanides** because they follow lanthanum (57). They are also called the rare earth elements.
- The 14 elements with atomic numbers 90 to 103 are called **actinides** because they follow actinium (89).
- Together, the lanthanides and actinides are the **inner transition metals**.

Link to ≫ ≫ ≫

Physics

In Mendeleev's periodic table, some elements seemed out of place. This problem was solved in 1914 by Henry Moseley. He measured the frequencies of X-rays emitted by various elements. From these frequencies, Moseley determined the atomic number for each element. Many inconsistencies in the periodic table were corrected when the elements were arranged by atomic number.

The word used for oxides in the 1700s was *earths*. Lanthanides were first discovered in their oxide forms and were believed to be rare. This is why they are sometimes called rare earth elements.

Several groups of elements are labeled in Figure 11.1.2. You will learn more about the families of the periodic table in Lesson 5.

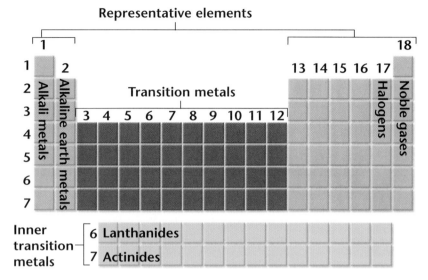

Figure 11.1.2 *The representative elements are the blue tiles, and the transition metals are the red tiles.*

When the elements are ordered by atomic number, from lowest to highest, their properties show a repeating pattern. Because the same sequence of properties appears in each row, the rows in the table are called **periods.** For example, sodium is in period 3. It is a soft, silvery metal that reacts vigorously with water and has a 1+ charge in ionic compounds. No other element in period 3 has this set of properties. However, in period 4, potassium has these properties. In period 5, rubidium has these properties. Sodium, potassium, and rubidium are part of the same family in column 1. The periodic table got its name because of this repeating pattern. In the rest of this chapter, you will see many other patterns in this useful table.

Procedure

Mendeleev predicted the properties of the element between calcium and titanium. This element was unknown at the time. He used properties of nearby elements to do this. Use the information in the table to predict the properties of this element.

Analysis

1. What is a likely density for the unknown element?

2. What is its likely atomic mass?

3. How many valence electrons might the unknown element have? Explain how you obtained your answer.

Element	Atomic Mass (amu)	Density (g/cm³)	Chlorine Compound
potassium	39.1	0.86	KCl
calcium	40.1	1.55	$CaCl_2$
unknown element			
titanium	47.9	4.51	$TiCl_4$

Chemistry in Your Life

Technology: Lanthanides in the Home

Although the lanthanide elements are called "rare earths," they are not all that rare. In the past, lanthanides did not have many applications. This has changed in recent years.

Television screens use certain lanthanide elements. The screens contain small dots called phosphors. These phosphors glow red, green, or blue when an electron beam strikes them. Adding europium (Eu) to a phosphor produces a bright red color. Terbium (Tb) causes a phosphor to glow bright green.

Portable compact disc players use lanthanides in several ways. Extremely strong magnets of iron, neodymium (Nd), and boron are used in headset speakers. Compact discs also contain lanthanides.

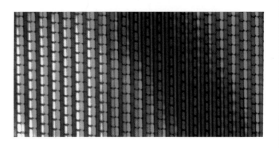

Dysprosium (Dy) and gadolinium (Gd) are used in the reflective coatings on the discs. By changing the optical properties of the disc, these elements allow more information to be stored. Lanthanides are also used in energy-saving lamps and optical fibers.

1. How are lanthanides used in televisions?

2. What lanthanide is used in the magnets of headsets?

Word Bank

octaves

periods

triads

On a sheet of paper, write the word from the Word Bank that completes each sentence.

1. Dobereiner used _____ to organize his version of the periodic table.

2. Newland used _____ to organize his version of the periodic table.

3. The rows of the periodic table are called _____.

On a sheet of paper, write the letter of the answer that completes each sentence.

4. Chlorine is a(n) _____.

   A noble gas   **C** transition metal
   B alkali metal   **D** halogen

5. Nickel is a(n) _____.

   A alkaline earth metal   **C** transition metal
   B alkali metal   **D** representative element

6. Californium is a(n) _____.

   A actinide   **C** lanthanide
   B representative element   **D** transition metal

Critical Thinking

On a sheet of paper, write the answer to each question.

7. In what part of the periodic table are the elements typically gases?

8. What is the name of barium's family?

9. What is true about elements in a family?

10. Explain how Mendeleev organized his periodic table. What was unusual about it?

Objectives

After reading this lesson, you should be able to

◆ explain that an atom shares, gains, or loses valence electrons in a bond to become more stable

◆ state the number of valence electrons in the most stable electron arrangement

◆ use electron configuration to predict the ionic charge of an element

Mendeleev placed elements in families based on their chemical properties. He did not know that these properties depend on valence electrons and energy levels. However, you know that the elements in a family have the same number of valence electrons. For example, alkali metals have 1 valence electron. Alkaline earth elements have 2, and halogens have 7. Their electron configurations end in a similar way.

How elements combine with other elements is one of the properties Mendeleev used to arrange elements in the periodic table. He combined some elements with oxygen to form compounds called oxides. He then determined the number of atoms of an element that combine with 1 oxygen atom. For example, 2 Na atoms combine with 1 O atom, while 1 Ca atom combines with 1 O atom. He placed elements with the same "combining power" in one family. This combining power is related to the number of valence electrons in an atom.

Remember that valence electrons are in the s and p orbitals of the highest energy level. An atom gains, loses, or shares its valence electrons to obtain a stable outer energy level. This level is stable when its four s and p orbitals each have 2 electrons. A set of 8 valence electrons is a stable electron arrangement—just like the noble gases.

To obtain a stable electron arrangement, some atoms *share* valence electrons in bonds. The elements in columns 14 and 15, for example, usually share electrons in bonds and rarely form ions. Other atoms *give* or *take* electrons in bonds, becoming ions with a charge. The alkali and alkaline earth metals almost always *give up* valence electrons to form cations in bonds. The elements in columns 16 and 17 often *take* valence electrons to form anions. In Chapter 12, you will learn more about bonds between atoms and why some atoms share electrons while others give or take them.

Atoms of metals tend to give away their valence electrons. As a result, they become positively charged cations. This empties their highest energy level. However, the level below is a stable set of s and p electrons. For example, look at calcium's electron configuration.

Ca: $1s^2 2s^2 2p^6 3s^2 3p^6 4s^2$

A calcium atom has 2 valence electrons, shown in red. It loses these to become a 2+ cation. Look at the cation's electron configuration.

Ca^{2+}: $1s^2 2s^2 2p^6 3s^2 3p^6 4s^0$ or $1s^2 2s^2 2p^6 3s^2 3p^6$

The cation has 8 valence electrons and a stable third energy level. Alkaline earth metals such as calcium have a 2+ charge in ionic compounds.

Atoms of most nonmetals have a valence energy level that is nearly filled. They tend to gain electrons and become negatively charged. Look at oxygen, for example.

O: $1s^2 2s^2 2p^4$

An oxygen atom has 6 valence electrons. It only needs 2 more to have a stable outer level. Gaining 2 electrons gives the atom a 2− charge.

O^{2-}: $1s^2 2s^2 2p^6$

Most other elements in oxygen's family (column 16) gain 2 electrons to form ionic compounds.

Technology and Society

Ion implantation is a technique for placing the ions of one substance into another solid substance. This changes the properties of the second substance. Ion implantation is especially useful in the manufacture of semiconductors. A semiconductor like silicon is exposed to a beam of boron, phosphorus, or arsenic ions. The implanted ions make silicon a better semiconductor.

			Atom's	Electrons		
Element	Atomic Number	Atom's Electron Configuration	Valence Electrons	Lost/ Gained	Ion's Electron Configuration	Ion and Charge

Example 1 — Write the electron configuration of sodium, fluorine, and aluminum. Then predict the ionic charge of each.

Read — You are asked to write electron configurations for three elements. By looking at these, you are asked to determine the likely ionic charge of each.

Plan — Na and Al are metals, and F is a nonmetal. Find the atomic number of each element. Then write their electron configurations using the diagonal chart (Figure 10.3.2) or the labeled periodic table (Figure 10.4.1). Identify the valence electrons. Metals usually give up these electrons, and nonmetals usually gain more. For each element, decide how many electrons should be lost or gained to get 8 valence electrons.

Solve — The results are shown below.

Element	Atomic Number	Atom's Electron Configuration	Atom's Valence Electrons	Electrons Lost/ Gained	Ion's Electron Configuration	Ion and Charge
Na	11	$1s^2 2s^2 2p^6 3s^1$	1	Gives up 1	$1s^2 2s^2 2p^6$	Na^{1+}
F	9	$1s^2 2s^2 2p^5$	7	Gains 1	$1s^2 2s^2 2p^6$	F^{1-}
Al	13	$1s^2 2s^2 2p^6 3s^2 3p^1$	3	Gives up 3	$1s^2 2s^2 2p^6$	Al^{3+}

Na and Al are metals with just a few valence electrons in energy level 3. By losing these, they obtain 8 valence electrons in energy level 2. F has 7 valence electrons. By gaining 1 electron, it has a set of 8. In each case, the number of electrons lost or gained determines the charge on the ion.

Reflect — After these atoms gain a charge, they have the same electron configuration. They are all isoelectronic with the noble gas, neon.

Practice — Use electron configuration to predict the ionic charge of tin, phosphorus, and neon.

Elements in the same column usually bond in similar ways. If the elements in one column typically form ions in bonds, they often have the same ionic charge. The ionic charges in Example 1 match the ones you used in Chapter 3 to determine formulas of ionic compounds. Figure 3.2.2 on page 93 shows the ionic charges of many elements. It also shows that ionic charge has a periodic pattern among the elements. Metals have positive ionic charges that, in general, increase across a row. Some nonmetals have negative ionic charges that, in general, decrease across a row.

Lesson 2   R E V I E W

Word Bank

the same number of

fewer

more

On a sheet of paper, write the word or phrase from the Word Bank that completes each sentence.

1. Compared to a neutral alkali metal atom, its ion has _____ valence electrons.

2. Compared to a neutral halogen atom, its ion has _____ valence electrons.

3. Elements in the same family usually have _____ valence electrons.

On a sheet of paper, write the letter of the correct answer to each question.

4. How many valence electrons does an arsenic atom have?

   A 2   **B** 3   **C** 5   **D** 8

5. How many valence electrons does a strontium atom have?

   A 1   **B** 2   **C** 3   **D** 8

6. How many valence electrons does a helium atom have?

   A 1   **B** 2   **C** 6   **D** 8

Critical Thinking

The following elements form ions. For each element, predict its most likely ionic charge. Then explain your answer in terms of electron configuration.

7. Ba   **8.** Rb   **9.** I   **10.** Ga

Research and Write

How does a toxic element interfere with elements that are essential to life? Research this question for one of these toxic elements: lead, mercury, or cadmium. The toxic element may be in the form of atoms or ions. Also find out how elements like calcium and zinc reduce the effects of toxic elements. Present your findings in a report or poster project.

Atomic radius

The distance from the nucleus of an atom to its outermost electron orbitals; a measure of the size of an atom

The periodic table holds a great deal of information, much more than the facts on each tile. With a little knowledge, you can predict many properties of the elements and many details about their atoms. Mendeleev used density and atomic mass to order the elements. To arrange them into families, he looked at how elements combine with other elements. There are other patterns hidden in this table.

Atomic Radius

One pattern in the periodic table involves atomic size. The size of an atom is measured by the **atomic radius**. This is an estimate of the distance from the nucleus to the outermost electron orbitals. Remember that the electrons in an atom move in energy levels. Each energy level consists of orbitals. Electrons in the first energy level are usually closest to the nucleus. Valence electrons in the outermost energy level are usually farthest from the nucleus. Atomic radius can be predicted from electron configuration. The more energy levels an atom has, the larger its radius.

For example, compare the electron configurations of lithium and rubidium.

Li: $1s^2 2s^1$

Rb: $1s^2 2s^2 2p^6 3s^2 3p^6 4s^2 3p^{10} 4p^6 5s^1$

Lithium has electrons in only the first two energy levels. Rubidium has electrons in five energy levels. As Figure 11.3.1 shows, energy level 5 is farther from the nucleus than level 2, and so rubidium has a larger atomic radius than lithium.

Figure 11.3.1
A lithium atom has two energy levels. A rubidium atom has five energy levels.

Li
atomic number 3

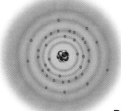

Rb
atomic number 37

Example 1	Compare the atomic radius of oxygen and selenium.
Read	You are asked to compare the size of two different atoms.
Plan	The atomic number of O is 8, and the atomic number of Se in 34. O is in period 2, and Se is in period 4.
Solve	Write their electron configurations. Then count the energy levels in each. O: $1s^2 2s^2 2p^4$ Se: $1s^2 2s^2 2p^6 3s^2 3p^6 4s^2 3d^{10} 4p^4$ Se has electrons in four energy levels, and O has electrons in only two levels. A Se atom has a larger radius than an O atom.
Reflect	O and Se are in the same family. Both have 6 valence electrons, but Se has more lower-level electrons (more energy levels below the valence level).
Practice	Compare the atomic radius of neon and krypton.

Atomic radius increases as you move from the top of the periodic table to the bottom. Elements in period (row) 1 have electrons only in energy level 1. Period 2 elements begin to fill energy level 2, and so on. This pattern in atomic radius occurs because of the increasing number of energy levels holding electrons.

Science Myth

Myth: All physical properties, such as atomic radius, gradually increase or decrease in a family or period.

Fact: Many physical properties vary in inconsistent ways. Electrical conductivity, for instance, can increase, then decrease, then increase again across a period. The same is true of melting point temperatures of elements in a period or family.

Elements at the bottom of a family are larger than elements at the top. Elements at the left of a period are larger than elements at the right.

How does atomic radius change across a period? Elements in the same period have electrons in the same energy level. As you go from left to right, each element has one more electron than the one before it. However, atomic size actually decreases, even though electron number increases. This is because each element also has one more proton than the element before it, while electrons keep filling the same energy level. The increased positive charge of the nucleus pulls the electrons in closer, and atomic size shrinks. As a result, elements at the left end of a period have a larger atomic size than elements at the right end. The exception is the noble gases, which are usually a bit larger than the halogens. Figure 11.3.2 compares the atomic sizes of elements in period 2.

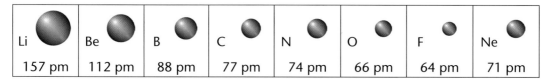

Li	Be	B	C	N	O	F	Ne
157 pm	112 pm	88 pm	77 pm	74 pm	66 pm	64 pm	71 pm

Figure 11.3.2 *The atomic radius of each element is given in picometers (pm).*

Example 2   Compare the atomic radius of magnesium and sulfur.

Read   You are asked to compare the size of two atoms.

Plan   Find the atomic number for each element: magnesium is 12, and sulfur is 16. Both are in the same period.

Solve   Write their electron configurations, then compare.

Mg: $1s^2 2s^2 2p^6 3s^2$
S: $1s^2 2s^2 2p^6 3s^2 3p^4$

Both have three energy levels, since they are both in period 3. However, S has 16 protons and Mg has only 12. S has a greater positive charge in its nucleus, which pulls its electrons in closer. Thus, an S atom is smaller than an Mg atom.

Reflect   Mg is in the same period as S, but farther to the left, so Mg is larger.

Practice   Compare the atomic radius of potassium and zinc.

Ionic Radius

Ionic radius is a distance like atomic radius, except it describes the size of an ion. When an atom loses its valence electrons to become a cation, it becomes smaller. Compare a Ca atom and a Ca^{2+} ion. Their electron configurations are

Ca: $1s^2 2s^2 2p^6 3s^2 3p^6 4s^2$ *larger*

Ca^{2+}: $1s^2 2s^2 2p^6 3s^2 3p^6$ *smaller*

It is easy to see that the Ca atom is larger. It has four energy levels, while the Ca^{2+} ion only has three.

When an atom gains valence electrons to become an anion, it becomes larger. The reason for this is not as simple. Compare the Cl atom with the Cl^{1-} anion.

Cl: $1s^2 2s^2 2p^6 3s^2 3p^5$ *smaller*

Cl^{1-}: $1s^2 2s^2 2p^6 3s^2 3p^6$ *larger*

Both have three energy levels. The anion has 1 more electron, making a set of 8 valence electrons. Both have 17 protons. The anion is larger for a couple of reasons.

- The anion has 1 more electron. Electrons have like charges, so they repel each other. There is more repulsion between 8 valence electrons than between 7. As a result, the set of 8 move slightly farther apart, even though they have a more stable arrangement.

- The anion's 17 protons are pulling on a total of 18 electrons. The 17 protons in the neutral atom are pulling on 17 electrons. The attraction between the nucleus and the 18 electrons is not as strong. As a result, the anion's electrons are a bit farther from the nucleus.

For elements that can have more than one charge, the greater the charge on a cation, the smaller it is. The greater the charge on an anion, the larger it is. The next example compares Sn, Sn^{2+}, and Sn^{4+}.

Ionic radius

The distance from the nucleus of an ion to its outermost electron orbitals; a measure of the size of an ion

Cations are smaller than neutral atoms of the same element. The greater the positive charge, the smaller the ion. Anions are larger than neutral atoms of the same element. The greater the negative charge, the larger the ion.

Example 3   Compare the radius of Sn, Sn^{2+}, and Sn^{4+}.

Read   You are asked to compare the radius of a neutral atom and two cations.

Plan   Tin has 50 protons. Find the electron configuration of the atom and cations.

Solve   Compare their electron configurations.

Sn: $1s^2 2s^2 2p^6 3s^2 3p^6 4s^2 3d^{10} 4p^6 5s^2 4d^{10} 5p^2$

Sn^{2+}: $1s^2 2s^2 2p^6 3s^2 3p^6 4s^2 3d^{10} 4p^6 5s^2 4d^{10}$

Sn^{4+}: $1s^2 2s^2 2p^6 3s^2 3p^6 4s^2 3d^{10} 4p^6 5s^2 4d^8$

The one with the smallest radius may not seem obvious at first, since all have five energy levels. In the Sn atom, 50 protons are pulling on 50 electrons. In Sn^{2+}, 50 protons are pulling on 48 electrons. And in Sn^{4+}, 50 protons are pulling on 46 electrons. The Sn^{4+} ion has the smallest radius because the protons can pull fewer electrons closer. The Sn^{2+} ion is a little larger, and the Sn atom is the largest.

Reflect   For a given element, the greater the positive charge, the smaller the ion. The greater the negative charge, the larger the ion.

Practice   Compare the radius of Ni, Ni^{1+}, and Ni^{2+}.

★ ★

Achievements in Science

The Discovery of Ions

Michael Faraday first suggested that ions exist. He used the idea of charged atoms to explain how current moves through some solutions. However, the exact nature of ions was unknown. Ions were not observed or correctly explained until the late 1800s. At that time, scientists studied how electric current behaves in cathode-ray tubes. They noticed phosphorescent rays moving from the negatively-charged cathode to the positively-charged anode. J. J. Thomson identified these rays as streams of negatively charged particles

(electrons). Later, scientists performed similar experiments using a cathode that had holes. Rays moved through the holes in a direction opposite the stream of electrons. These "canal rays" were studied by Wilhelm Wien. He measured how much the rays could be pulled from a straight path by an electric field. When different gases were placed in the cathode-ray tube, these rays deflected by different amounts. Wien realized that canal rays were atoms of gas that had a positive charge. This was the first sure evidence of ions.

On a sheet of paper, write the word or phrase from the Word Bank that completes each sentence.

Word Bank

anion

atomic radius

cation

1. The distance from an atom's nucleus to its outermost electron orbitals is the _____.

2. A(n) _____ is larger than a neutral atom of the same element.

3. A(n) _____ is smaller than a neutral atom of the same element.

On a sheet of paper, write the letter of the answer to each question.

4. Which of the following atoms has the largest radius?

   A Na   **B** Si   **C** S   **D** Ar

5. Which of the following ions has the largest radius?

   A F^{1-} **B** Cl^{1-} **C** Br^{1-} **D** I^{1-}

6. Which of the following has the smallest radius?

   A Fe   **B** Fe^{2+} **C** Fe^{3+} **D** K

Critical Thinking

On a sheet of paper, write the answer to each question.

7. Why is the atomic radius of barium larger than beryllium? Explain your answer by discussing energy levels.

8. Why is chlorine's atomic radius smaller than sodium's? Explain your answer by discussing protons and electrons.

9. Rank the following elements in order from smallest to largest radius: Ca, Be, O, Ba.

10. Rank the following in order from smallest to largest radius: Pb, Pb^{2+}, Pb^{4+}, C.

Materials
◆ compass
◆ pencil
◆ metric ruler
   (showing millimeters)
◆ worksheet

Periodic Change in Atomic Radius

Atomic radius differs with each element. How does atomic radius change across a period? How does it vary between periods? In this investigation, you will model data to show these changes.

Procedure

1. Look at the table on the next page. It lists the atomic radius for 21 elements in periods 2, 3, and 4. You will model the size of these atoms by drawing circles to represent them. The radius of each circle is listed under "Model Radius." For example, lithium's atomic radius is 157 pm. The radius of the circle representing this atom will be 16 mm.

2. Use the ruler and compass to draw your models in the table on the worksheet. Start with lithium. In the upper left square, draw a circle with a radius of 16 mm (a diameter of 32 mm). Write *Li* inside the circle. **Safety Alert: The compass has a very sharp point. Handle the compass with care.**

3. Complete the worksheet by repeating step 2 for each element listed. Label each model with its chemical symbol.

4. Check that the order of your
models reflects the order of
elements in periods 2, 3, and 4 of
the periodic table. The noble gases
are not modeled.

Cleanup/Disposal
Return all materials.

Analysis
1. What is the relationship
between atomic radius and the
corresponding model radius?

2. Some atoms are nearly the same
size. Do your models demonstrate
small size differences? Explain.

Conclusions
1. How does atomic radius change
from left to right across a period?

2. How does atomic radius change
for elements in a column as period
number increases?

3. Why does the radius increase at the
beginning of each new period?

Explore Further
Discuss other methods of modeling the
pattern of atomic size in the periodic
table. Using one of these methods,
model the atomic radius data provided
in this investigation. Compare the two
modeling methods.

Element	Period	Atomic Radius (pm)	Model Radius (mm)
Li	2	157	16
Be	2	112	11
B	2	88	9
C	2	77	8
N	2	74	7
O	2	66	7
F	2	64	6
Na	3	191	19
Mg	3	160	16
Al	3	143	14
Si	3	118	12
P	3	110	11
S	3	104	10
Cl	3	99	10
K	4	235	23
Ca	4	197	20
Ga	4	153	15
Ge	4	122	12
As	4	121	12
Se	4	117	12
Br	4	114	11

After reading this lesson, you should be able to

◆ explain the pattern of ionization energy in terms of distance

◆ describe the shielding effect and its effect on ionization energy

◆ define electron affinity and describe its pattern

◆ compare the ionization energies and electron affinities of two elements

Ionization energy

The amount of energy needed to remove a valence electron from an atom

Joule (J)

The SI unit for energy

So far, you have looked at the patterns of valence electrons and atomic size. You have seen how they change from element to element in the periodic table. This lesson introduces two more properties. These properties also create a pattern in the periodic table.

Ionization Energy

Ionization energy is the amount of energy needed to remove an electron from an atom. The harder it is to remove a valence electron, the higher the ionization energy is. Which family of elements has the highest ionization energies? Elements with the most stable electron configurations will hang on to their electrons the most tightly. These elements are, of course, the noble gases. They have a filled valence level of 8 electrons and will not easily give up one. Which family of elements has the lowest ionization energies? Elements that develop a noble gas configuration *after* losing an electron will easily give up that electron. These elements are the alkali metals. They readily become 1+ cations with 8 valence electrons. In general, ionization energy increases from left to right across a period.

For example, compare the valence electrons of chlorine and magnesium below. Neither has a completely filled valence energy level. Now compare their ionization energies. The SI unit for energy is the **joule** (J). The values below are in kilojoules per mole.

Cl: $1s^2 2s^2 2p^6 3s^2 3p^5$ ionization energy $= 1{,}251$ kJ/mol

Mg: $1s^2 2s^2 2p^6 3s^2$ ionization energy $= 738$ kJ/mol

A chlorine atom is only 1 electron away from having a complete set of 8 s and p electrons in energy level 3. It is far more likely to take an electron than lose one. A magnesium atom has 2 electrons in energy level 3. If it loses these 2 electrons, it will have a complete set of s and p electrons in energy level 2. You can conclude that more energy is needed to remove an electron from a chlorine atom. As you can see, chlorine has a higher ionization energy than magnesium.

How does ionization energy change within a family of the periodic table? Consider the electron configurations of lithium and rubidium, both alkali metals:

Li: $1s^2 2s^1$ ionization energy $= 520$ kJ/mol

Rb: $1s^2 2s^2 2p^6 3s^2 3p^6 4s^2 3d^{10} 4p^6 5s^1$ ionization energy $= 403$ kJ/mol

Lithium has only one energy level between its valence electron and the nucleus. The valence electron is close to the nucleus and held very tightly. In contrast, rubidium has four energy levels between its valence electron and the nucleus. This valence electron is farther away and much easier to remove than lithium's valence electron. Therefore, the smaller atom in a family—in this case, lithium—has the higher ionization energy. More energy is needed to remove an electron that is close to the nucleus. Look back at Figure 11.3.1 on page 432. You can see that lithium's valence electron is much closer to the positive charge of its nucleus.

Example 1	Which has the larger ionization energy, nitrogen or phosphorus?
Read	You are asked to compare the ionization energy of two elements in column 15.
Plan	Find the atomic number of each element and write their electron configurations. Then compare the distance between the nucleus and the valence electrons. N: $1s^2 2s^2 2p^3$ P: $1s^2 2s^2 2p^6 3s^2 3p^3$
Solve	Both have 5 valence electrons, but those of phosphorus are farther from the nucleus. Nitrogen, the smaller atom, has a larger ionization energy. Its valence electrons are held more tightly by the nearby nucleus. It would require more energy to remove an electron from a N atom than a P atom.
Reflect	Phosphorus has more protons than nitrogen. Even so, the longer distance from the nucleus has more effect on ionization energy than the stronger positive charge.
Practice	Which has the larger ionization energy, beryllium or oxygen?

From top to bottom within a family, ionization energy decreases. The attraction between protons and electrons decreases as the distance between them increases. It is easier to remove a valence electron when this attractive force is weak.

Besides distance, there is another reason why ionization energy is low near the bottom of a family. In a large atom, the lower-level electrons act as a shield. They partially block the valence electrons from the attractive force of the protons. This is called the **shielding effect.** The more electrons between the valence electrons and the nucleus, the stronger the shielding effect. For example, the 1 valence electron in rubidium is shielded by 36 other electrons. The valence electron has little attraction to the positive nucleus. It is easy to remove. As Figure 11.4.1 shows, both distance and shielding affect ionization energy.

Electron Affinity

Electron affinity is the opposite of ionization energy. It is the amount of energy released when an electron is added to an atom. Which family has the strongest electron affinities? The halogens (column 17). This family has a noble gas configuration after receiving an electron. In general, electron affinity increases from left to right within a period. From top to bottom within a family, electron affinity decreases. This pattern matches that of ionization energy.

Figure 11.4.1
Ionization energy decreases from top to bottom in a family. This is due to both the distance from the nucleus and the shielding effect.

Myth: Removing an electron becomes easier as the number of electrons in an atom increases.

Fact: Ionization energy depends on the number of electrons in a given energy level. For a given period, more electrons in the outermost energy level means more energy is required to remove one. Removing an electron becomes harder from left to right in a period. Noble gases therefore have the highest ionization energies.

One exception to the pattern of electron affinity is the noble gases. These elements have 8 electrons in their outermost *s* and *p* orbitals. They do not release energy, but actually require energy, to accept another electron. The noble gases are usually left out of a table showing electron affinity. The elements in columns 2 and 14 are also exceptions. As you move from left to right, electron affinity values drop a little at these columns. The exceptions at columns 2 and 14 are true for the pattern of ionization energy as well.

Figure 11.4.2 shows the patterns you have studied in this lesson. It also shows the pattern of atomic size from the last lesson.

- Both ionization energy and electron affinity usually increase from left to right within a period. They decrease from top to bottom within a family.
- Atomic size decreases from left to right within a period. It increases from top to bottom within a family.

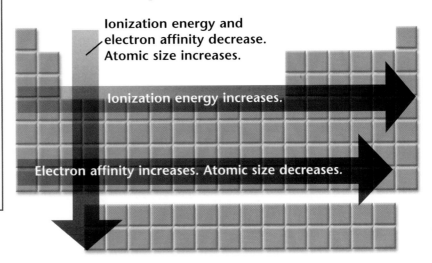

Figure 11.4.2 *In the periodic table, ionization energy usually increases from left to right. Electron affinity usually increases from left to right. Both decrease from top to bottom.*

Lesson 4   REVIEW

Word Bank

electron affinity

ionization energy

shielding effect

On a sheet of paper, write the phrase from the Word Bank that completes each sentence.

1. The amount of energy released when an electron is added to an atom is _____.

2. The _____ occurs when inner electrons block valence electrons from the attraction of the positively charged nucleus.

3. The energy required to remove a valence electron from an atom is _____.

On a sheet of paper, write the letter of the answer to each question.

4. Which atom has the highest ionization energy?

   A As   **B** P   **C** N   **D** Ne

5. Which atom has the highest electron affinity?

   A B   **B** N   **C** As   **D** Li

6. Which atom has the highest ionization energy?

   A Ba   **B** Ca   **C** Be   **D** F

Critical Thinking

On a sheet of paper, write the answer to each question.

7. Compare the shielding effect in a bromine atom to the shielding effect in a fluorine atom.

8. Which alkali metal has the highest ionization energy?

9. Rank the following elements in order from lowest to highest electron affinity: B, Al, O, C.

10. Which noble gas has the lowest ionization energy?

DISCOVERY INVESTIGATION 11

Materials
◆ graph paper
◆ red, blue, and green pens

Ionization Energy

The number of valence electrons and protons in an atom affect ionization energy. How does ionization energy change across a period and within a family? In this investigation, you will make a graph to show how ionization energy changes.

Procedure

1. Write a hypothesis predicting how ionization energy varies within a period and within a family.

2. Write a procedure that tells how to graph the data in the table below. The graph should show how ionization energy changes across a period and within a family. Plot all of the data on one graph. Use a different colored pen for each period.

Element	Valence Electrons	Ionization Energy (kJ/mol)	Element	Valence Electrons	Ionization Energy (kJ/mol)
Li	1	520	P	5	1,012
Be	2	899	S	6	1,000
B	3	801	Cl	7	1,251
C	4	1,086	Ar	8	1,520
N	5	1,402	K	1	419
O	6	1,314	Ca	2	590
F	7	1,681	Ga	3	579
Ne	8	2,081	Ge	4	762
Na	1	496	As	5	947
Mg	2	738	Se	6	941
Al	3	578	Br	7	1,140
Si	4	786	Kr	8	1,351

Continued on next page

3. Have your hypothesis and procedure approved by your teacher. Then construct your graph.

Cleanup/Disposal
Return any materials.

Analysis
1. Describe how you graphed the data. What units did you choose for the *x* axis and *y* axis? Explain your choices.

2. Does your graph show a steady change in ionization energy in a given period? If not, which elements do not follow the pattern?

3. Describe how ionization energy within a family changes as the period number increases. Explain this pattern in terms of atomic structure.

Conclusions
1. You graphed data for three periods. In each period, what element has the lowest ionization energy? Explain why these elements are easy to ionize.

2. Why do noble gases require so much energy to be ionized?

3. Why do you think alkaline earth metals have higher ionization energies than elements in the boron family?

Explore Further
Use reference books or the Internet to find ionization energies for the representative elements in period 5. Add these elements to your graph. Compare the trend you see in period 5 with the trends in periods 2, 3, and 4.

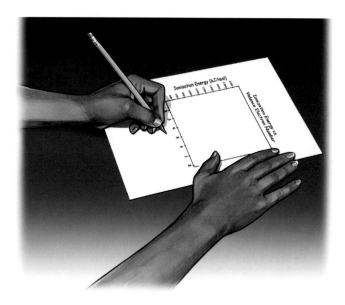

Objectives

After reading this lesson, you should be able to

◆ describe some properties of each family in the periodic table

◆ define allotrope and name an element that has allotropes

◆ list some common uses of elements

In Lesson 1, you learned the names of some families in the periodic table. The elements of a chemical family share common properties, just like the members of a human family share common traits. In this lesson, you will learn how each chemical family is unique. As you read, locate each family in the periodic table on the inside back cover of this book.

Alkali Metals

The alkali metals in column 1 have low densities, low melting points, and are good conductors of electricity. They are silver in color and soft enough to be cut. A newly cut surface is shiny, but it quickly reacts with oxygen in the air and becomes dull. Alkali metals are extremely active—they easily react with many other substances. These elements have 1 valence electron, which they readily give up to become a 1+ cation. The most active alkali metal is cesium.

Alkali metals react easily with oxygen and water. This is why they are not found in their elemental form in nature. They combine with oxygen in compounds called oxides, such as Li_2O and K_2O. All alkali metals react vigorously with water, producing a metal hydroxide solution, hydrogen gas, and heat. For any alkali metal A,

$$2A + 2H_2O \rightarrow 2AOH + H_2 + heat$$

If the reaction is fast enough, it will produce enough heat to cause the hydrogen gas to burn. This creates anything from a popping noise to a large explosion. As pure elements, alkali metals must be stored in a liquid such as oil to prevent contact with oxygen or water.

Alkali metals also combine with halogens to form salts. Sodium, for example, can be found in sodium chloride, NaCl. Potassium can be found in potassium iodide, KI, which is an important dietary ingredient.

Figure 11.5.1 *In 1937, the Hindenburg, a German dirigible, exploded. The H_2 gas it contained reacted with oxygen.*

Link to ➤➤➤

Language Arts

The name *alkaline earth metal* comes from the fact that most of these elements are found as compounds in mineral ores or "earths."

Hydrogen is placed at the top of column 1 because it has 1 valence electron. However, hydrogen is not a metal at all. When hydrogen reacts with a halogen, it shares an electron to form an HX molecule, where X is the halogen. Hydrogen gas, H_2, is very reactive and can quickly combust, as shown in Figure 11.5.1. Some periodic tables place hydrogen at the top of column 17. Like the halogens, hydrogen is only 1 electron short of the nearest noble gas (helium). Hydrogen reacts with alkali metals the same way halogens do: by forming a 1− ion. NaH and LiH are examples.

Alkaline Earth Metals

The alkaline earth metals in column 2 are like alkali metals in many ways. However, they are not as reactive and most do not need to be stored in oil. They are harder than alkali metals. Alkaline earth metals have 2 valence electrons and form ions with a 2+ charge. Like alkali metals, most react with water to produce a metal hydroxide solution and hydrogen gas, but the reaction is not as vigorous. When an alkaline earth metal reacts with oxygen, a hard oxide coating forms on its surface. For example,

$$2Mg + O_2 \rightarrow 2MgO$$

The oxide protects the metal from further reaction. Because of this, alloys containing magnesium are used as structural materials.

The Aluminum Family

The elements in column 13 include metals and semimetals. Boron, at the top, is a semimetal. Aluminum, gallium, indium, and thallium are metals. Each has 3 valence electrons and a 3+ charge in ionic compounds.

Aluminum is the most abundant metal in the earth's crust, but is not found in its elemental form. In the United States, aluminum is obtained from its ore, bauxite, which is processed to yield Al_2O_3. From this compound, aluminum is produced in a refining process that uses about 5% of the country's electricity.

Allotrope

A form of an element that has a different bonding arrangement than another form of the same element

Aluminum is obtained more easily by recycling aluminum cans. Aluminum's low density means it is lightweight. It conducts heat and electricity well. When exposed to oxygen or water, it forms a tough aluminum oxide coating that protects it from further reaction. In other words, it resists corrosion. These properties make aluminum one of the world's most used metals. Airplanes and many household products are made from it.

The Carbon Family

The elements in column 14 have a wide variety of properties. They all have 4 valence electrons in an ns^2np^2 configuration. Carbon is the only nonmetal in the family. Elemental carbon has many **allotropes**. Allotropes are forms of an element that have different bonding arrangements, as shown in Figure 11.5.2. Graphite is soft and is used as pencil lead and in lubricants. The carbon atoms in graphite are bonded to form separate layers that easily slide past each other. Diamond is the hardest natural substance. Besides its value as a gemstone, diamond is used in drilling and cutting equipment. The carbon atoms in diamond are bonded in a dense three-dimensional arrangement. Recently, scientists have discovered allotropes called fullerenes, such as C_{60} and C_{70}. They form molecules shaped like hollow balls or tubes. Fullerenes are being tested as structural materials and for uses in medicine and communications.

Figure 11.5.2 *Both graphite and diamond contain only carbon atoms. Because the atoms are bonded differently, the properties of these allotropes are very different.*

Charcoal is an allotrope of carbon that has no consistent structure or bonding arrangement.

Technology and Society

In the 1980s, a carbon allotrope of 60 atoms was discovered. This molecule is the most common fullerene. Fullerenes have high electron affinities. They form compounds with alkali metals, such as K_3C_{60}. These compounds have low electrical resistance at very low temperatures. In certain applications, fullerenes help convert light into electricity.

Silicon and germanium are semimetals that are widely used as semiconductors in computer technology. Semiconductors are solids that conduct electricity at high temperatures, but not at low temperatures. Silicon occurs naturally in silicon dioxide, or sand. Carbon, silicon, and germanium rarely form ionic compounds, so it is incorrect to assign them a 4− charge. Tin and lead are metals that form ions with a 4+ charge, but more often, a 2+ charge.

The Nitrogen Family

Within the group 15 elements, nitrogen and phosphorus are nonmetals, arsenic and antimony are semimetals, and bismuth is a metal. Each has 5 valence electrons. Nitrogen and phosphorus often share their outer electrons with other atoms. They can also form ions with a 3− charge. Nitrogen gas, N_2, makes up 78% of the earth's atmosphere. Nitrogen is essential to living things. It is part of proteins and deoxyribonucleic acid (DNA) molecules. Phosphorous comes in two allotropes. White phosphorous reacts immediately with oxygen. It is stored under water to prevent any exposure to air. Red phosphorous is less reactive and is used in matches.

The Oxygen Family

Most of the elements in column 16 are nonmetals. Polonium, at the bottom, is a semimetal. Each has 6 valence electrons. The nonmetals in this group readily take on 2 electrons to form ions with a 2− charge. They also share their valence electrons in bonds. Oxygen is the most abundant element on the earth. Oxygen gas, O_2, makes up about 21% of the earth's atmosphere. It is also present in water, carbon dioxide, and many compounds in living and nonliving things. Oxygen is the second most reactive nonmetal (after fluorine). It reacts with both metals and nonmetals. Elemental oxygen occurs as two allotropes: O_2 and O_3 molecules. O_3 is called ozone. Figure 11.5.3 compares these molecules.

Figure 11.5.3
O_2 and O_3 are allotropes: different molecular forms of oxygen.

O_2 O_3

Link to ➤➤➤

Biology

Nitrogen plays an important role in maintaining life on the earth. However, the nitrogen gas in the atmosphere cannot be used by plants or animals. This nitrogen must be combined with other elements to form compounds in order to be usable. This process is called nitrogen fixing. Nitrogen gas is naturally fixed in the soil, where bacteria convert it into ammonia (NH_3) or a nitrate compound. Nitrogen fixing also occurs from lightning and from plant and animal decomposition.

Although sulfur is known for its rotten-egg smell, elemental sulfur is odorless. The rotten-egg smell is caused by hydrogen sulfide gas. Sulfur has many allotropes. Sulfur in a solid state usually exists as an allotrope of crown-shaped S_8 molecules. A different crown-shaped allotrope, S_7, is responsible for sulfur's distinctive yellow color. Many ring-shaped allotropes have been prepared, including S_{12} and S_{18}.

Selenium is a poor conductor of electricity in the dark, but a good conductor in light. It is used in solar-powered devices, light-sensitive switches, and copy machines. Tellurium is very rare, and its compounds are toxic.

Halogens

The elements in column 17 make up the halogen family. All are nonmetals with 7 valence electrons. At room temperature, fluorine and chlorine are yellowish-green gases. Bromine is a dark red liquid, and iodine is a dark purple solid. In elemental form, halogens are diatomic. However, they do not occur as elements in nature because they are too reactive. Halogens have a 1− charge in ionic compounds. Halogens combine with alkali and alkaline earth metals to form salts such as KI and CaF_2. Fluoride ions are important for preventing tooth decay. Iodide ions play a big role in thyroid health. The thyroid is a gland that produces chemicals called hormones. Chloride ions are a necessary part of blood and other body fluids. Dilute chlorine solutions are used as bleaching agents (to remove color) and disinfectants (to kill germs on surfaces and in water).

Noble Gases

You already know about these unreactive elements. They have a set of 8 electrons in their outermost s and p orbitals. Thus, they do not accept or give up electrons. Helium has 2 valence electrons that fill energy level 1. Helium is less dense than air and is used in weather balloons. The rest of the noble gases have 8 valence electrons. Recently, chemists have been able to form compounds such as XeF_4, XeF_6, and KrF_4. Because xenon and krypton atoms are large, their valence electrons are far from the nucleus and can be removed with some effort.

Ductile

Having the ability to be pulled into a wire

Malleable

Having the ability to be rolled into sheets or hammered into shapes without breaking

Link to >>>

Art

Painters have long used pigments that contain metal compounds. Because many of these compounds contain toxic metals, the paints were dangerous to use. Despite this, metal pigments produce bright and beautiful colors. The names of some pigments, such as cadmium yellow, manganese violet, and cobalt green, indicate the metals they contain.

Transition Metals

The transition metals in columns 3–12 include the inner transition metals in the lanthanide and actinide series. Transition metals have properties of typical metals. Except for mercury, they are solids at room temperature. They are good conductors of heat and electricity. Most are **ductile,** which means they can be pulled into a wire. They are **malleable,** which means they can be rolled into sheets or hammered into shapes without breaking. Two transition metals have melting points close to or below room temperature. Mercury is a liquid at room temperature, and gallium melts at about 35°C. Table 11.5.1 lists some common transition metals and their uses.

Table 11.5.1 Some Transition Metals and Their Uses		
Metal	**Atomic Number**	**Use**
iron*	26	combined with other metals to form steel alloys
cobalt*	27	used to produce pigments in ceramics, paints, and inks
copper*	29	used as electrical wire because of its high conductivity
zinc*	30	used as a coating to protect steel from rusting
silver	47	used to make mirrors because of its reflective property; used in coins and jewelry because it does not react with oxygen or water
gold	79	used in coins, jewelry, and electrical contacts because it does not react with oxygen or water
uranium	92	used to produce energy from fission

These metals are also used by the body to maintain good health.

Research and Write

Among the elements predicted by Mendeleev were technetium (Tc) and rhenium (Re). Research the discovery of these elements. How were Ida Tacke and Walter Noddack involved in their discovery? Find out why the discovery of technetium, which they called masurium, was disputed. Present your findings in a report.

Spotlight on Gallium

31
Ga
Gallium
69.7

Gallium was the first element that Dmitri Mendeleev predicted from his periodic table. Mendeleev predicted its properties from the properties of nearby elements in the same period and family. When gallium was discovered in 1875, chemists who had doubted the usefulness of the periodic table changed their mind. Elements near gallium in the periodic table have low melting points. Knowing this, Mendeleev predicted that gallium would have a low melting point also. In fact, gallium has the lowest melting point of any stable metal, except mercury and cesium. If you held a piece of gallium in your hand, it would melt. Gallium also has a very high boiling point. Because of this property, gallium is used as the liquid in thermometers designed to check furnace temperatures. The temperature range in which gallium is a liquid spans 2,170°C! Compare this to water, which is a liquid for only a 100°C span. The main use of gallium is in semiconducting materials for computers. Gallium is also used to manufacture light-emitting diodes (LEDs).

Interesting Fact: Like water, gallium expands when it freezes.

Science at Work

Metallurgist

Metallurgy is the study of metals and ores. Metallurgists are scientists and engineers who perform a wide range of tasks. Metallurgists develop ways to remove metals from ores and refine these metals. They also develop ways to combine metals and form new alloys with particular properties. Metallurgists study how metals corrode. They find ways to make metals more durable. They also study and test the physical and chemical properties of metals and alloys.

Metallurgists are employed by industries that use metals or seek improvements in metals. These industries include the electronics, aerospace, and automotive industries. Research labs, government agencies, and universities also hire metallurgists. A metallurgist is usually trained as an engineer and has a strong background in chemistry and physics. Most metallurgists have at least a bachelor's degree in metallurgical engineering.

Lesson 5   R E V I E W

Word Bank

allotropes

ductile

malleable

On a sheet of paper, write the word from the Word Bank that completes each sentence.

1. Some elements exist naturally in different forms called _____.

2. A substance that bends without breaking is _____.

3. Elements that can be pulled into a wire are _____.

On a sheet of paper, write the letter of the answer to each question.

4. Which family of elements is most reactive with water?

    A the noble gases   **C** the alkaline earth metals

    B the boron family   **D** the alkali metals

5. Which family of elements contains the most abundant metal in the earth's crust?

    A the aluminum family   **C** the oxygen family

    B the nitrogen family   **D** the noble gases

6. Which family of elements contains the most abundant element on the earth?

    A the alkali metals   **C** the transition metals

    B the alkaline earth metals   **D** the oxygen family

Critical Thinking

On a sheet of paper, write the answer to each question.

7. Choose one halogen. Describe its state at room temperature. Then describe a biological function of its ion.

8. Which metals are so reactive that they are not found in nature as elements?

9. List three allotropes of carbon and describe each one.

10. Choose two transition metals and describe how each is used.

Arsenic and Semiconductors

Arsenic is not abundant, but it is widely spread throughout the earth's crust. Because it exists in ores containing gold and silver, arsenic was discovered by the oldest civilizations. The poisonous properties of arsenic make it an effective pesticide. Compounds of arsenic have been used to treat certain diseases. Today, arsenic is important in making electronics components that contain semiconductors. Semiconductors are substances that conduct electric charges better than insulators, but not nearly as well as metals. Germanium and silicon are semiconductors. However, these elements become more effective conductors when gallium or arsenic is added. Because of this, the electronics and computer industries use large quantities of arsenic. Much of this arsenic is washed away from the newly made semiconductors during cleaning. High concentrations of arsenic in wastewater from manufacturing plants can cause illness or even death. A solution is to recycle the wastewater and remove the arsenic. One way to do this is to use fine grains of iron oxide. Another way is to cause the arsenic in the water to become part of a solid compound. Recycling arsenic keeps it from reaching public water sources. The removed arsenic is used again to modify semiconductors.

The methods for removing arsenic are not limited to contaminated wastewater. In some areas, the drinking water has naturally high concentrations of arsenic. Removing the arsenic makes this water safe to drink.

1. How did early civilizations discover arsenic?

2. Why is arsenic important to the electronics and computer industries?

3. What are two advantages of removing arsenic from wastewater?

Chapter 11 SUMMARY

- The modern periodic table is organized so that elements with similar properties are in the same column.

- Understanding periodic patterns can help you make predictions about the properties of elements.

- Atomic radius increases from top to bottom within a family. Atomic radius decreases from left to right within a period.

- The radius of an anion is larger than the radius of the neutral atom. The radius of a neutral atom is larger than the radius of its cation.

- Ionization energy decreases from top to bottom within a family. Ionization energy usually increases from left to right within a period.

- Electron affinity decreases from top to bottom within a family. Electron affinity usually increases from left to right within a period.

- Elements in the same family usually have the same number of valence electrons. If they form ions, they usually have the same ionic charge.

- Metals typically lose their valence electrons to become cations. Nonmetals typically gain or share electrons to achieve a stable octet in their highest energy level. Many nonmetals become anions.

- The elements in the periodic table are diverse in many ways. The periodic table is organized so that elements within each family have some common physical and chemical properties. Every family of elements in the periodic table is unique in some way.

Vocabulary

actinide, 424	electron affinity, 442	joule, 440
alkali metal, 424	family, 424	lanthanide, 424
alkaline earth metal, 424	halogen, 424	malleable, 452
allotrope, 449	inner transition metal, 424	period, 425
atomic radius, 432	ionic radius, 435	shielding effect, 442
ductile, 452	ionization energy, 440	

Chapter 11 R E V I E W

Word Bank

alkali metals

alkaline earth
 metals

electron affinity

family

halogens

inner transition
 metals

ionization energy

lanthanides

noble gases

shielding effect

Vocabulary Review

On a sheet of paper, write the word or phrase from the Word Bank that completes each sentence.

1. The amount of energy needed to remove a valence electron is _____.

2. The _____ are extremely reactive and have a 1+ ionic charge.

3. The _____ occurs when inner electrons block valence electrons from the attraction of protons.

4. The _____ usually have an ionic charge of 2+.

5. The energy released when an electron is added to an atom is _____.

6. Elements with atomic numbers 58 through 71 are _____.

7. The _____ are very unreactive and have completely filled *s* and *p* orbitals in their highest energy level.

8. The _____ are reactive, diatomic nonmetals.

9. As a group, elements with atomic numbers 58–71 and 90–103 are the _____.

10. Elements in the same column of the periodic table are in the same _____.

Continued on next page

Concept Review

On a sheet of paper, write the chemical symbol of the element that fits each description. Use the periodic table.

11. a nonmetal with 5 valence electrons in energy level 3

12. a halogen with valence electrons in the fourth energy level

13. an alkali metal whose ion has the same electron configuration as xenon

14. a noble gas that does not have 8 valence electrons

15. the alkali metal with the lowest ionization energy

16. the noble gas with the smallest radius

On a sheet of paper, write the letter of the answer to each question.

17. For any period, the element with the highest ionization energy is in what family?

    A alkali metal   **C** halogen
    B alkaline earth metal   **D** noble gas

18. When alkaline earth metals form ions, what charge do they have?

    A 1+   **B** 2+   **C** 2−   **D** 1−

19. When halogens form ions, what charge do they have?

    A 1−   **B** 2−   **C** 1+   **D** 2+

20. Which of the following elements has chemical properties most like bromine?

    A selenium   **B** krypton   **C** chlorine   **D** oxygen

21. Which scientist is most responsible for developing the modern periodic table?

    A Dobereiner **B** Newlands **C** Mendeleev **D** Dalton

22. In a given period, which element has the largest atomic radius?

    A a transition metal   **C** the noble gas
    B the alkali metal   **D** a lanthanide

Critical Thinking

On a sheet of paper, write the answer to each question.

23. How does the shielding effect influence ionization energy within a family?

24. What is the pattern of atomic radius within a period? Explain your answer.

25. Which ion has a larger radius, Ca^{2+} or K^{1+}? Explain your answer.

Test-Taking Tip   To answer a multiple-choice question, read every choice before you answer the question. Cross out the choices you know are wrong. Then choose the best answer from the remaining choices.

12 Bonding

The photo shows the inner workings of a pocket watch. The gears have tiny teeth that fit together precisely. When one gear turns, energy is transferred to one or more other gears. Like the teeth on gears, atoms fit together when chemical bonds form. Energy is also transferred in the process. In Chapter 12, you will learn about types of chemical bonds and how they form.

Organize Your Thoughts

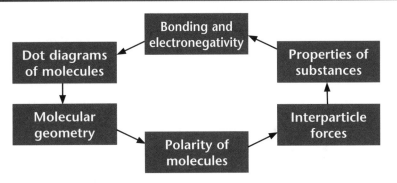

Goals for Learning

◆ To describe a bond between two atoms in terms of electronegativity

◆ To understand how valence electrons are arranged in the bonds of molecules

◆ To draw a dot diagram of a molecule or polyatomic ion

◆ To understand molecular geometry in terms of bonds and lone pairs

◆ To identify a polar molecule by its asymmetry and electronegativity values

◆ To explain five interparticle forces

Objectives

After reading this lesson, you should be able to

◆ explain how electrons are involved in chemical bonds

◆ describe three types of chemical bonds

◆ define electronegativity

◆ predict the bond type between two atoms using electronegativity values

Imagine that you are able to see two atoms of hydrogen, atom A and atom B. Each has 1 proton and 1 electron. As atoms A and B move close to each other, the proton from A begins to attract the electron from B. The proton from B begins to attract the electron from A. This attraction draws the atoms closer. Eventually, the atoms reach an ideal distance from each other. At this distance, their electrons are equally attracted to both protons. When two atoms reach this distance, a bond has formed, as shown in Figure 12.1.1. A chemical bond forms when two atoms share or transfer electrons.

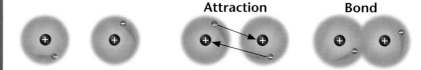

Attraction   **Bond**

Figure 12.1.1 *A chemical bond forms when electrons are shared between atoms.*

Bonds

In the H_2 example in Figure 12.1.1, the bonded atoms are identical. The attraction between an electron and either nucleus is the same. The electrons are shared equally by the atoms. However, in bonds between two *different* atoms, the electrons are not always shared equally. Because of this, there are two main types of bonds:

- covalent bonds
- ionic bonds

The atoms in molecular compounds are held together by **covalent bonds.** The bonds in all molecules are covalent. Their bonding electrons are shared equally or are somewhat shared. In ionic compounds, bonding electrons are hardly shared at all. In fact, in **ionic bonds,** electrons are completely transferred from one atom to another. This transfer creates the cations and anions in ionic compounds.

Covalent bond

A chemical bond in which electrons are shared between two atoms

Ionic bond

A chemical bond that results when electrons are transferred from one atom to another

> ***Electronegativity***
>
> *The ability of an atom to attract electrons in a chemical bond*

Electronegativity

How do you determine what type of bond is formed between two atoms? Chemists compare the **electronegativity** values of the atoms. Electronegativity is the ability of an atom to attract electrons in a chemical bond. Pretend that two different atoms come near each other and have a tug-of-war over electrons. The atom with the higher electronegativity attracts electrons more strongly. If the atoms form a bond, the electrons in the bond are held more closely by this atom. If the electronegativity difference is large enough, the more electronegative atom can pull electrons completely away from the other atom.

Each element has an electronegativity value, given in Figure 12.1.2. These values have no units. The halogens have high electronegativities. Fluorine has the highest value at 4.0. As you learned in Chapter 11, the halogens have a strong electron affinity. They are only 1 electron away from having a filled valence energy level. You would expect them to strongly attract a bonding electron. Elements that easily lose an electron have low electronegativities. Cesium and francium, both alkali metals, have the lowest values at 0.7. Elements toward the top and right of the periodic table (with the exception of the noble gases) have high electronegativities. Elements toward the bottom and left of the periodic table have low electronegativities.

1 **H** 2.1																	2 **He**
3 **Li** 1.0	4 **Be** 1.5											5 **B** 2.0	6 **C** 2.5	7 **N** 3.0	8 **O** 3.5	9 **F** 4.0	10 **Ne**
11 **Na** 0.9	12 **Mg** 1.2											13 **Al** 1.5	14 **Si** 1.8	15 **P** 2.1	16 **S** 2.5	17 **Cl** 3.0	18 **Ar**
19 **K** 0.8	20 **Ca** 1.0	21 **Sc** 1.3	22 **Ti** 1.5	23 **V** 1.6	24 **Cr** 1.6	25 **Mn** 1.5	26 **Fe** 1.8	27 **Co** 1.8	28 **Ni** 1.8	29 **Cu** 1.9	30 **Zn** 1.6	31 **Ga** 1.6	32 **Ge** 1.8	33 **As** 2.0	34 **Se** 2.4	35 **Br** 2.8	36 **Kr**
37 **Rb** 0.8	38 **Sr** 1.0	39 **Y** 1.2	40 **Zr** 1.4	41 **Nb** 1.6	42 **Mo** 1.8	43 **Tc** 1.9	44 **Ru** 2.2	45 **Rh** 2.2	46 **Pd** 2.2	47 **Ag** 1.9	48 **Cd** 1.7	49 **In** 1.7	50 **Sn** 1.8	51 **Sb** 1.9	52 **Te** 2.1	53 **I** 2.5	54 **Xe**
55 **Cs** 0.7	56 **Ba** 0.9	57 **La** 1.1	72 **Hf** 1.3	73 **Ta** 1.5	74 **W** 1.7	75 **Re** 1.9	76 **Os** 2.2	77 **Ir** 2.2	78 **Pt** 2.2	79 **Au** 2.4	80 **Hg** 1.9	81 **Tl** 1.8	82 **Pb** 1.9	83 **Bi** 1.9	84 **Po** 2.0	85 **At** 2.2	86 **Rn**
87 **Fr** 0.7	88 **Ra** 0.9	89 **Ac** 1.1	104 **Rf**	105 **Db**	106 **Sg**	107 **Bh**	108 **Hs**	109 **Mt**	110 **Ds**	111 **Rg**	112 **Uub**	113 **Uut**	114 **Uuq**	115 **Uup**	116 **Uuh**		

Figure 12.1.2 *Electronegativity values are shown in red. Atomic numbers are in black. The inner transition metals are not shown.*

Link to >>>

Biology

To function properly, the human body needs many different ions. For example, sodium and potassium ions allow the nervous system to send signals throughout the body. Calcium ions are involved in blood clotting and muscle contraction. Magnesium ions are needed for chemical reactions involving enzymes.

This pattern of electronegativity is similar to the pattern for electron affinity (Chapter 11). Both terms describe the same property: the attraction between an atom and the electrons of another atom. Electron affinity is the amount of released energy when an atom gains an electron, while electronegativity is a relative measure of attraction (with values from 0.7 to 4).

Bond Types

By comparing the electronegativity of two atoms, you can predict the type of bond between them.

When there is little or no difference in electronegativity, the bonding electrons are equally shared. In the H_2 example, both atoms have an electronegativity of 2.1. The difference is $2.1 - 2.1 = 0$. The bonding electrons are attracted to both atoms with the same force. They are equally shared in a covalent bond.

When the difference in electronegativity is large, the electrons are not equally shared. For a fluorine atom bonded to a cesium atom, the difference is $4.0 - 0.7 = 3.3$. This is the largest difference possible, so the bond is completely ionic. The bonding electrons are not shared at all. The fluorine atom removes an electron from the cesium atom. A fluoride anion and a cesium cation form.

The scale in Figure 12.1.3 shows how electronegativity differences can predict bond type. The scale represents the full range of electron sharing.

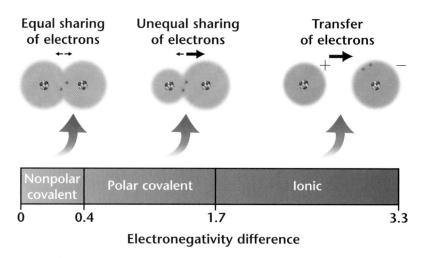

Figure 12.1.3 *As the electronegativity difference increases, the bonding electrons are more strongly attracted to one atom over the other.*

At the left end of Figure 12.1.3, bonding electrons form **nonpolar covalent bonds.** The electrons are shared equally—or somewhat equally—between the two atoms. The atoms are like two people of similar strength. The electron tug-of-war is basically a tie. Identical atoms always form nonpolar covalent bonds. Elements that are very close to each other on the periodic table usually form nonpolar covalent bonds. The electronegativity difference for nonpolar covalent bonds is typically less than 0.4.

As the electronegativity difference increases beyond 0.4, the covalent bond becomes more polar. In a **polar covalent bond,** the bonding electrons are shared, but not equally. They spend more time near the more electronegative atom. This bonding is like a tug-of-war between a big person and a smaller person. It is not a fair match, even though the smaller person has some pulling ability. Likewise, the more electronegative atom pulls more strongly on the bonding electrons than the less electronegative atom. Bonds with an electronegativity difference of 0.4 to 1.7 are considered polar covalent.

For electronegativity differences greater than 1.7, the bonding electrons spend all of their time near the more electronegative atom. In an ionic bond, the electrons are not shared at all. This is like a tug-of-war between a heavyweight fighter and a child. The match is not even close. The atom with the higher electronegativity takes the bonding electrons, gaining a negative charge. The less electronegative atom gets a positive charge. The two ions are held together by the attractive force between opposite charges. Ionic bonds usually occur between elements on opposite sides of the periodic table. Metals typically form ionic bonds with nonmetals.

It is best to understand bond types in terms of a range of electron sharing—not as three separate categories. For example, a bond with an electronegativity difference of 1.7 is considered polar covalent, but shows some ionic properties. The lines between categories cannot be sharply drawn.

Predicting Bond Types

To predict the bond type for two atoms in a compound, first find the electronegativity value of each element in Figure 12.1.2. Subtract the smaller value from the larger. Use this difference and Figure 12.1.3 to predict the bond type.

Example 1	Predict the type of bond in the compound, HCl.
Read	You are asked to predict the type of bond that occurs between the H atom and Cl atom in HCl.
Plan	Find the electronegativities of hydrogen and chlorine. In Figure 12.1.2, H has a value of 2.1 and Cl has a value of 3.0.
Solve	Subtract the smaller value from the larger: $3.0 - 2.1 = 0.9$. According to Figure 12.1.3, this difference indicates a polar covalent bond.
Reflect	Chlorine has a higher electronegativity than hydrogen. The bonding electrons spend most (but not all) of their time close to the chlorine atom.
Practice	Predict the type of bond in the compound, NaCl.

An electronegativity difference describes the bond between two atoms. For compounds of more than two atoms, such as CCl4, find the electronegativity difference between the C atom and one Cl atom.

Example 2	Predict the type of bond in the compound, CCl_4.
Read	You are asked to describe the bond between the C atom and one of the Cl atoms in CCl_4.
Plan	The electronegativity values are 2.5 for C and 3.0 for Cl.
Solve	The electronegativity difference is $3.0 - 2.5 = 0.5$. The bond type is polar covalent.
Reflect	Chlorine has a greater ability to attract an electron than carbon. As a result, the bonding electrons spend more time near the Cl atom.
Practice	Predict the type of bond in the compound, NH_3.

If you do not have electronegativity values, you can still predict the bond type for two atoms using these guidelines:

- Elements that are diatomic or polyatomic, such as O_2 or P_4, have nonpolar covalent bonds.
- Two nonmetals usually form a polar covalent bond. CO_2 is an example.
- A metal and a nonmetal usually form an ionic bond. NaCl is an example.

Once you know the type of bonding in a compound, you can begin to understand its properties.

Express Lab 12

Materials

- water faucet
- plastic comb

Procedure

1. Turn on the faucet so that a small stream of water flows.
2. Comb your hair with the plastic comb for 10 seconds.
3. Move the comb so that it is near, but not touching, the stream of water.

Analysis

1. Record your observations.
2. What type of bonding must be present in a water molecule? Explain your answer.

▼◀▲▼◀▲▼◀▲▼◀▲▼◀▲▼◀▲▼◀▲▼◀▲▼◀▲▼◀▲▼◀▲▼◀▲▼◀▲▼◀▲▼◀▲▼

Science at Work

Oncologist

An oncologist diagnoses and treats cancer. The three main specialties within oncology are clinical, surgical, and radiation oncology. Clinical oncologists use chemotherapy to treat cancer, and radiation oncologists use radiation. Surgical oncologists remove cancerous growths. The goal of each treatment is to eliminate cancer cells without damaging healthy cells. Chemotherapy and radiation break bonds

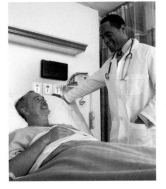

in molecules. This destroys cancer cell structures.

A career in oncology requires many years of training. After a college degree, four years of medical school are required. This is followed by an internship and a residency, including time spent studying oncology as a specialty. Practicing oncologists must study new advances made in cancer research and treatment.

On a sheet of paper, write the bond type from the Answer Bank that matches each description.

Answer Bank

ionic bond

nonpolar covalent bond

polar covalent bond

1. Electrons are shared fairly equally because the electronegativity difference is less than 0.4.

2. Electrons are shared unequally because the electronegativity difference is between 0.4 and 1.7.

3. Electrons are completely transferred to the more electronegative atom, creating a cation and an anion.

On a sheet of paper, write the letter of the answer that completes each sentence.

4. The type of bond between sulfur and oxygen in SO_3 is _____.

  A an ionic bond   **C** a nonpolar covalent bond
  B a polar covalent bond **D** an electronegative bond

5. The type of bond in N_2 gas is _____.

  A an ionic bond   **C** a nonpolar covalent bond
  B a polar covalent bond **D** an electronegative bond

6. When a chemical bond forms between two atoms, _____ are shared or transferred.

  A electrons   **B** protons   **C** neutrons   **D** ions

Critical Thinking

On a sheet of paper, write the answer to each question. Show any calculations.

7. What is the type of chemical bond in NO_2?

8. What is the type of chemical bond in MgF_2?

9. What is the type of chemical bond in I_2?

10. Compare the three types of chemical bonds by describing what happens to the electrons when each bond forms.

Objectives

After reading this lesson, you should be able to

◆ list four rules for drawing dot diagrams of compounds

◆ draw a dot diagram for a simple molecule

◆ describe single, double, and triple bonds

◆ draw a dot diagram for a polyatomic ion

Bonds are broken and formed during chemical reactions. Valence electrons are the electrons involved in bonds. They are responsible for most of the chemical properties of an atom. In Chapter 10, you learned how to draw the dot diagram of an atom. A dot diagram shows an atom's valence electrons. You can draw a dot diagram of a compound, too. This diagram shows how valence electrons are arranged in bonds. There are a few rules for dot diagrams of ionic and covalent compounds:

Rule 1. Atoms tend to transfer or share electrons to obtain 8 electrons in their outer energy level. Except for the smallest atoms (H, He, Li, Be, and B), a full valence level is 8 electrons, or an octet. This is the **octet rule.** It applies to both ionic and covalent compounds.

Rule 2. The number of dots in the diagram of a compound equals the sum of the valence electrons for each atom in the compound.

Rule 3. A covalent bond consists of 2, 4, or 6 shared electrons. In a **single bond,** 2 electrons (one pair) are shared. In a **double bond,** 4 electrons (two pairs) are shared. In a **triple bond,** 6 electrons (three pairs) are shared.

Rule 4. In an ionic bond, one atom or group of atoms gains enough electrons to fill its valence level. It becomes the anion. The other atom or group of atoms loses electrons and becomes the cation. The number of electrons transferred can be 1, 2, 3, 4, or, rarely, 5.

Octet rule

A rule that says atoms tend to transfer or share electrons to obtain 8 electrons in their outer energy level

Single bond

A covalent bond in which two atoms share one pair of electrons

Double bond

A covalent bond in which two atoms share two pairs of electrons

Triple bond

A covalent bond in which two atoms share three pairs of electrons

When you draw the dot diagram of a compound, remember that a covalent bond is different from an ionic bond. A covalent bond consists of 2, 4, or 6 shared electrons. In a covalent bond, the two atoms are held together because their nuclei attract the same shared electrons. An ionic bond forms when 1 or more electrons are transferred. In an ionic bond, the anion and cation are held together by the attraction between opposite charges.

Math Tip
Determine the total number of valence electrons for a compound before drawing its dot diagram.

Dot Diagrams of Simple Molecules

Diatomic chlorine, Cl_2, is a simple molecule with a nonpolar covalent bond. Each Cl atom has 7 valence electrons, so the total number of valence electrons in the molecule is 14. To draw its dot diagram, first write the symbol of each atom in the molecule.

Cl Cl

To be bonded covalently, these atoms must share at least one pair of electrons (rule 3). Place 2 dots between the symbols to represent this bond.

Cl:Cl

There are 12 more valence electrons to add to the diagram. Each atom must have a total of eight electrons around it (rule 1: the octet rule). Place pairs of electrons on the sides of the symbols so each atom has a total of 8.

:C̈l:C̈l:

There are 14 electrons total (rule 2), so this is the correct dot diagram of Cl_2. One pair is shared in a single bond. Three pairs in each atom are not shared. Valence electrons that are not involved in a bond are called **lone pairs.** In the dot diagram of Cl_2, there are a total of six lone pairs.

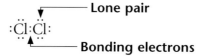

The two electrons in the single bond are shown in pink. As you might guess, the dot diagrams of F_2, Br_2, and I_2 are similar. All have a total of 14 valence electrons. But what about O_2? This molecule has a total of 12 valence electrons. Example 1 shows how to draw the dot diagram of O_2.

Example 1   Draw the dot diagram for O_2.

Read   You are asked to draw a diagram showing how the valence electrons are arranged to form the bond in O_2.

Plan   Oxygen has 6 valence electrons, so the total number of valence electrons in the molecule is 12. O_2 has an electronegativity difference of 0, so its bond is nonpolar covalent.

Solve   Write the element symbols of the two atoms. For a covalent bond, they must share at least one pair of electrons. Place 2 dots between the symbols. Then add enough lone pairs so that each atom has 8 valence electrons around it.

:Ö:Ö:

This dot diagram has 14 electrons. This is too many! Two electrons have to go. Remove one lone pair from each atom (remove 4 total). Then add another bonded pair (add 2 back).

:Ö::Ö:

There are 12 valence electrons now, and each atom has 8. Bonding rules 1, 2, and 3 are met.

Reflect   The bond in O_2 is a double bond. Four electrons, or 2 pairs, are shared in the double bond. Each atom also has two lone pairs.

Practice   Draw the dot diagram for Br_2.

To make dot diagrams simpler, chemists often show one pair of bonding electrons as a line between atoms. Double bonds are shown as two lines, and triple bonds are shown as three lines.

:Çl:Çl: or   :Çl—Çl:

:Ö::Ö: or   :Ö=Ö:

:N:::N: or   :N≡N:

Each line represents 2 bonding electrons.

Example 2   Draw the dot diagram for N_2.

Read   You are asked to draw a dot diagram showing the bond in N_2.

Plan   The total number of valence electrons in N_2 is $5 + 5 = 10$. N_2 is a nonpolar covalent bond.

Solve   Write the element symbols. Start by showing a bond of 2 electrons between the atoms. Then place lone pairs around the atoms so each has 8 electrons around it.

:N̈:N̈:

Although the octet rule is satisfied, there are too many valence electrons. Remove a lone pair from each atom and add a bonded pair.

:N̈::N̈:

Now there are 12 electrons—still too many. Again, remove a lone pair from each atom and add a bonded pair.

:N:::N: or   :N≡N:

Each atom has 8 electrons around it, and the total number of valence electrons is 10.

Reflect   This molecule contains a triple bond. The two atoms share 6 bonding electrons.

Practice   Draw the dot diagram for CO.

So far, you have learned how to represent molecules of two atoms. For molecules of three or more atoms, you need to think about how the atoms are arranged. If a molecule has only one atom of an element, that atom is usually in the center. The other atoms are bonded to the center atom. For example, in CH_4, the C atom is in the center. The four H atoms are bonded to the C atom, not to each other. The next example shows how to draw the dot diagram of CH_4.

Example 3	Draw the dot diagram for CH_4.
Read	You are asked to draw a dot diagram for a compound.
Plan	The total number of valence electrons is $4+1+1+1+1=8$. The electronegativity difference for a bond between C and H is $2.5-2.1=0.4$. This is a slightly polar covalent bond.
Solve	Arrange the element symbols so carbon is in the center, with the other atoms bonded to it. There are no bonds between H atoms. Place a pair of electrons between the C atom and each H atom.

```
         H                    H
         |                    |
   H:C:H       or      H — C — H
         ··                   |
         H                    H
```

This arrangement gives the molecule a total of 8 valence electrons. The C atom has 8 electrons around it. However, each H atom has only 2 electrons. For hydrogen, 2 valence electrons is a full set. The octet rule does not apply. In Chapter 10, you learned that hydrogen has one energy level consisting of the $1s$ orbital. There are no p orbitals in the first energy level. In a dot diagram, hydrogen must have exactly 2 valence electrons around it. The dot diagram above is correct.

Reflect	The four bonds in this molecule are single bonds.
Practice	Draw the dot diagram for NH_3.

As Example 3 shows, after a hydrogen atom forms a bond, it has a full set of 2—not 8—valence electrons. This is a full set because a hydrogen atom has only the $1s$ orbital. A helium atom already has this full set of 2 valence electrons, so it does not form bonds. There are other elements that are exceptions to the octet rule. Lithium has 1 valence electron in a $2s$ orbital. Lithium loses this single electron, forming a Li^{1+} ion. This ion has a complete set of 2 electrons in the $1s$ orbital. Beryllium and boron do not form ions. Beryllium typically forms only two covalent bonds by sharing the 2 electrons in the $2s$ orbital. Boron typically forms three bonds, obtaining a total of 6 electrons in its valence level. Many of the transition metals react as if they have 1, 2, or 3 valence electrons. They form ions that do not conform to the octet rule.

Example 4	Draw the dot diagram for CO_2.
Read	You are asked to draw a dot diagram of a compound.
Plan	In CO_2, the C atom is the center atom. The total number of valence electrons is $4+6+6=16$. The electronegativity difference for a bond between O and C is $3.5-2.5=1.0$. This is a polar covalent bond.
Solve	Arrange the element symbols so carbon is in the center. Place a pair of electrons between the C atom and each O atom. Then place lone pairs so each atom has 8 valence electrons. $:\ddot{O}:\ddot{C}:\ddot{O}:$ or $:\ddot{O}-\ddot{C}-\ddot{O}:$ This arrangement gives the molecule a total of 20 valence electrons. 4 electrons must go. To do this, remove one lone pair on each O atom and remove both lone pairs on the C atom. Then add a pair of electrons to each single bond, making double bonds. $:\ddot{O}::C::\ddot{O}:$ or $:\ddot{O}=C=\ddot{O}:$ This arrangement has a total of 16 valence electrons, and each atom has 8.
Reflect	The two bonds in this molecule are double bonds.
Practice	Draw the dot diagram for HCN. Place the C atom in the center.

❖ ❖

Technology and Society

The molecular compound, sulfur dioxide, SO_2, has been used to preserve food for hundreds of years. When this compound reacts with water, ionic compounds form. These compounds contain hydrogen sulfite (HSO_3^{1-}) and sulfite (SO_3^{2-}) ions. These ionic compounds keep foods, especially fruits, from spoiling and becoming discolored.

Dot Diagrams of Polyatomic Ions

From Chapter 3, you know that a polyatomic ion acts as a single cation or anion in an ionic compound. An anion and cation are held together by an ionic bond. However, the atoms within a polyatomic ion are held together by covalent bonds. Every polyatomic ion is just a molecule with a charge. Its dot diagram can be drawn. For example, $NaNO_3$ is an ionic compound. Its cation is Na^{1+}, and its anion is NO_3^{1-}. These two ions have an ionic bond between them. *Within* the NO_3^{1-} anion, however, are covalent bonds.

$$Na^{1+} \left[\begin{matrix} :\overset{\cdot\cdot}{O}: \\ | \\ N = \overset{\cdot\cdot}{O}: \\ | \\ :\overset{\cdot\cdot}{O}: \end{matrix} \right]^{1-}$$

When counting the valence electrons in a polyatomic ion, remember to adjust your count according to the charge. When the charge is negative, electrons are added to the total count. When the charge is positive, electrons are subtracted.

★ ★

Achievements in Science

The Octet Rule

Scientists are constantly developing theories that help them explain matter and its changes. The octet rule is a theory about how atoms react with each other to form compounds. It helps explain chemical reactions in terms of atomic structure. The octet rule is the result of the research of many scientists. An important step in the development of this theory came from the work of the chemist Gilbert N. Lewis.

Lewis imagined that an atom's nucleus and inner electrons are surrounded by a cube of valence electrons. The cube has eight corners, and each corner can contain one electron. This atomic model can be used to represent covalent bonds. A single bond is represented by two cubes sharing one edge (and two corners). A double bond is represented by two cubes sharing one side (and four corners). Lewis's cube model was simplified to dot diagrams. Dot diagrams are also known as Lewis structures.

Example 5	Draw the dot diagram for $CO_3{}^{2-}$.
Read	You are asked to draw the dot diagram for carbonate, a polyatomic ion. It has a charge of $2-$.
Plan	Carbon has 4 valence electrons, and oxygen has 6. The $2-$ charge indicates that there are 2 extra electrons. The total number of valence electrons is $4+6+6+6\,(+2)=24$. (For a positive ion like $NH_4{}^{1+}$, you would subtract 1 electron.)
Solve	Write the element symbols so the C atom is in the center. Each O atom is bonded to the C atom. Place a pair of electrons at each bond. Add lone pairs so that each atom is surrounded by 8 electrons.

$$:\ddot{O}:\ddot{C}:\ddot{O}:$$
$$:\ddot{O}:$$

Although each atom has 8 electrons, there are 26—too many. Remove a lone pair from the C atom and from one O atom. Add a bonding pair.

$$\left[:\ddot{O}:C::\ddot{O}\right]^{2-} \quad \text{or} \quad \left[:\ddot{O}-C=\ddot{O}\right]^{2-}$$
$$\quad\quad :\ddot{O}: \quad\quad\quad\quad\quad\quad :\underset{\cdot\cdot}{O}:$$

The total number of valance electrons is 24. One of the bonds in $CO_3{}^{2-}$ is a double bond.

Reflect	Always add brackets around the dot diagram of a polyatomic ion. Then write the charge outside.
Practice	Draw the dot diagram for $NO_2{}^{1-}$.

In the above example, it does not matter which oxygen atom has the double bond. There are actually three ways to correctly draw the dot diagram, depending on where the double bond goes.

$$\left[:\ddot{O}-C=\ddot{O}\right]^{2-} \quad \text{or} \quad \left[\ddot{O}=C-\ddot{O}:\right]^{2-} \quad \text{or} \quad \left[:\ddot{O}-C-\ddot{O}:\right]^{2-}$$
$$\quad :\ddot{O}: \quad\quad\quad\quad\quad\quad :\ddot{O}: \quad\quad\quad\quad\quad\quad :\ddot{O}:$$

Lesson 2   REVIEW

On a sheet of paper, write the phrase from the Word Bank that completes each sentence.

1. In a dot diagram, a bond containing 2 electrons can be drawn as a line, and a(n) _____ is drawn as two dots.

2. If two atoms share 4 electrons, the molecule contains a(n) _____.

3. The _____ states that almost all atoms form bonds to achieve a set of 8 electrons in their outermost energy level.

On a sheet of paper, write the letter of the answer that completes each sentence.

4. There are _____ electrons represented in the dot diagram of OH^{1-}.

   A 2   **B** 4   **C** 6   **D** 8

5. A triple bond involves the sharing of _____ electrons between two atoms.

   A 2   **B** 3   **C** 4   **D** 6

6. There are _____ electrons represented in the dot diagram of CCl_4.

   A 11   **B** 28   **C** 32   **D** 44

Critical Thinking

On a sheet of paper, write the answer to each question.

7. What is the total number of valence electrons in O_3? Draw its dot diagram.

8. What is the total number of valence electrons in NCl_3? Draw its dot diagram.

9. What is the total number of valence electrons in SiS_2? Draw its dot diagram.

10. What is the total number of valence electrons in CN^{1-}? Draw its dot diagram.

Dot diagrams on paper are flat, but the molecules they represent have three-dimensional shapes. By looking at the dot diagram for a molecule, you can predict its shape. The particular shape of a molecule is its **molecular geometry.** Once you know this geometry, you can understand some of the chemical properties of the molecule.

The key idea to molecular geometry is this: An atom's valence electron pairs repel each other. They tend to be as far away from each other as possible. This is true for all negatively charged objects. The correct shape of a molecule is the one that minimizes, or reduces, this repulsion. This idea is called **valence-shell electron-pair repulsion theory** (VSEPR theory, for short). Valence shell refers to the valence energy level. Think of a molecule with a center atom. The bonds to the center atom are positioned as far away as possible in three dimensions. When the distance between bonding electron pairs is greatest, the repulsion between them is smallest.

Molecular geometry

The particular shape of a molecule

Valence-shell electron-pair repulsion (VSEPR) theory

The idea that molecular geometry is determined by minimizing the repulsion between valence electron pairs

Linear

Having a flat, straight geometry

Linear Geometry

Look at the dot diagram for CO_2.

$$:\ddot{O}=C=\ddot{O}:$$

To minimize the electron-pair repulsion around the center atom, the electrons that make up each double bond are as far away from each other as possible. They are farthest apart when they are on opposite sides of the center atom. What shape is this? A straight line. The two double bonds are 180 degrees apart. A straight geometry is called **linear.**

180 degrees

Figure 12.3.1 *A CO_2 molecule is linear. The model on the left shows its three atoms, and the model on the right shows its two bonds.*

Molecules of only two atoms, like Cl_2 or CO, have no center atom and only one bond. Their molecular geometry is always linear.

It helps to use models to visualize the shapes of molecules. One type of model is called a space-filling model. It shows atoms as ball shapes. The balls are connected to show how atoms are arranged in a molecule. A second type of model shows the bonds of a molecule. This model uses tear shapes to represent bonding electrons as well as lone pairs on a center atom. CO_2 is modeled both ways in Figure 12.3.1. As you can see, CO_2 is a straight row of three atoms, or two bonds lined up end to end. A linear geometry like this is considered to be "flat." The atoms or bonds on the models do not "stick out of the page."

Trigonal Planar Geometry

A different molecular geometry is seen in the carbonate ion, $CO_3{}^{2-}$. Its dot diagram is

$$\left[:\ddot{O} - C = \ddot{O}: \atop { | \atop :\underset{\cdot\cdot}{O}:} \right]^{2-}$$

Dot diagrams usually show 90-degree or 180-degree angles between bond lines. However, this is not the greatest distance between the three bonds to carbon in this polyatomic ion. A better geometry, according to VSEPR theory, is a 120-degree angle between bonding electrons:

$$\left[{:\ddot{O} \ddot{O}: \atop \diagdown_{C}\diagup \atop {| \atop :\underset{\cdot\cdot}{O}:}} \right]^{2-}$$

The bonding electrons repel each other to a 120-degree separation. This molecular geometry is called **trigonal planar.** It has a flat, triangular shape, as the models in Figure 12.3.2 show.

Figure 12.3.2
A $CO_3{}^{2-}$ molecule is trigonal planar. The model on the left shows its four atoms, and the model on the right shows its three bonds.

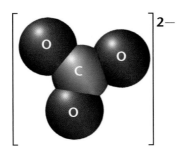

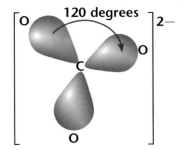

Tetrahedral Geometry

A third molecular geometry is shown by CH_4. In its dot diagram, the four bonds are drawn at 90-degree angles.

$$\begin{array}{c} H \\ | \\ H - C - H \\ | \\ H \end{array}$$

However, in a three-dimensional world, it is possible for the bonds to get even farther apart. This molecule has a **tetrahedral** shape. This shape is like a pyramid with four points (the H atoms) and four triangle-shaped sides, as shown in Figure 12.3.3. In a tetrahedral molecule, the four pairs of bonding electrons are 109.5 degrees apart. The molecule is not flat. The five atoms are not in the same plane.

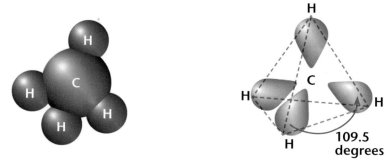

Figure 12.3.3 *A CH_4 molecule is tetrahedral. The model on the left shows its five atoms, and the model on the right shows its four bonds.*

Trigonal Pyramidal Geometry

You have looked at the shapes of three molecules so far: CO_2, CO_3^{2-}, and CH_4. In each case, the center atom, carbon, has no lone pairs. Look back at the dot diagrams of these molecules. All of the valence electrons around carbon are involved in bonds. When a molecule has a center atom *with a lone pair*, its geometry is affected. This is because the lone pair takes up space, just like bonding electrons would. The lone pair repels bonding electrons. As a result, the bond angles are slightly different. For example, look at the dot diagram of ammonia, NH_3.

$$H - \ddot{N} - H$$
$$\begin{array}{c} | \\ H \end{array}$$

The center nitrogen atom has four electron pairs around it—three pairs are in bonds and one is a lone pair. All four repel each other as far away as possible. The molecular geometry is close to a tetrahedral CH_4 molecule. However, only three atoms are bonded to nitrogen. As a result, the top point or leg of the pyramid is "missing" in a way. This molecular geometry is referred to as **trigonal pyramidal,** as shown in Figure 12.3.4.

Figure 12.3.4
_An NH_3 molecule is trigonal pyramidal. The model on the left shows its four atoms. In the model on the right, the three bonds are repelled by each other as well as by the "invisible" lone pair._

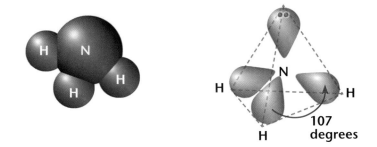

In a trigonal pyramidal molecule, the angles between bonds are slightly less than 109.5 degrees. The lone pair has more freedom of movement than electrons in a bond. Because of this freedom, it repels the three bonded pairs more strongly. As a result, the bonds are slightly closer to each other than the ones in a tetrahedral molecule. The angles between bonds are about 107 degrees.

Example 1	Draw the dot diagram of PF_3 and identify its molecular geometry.
Read	You are asked to draw the dot diagram of a molecule and then give the name of its molecular geometry, or shape.
Plan	P is the center atom. The total number of valence electrons in the molecule is $5+7+7+7=26$. Use the octet rule to distribute these elections. $:\ddot{F} - \ddot{P} - \ddot{F}:$ $\quad\ \ |$ $\quad\ :\ddot{F}:$
Solve	This molecule has three single bonds and one lone pair on the center atom. This is similar to NH_3, so the geometry is trigonal pyramidal.
Reflect	Because the lone pair can move more freely than the bonding electrons, it repels them more strongly. The angle between bonds is about 107 degrees.
Practice	Draw the dot diagram of PCl_3 and identify its molecular geometry.

Bent Geometry

There is one more type of geometry to learn. A water molecule has this geometry. The total number of valence electrons in H_2O is 8, since an oxygen atom has 6 and each hydrogen atom has 1. The dot diagram is

$$H-\ddot{\underset{..}{O}}-H$$

From this diagram, you might think that a H_2O molecule is linear. However, the center oxygen atom has two lone pairs, and both of these repel the two bonding pairs. A water molecule is close to a tetrahedral shape, but two points (atoms) are missing from the pyramid. This geometry is called **bent.** It is modeled in Figure 12.3.5.

Remember the geometry of NH_3? Its bond angles are slightly less than those of CH_4 due to one free-moving lone pair. Water has two free-moving lone pairs, so the angle between the two O-H bonds is affected even more so. The two lone pairs repel the two bonding pairs, making them even closer to each other. The bond angle in a H_2O molecule is about 104.5 degrees.

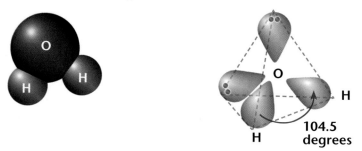

Figure 12.3.5 *An H_2O molecule has a bent geometry. The model on the left shows the three atoms. In the model on the right, the two O-H bonds are repelled by each other as well as by the two "invisible" lone pairs.*

Example 2	Draw the dot diagram of H_2S and identify its molecular geometry.
Read	You are asked to draw a dot diagram of a molecule and then name its geometry.
Plan	The total number of valence electrons is $1+1+6=8$. The S atom goes in the center, with an H atom on each side.
Solve	The dot diagram is $H - \ddot{S} - H$ Each H atom has two electrons around it. The S atom has four pairs of electrons around it: two bonding pairs and two lone pairs. This molecule has the same bent shape as water.
Reflect	H_2S has two single S-H bonds. The S atom has two lone pairs, giving the molecule its bent shape.
Practice	Draw the dot diagram of SCl_2 and identify its molecular geometry.

Some molecules have a center atom with two bonds and only one lone pair. These molecules are also described as bent. A good example is sulfur dioxide, SO_2. Its dot diagram is

$$:\ddot{O} - \ddot{S} = O:$$

The lone pair on the S atom pushes the two bonds closer together. The three atoms are not in a straight line. The angle between the two bonds is a little less than 120 degrees.

Table 12.3.1 summarizes the molecular geometries discussed in this lesson. There are many other molecular geometries that are more complex.

Table 12.3.1 Molecular Geometries				
Atoms Bonded to Center Atom	Lone Pairs on Center Atom	Molecular Geometry	Bond Angle (degrees)	Example
no center atom	no center atom	linear	180	Cl_2
2	0	linear	180	CO_2
3	0	trigonal planar	120	CO_3^{2-}
4	0	tetrahedral	109.5	CH_4
3	1	trigonal pyramidal	107	NH_3
2	2	bent	104.5	H_2O
2	1	bent	<120	SO_2

Spotlight on Phosphorus

15
P
Phosphorus
31.0

Phosphorus is an abundant element in nature. It is commonly found in the form of phosphate rock. Elemental phosphorus exists in three forms. These forms contain only phosphorus atoms, but they differ in how the atoms bond. Because of this, they have different properties. Red phosphorus consists of P_4 molecules shaped like a pyramid. White phosphorus also consists of P_4 molecules, but their structure is not stable. The third form is black phosphorus. Atoms in black phosphorus are arranged in a sheet.

Phosphorus is commonly used with nitrogen and potassium in fertilizers. Fertilizers are often described by a set of three numbers. The middle number is the percentage of phosphorus. For example, a 6-12-6 fertilizer contains 12% phosphorus and 6% each of nitrogen and potassium. Phosphorus helps green plants grow roots and flowers.

Interesting Fact: You use phosphorus when you light a match.

On a sheet of paper, write the word or phrase from the Word Bank that completes each sentence. Use Table 12.3.1 and dot diagrams to help you.

1. In a molecule with _____ geometry, the bond angle is 109.5 degrees.

2. The center atom in a molecule has no lone pairs and is bonded to three other atoms. The molecule's shape is _____.

3. The three-dimensional shape of a molecule is its _____ geometry.

4. The shape of a molecule of O_3 is _____.

5. The shape of a molecule of NCl_3 is _____.

6. The shape of a molecule of SiS_2 is _____.

Critical Thinking

On a sheet of paper, write the answer to each question.

7. Draw the dot diagram of OCl_2. What is its molecular geometry?

8. Draw the dot diagram of $SiBr_4$. What is its molecular geometry?

9. Draw the dot diagram of CH_2O (place carbon in the center). What is its molecular geometry?

10. Why does a H_2O molecule have bond angles slightly less than 109.5 degrees, even though it has a tetrahedral shape?

Objectives

After reading this lesson, you should be able to

◆ name the two characteristics of a polar molecule

◆ describe an asymmetric molecular geometry

◆ tell whether a molecule is polar or nonpolar

Both water and carbon dioxide have polar covalent bonds between a center atom and two other atoms. However, their properties are very different. H_2O is a liquid at room temperature. CO_2 is a gas. Water dissolves many substances, including carbon dioxide. Carbon dioxide rarely acts as a solvent. Why are these two molecules so different? The answer is related to their molecular geometry.

In an H_2O molecule, the shared electrons spend more time near the more electronegative O atom. This gives the O atom a slight negative charge. Each H atom has a slight positive charge. Because the molecule is bent, the center of the positive charges is toward the hydrogen end of the molecule. The center of negative charge is toward the oxygen end of the molecule.

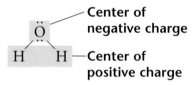

Polar molecule

A molecule with a slight positive charge on one end and a slight negative charge on the other end; also called a dipole

Nonpolar molecule

A molecule in which the positive charges and the negative charges are both balanced in the middle of the molecule

Water is a **polar molecule.** A polar molecule has a slight positive charge on one end and a slight negative charge on the opposite end.

In a CO_2 molecule, the shared electrons spend more time near each O atom. The O atoms are slightly negative, and the C atom is slightly positive. However, this molecule has a linear geometry. Because of this, the negative charge on one end balances the same negative charge on the other end. The center of these negative charges is in the middle of the molecule. The center of the positive charge is also in the middle.

Polar molecules are also called dipoles.

One end of the molecule is not more negative or positive than another end. The charges are balanced on the center atom. Because of its linear geometry, a CO_2 molecule is not polar. It is a **nonpolar molecule.**

Asymmetric

Having an unbalanced arrangement

A *bond* is ionic, nonpolar covalent, or polar covalent based on its electronegativity difference. A *molecule* is ionic, polar, or nonpolar based on bond type and molecular geometry. It is important to know whether you are talking about a bond or a molecule when using these terms.

How do you know if a molecule is polar or nonpolar? All polar molecules have *two* characteristics:

- They have at least one polar covalent bond.
- Their geometry is **asymmetric.**

A polar covalent bond has an electronegativity difference in the range of 0.4 to 1.7. Asymmetric means having an unbalanced arrangement. Asymmetric molecules have *one or both* of these characteristics:

- They have lone pairs on the center atom.
- They have different atoms bonded to the center atom.

In both cases, the center of the positive charges and the center of the negative charges are separated. Bent and trigonal pyramidal geometries have lone pairs, so they are always asymmetric. When the atoms bonded to a center atom are different, any geometry is asymmetric.

Example 1	Is CH_4 a polar molecule or a nonpolar molecule?
Read	You are asked if CH_4 is polar or nonpolar.
Plan	Check to see if CH_4 has the two characteristics of a polar molecule. Calculate the electronegativity difference between carbon and hydrogen. Then study the dot diagram for CH_4.

$$\begin{array}{c} H \\ | \\ H - C - H \\ | \\ H \end{array}$$

Solve	The electronegativity difference is $2.6 - 2.2 = 0.4$, so the C-H bond is polar covalent. In the dot diagram, there are no lone pairs on the center atom. All of the bonded atoms are H atoms. Thus, CH_4 is not asymmetric. It is a nonpolar molecule.
Reflect	CH_4 has a polar covalent bond. However, its geometry is not asymmetric.
Practice	Is SiS_2 a polar molecule or a nonpolar molecule?

Example 2	Is NH_3 a polar molecule or a nonpolar molecule?
Read	You are asked if NH_3 is polar or nonpolar.
Plan	Check to see if NH_3 has the two characteristics of a polar molecule. Calculate the electronegativity difference between nitrogen and hydrogen. Then study the dot diagram.

$$H-\overset{..}{N}-H$$
$$|$$
$$H$$ |
Solve	The N-H bond has an electronegativity difference of $3.0 - 2.2 = 0.6$, which means the bond is polar covalent. The molecule is asymmetric because there is a lone pair on the nitrogen atom. NH_3 is a polar molecule.
Reflect	This molecule has both characteristics of a polar molecule.
Practice	Is OCl_2 a polar molecule or a nonpolar molecule?

Example 3	Is HCN a polar molecule or a nonpolar molecule? Carbon is the center atom.
Read	You are asked if HCN is polar or nonpolar.
Plan	Calculate the electronegativity difference for the H-C bond and for the C-N bond. Then study the dot diagram.

$$H-C\equiv N:$$ |
Solve	The electronegativity differences are 0.4 for H-C and 0.5 for C-N. Both bonds are polar covalent. The molecule is asymmetric because the two atoms bonded to the center atom are different. The molecule is polar.
Reflect	Having two different atoms bonded to the center atom makes a molecule asymmetric. Having two different kinds of bonds (single and triple) does *not* make a molecule asymmetric.
Practice	Formaldehyde has the formula, CH_2O. Is it a polar or nonpolar molecule? Carbon is the center atom.

A polar molecule attracts other polar molecules. The attraction between polar molecules is discussed in the next lesson.

Word Bank

asymmetric

nonpolar

polar

On a sheet of paper, write the word from the Word Bank that completes each sentence.

1. O_2 is a(n) _____ molecule because it does not contain a polar covalent bond.

2. Molecules that are _____ have a polar covalent bond and are asymmetric.

3. A(n) _____ molecule has lone pair(s) of electrons on the center atom or has different atoms bonded to the center atom.

On a sheet of paper, write the answer to each question.

4. Draw the dot diagram of $SiBr_4$. Is it a polar molecule? Explain your answer.

5. Draw the dot diagram of water. Is it a polar molecule? Explain your answer.

6. Draw the dot diagram of NF_3. Is it a polar molecule? Explain your answer.

Critical Thinking

For each molecule, determine the bond type by calculating the electronegativity difference. Then draw the dot diagram and identify the molecular shape. Determine if the molecule is polar or nonpolar. Write your answers on a sheet of paper.

7. I_2 8. CO   9. PBr_3 10. SiO_2

Science Myth

Myth: All molecules that contain the same elements have the same polarity.

Fact: The polarity of a molecule depends on how many of each atom are present and how these atoms are arranged. For example, carbon and oxygen can form CO_2 and CO. The C-O bond is polar in each. However, CO_2 is not asymmetric and is nonpolar, while CO is asymmetric and polar.

Materials

- safety goggles
- lab coat or apron
- 600-mL beaker or other container
- isopropyl alcohol-water solution
- scissors
- chromatography paper
- pencil
- metric ruler
- 3 toothpicks
- red, blue, and green food dyes
- tape
- clear plastic wrap

Chromatography and Polarity

Chromatography is a method used to separate the substances in a mixture. Each substance is carried by a solvent at a different speed. This speed is based on how much attraction the substance has for the paper and for the solvent. A polar solvent attracts polar substances in a mixture more than nonpolar substances. How is separation by chromatography related to polarity? You will find out in this investigation.

Procedure

1. Put on safety goggles and a lab coat or apron.

2. Add the alcohol-water solution to the beaker until it is about 1 cm deep.

3. Cut three identical strips of paper. The three strips must be able to fit in the beaker as shown. Draw a pencil line 1 cm from the end of each paper strip. Using the toothpicks, center a spot of food dye on each line. Use a different color of dye for each strip.

4. Tape the strips to the pencil as shown, and place the pencil on top of the beaker. The ends of the strips must be barely in the solution. Cover the top of the beaker with clear plastic wrap to reduce evaporation.

5. Wait about 25 minutes while the solution moves up the paper. Then remove the strips from the solution. Allow them to dry overnight.

6. The next day, make a data table like the one below. Record in your table the colors that are in each dye. Also measure and record how far each color traveled up the paper.

Cleanup/Disposal

Pour the solution down the drain with running water. Wash the beaker and return all equipment. Clean your work area and wash your hands.

Analysis

1. Which substance in each dye traveled farthest?

2. Which substance in each dye traveled the least distance?

Conclusions

1. Which substance in each dye is likely to contain polar molecules?

2. Which substance in each dye is likely to contain molecules with little or no polarity?

Explore Further

Repeat the investigation using pure water as the solvent. Compare your results to those using the alcohol-water solution.

Dye Color	Colors of Substances in Dye	Distance Traveled from Line (cm)
red		
blue		
green		

Objectives

After reading this lesson, you should be able to

◆ list five kinds of attractive forces between particles

◆ tell when and why each force occurs

◆ explain the properties of some substances in terms of attractive forces

Interparticle force

An attractive force between particles in a substance

Polarity

The presence of separate areas of positive and negative charge

Dispersion force

A weak, temporary force of attraction between two particles that results from a temporary closeness of electrons within each particle

In the last three lessons, you have learned that the electron arrangement in covalent bonding affects the shape of a molecule. A molecule's shape affects the properties of the substance. There are other forces that act on particles of matter besides covalent bonds. These forces also affect the properties of substances. In fact, the variety of properties among substances is mostly due to the variation in forces that hold particles together.

There are five kinds of attractive forces between particles in substances. These forces are called **interparticle forces.** They can occur between atoms, molecules, or ions. All of these forces are caused by **polarity.** Polarity is the presence of separate positive and negative areas of charge. As you learned in the last lesson, polar molecules have this slight separation of charge. Polarity results from the arrangement or movement of valence electrons. Polarity can occur within a particle or between particles. Atoms can show polarity when their valence electrons are clustered together. Molecules can show polarity when the electrons in a bond spend more time near the more electronegative atom. Ionic compounds show an extreme form of polarity: the ions themselves are the positive and negative centers of charge.

Dispersion Forces

Dispersion forces are the weakest interparticle forces. A dispersion force is created by a temporary closeness of electrons within an atom or molecule. For example, a helium atom has two electrons in the $1s$ orbital. As these electrons move around, they may come near each other for a very short time. This temporary closeness creates a slight negative charge in that region of the atom. On the opposite side of the atom, a slight positive charge exists. This causes neighboring helium atoms to develop the same slight separation of charge. The positive end of one helium atom attracts the negative end of another helium atom. This attractive force between two or more atoms or molecules is a dispersion force, as shown in Figure 12.5.1.

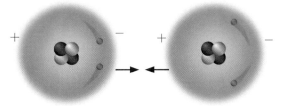

Dispersion force

Interparticle means "between particles." Interparticle forces are sometimes broadly called intermolecular forces. However, not all attractive forces occur between molecules. Some occur between atoms or ions.

Figure 12.5.1 *Two helium atoms are weakly attracted to each other because of a brief separation of charge in their electron cloud.*

Dispersion forces are very weak because they are temporary. However, as temperature decreases, dispersion forces get stronger. This explains why helium has such a low boiling point. Imagine the atoms in a sample of helium gas. Dispersion forces between gas particles are not very strong. For helium gas to become a liquid, the atoms must be held together by dispersion forces. At ordinary temperatures, these forces are not strong enough to do this. However, at −269°C or 4 K (just above absolute zero), the dispersion forces become strong enough to cause the helium atoms to stick together and become a liquid.

As particle size increases, dispersion forces also get stronger. I_2 is a nonpolar molecule with a relatively large mass. Because of the size of I_2 molecules, dispersion forces are strong enough to hold them together as a solid at room temperature.

Dispersion forces exist between all atoms and molecules. They are the only interparticle forces between nonmetal particles, such as helium and iodine. They are also the only interparticle forces between nonpolar molecules. Because dispersion forces are so weak, nonpolar molecules with a low molar mass are usually gases at room temperature.

Dipole-dipole force

A permanent attractive force between oppositely charged ends of two polar molecules

Hydrogen bonding

A strong attractive force between the hydrogen atom of one polar molecule and an oxygen, nitrogen, or fluorine atom of another polar molecule

Link to ➤➤➤

Earth Science

Water molecules are strongly affected by dipole-dipole forces and hydrogen bonding. As a result, water molecules arrange themselves in a definite pattern when ice forms. Ice is less dense than liquid water. In cold locations where lakes and ponds freeze, the ice floats on top of liquid water. This allows organisms in the water to survive below the surface and not be frozen in ice.

Dipole-Dipole Forces

Dipole-dipole forces are attractive forces between polar molecules. Recall that polar molecules have a slight negative charge on one end and a slight positive charge on the opposite end. This uneven distribution of charge is permanent, not temporary. As a result, a polar molecule has the ability to attract other polar molecules. The negative end of one polar molecule is attracted to the positive end of another polar molecule, as Figure 12.5.2 shows. This dipole-dipole force is much stronger than a dispersion force. Polar substances are more likely to be liquids or solids at room temperature than nonpolar substances. Atoms and nonpolar molecules do not have dipole-dipole forces.

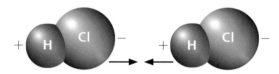

Dipole-dipole force

Figure 12.5.2 *In liquid hydrochloric acid, HCl, the molecules are attracted to each other because of dipole-dipole forces.*

Hydrogen Bonding

Hydrogen bonding is a force that occurs between polar molecules that have a hydrogen atom bonded to a nitrogen, oxygen, or fluorine atom. The electronegativity difference between hydrogen and any of these three elements is very large. Hydrogen's one electron spends almost all of its time near the more electronegative atom. The hydrogen atom, then, is basically a bare proton. This proton is attracted to the negative end of another molecule (the end with the nitrogen, oxygen, or fluorine atom). This attraction is a hydrogen bond. Hydrogen bonding is much stronger than most dipole-dipole forces. Figure 12.5.3 on page 495 shows the hydrogen bonding between water molecules. The dashed lines indicate hydrogen bonding. One water molecule can have hydrogen bonds to four other water molecules.

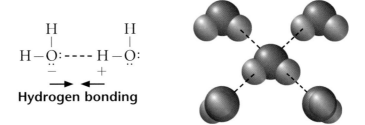

Hydrogen bonding

Figure 12.5.3 *Hydrogen bonding occurs between water molecules. The hydrogen end of the molecule is slightly positive, while the oxygen end is slightly negative. The dashed lines show hydrogen bonding.*

Science Myth

Myth: Hydrogen bonding is a covalent bond between hydrogen and another atom in the same molecule.

Fact: Hydrogen bonding is a strong dipole-dipole attractive force between a hydrogen atom in one molecule and a highly electronegative atom (oxygen, nitrogen, or fluorine) in another molecule. Hydrogen bonding is not a covalent or ionic bond.

Metallic Bonding

Metallic bonding occurs between the atoms in metals such as iron, copper, and tin. This interparticle force is stronger than the previous three forces. In elemental metals, the valence electrons are loosely held. As a result, they are able to delocalize, or spread out across all of the atoms. When electrons delocalize, they are not located in or between certain atoms. They are shared among all of the atoms. This creates a very strong attractive force between the atoms. It is often referred to as a sea of electrons. Figure 12.5.4 shows this sea of electrons for a metal that readily forms a 3+ ion.

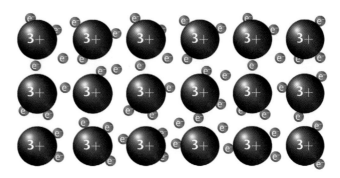

Figure 12.5.4 *Metal ions "float" in a sea of electrons. In this example, each metal atom releases three valence electrons into the sea.*

Metallic bonds are neither covalent nor ionic. There are no covalent or ionic bonds among the atoms of elemental metals.

Because valence electrons are delocalized in a metal sample, they move freely. As a result, metals conduct electricity and heat well. This is true of metals in a solid or liquid state. Metals conduct electricity well because electrons are free to move from one atom to the next. Metals conduct heat well because kinetic energy is rapidly transferred from one atom to the next. You will learn about electrons and electricity in Chapter 18.

Metals are ductile and malleable, as you learned in Chapter 11. They can be stretched or bent without breaking. Metals have these properties because of metallic bonding. The free-moving electrons form a strong connecting force among the atoms. Because of this force, metals usually have high melting and boiling points. It takes a lot of heat to separate atoms held together by metallic bonding.

Ionic Bonding

Ionic bonding occurs when the electronegativity difference between two atoms is greater than 1.7. In this range, valence electrons are no longer shared. Instead, some electrons are transferred from one atom to another. The result is two ions of opposite charge. Ionic bonding holds together ions in crystals made of repeating anions and cations. For this reason, ionic bonding is considered a bond type (determined by electronegativity difference) as well as an interparticle force. Ionic bonding is a very strong attractive force between positive and negative ions. Ionic bonding and metallic bonding are the strongest interparticle forces.

Cations and anions are held together very tightly by ionic bonds. Because of this strong attraction, most ionic compounds have high melting and boiling points. To break their ionic bonds by melting or boiling requires heating to a high temperature. Ionic compounds also dissolve fairly well in water. Many melted ionic compounds or solutions of ionic compounds are able to conduct electricity. These free-moving ions are similar to the free-moving electrons in metals. Ionic compounds are almost always solids at room temperature. Unlike metals, they are **brittle.** A brittle solid shatters when hit with force.

Table 12.5.1 summarizes the five attractive forces and the kinds of particles they act on.

Table 12.5.1 Interparticle Forces	
Force	Particles
dispersion force	all atoms and molecules
dipole-dipole force	polar molecules
hydrogen bonding	polar molecules that contain an H-N, H-O, or H-F bond
metallic bonding	atoms in elemental metals
ionic bonding	ions

Chemistry in Your Life

Consumer Choices: Microwave Cooking

You have probably used a microwave oven to cook food. Cooking food with microwaves is based on the polarity of the molecules in the food.

The energy field in a microwave oven has a certain polarity to it. Because of this, it attracts polar molecules. The polarity of the field changes more than a billion times each second. As the polarity changes, polar molecules in the food flip back and forth. Even the driest foods contain some water. A microwave oven cooks food primarily by increasing the speed of water molecules. Increased motion raises the temperature, and the food cooks.

In choosing a microwave oven, consumers might consider the wattage of the oven. The greater the wattage, the more quickly water molecules move, and the faster the food cooks.

1. Why does a microwave oven heat liquid water faster than it can melt an ice cube?

2. Many molecules in foods are nonpolar. Explain why these molecules are not affected by the energy field created by microwaves.

3. If you have a microwave oven, what is its wattage? Compare this to other values reported by classmates.

Word Bank
brittle
delocalized
interparticle

On a sheet of paper, write the word from the Word Bank that completes each sentence.

1. Substances that shatter when hit with a force are _____.

2. When electrons are shared among metal atoms, the electrons are _____.

3. There are five kinds of _____ forces.

On a sheet of paper, write the answer to each question.

4. What is the strongest interparticle force in a piece of copper?

5. What is the strongest interparticle force in a sample of NaCl?

6. What is the strongest interparticle force in a sample of I_2 gas?

Critical Thinking

Copy the chart below on a sheet of paper. For each compound, fill in the missing information. If a compound is not molecular, put an X in the spaces that cannot be answered.

	Compound	Bond Type	Dot Diagram	Molecular Geometry	Polar Molecule?	Interparticle Forces
7.	KI					
8.	CCl_4					
9.	NH_3					

On a sheet of paper, write the answer to the following question.

10. How are metals and ionic compounds able to conduct electricity?

Materials

- safety goggles
- lab coat or apron
- candle and holder
- matches
- 400-mL beaker
- beaker tongs
- 4 ice cubes
- strip of cobalt chloride paper

Forces Between Molecules

The properties of a molecular compound are affected by the attractive forces between its molecules. What can you conclude about these forces by observing the properties of the compound? In this investigation, you will examine a property of carbon dioxide and water vapor. These gases are formed by combustion.

Procedure

1. Using the materials provided, write a procedure to compare how easily CO_2 and H_2O change from a gas to a liquid. Both gases are produced by a burning candle. Include a hypothesis and safety alerts in your procedure. Cobalt chloride paper is used to detect the presence of liquid water.

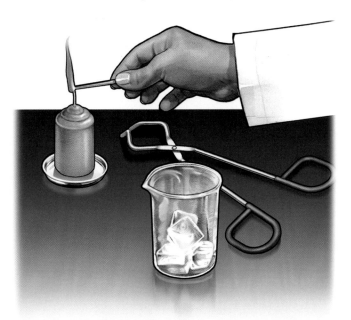

Continued on next page

2. Make a table to record your observations.

3. After your teacher approves your procedure, perform the investigation.

Cleanup/Disposal

Return the equipment and properly dispose of materials. Clean your work area and wash your hands.

Analysis

1. What did you observe when you cooled the gaseous products of the burning candle?

2. What did you learn by using the cobalt chloride paper?

3. Water boils at 100°C, while carbon dioxide is a gas at temperatures above −78°C. Use this information to explain your answers to questions 1 and 2.

Conclusions

1. What type of bond is present in a water molecule? In a carbon dioxide molecule?

2. Use dot diagrams to determine if the molecules of each substance are polar.

3. Based on your answers to questions 1 and 2, list the interparticle forces acting on each substance.

4. How do your answers to questions 1–3 help explain your results?

Explore Further

Dihydrogen sulfide, H_2S, is a poisonous gas with a boiling point of −60°C. Draw a dot diagram for H_2S and determine its geometry. Form a hypothesis explaining why H_2S boils at a much lower temperature than H_2O.

Petroleum and Its Molecules

Petroleum is a natural resource that supplies much of the world's energy needs. Many fuels, such as gasoline and heating oil, come from petroleum. Petroleum is also the source of most plastics and synthetic fibers. What plastic items do you use? Which pieces of clothing are made of synthetic fabrics? They all came from petroleum. Even items not made from petroleum are often produced using petroleum as an energy source.

Petroleum is a mixture of molecular compounds called hydrocarbons. As the name implies, hydrocarbons contain hydrogen and carbon. Some of the hydrocarbons in petroleum are small molecules, and some are extremely large molecules.

Not all compounds in petroleum are equally useful. When petroleum is refined, large molecules that are less useful may undergo a process known as cracking. Cracking involves breaking some covalent bonds in large molecules. Refiners use this process to change large molecules into smaller, more useful molecules.

Cracking is done by two different methods. Sometimes, heat and pressure are used to break the bonds. More commonly, a catalyst is added to the petroleum to help break large molecules into smaller ones.

Sometimes chemists join small hydrocarbons to create large molecules. Polymerization is one such process. In polymerization, small molecules from petroleum are placed under high pressure and heat. This causes the molecules to bond. The large molecules that form are used to make gasoline.

1. Explain the difference between cracking and polymerization.

2. Not all petroleum is the same. Petroleum from the United States may contain a different mixture of hydrocarbons than petroleum from Mexico. How do you think these differences might affect how the petroleum is refined?

Chapter 12 SUMMARY

- A bond forms when electrons are shared or transferred between two atoms.

- In nonpolar covalent bonds, electrons are shared equally between two atoms. The electronegativity difference of these bonds is less than 0.4.

- In polar covalent bonds, electrons are shared unequally between two atoms. The electronegativity difference of these bonds is in the range of 0.4 to 1.7.

- Ionic bonds form when electrons are completely transferred to the more electronegative atom. The electronegativity difference in an ionic bond is greater than 1.7.

- Dot diagrams illustrate how bonds and valence electrons are arranged in a molecule.

- The octet rule states that atoms transfer or share electrons to obtain a set of 8 electrons in their outer energy level. These electrons can be bonding electrons or lone pairs.

- Molecular geometry is the shape of a molecule. Five simple geometries are linear, trigonal planar, tetrahedral, trigonal pyramidal, and bent.

- Polar molecules contain a polar covalent bond and are asymmetric. They have a positively charged end and a negatively charged end.

- Bonds determine the arrangement of electrons, the shape of molecules, and the properties of substances.

- Besides covalent bonds, interparticle forces exist between atoms, ions, and molecules.

- Dispersion forces occur between all atoms and molecules. Dipole-dipole forces occur between polar molecules. Hydrogen bonding occurs between polar molecules in which a hydrogen atom is bonded to a nitrogen, oxygen, or fluorine atom. Metallic bonding occurs between atoms in metals. Ionic bonding occurs between ions.

Vocabulary

asymmetric, 487	interparticle force, 492	polarity, 492
bent, 482	ionic bond, 462	polar molecule, 486
brittle, 496	linear, 478	single bond, 469
covalent bond, 462	metallic bonding, 495	tetrahedral, 480
dipole-dipole force, 494	molecular geometry, 478	trigonal planar, 479
dispersion force, 492	nonpolar covalent bond, 465	trigonal pyramidal, 481
double bond, 469	nonpolar molecule, 486	triple bond, 469
electronegativity, 463	octet rule, 469	valence-shell electron-pair repulsion (VSEPR) theory, 478
hydrogen bonding, 494	polar covalent bond, 465	

Word Bank

bent

dipole-dipole
  forces

dispersion forces

double bond

electronegativity

hydrogen bonding

ionic bonding

metallic bonding

polarity

polar molecule

tetrahedral

trigonal planar

triple bond

Vocabulary Review

On a sheet of paper, write the word or phrase from the Word Bank that completes each sentence.

1. Two nonpolar molecules are attracted to each other by _____.

2. When two atoms share two pairs of electrons, it is called a(n) _____.

3. The presence of separate positive and negative areas of charge is _____.

4. Atoms in elements such as iron and zinc are attracted to each other because of _____.

5. A molecule with a positive end and a negative end is a(n) _____.

6. When two atoms share three pairs of electrons, it is called a(n) _____.

7. The attraction between two polar molecules is due to _____.

8. Compounds such as NaCl and KF are held together by _____.

9. A special dipole-dipole force called _____ occurs when polar molecules with an H-N, H-O, or H-F bond are attracted to each other.

10. The difference in _____ for two atoms determines the type of bond they form.

11. The shape of a molecule of SeF_2 is _____.

12. The shape of a molecule of $SiCl_4$ is _____.

13. The shape of the NO_3^{1-} ion is _____.

Continued on next page

Concept Review

On a sheet of paper, write the letter of the answer to each question. For some questions, it may help to draw a dot diagram.

14. Which of the following substances conducts electricity?

    A He   **C** Zn

    B CH_4 **D** SO_2

15. What is the molecular geometry of SiO_2?

    A linear   **C** tetrahedral

    B trigonal planar   **D** bent

16. What is the molecular geometry of PF_3?

    A trigonal planar   **C** tetrahedral

    B trigonal pyramidal   **D** bent

17. What type of bond exists between the atoms in O_2?

    A nonpolar covalent   **C** ionic

    B polar covalent   **D** electronegative

18. Which of the following substances dissolves in water to form a solution that conducts electricity?

    A O_2 **C** KF

    B $SiCl_4$ **D** SeF_2

19. Based on your knowledge of interparticle forces, which of the following substances is most likely a solid at room temperature?

    A O_2 **C** KF

    B $SiCl_4$ **D** SeF_2

Problem Solving

On a sheet of paper, write the answer to each question.

20. Which of the following molecules is polar: O_2, $SiCl_4$, or SeF_2? Explain your answer in terms of electronegativity difference and symmetry.

21. Use electronegativity difference to determine the bond type in N_2 gas, formaldehyde (CH_2O), and water. (Evaluate both kinds of bonds in CH_2O.)

22. Draw the dot diagrams of nitrogen (N_2), formaldehyde (CH_2O), and water (H_2O). In formaldehyde, carbon is the center atom.

Critical Thinking

On a sheet of paper, write the answer to each question.

23. Determine if each molecule in question 22 is polar or nonpolar. Explain your answer for each.

24. Name the interparticle forces in each substance listed in question 22.

25. N_2 gas has a boiling point of $-196°C$. Formaldehyde, CH_2O, has a boiling point of $-21°C$. Water's boiling point is $100°C$. Why are these boiling points so different? Explain your answer in terms of the strength of interparticle forces.

Test-Taking Tip Read a problem thoroughly before you begin to solve it. After you have calculated your answer, read the problem again to be sure your answer makes sense.

Thermodynamics

Flames warm the air inside this hot-air balloon, causing the balloon to rise. The balloon rises because the warmed air is lighter than the surrounding, cooler air. Warm air is lighter than cool air because it is less dense. It all comes down to the motion of air molecules. In Chapter 13, you will study heat and the movement of atoms and molecules. You will learn how heat is transferred.

Organize Your Thoughts

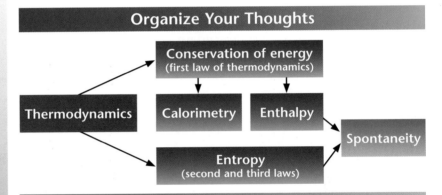

Conservation of energy
(first law of thermodynamics)

Thermodynamics

Calorimetry

Enthalpy

Spontaneity

Entropy
(second and third laws)

Goals for Learning

◆ To explain exothermic and endothermic processes in terms of heat transfer

◆ To understand specific heat and solve calorimetry problems

◆ To define enthalpy and calculate the heat of reaction for a chemical reaction

◆ To calculate the heat of reaction using standard heats of formation

◆ To explain entropy and give examples of changes that result in more entropy

◆ To understand how enthalpy and entropy changes determine spontaneity

Objectives

After reading this lesson, you should be able to

◆ explain endothermic and exothermic changes

◆ describe how heat is transferred

◆ explain what specific heat is

◆ use the heat equation to solve a calorimetry problem

Thermodynamics

The study of energy changes that accompany chemical and physical changes

Exothermic

Producing heat

Endothermic

Absorbing heat

Heat

The energy that is transferred between objects that have different temperatures

Specific heat (C_p)

The amount of heat needed to raise the temperature of 1 g of a substance by 1°C

Energy is essential to your way of life. Foods provide the energy you need to live, work, and play. Fuels provide the energy used to heat homes, run vehicles, and make products. Every chemical or physical change involves a change in energy. **Thermodynamics** is the study of these energy changes. When you light a match, a reaction takes place. This chemical change is **exothermic.** An exothermic change produces **heat.** When ice on a sidewalk melts on a sunny day, the ice is absorbing heat. This physical change is **endothermic.** An endothermic change absorbs heat. All exothermic and endothermic changes involve a transfer of heat between two or more substances.

Heat Transfer and Specific Heat

Heat is the energy that is transferred between objects that have different temperatures. Heat is always transferred from an object with a higher temperature to an object with a lower temperature. Temperature is a measure of average kinetic energy. When a warm object comes in contact with a colder object, kinetic energy is transferred from the higher-energy particles of the warm object to the lower-energy particles of the cold object. The higher-energy particles slow down (cool down), and the lower-energy particles speed up (warm up) until both are at the same temperature. The temperature change of an object depends on

• the amount of heat that is transferred to or from the object
• the mass of the object
• the **specific heat** of the object

Specific heat is the amount of heat needed to raise the temperature of 1 g of a substance by 1°C. Specific heat has the symbol C_p. It is a constant for a given substance at a certain pressure. The unit for specific heat is joule per gram per degree Celsius (J/g•°C). The SI unit of energy is the joule (J). Substances with a high specific heat act like a "heat sponge." They can absorb a lot of heat with just a small change in temperature.

In science, the Greek letter delta, Δ, means "change in."

Calorimetry is the measurement of heat transfer. Suppose a chemist wants to calculate the amount of heat transferred when the temperature of a sample changes by so many degrees. The amount of heat absorbed or released by the sample is q. It is calculated using this equation:

$$q = (m)(C_p)(\Delta T)$$

Here is what each symbol means:

- q is the symbol for heat. If q is a positive number, heat is absorbed by the sample and the change is endothermic. If q is a negative number, heat is released by the sample and the change is exothermic.
- m is the mass of the sample releasing or absorbing the energy.
- C_p is the specific heat of the substance. It is a constant.
- ΔT is the temperature change of the sample. ΔT is $T_2 - T_1$, where T_2 is the final temperature and T_1 is the starting temperature. If the temperature increases, ΔT is positive and the change is endothermic. If the temperature decreases, ΔT is negative and the change is exothermic.

If ΔT is negative, q is negative. If ΔT is positive, q is positive. The sign of q ($+$ or $-$) only tells if the change is exothermic or endothermic. The actual amount of energy transferred is never a negative number.

Science Myth

Myth: A small temperature change indicates that a small amount of heat has been transferred.

Fact: The amount of transferred heat does affect temperature. However, temperature depends on other factors, too. The mass and type of matter affect the size of a temperature change. A large amount of heat produces a small temperature change in a large mass.

Link to ➤➤➤

Earth Science

Air temperature does not change as much near a large lake or ocean. The reason is the specific heat of water. During the day, the body of water absorbs a large amount of energy. This tends to lower the air temperature. At night, the water slowly releases the stored energy and warms the air.

Example 1   What amount of heat is needed to increase the temperature of 10.00 mol of mercury by 7.50°C? The value of C_p for mercury is 0.139 J/g•°C.

Read   You are given a C_p value, an amount of mercury, and a temperature change.

Plan q is the amount of heat that must be absorbed by the mercury to raise its temperature. Use the equation, $q = (m)(C_p)(\Delta T)$, to solve for q. You will need to calculate m, the mass of the mercury. ΔT is given, so T_2 and T_1 are not needed. The temperature is increasing, so ΔT is positive.

Solve   Convert the 10.00 mol of mercury to grams. The molar mass of mercury is 200.6 g/mol.

$$m = 10.00 \text{ mol} \left(\frac{200.6 \text{ g}}{1 \text{ mol}} \right) = 2,006 \text{ g}$$

Now solve for q.

$$q = (m)(C_p)(\Delta T)$$

$$q = (2,006 \text{ g}) \left(\frac{0.139 \text{ J}}{\text{g}\cdot°\text{C}} \right) (7.50°\text{C}) = 2,090 \text{ J}$$

Reflect   The answer has been rounded to 3 significant figures. 2,090 J of heat is required to raise a 10.00-mol sample of mercury by 7.50°C. This physical change is endothermic.

Practice   What amount of heat is needed to increase the temperature of 22.4 g of nitrogen, N_2, by 9.5 K? The value of C_p for N_2 is 1.04 J/g•°C.

Link to ➤➤➤

Home and Career

Cooking utensils, such as pots and pans, are made from substances that have a low specific heat. The utensil heats quickly and requires a small amount of heat to reach a given temperature. Copper has a low specific heat, but is expensive. Aluminum and glass are inexpensive, but have higher specific heats. What material would make the best cooking utensils? Gold!

Heat Transfer in a Closed System

When heat is absorbed by a sample of matter, this heat must have been released by other matter. No heat is lost or created. The **first law of thermodynamics** states that the energy of the universe is constant. This is another way of stating the law of conservation of energy. Energy can be transferred or can change form, but it cannot be created or destroyed.

The first law of thermodynamics can be applied to a **system.** In chemistry, a system usually refers to all of the substances or objects involved in a change. When heat is transferred from substance 1 to substance 2, both substances are part of the same system. In a system, the heat absorbed by substance 1 equals the heat released by substance 2.

$$q_1 = -(q_2)$$
$$(m_1)(C_{p1})(\Delta T_1) = -(m_2)(C_{p2})(\Delta T_2)$$

In calorimetry experiments, a small amount of heat may be transferred to equipment or to the surrounding air. In calorimetry calculations, however, you may assume that no heat is transferred outside of the system. The system is considered to be "closed." All of the heat is transferred to the desired substance or object.

Suppose you want to measure the amount of heat transferred from a hot piece of metal to a sample of cooler water. If you know the specific heat of water, the water's mass, and the water's temperature change, you can calculate the amount of heat absorbed by the water. This equals the amount of heat released by the metal.

Technology and Society

A superinsulated window reduces energy transfer. The window consists of two panes of glass. The space between the panes contains a thin plastic film that reflects infrared radiation. The remaining space is often filled with argon or krypton gas. These gases are poor heat conductors compared to air.

Example 2   A 118-g piece of tin at 85.0°C is dropped into 100. g of water at 35.0°C. The final temperature of the mixture is 38.0°C. The specific heat of water is 4.18 J/g•°C. What amount of heat is absorbed by the water? What amount is released by the tin? What is the specific heat of tin?

Read   You are given the mass of a piece of tin and its starting and final temperatures. You are also given the mass of a sample of water, its starting and final temperatures, and its specific heat.

Plan   You are given several values. First, organize them into a table and identify which variables they represent in the heat equation, $q = (m)(C_p)(\Delta T)$.

	Tin	Water
m (g)	118	100.
T_1 (°C)	85.0	35.0
T_2 (°C)	38.0	38.0
ΔT (°C)	−47.0	3.0
C_p (J/g•°C)	?	4.18

Solve   Heat is always transferred from a warmer substance to a colder substance. In this system, the hot tin releases heat. This heat is transferred to the colder water. The amount released by the tin equals the amount absorbed by the water. The heat absorbed is

$$q_{water} = (100. \ g)\left(\frac{4.18 \ J}{g \cdot °C} \right)(3.0 \ °C) = 1,254 \ J$$

The value is positive because the heat is absorbed. This same amount of heat is released by the tin. However, when heat is released, its value is negative. So the heat released by the tin is

$$q_{tin} = -(q_{water}) = -1,254 \ J$$

To find the specific heat of tin, use the same equation, but for tin now, not water. You know $q_{tin} = -1,254$ J. You know the mass of tin. ΔT is negative because the tin dropped in temperature. Solve for C_p.

$$q_{tin} = -1,254 \ J = (118 \ g)(C_p)(-47.0°C)$$
$$C_p = 0.23 \ J/g•°C$$

Reflect   The answer has been rounded to 2 significant figures. The release of heat by tin is an exothermic change. The absorption of heat by water is an endothermic change.

Practice   A 66.3-g sample of beryllium at 89.0°C is dropped into 100. g of water at 22.0°C. The final temperature of the mixture is 37.0°C. The specific heat of water is 4.18 J/g•°C. Calculate the specific heat of beryllium.

The calorie (cal) is an energy unit equal to 4.18 J. The Calorie (Cal) is equal to 1,000 calories and is used to specify the energy content of food.

Whenever two substances of different temperatures are in contact with each other, heat is transferred. Heat continues to transfer from the warmer substance to a colder substance until both reach the same temperature.

Remember these things when using the heat equation, $q = (m)(C_p)(\Delta T)$:

- In a closed system, heat absorbed = heat released. Only the signs are different: $q_1 = -(q_2)$.
- A negative q means released heat, and positive q means absorbed heat.
- $\Delta T = $ (final temperature, T_2) $-$ (starting temperature, T_1).
- A positive ΔT means the temperature increased. A negative ΔT means the temperature decreased.

▼◄▲▼◄▲▼◄▲▼◄▲▼◄▲▼◄▲▼◄▲▼◄▲▼◄▲▼◄▲▼◄▲▼◄▲▼◄▲▼◄▲▼◄▲▼◄▲▼

Science at Work

Nutritionist

What do nutritionists have to do with thermodynamics? Nutritionists do many tasks. One of them is determining the energy content of food products. That information goes on the nutrition labels on packaging. The United States uses calories as a measure of energy content, while most other countries use kilojoules. Fats, carbohydrates, and proteins provide nearly all of the energy in food. For common foods, nutritionists may use known data to determine energy content. For less common foods, they may measure energy content using calorimetry. Nutritionists also inform patients about healthy dietary changes and work with hospital staff to plan menus.

Nutritionists often work for health clinics, hospitals, food manufacturers, or independent testing companies. They also work for the government agency responsible for food safety. Nutritionists usually have at least a bachelor's degree in nutrition, nursing, chemistry, food chemistry, or biology.

Example 3	A 125-g sample of iron at 93.5°C is dropped into an unknown mass of water at 25.0°C. The final temperature of the mixture is 32.0°C. The specific heat of iron is 0.451 J/g•°C. The specific heat of water is 4.18 J/g•°C. What is the mass of the water?	
Read	A hot iron sample is dropped into water. You are given several values for the iron and the water. You are asked to determine the mass of the water.	
Plan	Match the given values with the variables in $q=(m)(C_p)(\Delta T)$. Set up a data table.	

	Iron	Water
m (g)	125	?
T_1 (°C)	93.5	25.0
T_2 (°C)	32.0	32.0
ΔT (°C)	−61.5	7.0
C_p (J/g•°C)	0.451	4.18

Solve	You have all of the information to solve for q for the iron.

$$q_{iron}=(125\ g)\left(\frac{0.451\ J}{g\cdot °C}\right)(-61.5°C)=-3{,}467\ J$$

The negative value just means that 3,467 J of heat was released by the iron. This same heat was absorbed by the water.

$$q_{water}=-(q_{iron})=3{,}467\ J$$

Now use the data about the water in the heat equation.
$\Delta T=32.0°C-15.0°C=7.0°C$. Solve for m.

$$q_{water}=3{,}467\ J=(m)\left(\frac{4.18\ J}{g\cdot °C}\right)(7.0°C)$$
$$m=118\ g$$

Reflect	The answer has been rounded to 3 significant figures. As the temperature of the iron drops ($-\Delta T$), the temperature of the water rises ($+\Delta T$). In a closed system, an exothermic change occurs at the same time as an endothermic change.
Practice	A sample of aluminum at 87.2°C is dropped into 85.5 g of water at 27.2°C. The final temperature of the mixture is 32.5°C. The specific heat of aluminum is 0.899 J/g•°C, and the specific heat of water is 4.18 J/g•°C. What is the mass of the aluminum?

In Example 3, the mass of the water is close to the mass of the iron. However, their specific heats are very different. The temperature of the iron changed a lot (61.5°C). The same amount of heat changed the water temperature only 7.0°C.

Figure 13.1.1 *Take care when biting into a hot apple pie. Water has a high specific heat.*

As Example 3 shows, water is an excellent "heat sponge." It can absorb a great deal of heat without a large temperature change. When you eat an apple pie like the one in Figure 13.1.1, the filling can be very hot. This is because the filling contains water molecules that have absorbed a large amount of heat.

Chemistry in Your Life

The Environment: Coastal Climate Differences

The climates along the East and West Coasts of North America are very different. In summer, the East Coast has higher temperatures than the West Coast. In winter, the West Coast has higher temperatures than the East Coast. Two factors cause these differences. The first one is wind direction. Winds blow from west to east across North America and other world regions with similar latitudes. The other factor is the high specific heat of water compared to the low specific heat of land. In summer, land gets much hotter than ocean water. Winds blow in from the Pacific Ocean to cool the climate along the West Coast. Winds travel over hot land before reaching the East Coast, making the climate there hot. In winter, land cools quickly, but water does not. This means that the West Coast is warmed by the winds from the ocean. Along the East Coast, the winds come from the cold inland areas and make the climate cold, as the photo shows.

1. France is on the west coast of Europe, and Japan is along the east coast of Asia. Both cities are at about the same latitude as New York City. What can you conclude about the climate in these two countries, and why?

2. What changes in coastal climates would occur if the specific heat of land were greater than the specific heat of water? Explain.

3. Explain your climate in terms of the specific heats of land and water.

On a sheet of paper, write the word or phrase from the Word Bank that completes each sentence.

Word Bank

endothermic

exothermic

specific heat

1. A(n) _____ change releases heat.

2. A(n) _____ change absorbs heat.

3. The amount of heat needed to raise the temperature of 1 g of a substance by 1°C is _____.

On a sheet of paper, write the letter of the answer to each question. Use the C_p values in the box at the left if needed.

The following C_p values are in J/g•°C.

platinum	0.133
zinc	0.388
water	4.18
nickel	0.433
titanium	0.523

4. What amount of heat is needed to raise the temperature of 45.3 g of platinum from 17.0°C to 103°C?

    A −518 J   **B** 102 J   **C** 518 J   **D** 621 J

5. What amount of heat is released when 83.2 g of zinc cools from 75.2°C to 22.5°C?

    A 1,700 J   **B** 726 J   **C** −726 J   **D** −1,700 J

6. A certain mass of water cools from 52.5°C to 31.2°C. If 5,956 J of heat is released, what is the mass of the water?

    A 66.9 g   **B** 45.7 g   **C** 27.1 g   **D** 3.64 g

Critical Thinking

On a sheet of paper, write the answer to each question. Use the C_p values in the box above if needed.

7. A 128-g piece of iridium at 95.0°C is dropped into 45.2 g of water at 17.3°C. The final temperature of the mixture is 23.6°C. What is the specific heat of iridium?

8. A 63.2-g piece of nickel at 92.3°C is dropped into an unknown mass of water at 21.3°C. The final temperature of the mixture is 28.9°C. What is the mass of water?

9. A piece of titanium at 87.6°C is dropped into 53.1 g of water at 23.2°C. The final temperature of the mixture is 31.0°C. What is the mass of the titanium?

10. How does the first law of thermodynamics apply to a closed calorimetry system?

INVESTIGATION 13

Materials

- safety goggles
- lab coat or apron
- 2 foam cups
- balance
- 100-mL graduated cylinder
- water
- stirring rod
- 2 thermometers
- 400-mL beaker
- hot plate
- large test tube
- 2 known metal samples
- unknown metal sample
- ring stand
- test-tube clamp
- tongs

Determining the Specific Heat of Metals

In a closed system, the heat absorbed by one substance equals the heat released by another. Can you identify a substance from its specific heat? In this investigation, you will determine the specific heat for two known metals and one unknown metal.

Procedure

1. On a sheet of paper, make three tables like the one below, one for each metal sample.

2. Put on safety goggles and a lab coat or apron. Make a calorimeter by placing one foam cup inside another. Measure and record its mass.

3. Measure about 80 mL of water and pour this into the calorimeter. Measure and record the mass of the calorimeter and water. Place the stirring rod and one thermometer in the calorimeter.

4. Pour about 300 mL water into the 400-mL beaker. Place this on a hot plate. Turn on the hot plate. Bring the water to a boil. **Safety Alert: Be careful when working near a hot plate.**

5. Measure and record the mass of the large test tube. Place pieces of one known metal into it until it is half full. Measure and record the mass of the tube and contents.

Sample: _____	Data
mass of empty calorimeter	
mass of calorimeter and water	
mass of empty test tube	
mass of test tube and metal	
initial metal temperature	
initial water temperature	
final temperature	

Continued on next page

6. Support the test tube in the boiling water as shown. Heat the tube in boiling water for about 10 minutes. Turn off the hot plate. Measure the temperature of the boiling water. Record this as the initial temperature of the metal.

7. Stir the water in the calorimeter and measure its temperature. Record this as the initial temperature of the water.

8. Quickly transfer the metal from the test tube to the calorimeter without splashing. **Safety Alert: Be careful not to touch the water or the metal.** Stir the contents of the calorimeter for about 20 seconds. Record the final temperature of the water and metal (same temperature). Empty the calorimeter, saving the metal.

9. Repeat steps 3–8 for the other known metal and then for the unknown.

Cleanup/Disposal

Turn off the hot plate. Cool the water and then discard it, saving the metal samples. Dry and return the samples. Return all equipment. Wash your hands.

Analysis

1. Calculate the specific heat of each known metal.

2. What assumption is made about the initial temperature of the metal and the calorimeter?

3. Calculate the specific heat of the unknown metal.

Conclusions

1. Compare your calculated values for the known samples with the accepted specific heat of each metal.

2. What is the identity of your unknown metal?

3. Identify and explain possible sources of error in this investigation.

Explore Further

Suggest a way to determine the specific heat of a liquid substance.

Objectives

After reading this lesson, you should be able to

◆ define enthalpy and the heat of reaction

◆ calculate the enthalpy change for a given reaction

Enthalpy (H)

The amount of heat a sample has at a certain pressure and temperature; heat content

Heat of reaction (ΔH_{rxn})

The amount of heat released or absorbed in a chemical reaction per 1 mol of a reactant or product

In Lesson 1, you studied how a hot object transfers heat to a cooler sample of water, causing a temperature change in both substances. A change in temperature is a physical change. The substances themselves did not change. In this lesson, you will study the heat involved in chemical reactions. All chemical reactions either absorb or release energy.

Enthalpy is the amount of heat a sample has at a certain pressure and temperature. It is the sample's heat content. The symbol for enthalpy is H. It is sometimes used in place of the symbol for heat, q. However, enthalpy cannot be measured. Only changes in enthalpy can be measured. ΔH is the symbol for a change in enthalpy. ΔH can be calculated for a chemical reaction.

It is not always possible to use calorimetry to find the amount of heat absorbed or released by a chemical reaction. At the start of a reaction, each reactant has its own enthalpy, H. As the reaction progresses and atoms rearrange, heat is either released (an exothermic reaction) or absorbed (an endothermic reaction). This change in heat is called the **heat of reaction, ΔH_{rxn}**. It is the amount of heat released or absorbed in a chemical reaction, given 1 mol of a reactant or product. ΔH_{rxn} is the difference between the enthalpy of the reactants and the enthalpy of the products.

$$\Delta H_{rxn} = (H \text{ of products}) - (H \text{ of reactants})$$

If the enthalpy of the reactants is greater than the enthalpy of the products, heat is released and ΔH_{rxn} is negative. If the enthalpy of the reactants is less, heat is absorbed and ΔH_{rxn} is positive.

For a combustion reaction, the heat of reaction is called the **heat of combustion, ΔH_c.** Combustion reactions are always exothermic, so ΔH_c is always a negative value. The 1852 steam engine in Figure 13.2.1 burned wood. Some steam engines burned coal or oil. The enthalpy of the fuel is much greater than the enthalpy of the H_2O and CO_2 produced.

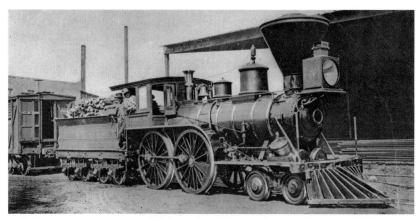

Figure 13.2.1
The Pioneer *was the first locomotive used in California. It used the energy released by burning wood to produce steam.*

Example 1	Carbon burns according to the equation, $C(s) + O_2(g) \rightarrow CO_2(g)$. $\Delta H_c = -393.5$ kJ/mol CO_2. If 2.00 mol of CO_2 forms, how much heat is released?
Read	You are given a combustion reaction and its ΔH_c. You are asked to calculate the amount of heat produced when 2.00 mol of CO_2 is produced.
Plan	The negative ΔH_c value means that 393.5 kJ of heat is released for each mole of CO_2 produced. You can use this value as a conversion factor. Notice the unit for ΔH_c: kilojoules per mole of CO_2.
Solve	Since 2.00 mol of CO_2 is produced, the amount of heat released is $$2.00 \text{ mol } CO_2 \left(\frac{-393.5 \text{ kJ}}{1 \text{ mol } CO_2} \right) = -787 \text{ kJ}$$ The enthalpy change for this reaction is -787 kJ.
Reflect	The ΔH_c value is specific for 1 mol of CO_2. However, all coefficients in this balanced equation happen to be 1. So $\Delta H_c = -393.5$ kJ is true for 1 mol of C, O_2, or CO_2.
Practice	For the combustion reaction below, $\Delta H_c = -1,390$ kJ/mol C_2H_4. If 7.50 mol of C_2H_4 reacts, how much heat is released? $C_2H_4(g) + 3O_2(g) \rightarrow 2CO_2(g) + 2H_2O(l)$

Sometimes the heat of reaction is written directly in a balanced chemical equation. If it is shown on the reactant side, heat is absorbed in an endothermic reaction. In this case, the heat of reaction, ΔH_{rxn}, is positive. If the heat of reaction is shown on the product side, heat is released in an exothermic reaction. In this case, ΔH_{rxn} is negative.

In Example 1, ΔH_c is -393.5 kJ/mol CO_2. The negative sign means the reaction is exothermic. ΔH_c could have been written on the product side of the equation:

$$C(s) + O_2(g) \rightarrow CO_2(g) + 393.5 \text{ kJ}$$

Even though this ΔH_{rxn} value is negative, it is added, not subtracted, as a product in the equation. When energy is shown on the product side, it is released energy, which has a negative value.

Express Lab 13

Materials

- safety goggles
- lab coat or apron
- 25–30 g of iron powder
- 1 g of sodium chloride (NaCl)
- plastic, self-sealing bag
- 1 large spoonful of vermiculite
- 5 mL of water

Procedure

1. Put on safety goggles and a lab coat or apron.

2. Place 25 to 30 g of iron powder into the plastic bag. Add 1 g of NaCl.

3. Seal the bag and shake to mix the contents.

4. Open the bag and add the vermiculite. Seal the bag and shake again to mix the contents.

5. Open the bag and add the water. Seal the bag and shake or squeeze it to mix the contents.

6. Wait about 1 minute. Record any observations.

Analysis

1. What did you observe after step 6?

2. How can you explain this observation?

Example 2 Natural gas, CH_4, burns according to this equation: $CH_4(g) + 2O_2(g) \rightarrow CO_2(g) + 2H_2O(l) + 890.2$ kJ. $\Delta H_c = -890.2$ kJ/mol CH_4. If 100. g of CH_4 burns, how much heat is released?

Read You are asked to find the amount of heat released by a reaction. You are given grams (not moles) of a reactant.

Plan ΔH_c is negative and is written on the product side of the equation. This means the reaction is exothermic. The unit for ΔH_c is kilojoules per mole. First use molar mass to convert the grams of CH_4 to moles. CH_4 has a molar mass of 16.0 g/mol. Then use the ΔH_c value to convert moles to kilojoules. Here is the conversion map:

mass of $CH_4 \rightarrow$ moles of $CH_4 \rightarrow$ energy released

Solve Use two conversion factors to convert the given mass to kilojoules. Place the desired unit in each factor on the top.

$$100. \text{ g } CH_4 \left(\frac{1 \text{ mol } CH_4}{16.0 \text{ g } CH_4} \right) \left(\frac{-890.2 \text{ kJ}}{1 \text{ mol } CH_4} \right) = -5,560 \text{ kJ}$$

The enthalpy change for this reaction is $-5,560$ kJ. In other words, 5,560 kJ of heat is released.

Reflect Review molar mass in Chapter 4 if needed.

Practice Carbon monoxide reacts with hydrogen to produce methanol, CH_3OH: $CO(g) + 2H_2(g) \rightarrow CH_3OH(g) + 90.5$ kJ. $\Delta H_{rxn} = -90.5$ kJ/mol CH_3OH. If 25.0 g of CH_3OH is produced, how much heat is released?

Word Bank

enthalpy

heat of combustion

heat of reaction

On a sheet of paper, write the word or phrase from the Word Bank that completes each sentence.

1. The heat content of a substance is its _____.

2. The amount of heat absorbed or released when 1 mol of a substance reacts is the _____.

3. When 1 mol of a substance burns in oxygen, the amount of heat released is the _____.

$$2SO_2(g) + O_2(g)$$
$$\rightarrow 2SO_3(g)$$
$\Delta H_{rxn} =$
-98.9 kJ/mol SO_3

$Fe_2O_3(s) + 2Al(s)$
$\rightarrow Al_2O_3(s) + 2Fe(l)$
$\Delta H_{rxn} =$
-853.9 kJ/mol Fe_2O_3

$CaCO_3(s)$
$\rightarrow CO_2(g) + CaO(s)$
$\Delta H_{rxn} =$
178.4 kJ/mol $CaCO_3$

On a sheet of paper, write the letter of the answer to each question. Use the equations and ΔH_{rxn} values in the box to the left.

4. 2.5 mol of SO_2 reacts with excess oxygen. How much heat is released?

  A -2.5 kJ   **B** $-40.$ kJ   **C** -98.9 kJ   **D** -250 kJ

5. If 3.50 mol of Fe_2O_3 reacts with excess aluminum, how much heat is released?

  A $-2,990$ kJ **B** $-1,490$ kJ **C** -853.9 kJ **D** -244 kJ

6. 0.250 mol of $CaCO_3$ decomposes. How much heat is absorbed?

  A 178.4 kJ   **B** 44.6 kJ   **C** -44.6 kJ   **D** -714 kJ

Critical Thinking

On a sheet of paper, write the answer to each question. Use the equations and ΔH_{rxn} values in the box.

7. 111 g of SO_3 is produced when SO_2 reacts with oxygen. How much heat is released?

8. 52.0 g of Fe_2O_3 reacts with excess aluminum. How much heat is released?

9. 150. g of $CaCO_3$ decomposes. How much heat is absorbed?

10. The value of ΔH_c for any combustion reaction is always negative. Why?

Objectives

After reading this lesson, you should be able to

◆ define standard state

◆ explain standard heat of formation

◆ calculate the heat of reaction, ΔH_{rxn}, using standard heats of formation

Enthalpy changes occur in all chemical reactions. In the last lesson, you learned that the enthalpy change for a combustion reaction is called the heat of combustion, ΔH_c. For a combination reaction, the enthalpy change is called the **standard heat of formation, ΔH_f.** This is the enthalpy change when 1 mol of a compound is formed from its elements in their **standard states.** Standard state is the state of an element at 1 atm and 25°C. For example, the standard state of sodium is a solid. Oxygen's standard state is a gas. Table 13.3.1 gives ΔH_f values for several compounds.

Table 13.3.1 Some Standard Heats of Formation

Compound	ΔH_f (kJ/mol)	Compound	ΔH_f (kJ/mol)
$Ba(OH)_2(s)$	−946	$HNO_3(aq)$	−207
$BaSO_4(s)$	−1,465	$H_2O(g)$	−241.8
$CH_4(g)$	−75	$H_2O(l)$	−285.8
$C_2H_6(g)$	−84	$H_3PO_4(l)$	−1,267
$CH_3OH(l)$	−239	$H_2SO_4(aq)$	−909
$CO(g)$	−110.5	$NH_3(g)$	−46.2
$CO_2(g)$	−393.5	$NO(g)$	+90
$Fe_2O_3(s)$	−822.1	$NO_2(g)$	+33.9
$HCN(g)$	+135	$SO_3(g)$	−396
$HCl(aq)$	−167	$SiCl_4(l)$	−687
$HCl(g)$	−92	$SiO_2(s)$	−911

Standard heat of formation (ΔH_f)

The enthalpy change when 1 mol of a compound is formed from its elements in their standard states

Standard state

The state of an element at 1 atm and 25°C

Standard state is not the same as standard temperature and pressure (STP) for gases.

For any chemical reaction, the enthalpy change can be calculated by this equation:

$$\Delta H_{rxn} = (\text{sum of } \Delta H_f \text{ of products}) - (\text{sum of } \Delta H_f \text{ of reactants})$$

When using this equation, follow these rules:

• $\Delta H_f = 0$ for an element in its standard state.

• If a reactant or product has a coefficient in the balanced equation, multiply its ΔH_f by its coefficient. Then enter this amount in the ΔH_{rxn} equation.

Example 1	Find the ΔH_{rxn} for the following balanced equation. Use the values of ΔH_f in Table 13.3.1. Iron's standard state is a solid.
	$2Fe(s) + 3CO_2(g) \rightarrow Fe_2O_3(s) + 3CO(g)$
Read	You are asked to calculate ΔH_{rxn}. You are given a balanced equation for the reaction. The reactant Fe is in its standard state.
Plan	Find the ΔH_f value for each compound in the reaction. They are listed in Table 13.3.1. Fe is in its standard state, so its $\Delta H_f = 0$. List the products and reactants separately.

Product	ΔH_f (kJ/mol)	Reactant	ΔH_f (kJ/mol)
$Fe_2O_3(s)$	-822.1	$CO_2(g)$	-393.5
$CO(g)$	-110.5	$Fe(s)$	0

Solve	Look at the coefficients in the balanced equation. Multiply each ΔH_f by the correct coefficient. Then add these values for each side.

$$\begin{aligned} \text{product sum} &= (1\ mol)(\Delta H_f\ Fe_2O_3) + (3\ mol)(\Delta H_f\ CO) \\ &= (1\ mol)(-822.1\ kJ/mol) + (3\ mol)(-110.5\ kJ/mol) \\ &= -1,153.6\ kJ \end{aligned}$$

$$\begin{aligned} \text{reactant sum} &= (2\ mol)(\Delta H_f\ Fe) + (3\ mol)(\Delta H_f\ CO_2) \\ &= (2\ mol)(0\ kJ/mol) + (3\ mol)(-393.5 kJ/mol) \\ &= -1,180.5\ kJ \end{aligned}$$

$$\begin{aligned} \Delta H_{rxn} &= (\text{product sum}) - (\text{reactant sum}) \\ &= (-1,153.6\ kJ) - (-1,180.5\ kJ) \\ &= +26.9\ kJ \end{aligned}$$

Reflect	The answer has only 1 significant figure to the right of the decimal point. ΔH_{rxn} is positive, so this reaction is endothermic.
Practice	Find the ΔH_{rxn} for the following balanced equation. Use the values of ΔH_f in Table 13.3.1. Oxygen's standard state is a gas.
	$4NH_3(g) + 7O_2(g) \rightarrow 4NO_2(g) + 6H_2O(g)$

Research and Write

The Swiss-Russian chemist G. H. Hess researched the amount of heat involved in chemical reactions. In 1840, he announced his findings. These findings are now called Hess's law. Use the Internet or reference books to find out what Hess's law is. Prepare a short presentation to explain it.

Word Bank

coefficient

standard heat of
formation

standard state

On a sheet of paper, write the word or phrase from the Word Bank that completes each sentence.

1. The _____ of nitrogen is a gas.

2. When a compound is formed from its elements, the enthalpy change is called the _____.

3. To calculate ΔH_{rxn} using heats of formation, make sure you multiply the ΔH_f value of each reactant and product by its _____ in the balanced equation.

On a sheet of paper, write the letter of the answer to each question. Use the data in Table 13.3.1.

4. What is ΔH_{rxn} for the following reaction?
$2H_2(g) + O_2(g) \rightarrow 2H_2O(l)$

   A -285.8 kJ   **B** -142.9 kJ   **C** -285.8 kJ   **D** -571.6 kJ

5. What is ΔH_{rxn} for the following reaction?
$2CH_3OH(l) + 3O_2(g) \rightarrow 2CO_2(g) + 4H_2O(l)$

   A -440.3 kJ   **B** $-1,452$ kJ   **C** $-1,691$ kJ   **D** $-2,408$ kJ

6. What is ΔH_{rxn} for the following reaction?
$SO_3(g) + H_2O(l) \rightarrow H_2SO_4(aq)$

   A $+799$ kJ   **B** $+227$ kJ   **C** -227 kJ   **D** -799 kJ

Critical Thinking

On a sheet of paper, write the answer to each question. Use the data in Table 13.3.1.

7. What is ΔH_{rxn} for the following reaction?
$3NO_2(g) + H_2O(l) \rightarrow 2HNO_3(aq) + NO(g)$

8. What is ΔH_{rxn} for the following reaction?
$4NH_3(g) + 5O_2(g) \rightarrow 4NO(g) + 6H_2O(g)$

9. What is ΔH_{rxn} for the following reaction?
$SiCl_4(l) + 2H_2O(l) \rightarrow SiO_2(s) + 4HCl(aq)$

10. $\Delta H_{rxn} = +175.8$ kJ for this reaction: $NH_4Cl(s) \rightarrow NH_3(g) + HCl(g)$. What is the ΔH_f value for NH_4Cl?

Objectives

After reading this lesson, you should be able to

◆ explain what entropy is

◆ state the second and third laws of thermodynamics

◆ give examples of changes in which entropy increases

Entropy

A measure of the disorder or randomness of a system

Entropy is the opposite of order and organization.

All physical and chemical changes are either endothermic or exothermic. When a *physical* change is exothermic, heat is released by a substance or object. The energy of that substance drops. When a *chemical* change is exothermic, the products have less energy than the reactants (ΔH_{rxn} is negative). For any exothermic change, the overall energy of the system drops. In general, *changes tend to occur so the lowest possible energy of a system is reached.* A system at a state of low energy is more stable than a system at a state of high energy. Why, then, would any change be endothermic?

This is a good question, because there are many endothermic changes. For example, melting ice is a physical change that is endothermic. Ice must absorb heat to become a liquid. This increases its kinetic energy. As a result, liquid water has more energy than ice. When a chemical change is endothermic, the products have more—not less—energy than the reactants. Endothermic changes occur because the system becomes more disordered. The system has an increased amount of **entropy.** Entropy is a measure of the disorder or randomness of a system. Molecules in liquid water have more entropy—more disorder—than molecules in ice. The scattered pieces in Figure 13.4.1 represent great entropy compared to the finished puzzle. In general, *changes tend to occur so the highest possible entropy is reached.*

Figure 13.4.1 *This puzzle models high and low entropy. After much effort, the randomly scattered pieces (high entropy) are moved into an ordered arrangement (low entropy).*

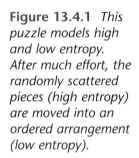

Entropy is not a form of energy. It is not conserved, like energy and matter. The **second law of thermodynamics** states that the entropy of the universe is always increasing. While systems tend to move toward a lower energy, they also tend to move toward a higher entropy. The entropy of a substance cannot be measured directly, but changes in entropy can be measured. Entropy values for elements and compounds have been calculated and are listed in reference tables. The **third law of thermodynamics** states that the entropy of an ideal solid at 0 K is zero. An ideal solid is a perfect crystal with no defects. It has no disorder at 0 K.

An endothermic change may occur if it results in more entropy. The following physical changes result in more entropy.

- When a solid becomes a gas, a liquid, or part of a solution, its entropy increases. When a liquid becomes a gas, entropy also increases. Figure 13.4.2 shows that a gas has more entropy than the same substance in its liquid state. The particles in a gas are more disorderly than the same particles in a liquid. For the same reason, a liquid (or solution) has more entropy than the same substance in its solid state. Ice melts because entropy increases.

- As the temperature of a substance increases, so does its entropy. This is because temperature is a measure of the average kinetic energy of the particles. More motion means more disorder. This explains why an ideal solid at 0 K has no entropy.

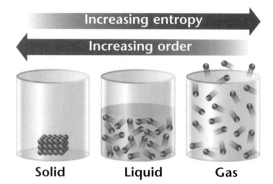

Figure 13.4.2 *Of the three states of matter, gas particles are the most random. Gases have more entropy than liquids. Liquids, in turn, have more entropy than solids.*

The following chemical changes also result in more entropy.

- In reactions, entropy usually increases when solid reactants produce liquids, solutions, or gases. Entropy increases when liquid reactants (or solutions) produce gases.
- In reactions, entropy increases when the number of particles increases. When a compound is broken into smaller parts, such as in a decomposition reaction, entropy increases. There are more moles of products than moles of reactants.

Endothermic changes occur because they are driven by the movement to greater entropy. Example 1 evaluates some physical and chemical changes in terms of entropy.

Example 1	Evaluate each change below. Which ones result in more entropy?
	A sugar dissolving in coffee
	B water freezing
	C $CaCO_3(s) \rightarrow CaO(s) + CO_2(g)$
Read	For each change, you are asked to decide if entropy increases or decreases.
Plan	Review the conditions that cause an increase in entropy (pages 528 and 529). If a change causes more disorder, entropy increases.
Solve	In **A**, the sugar is going from an orderly solid to a more disorderly solution. Entropy increases. In **B**, a liquid is becoming a solid. Since a solid state is more orderly, entropy decreases. In **C**, a solid compound decomposes into two smaller substances (and one is a gas). In the balanced equation, 1 mol of reactant yields 2 mol of products. Entropy increases.
Reflect	In **A** and **C**, entropy increases. In **B**, entropy decreases.
Practice	Evaluate each change below. Which ones result in more entropy?
	A a sugar cube being crushed
	B $2C_4H_{10}(l) + 13O_2(g) \rightarrow 8CO_2(g) + 10H_2O(g)$
	C carbon dioxide gas becoming a solid

The following ideas sum up the driving forces that cause changes in matter:

- Exothermic changes tend to occur because of a drop in energy.
- Endothermic changes tend to occur because of increased entropy.

However, a drop in energy does not guarantee that an exothermic change will occur. An increase in entropy does not guarantee that an endothermic change will occur. In the next lesson, you will learn why some changes happen and others do not.

Spotlight on Bismuth

83
Bi
Bismuth
209.0

Bismuth is a relatively scarce metal that has been known since ancient times. It is found in various ores. Occasionally, it is found as the free element. Bismuth looks similar to lead and tin and is sometimes confused with them. Until 2002, the common isotope of bismuth was considered stable. Now it appears that bismuth-209 has the longest half-life yet discovered, about 4×10^{19} years. This means that about one atom decays every hour in a mole of bismuth atoms.

Compared to other metals, bismuth does not conduct heat well. Most metals shrink when they solidify, but bismuth expands by 3%. Because of this property, bismuth and its alloys are used to make molded copies of objects because the metal completely fills the mold. Many bismuth alloys melt at low temperatures—some melt below 100°C. These alloys are used in fire protection devices such as overhead sprinklers.

Interesting Fact: Bismuth oxychloride is a white compound used in cosmetics because it is unreactive and insoluble.

On a sheet of paper, write the word from the Word Bank that completes each sentence.

Word Bank

decreases

entropy

increases

1. The disorder of a system is measured by _____.

2. When water boils, entropy _____.

3. When water freezes, entropy _____.

On a sheet of paper, write the letter of the answer to each question.

4. Which physical change represents a decrease in entropy?

    A a jar of marbles spilling   **C** nitrogen gas condensing
    B sugar dissolving in water   **D** butter melting on toast

5. Which chemical reaction represents an increase in entropy?

    A $CO_2(g) \rightarrow CO_2(s)$
    B $C_3H_8(g) + 5O_2(g) \rightarrow 3CO_2(g) + 4H_2O(g)$
    C $CaO(s) + SO_3(g) \rightarrow CaSO_4(s)$
    D $NaCl(l) \rightarrow NaCl(s)$

6. Which chemical reaction represents a decrease in entropy?

    A $N_2(g) + 3H_2(g) \rightarrow 2NH_3(g)$ **C** $H_2O(s) \rightarrow H_2O(g)$
    B $N_2(l) \rightarrow N_2(g)$ **D** $Br_2(l) \rightarrow Br_2(g)$

Critical Thinking

On a sheet of paper, write the answer to each question.

7. Dynamite explodes according to this equation:
$2C_6H_3(NO_2)_3(s) \rightarrow 12CO_2(g) + 3H_2(g) + 6NO_2(g)$.
Does entropy increase or decrease? Explain your answer.

8. Explain the change in entropy when steam condenses.

9. Octane burns according to this equation:
$2C_8H_{18}(l) + 25O_2(g) \rightarrow 16CO_2(g) + 18H_2O(g)$.
Does entropy increase or decrease? Explain your answer.

10. Compare the forces that drive exothermic and endothermic changes.

Materials

- 8 black checkers
- 8 red checkers
- tray

Simulating an Entropy Change

Many chemical and physical changes result in more disorder among particles of matter. In chemistry, the degree of disorder in a system is called entropy. How can you model changes in entropy? You will find out in this investigation.

Procedure

1. Place two rows of four black checkers in one corner of the tray. Place two rows of four red checkers next to the black checkers, as shown.

2. Find a way to cause a small increase in entropy among the checkers. Do not touch the checkers. Keep them flat on the tray.

3. Restore the checkers to the initial arrangement of four rows.

4. Find a way to cause a large entropy increase among the checkers. Again, do not touch the checkers and keep them flat on the tray.

Cleanup/Disposal

Return all materials. Clean your work area.

Analysis

1. How could you tell that entropy increased in step 2?

2. After step 2, how could you tell that the entropy of the checkers could increase further?

3. How could you tell that the entropy in step 4 was greater than the entropy in step 2?

Conclusions

1. Describe the entropy changes modeled in this investigation.

2. After step 4, do you think you could succeed in getting the checkers to return to their initial arrangement without touching them? Explain.

3. How could you get the checkers to return to their initial arrangement?

Explore Further

Use the tray and checkers to model the particle structure of a solid, a liquid, and a gas. Describe the entropy differences among the three states of matter.

After reading this lesson, you should be able to

◆ define a spontaneous change

◆ list three factors that affect spontaneity

◆ determine whether a change is spontaneous or nonspontaneous

Spontaneous

Occurring naturally as predicted

Nonspontaneous

Not occurring without the addition of energy

If you take an ice cube out of the freezer and leave it on the kitchen counter, what happens? If the air and the counter are above 0°C (the melting point of water), the ice spontaneously melts. **Spontaneous** changes occur naturally as predicted. Ice in a freezer will not spontaneously melt. The temperature is too low. However, water put in a freezer will spontaneously freeze. Spontaneous changes always happen on their own, although they may not happen fast.

For example, when iron is exposed to oxygen, iron(III) oxide, a type of rust, forms. The balanced equation is

$$4Fe(s) + 3O_2(g) \rightarrow 2Fe_2O_3(s)$$

This reaction is spontaneous, although it can take a long time to happen. Does rust ever spontaneously decompose to form iron under normal temperatures? No. The following reaction is **nonspontaneous.**

$$2Fe_2O_3(s) \rightarrow 4Fe(s) + 3O_2(g)$$

Nonspontaneous changes never happen on their own. However, they can be forced to happen by the addition of energy. When you recharge a dead battery using an electric recharger, you are forcing a nonspontaneous reaction to occur. A battery would never recharge on its own. Why are some changes spontaneous, while others are not?

The spontaneity of a change depends on three factors:

• enthalpy change—An exothermic change is more likely to be spontaneous than an endothermic change.

• entropy change—A change that results in more entropy is more likely to be spontaneous than a change in which entropy decreases.

• temperature—When the above two factors lead to differing predictions, temperature often determines whether a change is spontaneous or not.

Research and Write

Photosynthesis and respiration are chemical reactions that involve energy conversions. The two reactions are the reverse of each other. Use reference books or the Internet to find information on these reactions. Write the overall equation for each reaction. Prepare a short presentation that shows these equations. Tell whether each is endothermic or exothermic and whether there is an increase or a decrease in entropy.

Exothermic changes and increased entropy favor spontaneity. A change that is exothermic *and* results in increased entropy will always be spontaneous. An example is the combustion of propane:

$$C_3H_8(g) + 5O_2(g) \rightarrow 3CO_2(g) + 4H_2O(g)$$

Its ΔH_c is $-2{,}220$ kJ/mol C_3H_8—a very exothermic reaction. Entropy increases because 6 reactant molecules produce 7 product molecules. This reaction is always spontaneous.

Endothermic changes and decreased entropy do not favor spontaneity. A change that is endothermic *and* results in decreased entropy will never be spontaneous. Consider the reverse of the above reaction:

$$3CO_2(g) + 4H_2O(g) \rightarrow C_3H_8(g) + 5O_2(g)$$

The ΔH_{rxn} is $+2{,}220$ kJ/mol C_3H_8. This reaction is nonspontaneous because it is very endothermic and entropy decreases.

When a change is exothermic, but results in decreased entropy, it is sometimes spontaneous. The determining factor is temperature. If the temperature is low enough, the change is spontaneous. For example, when steam changes to liquid water, $H_2O(g) \rightarrow H_2O(l)$, the ΔH is -44 kJ/mol H_2O. This is an exothermic change. However, water as a gas has much more entropy than water as a liquid, so entropy decreases. This particular change is spontaneous if the temperature is 100°C or lower. 100°C is the boiling point of water. The temperature at which a change becomes spontaneous depends on the change.

When a change is endothermic, but results in increased entropy, it is sometimes spontaneous. Again, temperature determines spontaneity. If the temperature is high enough, the change is spontaneous. Ice melting, $H_2O(s) \rightarrow H_2O(l)$, is an endothermic change, absorbing 6.0 kJ/mol H_2O. However, the increased entropy of the liquid state allows this change to be spontaneous at 0°C or higher. 0°C is the melting point of ice. At -5°C, ice will not melt, and the change is not spontaneous. However, at 5°C (or any temperature above the melting point), ice will spontaneously melt.

Example 1	The reaction, $N_2(g) + 3H_2(g) \rightarrow 2NH_3(g)$, has a ΔH_{rxn} of -46 kJ/mol NH_3. Is it exothermic or endothermic? Does entropy increase or decrease? Is this reaction spontaneous always, sometimes, or never?
Read	You are asked to evaluate the enthalpy and entropy changes of a reaction. From this, you are asked to evaluate the spontaneity of the reaction.
Plan	Exothermic reactions have a negative ΔH_{rxn} value. Entropy increases when a change results in more disorder. Exothermic changes and increased entropy favor spontaneity.
Solve	Because ΔH_{rxn} is negative, this reaction is exothermic. However, entropy decreases because 4 mol of reactants produce 2 mol of product. This reaction is sometimes spontaneous.
Reflect	NH_3 is ammonia. In 1909, two chemists came up with a way to produce large amounts of ammonia using this reaction. Their process involved decreasing the temperature and increasing the pressure (see page 236).
Practice	The reaction, $SiO_2(s) \rightarrow Si(s) + O_2(g)$, has a ΔH_{rxn} of $+911$ kJ/mol SiO_2. Is it exothermic or endothermic? Does entropy increase or decrease? Is this reaction spontaneous always, sometimes, or never?

❋ ❋

Technology and Society

Ceramic items such as dishes are made from mixtures of solids. The mixture is shaped and then heated in a kiln. Heat causes the solids to react with one another and form the ceramic. Entropy decreases during this process because the ceramic is more ordered than the starting mixture.

To operate a machine or a mechanical system such as an engine, energy is required. This energy is always more than the energy (or work) produced by the machine. The difference between the energy input and the energy output is in the form of heat. Energy is conserved.

Table 13.5.1 summarizes how the spontaneity of a system is determined by enthalpy change, entropy change, and temperature.

Table 13.5.1 The Effect of Enthalpy, Entropy, and Temperature on Spontaneity		
Enthalpy	Entropy	Spontaneous?
decreases (exothermic)	increases	always
increases (endothermic)	decreases	never
decreases (exothermic)	decreases	only if temperature is low enough
increases (endothermic)	increases	only if temperature is high enough

★ ★

Achievements in Science

The Machine Age: The Beginning of Thermodynamics

As people used machines more and more in the 1800s, scientists and engineers became concerned with the efficiency of machines. They wanted to know how well the machines used energy. After all, energy cost money. Energy that was not doing useful work wasted money. For example, the firebox of a steam engine produced energy. This energy was used to do work—cause motion. But just how much energy was being used to heat the surroundings instead? Some way of measuring energy and work was needed.

In the late 1700s and early 1800s, James Watt performed experiments to measure the rate of doing work—the horsepower. Watt also made the steam engine about three times more efficient. In the first half of the 1800s, J. P. Joule proved that heat and work can be equal. Later, J. Willard Gibbs published his research on free energy, which is the energy available to do work. He used enthalpy, entropy, and temperature to calculate the free energy for a chemical reaction. He showed that this amount of free energy indicates whether the reaction will occur.

Lesson 5   R E V I E W

Word Bank

nonspontaneous

spontaneous

temperature

On a sheet of paper, write the word from the Word Bank that completes each sentence.

1. A reaction that proceeds as expected is _____.

2. Reactions that are _____ never happen on their own.

3. The spontaneity of a change depends on the enthalpy change, the entropy change, and the _____.

Match each reaction in the left column with a description in the right column. Write the letter of the answer on a sheet of paper.

4. $A(s) + \text{heat} \rightarrow A(l)$

5. $A(s) \rightarrow X(g) + Z(g) + \text{heat}$

6. $X(g) + Z(g) + \text{heat} \rightarrow A(s)$

A always spontaneous

B never spontaneous

C spontaneous only if the temperature is high enough

Critical Thinking

On a sheet of paper, write the answer to each question.

7. What two characteristics describe a reaction that is always spontaneous?

8. What does it mean when a reaction is described as spontaneous? Does it give any information about the speed of the reaction?

9. Consider the reaction, $X(g) + Z(g) \rightarrow A(s) + \text{heat}$. Is it always spontaneous, never spontaneous, or sometimes spontaneous? Explain your answer.

10. What does it mean when a reaction is described as nonspontaneous? Can a nonspontaneous reaction ever be made to be spontaneous?

Hydrogen Power

Most of the energy people use comes from burning fossil fuels. Petroleum is a fossil fuel. It is refined into gasoline and other products. Burning gasoline in vehicles produces water, carbon dioxide, and carbon monoxide. It also produces nitrogen compounds from the nitrogen gas in air. Most of these compounds contribute to air pollution.

To reduce this pollution, researchers are investigating the use of hydrogen as a fuel. Hydrogen burns cleanly, producing only water. A given mass of hydrogen produces about three times the energy as the same mass of gasoline. Furthermore, the earth's water provides a practically unlimited supply of hydrogen.

So, why isn't hydrogen power being used? The use of hydrogen fuel has several disadvantages. One is storage. Hydrogen gas has a low density of about 0.013 g/cm^3 at room temperature and a pressure of 160 atm. Even as a liquid, its density is only 0.071 g/cm^3. Liquid hydrogen must be stored below 20 K, which is not practical. Very large tanks and possibly very low temperatures would be required to store useful quantities. Another disadvantage is that hydrogen is highly reactive. Almost any mixture of hydrogen gas and air is explosive. Also, prolonged exposure to hydrogen causes many metals to become brittle.

In nature, almost all hydrogen occurs in compounds. Thus, elemental hydrogen must be manufactured. One way to manufacture hydrogen is to use electricity to break down water. However, most electricity comes from burning coal and oil. If you have to burn fossil fuels to produce hydrogen fuel, what's the point?

Hydrogen fuel holds great promise for the future. However, scientists and engineers must overcome its many disadvantages first.

1. What are some advantages of using hydrogen as a fuel?

2. Why is storage a disadvantage?

3. Besides fossil fuels, suggest other energy sources that could be used to produce hydrogen fuel. Which source do you think is best? Why?

Chapter 13 S U M M A R Y

- Heat is the energy that is transferred between objects at different temperatures.

- Heat always moves from a hotter object to a colder object.

- In a closed system, the heat released by one object is absorbed by another object.

- The heat absorbed or released by a certain amount of a substance can be calculated by the equation, $q = (m)(C_p)(\Delta T)$.

- A reaction in which heat is absorbed is endothermic, and ΔH is positive.

- A reaction in which heat is released is exothermic, and ΔH is negative.

- ΔH_{rxn} or ΔH_c can be used to calculate the amount of heat released or absorbed in a reaction, given a certain amount of reactant or product.

- The energy change for any reaction, ΔH_{rxn}, can be calculated using standard heats of formation.

- Entropy is a measure of the disorder of a system.

- Entropy increases when temperature increases, when the state of matter becomes more disorderly, or when the number of moles of product is greater than the number of moles of reactant.

- Exothermic changes favor spontaneity.

- Increased entropy favors spontaneity.

- Exothermic changes that result in increased entropy are always spontaneous.

- Endothermic changes that result in decreased entropy are never spontaneous.

- Exothermic changes that result in decreased entropy are spontaneous at low temperatures.

- Endothermic changes that result in increased entropy are spontaneous at high temperatures.

Vocabulary

calorimetry, 509
endothermic, 508
enthalpy, 519
entropy, 527
exothermic, 508
first law of thermodynamics, 511

heat, 508
heat of combustion, 520
heat of reaction, 519
nonspontaneous, 534
second law of thermodynamics, 528
specific heat, 508

spontaneous, 534
standard heat of formation, 524
standard state, 524
system, 511
thermodynamics, 508
third law of thermodynamics, 528

Chapter 13 REVIEW

Word Bank

calorimetry

endothermic

enthalpy

entropy

exothermic

heat

heat of combustion

heat of reaction

specific heat

spontaneous

standard heat of
  formation

standard state

system

thermodynamics

Vocabulary Review

On a sheet of paper, write the word or phrase from the Word Bank that completes each sentence.

1. The _____ of iron is a solid.

2. A reaction that proceeds as expected is _____.

3. The heat content of a substance is called _____.

4. In a(n) _____ reaction, the reactants have more energy than the products.

5. The amount of heat produced when a substance burns is the _____.

6. The measurement of heat transfer between two objects is _____.

7. The study of energy and its changes is _____.

8. The _____ of liquid water is greater than that of ice.

9. In a(n) _____ reaction, the products have more energy than the reactants.

10. The energy transferred between two objects at different temperatures is _____.

11. The amount of heat needed to raise the temperature of 1 g of a substance by 1°C is _____.

12. In a closed _____, the heat absorbed equals the heat released.

13. The _____ of an element in its standard state is zero.

14. The _____ of an exothermic reaction is negative.

Continued on next page

Concept Review

On a sheet of paper, write the letter of the answer to each question.

15. It takes 2,221 J of heat to raise the temperature of 75.0 g of chromium from 17.0°C to 83.0°C. What is the specific heat of chromium?

A 0.356 J/g•°C   **C** 1.74 J/g•°C

B 0.449 J/g•°C   **D** 2.23 J/g•°C

16. Carbon and water react as follows: $C(s) + H_2O(g) \rightarrow H_2(g) + CO(g)$. The heat of reaction is $+131$ kJ/mol C. How much heat is absorbed when 87.3 g of carbon reacts?

A 11,400 kJ   **C** 131 kJ

B 953 kJ   **D** 18.0 kJ

17. 93.2 g of Na_2CO_3 reacts according to this equation: $2HNO_3(aq) + Na_2CO_3(s) \rightarrow 2NaNO_3(aq) + H_2O(l) + CO_2(g) + 70.3$ kJ. What amount of heat is involved?

A -61.8 kJ   **C** -80.0 kJ

B -70.3 kJ   **D** $-6,550$ kJ

18. What is ΔH_{rxn} for the following reaction? Use the standard heats of formation in Table 13.3.1.

$Ba(OH)_2(s) + H_2SO_4(aq) \rightarrow BaSO_4(s) + 2H_2O(l)$

A $-2,250$ kJ   **C** -182 kJ

B -2.00×10^3 kJ   **D** 104.2 kJ

19. An endothermic change results in decreased entropy. How is this change best described?

A always spontaneous

B never spontaneous

C spontaneous at high temperatures

D spontaneous at low temperatures

Problem Solving

On a sheet of paper, write the answer to each problem.
Show your work.

20. A sample of nickel is heated to 99.8°C. Then it is added
to 150. g of water at 23.5°C. The final temperature of the
mixture is 45.2°C. The specific heat of water is 4.18 J/g•°C,
and the specific heat of nickel is 0.444 J/g•°C. What is the
mass of the nickel?

21. $\Delta H_{rxn} = -176$ kJ/mol NH_3 for this reaction:
$NH_3(g) + HCl(g) \rightarrow NH_4Cl(s)$. How much heat is released
when 75.2 g of NH_3 reacts?

22. What is ΔH_{rxn} for the following reaction? Use
the standard heats of formation in Table 13.3.1.
$2NH_3(g) + 3O_2(g) + 2CH_4(g) \rightarrow 2HCN(g) + 6H_2O(g)$

23. $\Delta H_{rxn} = -369.2$ kJ for the following reaction. What is
ΔH_f for P_4O_{10}? Use the standard heats of formation in
Table 13.3.1.
$P_4O_{10}(s) + 6H_2O(l) \rightarrow 4H_3PO_4(l)$.

Critical Thinking

On a sheet of paper, write the answer to each question.

24. Is the following reaction spontaneous always, sometimes,
or never? Explain your answer.
$2C_2H_6(g) + 7O_2(g) \rightarrow 4CO_2(g) + 6H_2O(g) + heat$

25. Substance A changes state as follows: $A(g) \rightarrow A(l) + heat$.
Is this change spontaneous always, sometimes, or never?
Explain your answer.

Test-Taking Tip Before a test, find out if you may use a calculator.

Solids and Liquids

The water shooting from this water fountain is "frozen" in time by the camera. But you can tell that this is liquid water, not ice. Water is the most abundant substance on the earth. Unlike most other substances, water easily exists on the earth in three states of matter. In Chapter 14, you will learn about states of matter. You will find out how matter changes from one state to another.

Organize Your Thoughts

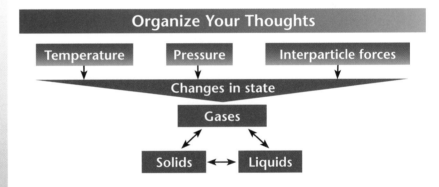

Goals for Learning

◆ To explain why a substance changes state in terms of interparticle forces

◆ To explain why the temperature is constant when a substance changes state

◆ To read a heating or cooling graph and calculate the total ΔH for a heating or cooling process

◆ To explain how temperature and interparticle forces affect vapor pressure

◆ To explain water's unique properties in terms of hydrogen bonding

◆ To understand a phase diagram and the effect of temperature and pressure on state

After reading this lesson, you should be able to

◆ define condensation, sublimation, boiling, freezing, and melting

◆ explain why a substance changes state in terms of interparticle forces

◆ compare crystals and amorphous solids

Condense

To change from a gas to a liquid

Only particles in ideal gases have no volume and no attraction for each other. As temperature decreases and pressure increases, gases do not act as ideal gases.

The attractive forces between particles hold many substances together as liquids or solids. Without interparticle forces, all matter would exist in a gas state!

Gases and Liquids

In Chapter 7, you studied gases. Gases consist of atoms or molecules that are widely spread out. These particles can collide with each other, but the attractive forces between them are overcome by the motion of the particles. However, as the temperature of a gas decreases, the average speed of the gas particles decreases. When the temperature drops low enough, the attractive forces take over and pull the particles close together. At this point, the gas becomes a liquid. When a substance **condenses,** it changes from a gas to a liquid.

The particles in a liquid are held close together by interparticle forces. The outside of a glass filled with an icy beverage often becomes wet, as shown in Figure 14.1.1. The beverage cools the air next to the glass, and some water in that air condenses. If you have cold winters where you live, you may have noticed that water in room air condenses on cold window panes.

Figure 14.1.1 *The formation of water droplets on a cold surface is evidence of condensation.*

You are also familiar with the opposite process. When a substance **boils,** it changes from a liquid to a gas. The temperature at which a substance boils is its boiling point. You will learn more about boiling point in Lesson 2. At temperatures *below* the boiling point, particles at the liquid's surface can gain enough kinetic energy to "escape" into the gas state. These particles have evaporated, not boiled. **Evaporation** occurs when particles at the surface of a liquid gain enough energy to leave the liquid and become a gas.

Liquids and Solids

Liquids have different properties than gases. The particles of a liquid are very close together and can slide past each other. Liquids take the shape of their container and, like gases, are fluid. Liquid and solid particles are much closer than gas particles. Liquids and solids are often referred to as **condensed states.**

As the temperature of a liquid drops, the particles move slower—just like in a gas. Eventually, at a certain temperature, the interparticle forces "lock" the particles in a specific geometric arrangement. The liquid **freezes,** or becomes a solid. The opposite process occurs when a solid **melts,** or becomes a liquid.

Some solids are capable of changing directly to a gas state. They do not become a liquid first. The process of changing from a solid directly to a gas is called **sublimation.** Solid carbon dioxide, also known as dry ice, can undergo sublimation. The opposite process is called **deposition.** Deposition occurs when a gas changes directly to a solid. Figure 14.1.2 summarizes the six possible changes in state.

Figure 14.1.2
Freezing and melting are opposite processes. Condensing and evaporating are opposite processes.

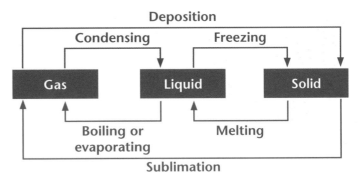

Crystals and Amorphous Solids

Crystal

A solid that has particles arranged in an orderly, repeating pattern

Crystal lattice

The three-dimensional pattern of particles in a crystal

A solid has a definite volume and a definite shape. The particles in a solid cannot move past each other. They only vibrate and rotate in place. True solid substances are **crystals.** In a crystal, the atoms, ions, or molecules are arranged in an orderly, repeating, three-dimensional pattern. This three-dimensional pattern is called a **crystal lattice.** There are many lattice shapes, from simple cubes to complex geometrical shapes. Figure 14.1.3 shows the cube-shaped lattice of solid sodium chloride, NaCl. When a crystal is broken, it splits into smaller crystals with the same repeating pattern. Many solid ionic compounds and metals are crystals.

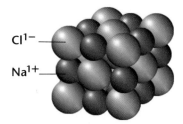

Cl^{1-}

Na^{1+}

Figure 14.1.3 *The crystal lattice of NaCl is made of Na^{1+} and Cl^{1-} ions. It is shaped like a cube.*

Express Lab 14

Materials

- safety goggles
- lab coat or apron
- solid air freshener, in small pieces
- small glass bowl with flat bottom
- 150-mL beaker
- plastic cup
- ice
- hot tap water

Procedure

1. Put on safety goggles and a lab coat or apron.

2. Place a few pieces of air freshener in the beaker, and fill the plastic cup with ice.

3. Place the cup with the ice inside the beaker. The cup should fit snugly inside the beaker but it should not touch the air freshener pieces.

4. Add hot water to the bowl to a depth of about 2.5 cm. Place the beaker assembly in the bowl.

Analysis

1. Describe your observations.

2. How can you explain your observations?

Amorphous

Having no orderly, repeating pattern of particles

Some materials appear to be solids, but have no crystal structure. Their particles are not arranged in an orderly, repeating pattern. These materials are called **amorphous** solids. An amorphous solid breaks into smaller pieces of varying shapes and sizes. Figure 14.1.4 shows an amorphous solid.

Figure 14.1.4 *Obsidian is an amorphous rock formed by volcanoes. Soot, glass, and some waxes are also amorphous solids.*

Science at Work

Glassmaker

Making the amorphous solid known as glass requires knowledge and skill. There are many types of glass, and they have different properties. Glassmakers need to know the use of each glass object they make. Common soda-lime glass is used for windows and containers. Silica glass can withstand extreme heat. Besides making glass, glassmakers shape glass into objects.

Most glassmakers specialize in a certain type of glass. For example, some work only with soda-lead glass, which is easy to melt and is beautiful when light passes through it. A glassmaker may specialize in either making the glass or forming it. Someone who makes the glass must have knowledge of math and chemistry. A glassmaker who forms glass usually learns the trade by working with a skilled glassmaker.

Iodine is a member of the halogen family. It has chemical properties similar to the other halogens, but its physical properties are quite different. Fluorine and chlorine are gases, and bromine is a reddish-brown liquid. Iodine, however, is a dark purple-black solid. One unique property of iodine is that it sublimes to form a purple vapor.

Iodine is an important element in the human body. It is part of a hormone produced by the thyroid gland. This hormone controls the rate at which the body grows and develops. Therefore, a lack of iodine in the diet can hinder growth. You may have noticed that the label on a container of table salt says "iodized salt." Small amounts of iodine compounds are added to table salt in geographic areas where the amount of iodine in the water supply is low. Solutions and compounds of iodine are used as antiseptics to prevent or treat infections.

You may have used iodine in a biology lab or other science course to test for the presence of starch in foods. A red-yellow iodine solution turns blue-black when it comes in contact with starch.

Interesting Fact: Silver iodide is used in photographic film.

Achievements in Science

Thin Films

A few decades ago, a typical calculator was as large as this book, a computer filled a room, and a radio was larger than a modern TV set. Advances in technology led to smaller and smaller versions of these devices. Part of this technology growth was the development of solids known as thin films. A thin film is a layer of atoms deposited on a surface. Thin films form crystals. Thin films can be conductors, insulators, or semiconductors, depending on what substances make up the film.

Thin films have many uses. Look at the shiny side of CDs and DVDs. These surfaces are thin films containing notches. The notches provide the information on the disk. Your calculator has layers of thin films that are used to make thousands of microcircuits. Without thin film technology, many of the conveniences you enjoy today would be impossible.

Lesson 1   R E V I E W

Word Bank

crystal

evaporation

sublimation

On a sheet of paper, write the word from the Word Bank that completes each sentence.

1. In a(n) _____, the particles are arranged in a repeating, orderly pattern.

2. When a solid changes directly to a gas, the process is called _____.

3. When particles at the surface of a liquid change to a gas, _____ occurs.

On a sheet of paper, write the answer to each question.

4. Which two states are called condensed states?

5. A gas changes to a liquid. What is this change called?

6. A solid changes to a liquid. What is this change called?

Critical Thinking

On a sheet of paper, write the answer to each question.

7. What is the difference between a crystal and an amorphous solid?

8. What is the difference between boiling and evaporating?

9. Describe how a gas condenses in terms of interparticle forces.

10. Describe how a liquid freezes in terms of interparticle forces.

❋ ❋

Technology and Society

The coldest substance known is liquid helium. Helium changes from a gas to a liquid at about −269°C, which is 4 K. Liquid helium is used in cryogenics, which is the study of extremely low temperatures. Scientists have been able to freeze and preserve certain body parts, such as corneas from human eyes, until they can be used.

Objectives

After reading this lesson, you should be able to

◆ explain how evaporation causes vapor pressure

◆ explain how temperature and interparticle forces affect vapor pressure

◆ compare normal boiling point and boiling point

◆ find the boiling point of a substance on a vapor pressure graph

Evaporated particles create pressure in a closed container, just as any gas would. The pressure created by an evaporated liquid is called **vapor pressure.** A liquid substance with a high vapor pressure evaporates easily.

Vapor pressure is directly related to temperature. As the temperature of a liquid substance increases, its vapor pressure increases. At a temperature where the vapor pressure equals the pressure of the surrounding air, the liquid boils. At the boiling point, particles in the liquid change to a gas state throughout the liquid. This is why you see gas bubbles forming inside a liquid during boiling. The **boiling point** of a liquid is the temperature at which its vapor pressure equals the atmospheric pressure. Atmospheric pressure varies, depending on geographic area. At a lower atmospheric pressure, water boils at a lower temperature. The **normal boiling point** of a liquid is the temperature at which its vapor pressure equals 1 atm. Figure 14.2.1 shows how temperature affects the vapor pressure of water.

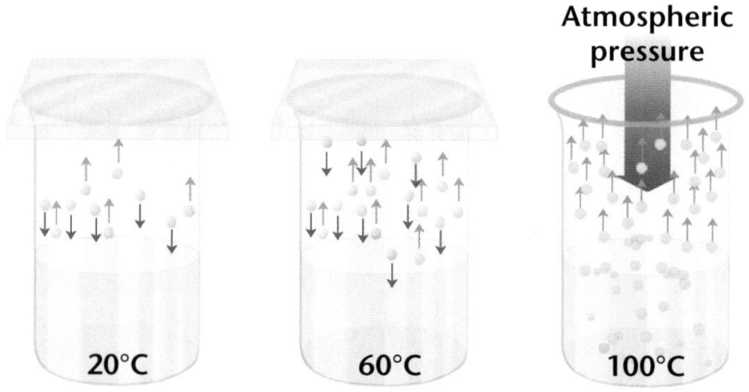

Vapor pressure

The pressure created by an evaporated liquid

Boiling point

The temperature at which the vapor pressure of a liquid equals the atmospheric pressure

Normal boiling point

The temperature at which the vapor pressure of a liquid equals 1 atm

Figure 14.2.1 *As the temperature of water increases, its vapor pressure increases. Water boils when its vapor pressure equals atmospheric pressure. The normal boiling point of water is 100°C.*

Water's normal boiling point is 100°C. However, it is possible to make water boil at lower temperatures by lowering the surrounding air pressure. If most of the air is removed from a container, the air pressure inside is very low. When water is heated in this container, its vapor pressure will not need to rise as high to equal the air pressure. The water will boil at a temperature less than 100°C. Under certain pressure conditions, it is possible to make room-temperature water boil.

Temperature is not the only factor that affects the vapor pressure of a liquid. Another important factor is the strength of the attractive forces between particles. If these forces are strong, the particles are held together tightly. A large amount of energy is required to break these forces, allowing the particles to evaporate. This results in a low vapor pressure and a high normal boiling point. Liquids with weak interparticle forces have low normal boiling points. Figure 14.2.2 is a graph of vapor pressure versus temperature for water and ethanol, C_2H_5OH. The attractive forces between ethanol molecules are weaker than the forces between water molecules. Ethanol's normal boiling point is 78.5°C, while water's is 100°C.

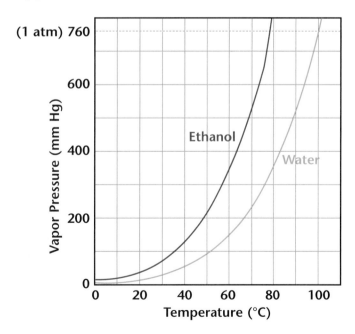

Figure 14.2.2 *The interparticle forces in liquid water are stronger than those in liquid ethanol. Water has a higher boiling point and a lower vapor pressure than ethanol.*

There are several important things to notice in Figure 14.2.2.

- As temperature increases, so does the vapor pressure of each liquid.
- A liquid boils when its vapor pressure equals the atmospheric pressure. When the atmospheric pressure is 1 atm (760 mm Hg), the liquid boils at its normal boiling point. The curve for water crosses the 1-atm line at 100°C, while the ethanol curve crosses this line at 78.5°C.
- To find the boiling point of a liquid at another pressure, find the point where its curve crosses the line for that pressure. Then find the corresponding temperature. For example, at 350 mm Hg, water boils at about 80°C.
- At any given temperature, ethanol has a higher vapor pressure than water. This means ethanol's interparticle forces are weaker. Ethanol molecules are not held together as tightly as water molecules. Ethanol evaporates more easily.

Example 1	What is the boiling point of water at a pressure of 400 mm Hg? What is the boiling point of ethanol at this pressure? Use Figure 14.2.2.
Read	You are asked to find the boiling point of two liquids at a pressure of 400 mm Hg.
Plan	A liquid will boil at 400 mm Hg when its vapor pressure is 400 mm Hg. Locate 400 mm Hg on the vapor pressure scale in Figure 14.2.2. Find the horizontal line representing this pressure.
Solve	Find the point where the water curve crosses this line. Look at the temperature scale and estimate the temperature at this point. The boiling point of water at 400 mm Hg is about 83°C. Repeat the process for ethanol. The boiling point of ethanol at 400 mm Hg is about 63°C.
Reflect	Compare these boiling points to the normal boiling points. As pressure decreases, the boiling point decreases.
Practice	What is the boiling point of water at a pressure of 600 mm Hg? What is the boiling point of ethanol at this pressure?

Chemistry in Your Life

Technology: Perspiration and Warmth

Water has an important role in controlling human body temperature. When you are active, you perspire. Perspiration prevents your body from overheating. Water in perspiration absorbs heat from the skin. This heat is used to evaporate the water. This process of evaporation cools the body.

In a hot climate, it is good that perspiration cools your body. In a cold climate, however, you want your body to be warm. Some fabrics are designed to pull moisture away from the body. Wearing clothing made of this fabric helps to keep you warm. For example, a shirt that contains a fiber called polypropylene pulls perspiration away from your skin. You stay warmer because no evaporation occurs next to your skin.

1. How does perspiring help your body?

2. A snow skier plans to wear a loose sweater, a polypropylene T-shirt, and a light jacket. In what order, from the skin outward, should these clothes be layered to stay warmest?

❀ ❀

Technology and Society

Materials known as liquid crystals do not change state in the typical manner. When they change from a solid to a liquid, they flow but still keep their crystal structure. Thin layers of liquid crystals change color when temperature changes. When a strip thermometer containing different liquid crystals is placed on someone's forehead, the resulting color indicates the person's body temperature.

Lesson 2 REVIEW

Word Bank

boiling point

normal boiling
 point

vapor pressure

On a sheet of paper, write the phrase from the Word Bank that completes each sentence.

1. The _____ is the temperature at which the vapor pressure of a liquid is 1 atm.

2. Particles that evaporate from a liquid create _____.

3. The _____ is the temperature at which the vapor pressure of a liquid equals atmospheric pressure.

On a sheet of paper, write the letter of the answer that completes each sentence. Use Figure 14.2.2 to help you.

4. Water boils at 80°C at about _____ mm Hg.

   A 40   **B** 200   **C** 275   **D** 350

5. At 100 mm Hg, the approximate boiling point of water is _____.

   A 30°C   **B** 50°C   **C** 100°C   **D** 125°C

6. Ethanol boils at 40°C at about _____ mm Hg.

   A 25   **B** 40   **C** 135   **D** 760

Critical Thinking

On a sheet of paper, write the answer to each question.

7. How does evaporation cause vapor pressure?

8. How does temperature affect the vapor pressure of a liquid?

9. The strongest interparticle force in carbon dioxide, CO_2, is dispersion forces. The strongest interparticle force in ammonia, NH_3, is hydrogen bonding. Which substance has the higher normal boiling point? Explain.

10. The atmospheric pressure in Denver is lower than the atmospheric pressure in Baltimore. Denver is a high-altitude city, and Baltimore is at sea level. In which city does water boil at a higher temperature? Explain.

Objectives

After reading this lesson, you should be able to

◆ explain why the temperature is constant when a substance changes state

◆ tell what kind of physical change each ΔH equation describes

◆ read a heating or cooling graph

◆ calculate the total ΔH for a heating or cooling process

When a substance changes state, heat is either absorbed or released. It is possible to calculate how much heat is involved in any change of state. In Chapter 13, you calculated the change in enthalpy (heat content) when a substance changes temperature. The enthalpy calculation when a substance changes state is different: The heat absorbed or released is used to change particle arrangements, not temperature.

- When a solid becomes a liquid, the absorbed heat moves the particles out of their fixed positions in the solid.

- When a liquid becomes a gas, the absorbed heat overcomes interparticle forces, moving the particles away from each other.

- When a gas becomes a liquid, heat is given off as interparticle forces take over, moving the particles close together.

- When a liquid becomes a solid, heat is given off as particles move into fixed positions.

During each state change above, the temperature stays constant.

Heating and Cooling Graphs

Suppose you have a sample of solid H_2O (ice) at $-15°C$. You begin to heat it. Every minute, you record the temperature. At first, the heat you are adding speeds up water molecules in the ice. The temperature (kinetic energy) of the ice increases. When the ice reaches its melting point of 0°C, the temperature holds for a time. Now the molecules have enough energy to overcome the interparticle forces locking them in place. At 0°C, the heat you are adding changes the solid into a liquid. The temperature stays at 0°C until the solid is completely melted. Look at the left part of the heating graph in Figure 14.3.1 on the next page. It shows how the temperature rises from $-15°C$ to 0°C, then stays at 0°C for a while.

Science Myth

Myth: The temperature of a substance changes during a change of state.

Fact: When energy is absorbed or released by a substance and no change of state occurs, the temperature of the substance changes. However, when a substance changes state, its temperature does not change.

You continue to heat your sample, which is now a liquid. The temperature rises again. The heat speeds up the molecules of the liquid. The molecules move faster and faster. More of the molecules are able to evaporate, which causes the vapor pressure to increase. Look at the graph in Figure 14.3.1 to see what happens when the water temperature reaches 100°C. This is the normal boiling point of water. The molecules have enough energy to overcome the interparticle forces holding them together. The heat is now used to move particles apart, changing the liquid into a gas. As the water boils, the temperature stays constant at 100°C. The temperature will not change while the water boils into steam. Once your sample is in a gas state (steam), the heat you are adding raises the temperature of the gas.

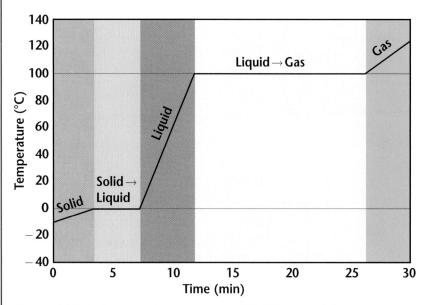

Figure 14.3.1 *In general, as a sample of H_2O is heated, its temperature rises. However, its temperature stays constant as its state changes.*

A cooling graph similar to Figure 14.3.1 can be drawn to show how the temperature of a substance changes as it is cooled.

Look at the ΔH_{vap} value for water in Table 14.3.1. When steam condenses, it releases a lot of energy. This is why steam causes severe burns.

Math Tip

It is helpful to use a calculator with the problems in this lesson. Remember the rules for significant figures when adding and subtracting.

Enthalpy Changes During Heating or Cooling

A change in temperature and a change in state are both physical changes. In either change, the substance does not become a different substance. When heating or cooling a substance, a temperature change and a state change do not occur at the same time. To calculate the total enthalpy change for a heating or cooling process, you will need three equations. The first equation gives ΔH when a substance changes temperature only (not state).

For a temperature change: $\Delta H = (m)(C_p)(\Delta T)$

You used this equation to find q, the heat transferred, in Chapter 13 (page 509). m is the mass of the sample. C_p is the specific heat of the substance in its current state (a constant). ΔT is the change in temperature. In this chapter, ΔT will always be positive.

The second equation gives ΔH when a substance melts or freezes.

For a liquid-solid state change: $\Delta H = (m)(\Delta H_{fus})$

ΔH_{fus} is a constant called the **heat of fusion**. It is the amount of heat transferred when 1 g of a substance melts or freezes.

The third equation gives ΔH when a substance boils or condenses.

For a liquid-gas state change: $\Delta H = (m)(\Delta H_{vap})$

ΔH_{vap} is a constant called the **heat of vaporization**. It is the amount of heat transferred when 1 g of a substance boils or condenses.

The total ΔH for a heating or cooling process is the sum of individual heat changes calculated using the above equations. Table 14.3.1 lists some constants needed for calculating total ΔH for water and benzene.

Table 14.3.1 Physical Constants for Water and Benzene					
Substance	Melting Point (°C)	Boiling Point (°C)	C_p (J/g·°C)	ΔH_{fus} (J/g)	ΔH_{vap} (J/g)
water, H_2O	0.0	100.0	2.06 (solid) 4.18 (liquid) 2.02 (gas)	334	2,260
benzene, C_6H_6	5.5	80.0	1.69 (liquid) 1.05 (gas)	126	567

Example 1   42.3 g of gaseous H_2O at 123.0°C is cooled to solid H_2O at -28.0°C. What is the total amount of heat released in this process? Refer to Table 14.3.1.

Read   You need to calculate the total ΔH for cooling a sample of water. You are given the sample's mass, starting temperature, and final temperature.

Plan   From the temperature range, you know that two state changes occur as the sample is cooled. Draw the cooling graph.

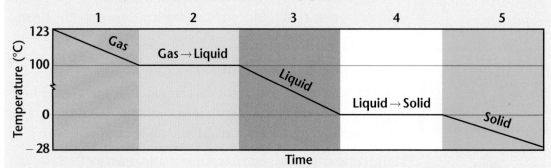

The five sections in the graph represent the five calculations you need to make.
Section 1: $\Delta H = (m)(C_p)(\Delta T)$
Section 2: $\Delta H = (m)(\Delta H_{vap})$
Section 3: $\Delta H = (m)(C_p)(\Delta T)$
Section 4: $\Delta H = (m)(\Delta H_{fus})$
Section 5: $\Delta H = (m)(C_p)(\Delta T)$

Solve   Use positive numbers to represent each ΔT. Find the constants in Table 14.3.1. The ΔH values are

Section 1: $\Delta H = (42.3\ g)(2.02\ J/g \cdot °C)(23.0°C) = 1{,}970\ J$
Section 2: $\Delta H = (42.3\ g)(2{,}260\ J/g) = 95{,}600\ J$
Section 3: $\Delta H = (42.3\ g)(4.18\ J/g \cdot °C)(100°C) = 17{,}700\ J$
Section 4: $\Delta H = (42.3\ g)(334\ J/g) = 14{,}100\ J$
Section 5: $\Delta H = (42.3\ g)(2.06\ J/g \cdot °C)(28.0°C) = 2{,}440\ J$

The total ΔH released in this cooling process is the sum of these values:

$1{,}970\ J + 95{,}600\ J + 17{,}700\ J + 14{,}100\ J + 2{,}440\ J = 131{,}810\ J \xrightarrow{round} 131{,}800\ J$

The answer is rounded to the least certain decimal place (the hundreds place).

Reflect   When a substance condenses from a gas to a liquid, or freezes from a liquid to a solid, heat is released. Cooling and freezing are exothermic processes.

Practice   17.1 g of gaseous H_2O at 115.0°C is cooled to solid H_2O at -35.0°C. What is the total amount of heat released in this process?

| *Example 2* | 22.0 g of liquid benzene at 8.0°C is heated to gaseous benzene at 105.0°C. What is the total amount of heat absorbed in this process? Refer to Table 14.3.1. |

Read You need to find the total heat absorbed when a sample of benzene is heated. You are given its mass, its starting temperature, and its final temperature.

Plan The temperature ranges from 8.0°C to 105.0°C. This includes the boiling point of benzene (80°C). The sample will increase in temperature, boil, and increase in temperature some more. Draw a heating graph to show what happens between these two temperatures.

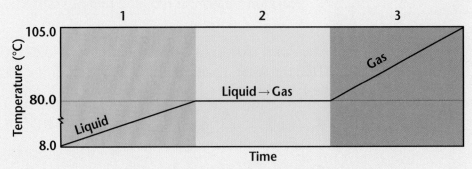

You will need to make three calculations, one for each graph section:
Section 1: $\Delta H = (m)(C_p)(\Delta T)$
Section 2: $\Delta H = (m)(\Delta H_{vap})$
Section 3: $\Delta H = (m)(C_p)(\Delta T)$

Solve Use positive numbers to represent each ΔT. Refer to Table 14.3.1 for constants. The ΔH values are

Section 1: $\Delta H = (22.0\ \text{g})(1.69\ \text{J/g•°C})(72.0°C) = 2{,}680\ \text{J}$
Section 2: $\Delta H = (22.0\ \text{g})(567\ \text{J/g}) = 12{,}500\ \text{J}$
Section 3: $\Delta H = (22.0\ \text{g})(1.05\ \text{J/g•°C})(25.0°C) = 578\ \text{J}$

The total ΔH for this heating process is the sum of these values:
$2{,}680\ \text{J} + 12{,}500\ \text{J} + 578\ \text{J} = 15{,}758\ \text{J} \xrightarrow{\text{round}} 15{,}800\ \text{J}$

The answer is rounded to the least certain decimal place (the hundreds place).

Reflect Raising the temperature of a liquid, boiling it, and raising the temperature of the gas requires the addition of heat. In this example, 15,800 J of heat is absorbed to do this work. Heating and boiling are endothermic processes.

Practice 32.0 g of benzene is heated from 15.0°C to 100.0°C. What is the total amount of heat absorbed in this process?

On a sheet of paper, write the phrase from the Word Bank that completes each sentence.

1. The amount of heat needed to raise the temperature of 1 g of a substance by 1°C is _____.

2. The amount of heat required to melt 1 g of a solid substance is the _____.

3. The amount of heat required to boil 1 g of a liquid substance is the _____.

Match each change in the first column with the equation for ΔH in the second column. Write the letter of the answer on a sheet of paper.

4. A substance changes temperature, not state.

5. A substance boils or condenses.

6. A substance melts or freezes.

A $\Delta H = (m)(C_p)(\Delta T)$

B $\Delta H = (m)(\Delta H_{fus})$

C $\Delta H = (m)(\Delta H_{vap})$

Critical Thinking

On a sheet of paper, write the answer to each problem.

7. A solid at 25°C is heated to 30°C. It is still a solid. How did the added energy affect the substance?

8. A solid at 0°C is heated to a liquid at 0°C. How did the added energy affect the substance?

9. Calculate the heat absorbed when 100. g of ice at −12.0°C is heated to a gas at 114.0°C. Refer to Table 14.3.1.

10. Calculate the heat absorbed when 50.0 g of liquid benzene at 10.0°C is heated to gaseous benzene at 90.0°C. Refer to Table 14.3.1.

The Heat of Fusion of Ice

When ice is added to warm water, the ice melts and the water cools. The mixture eventually reaches a final temperature. The heat released by the warm water equals the heat gained by the ice as it melts. Can you determine the heat of fusion of ice? Find out in this investigation.

Procedure

1. Make a data table like the one shown here.

Variable	Initial Value	Final Value
mass of empty cup (g)		
mass of cup and water (g)		
mass of water (g)		
temperature of water (°C)		

2. Put on safety goggles and a lab coat or apron.

3. Measure and record the mass of the empty cup.

4. Add 100 mL of warm water to the cup.

5. Measure the initial mass of the cup and warm water. Find the mass of the water. Measure the initial water temperature. Record all of these values.

6. Add the ice cubes to the warm water. Do not let any water splash out of the cup.

Continued on next page

7. Stir the water as shown until all of the ice melts.

8. Measure the final temperature of the water. Measure the final mass of the cup and water. Find the mass of the water. Record all of these values.

Cleanup/Disposal

Return all equipment. Clean your work area and wash your hands.

Analysis

1. Calculate how much heat the initial mass of water released as it cooled to the final temperature.

2. How many grams of ice melted? Explain your answer.

3. Calculate the amount of heat gained by the melted ice as it warmed from 0°C to the final temperature.

4. Subtract the amount of heat in question 3 from the amount in question 1. The result is the heat needed to melt the ice. Divide this amount by the number of grams of ice. The result is the heat of fusion of ice.

Conclusions

1. How does your value of the heat of fusion of ice compare with the accepted value of 334 J/g?

2. What might be some sources of error in the investigation?

Explore Further

Repeat the investigation with a larger cup and twice the amounts of warm water and ice. Is your heat of fusion value closer to the accepted value? Explain your answer.

Most liquid products containing water should be stored at temperatures above their freezing temperature. Water expands when it freezes, and the container may burst.

Earth is the only known planet to have liquid water on its surface. This is one reason why Earth can support life, while other planets cannot. About 70% of Earth's surface is water. Water is also found in Earth's atmosphere and crust. Water is a main component in plant and animal cells. Your body is about 60% water. Water has many unique physical properties that are essential for life. The hydrogen bonding between water molecules is the key to these properties.

Physical Properties of Water

As you learned in Chapter 13, *water has a high specific heat.* It can absorb a large amount of heat with just a small rise in temperature. When its temperature drops, a large amount of heat must be released. As a result, water heats up slowly and cools slowly. Because of water's specific heat, oceans and large lakes make nearby climates milder.

The density of solid water is less than the density of liquid water. This is not true of most substances. Usually, the solid state of a substance is denser than its liquid state. Again, the interparticle forces in water make it unique. More hydrogen bonding occurs in ice than in liquid water. However, instead of pulling the water molecules in ice closer together, the extra hydrogen bonding creates a more open arrangement of molecules. When water freezes, the molecules move into an open arrangement that pushes them farther apart, as Figure 14.4.1 shows. The volume of the water increases. As a result, ice is less dense liquid water. Ice floats on water. If ice sank in lakes and rivers, most aquatic animals in cold climates would not survive the winter.

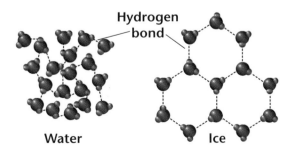

Figure 14.4.1
Molecules in liquid water are closer together than molecules in ice. This is why ice floats in water.

Water   **Ice**

Surface tension

The inward pull from hydrogen bonding that prevents a liquid from spreading out

Link to ➤➤➤

Biology

Water has a high specific heat. As a result, it takes a lot of heat to change the temperature of a large body of water. Many organisms that live in the ocean cannot tolerate large temperature changes. They survive because the oceans maintain a fairly constant temperature.

Water has an unusually high boiling point for its molecular mass. This is because of the strong hydrogen bonding between water's polar molecules. As a result, water is a liquid at room temperature. Other molecules of a similar mass, such as H_2S, do not have this strong hydrogen bonding and are gases at room temperature. Without water's high boiling point, living things could not function.

Water is often called the universal solvent. It is rare to find pure H_2O in nature because water can dissolve so many different substances. What makes water such a great solvent? A general rule in chemistry is "like dissolves like." Substances with a similar polarity dissolve fairly well in each other. Ionic compounds and polar molecules, like table salt and sugar, dissolve easily in water. These polar substances are attracted to the polar water molecules. Nonpolar substances like oil do not dissolve in water because the H_2O molecules attract each other more than they attract the oil molecules.

Water has fairly high **surface tension.** Surface tension is the inward pull from hydrogen bonding that tends to prevent water from spreading out. When you spill a little water on a flat surface, what happens? Tiny beads of water form—not a thin, wide puddle. Strong hydrogen bonds pull on the molecules at the liquid's surface. This inward force holds these molecules tightly and keeps the surface area of the liquid small. A liquid with high surface tension behaves as if its surface has a thin skin. Surface tension is what allows some bugs to walk on the surface of water, as Figure 14.4.2 shows.

Figure 14.4.2
Surface tension from strong hydrogen bonding allows this bug to walk on water.

The phase diagram
for water shows
that ice sublimes
at low temperature
and pressure. This
property is used
to remove water
from foods. The
foods are frozen.
Then a vacuum
pump lowers the
pressure below the
vapor pressure of
ice. The ice in the
foods sublimes,
leaving freeze-
dried foods that
are lightweight
and need no
refrigeration.

A Phase Diagram of Water

A phase diagram shows how the three phases, or states, of a substance are related to temperature and pressure. A phase diagram can tell you the state of a substance at a particular temperature and pressure. It can also tell you at what temperatures and pressures a substance will change from one state to another. Figure 14.4.3 is the phase diagram for water.

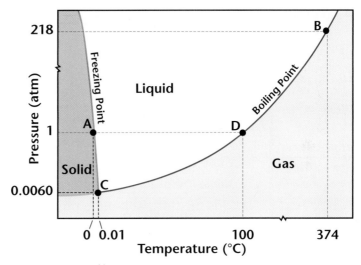

Figure 14.4.3 *This phase diagram shows the temperature and pressure limits of each state of water. The blue line is the freezing (melting) point. The pink line is the boiling (condensing) point. The green line is the sublimation point.*

In this diagram, pressure is plotted versus temperature. Each state—solid, liquid, and gas—is shown as an area on the diagram. The lines separating the three areas represent changes in state. The pink line, for example, represents the boiling point of water. Along this line, both liquid and gaseous water exist. The lettered points are explained on the next page.

Science Myth

Myth: When you add energy to ice at 0°C, it always melts.

Fact: Ice at 0°C usually melts when energy is added to it. However, the phase diagram for water shows that ice sublimes at low pressure. When it sublimes, ice changes directly to water vapor.

Find the points A, B, C, and D in Figure 14.4.3 on page 567.

Find the points A, B, C, and D in Figure 14.4.3 on page 567.

Normal melting point

The temperature at which a solid changes to a liquid at a pressure of 1 atm

Critical point

The critical pressure and critical temperature of a substance

Critical temperature

The temperature above which a gas cannot be condensed to a liquid

Critical pressure

The pressure required to condense a gas at the critical temperature

Triple point

The temperature and pressure at which all three states of a substance exist together

- A is the **normal melting point.** This is the temperature at which a solid changes to a liquid at a pressure of 1 atm. Water's normal melting point is 0°C.

- B is the **critical point.** This consists of two values: the **critical temperature** and the **critical pressure.** Above the critical temperature, a gas cannot be condensed into a liquid, no matter how much pressure is applied. The gas particles have too much energy. For water, the critical temperature is 374°C. The critical pressure is the pressure required to condense a gas at the critical temperature. For water, the critical pressure is 218 atm.

- C is the **triple point.** At this temperature and pressure, all three states exist together. For water, the triple point is a temperature of 0.01°C and a pressure of 0.0060 atm. Under these conditions, ice, liquid water, and water vapor exist at the same time.

- D is the normal boiling point. For water, the normal boiling point is 100°C.

Example 1	What state(s) of water exist at −10°C and 1 atm? Use Figure 14.4.3.
Read	You are given a temperature and a pressure. You need to determine if water is a solid, liquid, gas, or a combination of these at the given conditions.
Plan	On the phase diagram, locate −10°C on the temperature scale. Locate 1 atm on the pressure scale. Then find the point on the diagram that represents both values. An estimate is okay.
Solve	At −10°C and 1 atm, water is a solid.
Reflect	A pressure of 1 atm is a natural atmospheric pressure. At this temperature, you would expect water to be frozen.
Practice	What state(s) of water exist at 75°C and 0.0060 atm?

Example 2	What state(s) of water exist at 100°C and 1 atm? Use Figure 14.4.3.
Read	You need to determine if water is a solid, liquid, gas, or combination of these at the given temperature and pressure.
Plan	On the diagram, locate the point that represents 1 atm and 100°C.
Solve	This point is on the line separating the liquid state from the gas state. This line is the boiling point line. Both liquid and gas exist at 100°C and 1 atm.
Reflect	The normal boiling point of water is 100°C.
Practice	What state(s) of water exist at 0.01°C and 0.0060 atm?

A phase diagram can be drawn for any element or compound. Water's diagram is unusual in that the line for its melting/ freezing point slopes backwards. At a very high pressure, ice at a temperature of 0°C will melt.

Link to ➤➤➤

Health

Caffeine can cause nervousness and insomnia in some people. Carbon dioxide at its critical temperature and pressure is sometimes used to remove caffeine from coffee. The CO_2 acts as a liquid and dissolves the caffeine. Then, the CO_2 is easily changed to a gas, leaving the caffeine and coffee separated.

Research and Write

Some vitamins, such as vitamin B, are soluble in water. Other vitamins, such as vitamin E, are soluble in fats but not in water. Research the solubility of several vitamins. Create a table to summarize your findings.

On a sheet of paper, write the phrase from the Word Bank that completes each sentence.

1. At the _____, all states of a substance coexist.

2. Above the _____, a gas can no longer be condensed into a liquid, no matter how high the pressure is.

3. The inward pull from hydrogen bonding that prevents a liquid from spreading out is _____.

On a sheet of paper, write the letter of the answer that completes each sentence. Use Figure 14.4.3 to help you.

4. At 0°C and 1 atm, water exists as _____.

A a solid   **C** a solid and a liquid
B a liquid   **D** a solid, a liquid, and a gas

5. At 75°C and 15 atm, water exists as _____.

A a solid   **C** a gas
B a liquid   **D** a liquid and a gas

6. Water is a solid at −10°C and 1 atm. If the pressure drops to 0.0010 atm, the solid _____.

A melts   **C** freezes
B remains a solid **D** sublimes

Critical Thinking

On a sheet of paper, write the answer to each question.

7. Explain what "like dissolves like" means. Give an example.

8. Which state of water has the greatest density? Explain why this is unusual.

9. How are certain bugs able to walk on water without sinking?

10. You are given a phase diagram for an unknown substance. List at least three pieces of information that the diagram provides.

DISCOVERY INVESTIGATION 14

Materials

- safety goggles
- lab coat or apron
- transparent plastic cup
- room-temperature water
- scissors
- plastic pipet
- metric ruler
- thermal gloves
- small scoopula
- 2–3 g of dry ice (powdered or in small pieces)
- pliers

Melting Dry Ice

Solid carbon dioxide is called dry ice. It sublimes at room temperature and pressure, as the phase diagram below shows. However, CO_2 exists as a liquid at a pressure greater than its triple-point pressure. Can you observe liquid CO_2? You will explore this question in this investigation.

Procedure

1. Read the entire procedure. Study the phase diagram on the next page.

2. Make a table to record your observations. Write a hypothesis about what changes will occur during the investigation.

3. Put on safety goggles and a lab coat or apron.

4. Half-fill the cup with water.

5. Carefully cut the tip off the pipet so the stem is about 7 cm long.

6. Put on thermal gloves. Use the scoopula to place enough dry ice into the pipet to fill the bulb halfway. **Safety Alert: Do not touch dry ice. Wear thermal gloves when working with dry ice.**

7. Clamp the pliers over the open end of the pipet so that no gas escapes. Hold the pipet by the pliers and lower the bulb into the water. Observe and record what happens to the dry ice.

8. When you see liquid form in the bulb of the pipet, release the pressure on the pliers, while still holding the pipet in the water. Record your observations.

Continued on next page

9. Again clamp the pliers on the end of the pipet. Watch for liquid to form, then release the pressure. Repeat this step, observing and recording all changes that occur.

Cleanup/Disposal

Return or dispose of the materials. Clean your work area, and wash your hands.

Analysis

1. What was the purpose of the pliers?

2. Why was the bulb of the pipet placed in water?

3. How did the CO_2 change throughout the investigation?

Conclusions

1. Was the pressure inside the pipet greater than the triple-point pressure of CO_2? Explain your answer.

2. Describe what happens to dry ice as it warms at various pressures.

Explore Further

What do you predict will happen if you fill the pipet bulb three-quarters full with dry ice? Test your prediction.

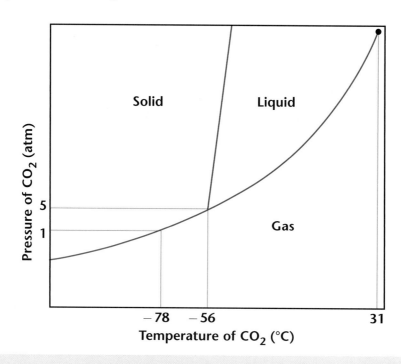

Phase-Change Materials

During a state change, energy is absorbed or released while temperature stays constant. Some products use the energy difference between a solid and a liquid to control temperature. These products contain materials known as phase-change materials.

For example, phase-change materials are sometimes added to wallboard. A common material in phase-change wallboard is paraffin, a waxy substance. When a room's temperature rises above normal, the paraffin melts slightly. As the paraffin melts, it absorbs and stores energy from the room. When the room's temperature drops below normal, at night for example, the paraffin freezes. As it freezes, it releases energy into the room. If the outdoor temperature stays below the indoor temperature, the wallboard can be heated by electricity at night, when electricity is not in high demand. This keeps the paraffin in a liquid state. The paraffin is then allowed to freeze during the day, releasing stored energy into the room.

Phase-change materials have many other uses. When packing a lunch, you may include a special pack to keep the food cold. This cold pack contains a phase-change material. It is stored in the freezer until it is needed.

Then, as the phase-change material melts, it absorbs energy from the lunch contents, keeping the lunch cold.

Phase-change materials are also used to keep food warm. You may have also seen or used pouches designed for this purpose. These pouches are first heated in a microwave oven, which melts the solid material inside. Then they release heat for hours as the phase-change material again becomes a solid.

1. What are phase-change materials?

2. Why might phase-change materials be used in flowerpots?

- A gas becomes a liquid when its temperature drops enough for attractive forces to hold the particles together. This process is called condensation.

- When a liquid boils, it changes into a gas. The change from liquid to gas also occurs when particles at the surface of a liquid evaporate. Evaporation can occur at any temperature.

- The particles in a liquid freeze when the temperature drops enough to cause the particles to lock into position as a solid. The opposite process is called melting.

- Most solids are crystals. Some solids are amorphous and form no crystals.

- To calculate the heat involved in a change between liquid and solid states, use the equation, $\Delta H = (m)(\Delta H_{fus})$.

- To calculate the heat involved in a change between liquid and gaseous states, use the equation, $\Delta H = (m)(\Delta H_{vap})$.

- To calculate the heat involved in changing the temperature when state does not change, use the equation, $\Delta H = (m)(C_p)(\Delta T)$.

- An evaporated liquid creates vapor pressure. When vapor pressure equals atmospheric pressure, the liquid boils. When vapor pressure equals 1 atm, the liquid is at the normal boiling point.

- A vapor pressure diagram relates the boiling point of a liquid to different pressure conditions.

- Water has unique properties because of its strong interparticle forces. It has a relatively high boiling point. Its solid state is less dense than its liquid state. Water has high surface tension. It makes an excellent solvent for polar substances.

- Phase diagrams can be used to determine the phase of a substance at a specific temperature and pressure.

Vocabulary

amorphous, 549
boil, 547
boiling point, 552
condensed state, 547
condense, 546
critical pressure, 568
critical temperature, 568
critical point, 568

crystal, 548
crystal lattice, 548
deposition, 547
evaporation, 547
freeze, 547
heat of fusion, 559
heat of vaporization, 559
melt, 547

normal boiling point, 552
normal melting point, 568
sublimation, 547
surface tension, 566
triple point, 568
vapor pressure, 552

Chapter 14 R E V I E W

Vocabulary Review

On a sheet of paper, write the word or phrase from the Word Bank that completes each sentence.

Word Bank

amorphous

condensed states

critical pressure

crystal lattice

vapor pressure

1. A(n) _____ solid has no repeating, orderly arrangement of particles.

2. The pressure required to condense a gas at the critical temperature is the _____.

3. The solid and liquid states are _____.

4. The pressure created when a liquid evaporates is _____.

5. The repeating, orderly pattern in a solid is a(n) _____.

Match the term in the first column with its definition in the second column. Write the letter of the answer on a sheet of paper.

6. freeze

7. condense

8. evaporate

9. sublimation

10. boiling point

A to change from gas to liquid

B temperature at which vapor pressure equals atmospheric pressure

C to change from liquid to solid

D to change from solid to gas

E to change from liquid to gas at any vapor pressure

Concept Review

On a sheet of paper, write the letter of the answer to each question. Use the vapor pressure diagram on the next page for questions 11–15.

11. Which substance has the weakest interparticle forces?

    A substance A
    B substance B
    C substance C
    D It is impossible to tell from this diagram.

Continued on next page

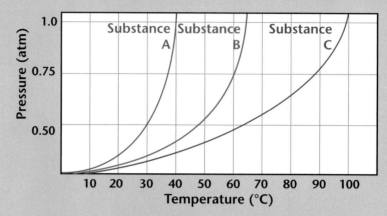

12. What is the normal boiling point of substance B?

    A 48°C   **B** 64°C   **C** 70°C   **D** 99°C

13. Estimate the boiling point of substance A at 0.75 atm.

    A 30°C   **B** 38°C   **C** 40°C   **D** 88°C

14. Which substance has the strongest interparticle forces?

    A substance A   **B** substance B   **C** substance C
    D It is impossible to tell from this diagram.

15. Estimate the boiling point of substance C at 0.50 atm.

    A 99°C   **B** 88°C   **C** 63°C   **D** 50°C

Problem Solving

On a sheet of paper, write the answer to each question. Use the phase diagram below for questions 16–18.

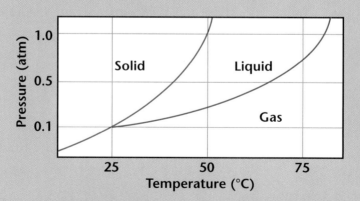

16. What is the normal melting point of this substance?

17. What change in state occurs as the pressure changes from 0.5 atm at 75°C to 1.0 atm at 75°C?

18. What is the temperature at the triple point?

On a sheet of paper, write the answer to each problem. Show all calculations. Use the constants in Table 14.3.1 on page 559.

19. Calculate the heat released when 45.3 g of gaseous H_2O at 112.0°C is cooled to a solid at -23.0°C.

20. Calculate the heat absorbed when 17.2 g of liquid benzene at 70°C is changed to gaseous benzene at 90°C.

Critical Thinking

On a sheet of paper, write the answer to each question.

21. How is evaporation different from boiling in terms of where it occurs?

22. When liquid benzene boils, what is in the gas bubbles that form?

23. What happens to the vapor pressure of a liquid as the temperature increases? Explain your answer.

24. Water in Baltimore (at sea level) boils at 100°C. Death Valley (below sea level) has a higher atmospheric pressure than Baltimore. Would the boiling point of water be higher in Baltimore or in Death Valley? Explain your answer.

25. The heat absorbed during melting or boiling does not increase the temperature of the substance. Why?

Test-Taking Tip When you review your notes to prepare for a test, use a marker to highlight key words, equations, and example problems.

15 Solutions

Colorful corals and sponges make up this Caribbean coral reef. Coral reefs form only in seawater, the most common kind of solution on the earth. In Chapter 15, you will learn about the parts of solutions and the property of solubility. You will also learn about different kinds of solutions and how they are made.

Organize Your Thoughts

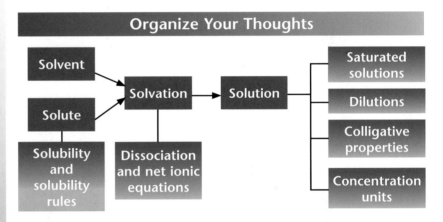

Solvent → Solvation → Solution
Solute → Solvation
Solubility and solubility rules → Solvation
Solvation → Dissociation and net ionic equations
Solution → Saturated solutions
Solution → Dilutions
Solution → Colligative properties
Solution → Concentration units

Goals for Learning

◆ To compare how ionic compounds and molecular compounds dissolve in water

◆ To explain what a saturated solution is and to read a solubility graph

◆ To use solubility rules to write the net ionic equation for a reaction

◆ To understand how dilute solutions are prepared from concentrated solutions

◆ To calculate molality, mass percent, and mole fraction

◆ To describe how the properties of a solution are different from the properties of a solvent

Objectives

After reading this lesson, you should be able to

◆ explain why an ionic compound dissolves in water

◆ explain why a polar molecular compound dissolves in water

◆ describe ways to increase the rate of solvation for a solid solute

◆ explain why colloids and suspensions are not solutions

Solvation

The process in which solvent particles attract and surround solute particles, causing them to dissolve

Soluble

A description of a solid that dissolves in a liquid

Insoluble

A description of a solid that does not dissolve in a liquid

Water is an excellent solvent for many solutes. Recall from Chapter 2 that a solute is a substance that is dissolved in a solvent to make a solution. The solute, solvent, and resulting solution may be solids, liquids, or gases. Most of the solutions discussed in this chapter are aqueous solutions made from a solid solute dissolved in water.

What happens when a solid solute dissolves in water? The ionic compound, NaCl, is a crystal in its solid state. Its lattice contains alternating Na^{1+} and Cl^{1-} ions. When placed in water, these ions are attracted by the polar water molecules. Attractive forces form between the water molecules and the ions. The negative ends of water molecules surround Na^{1+} ions,

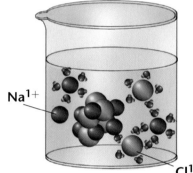

Figure 15.1.1 *When solid NaCl dissolves in water, the polar water molecules surround the ions.*

and the positive ends of water molecules surround Cl^{1-} ions. The ions are pulled away from their solid lattice. This process is called **solvation.** In solvation, solvent particles attract and surround solute particles, pulling them into solution. The solute dissolves, as shown in Figure 15.1.1. A solute that dissolves in a liquid is **soluble.** NaCl is soluble in water. A solute that does not dissolve in a liquid is **insoluble.**

Solvation of Ionic Compounds

A solute's polarity determines how well it dissolves in water. In general, polar solvents dissolve polar solutes, and nonpolar solvents dissolve nonpolar solutes. This is often summarized as "like dissolves like." A water molecule is polar, with a positive end and a negative end. Ionic compounds are also polar, since they consist of cations and anions. Ionic compounds usually dissolve very well in water.

When a solid ionic compound dissolves in water, it breaks apart and separates into individual ions. This is called **dissociation.** Sodium chloride dissociates in water, as shown in Figure 15.1.1. This can be expressed as an equation:

$$NaCl(s) \rightarrow Na^{1+}(aq) + Cl^{1-}(aq)$$

All ionic compounds that dissolve in water dissociate.

When an ionic compound dissociates in water, the ions are free to travel throughout the solution. The solution is capable of conducting electricity. Electricity is conducted by the movement of charged particles through matter. An **electrolyte** is a substance that can conduct electricity when melted or in aqueous solutions. Most ionic compounds are electrolytes.

Solvation of Molecular Compounds

Molecular compounds that dissolve in water do not dissociate. These molecules dissolve because they are polar, like water. Table sugar, $C_{12}H_{22}O_{11}$, is very soluble in water. Molecules of table sugar are polar because they have many O-H bonds. When table sugar is placed in water, the water molecules attract the O-H ends of the sugar molecules. This attractive force pulls the sugar molecules away from the solid and into solution. This solvation process can be expressed as

$$C_{12}H_{22}O_{11}(s) \rightarrow C_{12}H_{22}O_{11}(aq)$$

Many molecular compounds like sugar do not conduct electricity when melted or in aqueous solutions. They are **nonelectrolytes.** However, some molecular compounds, like sulfuric acid, are electrolytes.

Most nonpolar molecules are not soluble in water. Vegetable oil is a good example. Oil molecules contain many C-H bonds and are nonpolar. Water molecules are polar. Oil and water are **immiscible.** They do not dissolve in each other. When two liquids dissolve in each other, they are **miscible.** Oil and other nonpolar molecules, like gasoline, are miscible.

Link to ⪢⪢⪢

Health

During strenuous physical activity, your body loses important ions through perspiration. Sport drinks contain electrolytes like sodium chloride or potassium chloride. These ionic compounds replace the lost sodium, potassium, and chloride ions. Most of these ions can be replenished by a proper diet. Drinking water before, during, and after a workout is also important.

Factors Affecting Solvation

The rate of solvation depends on many factors. The following actions speed up the dissolving process for a soluble solid.

- Increase the temperature of the solution. This makes the solvent and solute particles move faster. Sugar dissolves much faster in hot tea than in iced tea.

- Increase the surface area of the solid solute. This can be done by breaking the solid into many small pieces. This allows more solute particles to be available to solvent particles. Granulated sugar dissolves faster than a sugar cube. There are more sugar molecules exposed to the solvent.

- Stir the solution. This moves solvated particles away so that new solute particles are exposed.

Express Lab 15

Materials
- safety goggles
- lab coat or apron
- 3 100-mL beakers
- 150 mL of distilled water
- 25 g of sugar ($C_{12}H_{22}O_{11}$)
- 25 g of calcium carbonate ($CaCO_3$)
- 25 g of table salt (NaCl)
- stirring rod

Procedure
1. Put on safety goggles and a lab coat or apron.

2. Pour 50 mL of distilled water into each beaker. **Safety Alert: Be careful when working with glassware.**

3. Pour the sugar into one beaker. Stir until all of the solute is dissolved.

4. Record your observations.

5. Repeat steps 3 and 4 with the other two solutes.

Analysis
1. Which solute was most soluble in water? Explain your answer.

2. Which solute was least soluble in water? Explain your answer.

Colloids and Suspensions

When solute particles are too large to completely dissolve, a **colloid** may form. A colloid is a mixture in which particles of one substance are evenly dispersed, or spread out, in another substance. The particles are small enough to remain dispersed and do not sink to the bottom of the container. A colloid is not a true solution. Milk, for example, is a colloid, not a solution. Milk is a mixture of fat and protein dispersed in a liquid called whey. Other examples of colloids are gelatin desserts, butter, whipped cream, and the household products shown in Figure 15.1.2. Mixtures called **suspensions** have even larger particles. These particles spread out evenly when the mixture is shaken, but they eventually settle out. A sample of muddy water is a suspension.

Sometimes it is hard to tell colloids from solutions. However, colloids show the **Tyndall effect.** The Tyndall effect is the scattering of light in all directions. When light passes through a solution, there is no scattering of light. A beam of light looks cloudy in colloids, but is not visible in solutions. For this reason, you can see the beams of car headlights when driving through fog. Fog, clouds, and mist are colloids of liquid water molecules dispersed in air.

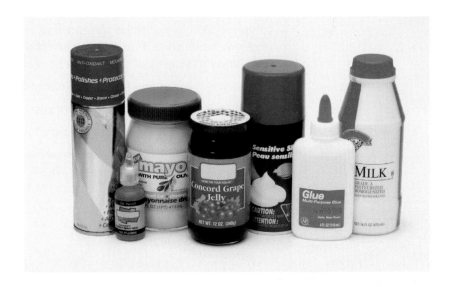

Figure 15.1.2
Aerosols, paint, mayonnaise, jelly, shaving cream, glue, and milk are colloids.

Consumer Choices: Household Solvents

Many of the household cleaners you use at home are solvents. The cleaners dissolve the substances that make a surface "dirty." There are many different kinds of cleaners. How do you choose the right one? You do not

need a different cleaner for every job. However, substances that stain or stick to a surface can have very different chemical compositions. Therefore, different solvents are needed to remove different categories of substances. The most effective and safest solvent is water. Water dissolves most polar compounds. However, some stains, such as grease and oil, are nonpolar compounds. These stains require nonpolar solvents, such as naptha or carbon tetrachloride. These solvents are often toxic and flammable. Safer alternatives are citrus or pine oils.

Did you ever remove a price tag and see a gummy substance left behind? This substance is an adhesive. Adhesives can be made from so many different compounds that no one solvent will remove them all. Many adhesives are made from nonpolar compounds. Oily nonpolar solvents that remove grease also tend to remove adhesives. But read the labels on cleaners—choose one that won't damage the surface beneath the adhesive.

1. When is water an effective household cleaner?

2. Why is grease dissolved by nonpolar solvents?

3. What cleaning solvents do you use at home?

Lesson 1   R E V I E W

Word Bank

dissociation

electrolyte

miscible

soluble

solvation

temperature

On a sheet of paper, write the word from the Word Bank that completes each sentence.

1. A substance that can conduct electricity when melted or in aqueous solutions is a(n) _____.

2. When two liquids dissolve in each other, they are _____.

3. When solid KI separates into K^{1+} and I^{1-} ions in water, it undergoes _____.

4. When a solid solute dissolves in a solvent, the solute is _____.

5. In most cases, you can increase the solubility of a solid in a liquid by increasing the _____.

6. In the process of _____, solvent particles attract the particles in a solid, pulling them into solution.

Critical Thinking

On a sheet of paper, write the answer to each question.

7. Describe in general how molecular compounds dissolve in water.

8. Why are oil and water immiscible?

9. Why does increasing temperature speed the dissolving process of a solid solute?

10. List two other ways to speed the dissolving process for a solid in water.

Objectives

After reading this lesson, you should be able to

◆ define a saturated, unsaturated, and supersaturated solution

◆ explain how temperature affects solid and gas solutes

◆ read a solubility graph

Suppose you add a heaping spoon of KCl to a liter of water. You stir, and the solute quickly dissolves. You add another spoonful and stir. Again, it dissolves. You continue adding solute and stirring. Is there a point when no more KCl will dissolve, no matter how much you stir? Yes. Eventually, the solution becomes "full" of solute.

Saturated Solutions

When a solution cannot dissolve more solute, it is **saturated.** A saturated solution contains the maximum amount of solute that is able to dissolve at a given temperature. If less than this maximum amount of solute is dissolved, the solution is **unsaturated.** An unsaturated solution is able to dissolve more solute.

The amount of solute needed to make a saturated solution depends on temperature. For most solid solutes, more can dissolve at a higher temperature. If a saturated solution is heated, it becomes unsaturated. It is able to dissolve additional solute—until it reaches the maximum solute amount at the new temperature.

It is possible to make a **supersaturated** solution of certain substances. A supersaturated solution contains more than the maximum amount of dissolved solute at a given temperature. How can it hold more than the maximum amount? This is achieved by making a saturated solution at a high temperature and then cooling it.

Saturated

Having the maximum amount of solute dissolved in a given amount of solvent at a specific temperature

Unsaturated

Having less than the maximum amount of solute dissolved in a given amount of solvent at a given temperature

Supersaturated

Having more than the maximum amount of solute dissolved in a given amount of solvent at a given temperature

❋ ❋

Technology and Society

Athletic trainers often use hot packs to treat sore muscles. Hot packs are plastic bags containing supersaturated solutions of sodium acetate or calcium chloride. When the bags are heated in water, the solute dissolves completely in the water. The solute does not crystallize in the supersaturated solution until it is disturbed. This is done by clicking a metal disk in the bag. The sudden crystallization of the solute releases energy as heat.

One substance that makes supersaturated solutions is sodium acetate, $NaC_2H_3O_2$. For example, at a certain temperature and volume, 119 g of sodium acetate makes a saturated solution. By heating this solution, an extra 51 g of sodium acetate (a total of 170 g) can dissolve, making a saturated solution at the new temperature. By carefully cooling this saturated solution, a supersaturated solution can be made. When the solution temperature drops, there is still 170 g of sodium acetate dissolved in the solution. A supersaturated solution is very unstable because the excess solute can easily crystallize out of solution, as shown in Figure 15.2.1. When this happens, the result is a saturated solution and the excess solid solute.

Figure 15.2.1 *A supersaturated solution of $NaC_2H_3O_2$ (left) is created by cooling a saturated solution. After the excess solute crystallizes, the solution becomes saturated (right).*

Science Myth

Myth: All solutions consist of liquid solvents.

Fact: Solvents can be solids, as long as their crystal structure remains unchanged. Examples of solid solutions are certain kinds of rocks, ceramics, and polymers. The most familiar solid solutions are alloys, in which one metal is dissolved in another metal.

Solubility

Solubility

The amount of solute that dissolves in a certain amount of solvent to create a saturated solution at a given temperature and pressure

Figure 15.2.2 shows the **solubility** of 10 substances. Solubility is the amount of solute that dissolves in a certain amount of solvent to create a saturated solution at a given temperature and pressure. In this particular graph, solubility is the mass of solute per 100. g of water. The curves in the graph are called solubility curves. Each represents one solute. As you can see, the amount of solute in a saturated solution depends on temperature. Look at the curve for $NaNO_3$. At 10°C, about 78 g can dissolve in 100. g of water. A solution containing less than 78 g at 10°C would be unsaturated. A solution containing more than 78 g at 10°C would be supersaturated.

For 7 of the 10 solutes (the red curves), their solubility increases as temperature increases. These solutes are solids. For three solutes (the blue curves), solubility decreases with temperature. These solutes are gases.

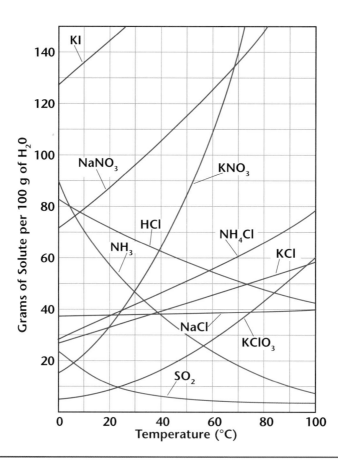

Figure 15.2.2
The solubility of a substance depends on temperature. The red curves represent solid solutes, and the blue curves represent gases.

Example 1	What is the solubility of KNO_3 at 50°C? Use Figure 15.2.2.
Read	You are asked to find the mass of KNO_3 that will make a saturated solution when dissolved in 100. g of water at 50°C.
Plan	Find the solubility curve for KNO_3 on the graph. Find where it intersects the line that represents 50°C.
Solve	At 50°C, the solubility of KNO_3 is about 85 g in 100. g of water.
Reflect	To make a saturated solution using 200. g of water at 50°C, you would need 2(85 g)=170 g of KNO_3.
Practice	50. g of NH_4Cl is dissolved in 100. g of water at 80°C. Is the solution saturated? If not, how much more NH_4Cl is needed to make the solution saturated?

Gas Solubility

Shaking or stirring a supersaturated solution of gas can cause gas particles to leave the solution. This happens when you open a can of soda after it was dropped or shaken. The dissolved gas particles suddenly leave the soda, causing some of the soda to spew out of the can.

Gas solutes act differently than solid solutes. The attractive forces between gas particles and solvent particles are relatively weak. As a result, gas particles tend not to stay dissolved. The following actions help keep gas solutes dissolved in a solution.

- Increase the pressure of the gas above the solution. More gas particles dissolve because they strike the surface of the solution more often. Carbonated beverages contain the gas solute, carbon dioxide. They are bottled under pressure. When you open a bottle, you hear a hissing sound as the pressure in the bottle drops to atmospheric pressure. If a carbonated beverage is left open too long, it goes "flat" because most of the carbon dioxide leaves the solution.

- Decrease the temperature of the solution. This decreases the kinetic energy of the solution particles. When the particles have less energy, attractive forces can hold more gas particles in solution. When temperature increases, the increased kinetic energy allows more gas particles to break away and leave the solution. If you have left an opened carbonated beverage in the sun, you may have noticed that it goes flat very quickly.

Word Bank

saturated

supersaturated

unsaturated

On a sheet of paper, write the word from the Word Bank that completes each sentence.

1. When the maximum amount of solute is dissolved in a volume of solvent, the solution is _____.

2. When more solute can dissolve in a solution, the solution is _____.

3. When more than the maximum amount of solute is dissolved in a volume of solvent, the solution is _____.

On a sheet of paper, write the letter of the answer to each question. Use the solubility graph in Figure 15.2.2.

4. Which of the following is the least soluble solid at 10°C?

A KI   **B** SO_2 **C** NaCl   **D** $KClO_3$

5. How much solute is needed to make a saturated solution of KNO_3 if the solvent (100 g of water) is at 30°C?

A 18 g   **B** 30 g   **C** 47 g   **D** 67 g

6. A solution of NH_4Cl contains 50 g of solute in 100 g of water at 10°C. How can this solution be described?

A saturated **B** unsaturated **C** insoluble **D** supersaturated

Critical Thinking

On a sheet of paper, write the answer to each question.

7. A gas is dissolved in water. How does the gas pressure above the solution affect the solubility of the gas?

8. A solution contains 100 g of water and 30 g of KCl at 70°C. How many more grams of KCl are needed to saturate the solution? Use Figure 15.2.2.

9. What mass of KCl is needed to saturate 200 g of water at 80°C? Use Figure 15.2.2.

10. Global warming refers to the increasing average temperature around the world. Many animals that live in oceans "breathe" the O_2 gas dissolved in the water. How might global warming affect these animals?

INVESTIGATION 15

Materials

- safety goggles
- lab coat or apron
- metal pan
- tap water
- hot plate
- ring stand
- beaker clamp
- thermometer clamp
- 100-mL beaker
- 65 g of potassium nitrate (KNO₃)
- balance
- distilled water
- stirring rod
- thermometer
- beaker tongs
- graph paper

Solubility and Temperature

Solubility usually varies with solvent temperature. How does water temperature affect the solubility of potassium nitrate? In this investigation, you will measure the temperatures at which quantities of KNO₃ dissolve. You will then construct a solubility curve from your data.

Procedure

1. Put on safety goggles and a lab coat or apron.

2. Pour tap water into the pan. Set the pan on the hot plate.

3. Set up the ring stand and clamps beside the hot plate as shown.

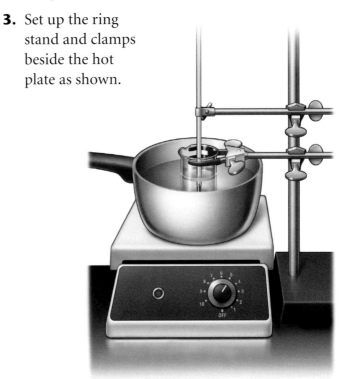

Continued on next page

4. Measure out one 25-g and four 10-g samples of KNO_3 on the balance. Set these samples aside. **Safety Alert: Keep the KNO_3 away from the hot plate even though the hot plate is turned off at this point.**

5. Pour 50 mL of distilled water into the beaker. Add the 25 g of KNO_3. Stir the solution with the stirring rod until no more solute dissolves. Some solute will not dissolve.

6. Place the beaker in its clamp and lower it halfway into the tap water. Place the thermometer in its clamp and lower the bulb into the solution. Turn on the hot plate to medium. **Safety Alert: Do not touch heated objects with your hands.**

7. Stir the solution until the solute has completely dissolved. Record the solution temperature.

8. Add a 10-g KNO_3 sample to the solution. Stir the solution until the solute has completely dissolved. Record the temperature.

9. Repeat step 8 for the remaining 10-g samples.

10. Turn off the hot plate and let the water in the pan cool.

11. Use your data to make a solubility curve on graph paper. Plot temperature on the x axis. Plot KNO_3 mass per 50 mL of water on the y axis.

Cleanup/Disposal

Use the beaker tongs to pour the solution into a proper waste container. Pour the water down the sink. Return equipment and clean your work area. Wash your hands.

Analysis

1. What does the shape of the solubility curve show?

2. Does the solubility curve show a large or small temperature dependence?

Conclusions

1. How much KNO_3 will dissolve in 50 mL of water at 55°C?

2. Is KNO_3 slightly soluble, soluble, or highly soluble in water? Justify your answer.

Explore Further

Repeat the investigation using sodium chloride, NaCl, as the solute.

Precipitate

A solid that forms out of a solution

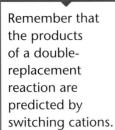

Remember that the products of a double-replacement reaction are predicted by switching cations.

In Chapter 5, you learned that the reactants in a double replacement are two ionic compounds. They are usually aqueous. A double-replacement reaction takes place only when one of the products is a solid or a molecular liquid or gas. Suppose you are told that two aqueous reactants switch cations, producing two aqueous products. Has a reaction really taken place? No. The same anions and cations are dissociated and moving freely in solution. Nothing has changed. However, if the reactant ions form a solid product or a molecular product like water or carbon dioxide, a reaction occurs.

Solubility Rules

How do chemists determine if two ionic reactants will cause a double-replacement reaction? First they predict the products. Then they determine if each product is molecular or ionic.

• If one possible product is a molecular compound (usually water or CO_2), the reaction occurs. An acid-base reaction occurs because water is produced.

• If both possible products are ionic compounds that are soluble, they remain dissociated and no reaction occurs.

• If both possible products are ionic compounds and one is insoluble, the reaction occurs.

When an ionic product is insoluble, it forms a solid. This solid is called a **precipitate** because it forms out of the solution. The forming of a precipitate forces the reaction to occur. Solubility rules are used to determine if an ionic product is soluble (aqueous) or insoluble (solid). These rules are listed on the next page. To find out if an ionic product is soluble or not, start with rule 1 and work down the list.

Water is a molecular compound and does not contain the H^{1+} ion. It is a liquid and is not aqueous.

Rule 1. Compounds containing nitrate ions (NO_3^{1-}) or acetate ions ($C_2H_3O_2^{1-}$) are *soluble*.

Rule 2. Compounds containing ammonium ions (NH_4^{1+}) or ions of alkali metals are *soluble*.

Rule 3. Compounds containing chloride ions (Cl^{1-}) are *soluble* except for $AgCl(s)$, $PbCl_2(s)$, and $Hg_2Cl_2(s)$.

Rule 4. Compounds containing sulfate ions (SO_4^{2-}) are *soluble* except for $BaSO_4(s)$, $PbSO_4(s)$, $Ag_2SO_4(s)$, $Hg_2SO_4(s)$, and $CaSO_4(s)$.

Rule 5. Most compounds containing hydroxide ions (OH^{1-}) are only slightly soluble in water. Assume that these products are *insoluble*. Exceptions are alkali metal and ammonium hydroxide compounds (soluble under rule 2).

Rule 6. Most compounds containing sulfide (S^{2-}), carbonate (CO_3^{2-}), or phosphate (PO_4^{3-}) ions are *insoluble*. Exceptions are compounds of these anions with sodium, potassium, or ammonium cations.

Spotlight on Chlorine

17
Cl
Chlorine
35.5

Chlorine is a yellow-green gas of the halogen family. It has the highest electron affinity of all elements. It is also one of the most reactive elements. This property explains why chlorine is never found in its gaseous state in nature. It also explains, in part, why nearly all metals form chlorine compounds. Chlorine is abundant in oceans. The presence of chloride and sodium ions gives seawater its salty taste. Another natural solution containing chloride ions is stomach acid. The stomach produces hydrochloric acid to digest food.

The applications of chlorine are vast. Chlorine has been used to manufacture plastics, solvents, bleaches, and antiseptics. Chlorine compounds are often added to drinking water to kill harmful bacteria. You can usually smell the chlorine coming from an indoor swimming pool. Nevertheless, chlorine is highly toxic. Health and environmental concerns have limited its applications in recent years.

Interesting Fact: Chlorine was the first halogen to be discovered, in 1774.

Spectator ion

An ion that remains aqueous and does not take part in a reaction

Research and Write

Research the use of salt domes for storing materials. Find out how they are used for storing petroleum and liquefied natural gas. Find out how the chemical properties of a substance determine if it can be safely stored. Present your findings in an oral or written report.

Example 1   Do the following reactants cause a reaction to occur? If so, write the balanced equation and include the state of each product.
$Ca(NO_3)_2(aq) + K_2SO_4(aq) \rightarrow$

Read   You are asked to determine if a double-replacement reaction occurs. If it does, you are asked to write the products, indicate their state, and balance the equation.

Plan   Identify the ions in each reactant. Find their charges (see pages 93 and 102).

$(Ca^{2+}$ and $NO_3^{1-}) + (K^{1+}$ and $SO_4^{2-})$

Predict the two products by switching cations. Make sure the positive charge equals the negative charge in each formula unit. Review Chapter 3 if you need help.

$Ca(NO_3)_2(aq) + K_2SO_4(aq) \rightarrow KNO_3 + CaSO_4$

Solve   According to rule 1, KNO_3 is soluble, so it is aqueous. According to rule 4, $CaSO_4$ is insoluble, so it is a solid. Because one product is a solid, the double replacement occurs. The balanced equation, including state symbols, is

$Ca(NO_3)_2(aq) + K_2SO_4(aq) \rightarrow 2KNO_3(aq) + CaSO_4(s)$

Reflect   Rules 1, 2, and 3 do not apply to $CaSO_4$, but rule 4 indicates it is a solid.

Practice   Do the following reactants cause a reaction to occur? If so, write a balanced equation and include the state of each product.
$Na_2CO_3(aq) + FeCl_2(aq) \rightarrow$

Net Ionic Equations

In the reaction in Example 1, the K^{1+} and NO_3^{1-} ions are in solution as aqueous reactants. They remain unchanged in solution as aqueous products. These two ions are not part of the reaction. They do not change state or combine with another substance. Ions that remain aqueous and do not take part in a reaction are called **spectator ions**. The K^{1+} and NO_3^{1-} ions are spectator ions in Example 1.

Sometimes chemists write a **net ionic equation** to show only the ions that take part in a reaction. The spectator ions are removed. The net ionic equation for Example 1 is

$$Ca^{2+}(aq) + SO_4^{2-}(aq) \rightarrow CaSO_4(s)$$

An easy way to determine a net ionic equation is to write only the precipitate or molecular product and the ions that form it. Net ionic equations are balanced with coefficients if needed.

Example 2	Do the following reactants cause a reaction? If so, write the net ionic equation, including state symbols. $CaCl_2(aq) + AgC_2H_3O_2(aq) \rightarrow$
Read	You need to determine if a double-replacement reaction occurs. If it does, you are asked to write the net ionic equation, which is a balanced equation without the spectator ions.
Plan	Identify the ions in each reactant: $(Ca^{2+}$ and $Cl^{1-}) + (Ag^{1+}$ and $C_2H_3O_2^{1-})$. Predict the two products by switching cations. $$CaCl_2(aq) + AgC_2H_3O_2(aq) \rightarrow Ca(C_2H_3O_2)_2 + AgCl$$
Solve	$Ca(C_2H_3O_2)_2$ is soluble, or aqueous (rule 1). AgCl is a solid (rule 3). The reaction occurs. The net ionic equation shows only the formation of $AgCl(s)$. $$Cl^{1-}(aq) + Ag^{1+}(aq) \rightarrow AgCl(s)$$
Reflect	The net ionic equation does not include Ca^{2+} and $C_2H_3O_2^{1-}$.
Practice	Do the following reactants cause a reaction? If so, write the net ionic equation, including state symbols. $HCl(aq) + NaOH(aq) \rightarrow$

Example 3	Do the following reactants cause a reaction? If so, write the net ionic equation, including state symbols. $BaCl_2(aq) + LiNO_3(aq) \rightarrow$
Read	You need to determine if a double-replacement reaction occurs. If it does, you are asked to write the net ionic equation.
Plan	Identify the ions in each reactant and predict the products. $$BaCl_2(aq) + LiNO_3(aq) \rightarrow Ba(NO_3)_2 + LiCl$$
Solve	$Ba(NO_3)_2$ is soluble (rule 1), and so is LiCl (rule 2). Both products are aqueous. No reaction occurs.
Reflect	All four ions are spectators. They remain dissociated in solution.
Practice	Do the following reactants cause a reaction? If so, write the net ionic equation, including state symbols. $NH_4Cl(aq) + Ca(C_2H_3O_2)_2(aq) \rightarrow$

Word Bank

net ionic equation

product

spectator ion

On a sheet of paper, write the word or phrase from the Word Bank that completes each sentence.

1. A _____ does not take part in a reaction.

2. A _____ shows only the formation of a solid or molecular product.

3. No replacement reaction occurs between $Ca(NO_3)_2(aq)$ and $AgC_2H_3O_2(aq)$ because each _____ is aqueous.

On a sheet of paper, write the letter of the answer to each question.

4. Which of the following compounds is soluble in water?

A $CaSO_4$ **B** $AgCl$ **C** $RbCl$ **D** $Ba(OH)_2$

5. Which of the following compounds is insoluble in water?

A $NaOH$ **B** HCl **C** $Al(C_2H_3O_2)_3$ **D** $CaCO_3$

6. Which net ionic equation represents this reaction: $HBr(aq) + KOH(aq) \rightarrow KBr(aq) + H_2O(l)$?

A $HBr(aq) + KOH(aq) \rightarrow KBr(aq) + H_2O(l)$
B $H^{1+}(aq) + OH^{1-}(aq) \rightarrow H_2O(l)$
C $Br^{1-}(aq) + K^{1+}(aq) \rightarrow KBr(aq)$
D $HBr(aq) + KOH(aq) \rightarrow H_2O(l)$

Critical Thinking

Predict the products of each reaction. On a sheet of paper, write the net ionic equation. If no reaction occurs, write *no reaction*.

7. $Na_2SO_4(aq) + Pb(NO_3)_2(aq) \rightarrow$

8. $2KOH(aq) + BaCl_2(aq) \rightarrow$

9. $HBr(aq) + LiOH(aq) \rightarrow$

On a sheet of paper, write the answer to the following question.

10. How do you determine which ions are included in a net ionic equation?

After reading this lesson, you should be able to

◆ give the equation used for dilutions

◆ describe how to make a solution of a given molarity from a more concentrated solution

In Chapter 4, you learned that molarity, *M*, is

$$M = \frac{\text{moles of solute}}{\text{liters of solution}}$$

This equation involves three variables: molarity, moles of solute, and volume of solution. If you know two of these, you can solve for the third one. Review the examples on pages 141–143.

Describing a solution as saturated or unsaturated, or dilute or concentrated, is a qualitative observation. Most of the time, chemists use specific concentrations of solutions. Concentration is a quantitative description. It gives the amount of solute in a certain volume of solution. Preparing aqueous solutions of specific concentrations is a common task in chemistry research. To make an aqueous solution from a solid solute, you measure a specific mass of solute, then dissolve it in enough water to make a specific volume of solution.

However, not all solutions are made from solid solutes. Solutions are often made by diluting more concentrated solutions. This process is called dilution. For example, acid solutions are usually made by adding a certain volume of a concentrated acid solution to water. The molarity of the concentrated solution is known. The molarity of the new, dilute solution is related, according to this equation:

$$M_1 V_1 = M_2 V_2$$

M_1 and V_1 are the molarity and volume of the concentrated solution. M_2 and V_2 are the molarity and volume of the dilute solution. The two volumes must have the same unit. This unit does not necessarily have to be liters.

Example 1	A 12.0 *M* solution of HCl is diluted with water. The original volume is 0.0400 L, and the final volume is 2.00 L. What is the molarity of the new solution?
Read	This is a dilution problem. It involves two solutions. You know two things about the concentrated solution: its molarity and volume. You know one thing about the dilute solution: its volume.
Plan	You are given three of the four values in the equation $M_1 V_1 = M_2 V_2$. M_1 is 12.0 *M*, V_1 is 0.0400 L, and V_2 is 2.00 L.

Solve   Use these values in the equation. Solve for M_2, the molarity of the new solution.

$$M_1 V_1 = M_2 V_2$$
$$(12.0\ M)(0.0400\ L) = (M_2)(2.00\ L)$$
$$M_2 = 0.240\ M$$

The original 12.0 M solution is diluted to a 0.240 M solution.

Reflect   In a dilution problem, you are multiplying and dividing measurements. Always check the significant figures in your answer.

Practice   3.25 L of an acid solution is diluted with water to make 4.00 L. If the new concentration is 0.95 M, what is the concentration of the original solution?

Example 2   A chemist has 10.0 M HNO_3, but needs 6.00 M HNO_3. What volume of the concentrated solution should be used to make 150. mL of the dilute solution?

Read   You are asked to find the volume of a concentrated acid solution. You know its molarity. You also know the molarity and volume of the dilute solution to be made from it.

Plan   Identify the variables in the dilution equation: M_1 is 10.0 M, M_2 is 6.00 M, and V_2 is 150. mL. V_1 is the unknown.

Solve   Use these values to solve for V_1. Since V_2 is given in milliliters, V_1 will be in milliliters.

$$M_1 V_1 = M_2 V_2$$
$$(10.0\ M)(V_1) = (6.00\ M)(150.\ mL)$$
$$V_1 = 90.0\ mL$$

Reflect   To make this dilution, the chemist would measure 90.0 mL of the concentrated acid, then add this to enough water to make exactly 150. mL.

Practice   A chemist needs to make 100. mL of 1.00 M H_2SO_4 from an 18.0 M H_2SO_4 solution. Describe how to make the solution.

In Example 2, what if you used 0.150 L for V_2 instead of 150. mL? Then the answer, V_1, would also be in liters. Try it:

$$(10.0\ M)(V_1) = (6.00\ M)(0.150\ L)$$

$$V_1 = 0.090\ L$$

This is the same as 90.0 mL. Either way, you get the correct answer. Remember that V_1 and V_2 always have the same unit.

Link to ➤➤➤

Home and Career

Many solutions in your home are dilutions. Vinegar, for instance, is dilute acetic acid, $HC_2H_3O_2$. Household ammonia is a dilute solution of ammonium hydroxide, NH_4OH. Most of these compounds are extremely corrosive in their concentrated forms.

▼◄ ▲ ▼◄ ▲ ▼◄ ▲ ▼◄ ▲ ▼◄ ▲ ▼◄ ▲ ▼◄ ▲ ▼◄ ▲ ▼◄ ▲ ▼◄ ▲ ▼◄ ▲ ▼◄ ▲ ▼◄ ▲ ▼◄ ▲ ▼◄ ▲ ▼◄ ▲ ▼◄ ▲ ▼

Science at Work

Environmental Field Technician

Environmental field technicians use chemistry to study the movement of pollutants in the environment. The field technician is often responsible for analyzing the water or air at a particular site. This person sets up the analysis equipment, keeps it operating properly, and collects the data. If there are several sites being monitored, the technician may store the data for all sites in a database. Sometimes, the technician collects samples to bring back to a lab for analysis. The field technician is often responsible for organizing and maintaining the lab.

Environmental field technicians must know about computers and database software. They need the mechanical ability to use and fix equipment. Knowledge of chemistry, geology, and environmental science is essential. However, most entry-level positions require only two years of college. Positions are available in industry, government, consulting firms, and universities.

Word Bank

dilute

molarity

unit

On a sheet of paper, write the word from the Word Bank that completes each sentence.

1. In a dilution problem, the two volumes must have the same _____.

2. Moles of solute divided by liters of solution is _____.

3. An aqueous solution can be made more _____ by adding water.

Critical Thinking

On a sheet of paper, write the answer to each problem.

4. A chemist needs to prepare 500.0 mL of 1.50 *M* HCl from a concentrated solution of 12.0 *M* HCl. What volume of concentrated acid is needed?

5. A chemist measures out 75.0 mL of 6.0 *M* HNO_3 and adds it to enough water to make 1.0 L of solution. What is the molarity of the new solution?

Molarity is only one way to describe the amounts of solute and solvent in a solution. In this lesson, you will learn three other quantitative ways to describe a solution.

Molality

Another common unit of concentration is **molality.** It has the symbol m. Molality is defined as

$$m = \frac{\text{moles of solute}}{\text{kilograms of solvent}}$$

It is important to understand the difference between molality (m) and molarity (M)—especially when their definitions, spellings, and symbols are so similar.

$$m = \frac{\text{moles of solute}}{\text{kilograms of solvent}} \qquad M = \frac{\text{moles of solute}}{\text{liters of solution}}$$

Both units have moles of solute as their numerator. However, their denominators are different.

Example 1	117 g of $AgNO_3$ dissolves in 350. g of water. What is the molality of the solution?
Read	You are given the mass of a solute ($AgNO_3$) and the mass of a solvent (water). You are asked to calculate the solution's molality.
Plan	Molality is moles of solute per kilograms of solvent. Convert grams of solute to moles using molar mass. Then convert grams of water to kilograms.

$$117 \text{ g AgNO}_3 \left(\frac{1 \text{ mol AgNO}_3}{169.9 \text{ g AgNO}_3} \right) = 0.689 \text{ mol AgNO}_3$$

$$350. \text{ g H}_2\text{O} \left(\frac{1 \text{ kg H}_2\text{O}}{1 \times 10^3 \text{ g H}_2\text{O}} \right) = 0.350 \text{ kg water}$$

Solve	Calculate the molality of the solution using these values.

$$m = \frac{0.689 \text{ mol AgNO}_3}{0.350 \text{ kg water}} = 1.97 \text{ } m$$

Reflect	In molality calculations, water is almost always the solvent. Remember that molality requires the mass of solvent in kilograms, not grams.
Practice	35.7 g of $Cu(NO_3)_2$ dissolves in 250. g of water. What is the molality of the solution?

Mass Percent

If you know the mass of a solution and the mass of solute dissolved in it, you can find the solution's **mass percent.** Mass percent tells what percentage of a solution's mass is due to the solute. It is calculated as follows:

$$\text{mass percent} = \left(\frac{\text{grams of solute}}{\text{grams of solution}} \right) 100\%$$

Mass percent can be calculated for solutions made from solid solutes. It cannot be calculated for solutions made by dilution. Mass percent is also called weight percent.

Example 2	37.5 g of $CaCl_2$ dissolves in 112.5 g of water. What is the mass percent of the solution?
Read	You are given the mass of a solute and the mass of a solvent. You are asked to calculate the mass percent.
Plan	To calculate mass percent, you need the mass of the solution, not solvent. To find the solution's mass, add the solute mass and the solvent mass. 37.5g + 112.5 g = 150. g of solution. This is true because of the law of conservation of mass.
Solve	Set up and solve the equation for mass percent. $$\text{mass percent} = \left(\frac{37.5 \text{ g } CaCl_2}{150. \text{ g solution}} \right) 100\%$$ $$= 25.0\% \ CaCl_2$$
Reflect	The unit for mass percent is a percent sign.
Practice	18.2 g of KNO_3 dissolves in 123.2 g of water. What is the mass percent of the solution?

The solution in Example 2 is 25% solute by mass, as Figure 15.5.1 shows.

Figure 15.5.1 *Mass percent tells how much of the solution's mass is solute. In this example, the solution is 25% $CaCl_2$ by mass.*

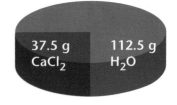

Mole Fraction

Another way to compare solute and solution amounts is to calculate a **mole fraction.** A mole fraction is similar to a percentage. It is a ratio comparing two molar amounts: the moles of one substance in a mixture and the total moles of all substances in the mixture. Unlike a percentage, this ratio is not multiplied by 100%. It is expressed as a decimal and has no units. Mole fraction has the symbol X.

$$X = \frac{\text{moles of one substance in mixture}}{\text{total moles of all substances in mixture}}$$

Example 3	75.0 g of HCl dissolves in 100. g of water. What is the mole fraction of each substance in the solution?
Read	You are given a mixture of two substances: a solute and a solvent. You are asked to calculate a mole fraction for each.
Plan	First calculate the number of moles of each substance using molar mass.

$$75.0 \text{ g HCl} \left(\frac{1 \text{ mol HCl}}{36.5 \text{ g HCl}} \right) = 2.05 \text{ mol HCl}$$

$$100. \text{ g H}_2\text{O} \left(\frac{1 \text{ mol H}_2\text{O}}{18.0 \text{ g H}_2\text{O}} \right) = 5.56 \text{ mol H}_2\text{O}$$

Solve	Now use these values to find two mole fractions. The denominator for both is the total moles: 2.05 mol + 5.56 mol = 7.61 mol.

$$X_{\text{HCl}} = \frac{2.05 \text{ mol HCl}}{7.61 \text{ mol total}} = 0.269$$

$$X_{\text{H}_2\text{O}} = \frac{5.56 \text{ mol H}_2\text{O}}{7.61 \text{ mol total}} = 0.731$$

Reflect	The mole fractions should add up to 1 (or close to it). 26.9% of the moles in this mixture are HCl and 73.1% are H₂O.
Practice	17.2 g of NiSO₄ dissolves in 453 g of water. What is the mole fraction of each substance in the solution?

Molarity, molality, mass percent, and mole fraction are four ways to express concentration. The first two are the most common. In the next lesson, you will use molality.

Word Bank

mass percent

molality

mole fraction

On a sheet of paper, write the word or phrase from the Word Bank that completes each sentence.

1. To calculate _____, divide the moles of one substance by the total moles of all substances.

2. To calculate _____, divide the mass of solute by the mass of solution, then multiply by 100%.

3. To calculate _____, divide the moles of solute by the kilograms of solvent.

On a sheet of paper, write the letter of the answer to each question.

4. 12.5 g of $Al_2(SO_4)_3$ dissolves in 150.0 g of water. What is the mass percent of the solution?

    A 7.69%   **B** 8.33%   **C** 9.09%   **D** 12.5%

5. A solution is made by dissolving 17.7 g of $Ca(ClO_3)_2$ in 125 g of water. What is the mole fraction of $Ca(ClO_3)_2$?

    A 0.0122   **B** 0.124   **C** 0.142   **D** 0.988

6. A solution is made by dissolving 42.3 g of MgI_2 in 275 g of water. What is its molality?

    A 0.00985 m **B** 0.133 m **C** 0.553 m **D** 1.81 m

Critical Thinking

On a sheet of paper, write the answer to each problem.

7. A solution is made by dissolving 87.5 g of $C_{12}H_{22}O_{11}$ in 450. g of water. What is its mass percent?

8. 53.5 g of KOH dissolves in 275 g of water. What is the mole fraction of KOH?

9. What is the molality of a solution made by dissolving 53.5 g of KOH in 275 g of water?

10. What is the molality of a solution made by dissolving 15.3 g of NH_4Cl in 135 g of water?

Objectives

After reading this lesson, you should be able to

◆ list and describe three colligative properties

◆ calculate boiling-point elevation and freezing-point depression

Colligative property

A physical property of a solution that depends on the number of dissolved solute particles

Dissolving salt in water creates a solution that has different properties than pure water. This is true when any solute is dissolved in any solvent. Some physical properties of the solution differ from those of the pure solvent. These physical properties are called **colligative properties.** There are three main physical properties of solutions that depend on the number of dissolved solute particles. One colligative property is the lowering of vapor pressure.

Vapor-Pressure Lowering

Solute particles occupy space throughout a solution, including space at the solution's surface. The solute particles at the surface interfere with the ability of solvent particles to evaporate. These solute particles prevent some solvent particles from leaving the solution and entering the gas state. As a result, the vapor pressure of a solution is lowered by the addition of a solute.

For example, when NaCl is added to water, the Na^{1+} and Cl^{1-} ions reduce the ability of the water molecules to evaporate. This decreases the vapor pressure of the solution, as Figure 15.6.1 shows. There are fewer evaporated water molecules "pressing" on the solution. As a result, an aqueous solution has a lower vapor pressure than pure water at the same temperature.

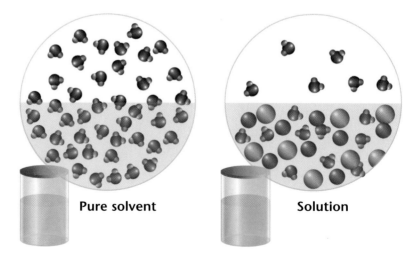

Figure 15.6.1 *Fewer solvent molecules can evaporate when there are solute particles in their way.*

Pure solvent   **Solution**

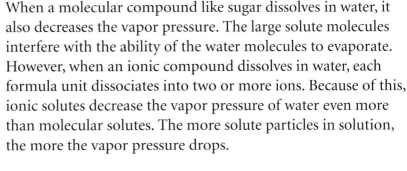

Boiling-point elevation (ΔT_b)

The temperature difference between the boiling point of a solution and the boiling point of the pure solvent

Atmospheric pressure decreases as elevation increases. At higher elevations, a solvent boils with a lower vapor pressure and thus, has a lower boiling point. This effect offsets the increase in boiling point due to the addition of a solute.

When a molecular compound like sugar dissolves in water, it also decreases the vapor pressure. The large solute molecules interfere with the ability of the water molecules to evaporate. However, when an ionic compound dissolves in water, each formula unit dissociates into two or more ions. Because of this, ionic solutes decrease the vapor pressure of water even more than molecular solutes. The more solute particles in solution, the more the vapor pressure drops.

Boiling-Point Elevation

Boiling point is the temperature at which the vapor pressure of a liquid equals atmospheric pressure. A solute added to a solvent lowers the vapor pressure. When the vapor pressure is lowered, the solution must be heated to a higher temperature in order for the vapor pressure to equal atmospheric pressure. Then the solution boils. This means that the boiling point of the solution is higher than the boiling point of the pure solvent. The temperature difference between the boiling point of a solution and the boiling point of the pure solvent is called the **boiling-point elevation.** The presence of a solute elevates, or increases, the boiling point. As the number of dissolved solute particles increases, the boiling point increases.

When a solution boils, only the solvent changes to a gaseous state. When saltwater boils, water molecules leave the liquid as steam. The salt remains in solution. This loss of solvent particles causes the molality of the solution to increase. As a solution continues to boil, there are fewer and fewer solvent particles compared to solute particles. The vapor pressure drops. The boiling point increases until all of the solvent has boiled off, leaving behind the solid solute.

Science Myth

Myth: Adding salt to boiling water raises the boiling point significantly.

Fact: Adding a handful of table salt, NaCl, does raise the boiling point of water. However, 1 mol of NaCl raises the boiling point of 1 kg of water by just 1.02°C. A handful of salt added to 5 kg of water raises the boiling point by about 0.2°C.

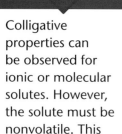

Colligative properties can be observed for ionic or molecular solutes. However, the solute must be nonvolatile. This means that the solute must not evaporate easily.

You can calculate the boiling-point elevation, ΔT_b, of a solution. This temperature difference depends on the amount of solute (the molality of the solution). For ionic solutes, ΔT_b also depends on the number of ions in a formula unit.

$$\Delta T_b = (K_b)(m)(i)$$

In this equation, ΔT_b is the change in boiling point (not the new boiling point). K_b is a constant that is unique to the solvent. m is molality of the solution. i is the number of ions formed when one formula unit of solute dissociates. If the solute is a molecular compound, $i = 1$. Some values of i are given in Table 15.6.1.

Table 15.6.1 Some Solutes and Their *i* Values

Solute	Type of Compound	Dissociation	*i* Value
$C_{12}H_{22}O_{11}$	molecular	no dissociation	1
NaCl	ionic	$Na^{1+} + Cl^{1-}$	2
MgF_2	ionic	$Mg^{2+} + 2(F^{1-})$	3
$Al(NO_3)_3$	ionic	$Al^{3+} + 3(NO_3^{1-})$	4

Once you calculate ΔT_b, you can find the boiling point of the solution. Just add ΔT_b to the boiling point of the pure solvent. The solution's boiling point is always higher.

Example 1 23.2 g of $MgCl_2$ dissolves in 175 g of water. $K_b = 0.51°C/m$ for water. Water boils at 100.0°C. What is the boiling point of the solution?

Read You are asked to find the boiling point of an aqueous solution of $MgCl_2$.

Plan Use the equation for boiling-point elevation: $\Delta T_b = (K_b)(m)(i)$. K_b is given. You need to calculate m, the molality of the solution. You also need to determine i.

Solve Molality is moles of solute per kilogram of solvent. To calculate m, first find the number of moles of solute.

$$23.2 \text{ g } MgCl_2 \left(\frac{1 \text{ mol } MgCl_2}{95.3 \text{ g } MgCl_2} \right) = 0.243 \text{ mol } MgCl_2$$

Solve   The molality of the solution is
$$m=\frac{0.243 \text{ mol MgCl}_2}{0.175 \text{ kg H}_2\text{O}}=1.39 \text{ m}$$

$MgCl_2$ is an ionic compound. It dissociates into one Mg^{2+} cation and two Cl^{1-} anions. This means $i=3$. The change in boiling point is

$$\Delta T_b=(0.51°C/m)(1.39 \text{ m})(3)=2.1°C$$

Since the boiling point of pure water is 100.0°C, the boiling point of the solution is
100.0°C+2.1°C=102.1°C

Reflect ΔT_b is the change in the boiling point. To find the new boiling point, add ΔT_b to the boiling point of the pure solvent. The value of i is a counting number, not a measurement.

Practice   34.1 g of $Fe(NO_3)_2$ dissolves in 350. g of water. $K_b=0.51°C/m$ for water. What is the boiling point of the solution?

Example 2   75.6 g of sucrose, $C_{12}H_{22}O_{11}$, dissolves in 200. g of water. $K_b=0.51°C/m$ for water. Water boils at 100.0°C. What is the boiling point of the solution?

Read   You are asked to find the boiling point for an aqueous solution of a molecular compound.

Plan   Use the equation for boiling-point elevation: $\Delta T_b=(K_b)(m)(i)$. K_b is given. You need to calculate m and determine i.

Solve   The number of moles of solute is
$$75.6 \text{ g } C_{12}H_{22}O_{11}\left(\frac{1 \text{ mol } C_{12}H_{22}O_{11}}{342.0 \text{ g } C_{12}H_{22}O_{11}}\right)=0.221 \text{ mol } C_{12}H_{22}O_{11}$$

The molality of the solution is
$$m=\left(\frac{0.221 \text{ mol } C_{12}H_{22}O_{11}}{0.200 \text{ kg H}_2\text{O}}\right)=1.11 \text{ m}$$

Because $C_{12}H_{22}O_{11}$ is molecular, $i=1$. The boiling-point elevation is
$$\Delta T_b=(0.51°C/m)(1.11 \text{ m})(1)=0.57°C$$

The boiling point of the solution is
100.0°C+0.57°C=100.6°C

Reflect   The mass of solute in this example is larger than in Example 1. However, the boiling point changed less because $C_{12}H_{22}O_{11}$ is molecular, with $i=1$.

Practice   47.5 g of $C_6H_{12}O_6$ dissolves in 93.6 g of water. $K_b=0.51°C/m$ for water. What is the boiling point of the solution?

Link to ➤➤➤

Earth Science

Carbon dioxide combines with water in the air to form carbonic acid, H_2CO_3. Carbonic acid slowly reacts with calcium and magnesium in rocks to form carbonates. Rivers wash the carbonates into the ocean, where they settle to the bottom. Over millions of years, the carbonates may form rock or return to the atmosphere during volcanic eruptions. These processes are part of the earth's carbon cycle.

Freezing-Point Depression

Solute particles also interfere when a solvent freezes or melts. When a solute is added to a solvent, the freezing/melting temperature drops. The difference between the freezing point of a solution and the freezing point of the pure solvent is called the **freezing-point depression.** For a liquid solvent to freeze, the particles must slow down enough to "lock" in place in a crystal lattice. When a solute is added, the solute particles get in the way of solvent particles locking together. The temperature of the solution must be lower—slowing the particles further— for the solvent to freeze. When most solutions freeze, only the solvent changes to a solid state. The solute particles usually do not freeze with the solvent, but are pushed out as the solid solvent forms. When salty ocean water freezes into an iceberg, the iceberg is nearly free of salt.

Salt is scattered on an icy sidewalk to make walking safer. How does the salt clear the sidewalk of ice? The salt dissolves in the surface of the ice, lowering its freezing point. That portion of ice melts and dissolves more salt. As more ice melts and dissolves more salt, less ice remains on the sidewalk.

To determine the freezing-point depression, you use an equation similar to the one for boiling-point elevation.

$$\Delta T_f = (K_f)(m)(i)$$

ΔT_f is the change in freezing point. K_f is a constant that is unique for the solvent. m is the molality of the solution. i is the number of ions formed when one formula unit of solute dissociates. For molecular solutes, $i = 1$.

To find the freezing point of the solution, subtract ΔT_f from the freezing point of the pure solvent. Remember that ΔT_b, the boiling-point elevation, is *added* to the solvent's boiling point. However, ΔT_f *is subtracted* because the freezing point of the solvent is depressed, or lowered.

Example 3 174.6 g of sucrose, $C_{12}H_{22}O_{11}$, dissolves in 450. g of water. $K_f = 1.86°C/m$ for water. Water freezes at 0.0°C. What is the freezing point of the solution?

Read   You are asked to find the freezing point of a solution containing a molecular compound.

Plan   Use the equation for freezing-point depression: $\Delta T_f = (K_f)(m)(i)$. Determine the molality of the solution and the value of i.

Solve   The number of moles of solute is

$$174.6 \text{ g } C_{12}H_{22}O_{11}\left(\frac{1 \text{ mol } C_{12}H_{22}O_{11}}{342.0 \text{ g } C_{12}H_{22}O_{11}}\right) = 0.5105 \text{ mol } C_{12}H_{22}O_{11}$$

The molality of the solution is

$$m = \frac{0.5105 \text{ mol } C_{12}H_{22}O_{11}}{0.450 \text{ kg } H_2O} = 1.13 \text{ } m$$

Because sucrose is molecular, $i = 1$. The change in freezing point is

$$\Delta T_f = (1.86°C/m)(1.13 \text{ } m)(1) = 2.10°C$$

The freezing point of the solution is $0.0°C - 2.10°C = -2.1°C$.

Reflect   When a solution contains a molecular solute, the freezing point does not drop as much as it does with an ionic solute.

Practice   58.5 g of NaCl dissolves in 1,000. g of water. $K_f = 1.86°C/m$ for water. What is the freezing point of the solution?

★✦★

Achievements in Science

Colligative Properties

The first detailed analysis of colligative properties was performed in the late 1800s. The Dutch chemist Jacobus van't Hoff studied how colligative properties vary with solute concentration. He found that the freezing-point depression equals the solute molality multiplied by a constant. This constant is a physical property of the solvent. A similar formula describes boiling-point elevation. The amount of solute actually in solution depends on whether the solute dissociates into ions. It also depends on how many ions form, and how complete the dissociation is.

Colligative properties also vary with the size of the solute particle. The larger the solute particle, the less the freezing point is depressed—and the less the boiling point is elevated. Because of this, colligative properties can be used to determine the molecular mass of a solute. In fact, this method provided the first proof that very large molecules exist. When such molecules are in solution, the freezing point of the solution is nearly unchanged.

Lesson 6   R E V I E W

Word Bank

boiling point

colligative
 properties

freezing point

On a sheet of paper, write the phrase from the Word Bank that completes each sentence.

1. When a solute is added to a solvent, _____ change.

2. When a solute is added to a solvent, the _____ decreases.

3. When a solute is added to a solvent, the _____ increases.

On a sheet of paper, write the letter of the answer to each question.

4. Adding solute causes which solvent property to decrease?

    A density   **C** boiling point

    B vapor pressure   **D** temperature

5. As saltwater boils, what property of the solution increases?

    A K_b **B** mass   **C** molality   **D** the ion number, i

6. What is the i value for the compound, $AlCl_3$?

    A 1   **B** 2   **C** 3   **D** 4

Critical Thinking

On a sheet of paper, write the answer to each question.

7. A solution is made by dissolving 42.3 g of $Ca(NO_3)_2$ (an ionic compound) in 0.25 kg of water. For water, $K_f = 1.86°C/m$. What is the freezing point of the solution?

8. A solution is made by dissolving 85.6 g of $C_6H_{12}O_6$ (a molecular compound) in 150. g of water. For water, $K_b = 0.51°C/m$. What is the boiling point of the solution?

9. 1.72 g of ethylene glycol, $C_2H_6O_2$ (a molecular compound) dissolves in 100. g of butanol. For butanol, $K_f = 8.37°C/m$ and its freezing point is 25.5°C. What is the freezing point of the solution?

10. North of the Arctic Circle, the temperature rarely rises above freezing, yet the ocean never completely freezes. Explain this using your knowledge of colligative properties.

Materials

- safety goggles
- lab coat or apron
- 600-mL beaker
- small ice cubes or crushed ice
- rock salt
- ring stand
- test-tube clamp
- 4 large test tubes
- test tube rack
- 25 g of calcium chloride (CaCl$_2$)
- balance
- 200 mL of distilled water
- stirring rod
- thermometer
- graph paper

Freezing-Point Depression

A solution does not freeze at the same temperature as the pure solvent. This is because solute and solvent particles interact, reducing the ability of the solvent particles to freeze. How much does solute concentration affect the freezing point of a solution? In this investigation, you will measure the freezing point of solutions of different concentrations.

Procedure

1. Write a hypothesis predicting how the freezing point will vary for four different aqueous solutions of CaCl$_2$.

Continued on next page

2. Write a procedure to test your hypothesis. In your procedure, describe how you plan to vary the $CaCl_2$ concentration. Also describe how you plan to use ice and rock salt to freeze the test solutions. Include any safety alerts.

3. Have your hypothesis and procedure approved by your teacher.

4. Perform your procedure and record your data. Be sure to wear safety goggles and a lab coat or apron.

5. Graph your data. Plot concentration on the x axis and temperature on the y axis.

Cleanup/Disposal

Pour the solutions into the proper waste container. Pour the ice and saltwater mixture down the sink. Wash and dry the glassware and return all equipment. Wash your hands.

Analysis

1. What information does your graph show?

2. How does freezing point vary with concentration? Is your plot a straight line or a curve?

3. How were you able to make the ice bath colder than the freezing point of ice?

Conclusions

1. Suppose a 50-mL aqueous solution contains 12.5 g of $CaCl_2$. At what temperature do you predict this solution will freeze? Use your graph to find your answer.

2. Suppose your graph was flatter (more horizontal). What would this show?

3. Suppose you measured the boiling point of the four solutions. Which solution would you expect to have the highest boiling point?

Explore Further

Using ice and different amounts of rock salt, measure freezing-point depressions for the ice bath. Try to find the lowest temperature to which the freezing point can be reduced.

Artificial Blood

A main concern of hospitals is whether they have enough blood for transfusions. Even if blood is available, it may not match the blood type of the patient. Blood for transfusions is rarely available in remote locations. Also, blood can only be stored for about 42 days. So a blood surplus can soon become a blood shortage.

In the 1960s, researchers began to develop blood substitutes that could be used during blood shortages. The first compounds developed were perfluorocarbons. Oxygen is 100 times more soluble in perfluorocarbons than in blood plasma. This meant that perfluorocarbons could deliver oxygen to body tissues more efficiently than the hemoglobin in real blood. However, these early blood substitutes caused health problems in many patients. Some even died.

Learning from early failures, scientists improved artificial blood. Better technologies and new molecules have led to safer blood substitutes. One promising blood substitute is being tested. Another form of artificial blood is derived from real blood. This artificial blood is a powder that can be mixed into liquid when needed.

Artificial blood has some advantages over stored natural blood. It has a shelf life of nearly two years. It can be given to any

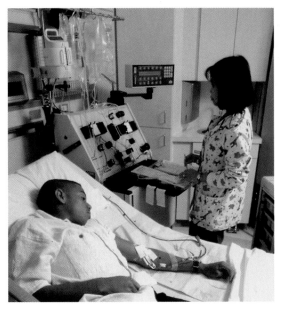

patient, regardless of their blood type. Infectious diseases cannot be transferred to a patient from artificial blood.

However, blood substitutes have drawbacks. Artificial blood only transfers oxygen, as hemoglobin does in real blood. It lacks the other components of real blood. Artificial blood can only be used for short times. Also, because of the cost of research, artificial blood is expensive.

1. Why is artificial blood needed?

2. What property of perfluorocarbons made them promising blood substitutes?

3. What are two advantages and two disadvantages of artificial blood?

Chapter 15 S U M M A R Y

- Solutes that are able to dissolve in a solvent are called soluble.

- If a soluble solute is ionic, it dissociates into ions.

- The rate of solvation for a solid solute increases by increasing the solution temperature, increasing the surface area of the solute, or stirring.

- Colloids and suspensions are mixtures that are not solutions.

- Saturated solutions contain the maximum amount of solute that can dissolve at a given temperature. Unsaturated solutions contain less than this amount, and supersaturated solutions contain more than this amount.

- Solubility graphs show the amount of solute necessary to create a saturated solution at various temperatures.

- The solubility of a gaseous solute increases by decreasing the solution temperature or increasing the solution pressure.

- Solubility rules are used to determine if an ionic product is soluble or not.

- Net ionic equations include only the liquid, solid, or gas product of a reaction and the ions that produce it.

- Diluting a solution results in a solution of lower concentration, according to the equation, $M_1 V_1 = M_2 V_2$.

- Molarity is a common unit of concentration. However, solution concentration can also be expressed in molality (m), mass percent, and mole fractions (X).

- Adding solute to a solvent lowers the vapor pressure, lowers the freezing point, and raises the boiling point.

- To calculate the boiling-point elevation, use $\Delta T_b = (K_b)(m)(i)$. To calculate the freezing-point depression, use $\Delta T_f = (K_f)(m)(i)$.

Vocabulary

Chapter 15 R E V I E W

Vocabulary Review

On a sheet of paper, write the word or phrase from the
Word Bank that completes each sentence.

1. When two liquids do not dissolve in each other, the liquids
   are _____.

2. The solute particles in a mixture are too large to
   completely dissolve, but remain dispersed evenly
   throughout the mixture. This is a(n) _____.

3. The process in which solvent particles attract and
   surround solute particles, causing them to dissolve, is
   called _____.

4. When the moles of one substance in a mixture are divided
   by the total moles of all substances in the mixture, the
   quantity obtained is a(n) _____.

5. A(n) _____ solution has more than the maximum amount
   of solute that can dissolve at a specific temperature.

6. In a net ionic equation, each _____ is eliminated.

7. A(n) _____ is able to conduct electricity when dissolved in
   water.

8. A(n) _____ shows only the solid, liquid, or gas product of
   a reaction and the ions that form it.

9. A(n) _____ solution has the maximum amount of solute
   that can dissolve at any particular temperature.

10. One colligative property is _____.

Concept Review

On a sheet of paper, write the letter of the answer to each
question.

11. In Figure 15.2.2, which solid is the least soluble at 10°C?

    A KI   **B** SO_2 **C** $KClO_3$ **D** KNO_3

Continued on next page

12. According to Figure 15.2.2, what mass of KCl will saturate 100 g of water at 60°C?

A 28 g   **B** 39 g   **C** 45 g   **D** 55 g

13. A solution contains 140 g of $NaNO_3$ in 200 g of water at 20°C. How can this solution be described?

A saturated   **C** supersaturated
B unsaturated   **D** dilute

14. What is the net ionic equation for the following reaction?
$HBr(aq) + KOH(aq) \rightarrow H_2O + KBr$

A No reaction occurs, so there is no net ionic equation.
B $Br^{1-} + OH^{1-} \rightarrow KBr$
C $H^{1+} + OH^{1-} \rightarrow H_2O$
D $H^{1+} + Br^{1-} + K^{1+} + OH^{1-} \rightarrow H^{1+} + Br^{1-} + K^{1+} + OH^{1-}$

15. What is the net ionic reaction for the following reaction?
$CaCl_2(aq) + 2AgC_2H_3O_2(aq) \rightarrow Ca(C_2H_3O_2)_2 + 2AgCl$

A No reaction occurs, so there is no net ionic equation.
B $Ca^{2+} + C_2H_3O_2^{1-} \rightarrow Ca(C_2H_3O_2)_2$
C $Ca^{2+} + 2Cl^{1-} \rightarrow 2Ag^{1+} + 2Cl^{1-}$
D $Cl^{1-} + Ag^{1+} \rightarrow AgCl$

16. What is the net ionic reaction for the following reaction?
$Na_2SO_4(aq) + 2NH_4Cl(aq) \rightarrow (NH_4)_2SO_4 + 2NaCl$

A No reaction occurs, so there is no net ionic equation.
B $Na^{1+} + Cl^{1-} \rightarrow NaCl$
C $SO_4^{2-} + 2NH_4^{1+} \rightarrow (NH_4)_2SO_4$
D $2Na^{1+} + SO_4^{2-} \rightarrow 2NH_4^{1+} + 2Cl^{1-}$

17. Which of the following substances is not soluble in water?

A $CaCl_2$ **B** $CuSO_4$ **C** NaOH   **D** $PbSO_4$

Problem Solving

On a sheet of paper, write the answer to each problem.
Show your work.

18. 17.5 g of $CaCl_2$ dissolves in 153 g of water. What is the molality of the solution?

19. A solution is made when 45 g of $C_6H_{12}O_6$ dissolves in 100. g of water. What is the mass percent of the solution?

20. A solution is made with 12.3 g NiCl and 153 g of water. What is the mole fraction of NiCl?

21. 22.4 g of $Fe(NO_3)_2$ (an ionic compound) dissolves in 250.0 g of water. For water, $K_f = 1.86°C/m$. What is the freezing point of this solution?

22. 22.4 g of $Fe(NO_3)_2$ (an ionic compound) dissolves in 250.0 g of water. For water, $K_b = 0.51°C/m$. What is the boiling point of this solution?

23. Ethylene glycol, $C_2H_6O_2$, is a molecular compound. A solution is made by dissolving 3.75 g of $C_2H_6O_2$ in 75.3 g of butanol. Butanol has a freezing point of 25.5°C and a K_f of 8.37°C/m. What is the freezing point of the solution?

Critical Thinking

On a sheet of paper, write the answer to each question.

24. Why is the boiling point of a solution higher than the boiling point of the pure solvent?

25. A student measures a solid solute and adds it to water. What could the student do to speed up the dissolving process?

Test-Taking Tip When choosing answers from a Word Bank, complete the items you know first. Then study the remaining answers to complete the items you are not sure about.

16

Reaction Rates and Equilibrium

Rust covers this sunken ship. A chemical reaction between iron and oxygen produced the rust. Scientists were surprised that sunken steel ships rust as quickly as they do. They found that bacteria in seawater create an acidic environment, which increases the rate of rusting. In Chapter 16, you will learn about factors that affect the rate of chemical reactions. You also will learn about reversible reactions.

Organize Your Thoughts

```
                    Rate                    Equilibrium
Activation      mechanisms and          expressions and
energy          rate laws               constants

        Reaction rates              Equilibrium

Collision           Potential energy            Stress and
theory              diagrams                    Le Chatelier's
                                                principle
```

Goals for Learning

◆ To explain factors affecting reaction rate in terms of collision theory

◆ To explain an activated complex and interpret a potential energy diagram

◆ To explain a reaction mechanism

◆ To describe a reversible reaction at equilibrium

◆ To calculate K and explain what its value means

◆ To describe how an equilibrium system shifts under stress

After reading this lesson, you should be able to

◆ list the requirements for a reaction to occur, according to collision theory

◆ define activation energy

◆ explain four ways to increase reaction rate

Reaction rate

The speed of a reaction; the rate at which a product forms or a reactant is used up

Collision theory

The idea that a reaction occurs when particles of matter collide with enough energy to break bonds and form new bonds

Activation energy (E_a)

The minimum amount of energy needed to break bonds in reactants and cause a reaction to occur

Chapter 13 discussed spontaneous reactions. These reactions occur naturally as expected. They happen on their own. The spontaneity of a reaction, however, says nothing about the speed of the reaction. A spontaneous reaction can happen very quickly, as in the combustion of gasoline. A spontaneous reaction can happen very slowly, as in the rusting of iron. Both reactions are spontaneous, but they occur at different rates, or speeds. **Reaction rate** is the speed of a reaction. It is the rate at which a product forms or a reactant is used up. Why do some reactions take place quickly and some take many years to occur?

Collision Theory

For a reaction between two or more particles to take place, the particles must collide with each other, causing old bonds to break and new bonds to form. This idea is called **collision theory.** Collision theory states that

• A reaction takes place only when reactant particles collide with sufficient energy to break one or more existing bonds. The minimum amount of energy needed to break the bonds in reactants is called **activation energy**, E_a. Activation energy varies, depending on the reaction.

• A reaction takes place only when reactant particles collide in a favorable position. When existing bonds break, it must become easier, not harder, for new bonds to form.

Consider this combination reaction, which produces hydrogen fluoride gas:

$$H_2(g) + F_2(g) \rightarrow 2HF(g)$$

What bonds are broken? What bonds form? Look at the dot diagrams of the reactants and product:

$$H-H \ + \ :\overset{..}{F}-\overset{..}{F}: \ \rightarrow \ 2(H-\overset{..}{F}:)$$

Link to ≻≻≻

Art

Some art, such as paintings, written documents, and books, can be ruined if not properly cared for. One method used at museums to preserve art is to control the environment. Cool temperatures slow the rate of chemical reactions. Low humidity slows chemical reactions that involve water.

In this balanced equation, two molecules collide to form two new molecules. Two bonds are broken: one H-H bond and one F-F bond. Two H-F bonds form. For the two reactants to collide in a favorable position, each H atom must be close to an F atom:

$$H-H$$
$$:\ddot{F}-\ddot{F}:$$

In the formation of ammonia, what bonds are broken and what bonds form?

$$N_2 + 3H_2 \rightarrow 2NH_3$$

$$:N\equiv N: \;+\; 3(H-H) \;\rightarrow\; 2\left[\begin{array}{c} H-\ddot{N}-H \\ | \\ H \end{array}\right]$$

Four bonds are broken: one N-N bond and three H-H bonds. Two molecules form; each one has three N-H bonds.

Factors Affecting Reaction Rate

In collision theory, reactions take place because reactant particles collide and bonds rearrange. There are several ways to increase the rate of a spontaneous reaction.

- Increase the temperature of the reactants. This means the reactant particles have more energy. They are more likely to have the activation energy needed for the reaction to occur. *As more particles have the required activation energy, the reaction rate increases.* When reactant particles have more energy, they move faster and collide more often. *As particles collide more often, the reaction rate increases.*

- Increase the concentration of the reactants. A greater concentration means there are more reactant particles available to collide. *As more particles collide, the reaction rate increases.*

- Increase the surface area of a solid reactant. If a solid reactant is crushed into smaller pieces, more surface area is exposed. Therefore, more particles are available to collide. *As more particles collide, the reaction rate increases.*

- Add a **catalyst.** A catalyst is a substance that increases the reaction rate without taking part in the reaction.

Enzyme

A biological catalyst

Enzymes affect the rates of reactions. The first successful attempt to describe the way enzymes determine reaction rates was made in 1913 by Leonor Michaelis and Maud Menten.

A catalyst is not a reactant or product. The formula of a catalyst is often written above the arrow in a chemical equation. For example, hydrogen peroxide quickly decomposes in the presence of powdered manganese dioxide, as shown in Figure 16.1.1.

$$2H_2O_2(aq) \xrightarrow{\text{MnO}_2} 2H_2O(l) + O_2(g)$$

Enzymes are biological catalysts. They speed up reactions that occur in living things. For example, enzymes allow the human body to quickly release energy by breaking down food molecules into energy.

Figure 16.1.1
Hydrogen peroxide decomposes quickly when mixed with a catalyst (in the beaker at left).

Express Lab 16

Materials

- safety goggles
- lab coat or apron
- 3 effervescent antacid tablets
- 3 plastic cups
- cold, hot, and room-temperature water
- watch or clock with a second hand

Procedure

1. Put on safety goggles and a lab coat or apron.
2. Fill one plastic cup with hot water, one with room-temperature water, and one with cold water.
3. Drop an antacid tablet in the cup of hot water. Record the time.
4. Wait until the tablet has disappeared, then record the time again.
5. Repeat steps 3 and 4 with the other cups.

Analysis

1. How did the water temperature affect the amount of time required for each tablet to disappear?
2. What result would you expect if you placed a tablet in ice water? In boiling water?

---

624 *Chapter 16 Reaction Rates and Equilibrium*

Consumer Choices: Bad Food or Good Food?

Scientists have developed substances that help prevent food from spoiling. These substances are of two basic types. One type slows or prevents the growth of bacteria, fungi, and yeasts. The other type slows the reaction between food and oxygen.

INGREDIENTS: WHOLE GRAIN WHEAT, SUGAR, SALT, CALCIUM CARBONATE, BARLEY MALT EXTRACT, TRISODIUM PHOSPHATE, IRON AND ZINC (MINERAL NUTRIENTS), VITAMIN C (SODIUM ASCORBATE), B VITAMIN (NIACINAMIDE), VITAMIN B_1 (THIAMIN MONONITRATE), VITAMIN B_6 (PYRIDOXINE HYDROCHLORIDE), VITAMIN A (PALMITATE), VITAMIN B_2 (RIBOFLAVIN), B VITAMIN (FOLIC ACID), VITAMIN B_{12}, VITAMIN D. FRESHNESS PRESERVED BY BHT.

Substances of this second type are called antioxidants. Oxidized foods taste bad and may have a brownish color. Antioxidants help to preserve food. Examples of antioxidants include vitamin C, BHA, and BHT. BHT is listed as a preservative in the label above.

Substances added to food must be safe to eat. In most countries, new substances are tested and approved by a government agency. The agency considers the amount to be used in food, whether eating this amount for long periods is safe, and any toxic effects.

1. Some people prefer to avoid foods that contain preservatives. What are the advantages and disadvantages of eliminating these foods from your diet?

2. Besides using antioxidants, what are some other ways to slow the reaction between food and oxygen?

3. What foods do you eat that contain added antioxidants?

On a sheet of paper, write the word or phrase from the Word Bank that completes each sentence.

1. A(n) _____ increases the rate of a reaction without taking part in the reaction.

2. The minimum amount of energy necessary for a reaction to occur is the _____.

3. According to _____, a chemical reaction occurs when reactant particles come together and bonds rearrange.

On a sheet of paper, write the letter of the answer to each question.

4. Which set of reactants will react the fastest?

  A 10 mL of 0.5 *M* HCl and a 5-g chunk of Mg
  B 10 mL of 0.5 *M* HCl and 5 g of powdered Mg
  C 10 mL of 0.1 *M* HCl and a 5-g chunk of Mg
  D 10 mL of 0.1 *M* HCl and 5 g of powdered Mg

5. The rate of a chemical reaction decreased. Which explanation is possible?

  A More reactant was added.   **C** The temperature decreased.
  B A catalyst was added.   **D** The temperature increased.

6. A reaction occurs when particles collides with enough energy and in a favorable _____?

  A rate   **B** size   **C** amount   **D** position

Critical Thinking
Determine if each change would increase or decrease a reaction rate. On a sheet of paper, write *increase* or *decrease*. Then explain your answer.

7. lowering the temperature of a reaction

8. decreasing the concentration of a reactant

9. increasing the surface area of a solid reactant

10. adding a catalyst

When two or more reactant particles collide, they temporarily form an **activated complex.** An activated complex is the group of atoms that forms at the moment of collision. In an activated complex, all reactant atoms are together in a group. An activated complex has a great deal of potential energy because the atoms are so close to each other. For a reaction to take place, the reactant particles must collide with enough energy to form this high-energy complex. The amount of energy needed to form an activated complex is the activation energy. If the reactant particles do not collide with enough energy, the complex does not form and the reaction does not occur.

Consider again the formation of hydrogen fluoride, HF:

$$H_2(g) + F_2(g) \rightarrow 2HF(g) + heat$$

This reaction is exothermic. The reactants have more energy than the products. The difference in energy is released as heat. The activated complex is a group of all four reactant atoms.

$$\begin{array}{c} H \cdots H \\ \vdots \quad \vdots \\ F \cdots F \end{array}$$

Activated complexes are not shown in chemical equations.

Activated complex

A group of atoms that temporarily forms when two or more reactant particles collide

★ ✦ ★ ✦ ★ ✦ ★ ✦ ★ ✦ ★ ✦ ★ ✦ ★ ✦ ★ ✦ ★ ✦ ★ ✦ ★ ✦ ★ ✦ ★ ✦ ★ ✦ ★ ✦ ★ ✦ ★ ✦ ★

Achievements in Science

Biotechnology

A relatively new application of science is biotechnology. Biotechnology is the use of living cells to create substances or solve problems. For example, small organisms are used to produce pharmaceuticals, vitamins, dyes, and flavoring compounds. Organisms are also used to clean up spilled oil and toxic wastes.

Fungi, bacteria, and microbes are commonly used for these purposes. They grow easily and multiply rapidly.

Changing their food supply may cause them to produce a desired substance. Some naturally produce a desired substance with no modifications. Other organisms can use toxic wastes as their food.

The most common way to make an organism produce a specific substance is to alter its genetic makeup. This changes how the cells function. The drugs insulin and interferon are produced by organisms with altered genes.

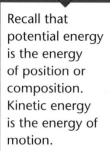

Recall that potential energy is the energy of position or composition. Kinetic energy is the energy of motion.

Figure 16.2.1 is a potential energy diagram for this reaction. It shows how potential energy changes from the reactants to the activated complex to the products. The reactants have more energy than the products. The peak of the curve represents the activated complex, which has even more energy than the reactants. The numbered arrows represent changes in energy.

- Arrow 1 is the potential energy of the reactants before they collide. It is the amount of energy the reactants have because of their bonds.

- Arrow 2 is the difference in energy between the reactants and the activated complex. This energy difference is the activation energy, E_a, for the reaction. For the reactants to form the activated complex and then the products, they must achieve this amount of energy.

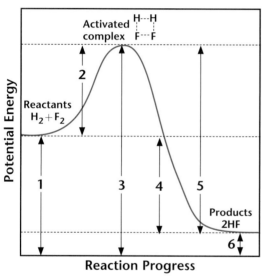

Figure 16.2.1 *During the formation of HF, the potential energy peaks at the activated complex, then drops when the products form.*

- Arrow 3 is the potential energy of the activated complex. The activated complex has much more potential energy than either the reactants or products.

- Arrow 4 is the difference in energy between the reactants and the products. This difference is the heat of reaction, ΔH_{rxn} (see Chapter 13).

- Arrow 5 is the difference in energy between the products and the activated complex.

- Arrow 6 is the potential energy of the products. Because the products have less energy than the reactants, this is an exothermic reaction.

Think of a potential energy diagram as a hill. The reactants are bowling balls that have to go over the hill to the other side. The bowling balls need to gain enough energy (activation energy) to make it over the hill. Use this hill analogy to understand how the factors listed on page 623 increase reaction rate.

- Increasing reactant temperature results in particles that have more energy. They move faster and collide more often. As a result, they are more likely to make it over the hill.

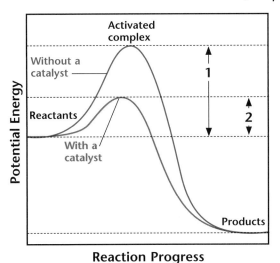

Figure 16.2.2 *A catalyst provides a shortcut to the activated complex, increasing the reaction rate.*

- Increasing reactant concentration or surface area increases the number of particles available to react. This increases the number of collisions. As a result, more particles are likely to make it over the hill.

- Adding a catalyst has a different effect. A catalyst lowers the activation energy, making it easier for reactant particles to go over the hill. This is like making the hill lower, as shown in Figure 16.2.2. With a lower activation energy, more reactant particles have enough energy to make it over the hill. Arrow 1 is the activation energy, E_a, without a catalyst. Arrow 2 is E_a when a catalyst is present.

Link to ➢➢➢

Environmental Science

Catalytic converters are required on automobiles to reduce pollution. The combustion process leaves some fuel partially burned. It also produces carbon monoxide and unwanted nitrogen oxides. In a catalytic converter, a catalyst increases reaction rates and lowers activation energies. Nitrogen oxides are broken down into nitrogen and oxygen gases. Partially burned fuel and carbon monoxide are converted to carbon dioxide.

Example 1 | The potential energy diagram below is for the reaction between nitrogen and oxygen, producing nitrogen monoxide. Is the reaction exothermic or endothermic? What does each numbered arrow represent?

Read | You are asked to determine if this reaction is exothermic or endothermic. You are asked to explain the energy differences in the diagram.

Plan | Notice the general shape of the curve, with reactants having a lower energy than products. Determine where each arrow starts and ends.

Solve | **Arrow 1** is the potential energy of the reactants.

Arrow 2 is the energy difference between the reactants and the activated complex. This is the activation energy, E_a—the amount of energy needed for reactants to form the activated complex.

Arrow 3 is the potential energy of the activated complex.

Arrow 4 is the energy difference between the reactants and the products. It is the heat of reaction, ΔH_{rxn}. The products have more energy than the reactants, so the reaction is endothermic.

Arrow 5 is the energy difference between the products and the activated complex.

Arrow 6 is the potential energy of the products.

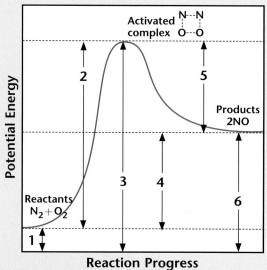

Reflect | Endothermic reactions absorb energy because the products have more energy than the reactants. Exothermic reactions release energy because the reactants have more energy than the products.

Practice | What effect would a catalyst have on the above diagram? Which numbered arrows would change in size?

Suppose the reverse reaction in Example 1 were to occur: $2NO \rightarrow N_2 + O_2$. Arrow 5 in the potential energy diagram would represent its activation energy. This would be the amount of energy needed for two NO molecules to form an N_2 molecule and an O_2 molecule. In Lesson 4, you will learn about reactions that can go in the forward and reverse direction.

▼◄▲▼◄▲▼◄▲▼◄▲▼◄▲▼◄▲▼◄▲▼◄▲▼◄▲▼◄▲▼◄▲▼◄▲▼◄▲▼

Science at Work

Catalyst Chemist

A relatively new specialty within chemistry is catalyst chemistry. Some catalyst chemists perform experiments to find out how a particular catalyst works. Others find new applications for an existing catalyst. One of the fastest growing areas of catalyst chemistry is research to develop new catalysts.

Catalyst chemists may work for pharmaceutical companies or national laboratories. Other employers include the petroleum and automotive industries, as well as companies whose primary business is developing new catalysts.

Most scientists in this field have chemistry degrees ranging from a bachelor's degree to a Ph.D. Many catalyst chemists also have chemical engineering or industrial engineering experience.

Refer to the potential energy diagram. It shows a reaction with and without a catalyst. On a sheet of paper, write the arrow letter that matches each description.

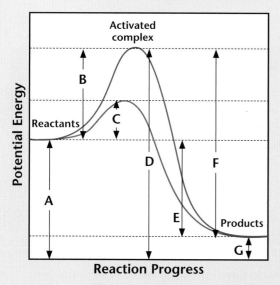

1. The heat of reaction for the uncatalyzed reaction

2. The activation energy for the uncatalyzed reaction

3. The activation energy for the catalyzed reaction

4. The potential energy of the reactants

5. The potential energy of the products

6. The potential energy of the uncatalyzed activated complex

Critical Thinking

On a sheet of paper, write the answer to each question.

7. Is the reaction shown in the above diagram exothermic or endothermic? How do you know?

8. Does a catalyst change the products of a chemical reaction? Explain.

9. What is the result when reactant particles first collide in a chemical reaction? How is this different from the final product(s)?

10. What amount of energy must the reactants have for a chemical reaction to take place?

INVESTIGATION 16

Materials

- safety goggles
- lab coat or apron
- 50 mL of 3% hydrogen peroxide (H_2O_2) solution in a 100-mL beaker
- 0.1 g of manganese dioxide (MnO_2)
- radish or potato, finely chopped
- wood splints
- matches
- 3 medium test tubes
- test-tube rack
- spatula
- grease pencil
- metric ruler

How a Catalyst Affects a Chemical Reaction

Catalysts change the behavior of chemical reactions. One catalyst is manganese dioxide. It is insoluble in water. Another catalyst is an enzyme called catalase or peroxidase. This enzyme is in animal tissues and certain vegetables. How do these catalysts affect the decomposition of hydrogen peroxide? Find out in this investigation.

Procedure

1. Put on safety goggles and a lab coat or apron.

2. Using the grease pencil, place a line about 3 cm from the bottom of each test tube. Label the test tubes 1, 2, and 3. Place them in the rack.

3. Use the spatula to place enough of the chopped vegetable into test tube 1 to reach the line.

4. Add the manganese dioxide to test tube 2. Leave test tube 3 empty.

5. Slowly pour hydrogen peroxide solution into tube 1 until it reaches the line. **Safety Alert: Hydrogen peroxide can bleach clothing. Handle it carefully.**

6. Observe the contents in the test tube and record your observations.

7. Wait until any observed reaction slows down. Then light the end of a splint with a match. Blow out the flame, leaving the end of the splint glowing. **Safety Alert: Be careful with the match and flame.**

Continued on next page

8. Quickly place the glowing splint into the mouth of test tube 1. Observe and record the result. If a flame is produced, completely extinguish the splint before proceeding.

9. Repeat steps 5 through 8 with test tube 2 and then with test tube 3.

Cleanup/Disposal
Dispose of the cooled matches and splints. Dispose of the test tube contents as your teacher directs. Clean and return the other materials. Wash your hands.

Analysis
1. Describe what happened when hydrogen peroxide was added to each test tube.

2. What happened when the glowing splint was put into each tube?

Conclusions
1. What was the purpose of test tube 3, which contained only hydrogen peroxide?

2. What was given off by the catalyzed reactions? How do you know?

3. Write the balanced equation for the decomposition of hydrogen peroxide.

Explore Further
Repeat the experiment with other fresh plant materials. Which ones produce results similar to the plant material you used in the above investigation, and which ones do not?

Objectives

After reading this lesson, you should be able to

◆ define a reaction mechanism

◆ identify the rate-determining step in a reaction

◆ tell how reactant concentration affects reaction rate

◆ write a rate law for a reaction mechanism

Reaction mechanism

A series of small reaction steps that describe how a chemical reaction occurs

Intermediate

A particle in a reaction mechanism that is not an initial reactant or a final product

Rate-determining step

The step in a reaction mechanism with the highest activation energy; it is the slowest step and determines the reaction rate

Collision theory states that reactant particles must collide with sufficient energy to form products. What if there are 11 reactant particles? Do they all have to collide at the same time? The following balanced reaction is spontaneous.

$$4NH_3(g) + 7O_2(g) \rightarrow 4NO_2(g) + 6H_2O(g)$$

According to collision theory, this reaction takes place only if 4 ammonia molecules collide with 7 oxygen molecules *at the same time*. What are the chances of that happening?

Reaction Mechanisms

It is unlikely that more than 2 or 3 particles could collide at the same time. To explain reactions involving more than 3 reactant particles, chemists use reaction mechanisms. A **reaction mechanism** is a series of small reactions called steps. Each step involves only 1, 2, or 3 reactant particles. Together, the steps describe the overall balanced equation. Some particles that are part of a reaction mechanism are called **intermediates.** They are neither the initial reactants nor the final products. They help explain how the reaction takes place.

One step in a reaction mechanism is always slower than the rest. This step is called the **rate-determining step.** It has a higher activation energy than the other steps, so it takes longer. This step determines the rate of the overall reaction.

Imagine a large family eating dinner. At the end of the meal, five people are given the task of cleaning up. This task consists of three steps: clearing the table, washing and drying the dishes, and putting away the dishes. Suppose two people clear the table, one person washes and dries the dishes, and two people put them away. Which step do you think will be the rate-determining step?

Figure 16.3.1 *In this cleanup scenario, the second step is the rate-determining step.*

In a reaction mechanism, each step has its own activated complex. Activated complexes are not shown in these steps or in the overall balanced equation. Activated complexes are not the same as intermediates. Every reaction mechanism has at least one intermediate. The intermediate is shown in the steps, but not in the overall equation.

The second step, as Figure 16.3.1 shows, will be the slowest. It may take a while to clear the table, but eventually the dishes will pile up at the sink. As a dish is dried, it will immediately be put away. The washing and drying step will determine how fast the task is finished.

In chemical reactions, the rate-determining step requires the most time to form its product. As soon as its product is made, however, any remaining steps quickly use up this product to complete the reaction. A catalyst lowers the activation energy of the rate-determining step. When a catalyst is present, the slowest step goes faster, causing the overall reaction to go faster.

Look at this two-step mechanism for a reaction:

Step 1 $2NO \rightarrow N_2O_2$

Step 2 $N_2O_2 + H_2 \rightarrow N_2O + H_2O$

Each step is balanced. To find the balanced equation for the overall reaction, first add the steps together. Then cancel any substance that is exactly the same on both sides. This substance is an intermediate.

$$2NO \rightarrow N_2O_2$$
$$N_2O_2 + H_2 \rightarrow N_2O + H_2O$$
$$\overline{2NO + \cancel{N_2O_2} + H_2 \rightarrow \cancel{N_2O_2} + N_2O + H_2O}$$

N_2O_2 is an intermediate in this reaction mechanism. It is neither a reactant nor a product, so it is not shown in the overall balanced equation:

$$2NO + H_2 \rightarrow N_2O + H_2O$$

In this reaction, dinitrogen oxide and water are the final products. The first step—the formation of the intermediate N_2O_2—is the slowest, so it is the rate-determining step.

Math Tip

Adding two steps
of a mechanism is
similar to adding
two algebra
equations.

Example 1 Study the following reaction mechanism. What is the overall balanced equation? What is the intermediate? Which step is rate-determining?

Step 1 $NO + Cl_2 \rightarrow NOCl_2$ *fast*
Step 2 $NOCl_2 + NO \rightarrow 2NOCl$ *slow*

Read You are asked to give some information about a two-step reaction mechanism. The second step is the slowest.

Plan Check that each step is balanced. Then add them together.

Solve The combined equation is

$NO + Cl_2 + \overline{NOCl_2} + NO \rightarrow \overline{NOCl_2} + 2NOCl$

After removing $NOCl_2$ from each side, the overall equation is

$2NO + Cl_2 \rightarrow 2NOCl$

$NOCl_2$ is the intermediate since it was canceled. The rate-determining step is the slowest step. In this case, it is the second step.

Reflect If a catalyst were added to this reaction, it would have the greatest effect on the rate-determining step. It would speed up the second step, causing the overall reaction rate to increase.

Practice Study the following reaction mechanism. What is the overall balanced equation? What are the two intermediates? Which step is rate-determining?

Step 1 $Cl_2 \rightarrow 2Cl$ *fast*
Step 2 $Cl + CHCl_3 \rightarrow HCl + CCl_3$ *slow*
Step 3 $CCl_3 + Cl \rightarrow CCl_4$ *fast*

The steps of a reaction mechanism add up to the overall balanced equation. Reaction rate data obtained from experiments support reaction mechanisms.

Rate Laws

Chemists conduct experiments to determine the **rate law** for a chemical reaction. A rate law is a mathematical equation that shows how the reaction rate is related to the concentrations of the reactants. From collision theory (Lesson 1), you know that one way to speed up a reaction is to increase reactant concentrations. For two reactants, a rate law has this form:

$$\text{rate} = k[\text{reactant A}]^m[\text{reactant B}]^n$$

The term k is the **rate constant.** It is a number that is unique to each reaction. It is determined by experimentation. Each [reactant] term is a reactant concentration. Remember that brackets are used in chemistry to indicate concentration, usually molarity. The exponents m and n are the coefficients of the reactants in a balanced equation. They indicate the order of each reactant in the reaction. For example, an exponent of 1 means the reaction is first order with respect to the given reactant. A reaction rate depends on both the concentration of each reactant and the order of each reactant. A reactant with an order of 2 has a much greater effect on the rate than a reactant with an order of 1.

The rate of a reaction is determined by the slowest step in the reaction mechanism. Because of this, a rate law is written only for the rate-determining step. To write a rate law, refer to a balanced equation for the rate-determining step. Write the rate constant k. Then write the formula of each reactant in brackets. The rate law has as many [reactant]^n terms as there are reactants. If there is only one reactant, the rate law has this form: rate $= k[\text{reactant}]^n$. Write the equation coefficient of each reactant as an exponent.

Example 2 Look at the reaction mechanism from Example 1 on page 637. Write a rate law based on the rate-determining step. What is the order of the reaction with respect to each reactant?

Read You need to write a rate law for one step in a reaction mechanism. You also need to determine the order of the reaction with respect to each reactant.

Plan The rate-determining step in the mechanism in Example 1 is

Step 2 $NOCl_2 + NO \rightarrow 2NOCl$ *slow*

The reactants in this step are $NOCl_2$ and NO. Both have coefficients of 1 in this balanced equation.

Solve The rate law is rate $= k[NOCl_2]^1[NO]^1$.
This is a first-order reaction with respect to both $NOCl_2$ and NO.

Reflect The exponents are the coefficients of the reactants in the balanced equation.

Practice Write a rate law for the rate-determining step in the reaction mechanism below. What is the order of the reaction with respect to HBr and O_2?

Step 1 $HBr + O_2 \rightarrow HBrO_2$ *slow*
Step 2 $HBrO_2 + HBr \rightarrow 2HOBr$ *fast*
Step 3 $HOBr + HBr \rightarrow H_2O + Br_2$ *fast*
Step 4 $HOBr + HBr \rightarrow H_2O + Br_2$ *fast*

Spotlight on Bromine

35
Br
Bromine
79.9

Bromine is one of the halogens. It was first isolated in 1826 from water taken from a salt marsh. Bromine is a reddish-brown liquid and easily vaporizes to produce a dense gas of the same color. It is the only nonmetal that is a liquid at room temperature. Bromine has an unpleasant odor. In fact, its name comes from a Greek word meaning "stench." Bromine dissolves in water and can be used in place of chlorine for water sanitation. Several bromine compounds are used as pesticides. One is almost a universal pesticide, since it is effective against insects, fungi, and plants. Most traditional photographic films and prints use silver bromide as the light-sensitive material. Bromine compounds are used to study reaction mechanisms and reaction rates. Organic chemists use bromine and its compounds to create new compounds.

Interesting Fact: Bromine compounds make fabrics fire resistant.

Lesson 3   R E V I E W

Word Bank

intermediate

rate-determining
step

reaction
mechanism

On a sheet of paper, write the word or phrase from the Word Bank that completes each sentence.

1. The slowest part of a reaction mechanism is the _____.

2. A(n) _____ is a series of steps that each involve only 1, 2, or 3 reactant particles.

3. A(n) _____ is a particle in a reaction mechanism that is not shown in the overall balanced equation.

On a sheet of paper, write the letter of the answer to each question. Refer to the reaction mechanism at the left.

Step 1   *slow*
$A + B \rightarrow C$

Step 2   *fast*
$C + B \rightarrow D$

Step 3   *fast*
$D + B \rightarrow E$

4. What is the overall balanced equation?

   A $A + 3B + C + D \rightarrow C + D + E$
   B $A + 3B \rightarrow E$
   C $A + 3B \rightarrow 2C + 2D + E$
   D $A + 3B + 2C + 2D \rightarrow E$

5. What is the rate law for this mechanism?

   A $k[A]^1[B]^3$ **B** $k[C]^2[D]^2$ **C** $k[E]^1$ **D** $k[A]^1[B]^1$

6. What is an intermediate in this reaction?

   A A   **B** B   **C** C   **D** E

Critical Thinking

On a sheet of paper, write the answer to each question. Questions 7–9 refer to the reaction mechanism at the left.

Ozone, O_3, decomposes in the upper atmosphere, where oxygen atoms can exist uncombined.

Step 1   *slow*
$Cl + O_3 \rightarrow$
$ClO + O_2$

Step 2   *fast*
$O + ClO \rightarrow Cl + O_2$

7. What is the overall balanced equation?

8. What is the rate law?

9. Which step would be most affected by a catalyst? Why?

10. Why is the reaction, $N_2 + 3H_2 \rightarrow 2NH_3$, not an acceptable step in a reaction mechanism?

Reversible reaction

A reaction in which the products can react to form the reactants

Chemical equilibrium

The state of a reversible reaction when the rate of the forward reaction equals the rate of the reverse reaction

Equilibrium system

A reaction that is in a state of chemical equilibrium

Some reactions can occur in the reverse direction. The products can react to form the reactants. Collision theory is true for these **reversible reactions.** The products must achieve enough energy to form the activated complex and then the reactants. A reaction that is reversible consists of two reactions taking place at the same time. This is true of the formation of gaseous hydrogen fluoride.

$$H_2(g) + F_2(g) \rightleftarrows 2HF(g)$$

The double arrow in the equation indicates that both the forward and reverse reactions occur. Suppose you start with 1 mol of H_2 gas and 1 mol of F_2 gas in an empty container. When one molecule of H_2 reacts with one molecule of F_2, two molecules of HF gas form.

$$H_2 + F_2 \rightarrow 2HF$$

As more HF molecules are produced, some decompose to H_2 and F_2 molecules.

$$2HF \rightarrow H_2 + F_2$$

Both reactions occur at the same time. Eventually, the reaction reaches a state of **chemical equilibrium.** Chemical equilibrium is reached when the rate of the forward reaction equals the rate of the reverse reaction. A reaction that is at equilibrium is often called an **equilibrium system.** The forward reaction makes up half of the system, and the reverse reaction makes up the other half.

Equilibrium

When a system reaches equilibrium, the amount of each reactant and product remains constant with time. Equilibrium occurs in the above reaction when the amounts of H_2 gas, F_2 gas, and HF gas stop changing. At equilibrium, does the reaction stop? No. Both the forward and reverse reactions continue, but at the same rate. At equilibrium, the total number of reactant particles stays the same, and the total number of product particles stays the same. However, individual particles continue to react in both directions.

At equilibrium, the system usually does not consist of 50% reactants and 50% products. These equilibrium amounts vary greatly with each reaction and also with temperature.

For example, consider again the reaction of 1 mol of H_2 with 1 mol of F_2. When this reaction reaches equilibrium at a certain temperature, there may be 0.997 mol of H_2, 0.997 mol of F_2, and 0.006 mol of HF. In this case, the equilibrium lies to the left, with the reactants. There are many more reactant molecules than product molecules. The reactants are favored. At a different temperature, the equilibrium amounts may be 0.003 mol of H_2, 0.003 mol of F_2, and 1.994 mol of HF. In this case, the equilibrium lies to the right. The products are favored.

Equilibrium Expressions

To describe an equilibrium system, chemists use an **equilibrium expression.** This is a mathematical equation relating the concentrations of products to the concentrations of reactants at equilibrium. These concentrations may be expressed as gas pressures or molarities. In this chapter, molarities are used. You can write an equilibrium expression for any balanced equation,

$$aA + bB + \cdots \rightleftarrows cC + dD + \cdots$$

A, B, C, D, etc. are substances and a, b, c, d, etc. are their coefficients. The equilibrium expression is

$$K = \frac{[C]^c[D]^d}{[A]^a[B]^b}$$

Each term in brackets is the molarity of a reactant or product at equilibrium. The products (C, D, etc.) are written in the top of the fraction. The reactants (A, B, etc.) are written in the bottom. An easy way to remember this expression is to think, "K equals products over reactants." When setting up an equilibrium expression, you can eliminate state symbols. The equilibrium expression for $H_2 + F_2 \rightleftarrows 2HF$ is

$$K = \frac{[HF]^2}{[H_2][F_2]}$$

Any number raised to the power of 1 equals itself. For example, $[H_2]^1 = [H_2]$. An exponent of 1 does not need to be written.

Example 1 What is the equilibrium expression for the following equation?
$N_2(g) + 3H_2(g) \rightleftharpoons 2NH_3(g)$

Read You are asked to write the equilibrium expression for a reversible reaction.

Plan Use the equilibrium expression below.
$$K = \frac{[C]^c[D]^d}{[A]^a[B]^b}$$

Solve Replace the A and B with the formulas of the two reactants. Replace the C with NH_3. There is no D since there is only one product. Check that the given equation is balanced. Then use the coefficients to replace a, b, and c. An exponent of 1 does not need to be written.
$$K = \frac{[NH_3]^2}{[N_2][H_2]^3}$$

Reflect It does not matter which reactant term is written first.

Practice What is the equilibrium expression for the following equation?
$2CO(g) + O_2(g) \rightleftharpoons 2CO_2(g)$

Solid and liquid substances are not included in equilibrium expressions. Only gaseous and aqueous substances are considered in the equilibrium of a reaction.

Example 2 What is the equilibrium expression for the following equation?
$CaCO_3(s) \rightleftharpoons CaO(s) + CO_2(g)$

Read You are asked to write the equilibrium expression for a reversible reaction.

Plan The reactant, calcium carbonate, is a solid. One of the products, calcium oxide, is also a solid. This equilibrium system is not affected by the amount of $CaCO_3$ or CaO, so they are left out of the expression.

Solve The only term in the expression is the molarity of the CO_2 gas.
$K = [CO_2]$

Reflect The reverse reaction, $CaO(s) + CO_2(g) \rightleftharpoons CaCO_3(s)$, has this equilibrium expression: $K = \frac{1}{[CO_2]}$.

Practice What is the equilibrium expression for the following equation?
$2H_2O(l) \rightleftharpoons 2H_2(g) + O_2(g)$

In the next lesson, you will learn what the value of a calculated equilibrium expression means.

Word Bank

chemical
equilibrium

equilibrium
expression

reversible reaction

On a sheet of paper, write the phrase from the Word Bank
that completes each sentence.

1. In a(n) _____, the products form the reactants.

2. During _____, the number of reactant particles and the
number of product particles do not change.

3. To set up a(n) _____, product concentrations are divided
by reactant concentrations, with coefficients written as
exponents.

On a sheet of paper, write the letter of the equilibrium
expression for each reaction.

4. $2NO_2(g) \rightleftarrows N_2O_4(g)$

A $\dfrac{2[NO_2]}{[N_2O_4]}$ **B** $\dfrac{[NO_2]^2}{[N_2O_4]}$ **C** $\dfrac{[N_2O_4]}{[NO_2]^2}$ **D** $\dfrac{[N_2O_4]}{[2NO_2]}$

5. $2SO_2(g) + O_2(g) \rightleftarrows 2SO_3(g)$

A $\dfrac{[SO_3]^2}{[SO_2]^2[O_2]}$ **B** $\dfrac{[SO_3]^2}{[SO_2]^2+[O_2]}$ **C** $\dfrac{2[SO_3]^2}{2[SO_2][O_2]}$ **D** $\dfrac{[SO_2]^2[O_2]}{[SO_3]^2}$

6. $C(s) + H_2O(g) \rightleftarrows CO(g) + H_2(g)$

A $\dfrac{[CO][H_2]}{[C][H_2O]}$ **B** $\dfrac{[CO][H_2]}{[H_2O]}$ **C** $\dfrac{[H_2O][C]}{[CO][H_2]}$ **D** $\dfrac{[H_2O]}{[CO][H_2]}$

Critical Thinking

On a sheet of paper, write the equilibrium expression for
each reaction.

7. $4HCl(g) + O_2(g) \rightleftarrows 2Cl_2(g) + 2H_2O(g)$

8. $Na_2CO_3(s) \rightleftarrows Na_2O(s) + CO_2(g)$

9. $PCl_5(g) \rightleftarrows PCl_3(g) + Cl_2(g)$

10. $PCl_3(g) + Cl_2(g) \rightleftarrows PCl_5(g)$

Objectives

After reading this lesson, you should be able to

◆ explain what the value of an equilibrium constant means

◆ use the equilibrium expression to calculate *K*

Equilibrium constant (K)

A unique constant that describes the equilibrium of a specific reaction at a certain temperature

In the last lesson, you were introduced to the equilibrium expression. It shows that the equilibrium of a reaction is affected by the reactant and product concentrations.

$$K = \frac{[C]^c[D]^d}{[A]^a[B]^b}$$

[A] and [B] represent reactant concentrations, and [C] and [D] represent product concentrations. When these concentration terms are replaced with actual molarity values measured at equilibrium, you can solve for *K*. *K* is the **equilibrium constant.** It is a unique constant that describes a specific equilibrium system at a certain temperature. Equilibrium constants are sensitive to temperature changes. They have no units.

An equilibrium constant provides information about an equilibrium system.

- If *K* is greater than 1, there are more product particles than reactant particles. The reaction tends to proceed (although you do not know how fast it will proceed). The products are favored.

- If *K* is less than 1, there are more reactant particles than product particles. The reaction does not proceed to a great extent, so the reactants are favored.

Link to ≻≻≻

Health

Many cleaning products carry a warning that mixing them with chlorine bleach will produce hazardous chlorine gas. Chlorine bleach is an equilibrium mixture of chlorine gas in a base, usually sodium hydroxide. Mixing bleach with an acidic substance disrupts the equilibrium. As a result, chlorine gas comes out of the solution.

Math Tip

A large number divided by a small number is a very large number.
A small number divided by a large number is a very small number.

$$\frac{\text{LARGE}}{\text{SMALL}} = \text{VERY LARGE}$$

$$\frac{\text{SMALL}}{\text{LARGE}} = \text{VERY SMALL}$$

Example 1   The following reaction is at equilibrium: $H_2(g) + F_2(g) \rightleftharpoons 2HF(g)$. The concentrations of H_2 and F_2 are 0.472 M each. The concentration of HF is 5.056 M. What is the value of the equilibrium constant, K? Are the products or reactants favored?

Read   You are asked to calculate K using the given reactant and product concentrations at equilibrium.

Plan   Set up the equilibrium expression. All substances are gases, so all are involved in the expression. One product term is in the numerator, and two reactant terms are in the denominator. In the balanced equation, the coefficients of both reactants are 1, and the product's coefficient is 2.

$$K = \frac{[HF]^2}{[H_2][F_2]}$$

Solve   Replace the concentration terms with the given values and solve for K. To do this correctly, multiply the values in the denominator first. Then divide the numerator by the denominator. Equilibrium constants have no unit, so the concentration unit in each term can be ignored.

$$K = \frac{(5.056\ M)^2}{(0.472\ M)(0.472\ M)} = \frac{25.6}{0.223} = 115$$

The value of K is much greater than 1. This means the products are favored over the reactants. There are more product particles than reactant particles at equilibrium.

Reflect   The concentration of the product is more than 10 times larger than the individual concentrations of the reactants. This also tells you that the products are favored.

Practice   The following reaction is at equilibrium: $N_2(g) + 3H_2(g) \rightleftharpoons 2NH_3(g)$. The concentrations are $[N_2] = 1.05\ M$, $[H_2] = 2.13\ M$, $[NH_3] = 0.778\ M$. What is the value of the equilibrium constant, K? Are the products or reactants favored?

A known K value can be used to determine if a given set of concentrations represents an equilibrium system. A known K value can also be used to find an unknown concentration of a reactant or product, as the next example shows.

Math Tip

To see the algebra steps for solving for $[O_2]$ in Example 2, turn to page 795 in Appendix B.

Example 2 The reaction, $2SO_2(g) + O_2(g) \rightleftarrows 2SO_3(g)$, is at equilibrium. $K = 278$, $[SO_2] = 0.575\ M$, and $[SO_3] = 3.53\ M$. What is the equilibrium concentration of oxygen?

Read You are asked to find $[O_2]$. You are given K and the other two concentrations.

Plan Set up the equilibrium expression.

$$K = \frac{[SO_3]^2}{[SO_2]^2[O_2]}$$

Solve Use the known values in the expression.

$$278 = \frac{(3.53)^2}{(0.575)^2[O_2]}$$

Solve for the unknown value, $[O_2]$. This involves some algebra.

$$91.9[O_2] = 12.5$$
$$[O_2] = 0.136\ M$$

Reflect The answer is a concentration. It needs the unit, molarity.

Practice The reaction, $H_2O(g) + Cl_2O(g) \rightleftarrows 2HOCl(g)$, is at equilibrium. $K = 0.0900$, $[H_2O] = 0.49\ M$, and $[Cl_2O] = 0.040\ M$. What is the equilibrium concentration of HOCl?

Science Myth

Myth: Reactions at equilibrium have equal concentrations of reactants and products.

Fact: Any concentration of a reactant and any concentration of a product is possible at equilibrium. Equilibrium means that the concentration of each individual reactant or product is not changing. This does not mean that the concentrations of reactants and products are equal.

Lesson 5   R E V I E W

On a sheet of paper, write the word or phrase from the Word Bank that completes each sentence.

Word Bank

equilibrium constant

products

reactants

1. If an equilibrium constant is greater than 1, the _____ are favored.

2. If an equilibrium constant is less than 1, the _____ are favored.

3. Each reversible chemical reaction has a unique _____.

Calculate K for each reaction. Use the given concentrations. On a sheet of paper, write your answer.

4. $2NO_2(g) \rightleftarrows N_2O_4(g)$
   $[NO_2] = 0.235\ M, [N_2O_4] = 6.01\ M$

5. $2SO_2(g) + O_2(g) \rightleftarrows 2SO_3(g)$
   $[SO_2] = 0.115\ M, [O_2] = 0.088\ M, [SO_3] = 1.63\ M$

6. $4HCl(g) + O_2(g) \rightleftarrows 2Cl_2(g) + 2H_2O(g)$
   $[HCl] = 2.53\ M, [O_2] = 0.56\ M, [Cl_2] = 0.311\ M,$
   $[H_2O] = 1.06\ M$

Critical Thinking

On a sheet of paper, write the answer to each question.

7. Write the equilibrium expression for the reaction below. Then calculate K using these concentrations: $[PCl_5] = 0.000421\ M, [PCl_3] = 6.96\ M,$ and $[Cl_2] = 3.47\ M.$
   $PCl_5(g) \rightleftarrows PCl_3(g) + Cl_2(g)$

8. Write the equilibrium expression for the reaction below. Then calculate K using these concentrations: $[NH_3] = 1.35\ M, [N_2] = 5.25\ M,$ and $[H_2] = 3.47\ M.$
   $N_2(g) + 3H_2(g) \rightleftarrows 2NH_3(g)$

9. For the reaction, $2NO_2(g) \rightleftarrows 2NO(g) + O_2(g), K = 175.$ If $[NO_2] = 0.575\ M$ and $[NO] = 2.96\ M,$ what is $[O_2]$?

10. For the reaction, $2HI(g) \rightleftarrows H_2(g) + I_2(g), K = 0.75.$ If $[H_2] = 1.42\ M$ and $[I_2] = 2.05\ M,$ what is $[HI]$?

After reading this lesson, you should be able to

◆ state Le Chatelier's principle

◆ list three stresses that affect a system at equilibrium

◆ describe how the equilibrium of a reaction shifts under a given stress

Le Chatelier's principle

A principle that states that a reversible reaction at equilibrium will shift to relieve a stress

Stress

A change in the conditions of a system at equilibrium

An equilibrium system is a system in balance. The concentration of each reactant is constant, and the concentration of each product is constant. It is possible to upset this balance. A chemist named Henri Louis Le Chatelier studied how equilibrium systems change. He observed this principle, called **Le Chatelier's principle**: If a **stress** is applied to a system at equilibrium, the equilibrium shifts to establish a new equilibrium that relieves the stress. A stress is a change in the conditions of an equilibrium system. What are some stresses that can be applied to a system?

• A change in the concentration of a reactant or product
• A temperature change
• A pressure change in an equilibrium system of gases

According to Le Chatelier's principle, each of these stresses causes a reaction to shift in one direction or another to regain equilibrium. It is helpful to think of an equilibrium system as a perfectly balanced seesaw.

Reactants ⇌ Products

Adding Reactants or Removing Products

How does this seesaw shift when more reactants are added? It moves like this:

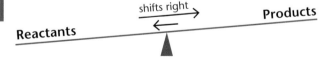

More reactant particles are available to react. As a result, more products are formed. Soon, the rates of the forward and reverse reactions are again the same. A new equilibrium is established. The equilibrium shifted to the right—to the product side of the equation. Removing products has the same effect as adding reactants. The seesaw regains balance by forming more products and shifting right.

Adding Products or Removing Reactants

How does the seesaw shift when more products are added? It moves like this:

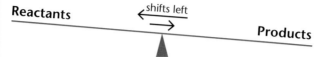

More product particles are now available to react. As a result, more reactants form. Soon, the rates of the forward and reverse reactions are again the same. Equilibrium is restored. The new equilibrium represents a shift to the left—to the reactant side of the equation. A similar shift occurs when some reactants are removed. More reactants will form as the equilibrium shifts left.

Compare the effect of adding more reactant to the effect of adding more product. Adding reactant causes the equilibrium to shift to the right. Adding product causes the equilibrium to shift to the left. This is true for all stresses: an opposite stress will cause an opposite shift.

Changing the Temperature

Changing the temperature of an equilibrium system also causes the equilibrium to shift. Increasing the temperature of any equilibrium system shifts the equilibrium in the direction that absorbs energy. Decreasing the temperature of any system shifts the equilibrium in the direction that releases energy. The direction of the shift depends on whether the reaction is endothermic or exothermic.

❋❋❋❋❋❋❋❋❋❋❋❋❋❋❋❋❋❋❋❋❋❋❋❋❋❋❋❋❋❋❋

Technology and Society

The cost of processing raw materials into other substances is a concern for chemical companies. One way to reduce cost is to shift the equilibrium of a reaction. Removing product as it is produced shifts the equilibrium so that more product is formed. The production cost is lowered, which lowers the cost of the product and the goods made from it.

In an endothermic reaction, energy is like a reactant. Increasing temperature has the same effect as adding more reactant. The balance looks like this:

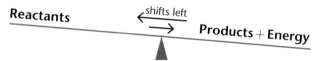

More energy is available on the reactant side, so more products form. This absorbs the added energy, restoring equilibrium. As temperature increases, an endothermic reaction shifts in the forward direction—the direction that absorbs the added energy. The new equilibrium is farther to the right. Decreasing the temperature of an endothermic reaction has the opposite effect.

In an exothermic reaction, energy is like a product. Increasing temperature has the same effect as adding more product. The balance looks like this:

More energy is available on the product side, so more reactants form, absorbing the added energy. An exothermic reaction shifts in the reverse direction—the direction that uses up the added energy. The new equilibrium is farther to the left. Decreasing the temperature has the opposite effect.

The equilibrium constant, *K*, is very sensitive to temperature. How is *K* affected by a temperature change? Recall that *K* is the product concentrations divided by the reactant concentrations for any reaction, $aA + bB \rightleftharpoons cC + dD$.

$$K = \frac{[C]^c[D]^d}{[A]^a[B]^b}$$

When the temperature of an endothermic system is increased, the equilibrium shifts right. The amount of products (C and D) increases and the amount of reactants (A and B) decreases. A shift to the right increases the value of *K*. When the temperature of an exothermic reaction is increased, the equilibrium shifts left. The amount of products decreases and the amount of reactants increases. A shift to the left decreases the value of *K*.

Changing the Pressure on a System of Gases

Increasing the pressure (or decreasing the volume) on an equilibrium system of gases shifts the equilibrium to the side with fewer moles of gas. This is because increasing the pressure forces the particles closer together. As a result, the gas particles collide more often and react. Soon, the rates of the forward and reverse reactions are again the same, and equilibrium is restored. Decreasing the pressure (or increasing the volume) has the opposite effect: it shifts the equilibrium to the side with more moles of gas. If both sides of the reaction have the same total number of moles of gas, the equilibrium does not change.

Table 16.6.1 summarizes the effect of different stresses on chemical equilibrium.

Table 16.6.1 Stresses and Their Effect on Equilibrium Systems	
Stress	**Shift**
Increase reactant concentration (or decrease product concentration).	right, toward products
Increase product concentration (or decrease reactant concentration).	left, toward reactants
Increase temperature of exothermic reaction (or decrease temperature of endothermic reaction).	left, toward reactants
Increase temperature of endothermic reaction (or decrease temperature of exothermic reaction).	right, toward products
Increase pressure (or decrease volume) of a gas system.	toward side with fewer moles of gas

❋ ❋

Technology and Society

Diamonds and graphite are two different forms of carbon. Synthetic diamonds are produced from graphite using a high-temperature, high-pressure method. Graphite is heated to about 2,500°C and squeezed at 10,000 atm of pressure to produce small diamonds. These diamonds are used in cutting tools and grinding wheels. At atmospheric pressure and 1,200°C, diamonds turn back into graphite.

Example 1   The reaction, $PCl_5(g) + energy \rightleftharpoons PCl_3(g) + Cl_2(g)$, is at equilibrium. How will the equilibrium shift under the following stresses?
A   an increase in Cl_2 concentration
B   a decrease in PCl_5 concentration
C   an increase in temperature
D   a decrease in pressure

Read   You are asked to describe how the equilibrium will shift for each of four conditions.

Plan   Use Le Chatelier's principle and the seesaw analogy to predict the effect of each stress.

Solve   For each stress, the system shifts to regain its equilibrium.
A: Cl_2 is a product, so increasing its concentration shifts the equilibrium to the left (toward the reactants).
B: PCl_5 is a reactant, so decreasing its concentration also causes a shift to the left.
C: The reaction is endothermic, since energy is a reactant. Increasing the temperature shifts the equilibrium toward the products, to the right.
D: All of the substances are gases, so decreasing the pressure shifts the equilibrium to the side with the most gas moles. In the balanced equation, there are 2 mol of products and 1 mol of reactant. The equilibrium shifts to the right.

Reflect   A pressure change has no effect if no reactants or products are gases or if there are equal moles of gases on both sides of the balanced equation.

Practice   The following reaction is at equilibrium. How will the equilibrium shift under the following stresses?
$4HCl(g) + O_2(g) \rightleftharpoons 2Cl_2(g) + 2H_2O(g) + energy$
A   a decrease in Cl_2 concentration
B   a decrease in HCl concentration
C   an increase in pressure
D   a decrease in temperature

On a sheet of paper, write the word from the Word Bank that completes each sentence.

Word Bank
left
right
stress

1. If a _____ is applied to an equilibrium system, the system shifts to establish a new equilibrium.

2. Decreasing the temperature of an endothermic reaction shifts the equilibrium to the _____.

3. Decreasing a product concentration in an equilibrium shifts the equilibrium to the _____.

On a sheet of paper, write the letter of the answer that completes each sentence.

4. The pressure is increased on the equilibrium system below. The equilibrium _____ .
$$H_2(g) + I_2(g) \rightleftarrows 2HI(g)$$

  A shifts right   **C** does not shift

  B shifts left   **D** cannot be restored

5. The equilibrium system below shifts right. This could be caused by _____.
$$4HCl(g) + O_2(g) \rightleftarrows 2Cl_2(g) + 2H_2O(g) + energy$$

  A a decrease in $[O_2]$ **C** a decrease in pressure

  B a temperature increase   **D** a decrease in $[H_2O]$

6. The equilibrium system below shifts left. This could be caused by _____. $2NO_2(g) + energy \rightleftarrows N_2O_4(g)$

  A a temperature increase   **C** a decrease in $[N_2O_4]$

  B a drop in pressure   **D** an increase in $[NO_2]$

Critical Thinking

For each stress, determine the direction of shift for this system:
$$4NH_3(g) + 5O_2(g) \rightleftarrows 4NO(g) + 6H_2O(g) + energy$$
On a sheet of paper, write *left* or *right*. Then explain your answer.

7. $[H_2O]$ decreases.

8. Temperature increases.

9. Pressure increases.

10. Oxygen is added.

Materials

- safety goggles
- lab coat or apron
- gloves
- 2 250-mL beakers
- 2 mL of 0.1 M cobalt(II) chloride ($CoCl_2$) solution in a medium test tube
- test-tube rack
- concentrated hydrochloric acid (HCl) in a dropper bottle
- 10 mL of distilled water
- eyedropper
- hot plate
- tap water
- cup of ice

Le Chatelier's Principle

According to Le Chatelier's principle, when a stress is applied to a reaction at equilibrium, the equilibrium changes to relieve the stress. How can you demonstrate Le Chatelier's principle? In this investigation, you will apply stress to an equilibrium system and observe what happens.

Procedure

1. Put on safety goggles, a lab coat or apron, and gloves.

2. Record the color of the $CoCl_2$ solution.

3. Add concentrated HCl to the $CoCl_2$ solution, one drop at a time, until a color change occurs. Then add 5 more drops of HCl. Record your observations. **Safety Alert: Concentrated HCl can burn skin and clothing. Handle it carefully. Report any spills immediately. Do not inhale the HCl vapor.**

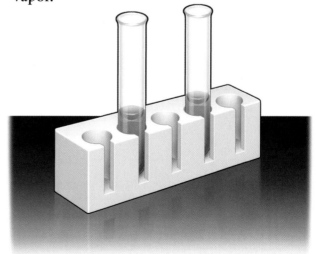

Continued on next page

4. Add distilled water to the same solution, drop by drop, until the color changes again. Record your observations.

5. Slowly add drops of concentrated HCl just until the solution becomes purple. This color should be about halfway between the two colors you observed already.

6. Remove your gloves and goggles. Write a procedure to test the effect of temperature on this solution. Use the materials provided. Include safety alerts.

7. Have your procedure approved by your teacher. Then put on gloves and goggles. Carry out your procedure and record your results.

Cleanup/Disposal

Turn off the hot plate and allow it to cool. Dispose of the solution in a proper waste container. Then clean the glassware and return all materials. Wash your hands.

Analysis

1. What was the color of the starting solution (step 2)?

2. What was the solution color after HCl was added (step 3)?

3. What was the solution color after water was added (step 4)?

4. What was the solution color at equilibrium (step 5)?

5. How did temperature affect the color of the solution?

Conclusions

The equation for the equilibrium reaction is as follows:

$$CoCl_4^{2-}(aq) + 6H_2O(l) \rightleftharpoons$$
$$Co(H_2O)_6^{2+}(aq) + 4Cl^{1-}(aq) + heat$$

1. There are two cobalt-containing ions in this reaction. How does each one affect the color of the solution? Explain your answer.

2. Why is the solution color affected by temperature?

3. Silver nitrate reacts with chloride ions to form insoluble silver chloride (AgCl). How would adding silver nitrate change the equilibrium of the above reaction? Explain your answer.

Explore Further

A simple weather indicator consists of a strip of paper that has been soaked in $CoCl_2$ solution and allowed to dry. The color of the paper changes according to the humidity. Predict the color of the indicator in moist air and in dry air. Explain your predictions.

More Gasoline with Catalysts

Petroleum, or crude oil, is a mixture of many different compounds. These compounds vary from simple ones containing a few atoms to complex ones containing hundreds of atoms. Some of the products obtained from crude oil are gasoline, kerosene, diesel oil, and heating oil. These products contain different mixtures of compounds.

Crude oil is distilled to separate it into its components. This separation works because each compound has a particular boiling point. The compounds with the highest boiling points consist of the largest molecules. These compounds, called the residue, are the least useful as fuel. Rather than throw the residue away, it is processed to produce additional gasoline and other useful products.

The residue from the distillation is mixed with a catalyst and heated. This process is called catalytic cracking. The heat and the catalyst cause the large molecules to break apart. The result is a mixture of smaller molecules, such as those used in gasoline. Some carbon atoms are also produced. The carbon atoms stop the catalyst from working because they cling to it. The catalyst is restored by heating it to burn off the carbon.

The mixture produced by cracking is then distilled as if it were crude oil. The resulting compounds are mixed with those produced by the crude oil distillation. By using catalysts, refineries like the one shown can produce more gasoline and other products from a barrel of oil. Catalysts also allow refineries to produce these products with less waste and at a lower cost.

1. What process is used to separate gasoline from crude oil, and how does it work?

2. Is gasoline the only product produced by catalytic cracking? Explain.

3. Why do refineries use catalytic cracking?

- Collision theory can be used to explain how to increase the rate of a reaction.

- For a reaction to proceed, the reactants must achieve a level of energy called the activation energy.

- Increasing the temperature increases the reaction rate because the particles have more energy and collide more often.

- Increasing the concentration of a reactant increases the reaction rate because more particles are available to collide. Increasing the surface area of a solid has the same effect.

- A catalyst increases the reaction rate by lowering the activation energy.

- An activated complex is a temporary particle created when reactants collide

- A potential energy diagram shows how potential energy changes from reactants to activated complex to products.

- A reaction mechanism describes a reaction as a series of steps. These steps include one or more intermediates.

- The slowest step in a reaction mechanism is called the rate-determining step. A rate law can be written for this step.

- Chemical equilibrium occurs when the concentrations of the reactants and the concentrations of the products remain constant over time.

- The equilibrium expression for the reaction, $aA + bB \rightleftarrows cC + dD$, is
$$K = \frac{[C]^c[D]^d}{[A]^a[B]^b}$$

- The equilibrium constant, K, is found by solving the equilibrium expression using equilibrium concentrations.

- For K values greater than 1, the products are favored. For K values less than 1, the reactants are favored.

- The equilibrium of a system shifts when a stress is applied. Such stresses include changes in reactant and product concentrations, temperature, and pressure.

Vocabulary

activated complex, 627	enzyme, 624	intermediate, 635	reaction mechanism, 635
activation energy, 622	equilibrium constant, 645	Le Chatelier's principle, 649	reaction rate, 622
catalyst, 623	equilibrium expression, 642	rate constant, 638	reversible reaction, 641
chemical equilibrium, 641	equilibrium system, 641	rate-determining step, 635	stress, 649
collision theory, 622		rate law, 638	

Chapter 16 REVIEW

Word Bank

activated complex

activation energy

catalyst

chemical equilibrium

equilibrium expression

rate-determining step

reaction mechanism

reaction rate

reversible reaction

stress

Vocabulary Review

On a sheet of paper, write the word or phrase from the Word Bank that completes each sentence.

1. The minimum amount of energy needed for a reaction to take place is the _____.

2. In a reaction mechanism, the _____ has the highest activation energy.

3. A reversible reaction reaches _____ when the concentration of each reactant and product remains constant over time.

4. A(n) _____ is a temporary particle created when reactant particles collide.

5. A(n) _____ is a series of small steps that add up to the overall balanced equation.

6. A(n) _____ speeds up a reaction without taking part in it.

7. The number of reactant particles that react in a given period of time is the _____.

8. In a(n) _____, the products can react to form the reactants.

9. A(n) _____ is a change in the conditions of a system at equilibrium.

10. To set up a(n) _____, place product concentrations in the numerator and reactant concentrations in the denominator. Use equation coefficients as exponents for the concentrations.

Continued on next page

Concept Review

On a sheet of paper, write the letter of the answer to each question. Questions 11–13 refer to the diagram at the left.

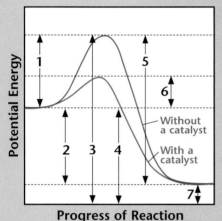

Potential Energy / 1 / 5 / 6 / 2 / 3 / 4 / Without a catalyst / With a catalyst / 7 / **Progress of Reaction**

11. Which arrow represents the activation energy for the uncatalyzed reaction?

    A 1   **B** 2   **C** 3   **D** 4

12. Which arrow represents the heat of reaction?

    A 1   **B** 2   **C** 4   **D** 7

13. Which arrow represents the activation energy for the catalyzed reaction?

    A 7   **B** 6   **C** 5   **D** 4

Questions 14–16 refer to the reaction mechanism at the left.

Step 1   *fast*
$A + B \rightarrow C$

Step 2   *slow*
$A + D \rightarrow E$

Step 3   *fast*
$C + E \rightarrow F$

14. What is the overall balanced equation?

    A $B + D \rightarrow F$ **C** $C + D + E \rightarrow C + E + F$

    B $2A + B + D \rightarrow F$ **D** $A + D \rightarrow E$

15. What is the rate law for this reaction mechanism?

    A $rate = k[A][D]$ **C** $rate = k[E]$

    B $rate = k[A]^2[B][D]$ **D** $rate = k[A][B]$

16. The highest activation energy is in which step(s)?

    A 1   **B** 2   **C** 3   **D** 1 and 3

17. Which stress could shift the following equilibrium to the right? $4NH_3(g) + 5O_2(g) \rightleftharpoons 4NO(g) + 6H_2O(g) + energy$

    A a temperature increase   **C** the removal of $O_2(g)$

    B more $NO(g)$ **D** a drop in pressure

18. Which stress could shift the following equilibrium to the left? $H_2(g) + I_2(g) \rightleftharpoons 2HI(g) + energy$

    A a temperature decrease   **C** a pressure increase

    B more $HI(g)$ **D** more $I_2(g)$

Problem Solving

On a sheet of paper, write the answer to each problem. Show all calculations.

19. What is the equilibrium expression for the following reaction? $CO_2(g) + CaO(s) \rightleftharpoons CaCO_3(s)$

20. Calculate the equilibrium constant for the following reaction. Use these equilibrium concentrations: $[NOCl] = 0.50\ M$, $[NO] = 0.020\ M$, and $[Cl_2] = 0.010\ M$.
$2NOCl(g) \rightleftharpoons 2NO(g) + Cl_2(g)$

21. At a certain temperature, $K = 198$ for the following reaction at equilibrium. If $[NH_3] = 0.070\ M$, $[P(NH_2)_3] = 0.435\ M$, and $[HCl] = 0.225\ M$, what is $[PCl_3]$?
$PCl_3(g) + 3NH_3(g) \rightleftharpoons P(NH_2)_3(g) + 3HCl(g)$

22. At a certain temperature, $K = 9.3 \times 10^{-3}$ for the following reaction. If $[HBr] = 0.55\ M$, what are $[H_2]$ and $[Br_2]$?
$2HBr(g) \rightleftharpoons H_2(g) + Br_2(g)$

Critical Thinking

On a sheet of paper, write the answer to each question.

23. Why does milk spoil faster when left out of the refrigerator?

24. The following reversible reaction was used by Fritz Haber in 1909 to produce ammonia (NH_3) from atmospheric nitrogen. List three ways to increase the production of ammonia. $N_2(g) + 3H_2(g) +$ energy $\rightarrow 2NH_3(g)$

25. For the equilibrium system in question 24, consider the equilibrium expressions for the forward reaction and the reverse reaction. How are the two expressions related to each other? Explain.

Test-Taking Tip   When studying for a test, work with a partner to write your own test problems. Then solve the problems. Check your answers.

17

Acids and Bases

The water in this swimming pool is beautiful and clear. You can see the tiles that make up the floor of the pool. Did you know you have to be an amateur chemist to keep pool water this clear? When you add chemicals to pools, you are conducting an acid-base reaction. In Chapter 17, you will study acids and bases and how they react. You will also learn about the pH scale and the strength of acids and bases.

Organize Your Thoughts

```
        Acids  ——  pH  ——  Bases
          │          │          │
          ▼          ▼          ▼
   Strong and   Neutralization   Strong and
   weak acids   reactions and    weak bases
                  titrations
          │          │          │
          └───────── ▼ ─────────┘
                   Salts
                     │
                     ▼
                  Buffers
```

Goals for Learning

◆ To understand acids and bases as donors and acceptors of protons in acid-base reactions

◆ To explain the equivalence point in a neutralization reaction and to calculate the molarity or volume of an acid or base in a titration

◆ To explain the pH scale and calculate the pH, $[H^{1+}]$, and $[OH^{1-}]$ of a solution

◆ To understand how strong and weak acids and bases ionize in water

◆ To describe a buffer and explain how it reacts when an acid or base is added

Objectives

After reading this lesson, you should be able to

◆ compare Arrhenius and Brønsted-Lowry definitions of an acid and base

◆ identify the acid and base in an acid-base reaction

◆ identify the conjugate acid and conjugate base in an acid-base reaction

Acid

A compound that is a proton (H^{1+}) donor

Base

A compound that is a proton (H^{1+}) acceptor

Acids and bases are an important part of everyday life. Vinegar is a solution of acetic acid ($HC_2H_3O_2$). Citrus fruits contain citric acid, and vitamin C is ascorbic acid. Ammonia (NH_3) is a base commonly used for cleaning. Sodium hydroxide (NaOH) is also called lye. This base is a common drain cleaner. Milk of magnesia ($Mg(OH)_2$) is a base that is sometimes used to soothe an upset stomach. Both acids and bases are important substances in industry as well.

Acids and bases have very different chemical properties. Acids are usually liquids or gases, and bases are often solids. Many acids and some bases are soluble and are commonly used in aqueous solutions. In Chapter 3, an acid was defined as a compound that produces H^{1+} ions when dissolved in water. A base was defined as a compound that produces OH^{1-} ions when dissolved in water. These definitions were developed by Svante Arrhenius around 1890. According to Arrhenius's definitions, HCl is an acid and NaOH is a base. They react to form water and a salt.

$$HCl + NaOH \rightarrow H_2O + NaCl$$

 acid   base   water   salt

While Arrhenius's definitions are true, they are somewhat limiting.

A broader definition of an **acid** is a compound that is a proton donor. Likewise, a **base** is a compound that is a proton acceptor. The hydrogen ion, H^{1+}, is a proton. Acids donate H^{1+} ions, while bases accept H^{1+} ions. These definitions are Brønsted-Lowry definitions, named after the chemists who developed them.

All Arrhenius acids are Brønsted-Lowry acids, and all Arrhenius bases are Brønsted-Lowry bases. However, some Brønsted-Lowry bases do not qualify as Arrhenius bases. For this reason, Brønsted-Lowry definitions are used throughout most of this chapter.

Water is an H^{1+} acceptor in the acid-base reaction below. It acts as a base even though it does not produce OH^{1-} ions.

$$H^{1+} + H_2O \rightleftharpoons H_3O^{1+}$$
$$\text{acid} \quad \text{base}$$

The product is the hydronium ion, H_3O^{1+}. When a Brønsted-Lowry acid and base react, they do not necessarily form water and a salt.

An easy way to identify the acid and base in an acid-base reaction is to count the number of hydrogen atoms in each reactant and product. Look at this acid-base reaction:

$$HC_2H_3O_2 \quad + \quad NH_3 \quad \rightleftharpoons \quad NH_4^{1+} \quad + \quad C_2H_3O_2^{1-}$$
$$\text{4 H atoms} \quad \text{3 H atoms} \quad \text{4 H atoms} \quad \text{3 H atoms}$$

$HC_2H_3O_2$ has 4 H atoms. It loses one—in the form of a proton—to become $C_2H_3O_2^{1-}$. NH_3 has 3 H atoms. It gains one–in the form of a proton—to form NH_4^{1+}. This shows you that $HC_2H_3O_2$ donates an H^{1+} ion (a proton) to NH_3, so $HC_2H_3O_2$ is the acid (acetic acid). Ammonia, NH_3, is the base.

This reaction is reversible. The products, NH_4^{1+} and $C_2H_3O_2^{1-}$, can react to produce NH_3 and $HC_2H_3O_2$. In the reverse reaction, NH_4^{1+} acts as an acid. It donates a proton to $C_2H_3O_2^{1-}$, which acts as a base. In the original reaction, the base (NH_3) becomes a **conjugate acid** (NH_4^{1+}). A conjugate acid is the molecule or ion formed when a base accepts a proton. The acid ($HC_2H_3O_2$) becomes a **conjugate base** ($C_2H_3O_2^{1-}$). A conjugate base is the molecule or ion formed when an acid donates a proton.

$$HC_2H_3O_2 \quad + \quad NH_3 \quad \rightleftharpoons \quad NH_4^{1+} \quad + \quad C_2H_3O_2^{1-}$$
$$\text{acid} \qquad\qquad \text{base} \qquad \text{conjugate} \qquad \text{conjugate}$$
$$\text{acid} \qquad\qquad \text{base}$$

accepts proton

donates proton

Most acid-base reactions have two conjugate acid-base pairs. In the reaction above, $HC_2H_3O_2$ and $C_2H_3O_2^{1-}$ are a conjugate acid-base pair. NH_3 and NH_4^{1+} make up the other pair.

Example 1

Identify the acid and base in the following reaction. Use Brønsted-Lowry definitions.
$$CH_3NH_2 + HNO_3 \rightarrow NO_3^{1-} + CH_3NH_3^{1+}$$

Read

You are asked to identify the acid and base in a reaction.

Plan

An acid is a proton (H^{1+}) donor. A base is a proton ($H1^+$) acceptor.

Solve

Count the number of H atoms in each reactant and product.

$$CH_3NH_2 + HNO_3 \rightarrow NO_3^{1-} + CH_3NH_3^{1+}$$
5 H atoms   1 H atom   no H atoms   6 H atoms

By comparing these counts, you can tell that CH_3NH_2 gains an H^{1+} ion (a proton), so it is the base. This proton is donated by HNO_3, which loses an H^{1+} ion (a proton) to become NO_3^{1-}. HNO_3 is the acid.

Reflect

The NO_3^{1-} anion is the conjugate base, and the $CH_3NH_3^{1+}$ cation is the conjugate acid. HNO_3 fits the Arrhenius definition of an acid: it produces and donates an H^{1+} ion. However, CH_3NH_2 is not an Arrhenius base: no OH^{1-} ions are produced.

Practice

Identify the acid and base in the following reaction.
$$OH^{1-} + HF \rightarrow F^{1-} + H_2O$$

Example 2

Identify the acid, base, conjugate acid, and conjugate base in the following reaction.
$$HCO_3^{1-} + H_2O \rightleftarrows CO_3^{2-} + H_3O^{1+}$$

Read

You are asked to identify the acid, base, conjugate acid, and conjugate base in a reaction.

Plan

An acid is a proton donor. It is the reactant that donates an H^{1+} ion (a proton) to the base. A base is a proton acceptor. It is the reactant that accepts this proton from the acid. The acid becomes the conjugate base, and the base becomes the conjugate acid. The conjugate base and conjugate acid are the products.

Solve	Count the number of H atoms.

$$HCO_3^{1-} + H_2O \rightleftharpoons CO_3^{2-} + H_3O^{1+}$$

1 H atom 2 H atoms no H atoms 3 H atoms

HCO_3^{1-} loses a proton to become CO_3^{2-}. HCO_3^{1-} is the acid, and CO_3^{2-} is the conjugate base. Water gains a proton to become H_3O^{1+}. Water is the base, and H_3O^{1+} is the conjugate acid.

Reflect	Count H atoms carefully. Make sure the acid and base are matched to their correct conjugate.
Practice	Identify the acid, base, conjugate acid, and conjugate base in the following reaction. $HS^{1-} + H_2O \rightleftharpoons H_2S + OH^{1-}$

In the reaction in Example 2, water acts as the base. In the reaction given in the practice problem, water acts as the acid. Water is able to act as an acid or a base, depending on the other reactant.

Express Lab 17

Materials

- safety goggles
- lab coat or apron
- 6 test tubes
- test-tube rack
- 30 mL of 3 M HCl
- 10-mL graduated cylinder
- bromthymol blue
- blue litmus strip
- zinc piece
- aluminum piece
- marble chip
- raw egg white
- grease pencil

Procedure

1. Put on safety goggles and a lab coat or apron.
2. Pour 5 mL of HCl into each test tube. Place the test tubes in the rack. Number the tubes 1 to 6.
3. Dip the litmus strip into tube 1.
4. Add a drop of bromthymol blue to tube 2.
5. Add a piece of zinc to tube 3.
6. Add a piece of aluminum to tube 4.
7. Marble is a carbonate. Add a marble chip to tube 5.
8. Egg white is protein. Add egg white to tube 6.

Analysis

1. Describe your observations of each tube.
2. How can you explain your observations?

Word Bank

acid

base

conjugate acid

Research and Write

In addition to Arrhenius and Brønsted-Lowry definitions, acids and bases are also defined using Lewis definitions. Find out about Lewis acids and bases. Present your findings in a concept map that includes all three definitions of acids and bases.

On a sheet of paper, write the word or phrase from the Word Bank that completes each sentence.

1. A substance that is a proton acceptor is a(n) _____.

2. A substance that is a proton donor is a(n) _____.

3. When a substance accepts a proton, it becomes a(n) _____.

On a sheet of paper, write the letter of the answer to each question. Refer to the following reaction.

$$H_3PO_4 + H_2O \rightleftharpoons H_2PO_4^{1-} + H_3O^{1+}$$

4. Which substance is the acid?

   A H_3PO_4 **B** H_2O **C** $H_2PO_4^{1-}$ **D** H_3O^{1+}

5. Which substance is the base?

   A H_3PO_4 **B** H_2O **C** $H_2PO_4^{1-}$ **D** H_3O^{1+}

6. Which substance is the conjugate acid?

   A H_3PO_4 **B** H_2O **C** $H_2PO_4^{1-}$ **D** H_3O^{1+}

Critical Thinking

On a sheet of paper, write the answer to each question.

7. Explain why NaOH is both an Arrhenius base and a Brønsted-Lowry base.

8. What is the major difference between the Arrhenius definitions of an acid and base and the Brønsted-Lowry definitions?

9. What is the Brønsted-Lowry base in the following reaction? Explain your answer.
   $$C_2H_5NH_2 + H_2CO_3 \rightleftharpoons HCO_3^{1-} + C_2H_5NH_3^{1+}$$

10. Explain why HCO_3^{1-} can act as either a Brønsted-Lowry acid or a Brønsted-Lowry base.

Neutralization reaction

An acid-base reaction

Equivalence point

The point in a neutralization reaction at which all of the acid has reacted with all of the base

One property of acids and bases is their ability to react with each other. When an acid and base react, they neutralize each other. An acid-base reaction is also called a **neutralization reaction**. In the neutralization reaction below, an Arrhenius acid and base produce water and KCl, a salt.

$$HCl + KOH \rightarrow H_2O + KCl$$

Suppose you have a flask containing a solution of hydrochloric acid, HCl. Drop by drop, you add a solution of potassium hydroxide, KOH. When all of the acid has reacted with all of the base, you have reached the **equivalence point.** The acid and base have exactly neutralized each other. The resulting solution does not have the properties of either the acid or base. In the reaction between HCl and KOH, the equivalence point is reached when the moles of added KOH equal the moles of HCl. This is because 1 mol of HCl reacts with 1 mol of KOH—the mole ratio is 1:1. In the reaction between H_2SO_4 and KOH, however, 1 mol of H_2SO_4 reacts with 2 mol of KOH.

$$H_2SO_4 + 2KOH \rightarrow K_2SO_4 + 2H_2O$$

Because of the 1:2 mole ratio, the equivalence point in this reaction is reached when there are twice as many moles of KOH as there are moles of H_2SO_4. The majority of acid-base reactions in this chapter have a 1:1 mole ratio between the acid and base.

❋ ❋

Technology and Society

Paper often contains a compound called alum. Alum keeps ink from spreading and paper from absorbing water. However, alum makes paper acidic. Over time, the acid attacks fibers in the paper, and the paper decays. To remove the acid in paper, the paper is placed in a fluid and then dried in a vacuum.

Chemists use neutralization reactions to determine the molarity of an acid or base solution. This process is called **titration.** For example, suppose you have a 1 *M* KOH solution. You also have an HCl solution, but you do not know its molarity. You can use titration to find the unknown concentration. A titration usually involves these steps:

1. Measure a specific volume of the acid (or base) of unknown concentration. Pour it into a flask.

2. Add a small amount of a substance called an **indicator.** An indicator is one color in an acid and another color in a base. The small amount does not affect the neutralization reaction to any great extent.

3. Add small, measured amounts of a base (or acid) of known concentration. This solution is called the **standard solution.** It is typically dispensed from a glass column called a buret, as Figure 17.2.1 shows.

4. Continue adding the standard solution until the indicator changes color. This signals that the neutralization reaction has reached the equivalence point. In a titration, this color change is called the **end point.**

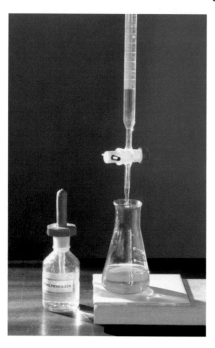

5. Record the volume of base (or acid) that was added. Then determine the concentration of the acid (or base). For reactions that have a 1:1 mole ratio between the acid and base, use this equation:

$$M_a V_a = M_b V_b$$

M_a is the molarity of the acid, and M_b is the molarity of the base. V_a and V_b are their volumes. They must have the same unit. (For mole ratios other than 1:1, coefficients must be added to the above equation.)

Figure 17.2.1 *In this titration, the end point occurred when the colorless solution in the flask became faint pink.*

Example 1	In a titration, a 25.0-mL sample of an HCl solution is neutralized by 17.5 mL of 1.00 M KOH. The reaction is $HCl + KOH \rightarrow H_2O + KCl$. What is the molarity of the HCl?
Read	You are asked to determine the molarity of an acid using a neutralization reaction.
Plan	Use the equation, $M_a V_a = M_b V_b$. Identify the given values: $V_a = 25.0$ mL, $M_b = 1.00$ M, $V_b = 17.5$ mL, and M_a is unknown. V_a and V_b have the same unit.
Solve	Use algebra to solve for M_a, the HCl concentration. $(M_a)(25.0 \text{ mL}) = (1.00 \ M)(17.5 \text{ mL})$ $M_a = 0.700 \ M$ HCl
Reflect	Since a smaller base volume neutralized a larger acid volume, you would expect the concentration of the acid to be less than 1 M.
Practice	In a titration, a 50.0-mL sample of NaOH is neutralized by 63.5 mL of 0.750 M HNO_3. The reaction is $HNO_3 + NaOH \rightarrow NaNO_3 + H_2O$. What is the concentration of the NaOH?

Example 2	A 1.00 M solution of LiOH is neutralized by 75.3 mL of 0.865 M HCl. The reaction is $LiOH + HCl \rightarrow H_2O + LiCl$. What is the volume of the LiOH?
Read	You are asked to calculate the volume of a base.
Plan	Use the equation, $M_a V_a = M_b V_b$. Identify the given values: $M_a = 0.865$ M, $V_a = 75.3$ mL, and $M_b = 1.00$ M. V_b is unknown.
Solve	Solve for the LiOH volume. $(0.865 \ M)(75.3 \text{ mL}) = (1.00 \ M)(V_b)$ $V_b = 65.1$ mL
Reflect	The units for V_a and V_b must match. Since V_a is in milliliters, V_b must be in milliliters.
Practice	A 0.725 M solution of HF is neutralized by 0.322 L of 0.150 M LiOH. The reaction is $HF + LiOH \rightarrow LiF + H_2O$. What is the volume of the acid?

A common indicator is phenolphthalein. In an acid solution, phenolphthalein is colorless. In a base solution, it is bright pink. When a base is added to an acid in titration, the phenolphthalein temporarily turns the solution pink. The added base is quickly neutralized by the acid, and the solution becomes colorless again. At the end point, the solution stays slightly pink, as Figure 17.2.1 on page 670 shows. The color change indicates that all of the acid has reacted with all of the base.

There are other indicators besides phenolphthalein. Each one has a unique color change at the end point.

Chemistry in Your Life

Consumer Choices: Antacids

Do you ever get an "acid stomach?" The stomach secretes hydrochloric acid to help digest food. Normally, the stomach lining is protected from the acid by a layer of mucus. However, sometimes you eat acidic foods or the stomach secretes too much acid. Some of this acid needs to be neutralized to return the acidity of the stomach to normal levels.

Over-the-counter and prescription antacids help to reduce the amount of acid in the stomach. Some antacids contain insoluble hydroxides, such as $Mg(OH)_2$. These antacids neutralize stomach acid, forming water and a salt. Other antacids contain carbonates. These compounds react with acid, forming a salt, carbon dioxide, and water. Some medications work by decreasing the amount of stomach acid produced.

All antacids reduce the amount of acid, bringing relief.

1. Write a balanced chemical equation for the reaction between magnesium hydroxide and stomach acid.

2. Why do you think you should be careful not to use too many antacids?

On a sheet of paper, write the word or phrase from the Word Bank that completes each sentence.

1. A(n) _____ has a known concentration.

2. A(n) _____ is a method for determining the molarity of an acid or base.

3. When all of the acid in a neutralization reaction has reacted with all of the base, the reaction is at the _____.

On a sheet of paper, write the letter of the answer to each question. Refer to the following neutralization reaction.

$$KOH + HClO_4 \rightarrow H_2O + KClO_4$$

4. 75.0 mL of 0.250 M KOH is needed to neutralize 150. mL of $HClO_4$. What is the molarity of the $HClO_4$?

    A 0.250 M **B** 0.500 M **C** 0.125 M **D** 2.50 M

5. What volume of 0.300 M $HClO_4$ is needed to neutralize 82.4 mL of 0.150 M KOH?

    A 82.4 mL   **B** 41.2 mL   **C** 164.8 mL   **D** 0.300 L

6. 48.6 mL of 1.00 M $HClO_4$ is needed to neutralize 24.3 mL of KOH. What is the molarity of the KOH?

    A 2.00 M **B** 1.00 M **C** 0.500 M **D** 1.18 M

Critical Thinking

On a sheet of paper, write the answer to each question.

7. Describe the steps involved in a titration.

8. What is an indicator, and how is it used?

9. Predict the products of the following acid-base reaction. Write the name and formula of each product.
$$Mg(OH)_2 + 2HNO_3 \rightarrow$$

10. In a titration using phenolphthalein, a chemist places a piece of white paper under the flask. Why?

Materials

- safety goggles
- lab coat or apron
- gloves
- 3 125-mL Erlenmeyer flasks
- 2 100-mL beakers
- 2 50-mL burets
- buret clamp
- ring stand
- 80 mL of distilled white vinegar
- phenolphthalein solution in a dropper bottle
- 80 mL of standardized NaOH solution
- piece of white paper
- grease pencil
- distilled water
- 10-mL graduated cylinder

Titrating the Acid in Vinegar

When apple cider ferments, it sometimes forms acetic acid, $HC_2H_3O_2$. Vinegar is dilute acetic acid. Can you use titration to find the molarity of the acetic acid in vinegar? You will find out in this investigation.

Procedure

1. To record your data, make a data table like the one shown at the top of the next page.

2. Put on safety goggles, a lab coat or apron, and gloves.

3. Label one beaker and one buret *NaOH*; label the other beaker and buret *vinegar*. Use the two beakers to get about 80 mL each of the vinegar and the NaOH solution. Set up the burets as shown on the next page. Fill them according to your teacher's instructions. **Safety Alert: Be careful when working with glassware and the solutions. Avoid skin contact with the solutions.**

4. In your data table, record the initial readings of both burets. Use the vinegar buret to add approximately 10 mL of vinegar to a flask. Record the final reading of this buret. Add about 10 mL of distilled water and two drops of phenolphthalein to the vinegar in the flask.

5. Use the NaOH buret to add the standardized solution to the vinegar solution in a slow, steady stream of drops, while gently swirling the flask. When the pink color in the flask begins to last longer, add the NaOH solution one drop at a time, swirling the flask between drops.

Trial	Vinegar (mL)			NaOH Solution (mL)		
	Initial Buret Reading	Final Buret Reading	Volume Used	Initial Buret Reading	Final Buret Reading	Volume Used
1						
2						
3						

6. When the pink color remains in the solution, stop adding NaOH. You have reached the end point. Record the final reading of the NaOH buret.

7. Repeat the procedure two more times using the other flasks.

Cleanup/Disposal

Clean the glassware and return the equipment. Dispose of the solutions in a proper waste container. Clean your work area and wash your hands.

Analysis

1. From the buret readings, calculate the NaOH volume and vinegar volume used in each trial.

2. What is the molarity of the standardized NaOH? For each trial, calculate the molarity of the vinegar.

3. What is the average molarity of the vinegar? Why is it useful to have more than one trial and average the results?

Conclusions

1. Why is it important for a producer of vinegar to check its molarity?

2. Why could you add water to the vinegar sample without changing the results?

Explore Further

Repeat the investigation with wine vinegar or cider vinegar. What problem do you have that you did not have with white vinegar?

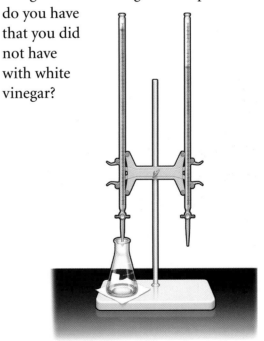

pH

A way of describing the H^{1+} concentration of a solution; the pH scale ranges from 0 to 14

Math Tip

Log is short for "logarithm." The log of a number is the exponent to which a base number (usually 10) is raised to equal the original number. For example, the log of 3 is 0.48 because $10^{0.48} = 3$.

You may have heard that acids and bases have something to do with **pH.** What is pH? It is a way of describing the H^{1+} concentration of a solution. pH values usually range from 0 to 14. Acids have a pH less than 7, and bases have a pH greater than 7. pH values have no unit, so what do they mean?

pH values describe only aqueous solutions. Water can act as an acid or a base. Recall that acids are proton (H^{1+}) donors, and bases are proton (H^{1+}) acceptors. In any aqueous solution, a small number of water molecules ionize, or break apart into ions. This is a reversible reaction:

$$H_2O(l) \rightleftharpoons H^{1+}(aq) + OH^{1-}(aq)$$

The equilibrium concentrations of H^{1+} and OH^{1-} ions are related by an equilibrium constant called K_w. The equilibrium expression for the ionization of water is

$$K_w = [H^{1+}][OH^{1-}]$$

Remember that brackets indicate the molarity of whatever is written inside the brackets. Water, a liquid, is left out of the expression. At 25°C, $K_w = 1.00 \times 10^{-14}$. In pure water, the concentration of H^{1+} ions equals the concentration of OH^{1-} ions. If $K_w = 1.00 \times 10^{-14}$, this means that $[H^{1+}] = 1.00 \times 10^{-7}\ M$ and $[OH^{1-}] = 1.00 \times 10^{-7}\ M$.

$$1.00 \times 10^{-14} = (1.00 \times 10^{-7}\ M)(1.00 \times 10^{-7}\ M)$$

In solutions of acids, $[H^{1+}]$ is very large since acids donate these ions. How does this affect the equilibrium between water and its ions? According to Le Chatelier's principle, a large $[H^{1+}]$ means $[OH^{1-}]$ is very small. In solutions of bases, $[OH^{1-}]$ is very large, so $[H^{1+}]$ is very small. Because many H^{1+} and OH^{1-} concentrations are expressed in scientific notation with negative exponents, the pH scale was developed. pH is a simple way to describe the very wide range of H^{1+} concentration among acid and base solutions. pH is the negative logarithm of $[H^{1+}]$. This is expressed as

$$pH = -\log[H^{1+}]$$

Acidic

Having a pH below 7

Basic

Having a pH above 7; alkaline

Basic solutions are also called alkaline solutions because alkali metals react with water to form bases. For example, sodium reacts with water to form sodium hydroxide and hydrogen.

pH values have no unit. However, to calculate pH, $[H^{1+}]$ must be in molarity. If you know $[H^{1+}]$, you can find the pH. To calculate the log of a number, you will need a calculator with a log button.

What is the pH of pure water? You know that pure water has an H^{1+} concentration of 1.00×10^{-7} M. This means that

$$pH = -\log[H^{1+}] = -\log(1.00 \times 10^{-7} \, M) = 7$$

The pH of pure water is 7. A pH of 7 is a neutral pH. Acids have pH values below 7, and bases have pH values above 7. Any substance that has a pH below 7 in aqueous solution is considered **acidic,** as Figure 17.3.1 shows. Any substance with a pH above 7 in aqueous solution is **basic.** Substances with a pH of exactly 7 are neither acidic nor basic—they are neutral.

A solution of pH 5 and a solution of pH 4 are both acidic. However, the pH 4 solution has 10 times the H^{1+} concentration of the pH 5 solution.

pH = 4 means: $[H^{1+}] = 10^{-4} \, M = 0.0001 \, M$

pH = 5 means: $[H^{1+}] = 10^{-5} \, M = 0.00001 \, M$

Each difference of 1 unit on the pH scale represents a tenfold decrease or increase in $[H^{1+}]$.

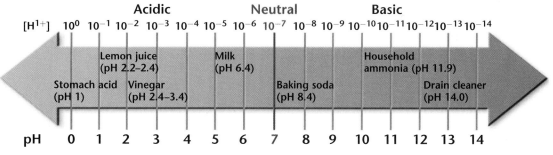

Figure 17.3.1 *Pure water has a pH of 7. Compared to water, acids have lower pH values, and bases have higher pH values.*

Link to >>>

Health

The pH of a spa or swimming pool must be slightly basic, between 7.3 and 7.6. The pH must be high enough to prevent the growth of potentially harmful organisms and low enough to not irritate human tissue. The effectiveness of water sanitizers, such as chlorine, is also affected by the pH of the solution.

Example 1 In a solution of 0.0100 *M* HCl, $[H^{1+}] = 0.0100$ *M*. What is the pH of the solution?

Read You are asked to calculate the pH of an HCl solution.

Plan Use the given molarity in the equation, $pH = -\log[H^{1+}]$.

Solve Use a calculator to find the negative log of 0.0100. The unit is dropped.
$$pH = -\log[H^{1+}] = -\log(0.0100) = 2$$

Reflect The answer makes sense. The pH of an acid solution is less than 7.

Practice A basic solution has an H^{1+} concentration of 1.0×10^{-11} *M*. What is its pH?

The two concentrations, $[H^{1+}]$ and $[OH^{1-}]$, are related by the equilibrium expression for the ionization of water:

$$K_w = [H^{1+}][OH^{1-}] = 1.00 \times 10^{-14}$$

If you know $[OH^{1-}]$ for a solution, you can calculate $[H^{1+}]$.

Example 2 A solution has a hydrogen ion concentration of 0.0100 *M*. What is its hydroxide ion concentration in molarity? Is the solution acidic or basic?

Read You are given $[H^{1+}]$ for a solution. You are asked to calculate $[OH^{1-}]$ and tell if the solution is acidic or basic.

Plan Use the equation for K_w. Substitute the value 0.0100 *M* for $[H^{1+}]$. Its unit can be dropped. However, add the unit molarity to your answer.

Solve Solve for $[OH^{1-}]$ using a calculator.
$$1.00 \times 10^{-14} = (0.0100)[OH^{1-}]$$
$$[OH^{1-}] = 1.00 \times 10^{-12} \text{ } M$$

This is not a solution of pH 12! Since $pH = -\log[H^{1+}]$, the pH of the solution is $pH = -\log(0.0100) = 2$. The solution is very acidic.

Reflect You would expect $[H^{1+}]$ to be much larger than $[OH^{1-}]$ in an acidic solution.

Practice A solution has an H^{1+} concentration of 1.0×10^{-11} *M*. What is its $[OH^{1-}]$? Is the solution acidic or basic?

Math Tip

Most scientific calculators have a button labeled "log." The second function of this same button is often labeled "10^x." It is easy to confuse the log and 10^x functions on a calculator. To enter a number that has an exponent, such as $10^{-2.5}$, use the 10^x function. To calculate a log, such as $\log(0.0100)$, use the log function.

Litmus is a mixture of dyes extracted from a species of lichen. It is blue when placed in a basic solution and red when placed in an acidic solution. Remember "blue in base" and "red in acid." Litmus paper is made by soaking paper in a litmus solution and allowing it to dry.

If you are given the pH of a solution, you can calculate its $[H^{1+}]$. The equation $pH = -\log[H^{1+}]$ can be rewritten as
$$[H^{1+}] = 10^{-pH}$$

To use this equation, you will need a calculator with a "10^x" button. This is often the second function of the log button.

Example 3   What is $[H^{1+}]$ for a solution with a pH of 2.5? Is the solution acidic or basic?

Read   You are given a pH value. You are asked to calculate $[H^{1+}]$ and tell if the solution is acidic or basic.

Plan   Use the equation, $[H^{1+}] = 10^{-pH}$.

Solve   Substitute the given pH into the equation. Use a calculator to solve. The answer is a concentration, so include the unit molarity.

$[H^{1+}] = 10^{-2.5}$
$[H^{1+}] = 0.0032\ M$

Since the solution's pH is 2.5, it is acidic.

Reflect   When calculating a concentration from a pH value, the number of significant figures in the answer should equal the number in the pH value. In this example, $[H^{1+}]$ has 2 significant figures because the given pH value has 2 significant figures.

Practice   What is $[H^{1+}]$ for a solution with a pH of 9.8? Is the solution acidic or basic?

Link to ➤➤➤

Biology

Plants are sensitive to soil pH. Most crop plants, such as potatoes, grow best in slightly acidic soil. Some plants, such as blueberries, require a more acidic soil. Clematis is one of the few plants that grow best in basic soil. Lime can be added to neutralize the acid in soil that is too acidic. Decomposing plant material, such as peat moss, makes soil more acidic.

Hydrogen ion concentrations can vary from 18 M to 1×10^{-15} M. This means that pH values can actually vary from -1.3 to 15.

For any aqueous solution, you can use the following equations to calculate pH, $[H^{1+}]$, and $[OH^{1-}]$.

$$pH = -\log[H^{1+}]$$

$$[H^{1+}] = 10^{-pH}$$

$$[H^{1+}] = \frac{1.00 \times 10^{-14}}{[OH^{1-}]}$$

$$[OH^{1-}] = \frac{1.00 \times 10^{-14}}{[H^{1+}]}$$

▼◄ ▲ ▼◄ ▲ ▼◄ ▲ ▼◄ ▲ ▼◄ ▲ ▼◄ ▲ ▼◄ ▲ ▼◄ ▲ ▼◄ ▲ ▼◄ ▲ ▼◄ ▲ ▼◄ ▲ ▼◄ ▲ ▼◄ ▲ ▼◄ ▲ ▼◄ ▲ ▼◄ ▲ ▼

Science at Work

Cosmetic Chemist

Cosmetic chemists are involved in all areas of cosmetics development. They control dyes and scents, making sure the products are appealing, but safe. They make sure the products do what they are supposed to do.

One important job of cosmetic chemists is to control the pH of cosmetics. A cosmetic with an incorrect pH can damage skin or hair. For example, it is important that shampoos be slightly acidic. Shampoos with too high of a pH cause the hair shaft to swell. This pushes out the outer layer of hair, called the cuticle. Basic ingredients in hair products can also dissolve some of the cuticle. Acidic ingredients shrink the hair shaft, making

the cuticle lie flat. When a hair product is labeled "pH balanced," it does not mean that the product is neutral. It means that the pH is correct for healthy hair.

Cosmetic chemists need a college education with courses in biology and chemistry. Additional training on the job is also necessary.

Lesson 3   R E V I E W

Word Bank

acidic

basic

pH

On a sheet of paper, write the word from the Word Bank that completes each sentence.

1. A solution with a pH of 4 is _____.

2. A measure of the concentration of H^{1+} ions in solution is _____.

3. If the OH^{1-} ion concentration in a solution is 10^{-3} M, the solution is _____.

On a sheet of paper, write the letter of the answer to each question.

4. What is the pH of a solution with $[H^{1+}] = 5.7 \times 10^{-5}$ M?

    A 1.8×10^{-10} **B** 9.8   **C** 14   **D** 4.2

5. What is the $[OH^{1-}]$ of a solution that has a $[H^{1+}]$ of 8.3×10^{-11} M?

    A 3.9 M **B** 1.2×10^{-4} M **C** 10.1 M **D** 1×10^{-14} M

6. What is the pH of a solution with $[OH^{1-}] = 7.1 \times 10^{-3}$ M?

    A 2.1   **B** 1.4×10^{-12} **C** 11.9   **D** 14

Critical Thinking

On a sheet of paper, write the missing information in each row of the table. Then write the answer to question 10.

	Solution pH	$[H^{1+}]$ (M)	$[OH^{1-}]$ (M)	Acidic or Basic?
7.	2			
8.	6			
9.	8			

10. How did you determine whether the solutions in the above table were acidic or basic? Explain in terms of pH and ion concentration.

Objectives

After reading this lesson, you should be able to

◆ describe what happens when strong acids and bases dissolve in water

◆ describe what happens when weak acids and bases dissolve in water

◆ compare strong and weak acids and bases in terms of pH

Strong acid

An acid that completely ionizes in water

Strong base

A base that completely dissociates in water

When molecules form ions, the process is called ionization. When ionic compounds break apart into ions, the process is called dissociation.

Certain acids and bases are stronger than others. Vinegar and hydrochloric acid are both acids. Vinegar is often used to make salad dressings. However, hydrochloric acid is most definitely not safe to consume.

Strong Acids and Bases

The strength of an Arrhenius acid is based on its ability to ionize, or break apart into H^{1+} ions and anions. There is a strong attraction between acid molecules and water molecules. Both are polar. This attraction causes acid molecules to ionize in water. Acids that completely ionize in water are **strong acids.** In an aqueous solution of a strong acid, there are few acid molecules—nearly all of them have ionized. There are six well-known strong acids. Their ionization reactions are given below.

$$HCl(aq) \rightarrow H^{1+}(aq) + Cl^{1-}(aq)$$
$$HBr(aq) \rightarrow H^{1+}(aq) + Br^{1-}(aq)$$
$$HI(aq) \rightarrow H^{1+}(aq) + I^{1-}(aq)$$
$$HNO_3(aq) \rightarrow H^{1+}(aq) + NO_3^{1-}(aq)$$
$$HClO_4(aq) \rightarrow H^{1+}(aq) + ClO_4^{1-}(aq)$$
$$H_2SO_4(aq) \rightarrow H^{1+}(aq) + HSO_4^{1-}(aq)$$

Most acids are molecular compounds. Their molecules ionize when dissolved in water. Many bases are ionic compounds. Their formula units dissociate when dissolved in water. A few bases, such as ammonia, are molecular compounds that ionize when dissolved in water.

Dissolved **strong bases** dissociate completely in water. For example, when dissolved in water, the formula units of sodium hydroxide completely dissociate into Na^{1+} and OH^{1-} ions. Some strong bases are not very soluble in water, so few formula units dissolve. However, these bases are still considered strong because all of the formula units that do dissolve completely dissociate. The dissociation reactions of some strong Arrhenius bases are given on the next page.

$$LiOH(aq) \rightarrow Li^{1+}(aq) + OH^{1-}(aq)$$
$$NaOH(aq) \rightarrow Na^{1+}(aq) + OH^{1-}(aq)$$
$$KOH(aq) \rightarrow K^{1+}(aq) + OH^{1-}(aq)$$
$$Ca(OH)_2(aq) \rightarrow Ca^{2+}(aq) + 2OH^{1-}(aq)$$
$$Sr(OH)_2(aq) \rightarrow Sr^{2+}(aq) + 2OH^{1-}(aq)$$
$$Ba(OH)_2(aq) \rightarrow Ba^{2+}(aq) + 2OH^{1-}(aq)$$
$$Mg(OH)_2(aq) \rightarrow Mg^{2+}(aq) + 2OH^{1-}(aq)$$

The last four bases are only partially soluble in water.

Weak Acids and Bases

The strength of acids and bases varies greatly. All acids and bases that are not considered strong are called weak. When dissolved in water, **weak acids** and **weak bases** do not ionize as much as strong acids and strong bases. Because of this, any solution of a weak acid or base is an equilibrium system. An equilibrium exists between the weak acid or base and its conjugate. In solutions of strong acids or bases, there is no equilibrium since ionization is complete.

A good example of a weak acid is acetic acid, $HC_2H_3O_2$. Vinegar is a dilute solution of this acid. In a 1.0 M solution of acetic acid, only about 0.5% of the acid molecules ionize. In other words, only 5 out of 1,000 acid molecules break apart into H^{1+} and $C_2H_3O_2^{1-}$ ions.

Figure 17.4.1 compares acetic acid to hydrochloric acid, a strong acid. In water, almost all HCl molecules ionize into H^{1+} and Cl^{1-} ions. A 1.0 M solution of HCl has a pH of 0, but a 1.0 M solution of acetic acid has a pH of 2.4. Weak acids do not produce nearly as many hydrogen ions as strong acids. The pH of a weak acid is higher than the pH of a strong acid with the same concentration. No matter how weak, acid solutions always have pH values under 7. Other common weak acids are citric acid (used in many soft drinks) and ascorbic acid (vitamin C).

Figure 17.4.1
Strong acids like HCl completely ionize in water. Weak acids like $HC_2H_3O_2$ do not ionize much in water.

Weak acid

An acid that partially ionizes in water

Weak base

A base that partially dissociates in water

Because they form ions in solution, both acids and bases are electrolytes. Remember that an electrolyte is a substance that conducts electricity when dissolved in water. The electricity is conducted by ions in the solution. Strong acids and bases are strong electrolytes. Weak acids and bases are weak electrolytes.

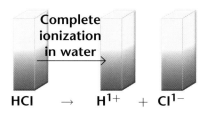

Myth: All hydrogen atoms in an acid molecule form H^{1+} ions in solution.

Fact: In some acids that contain only carbon, oxygen, and hydrogen, some of the hydrogen atoms are bonded to carbon atoms. These hydrogen atoms do not form H^{1+} ions in solution. An example is acetic acid, $HC_2H_3O_2$. Three of the hydrogen atoms are bonded to a carbon atom, and they do not form H^{1+} ions.

Like weak acids, weak bases do not completely ionize in solution. Ammonia, NH_3, is a good example. In a 1.0 *M* NH_3 solution, only about 0.5% of ammonia molecules ionize. 1.0 *M* NH_3 has a pH of 11.6. Compare this to a 1.0 *M* solution of NaOH, a strong base. Its pH is 14.0. The pH of a weak base is lower than the pH of a strong base with the same concentration. All solutions of bases, however, have a pH above 7. Figure 17.4.2 compares the pH values of strong and weak acids and bases of the same concentration.

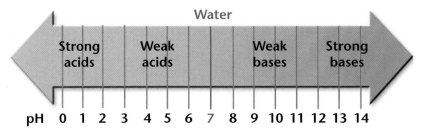

Figure 17.4.2 *A strong base always has a higher pH than a weak base of the same molarity.*

Although weak acids and weak bases do not completely ionize, they are extremely important, especially in biological systems. The pH of the blood in your body is based on the behavior of weak acids and bases. The pH of your favorite shampoo or soft drink depends on weak acids and bases as well. The venom of fire ants is formic acid. Erupting volcanoes, such as the one in Figure 17.4.3, often release hydrogen sulfide gas into the atmosphere. Both formic acid and hydrogen sulfide are weak acids. *Weak* does not mean unimportant when it refers to acids and bases.

Figure 17.4.3 *Sulfur is dissolved in magma deep inside a volcano. As the magma works its way upward, the dissolved sulfur can escape in the form of hydrogen sulfide, H_2S, a weak acid.*

Lesson 4   R E V I E W

Word Bank

dissociates

strong base

weak acid

On a sheet of paper, write the word or phrase from the Word Bank that completes each sentence.

1. When an ionic compound breaks apart into ions, it _____.

2. $Ca(OH)_2$ is an example of a _____.

3. HF is an example of a _____.

On a sheet of paper, write the letter of the answer to each question.

4. Which substance could be used to make a 1.0 *M* solution that has a pH near 14?

   A HI   **B** $Al(OH)_3$ **C** KOH   **D** H_2S

5. Which substance could be used to make a 0.1 *M* solution that has a pH of 1?

   A NaOH   **B** $HClO_4$ **C** NH_3 **D** H_3PO_4

6. Which substance could be used to make a 1.0 *M* solution with a pH close to 5?

   A HCN   **B** HNO_3 **C** NH_3 **D** $Mg(OH)_2$

Critical Thinking

On a sheet of paper, write the answer to each question.

7. How are weak acids different from strong acids?

8. Strong acids have a pH that is fairly low. Why do weak acids have higher pH values?

9. How are weak bases different from strong bases?

10. Strong bases have a high pH. Why do weak bases have lower pH values?

Materials

- safety goggles
- lab coat or apron
- gloves
- 100 mL of 2.0 M acetic acid ($HC_2H_3O_2$)
- 100 mL of 2.0 M hydrochloric acid (HCl)
- 6 100-mL beakers
- 50-mL graduated cylinder
- distilled water
- wash bottle
- conductivity tester
- grease pencil

Strong and Weak Acids

Strong acids completely ionize in water. Weak acids ionize only slightly. How well do acidic solutions conduct an electric current? In this investigation, you will relate the strengths and concentrations of acids to their electrical conductivity.

Procedure

1. You will determine how well six acid solutions conduct a current by whether a lightbulb in a circuit lights up brightly, dimly, or not at all. Read the entire procedure. Then make a table you can use to record your data.

2. The equation, $M_1V_1 = M_2V_2$, can be used to make dilutions. Write a procedure to show how you can make 100. mL each of 1.0 M HCl and 1.0 M $HC_2H_3O_2$ from the 2.0 M solutions. Then write a procedure for making 100. mL each of 0.10 M HCl and 0.10 M $HC_2H_3O_2$ from the 1.0 M solutions. Include safety alerts in your procedure.

3. Have your teacher approve your procedure.

4. Put on safety goggles, a lab coat or apron, and gloves. **Safety Alert: Acids can damage skin and clothing.**

5. Prepare the four new solutions according to your procedure. Use labeled beakers to store the six solutions.

6. Use the conductivity tester to test each solution, as shown. For each test, record the brightness of the bulb in your data table. Wash the wires of the tester with distilled water between tests.

Cleanup/Disposal

Wash the glassware and return all equipment. Dispose of the solutions according to your teacher's instructions. Clean your work area and wash your hands.

Analysis

1. For which solutions did the bulb burn brightly?

2. As the concentration of the HCl and $HC_2H_3O_2$ decreased, what happened to the conductivity?

Conclusions

1. Explain why the concentration of an acid affects its conductivity.

2. Based on your data, is hydrochloric acid strong or weak? Is acetic acid strong or weak?

Explore Further

List common acidic solutions you have at home. Predict whether these acids are strong or weak. If your teacher approves, use the conductivity tester to test these solutions.

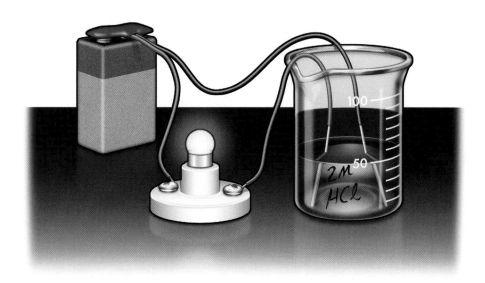

NaCl is the main substance in common table salt. Most table salt also contains KI. This is added because iodine helps to maintain thyroid function. People who are concerned about the amount of sodium in table salt may choose a "no-salt" salt substitute. The main substance in a salt substitute is KCl. However, NaCl, KI, and KCl are all salts in the world of chemistry. Salts are composed of the cation of a base and the anion of an acid.

Neutral Salts

In a reaction between a strong acid and a strong base, the products are water and a salt. When this salt is dissolved in water, it has a pH near 7.0. The salt produced from a strong acid and a strong base is a **neutral salt.** An example of a neutral salt is NaCl, common table salt. NaCl is produced from the reaction between HCl and NaOH:

$$HCl + NaOH \rightarrow H_2O + NaCl$$

Because both the acid and the base are strong, the salt is neutral. When either the acid or the base is weak, the salt produced is not neutral.

Acidic Salts

The salt formed by a strong acid and weak base is an **acidic salt.** An example is ammonium chloride, NH_4Cl. It forms when HCl (a strong acid) reacts with NH_3 (a weak base). This salt is soluble in water, so it quickly dissociates into its ions.

$$H^{1+}(aq) + Cl^{1-}(aq) + NH_3(aq) \rightarrow NH_4^{1+}(aq) + Cl^{1-}(aq)$$

In this reaction, the chloride ion is a spectator ion. The overall reaction, without the spectator ion, can occur in reverse. In the reverse reaction, the acidic salt produces a slightly acidic solution.

$$NH_4^{1+} \rightleftharpoons NH_3 + H^{1+}$$

Only the NH_4^{1+} ion reacts. At equilibrium, the amount of H^{1+} is very small. This H^{1+} concentration creates a slightly acidic solution.

Neutral salt

The salt produced from a strong acid and a strong base

Acidic salt

The salt produced from a strong acid and a weak base

Basic salt

The salt produced from a weak acid and a strong base

Link to ➤➤➤

Earth Science

The flowers on hydrangea plants are blue when the soil is acidic. They are pink in basic soil. The difference in color depends on the amount of available aluminum in the soil. The earth's crust contains a large amount of aluminum. Because acids react with aluminum, more aluminum is available in solution in acidic soil. Hydrangeas are blue when more aluminum is present.

Basic Salts

The salt formed by a weak acid and strong base is a **basic salt.** An example is magnesium carbonate, $MgCO_3$. This salt is used in some antacids. It is also used as a sweat absorber in sports such as gymnastics and rock climbing. $MgCO_3$ forms when $Mg(OH)_2$ (a strong base) reacts with H_2CO_3 (a weak acid). When a basic salt reacts in the reverse reaction in this equilibrium system, a slightly basic solution forms.

$$CO_3{}^{2-} + H_2O \rightleftharpoons HCO_3{}^{1-} + OH^{1-}$$

In this reverse reaction, Mg^{2+} is a spectator ion and is not shown. The $CO_3{}^{2-}$ ion reacts with water. At equilibrium, the concentration of OH^{1-} is very small. The solution is slightly basic.

In general, a weak acid and a weak base do not react much at all, so not much salt forms.

★★★★★★★★★★★★★★★★★★★★★★★★★★★★★★★★★★★★

Achievements in Science

Salts That Clean

Soaps are salts formed by the reaction of a strong base and a fatty acid. The process of making soap involves heating a fat with the sodium hydroxide from ashes. This process has been used for thousands of years. Scientists have found soaplike materials that were made about 2800 B.C.

Although soap was used in isolated cultures, its use was not widespread until about 2,000 years ago. Roman civilization greatly valued cleanliness and the use of soap. After the fall of Rome, bathing declined. The resulting unsanitary conditions contributed to the plagues of the Middle Ages. By the 1600s, cleanliness and bathing once again became important. By the mid-1800s, soapmaking was one of the fastest growing industries in the United States.

One problem with using soap in hard water is the formation of soap scum. Detergents were developed in the early 1900s. The products that detergents form with hard water are more soluble than products formed by soaps. As a result, detergents have now replaced most soaps.

Example 1 What salt is produced by each set of reactants? Is the salt acidic, basic, or neutral?

$$HCN + LiOH \rightarrow$$
$$HNO_3 + CuOH \rightarrow$$
$$HI + KOH \rightarrow$$

Read You need to predict the salt formed in three acid-base reactions. You also need to determine if each salt is acidic, basic, or neutral.

Plan Recall the acid-base combination that produces each kind of salt:

strong acid + strong base → neutral salt
weak acid + strong base → basic salt
strong acid + weak base → acidic salt

Strong acids and bases are listed in Lesson 4. If an acid or base is not listed there, it is considered weak.

Solve The products of many acid-base reactions are water and a salt. To determine the formula of the salt, combine the cation of the base and the anion of the acid.

$$\underset{\text{weak}}{HCN} + \underset{\text{strong}}{LiOH} \rightarrow H_2O + \underset{\text{basic salt}}{LiCN}$$

$$\underset{\text{strong}}{HNO_3} + \underset{\text{weak}}{CuOH} \rightarrow H_2O + \underset{\text{acidic salt}}{CuNO_3}$$

$$\underset{\text{strong}}{HI} + \underset{\text{strong}}{KOH} \rightarrow H_2O + \underset{\text{neutral salt}}{KI}$$

Reflect Of the three salts, only KI has no effect on the pH of the solution at equilibrium.

Practice What salt is produced by the reactants HF and $Mg(OH)_2$? Is the salt acidic, basic, or neutral?

Buffers

A **buffer** is a solution that resists a change in pH when a small amount of an acid or base is added. A buffer contains particles that react with H^{1+} ions as well as particles that react with OH^{1-} ions. There are two ways to create a buffer:

- Mix a weak acid with one of its basic salts.
- Mix a weak base with one of its acidic salts.

For example, NH_3 (a weak base) and NH_4Cl create a buffer.

Link to ⪢⪢⪢

Biology

If medications are acidic or basic, they can cause stomach upset or other problems. As a result, buffers are sometimes added to medications. Aspirin is an acid that is commonly buffered. When buffered aspirin is ingested, the pH of the digestive system is nearly unchanged.

Another buffer is the mixture of acetic acid, $HC_2H_3O_2$, and sodium acetate, $NaC_2H_3O_2$. In this buffer, an equilibrium exists between the acid and its conjugate base, $C_2H_3O_2{}^{1-}$ (from the salt). The sodium cation is a spectator ion.

$$HC_2H_3O_2 \rightleftharpoons C_2H_3O_2{}^{1-} + H^{1+}$$

If an acid is added to this buffer, the acetate ion reacts with the extra hydrogen ions:

$$C_2H_3O_2{}^{1-} + H^{1+} \rightarrow HC_2H_3O_2$$

By "capturing" the extra H^{1+} ions, the pH of the solution does not change much, even if moderate amounts of acid are added. If a base is added to this buffer, the acetic acid reacts with the extra OH^{1-} ions:

$$HC_2H_3O_2 + OH^{1-} \rightarrow H_2O + C_2H_3O_2{}^{1-}$$

Again, the pH does not change greatly, even if moderate amounts of base are added. If the same amount of an acid or base were added to pure water, the pH would change significantly. There is no buffer system in pure water to counteract the acid or base.

Spotlight on Sodium

11
Na
Sodium
23.0

Sodium is a very active alkali metal. Sodium is so active that it is found in nature only in compounds. It is never found as a free element. Sodium conducts electricity well and has other metallic properties, such as luster. However, it cannot be used in many of the ways other metals are used because it is too soft and reactive.

Sodium forms ionic compounds with nonmetals and polyatomic anions. All sodium compounds are soluble in water, and these compounds dissociate to form sodium cations and other anions. Sodium ions are essential for good health. Sodium and potassium ions are necessary for proper motion of nerve impulses and water retention by cells.

All alkali metals form water-soluble bases when placed in water. Sodium reacts with water to form sodium hydroxide and hydrogen gas.

Interesting Fact: Sodium is so reactive that it is often stored in kerosene.

Lesson 5   R E V I E W

Word Bank

acidic salt

buffer

neutral salt

On a sheet of paper, write the word or phrase from the Word Bank that completes each sentence.

1. The salt produced from a reaction between a strong acid and a weak base is a(n) _____.

2. The salt produced from a reaction between a strong acid and a strong base is a(n) _____.

3. A solution that resists a change in pH when a small amount of an acid or base is added is a(n) _____.

For each acid-base pair, determine the kind of salt formed when they react. On a sheet of paper, write *neutral salt*, *acidic salt*, or *basic salt*. If both the acid and base are weak, write *cannot determine*.

4. H_2S and KOH

5. HI and $Ca(OH)_2$

6. HF and NH_3

Critical Thinking

On a sheet of paper, write the answer to each question.

7. Why is a buffer able to withstand the addition of a small amount of acid or base without changing pH?

8. Predict the products of the following neutralization reaction. What kind of salt is produced?
$H_2SO_4 + LiOH \rightarrow$

9. Predict the products of the following neutralization reaction. What kind of salt is produced?
$HNO_3 + Al(OH)_3 \rightarrow$

10. What forms when a weak acid and a weak base are mixed together?

Acid Precipitation

All rain is slightly acidic because carbon dioxide and water form carbonic acid in rainwater. This acid is weak, and the solution is dilute. Normal rain has a pH of about 5.6. Substances in the environment can neutralize this amount of acid. This precipitation is not acidic enough to harm the environment. However, some rain is acidic enough to damage organisms and other parts of the environment. Acid precipitation is the name given to rain, snow, or sleet that is more acidic than normal rain.

Acid precipitation forms when certain pollutants in the air dissolve in rainwater. Most of these pollutants are oxides of nitrogen and sulfur that are produced when fossil fuels burn. When these oxides dissolve in rainwater, they form sulfuric acid and nitric acid.

Acid precipitation can make water in lakes and streams acidic, killing organisms that live in the water. It can also damage plant life and react with many types of stone. Acid rain damaged this forest on Mt. Mitchell in North Carolina.

The best solution is to prevent acid precipitation from occurring. Areas where air pollutants are strictly controlled have less acid precipitation. Materials that neutralize the acids may also be used. For example, lime, CaO, neutralizes acids. Sometimes lime is added to soil and water to reduce the effects of acid rain.

1. A sample of rainwater is tested and found to have a pH of 5.9. Another sample from a different location has a pH of 4.5. Which sample is an example of acid rain? Explain your answer.

2. List two things that citizens can do to reduce the amount of acid precipitation.

- In solution, an Arrhenius acid produces H^{1+} ions, and Arrhenius bases produce OH^{1-} ions. Brønsted-Lowry acids donate protons and become conjugate bases. Brønsted-Lowry bases accept protons and become conjugate acids.

- The reaction of an acid and a base is called a neutralization reaction.

- A titration uses a neutralization reaction to determine the molarity of an unknown acid or base. For a 1:1 acid:base mole ratio, the equation $M_aV_a = M_bV_b$ is used to determine the unknown molarity.

- The equilibrium expression for the ionization of water is
$K_w = [H^{1+}][OH^{1-}]$
At 25°C, $K_w = 1.00 \times 10^{-14}$.

- The pH scale ranges from 0 to 14 and shows how acidic or basic a solution is. A solution with a pH below 7 is acidic; a solution with a pH above 7 is basic; a solution with a pH of 7 is neutral.

- The following equations can be used for any aqueous solution at 25°C:
$pH = -\log[H^{1+}]$
$[H^{1+}] = 10^{-pH}$
$[OH^{1-}] = \dfrac{1.00 \times 10^{-14}}{[H^{1+}]}$

- Most acids are molecular compounds. Strong acids completely ionize in water. Weak acids partially ionize in water.

- Most bases are ionic compounds. Strong bases completely dissociate in water. Weak bases partially dissociate in water.

- A strong acid and a strong base produce a neutral salt. A strong acid and a weak base produce an acidic salt. A weak acid and a strong base produce a basic salt.

- When a small amount of acid or base is added to a buffer, its pH changes little or not at all. Buffers are made by mixing a weak acid with a basic salt, or a weak base with an acidic salt.

Vocabulary

acid, 664	buffer, 690	indicator, 670	strong acid, 682
acidic, 677	conjugate acid, 665	neutral salt, 688	strong base, 682
acidic salt, 688	conjugate base, 665	neutralization reaction, 669	titration, 670
base, 664	end point, 670		weak acid, 683
basic, 677	equivalence point, 669	pH, 676	weak base, 683
basic salt, 689		standard solution, 670	

Chapter 17 R E V I E W

Vocabulary Review

Continued on next page

Word Bank

acid
base
basic salt
buffer
conjugate base
end point
indicator
neutral salt
pH
standard solution
strong base
titration
weak acid

1. The solution of known concentration in a titration is called a(n) _____.

2. A(n) _____ is a proton donor.

3. A measure of the concentration of hydrogen ions in solution is _____.

4. When the indicator changes color in a titration, the titration has reached the _____.

5. When an acid loses a proton, it becomes a(n) _____.

6. A strong acid and a strong base react to form a(n) _____.

7. A substance that changes color in the presence of an acid or base is a(n) _____.

8. A(n) _____ resists a change in pH when a small amount of an acid or base is added.

9. A(n) _____ is a proton acceptor.

10. A(n) _____ involves an indicator and a standard solution and is used to determine the concentration of an unknown acid or base.

11. A(n) _____ completely dissociates in water and has a high pH value.

12. A(n) _____ forms from the reaction between HNO_2 and $Ca(OH)_2$.

13. A(n) _____ ionizes only partially in solution.

Concept Review

On a sheet of paper, write the letter of the answer to each question. For questions 14–16, refer to the following equation.

$$C_5H_5N + HClO_2 \rightarrow C_5H_5NH^{1+} + ClO_2^{1-}$$

14. Which substance in the equation is the acid?

    A C_5H_5N **B** $HClO_2$ **C** $C_5H_5NH^{1+}$ **D** ClO_2^{1-}

15. Which substance in the equation is the conjugate acid?

    A C_5H_5N **B** $HClO_2$ **C** $C_5H_5NH^{1+}$ **D** ClO_2^{1-}

16. Which substance in the equation is the base?

    A C_5H_5N **B** $HClO_2$ **C** $C_5H_5NH^{1+}$ **D** ClO_2^{1-}

For questions 17–19, refer to the following equation.

$$KOH(aq) + HBr(aq) \rightarrow H_2O(l) + KBr(aq)$$

17. If 17.5 mL of 0.553 M KOH is needed to neutralize 25.0 mL of an HBr solution, what is the molarity of the HBr solution?

    A 242 M **B** 1.27 M **C** 0.790 M **D** 0.387 M

18. If 0.0812 L of 0.158 M KOH is needed to neutralize a sample of 0.275 M HBr, what is the sample's volume?

    A 0.0467 L   **B** 0.128 L   **C** 0.141 L   **D** 0.535 L

19. Which substance is the salt, and what kind of salt is it?

    A KOH, basic salt   **C** HBr, acidic salt

    B KBr, neutral salt   **D** KOH, neutral salt

Problem Solving

On a sheet of paper, write the answer to each problem.
Show any calculations.

20. Calculate the pH of a solution when
$[H^{1+}] = 2.5 \times 10^{-9}\ M$.

21. Calculate the pH of a solution that has
$[OH^{1-}] = 3.7 \times 10^{-3}\ M$.

22. 27.5 mL of 0.105 M NaOH is needed to neutralize 35.3 mL
of an HI solution. What is the molarity of the HI solution?
Show your work, including the balanced equation.

Critical Thinking

On a sheet of paper, write the answer to each question.

23. Fill in the missing data in the following table.

Solution pH	$[H^{1+}]$	$[OH^{1-}]$	Acidic or Basic?
	$3.7 \times 10^{-2}\ M$		
		$8.1 \times 10^{-5}\ M$	
5.3			
9.7			

24. What is the difference between a strong acid and a weak
acid? How does this difference affect the pH of acids?

25. What is the purpose of an indicator in a titration? What
would happen if an indicator were not added before
beginning a titration?

Test-Taking Tip When studying for a test, use a marker to highlight key words and
important concepts in your notes. For a final review, read what you
highlighted.

18 Electrochemistry

This blast furnace separates the element iron from iron ore. Iron ore contains iron oxides such as Fe_2O_3. The oxygen must be removed from these oxides by changing the iron cations to neutral atoms. This process is called reduction. At the same time, another substance must take on oxygen atoms, a process called oxidation. In Chapter 18, you will learn about oxidation and reduction reactions. You will also learn about many applications of these reactions.

Organize Your Thoughts

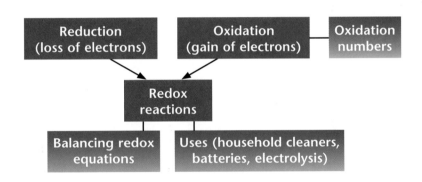

Reduction (loss of electrons)

Oxidation (gain of electrons)

Oxidation numbers

Redox reactions

Balancing redox equations

Uses (household cleaners, batteries, electrolysis)

Goals for Learning

◆ To define a redox reaction and assign oxidation numbers

◆ To use oxidation numbers to identify the oxidized and reduced reactants in a redox reaction

◆ To balance a redox reaction

◆ To describe some common uses of redox reactions

◆ To explain voltaic cells and predict their half-reactions

◆ To compare a voltaic cell and an electrolytic cell

◆ To describe how electrolysis is used in industry

Objectives

After reading this lesson, you should be able to

◆ define oxidation and reduction

◆ give the rules for determining oxidation numbers

◆ determine the oxidation number of each atom in a compound

Oxidation

A chemical reaction in which an atom or ion loses electrons

Reduction

A chemical reaction in which an atom or ion gains electrons

Redox reaction

An oxidation-reduction reaction

What do a battery, the Statue of Liberty, and bleach have in common? Each one involves the same kind of chemical reaction. When the early chemists were studying chemical reactions, they found that oxygen readily reacts with most other elements. Chemists referred to a reaction with oxygen as an oxidation reaction.

An oxygen atom is very electronegative—it has a strong ability to attract electrons of other atoms to itself, forming a negative charge. Other electronegative elements behave like oxygen. Today, chemists use the term **oxidation** to refer to any chemical reaction in which an atom or ion loses electrons. **Reduction** is just the opposite: It is a reaction in which an atom or ion gains electrons. Oxidation and reduction always occur together in a reaction. The electrons lost in oxidation are the same electrons gained in reduction. This kind of reaction is an oxidation-reduction reaction, often called a **redox reaction.** Many familiar reactions are redox reactions, as Figure 18.1.1 shows. Redox reactions take place on the surface of the Statue of Liberty and inside a battery. The rusting of iron, the combustion of fuel, the effect of bleach, and the browning of fruit are all redox reactions.

Figure 18.1.1
Redox reactions are responsible for color changes on the surface of these objects.

How do chemists determine which reactants lose and gain electrons in a redox reaction? Chemists assign an **oxidation number** to every atom in the reactants and products. An oxidation number is the charge that an atom in a compound would have if its bonds were ionic. Oxidation numbers show the general distribution of electrons among bonded atoms. By looking at how oxidation numbers change from the reactant side to the product side, chemists can identify what is oxidized and reduced in a redox equation.

In Chapter 3, you learned that some elements can have more than one charge as ions. For example, an iron atom can form a 2+ or 3+ ion, depending on the compound it is in. The correct charge for the iron ion is the one that results in an overall charge of 0 for the formula unit. Oxidation numbers for atoms in compounds are determined in a similar way. There are a few rules for determining oxidation numbers. The first two rules are for neutral and charged atoms.

Rule 1. Atoms of all monatomic, diatomic, or polyatomic elements have an oxidation number of 0. For example, single Na and Fe atoms and the atoms in O_2 and P_4 molecules have an oxidation number of 0.

Rule 2. All monatomic ions have an oxidation number equal to their ionic charge. For example, the Zn^{2+} ion has an oxidation number of 2+, and the Cl^{1-} ion has an oxidation number of 1−.

Rule 3. In compounds, oxygen has an oxidation number of 2−.

Rule 4. In compounds, hydrogen has an oxidation number of 1+.

Rule 5. In compounds, alkali metals have an oxidation number of 1+, alkaline earth metals have an oxidation number of 2+, and fluorine has an oxidation number of 1−.

Rule 6. For a compound, the sum of the oxidation numbers of each atom must equal 0. For a polyatomic ion, the sum of the oxidation numbers of each atom must equal the ion's charge.

Example 1	What is the oxidation number of each atom or ion in the following substances: Cl_2, Sn^{4+}, CO, CH_4?	

Read   You are asked to find oxidation numbers for four substances.

Plan   For each substance, apply the rules for oxidation numbers in the order the rules are listed.

Solve   The oxidation numbers and the rules used to determine them are given below.

Cl_2 is a diatomic element.	oxidation number of each Cl$=0$ (rule 1)
Sn^{4+} is an ion.	oxidation number of $Sn^{4+}=4+$ (rule 2)
CO is a compound.	oxidation number of O$=2-$ (rule 3)
	oxidation number of C$=2+$ (rule 6)
CH_4 is a compound.	oxidation number of each H$=1+$ (rule 4)
	oxidation number of C$=4-$ (rule 6)

Reflect   To find the oxidation number for the C atom in CO and CH_4, remember that the sum of the oxidation numbers of the atoms must equal 0 (rule 6). For example, there are 4 H atoms and 1 C atom in CH_4, so the sum of 5 oxidation numbers must be 0. Let x be the oxidation number of the C atom. You know that $x+4(1+)=0$, so $x=4-$.

Practice   What is the oxidation number of each atom or ion in the following substances: MnO_2, CH_3OH, Fe^{3+}?

In Example 1, you saw that the C atom in CO has a different oxidation number than the C atom in CH_4. A given atom in different compounds may have different oxidation numbers. However, the oxidation number of O and H atoms does not vary from compound to compound. The same is true for the oxidation number of alkali metals, alkaline earth metals, and fluorine.

Example 2	What is the oxidation number of each atom in MnO_4^{1-} and $Na_2S_2O_3$?

Read   You are asked to find the oxidation numbers for two substances.

Plan   Apply the rules for oxidation numbers in the order the rules are listed. Sodium is an alkali metal. Remember that the sum of the oxidation numbers for MnO_4^{1-} does not equal 0; it equals the ion's charge of $1-$.

Solve   The oxidation numbers and the rules used are listed below.

MnO_4^{1-} is a polyatomic ion.   oxidation number of each $O = 2-$ (rule 3)

oxidation number of $Mn = 7+$ (rule 6)

$Na_2S_2O_3$ is a compound.   oxidation number of each $O = 2-$ (rule 3)

oxidation number of each $Na = 1+$ (rule 5)

oxidation number of each $S = 2+$ (rule 6)

For MnO_4^{1-}, the sum of the oxidation numbers must be $1-$. Set up an algebra equation. Let x be the oxidation number of the Mn atom. $x + 4(2-) = 1-$, so $x = 7+$.

For $Na_2S_2O_3$, the sum of the oxidation numbers must equal 0. Set up an equation, letting x be the oxidation number of an S atom: $2(1+) + 2(x) + 3(2-) = 0$. Solving gives $x = 2+$.

Reflect   When setting up an equation for a compound or polyatomic ion, account for every atom. For $Na_2S_2O_3$, you need to account for 7 oxidation numbers. To do this, multiply oxidation numbers by the appropriate subscripts in the formula.

Practice   What is the oxidation number of each atom in N_2O, $Na_2C_2O_4$, and ClO_3^{1-}?

Within a compound, identical atoms are assigned the same oxidation number. In $Na_2S_2O_3$, the two S atoms cannot have two different oxidation numbers.

Now that you know how to assign oxidation numbers, you are ready to interpret them. In the next lesson, you will learn how oxidation numbers indicate what is oxidized and reduced in a redox reaction.

Express Lab 18

Procedure

1. In this lab, you will practice using the rules for determining oxidation numbers. On a sheet of paper, copy the table below.

2. Fill in the missing oxidation numbers.

Analysis

1. Iodine typically has an oxidation number of $1-$. Explain why this is or is not true for I_2.

2. Chlorine typically has an oxidation number of $1-$. Explain why this is or is not true for $NaClO_4$.

Substance	Oxidation Numbers
I_2	$I = ?$
H_2O	$O = ?, H = ?$
$NaClO_4$	$O = ?, Na = ?, Cl = ?$
$Ca_3(PO_4)_2$	$Ca = ?, P = ?, O = ?$

Link to ≫≫≫

Language Arts

Clues to the meanings of scientific terms are often included within the term. For example, *oxidation* originally described any reaction that occurs with oxygen. These reactions typically involve oxygen removing electrons from, or oxidizing, another substance. Similarly, *reduction* originally referred to a decrease in the amount of elemental oxygen. When oxygen accepts electrons from another substance, it typically becomes part of a compound. Thus, the amount of elemental oxygen is reduced.

Word Bank

oxidation

oxidation number

reduction

On a sheet of paper, write the word or phrase from the Word Bank that completes each sentence.

1. A reaction in which an atom or ion loses electrons is called _____.

2. A(n) _____ is the charge an atom in a compound would have if all bonds were ionic.

3. A reaction in which an atom or ion gains electrons is called _____.

On a sheet of paper, write the letter of the answer to each question.

4. What is the oxidation number of iron in Fe_2O_3?

    A 2+   **B** 3+   **C.** 6+   **D** 3−

5. What is the oxidation number of phosphorus in P_4O_{10}?

    A 20+   **B** 4+   **C** 5+   **D** 3−

6. What is the oxidation number of fluorine in PF_3?

    A 1−   **B** 3−   **C** 3+   **D** 1+

Critical Thinking

On a sheet of paper, write the answer to each question.

7. Why is it impossible to have oxidation without reduction?

8. Compare the oxidation numbers of a tin atom, an Sn^{2+} ion, and an Sn^{4+} ion. Why is there a difference in these numbers?

9. Determine the oxidation number of each atom in $Bi(OH)_3$.

10. Determine the oxidation number of each atom in $Na_2Cr_2O_7$.

After reading this lesson, you should be able to

◆ explain what a change in oxidation number means in terms of electrons

◆ identify the oxidized reactant and the reduced reactant in a redox reaction

◆ identify the reducing agent and the oxidizing agent in a redox reaction

In a redox reaction, particular atoms or ions in the reactants lose or gain electrons. However, chemists often refer to whole reactants as the substances that are oxidized or reduced. One reactant is oxidized while another reactant is reduced. An easy way to remember the definitions of oxidation and reduction is to think of the sentence, LEO the lion says "GER."

• LEO: **L**oss of **E**lectrons is **O**xidation.
• GER: **G**ain of **E**lectrons is **R**eduction.

Recall that electrons are negatively charged. In a redox reaction, the reactant that is oxidized loses electrons. For one element in this reactant, the oxidation number increases. The reactant that is reduced gains these electrons. For one element in this reactant, the oxidation number decreases.

• The reactant that is oxidized loses electrons. One oxidation number increases.
• The reactant that is reduced gains electrons. One oxidation number decreases.

Most redox reactions take place in an aqueous acidic solution. The symbol (*aq*) is often written after an ion in a redox reaction. The hydrogen ion, $H^{1+}(aq)$, is often a reactant. This indicates that the reaction is occurring in an acidic solution.

To determine the oxidized and reduced reactants, compare the oxidation numbers of elements on each side of the redox equation. The oxidation numbers that change indicate which reactants lose and gain electrons. If no oxidation numbers change from the left side to the right, the equation is not a redox reaction. Most double-replacement reactions are not redox reactions.

Example 1   In the following unbalanced redox equation, which reactant is oxidized and which reactant is reduced?
$$H^{1+}(aq) + As_2O_3(s) + NO_3^{1-}(aq) \rightarrow$$
$$H_3AsO_4(aq) + NO(g)$$

Read   You are asked to identify the substances that are oxidized and reduced in a redox reaction.

Plan   First determine the oxidation number for each atom in the reactants and products. Use the rules in Lesson 1 to do this.

Solve   Write the oxidation numbers below the redox reaction. If a formula has two or more atoms of an element, write the oxidation number for *just one atom*. Drop the state symbols for now.

$$H^{1+} + As_2O_3 + NO_3^{1-} \rightarrow H_3AsO_4 + NO$$
$$1+ \quad\; 3+\; 2- \quad 5+\; 2- \quad\; 1+\; 5+\; 2- \quad 2+\; 2-$$

Now compare the oxidation numbers on each side of the equation. The oxidation number of As increased from 3+ to 5+. Each As atom lost 2 electrons. The oxidation number of N decreased from 5+ to 2+. The N atom gained 3 electrons. In this redox reaction, As_2O_3 was oxidized and NO_3^{1-} was reduced.

Reflect   In this redox reaction, each As atom lost 2 electrons. However, the whole reactant, As_2O_3, is identified as being oxidized.

Practice   In the following redox equation, which reactant is oxidized and which reactant is reduced?
$$C_2H_4(g) + O_2(g) \rightarrow CO_2(g) + H_2O(g)$$

In Example 1, you may have wondered how the N atom gained 3 electrons if each As atom lost 2. The given equation was not balanced. In a balanced equation, the number of electrons lost equals the number gained. You will learn how to balance a redox equation in Lesson 3. However, the coefficients in redox equations do not affect the assigning of oxidation numbers. You can identify the oxidized and reduced reactants without balancing the equation.

In a redox reaction, chemists also refer to the **reducing agent** and the **oxidizing agent**. The reducing agent is the reactant that causes another reactant to be reduced. It is the reactant that is oxidized. The oxidizing agent is the reactant that causes another reactant to be oxidized. It is the reactant that is reduced. In other words, chemists use two different terms for the same reactant:

Reducing agent

The reactant that causes another reactant to be reduced; the oxidized reactant

Oxidizing agent

The reactant that causes another reactant to be oxidized; the reduced reactant

- Reducing agent = reactant that is oxidized (loses electrons)
- Oxidizing agent = reactant that is reduced (gains electrons)

Example 2	In the following redox equation, identify the oxidized reactant, the reduced reactant, the reducing agent, and the oxidizing agent. $Br^{1-}(aq) + MnO_4{}^{1-}(aq) \rightarrow Br_2(l) + Mn^{2+}(aq)$
Read	You are asked to identify which reactant 1) is oxidized, 2) is reduced, 3) is doing the reducing, and 4) is doing the oxidizing.
Plan	First find the oxidation number of each atom in the equation. Then compare the numbers on each side of the equation. Identify the ones that change. You do not need to balance the equation.
Solve	Write the oxidation numbers below the redox reaction. Each number should represent *just one atom*.

$$Br^{1-} + MnO_4{}^{1-} \rightarrow Br_2 + Mn^{2+}$$
$$1- \qquad 7+\ 2- \qquad 0 \qquad 2+$$

The Br^{1-} ion has a different oxidation number than diatomic Br_2. The number changes from 1− to 0, so the Br^{1-} ion is oxidized. This means it is the reducing agent. When the Mn atom becomes an ion, its oxidation number changes from 7+ to 2+. $MnO_4{}^{1-}$ is reduced, which means it is the oxidizing agent.

Br^{1-} = oxidized reactant = reducing agent
$MnO_4{}^{1-}$ = reduced reactant = oxidizing agent

Reflect	When there are only two reactants, you may be tempted to identify the first reactant's role and then assume the second reactant's role. However, it is best to determine oxidation numbers for all atoms before identifying each reactant's role.
Practice	In the following redox equation, identify the oxidized reactant, the reduced reactant, the reducing agent, and the oxidizing agent. $Cr_2O_7{}^{2-}(aq) + Fe^{2+}(aq) \rightarrow Cr^{3+}(aq) + Fe^{3+}(aq)$

On a sheet of paper, write the word or phrase from the Word Bank that completes each sentence.

Word Bank

decreases

increases

oxidizing agent

reducing agent

1. The reactant that is oxidized is the _____.

2. The reactant that is reduced is the _____.

3. When an element is oxidized, its oxidation number _____.

4. When an element is reduced, its oxidation number _____.

On a sheet of paper, write the answer to each question.

5. What is the oxidizing agent in the following redox reaction?
$N_2(g) + 3H_2(g) \rightarrow 2NH_3(g)$

6. What is the reducing agent in the following redox reaction?
$2Li(s) + 2H_2O(l) \rightarrow 2LiOH(aq) + H_2(g)$

Critical Thinking

For each equation, use oxidation numbers to determine which reactant is oxidized and which is reduced. Some equations are unbalanced. Write your answers on a sheet of paper.

7. $MnO_2(s) + H_2C_2O_4(aq) \rightarrow Mn^{2+}(aq) + CO_2(g) + H_2O(l)$

8. $I_2O_5(s) + CO(g) \rightarrow I_2(s) + CO_2(g)$

9. $Mg(s) + Cu(NO_3)_2(aq) \rightarrow Mg(NO_3)_2(aq) + Cu(s)$

10. $Al(s) + HCl(aq) \rightarrow Al^{3+}(aq) + Cl^{1-}(aq) + H_2(g)$

Link to ➤➤➤

Biology

Some of the most important processes in biology are redox reactions. Photosynthesis is a redox reaction. In photosynthesis, plants reduce carbon dioxide to produce sugars. Water is then oxidized to form oxygen. The reverse of this reaction, respiration, is also a redox reaction. During respiration, sugars are oxidized to produce carbon dioxide, and oxygen is reduced to form water.

In Lesson 2, you learned how to identify the oxidized and reduced reactants in a redox reaction. The equations you studied were not balanced. The number of the electrons lost by the oxidized reactant was not the same number gained by the reduced reactant. In this lesson, you will learn how to balance redox reactions. There are two very important things to remember when balancing redox reactions:

- The number of atoms of each element must be the same on both sides of the equation. This is true for any balanced chemical equation.
- The sum of the ionic charges on each side must be the same. Compounds and elements have a charge of 0. Only ions have a charge.

Some redox equations can be balanced quickly. Look at the oxidation of zinc:

$$Zn(s) + H^{1+}(aq) \rightarrow Zn^{2+}(aq) + H_2(g)$$

This equation can be balanced by adding a coefficient of 2 to the left of the hydrogen ion. Then the numbers of atoms are balanced, and the charges are also balanced.

$$Zn + 2H^{1+} \rightarrow Zn^{2+} + H_2$$

Other redox equations take more time to balance. The following equation shows the oxidation of the Fe^{2+} ion by the $Cr_2O_7^{2-}$ ion.

$$Cr_2O_7^{2-}(aq) + Fe^{2+}(aq) \rightarrow Cr^{3+}(aq) + Fe^{3+}(aq)$$

It cannot be balanced as easily. There are oxygen atoms on the reactant side, but none on the product side. Redox equations like this one are balanced by following a series of steps. If each step is followed properly, the equation is balanced at the end. The steps for balancing a redox equation are listed on the next page.

Half-reaction

One of two reactions that together make up a complete redox equation

The steps for balancing redox equations are summarized below.

1. Split into half-reactions.

2. Balance atoms except O and H.

3. Balance O atoms by adding H_2O.

4. Balance H atoms by adding H^{1+}.

5. Balance charges by adding e^{1-}.

6. Make electrons lost = electrons gained.

7. Add half-reactions. Cancel identicals.

8. Check atoms and charges.

Step 1. Split the redox equation into two **half-reactions.** A half-reaction shows only one reactant and one product. One half-reaction will show the oxidized reactant and the product of oxidation. The other half-reaction will show the reduced reactant and the product of reduction.

Step 2. For each half-reaction, balance the number of atoms of each element—except oxygen and hydrogen.

Step 3. For each half-reaction, balance the number of oxygen atoms by adding one H_2O molecule for each missing oxygen atom.

Step 4. For each half-reaction, balance the number of hydrogen atoms by adding one H^{1+} ion for each missing hydrogen atom.

Step 5. For each half-reaction, balance the ionic charges by adding electrons (e^{1-}). The sum of the charges on each side must be the same. The charge on an electron is $1-$, so adding an electron will *decrease* the charge sum. You will add electrons to the reactant side of one half-reaction and to the product side of the other half-reaction. You *cannot* add electrons to the same side of both half-reactions.

Step 6. Multiply one or both half-reactions by a whole number to make the electrons lost equal the electrons gained. Make sure you multiply the entire half-reaction by this number, not just the electrons.

Step 7. Add the half-reactions. Cancel any substances that appear on both sides of the equation. The electrons must cancel.

Step 8. Check that the numbers of atoms on both sides are equal *and* the sums of the charges on both sides are equal.

Whew! That looks a lot harder than it actually is. A summary of these steps is shown in the left margin. You may want to memorize this list and practice using it. These steps will work for balancing any redox equation.

Example 1	Balance the following redox equation.

$$Ce^{4+}(aq) + Sn^{2+}(aq) \rightarrow Ce^{3+}(aq) + Sn^{4+}(aq)$$

Read   You are asked to balance a redox equation.

Plan   Since there are no O or H atoms, it can be balanced quickly.

Solve   Follow the eight steps for redox balancing.

Step 1. Split into half-reactions.

$$Ce^{4+} \rightarrow Ce^{3+} \qquad \text{and} \qquad Sn^{2+} \rightarrow Sn^{4+}$$

Step 2. Balance atoms except O and H. The atoms are already balanced.

Step 3. Balance O atoms. Skip this step.

Step 4. Balance H atoms. Skip this step.

Step 5. Balance charges by adding electrons. Remember that adding electrons decreases the charge. In the first half-reaction, add $1e^{1-}$ to the reactant side. This reduces the charge on that side from 4+ to 3+. In the second half-reaction, add $2e^{1-}$ to the product side. This reduces the charge on that side from 4+ to 2+.

$$Ce^{4+} + 1e^{1-} \rightarrow Ce^{3+} \qquad\qquad Sn^{2+} \rightarrow Sn^{4+} + 2e^{1-}$$

Step 6. Make electrons lost = electrons gained. Multiply *everything* in the first half-reaction by 2. This makes $2e^{1-}$ gained in reduction = $2e^{1-}$ lost in oxidation.

$$2e^{1-} + 2Ce^{4+} \rightarrow 2Ce^{3+} \qquad\qquad Sn^{2+} \rightarrow Sn^{4+} + 2e^{1-}$$

By looking at these half-reactions, you can tell that the cerium cation is reduced because it gains $2e^{1-}$. The tin cation is oxidized because it loses $2e^{1-}$.

Step 7. Add the half-reactions. Cancel identicals. (Make sure that you do not cancel the Ce^{4+} with the Ce^{3+} or the Sn^{2+} with the Sn^{4+}. These ions are not identical.) Add the reactants from both half-reactions, then add the products from both.

$$\cancel{2e^{1-}} + 2Ce^{4+} + Sn^{2+} \rightarrow 2Ce^{3+} + Sn^{4+} + \cancel{2e^{1-}}$$

The balanced equation is

$$2Ce^{4+} + Sn^{2+} \rightarrow 2Ce^{3+} + Sn^{4+}$$

Step 8. Check atoms and charges. There are 2 Ce atoms and 1 Sn atom on each side. The total charge on each side is 10+.

Reflect   Electrons were added as reactants in one half-reaction and as products in the other half-reaction. This is true for any redox reaction.

Practice Balance the following redox equation.

$$Cu(s) + Ag^{1+}(aq) \rightarrow Cu^{2+}(aq) + Ag(s)$$

In Example 1, the charges on the ions made it easy to tell which reactant is reduced and which is oxidized. At the start of the next example, this is not as obvious. However, in step 5, you can always identify the reduced and oxidized reactants. The reduced reactant gains electrons, and the oxidized reactant loses them.

Example 2 Balance the following redox equation.
$$MnO_4^{1-}(aq) + Fe^{2+}(aq) \rightarrow Fe^{3+}(aq) + Mn^{2+}(aq)$$

Read You are asked to balance a redox equation.

Plan This reaction contains oxygen, so step 3 is needed.

Solve Follow each step carefully.

Step 1. The half-reactions are

$$MnO_4^{1-} \rightarrow Mn^{2+}$$ and $$Fe^{2+} \rightarrow Fe^{3+}$$

Step 2. The atoms are already balanced.

Step 3. To balance the O atoms in the first half-reaction, add $4H_2O$ to the product side.

$$MnO_4^{1-} \rightarrow Mn^{2+} + 4H_2O$$ $$Fe^{2+} \rightarrow Fe^{3+}$$

Step 4. Since water molecules were added in step 3, the first half-reaction now has 8 H atoms. Add $8H^{1+}$ to the reactant side.

$$MnO_4^{1-} + 8H^{1+} \rightarrow Mn^{2+} + 4H_2O$$ $$Fe^{2+} \rightarrow Fe^{3+}$$

Step 5. Total the ionic charges on each side of each half-reaction. Then add electrons to balance the charges.

$$MnO_4^{1-} + 8H^{1+} + 5e^{1-} \rightarrow Mn^{2+} + 4H_2O$$ $$Fe^{2+} \rightarrow Fe^{3+} + 1e^{1-}$$

In the first half-reaction, the total charge on each side is now $2+$. (Remember that $8H^{1+}$ contributes a charge of $8+$.) In the second half-reaction, the total charge on each side is $2+$. Check these sums.

Step 6. To make electrons lost = electrons gained, multiply everything in the second half-reaction by 5.

$$MnO_4^{1-} + 8H^{1+} + 5e^{1-} \rightarrow Mn^{2+} + 4H_2O$$ $$5Fe^{2+} \rightarrow 5Fe^{3+} + 5e^{1-}$$

Step 7. Add the half-reactions. The electrons cancel out, as they should.

$$MnO_4^{1-} + 8H^{1+} + 5e^{1-} + 5Fe^{2+} \rightarrow Mn^{2+} + 4H_2O + 5Fe^{3+} + 5e^{1-}$$

Step 8. There is the same number of each kind of atom on both sides. The total charge on each side is $17+$. The equation is balanced.

Reflect The MnO_4^{1-} ion is reduced. The Fe^{2+} ion is oxidized.

Practice Balance the following redox equation.
$$Cu(s) + NO_3^{1-}(aq) \rightarrow Cu^{2+}(aq) + NO(g)$$

In Example 2, notice that H_2O is not in the original equation. The presence of oxygen on the left side of the equation—but not on the right—is a clue that H_2O will need to be added.

Sometimes a redox equation includes H_2O molecules or H^{1+} ions. Unless H_2O is oxidized to O_2 gas, or H^{1+} is reduced to H_2 gas, you can omit them in half-reactions, as Example 3 shows.

Example 3   Balance the following redox equation.
$$H^{1+} + As_2O_3(s) + NO_3{}^{1-}(aq) \rightarrow H_3AsO_4(aq) + NO(g)$$

Read   You are asked to balance a redox equation.

Plan   There is no H_2 product, so omit H^{1+} when writing half-reactions. Make sure you follow step 2: Balance the As atoms *before* balancing anything else.

Solve   For the steps below, only the equations are shown.

1. $As_2O_3 \rightarrow H_3AsO_4$ $NO_3{}^{1-} \rightarrow NO$
2. $As_2O_3 \rightarrow 2H_3AsO_4$ $NO_3{}^{1-} \rightarrow NO$
3. $5H_2O + As_2O_3 \rightarrow 2H_3AsO_4$ $NO_3{}^{1-} \rightarrow NO + 2H_2O$
4. $5H_2O + As_2O_3 \rightarrow 2H_3AsO_4 + 4H^{1+}$ $4H^{1+} + NO_3{}^{1-} \rightarrow NO + 2H_2O$
5. $5H_2O + As_2O_3 \rightarrow 2H_3AsO_4 + 4H^{1+} + 4e^{1-}$ $3e^{1-} + 4H^{1+} + NO_3{}^{1-} \rightarrow NO + 2H_2O$
6. $15H_2O + 3As_2O_3 \rightarrow 6H_3AsO_4 + 12H^{1+} + \cancel{12e^{1-}}$ $\cancel{12e^{1-}} + 16H^{1+} + 4NO_3{}^{1-} \rightarrow 4NO + 8H_2O$
7. $4\,\cancel{16}H^{1+} + 4NO_3{}^{1-} + 7\,\cancel{15}H_2O + 3As_2O_3 \rightarrow 6H_3AsO_4 + \cancel{12}H^{1+} + 4NO + \cancel{8}H_2O$

In the equation above, there are H^{1+} ions and H_2O molecules on both sides. Subtract the smaller number of H^{1+} ions from both sides, leaving $4H^{1+}$ as a reactant only. Subtract the smaller number of H_2O molecules from both sides, leaving $7H_2O$ as a reactant only.

$$4H^{1+} + 4NO_3{}^{1-} + 7H_2O + 3As_2O_3 \rightarrow 6H_3AsO_4 + 4NO$$

Step 8. The atoms are balanced. The sum of the charges on each side is 0.

Reflect   Always follow the steps in the correct order. Step 2—balancing atoms other than O and H—is crucial in this example and in the practice problem below.

Practice   Balance the following redox equation.
$$H^{1+}(aq) + Br^{1-}(aq) + MnO_4{}^{1-}(aq) \rightarrow Br_2(l) + MnO_2(s) + H_2O$$

Although this balancing procedure may seem long at first, it will go faster with practice. You do not need to rewrite the equations at each step.

Lesson 3   R E V I E W

On a sheet of paper, write the equation(s) that answer each question. Start with the following *unbalanced* redox equation. Use the steps explained in the lesson.

$$MnO_2(s) + H^{1+}(aq) + C_2O_4^{2-}(aq) \rightarrow Mn^{2+}(aq) + CO_2(g) + H_2O(l)$$

1. What are the two half-reactions for this redox reaction? (Follow step 1.)

2. What are the half-reactions after balancing all atoms except O and H? (Follow step 2.)

3. What are the half-reactions after balancing the O atoms? (Follow step 3.)

4. What are the half-reactions after balancing the H atoms? (Follow step 4.)

5. What are the half-reactions after balancing the charges? (Follow step 5. Then step 6 will already be done.)

6. What is the final balanced equation after adding the half-reactions and canceling identicals? (Follow steps 7 and 8.)

Critical Thinking

On a sheet of paper, write the answer to each question.

7. When balancing a redox equation, why is it important to follow the steps in order?

8. How can you be sure that a redox equation is balanced?

9. Balance the following redox equation.
$$Cr_2O_7^{2-}(aq) + H^{1+}(aq) + Cl^{1-}(aq) \rightarrow$$
$$Cr^{3+}(aq) + H_2O(l) + Cl_2(g)$$

10. Balance the following redox equation.
$$MnO(s) + PbO_2(s) \rightarrow Pb^{2+}(aq) + MnO_4^{1-}(aq)$$

INVESTIGATION 18

Materials

- safety goggles
- lab coat or apron
- gloves
- 3 medium test tubes
- grease pencil
- test-tube rack
- 10-mL graduated cylinder
- 15 mL of 0.20 M potassium iodide (KI) solution
- 8 mL of KI solution of unknown concentration in a medium test-tube
- 50 mL of distilled water
- stirring rod
- 40 mL of 0.20 M iron(III) chloride ($FeCl_3$) solution
- 50-mL beaker

Concentration in a Redox Reaction

The oxidation or reduction of a reactant causes its properties to change. How does this change relate to concentration? In this investigation, you will observe the reaction given by this unbalanced equation:

$$Fe^{3+} + I^{1-} \rightarrow Fe^{2+} + I_2$$

Procedure

1. Put on safety goggles, gloves, and a lab coat or apron.

2. Use the grease pencil to label the test tubes 1, 2, and 3. Place the test tubes in the rack.

3. Measure 2 mL of 0.20 M KI solution in the graduated cylinder. Pour it into tube 1. Stir in 6 mL of distilled water. **Safety Alert: Handle glassware with care. Dispose of broken glass properly.**

4. Measure 4 mL of 0.20 M KI solution and pour it into tube 2. Stir in 4 mL of distilled water.

5. Measure 8 mL of 0.20 M KI solution and pour it into tube 3.

6. Rinse the graduated cylinder with distilled water.

7. Measure 10 mL of $FeCl_3$ solution and pour it into the beaker. **Safety Alert: Iron(III) chloride is a skin irritant. Handle the solution carefully.**

8. Slowly pour the 10 mL of $FeCl_3$ solution from the beaker into tube 1. Stir the mixture and record your observations.

9. Repeat steps 7 and 8 for tubes 2 and 3 and for the solution of unknown concentration.

Cleanup/Disposal

Pour the solutions into the proper waste containers. Wash, dry, and return the equipment. Then wash your hands.

Analysis

1. How do you know that diatomic iodine, I_2, is produced in this reaction?

2. Compare the colors of the liquids in the four tubes after adding the $FeCl_3$.

Conclusions

1. What are the molarities of the KI solutions in tubes 1, 2, and 3?

2. Estimate the unknown KI molarity. Explain your answer.

3. Write the half-reactions for this redox reaction.

4. Which element is oxidized? Which is reduced?

Explore Further

Find the overall balanced redox equation for the reaction that occurred in this investigation. Do potassium and chlorine appear in the equation? Explain your answer.

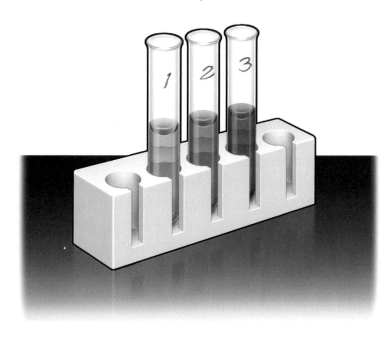

Redox chemistry is part of your everyday life. If you have ever used bleach to remove a stain, taken vitamin C to improve your health, or used a battery, you have used redox reactions.

Bleach and Other Oxidizing Cleaners

Bleach is used to "remove" stains from clothing or other items. Where do the stains go? Actually, bleach does not make a stain leave the fabric. Instead, it reacts with the stain to form a colorless compound. Most bleaches contain sodium hypochlorite, $NaOCl$. This compound decomposes to form sodium chloride and an oxygen atom.

$$NaOCl(aq) \rightarrow NaCl(aq) + O(aq)$$

Atomic oxygen is very reactive and an extremely strong oxidizing agent. It oxidizes the stain molecules to form colorless molecules. Although bleach is often called chlorine bleach, it is oxygen that does the bleaching. Bleach must be used carefully because of its oxidizing power. Most bleach labels warn the user to test a small piece of fabric first.

Bleaches are also used to purify water and disinfect swimming pools. Bacteria are killed when they are oxidized by bleach. Bleach can be harmful to the human body and the environment depending on the amount used.

Other cleaning agents use redox reactions, too. Some cleaners contain a compound called sodium percarbonate, $Na_2CO_3 \cdot 3H_2O_2$. When dissolved in water, it releases concentrated hydrogen peroxide, H_2O_2. The hydrogen peroxide decomposes, producing water and an oxygen atom:

$$H_2O_2(aq) \rightarrow H_2O(l) + O(aq)$$

Again, atomic oxygen oxidizes stain molecules, changing them from colored to colorless compounds. Compared to bleach, these kinds of cleaners are safer for the environment.

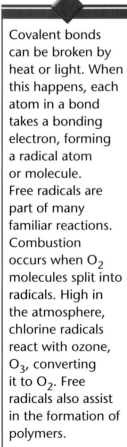

Antioxidants

A popular health topic is the importance of **antioxidants** in a healthy diet. Antioxidants are stable molecules that react with **free radicals** and reduce their effect. Free radicals are particles that contain an atom with an unpaired electron in its outermost level. As a result, they are extremely reactive. Free radicals can damage cells and body tissues by stealing electrons from biological molecules. This causes the molecules to become free radicals. A chain reaction begins as one free radical reacts to form another free radical. Sometimes, the human body purposely creates free radicals to fight viruses or bacteria. However, cigarette smoke, pollution, and radiation create harmful free radicals.

How do an antioxidant and a free radical react? The antioxidant gives an electron to the free radical. The antioxidant is oxidized, and the radical is reduced. The antioxidant stops the chain reaction by changing the free radical to a stable atom or molecule. Unlike other molecules, the antioxidant remains stable even after being oxidized.

Vitamin C is a powerful antioxidant because it readily reacts with oxygen in the air. For example, lemon juice contains vitamin C. A little lemon juice sprinkled on freshly cut fruit prevents the fruit from turning brown. The vitamin C reacts with nearby oxygen, thus preventing the oxygen from oxidizing the fruit.

Antioxidant

A stable molecule that reacts with a free radical, reducing its effect

Free radical

An extremely reactive particle containing an atom with an unpaired electron

Covalent bonds can be broken by heat or light. When this happens, each atom in a bond takes a bonding electron, forming a radical atom or molecule. Free radicals are part of many familiar reactions. Combustion occurs when O_2 molecules split into radicals. High in the atmosphere, chlorine radicals react with ozone, O_3, converting it to O_2. Free radicals also assist in the formation of polymers.

❋ ❋

Technology and Society

Certain redox reactions produce light. This process is called chemical luminescence. There are many applications of chemical luminescence. Luminol, for instance, is used to indicate the presence of blood. Cyalume is used in toy light sticks—the kind you might buy at a concert. The compound luciferin, the glowing substance in fireflies, is used in tuberculosis research.

Corrosion

The weakening of a metal by oxidation

Rocket Fuel

The power of a rocket engine comes from redox reactions. The fuel for the main engines of a space shuttle is liquid hydrogen. The shuttle also carries tanks of liquid oxygen. When the hydrogen and oxygen are sprayed into the engine, the mixture reacts to produce water and energy.

$$2H_2(l) + O_2(l) \rightarrow 2H_2O(g) + \text{energy}$$

This is a redox reaction. A different redox reaction takes place in the booster rocket when a space shuttle is launched:

$$10Al(s) + 6NH_4ClO_4(s) \rightarrow 4Al_2O_3(s) + 2AlCl_3(s) + 12H_2O(g) + 3N_2(g)$$

Both reactions are used to produce the energy needed to put the rocket shown in Figure 18.4.1 into space.

Corrosion

Each year, governments and individuals spend millions of dollars to clean up after a special group of redox reactions: the **corrosion** of metals. Corrosion is the weakening of a metal by oxidation. Corrosion occurs when the metal is exposed to oxygen in water, air, or other substances. Iron and iron alloys like steel are common construction materials. When iron is oxidized, iron ions in the form of iron oxides are produced. The corrosion of iron often occurs in two steps:

$$Fe(s) + O_2(g) + 2H_2O(l) \rightarrow 2Fe(OH)_2(s)$$
$$4Fe(OH)_2(s) + O_2(g) + 2H_2O(l) \rightarrow 4Fe(OH)_3(s)$$

In the first step, iron is oxidized to Fe^{2+} ions. In the second step, Fe^{2+} ions are further oxidized to Fe^{3+} ions. When the system dries, iron(III) oxide, or rust, is formed:

$$2Fe(OH)_3(s) \rightarrow Fe_2O_3(s) + 3H_2O(l)$$

The rust eventually flakes off the iron structure, exposing more iron to oxygen. Corrosion occurs more quickly in the presence of salts and acids because these substances help transfer electrons.

Some metals, like gold and platinum, resist corrosion. They do not corrode over time, and people value their beauty. Therefore, they are valuable metals.

Figure 18.4.1 *More than 2.5 million pounds of thrust is needed to launch a space shuttle.*

Other metals, like aluminum, zinc, and magnesium, oxidize fairly easily. However, the product of oxidation, a metal oxide, forms a protective coating on the surface of these metals. This coating does not flake off and prevents the metal atoms under the surface from oxidizing. A layer of aluminum or zinc is added to some iron surfaces to protect the reactive iron underneath.

Metals that oxidize easily can also be protected by a coating of paint, plastic, or oil. These coatings prevent oxidation until they are scratched. When this happens, the exposed metal begins to react with the oxygen in surrounding air or water. Large steel pieces that are underwater or buried in the earth, such as bridge supports or pipelines, are sometimes connected to a piece of magnesium or zinc. When iron atoms on the surface lose electrons in oxidation, the magnesium or zinc immediately transfers some of its own electrons to the iron atoms. The magnesium or zinc is oxidized, saving the iron from oxidizing. It is much easier to replace a piece of magnesium or zinc than a bridge support or a pipeline.

Spotlight on Mercury

80
Hg
Mercury
200.6

In terms of atomic mass, mercury is the heaviest of the nonradioactive transition metals. Mercury is a liquid between −39°C and 357°C. For this reason, it is used in thermometers and barometers.

Because it is a metal, mercury is used in applications that require metallic properties. It is a good electrical conductor and is used in switches and electrical components. Mercury can be combined with other metals in alloys. Its ability to form an alloy with gold makes it essential for extracting gold from ore. Mercury vapor is used in streetlights and fluorescent lamps.

Unfortunately, the usefulness of mercury is matched by its toxicity. The element mercury is mostly hazardous as a gas. When inhaled, mercury can damage the nervous system and kidneys. Compounds of mercury and carbon are especially poisonous. Because of health concerns, the use of mercury is being reduced.

Interesting Fact: Mercury's chemical symbol, Hg, comes from the Greek word *hydrargyrum*, which means "quick silver."

Word Bank

antioxidants

corrosion

free radicals

On a sheet of paper, write the word or phrase from the Word Bank that completes each sentence.

1. Extremely reactive particles containing an atom with an unpaired electron are _____.

2. Stable molecules that donate an electron, yet remain stable, are _____.

3. The deterioration of a metal due to oxidation is _____.

On a sheet of paper, write the letter of the answer to each question.

4. Which of the following is a powerful antioxidant?

A sodium hypochlorite   **C** free radicals
B bleach   **D** vitamin C

5. Which of the following will protect metals from corrosion?

A zinc coatings   **C** liquid hydrogen
B sodium hypochlorite   **D** vitamin C

6. Which metals are very resistant to corrosion?

A gold and iron   **C** iron and magnesium
B gold and platinum   **D** zinc and platinum

Critical Thinking

On a sheet of paper, write the answer to each question.

7. Explain how antioxidants stop free radicals from causing cell and tissue damage.

8. Explain how bleach "removes" stains from clothing.

9. What are some ways that metals are protected from corrosion? How does each work?

10. Look at the two reactions on page 720 that are used by space shuttles to produce energy. Identify the oxidizing agent in each.

Electrochemistry

The study of the relationship between electrical energy and chemical reactions

Electric current

The flow of electrons

Voltaic cell

A device that converts chemical energy into electrical energy

Chemical changes can cause electrical activity, and electrical activity can cause chemical changes. **Electrochemistry** is the study of the relationship between electrical energy and chemical reactions. In a redox reaction, electrons are transferred from one substance to another. For example, when a piece of zinc is placed in a solution containing copper(II) ions, the following spontaneous reaction takes place:

$$Zn(s) + Cu^{2+}(aq) \rightarrow Zn^{2+}(aq) + Cu(s)$$

The spectator anions are not shown. The zinc atoms are oxidized, forming Zn^{2+} ions in solution. The Cu^{2+} ions are reduced, forming a thin coating of solid copper on the piece of zinc. This coating of solid metal over another piece of metal is called a plating.

Voltaic Cells

The half-reactions for the above redox reaction are

$$Zn(s) \rightarrow Zn^{2+}(aq) + 2e^{1-}$$
$$Cu^{2+}(aq) + 2e^{1-} \rightarrow Cu(s)$$

Imagine that you could physically separate the oxidation half-reaction from the reduction half-reaction. Imagine that the electrons could travel through a wire from the oxidized reactant to the reduced reactant. This is what happens in a battery. A battery converts the chemical energy of a redox reaction into electrical energy. When electrons flow, they create an **electric current.** When you turn on a flashlight, the electricity produced by the batteries is used to do work—produce light. Many redox reactions are used in batteries. All of them are spontaneous.

When two half-reactions are separated into different containers and connected by a wire, a **voltaic cell** is created. A voltaic cell is a device that converts chemical energy into electrical energy. A voltaic cell is also called an electrochemical cell. A simple voltaic cell is shown in Figure 18.5.1 on the next page.

Electrode

A metal object used for the purpose of conducting electric current into or out of an electrochemical cell

Half-cell

A single electrode immersed in a solution of its ions

Anode

The half-cell of a voltaic cell in which oxidation takes place; the electrode from which electrons move

Cathode

The half-cell of a voltaic cell in which reduction takes place; the electrode toward which electrons move

A voltmeter is an instrument that measures the amount of volts associated with an electrical device.

There are several parts to the voltaic cell in Figure 18.5.1. The pieces of metal in each beaker are **electrodes.** An electrode is a metal object used for the purpose of conducting electric current into or out of a voltaic cell. Each electrode is immersed in an electrolyte solution that contains ions of that metal. A single electrode and its solution make up a **half-cell.** The two half-cells are connected by a wire through which electrons can travel. The half-cell in which oxidation takes place is called the **anode.** The half-cell in which reduction takes place is called the **cathode.** The oxidation half-reaction occurs at the anode, and the reduction half-reaction occurs at the cathode. To remember this, think of a

> **red cat** (**red**uced **cat**hode)
>
> **an ox** (**an**ode **ox**idized)

In one half-cell, the zinc electrode is slowly oxidizing into Zn^{2+} cations. The beaker contains a solution of $ZnSO_4$, but the SO_4^{2-} ions are spectator ions. As the reaction spontaneously progresses, the concentration of Zn^{2+} ions increases. Thus, the positive charge in the anode *increases*. In the other half-cell, the Cu^{2+} ions in solution are slowly plating the solid copper electrode. The beaker contains a solution of $CuSO_4$, but the SO_4^{2-} anions are spectators. As the reaction progresses, the positive charge in the cathode *decreases*.

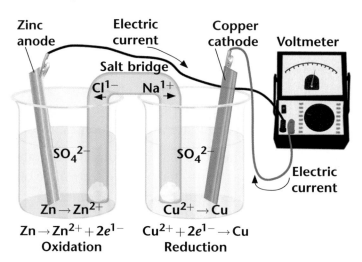

Figure 18.5.1 *In this voltaic cell, zinc metal is in a solution of $ZnSO_4$ (left half-cell), and copper metal is in a solution of $CuSO_4$ (right half-cell).*

This change in charge in the anode and cathode will quickly stop the redox reaction. To allow the reaction to proceed, a **salt bridge** is added to balance the charges. The salt bridge contains spectator cations and anions. The anions move into the anode and decrease its positive charge. The cations move into the cathode and increase its positive charge. The salt bridge maintains a balance of charge in the half-cells. The electrons travel through the wire from the anode to the cathode, producing a current. To remember the direction of electron flow, think of this:

Electrons travel from A (anode) to C (cathode).

Table 18.5.1 Ease of Oxidation for Common Metals	
Easily oxidized	
lithium	$Li \rightarrow Li^{1+} + 1e^{1-}$
potassium	$K \rightarrow K^{1+} + 1e^{1-}$
calcium	$Ca \rightarrow Ca^{2+} + 2e^{1-}$
sodium	$Na \rightarrow Na^{1+} + 1e^{1-}$
magnesium	$Mg \rightarrow Mg^{2+} + 2e^{1-}$
aluminum	$Al \rightarrow Al^{3+} + 3e^{1-}$
manganese	$Mn \rightarrow Mn^{2+} + 2e^{1-}$
zinc	$Zn \rightarrow Zn^{2+} + 2e^{1-}$
chromium	$Cr \rightarrow Cr^{3+} + 3e^{1-}$
iron	$Fe \rightarrow Fe^{2+} + 2e^{1-}$
nickel	$Ni \rightarrow Ni^{2+} + 2e^{1-}$
tin	$Sn \rightarrow Sn^{2+} + 2e^{1-}$
lead	$Pb \rightarrow Pb^{2+} + 2e^{1-}$
copper	$Cu \rightarrow Cu^{2+} + 2e^{1-}$
silver	$Ag \rightarrow Ag^{1+} + 1e^{1-}$
mercury	$Hg \rightarrow Hg^{2+} + 2e^{1-}$
platinum	$Pt \rightarrow Pt^{2+} + 2e^{1-}$
gold	$Au \rightarrow Au^{3+} + 3e^{1-}$
Not easily oxidized	

Predicting Half-Reactions

Besides the zinc-copper redox reaction, other reactions can spontaneously produce electricity. How do chemists know which ones? Table 18.5.1 ranks some common metals according to how easily they are oxidized. For any pair of metals, the one listed higher in the table is oxidized. Its half-reaction is shown in the table. The one lower in the table is reduced. Its half-reaction is the reverse of the one shown.

Silver, platinum, and gold are at the bottom of the table. These metals are not easily oxidized and, thus, resist corrosion. This property accounts, in part, for their value and use in jewelry.

Example 1   A voltaic cell is made with magnesium, tin, and solutions containing their cations. What is the half-reaction in each half-cell?

Read   You are asked to determine the half-reactions for a voltaic cell.

Plan   Locate magnesium and tin on Table 18.5.1. The one that is closer to the top is more easily oxidized. Use the table to write the half-reactions.

Solve   Magnesium is above tin, so magnesium is oxidized. As given in the table, the oxidation half-reaction in the anode is
$$Mg(s) \rightarrow Mg^{2+}(aq) + 2e^{1-}$$
Tin is reduced. Its half-reaction in the cathode is the reverse of the one given for tin in the table.
$$Sn^{2+}(aq) + 2e^{1-} \rightarrow Sn(s)$$

Reflect   The electrons travel from the magnesium half-cell to the tin half-cell. The cations in the salt bridge move to the tin half-cell, and the anions move to the magnesium half-cell.

Practice A voltaic cell is made with nickel, aluminum, and solutions containing their cations. What is the half-reaction in each half-cell? Which direction do the electrons travel between the electrodes? Which half-reaction needs cations from the salt bridge?

★ ✦ ★

Achievements in Science

Voltammetry

Voltammetry is the study of redox reactions by measuring the electricity they produce. In voltammetry, the voltage between the electrodes in the half-cells is varied. This affects the transfer of electrons, which is measured as electric current. From these measurements, scientists can learn about the process of the reaction or the concentration of substances involved in the reaction.

The first important development in voltammetry was polarography. Invented by Jaroslav Heyrovsky in 1922, polarography used drops of mercury for the cathode. Because the mercury dripped continuously, a clean, smooth reaction surface was repeatedly provided. This made it possible to observe the reaction many times during the experiment.

Later methods for changing the voltage in cycles or pulses improved voltammetry. One important technique was square-wave voltammetry, developed by Geoffrey Barker and Robert and Janet Osteryoung. In square-wave voltammetry, the voltage goes from a maximum to a minimum value suddenly instead of gradually. This produces a faster, more sensitive, and more accurate way to analyze redox reactions.

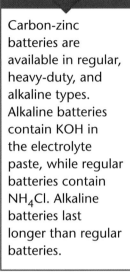

Dry cell

A voltaic cell in which the half-cells contain an electrolyte that is a paste instead of a solution

Carbon-zinc batteries are available in regular, heavy-duty, and alkaline types. Alkaline batteries contain KOH in the electrolyte paste, while regular batteries contain NH_4Cl. Alkaline batteries last longer than regular batteries.

Batteries

Voltaic cells are also called galvanic cells. Portable voltaic cells are usually called batteries. There are many types of batteries. The cell phone in Figure 18.5.2 uses a lithium battery. Most batteries use redox reactions to produce electrical energy.

Although the voltaic cells described earlier do produce electricity, they would be very messy in a flashlight on a camping trip. The electrolytes in each half-cell would spill easily. The batteries in a flashlight are **dry cells.** Their half-cells contain a moist paste instead of a solution. One inexpensive type of dry cell has a zinc electrode in the anode and a carbon electrode in the cathode. The electrodes are surrounded by a thick paste containing MnO_2, $ZnCl_2$, KOH, and water. A paper liner keeps the contents of the paste from freely mixing. The half-reactions are

$$Zn(s) \rightarrow Zn^{2+}(aq) + 2e^{1-}$$
$$2MnO_2(s) + H_2O(l) + 2e^{1-} \rightarrow Mn_2O_3(s) + 2OH^{1-}(aq)$$

In this cell, the carbon does not actually undergo reduction; the MnO_2 in the paste is the reduced substance. The ability of these cells to produce electricity decreases with use. This kind of dry cell is not rechargeable.

Figure 18.5.2 *Besides cell phones, many cameras and medical implants use lithium batteries as their power source.*

An example of a rechargeable voltaic cell is a car battery. The most common battery used in cars is a lead storage battery. In a battery of this type, six voltaic cells are connected. Each cell contains two electrodes. The anode is packed with a spongy lead, and the cathode contains PbO_2. They are placed in a solution of sulfuric acid. The half-reactions are

$$Pb(s) + SO_4{}^{2-}(aq) \rightarrow PbSO_4(s) + 2e^{1-}$$
$$PbO_2(s) + 4H^{1+}(aq) + SO_4{}^{2-}(aq) + 2e^{1-} \rightarrow PbSO_4(s) + H_2O(l)$$

The overall reaction is

$$Pb(s) + PbO_2(s) + 2H_2SO_4(aq) \rightarrow 2PbSO_4(s) \rightarrow 2H_2O(l)$$

When this redox reaction occurs in a lead storage battery, electrical energy is produced. This energy is used to start the car. As the battery is used, the reactant amounts decrease while the amount of $PbSO_4$ increases.

A car battery is recharged by the car's alternator. If this were not the case, the redox reaction in the battery would eventually stop and the battery would die. When the battery is recharged, the reverse reaction is forced to take place. The reverse reaction is nonspontaneous, so recharging the battery requires energy. Theoretically, a lead storage battery could be recharged forever. However, over time, some $PbSO_4$ falls to the bottom of the battery and is removed from the reaction. Eventually, the battery can no longer be recharged.

❋ ❋

Technology and Society

Voltammetric techniques use electrical measurements to study redox reactions. These techniques are even used to study chemical reactions in humans. This area of research, called *in vivo* voltammetry, has been developed over the last 30 years. One important application is the study of neurotransmitters in the brain. This requires placing tiny electrodes within the brain.

Batteries are available in different voltages. You may have used a 9-volt battery for a radio or smoke detector. Many car batteries are 12-volt batteries. The **volt (V)** is a unit of **electrical potential difference.** This is the difference in electron pressure between two points. In a voltaic cell, these points are the anode and cathode. Electrons are given up by oxidation at the anode, so the anode has a high electron pressure—a large negative potential. Electrons are removed by reduction at the cathode, so the cathode has a low electron pressure—a large positive potential. The difference between these potentials is the "force" that pushes electrons from the anode to the cathode. If there is no potential difference between the electrodes, there is no electron flow. If there is a large potential difference, the voltage is large.

Chemistry in Your Life

The Environment: Selecting Batteries

Household batteries are voltaic cells. They are used in various home appliances and devices. Different devices require different kinds of batteries. That's because different combinations of substances in batteries produce different voltages. These substances also affect how long the battery lasts, and whether it can be recharged.

Recently, concerns have been raised about the substances in batteries, especially mercury compounds. Mercury oxide batteries are small disks. They are used in appliances that require steady voltages, such as watches, hearing aids, and some calculators. Because mercury is toxic, the

use of these batteries is becoming more limited. Also, new regulations require that these batteries be recycled.

To reduce the number of disposable batteries, manufacturers have developed rechargeable batteries. A common type is a nickel-cadmium cell. While these can be used up to 1,000 times longer than disposable batteries, they do wear out eventually. These batteries must be recycled because cadmium is toxic.

1. In what kinds of appliances are mercury oxide batteries used?
2. Why must mercury oxide and nickel-cadmium batteries be recycled?
3. What types of batteries do you use at home?

Word Bank

anode

cathode

dry cell

electric current

salt bridge

voltaic cell

On a sheet of paper, write the word or phrase from the Word Bank that completes each sentence.

1. A(n) _____ is used to maintain the charge balance between two half-cells.

2. The half-cell in which reduction takes place is the _____.

3. A(n) _____ uses pastes instead of solutions as electrolytes.

4. A device that converts chemical energy to electrical energy is a(n) _____.

5. When two half-cells are connected by a wire, a(n) _____ is produced.

6. Electrons leave a voltaic cell at the _____.

Critical Thinking

On a sheet of paper, write the answer to each question.

7. What is the purpose of the salt bridge in a voltaic cell? How does it work?

8. How can you identify which electrode is the anode and which is the cathode in a voltaic cell?

9. What happens when a car battery is recharged?

10. A voltaic cell is made with chromium and copper and solutions of their cations, Cr^{3+} and Cu^{2+}. What reaction takes place at the anode? At the cathode? To which electrode will the cations in the salt bridge move? To which electrode will the anions in the bridge move?

Research and Write

Research how scientists determine how easily certain elements are oxidized. Find out about the equipment used for this purpose, especially the standard hydrogen electrode (SHE). Learn why hydrogen is used to establish a point of reference for oxidation or reduction strength. Present your findings in a short written report.

Objectives

After reading this lesson, you should be able to

◆ define electrolysis

◆ compare a voltaic cell and an electrolytic cell

◆ describe three ways that electrolysis is used in industry

Electrochemical process

A process that converts electrical energy into chemical energy, or chemical energy into electrical energy

Electrolysis

The use of electrical energy to cause a chemical change

Electrolytic cell

A cell in which electrons are forced to move from the anode to the cathode by an external source of electricity

In Lesson 5, you learned that voltaic cells use spontaneous redox reactions to produce electricity. An outside source of electric current, such as a battery recharger, can be used to force nonspontaneous chemical reactions. Both reactions are **electrochemical processes.** Electrochemical processes convert chemical energy into electrical energy, or electrical energy into chemical energy. This lesson discusses the use of electrical energy to produce chemical energy.

Many nonspontaneous reactions can be forced to occur by the addition of energy. **Electrolysis** is the use of electrical energy to cause a chemical change. Electrolysis occurs in **electrolytic cells.** These cells are similar to voltaic cells.

- Oxidation takes place in the anode.
- Reduction takes place in the cathode.
- Electrons travel from the anode to the cathode.

The main difference is that, in an electrolytic cell, the electrons are forced to move from the anode to the cathode by an external source of electricity. Recharging a car battery is one example of electrolysis. Electrolysis is also used in industry to produce substances, purify metals from their ores, and plate one metal onto another.

Link to ≫≫≫

Physics

A rechargeable battery is both a voltaic cell and an electrolytic cell. When a charged battery is used, it is a voltaic cell. When the battery loses its charge, the spontaneous redox reaction has reached equilibrium. By passing a current through the battery, electrolysis redeposits the metals on their electrodes. During recharging, the chemical reaction is reversed to some extent.

Industrial Production of Substances

Many alkali metals and alkaline earth metals are too easily oxidized to exist in nature as free elements. They exist only in compounds. An electrolytic cell can isolate these reactive elements from their compounds. For example, liquid sodium is produced in the electrolytic reaction of liquid sodium chloride.

$$2Na^{1+}(l) + 2Cl^{1-}(l) \rightarrow 2Na(l) + Cl_2(g)$$

Using electrolysis, a chemist named Humphry Davy discovered metallic sodium, potassium, magnesium, strontium, barium, and calcium.

As you have learned, pure water does not conduct an electric current. However, add an electrolyte such as sulfuric acid to water. When this solution is used in an electrolytic cell, bubbles begin to form at both electrodes. The water is reduced, producing hydrogen gas at the cathode. At the anode, the water is oxidized, producing oxygen gas.

$$2H_2O(l) \rightarrow 2H_2(g) + O_2(g)$$

This is an easy way to produce oxygen gas in a laboratory.

Ore Refining

At one time, aluminum was more valuable than gold or silver because it was so difficult to isolate from its ore. In 1886, two scientists discovered a way to produce aluminum in an electrolytic cell. The reaction is

$$2Al_2O_3(s) + 3C(s) \rightarrow 4Al(l) + 3CO_2(g)$$

To force this reaction, the electrolytic cell must be about 1,000°C. Recycling aluminum takes only about 10% of the energy required to isolate aluminum from its ore. It is a much cheaper way to form new aluminum products.

Copper is used in water pipes, electrical wires, and cookware. It can be found in its elemental form in many places in the world. However, most natural copper exists as an ore and needs to be refined in order to be used. Refining copper ore involves many steps. One step requires an electrolytic cell. The cell can produce copper that is 99.95% pure. The copper is then available to be melted into sheets or rods. Copper rods can be drawn into wire for electrical uses.

Electroplating

Electroplating is the process of depositing a thin layer of metal on an object in an electrolytic cell. Lesson 5 discussed how a copper plating forms on zinc when it is placed in a solution of copper ions. That redox reaction is spontaneous, but the copper plating tends to flake off. Electroplating can produce the same copper plating, but it can be controlled so that the plating is more permanent. Many car makers electroplate zinc onto steel before making steel car parts. A piece of steel is dragged across the surface of a zinc solution in an electrolytic cell. A zinc plating forms on one side of the steel. When car parts are made, the zinc-plated side is used on the exterior of the car. Zinc-plated steel is less likely to rust in the presence of air, water, and salts.

▼◄ ▲▼◄ ▲▼◄ ▲▼◄ ▲▼◄ ▲▼◄ ▲▼◄ ▲▼◄ ▲▼◄ ▲▼◄ ▲▼◄ ▲▼◄ ▲▼◄ ▲▼◄ ▲▼◄ ▲▼◄ ▲▼

Science at Work

Electroplater

An electroplater specializes in coating metal objects using electrolysis. Common elements for electroplating are silver, nickel, copper, chromium, and zinc. Electroplating is used in many industries. Electroplaters work for manufacturers of cars, circuit boards, and cans. Some electroplaters operate their own electroplating shop. Often, an electroplater will specialize in a particular operation, such as anodizing or metal preparation.

Electroplaters adjust the electric current between the anode and cathode to the correct amount. They also prepare and maintain the plating solutions and clean the electrodes and vats. This maintenance involves the use of cleaning solutions, strong acids or bases, and specialized scouring equipment. The electroplater must know the properties and hazards of these materials and techniques.

Technical training is required to be an electroplater. Experience and additional study allow an electroplater to advance to higher positions.

Lesson 6   R E V I E W

Word Bank

electrolysis

electrolytic cell

electroplating

On a sheet of paper, write the word or phrase from the Word Bank that completes each sentence.

1. An _____ can be used to separate a metal like copper from its ore.

2. The process of depositing a thin layer of one metal onto another is called _____.

3. The process of _____ uses electrical energy to force a nonspontaneous chemical reaction.

On a sheet of paper, write the letter of the answer that completes each sentence.

4. Electrolysis can be used to isolate _____.

   A noble gases   **C** metal ores

   B reactive metals   **D** liquid NaCl

5. The element _____ was *not* discovered using an electrolytic cell.

   A sodium   **B** barium   **C** magnesium   **D** neon

6. An electrolytic cell requires a(n) _____.

   A outside electricity source   **C** rechargeable battery

   B spontaneous reaction   **D** very high temperature

Critical Thinking

On a sheet of paper, write the answer to each question.

7. How is electroplating used to protect metal car parts?

8. What is the advantage of recycling aluminum over obtaining it from the ore?

9. Compare a voltaic cell and an electrolytic cell.

10. Using what you know about electroplating, hypothesize how gold-plated jewelry is made.

Materials

- safety goggles
- lab coat or apron
- 9-V battery
- 2 wires with alligator clips on each end
- 2 graphite (carbon) rods
- petri dish
- distilled water
- 0.1 M copper sulfate ($CuSO_4$) solution
- 0.1 M potassium iodide (KI) solution
- 0.1 M sodium chloride (NaCl) solution
- 0.1 M acetic acid ($HC_2H_3O_2$) solution

Electrolysis

Electricity can be used to produce or reverse redox reactions. The nature of these reactions depends on the amount of electricity used. It also depends on the properties of the electrolyte and its concentration. What reaction will occur when electric current is passed through a given electrolyte? In this investigation, you will observe electrolysis using several electrolytes.

Procedure

1. Predict what reactions will occur during electrolysis using distilled water and using each of the four electrolyte solutions. The graphite rods are the electrodes. Write your hypotheses. Then write a procedure for testing them. Include safety alerts.

2. Have your hypotheses and procedure approved by your teacher. Then construct your testing apparatus, shown on the next page.

3. Put on safety goggles and a lab coat or apron.

4. Perform your investigation. Record your observations for each solution tested.

Cleanup/Disposal

Pour the $CuSO_4$ and KI solutions into proper waste containers. Pour the NaCl and $HC_2H_3O_2$ solutions down the sink with plenty of running water. Wash and return the equipment. Wash your hands.

Continued on next page

Analysis

1. Did the electrolysis using distilled water produce the result you expected? Explain your answer.

2. What evidence of a reaction occurred when you used the $CuSO_4$ solution as an electrolyte? When you used the KI solution?

3. Compare the reactions that occurred when you used the NaCl and $HC_2H_3O_2$ solutions as electrolytes.

Conclusions

1. Was the cathode connected to the positive or negative terminal of the battery? Explain your answer.

2. For the reactions that produced bubbles at the electrodes, which gas was produced at the anode? At the cathode? Explain your answers.

3. Which of the four electrolytes produced the slowest reaction? Explain your answer.

4. The reaction at the cathode was different in the $CuSO_4$ solution than in the other solutions. Use Table 18.5.1 to explain why.

Explore Further

Repeat the investigation using a sodium carbonate (Na_2CO_3) solution. Compare how much gas is produced at the anode and at the cathode. Explain your results.

Bioremediation

Many scientists and engineers look for ways to eliminate harmful substances from the environment. These substances range from stored toxic waste (shown in photo) to oil spills at sea. One way to solve these problems is bioremediation.

Bioremediation uses redox reactions that small organisms perform. These redox reactions change the chemical makeup of the pollutant, making it less reactive or breaking it down into safer compounds. By speeding up these usually slow reactions, the pollutant is destroyed quickly.

Aerobic microorganisms are used to treat oil spills. They use oxygen to decompose the hydrocarbons in the oil. Added nutrients keep the microorganisms alive.

Some pesticides and solvents contain carbon-halogen compounds. These compounds create health risks in underground water supplies. They are difficult and costly to remove directly. However, certain microorganisms obtain energy by decomposing these pollutants. When these microorganisms and hydrogen are added to a water supply, the pollutants are safely removed.

Bioremediation is also used to remove toxic hydrocarbons from soil. For example, some types of fungus produce enzymes. These enzymes break down certain hydrocarbons. Some plants are able to decompose hydrocarbons in soil. Certain microorganisms that break down hydrocarbons are kept alive with nutrient-rich organic matter.

Bioremediation can be applied to many contamination problems. It can be used where the contamination is difficult to reach. In general, bioremediation techniques are safe and inexpensive. However, they cannot solve all contamination problems. In situations requiring the removal of heavy metals, for example, living organisms work poorly.

1. In general, how does bioremediation eliminate pollutants?

2. What type of bioremediation works well on carbon-halogen compounds?

3. What three bioremediation sources remove hydrocarbons from soil?

■ Oxidation occurs when an atom or ion loses electrons. Reduction occurs when an atom or ion gains electrons.

■ Oxidation and reduction occur together in a redox reaction.

■ In a redox reaction, the oxidized reactant is the reducing agent. The reduced reactant is the oxidizing agent. The electrons lost by the reducing agent are gained by the oxidizing agent.

■ Oxidation numbers are used to determine which reactant is oxidized and which is reduced. The oxidation number of an atom in the oxidized reactant increases. The oxidation number of an atom in the reduced reactant decreases.

■ Balancing a redox equation requires a series of eight steps. The first step is to split the equation into two half-reactions. Each side of a balanced redox equation has the same numbers of atoms and the same total charge.

■ Bleaches contain oxidizing agents. Antioxidants react with free radicals by a redox reaction. Rocket engines use redox reactions to create energy. Corrosion is the oxidation of metal.

■ A voltaic cell uses a spontaneous redox reaction to produce electrical energy. It consists of two metal electrodes, each immersed in an electrolyte solution that contains ions of that metal.

■ Each electrode and its solution form one half-cell. The half-cells are connected by a wire through which electrons can travel. Oxidation occurs in the anode. Reduction occurs in the cathode.

■ Metals are ranked by how easily they are oxidized. This ranking is used to predict which electrode is oxidized and which is reduced.

■ Batteries are portable voltaic cells. Most are dry cells, in which the electrolyte is a paste.

■ Electrolysis occurs in electrolytic cells. These cells are similar to voltaic cells, except they require electrical energy to force a nonspontaneous redox reaction.

Vocabulary

anode, 724	electric current, 723	electroplating, 733	oxidizing agent, 708
antioxidant, 719	electrochemical process, 731	free radical, 719	redox reaction, 700
cathode, 724		half-cell, 724	reducing agent, 708
corrosion, 720	electrochemistry, 723	half-reaction, 711	reduction, 700
dry cell, 727	electrode, 724	oxidation, 700	salt bridge, 725
electrical potential difference, 729	electrolysis, 731	oxidation number, 701	volt, 729
	electrolytic cell, 731		voltaic cell, 723

Word Bank

electrolysis

electrolytic cell

electroplating

free radical

half-cell

half-reaction

oxidation

oxidation number

oxidizing agent

reducing agent

reduction

voltaic cell

Vocabulary Review

On a sheet of paper, write the word or phrase from the Word Bank that completes each sentence.

1. A(n) _____ consists of a single electrode immersed in a solution of its ions.

2. When a substance gains electrons, _____ occurs.

3. A(n) _____ indicates the charge an atom would have if all bonds in a substance were ionic.

4. In _____, electrical energy is used to force a nonspontaneous redox reaction.

5. The reactant that is reduced in a redox reaction is the _____.

6. In the process of _____, a thin layer of metal is deposited onto a different metal.

7. A(n) _____ is one of two equations that make up a complete redox equation.

8. A(n) _____ is an extremely reactive particle containing an atom with an unpaired electron.

9. When a substance loses electrons, _____ occurs.

10. In a(n) _____, electrons are forced to move from the anode to the cathode by an external source of electricity.

11. The reactant in a redox reaction that is oxidized is the _____.

12. In a(n) _____, the flow of electrons from the anode to the cathode occurs spontaneously.

Continued on next page

Concept Review

On a sheet of paper, write the letter of the answer to each question.

13. What is used in a voltaic cell to maintain the charge balance between the two half-cells?

A anode   **B** cathode   **C** electrode   **D** salt bridge

14. Which of the following is a voltaic cell that contains an electrolyte paste?

A car battery   **C** electrolytic cell
B dry cell   **D** antioxidant

15. What is the oxidation number of chromium in $Cr_2O_7^{2-}$?

A 14+   **B** 12+   **C** 6+   **D** 3+

16. What is the reducing agent in the following reaction?
$$Zn + 2MnO_2 + 2NH_4^{1+} + 2Cl^{1-} \rightarrow$$
$$Zn^{2+} + Mn_2O_3 + 2NH_3 + 2Cl^{1-} + H_2O$$

A Zn   **B** MnO_2 **C** NH_4^{1+} **D** Cl^{1-}

17. What is the oxidizing agent in the reaction given in question 16?

A Zn   **B** MnO_2 **C** NH_4^{1+} **D** Cl^{1-}

18. What is the oxidation number of carbon in $Na_2C_2O_4$?

A 6−   **B** 3−   **C** 3+   **D** 4+

19. What is the oxidation number of selenium in $NaHSeO_3$?

A 1−   **B** 1+   **C** 3+   **D** 4+

20. Which pair of metals will most likely produce electricity spontaneously in a voltaic cell?

A silver and gold   **C** nickel and cadmium
B gold and platinum   **D** silver and mercury

Problem Solving

On a sheet of paper, write the letter of the answer to each question.

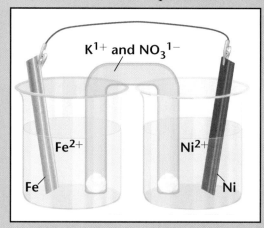

K^{1+} and NO$_3$$^{1-}$

Fe^{2+}

Ni^{2+}

Fe

Ni

21. Which statement describes the voltaic cell shown at the left?

A The anode contains the reaction,
$Fe^{2+}(aq) + 2e^{1-} \rightarrow Fe(s)$.

B The anode contains the reaction,
$Ni(s) \rightarrow Ni^{2+}(aq) + 2e^{1-}$.

C The cathode contains the reaction,
$Fe^{2+}(aq) + 2e^{1-} \rightarrow Fe(s)$.

D The cathode contains the reaction,
$Ni^{2+}(aq) + 2e^{1-} \rightarrow Ni(s)$.

22. Refer to the voltaic cell shown above. Which statement describes the nitrate ion (NO_3^{1-}) in the salt bridge?

A It moves to the cathode to reduce the positive charge.

B It moves to the anode to reduce the positive charge.

C It moves to the cathode to increase the positive charge.

D It moves to the anode to increase the positive charge.

Critical Thinking

Balance the following redox equations. Show your work on a sheet of paper.

23. $Sn^{4+} + Fe^{2+} \rightarrow Fe^{3+} + Sn$

24. $Cu + NO_3^{1-} \rightarrow Cu^{2+} + NO_2$

25. $HNO_3 + HI \rightarrow NO + I_2 + H_2O$

Test-Taking Tip After solving a problem, recheck your work. Make sure you did not make a calculation error.

19 Organic Chemistry

This leopard keeps a watchful eye on the photographer while enjoying a drink of water. Like all matter, living things are made of elements, mixtures, and compounds. Different compounds create the qualities and diversity of life. But it is the unique bonding patterns of carbon that make this diversity possible. In Chapter 19, you will learn about the carbon compounds that make up living things and many of the products you use every day.

Organize Your Thoughts

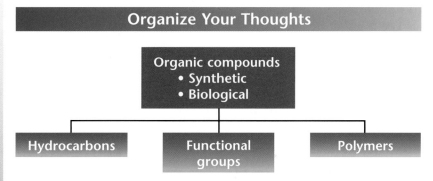

Organic compounds
• Synthetic
• Biological

Hydrocarbons   Functional groups   Polymers

Goals for Learning

◆ To describe alkanes, alkenes, alkynes, and aromatic compounds

◆ To identify the functional group and general structure of halogenated hydrocarbons, alcohols, carboxylic acids, esters, and ethers

◆ To identify the functional group and general structure of ketones, aldehydes, amines, and amides

◆ To explain polymers and how they are formed

◆ To describe carbohydrates and lipids and their functions in the body

◆ To describe proteins and nucleic acids and their functions in the body

743

Look at the label of your favorite shampoo. You are likely to find an ingredients list with words like *sodium laureth sulfate*, *cocomidopropyl betaine*, and *sodium benzoate*. These substances belong to a category of compounds called **organic compounds.** Organic compounds are all compounds that contain carbon atoms, except for carbon oxides, carbides, cyanides, and carbonates. The carbon atoms in organic compounds are covalently bonded to each other and to other atoms, usually hydrogen, nitrogen, oxygen, sulfur, or halogens. Most of the compounds described so far in this book are **inorganic compounds.** Inorganic compounds are all compounds that are not organic compounds.

Organic chemistry is the study of the structures, properties, and reactions of organic compounds. There are millions of organic compounds. This is because carbon has the ability to bond with other carbon atoms to form long chains. Every carbon atom can bond to as many as four other atoms, so these chains can have branches and ring structures. Other atoms can be part of these chains, making the variety of organic compounds almost endless.

Organic compounds are molecular, so they have molecular formulas. Organic molecules are often represented by **structural formulas.** Structural formulas use element symbols and bond lines to model molecules. They are similar to dot diagrams, except only bonds are shown. Compare ethane's molecular formula with its structural formula:

Organic compound

Any compound that contains carbon, except for carbon oxides, carbides, cyanides, and carbonates

Inorganic compound

Any compound that is not organic

Organic chemistry

The study of the structures, properties, and reactions of organic compounds

Structural formula

A model that uses element symbols and bond lines to represent a molecule

$$\begin{array}{ccccc} & & H & H & \\ & & | & | & \\ H & - & C & - & C & - & H \\ & & | & | & \\ & & H & H & \end{array}$$

C_2H_6

Molecular formula   **Structural formula**

To study such a large number of organic compounds, chemists have classified them into groups. One group is hydrocarbons. Hydrocarbons were mentioned in Chapter 5 when you studied combustion reactions. Hydrocarbons are organic compounds that contain only carbon and hydrogen atoms. Many hydrocarbons are fuels that produce heat when burned. There are four major types of hydrocarbons.

Alkanes

The simplest hydrocarbons are **alkanes.** In alkanes, the carbon atoms are bonded to each other with single bonds. Alkanes can be straight chains, chains with branches, or even rings. Some common fuels are straight-chain hydrocarbons:

Methane, CH_4 Ethane, C_2H_6 Propane, C_3H_8 Butane, C_4H_{10}

Each structural formula above differs from the one before it by the addition of a $H-C-H$ link. Each molecular formula differs from the one before it by 1 C atom and 2 H atoms.

Some alkanes contain one or more branches off the main chain of carbon atoms. A branched alkane has the same molecular formula as a straight-chain alkane. Compounds that have the same molecular formula, but different structural formulas, are **isomers.** An isomer of butane is methylpropane.

Butane, C_4H_{10} Methylpropane, C_4H_{10}

If you count the carbon and hydrogen atoms in each compound, they are the same. However, they are different compounds because their structures are different.

Originally, organic chemistry was the study of organic compounds found in living things. As technology improved, chemists have been able to create millions of organic compounds. Today, organic chemistry includes both biological and synthetic compounds.

To simplify structural formulas of rings, chemists often do not draw the carbon atoms. Cyclopentane can be drawn like this:

To simplify ring structures even more, the hydrogen atoms can be dropped:

Alkanes form rings when the carbon atoms at each end of a chain bond. These alkanes are called cycloalkanes. Two common cycloalkanes are cyclopentane and cyclohexane.

Cyclopentane, C_5H_{10} Cyclohexane, C_6H_{12}

Alkanes are nonpolar molecules, so they do not dissolve in water. However, alkanes are good solvents for other nonpolar substances like varnish, oil, and grease. Alkanes with long chains have higher melting and boiling points than those with short chains. As the molecular mass of an alkane increases, dispersion forces become stronger. At room temperature, methane, ethane, propane, and butane are gases. Straight-chain alkanes with 5 to 17 carbon atoms are liquids, and those with 18 or more carbon atoms are solids.

Alkanes are very stable compounds. They generally do not react with metals or acids. Alkanes react with halogens. They also react with oxygen. Alkanes are often used as an energy source because they produce heat and light when they burn. Methane, ethane, propane, and butane are used as fuels. Natural gas is mostly methane. Gasoline is a mixture of small hydrocarbons, most having from 5 to 12 carbon atoms. Paraffin wax is an alkane.

Alkanes are the only hydrocarbons that are **saturated.** In organic chemistry, *saturated* means that all of the bonds between carbon atoms are single bonds. All of the other types of hydrocarbons are **unsaturated.** Unsaturated hydrocarbons contain at least one double or triple bond between carbon atoms.

Alkenes

Alkenes are hydrocarbons that have at least one double bond between carbon atoms. They are unsaturated. A common alkene is ethene, although it is better known as ethylene.

$$H\diagdown \quad \diagup H$$
$$C = C$$
$$H \diagup \quad \diagdown H$$

Ethene, C_2H_4

Ethene gas is naturally produced when fruit ripens. It is often used to treat fruits and vegetables so they ripen at the same time. Ethene is also used heavily in the plastics industry. It is used to make car antifreeze, or ethylene glycol. Propene (or propylene) and 2-methylpropene (or isobutylene) are also alkenes.

Alkenes are similar to alkanes. They are nonpolar and insoluble in water, but soluble in nonpolar solvents. Their melting and boiling points depend in part on their size (their molecular mass). Alkenes with 1 to 4 carbon atoms are gases at room temperature. As the number of carbon atoms increases, dispersion forces become strong enough to keep the alkene in a liquid or even a solid state.

Electrons in double bonds are more loosely held than those in single bonds. As a result, alkenes are more reactive than alkanes. Alkenes react very easily with halogens. One halogen atom bonds to each carbon atom in the double bond. The result is a single C—C bond. For example, ethene and bromine react as follows:

$$H - C = C - H \quad + \quad Br - Br \quad \rightarrow \quad H - C - C - H$$

A similar reaction occurs when H_2 reacts with an alkene. An H atom bonds to each carbon atom in the double bond, forming an alkane. When an alkene reacts with water, an —OH group and an H atom bond to the carbon atoms.

Alkynes

Another type of unsaturated hydrocarbon is an alkyne. **Alkynes** contain at least one triple bond between carbon atoms. The most common alkyne is ethyne, also known as acetylene.

$$H - C \equiv C - H$$

Ethyne, C_2H_2

Ethyne is used as a fuel in welding torches. Ethyne's triple bond is unstable, resulting in high temperatures when ethyne burns. Ethyne is also used in the production of some vinyl and acrylic materials. Another alkyne is propyne.

Alkynes are nonpolar molecules. They are insoluble in water, but soluble in nonpolar solvents. Their melting and boiling points rise with increasing chain length (molecular mass). Their triple bonds are extremely unstable, so alkynes easily react with other substances. Alkynes react in a similar manner as alkenes.

Alkyne

A hydrocarbon that has at least one triple bond between carbon atoms

Because alkynes are extremely reactive, not many exist naturally.

Express Lab 19

Materials
◆ gumdrops, plastic foam balls, or a ball-and-stick model kit
◆ toothpicks or sticks from model kit

Procedure
1. Put on safety goggles. You will model and sketch the isomers of heptane, C_7H_{16}. For each model, use 7 carbon atoms and 16 hydrogen atoms. Every carbon atom must be bonded to four atoms.

2. Isomers differ in the way they branch. Start with a chain of 7 carbon atoms. Then model as many different heptane isomers as you can using chains of 6, 5, and 4 carbon atoms. Sketch each model you make.

Analysis
1. How many isomers of heptane are there?

2. After creating the isomers in step 2, can you create any new isomers if you start with a 3-carbon chain and add branches? Explain your answer.

Aromatic Compounds

Aromatic
compound

A hydrocarbon that
contains at least one
benzene ring

Aromatic compounds make up the last type of hydrocarbons. The smallest compound in this group is benzene, C_6H_6. Benzene is a single ring. All aromatic compounds contain at least one benzene ring. Chemists originally thought benzene had alternating single and double bonds between the carbon atoms, like the structural formula on the left below. However, research has shown that 6 electrons from the three double bonds are shared equally between all 6 carbon atoms. These 6 shared electrons are represented by a circle in the structural formula at the right. All of the carbon atoms are bonded to each other with a single bond.

Incorrect

Benzene, C_6H_6

Correct

Benzene, C_6H_6

The structural formula of benzene can also be drawn as a hexagon with a circle inside it, as shown above. Each corner of the hexagon represents a carbon atom.

The sharing of bonding electrons in a 6-carbon ring structure makes aromatic compounds unique. Larger aromatic compounds contain carbon chains and/or more than one benzene ring. The name *aromatic* comes from the fact that these compounds were first found in sweet-smelling oils from spices and fruits. Naphthalene (used in mothballs), trinitrotoluene (known as TNT), and acetylsalicylic acid (aspirin) are aromatic compounds.

Aromatic compounds are nonpolar compounds and are generally liquids or solids at room temperature. Benzene reacts with halogens. In the reaction, a halogen atom replaces a hydrogen atom on the ring.

Example 1   Classify each structure as an alkane, alkene, alkyne, or aromatic compound.

Structure A   **Structure B**

Structure C   **Structure D**   **Structure E**

Read   You are asked to classify five hydrocarbon structures.

Plan   Look for the identifying features of each hydrocarbon type. Alkanes have
              only single C—C bonds; alkenes have one or more double C=C bonds;
              alkynes have one or more triple C≡C bonds, and aromatic compounds
              have one or more benzene rings.

Solve   **Structure A** has a triple bond, which makes it an alkyne. **Structure B** has a
              double bond, which makes it an alkene. The branching of a compound does
              not determine which hydrocarbon type it is. **Structure C** has a benzene
              ring, which makes it an aromatic compound. **Structure D** has all single
              C—C bonds, which makes it an alkane—a cycloalkane. **Structure E** has one
              double bond, which makes it an alkene—a cycloalkene.

Reflect   Even though structures D and E contain rings, they are not aromatic.
              Aromatic compounds contain a benzene ring.

Practice Classify each structure as an alkane, alkene, alkyne, or aromatic compound.

Structure A   **Structure B**

Structure C

Sometimes groups of atoms in structural formulas are shown in a condensed form. For example, $-CH_3$ means

$$-\overset{\displaystyle H}{\underset{\displaystyle H}{C}}-H$$

Table 19.1.1 summarizes the four main hydrocarbon types.

Table 19.1.1 Hydrocarbon Types	
Hydrocarbon	Common Feature
alkane	single bonds between all carbon atoms
alkene	at least one double bond between carbon atoms
alkyne	at least one triple bond between carbon atoms
aromatic compound	at least one benzene ring (C_6H_6)

Spotlight on Carbon

6
C
Carbon
12.0

Carbon is one of two nonmetals in column 14 of the periodic table. It has several allotropes, including diamond, graphite, charcoal, and fullerenes. The earth's crust contains only a tiny percentage of carbon by mass. However, carbon is part of almost every molecule in plants and animals. A whole field of science called organic chemistry is devoted to carbon compounds.

The number of biological and synthetic organic compounds is almost endless. This is because of carbon's ability to bond with other carbon atoms to form chains and rings of varying size. Many other atoms and functional groups can be added to these chains and rings. The result is millions of possible molecular structures. DNA, proteins, carbohydrates, and lipids are some of the organic molecules essential to cells. Many other organic molecules are important to industry. Plastics are synthetic polymers that are used to make many products.

Carbon reacts with oxygen to form two different oxides, CO and CO_2. These oxides are inorganic. Carbon dioxide is a product of burning any fuel. If oxygen is limited, CO forms instead of CO_2. Carbon monoxide can be dangerous to inhale because it bonds with hemoglobin, a protein in blood. This keeps the hemoglobin from bonding with oxygen and delivering oxygen to the body's cells. The concentration of CO_2 gas in the atmosphere is increasing because of fossil fuel use. The warming effect associated with this buildup is called the "greenhouse effect."

Interesting Fact: Frozen carbon dioxide is called dry ice.

Word Bank

alkenes

inorganic compounds

isomers

On a sheet of paper, write the word or phrase from the Word Bank that completes each sentence.

1. Two substances that have the same molecular formula, but different structural formulas, are _____.

2. Hydrocarbons that contain at least one double bond between carbon atoms are _____.

3. Carbon dioxide and calcium carbonate are _____.

Refer to the four structural formulas in the left margin. On a sheet of paper, answer each question by writing the letter of the structure.

Structure A

4. Which one is benzene?

5. Which one is a straight-chain hydrocarbon?

Structure B

6. Which one is saturated?

Critical Thinking

On a sheet of paper, write the answer to each question.

7. Compare the physical properties of alkanes, alkenes, and alkynes.

Structure C

8. Is the structure to the right an alkane, alkene, alkyne, or aromatic compound? How do you know?

Structure D

9. Is the structure to the right an alkane, alkene, alkyne, or aromatic compound? How do you know?

10. Is the structure to the right an alkane, alkene, alkyne, or aromatic compound? How do you know?

Many hydrocarbons can react with other compounds to produce a variety of new organic compounds. A good example is the reaction between methane, CH_4, and chlorine gas, Cl_2. This reaction can produce several compounds, all of which have a chlorine atom in place of a hydrogen atom:

$$
\begin{array}{cccc}
\text{Cl} & \text{Cl} & \text{Cl} & \text{Cl} \\
| & | & | & | \\
\text{H}-\text{C}-\text{H} & \text{H}-\text{C}-\text{Cl} & \text{Cl}-\text{C}-\text{Cl} & \text{Cl}-\text{C}-\text{Cl} \\
| & | & | & | \\
\text{H} & \text{H} & \text{H} & \text{Cl}
\end{array}
$$

When one or more hydrogen atoms are replaced with a different atom or group of atoms, the result is a **substituted hydrocarbon.** The new atom or group of atoms is responsible for any change in chemical properties. The atoms and groups of atoms that can replace hydrogen are called **functional groups.** A functional group can be one atom, a group of atoms, or even a double or triple bond. Substituted hydrocarbons are classified by their functional groups. You have already learned about three functional groups: alkenes, alkynes, and aromatic compounds. There are many other functional groups.

Halogenated Hydrocarbons

Substituted hydrocarbon

An organic compound in which one or more hydrogen atoms are replaced by a functional group

Functional group

An atom or group of atoms that replaces a hydrogen atom in a hydrocarbon

Halogenated hydrocarbon

An organic compound that contains one or more halogen atoms

Several years ago, many countries agreed to ban CFCs to help protect the earth's ozone layer. CFC stands for chlorofluorocarbon. CFCs are **halogenated hydrocarbons.** In a halogenated hydrocarbon, one or more of the hydrogen atoms on a hydrocarbon chain are replaced by a halogen atom. In these compounds, the functional group is one atom: F, Cl, Br, or I. The reaction between a halogen and an alkane often requires heat and light. The general structure of a halogenated hydrocarbon is

$\boxed{R-X}$ where $X = F$, Cl, Br, or I

The functional group is in the yellow box. The abbreviation R represents the hydrocarbon part of the molecule. Throughout this chapter, R and R′ represent any hydrocarbon structure.

Halogenated hydrocarbons have high densities. They are used as solvents. They are also used to make a variety of other useful compounds. Carbon tetrachloride (CCl_4), freon (CCl_2F_2), and chloroform ($CHCl_3$) are halogenated hydrocarbons. Polyvinyl chloride (abbreviated PVC), known as vinyl plastic, is another halogenated hydrocarbon.

Alcohols

Alcohols contain the functional group $-OH$, which is called a **hydroxyl group.** The hydroxyl group is not necessarily at the end of a hydrocarbon chain. It can substitute for any hydrogen atom in any hydrocarbon.

$$R - O - H$$

Because the hydrogen atom in the hydroxyl group is bonded to an oxygen atom, most alcohols are somewhat polar. The longer the chain, the less polar the alcohol is. Alcohols of 5 carbon atoms or fewer are soluble in water. They have high boiling points and are used in disinfectants, mouthwash, solvents, and antifreeze. Ethanol is commonly known as grain alcohol. Isopropanol is the alcohol in rubbing alcohol.

Ethanol, C_2H_5OH Isopropanol, C_3H_7OH

* * *

Technology and Society

Methanol and ethanol are alcohols that are sometimes added to gasoline. They burn more completely than gasoline does, so they produce less pollution. They are made from plant sources and, therefore, reduce the amount of fossil fuel used. However, their combustion releases less energy than gasoline does. They also are more likely to corrode gas tanks.

Carboxylic Acids

Carboxylic acids are substituted hydrocarbons that contain a **carboxyl group.** This functional group is a group of four atoms, $-COOH$. Carboxylic acids have this structure:

O
||
$R-C-O-H$

Carboxyl groups are substituted at the ends of hydrocarbon chains. They are called acids because the hydrogen atom in the carboxyl group is loosely held and can be donated to a base, such as water. Carboxylic acids are weak acids. Ethanoic acid, commonly called acetic acid, is a carboxylic acid. Vinegar is a dilute solution of acetic acid.

H   O
| ||
$H-C-C-O-H$
|
H

Acetic acid, CH_3COOH or $HC_2H_3O_2$

Carboxylic acids are weakly acidic. Those with a low molecular mass dissolve well in polar solvents like water. The hydroxyl group is very polar and hydrogen-bonds to other oxygen-containing molecules. Carboxylic acids have high melting and boiling points because of the strength of hydrogen bonding. Many carboxylic acids have a strong odor and are used in flavorings, soaps, oils, and preservatives. Formic acid, $HCOOH$, is found in the venom of fire ants. Citric acid, $C_6H_8O_7$, is responsible for the sour taste of citrus fruits and some candy.

Esters

When an alcohol and a carboxylic acid react, a water molecule and an **ester** form. An ester is made by the bonding of an alcohol chain (R') to a carboxylic acid chain (R) at the oxygen atom in each functional group. The H atom from the alcohol and the $-OH$ group from the carboxylic acid are removed as water. The functional group is in the middle of the hydrocarbon. It consists of a C atom and 2 O atoms.

O
||
$R-C-O-R'$

Volatile and *flammable* are not the same thing. Volatile substances are not necessarily flammable.

The functional group in an ester is a modified carboxyl group. The H atom in $-COOH$ is replaced with a hydrocarbon: $-COOR$.

Esters are mildly polar molecules. A few esters of low molecular mass dissolve in water. The melting and boiling points of esters are similar to other hydrocarbons of the same size. Most esters have a strong but pleasant odor. Many natural and artificial aromatic oils contain esters. Oil of wintergreen and many fruit flavorings are examples of esters. Oil of banana is shown below. Perfumes and polyester fabrics also contain esters.

Oil of banana (isopentyl acetate), $C_7H_{14}O_2$

Ethers

Ethers contain two hydrocarbon chains connected to an oxygen atom. Their functional group is the connecting O atom. Their general structure is

$$R-O-R'$$

Ethers are nonpolar molecules with fairly low melting and boiling points. Because they are nonpolar, they are usually **volatile** and **flammable,** like alkanes. Volatile substances evaporate easily. Flammable substances burn easily. Ethers react with halogens, but with little else. Diethyl ether (also called ether), shown below, was used for many years as an anesthetic. Penthrane, $C_3H_4OF_2Cl_2$, and enthrone, $C_3H_2F_5ClO$, are also anesthetics.

Diethyl ether, $C_4H_{10}O$

Example 1   Identify the functional group in each organic molecule. Then identify the type of substituted hydrocarbon.

$$H-\overset{\overset{\displaystyle H}{|}}{\underset{\underset{\displaystyle H}{|}}{C}}-\overset{\overset{\displaystyle H}{|}}{\underset{\underset{\displaystyle H}{|}}{C}}-\overset{\overset{\displaystyle H}{|}}{\underset{\underset{\displaystyle H}{|}}{C}}-O-\overset{\overset{\displaystyle O}{\|}}{C}-\overset{\overset{\displaystyle H}{|}}{\underset{\underset{\displaystyle H}{|}}{C}}-H$$

Structure A

$$H-\overset{\overset{\displaystyle H}{|}}{\underset{\underset{\displaystyle H}{|}}{C}}-O-\overset{\overset{\displaystyle H}{|}}{\underset{\underset{\displaystyle H}{|}}{C}}-\overset{\overset{\displaystyle H}{|}}{\underset{\underset{\displaystyle H}{|}}{C}}-H$$

Structure B

$$H-\overset{\overset{\displaystyle H}{|}}{\underset{\underset{\displaystyle H}{|}}{C}}-\overset{\overset{\displaystyle H}{|}}{\underset{\underset{\displaystyle H}{|}}{C}}-\overset{\overset{\displaystyle H}{|}}{\underset{\underset{\displaystyle O}{|}}{C}}-\overset{\overset{\displaystyle H}{|}}{\underset{\underset{\displaystyle H}{|}}{C}}-\overset{\overset{\displaystyle H}{|}}{\underset{\underset{\displaystyle H}{|}}{C}}-H$$

Structure C

$$H-\overset{\overset{\displaystyle H}{|}}{\underset{\underset{\displaystyle H}{|}}{C}}-\overset{\overset{\displaystyle H}{|}}{\underset{\underset{\displaystyle H}{|}}{C}}-\overset{\overset{\displaystyle O}{\|}}{C}-O-H$$

Structure D

$$H-\overset{\overset{\displaystyle H}{|}}{\underset{\underset{\displaystyle H}{|}}{C}}-\overset{\overset{\displaystyle H}{|}}{\underset{\underset{\displaystyle Cl}{|}}{C}}-\overset{\overset{\displaystyle H}{|}}{\underset{\underset{\displaystyle Cl}{|}}{C}}-\overset{\overset{\displaystyle H}{|}}{\underset{\underset{\displaystyle H}{|}}{C}}-H$$

Structure E

Read   You are asked to identify the functional group in each molecule. You are also asked to identify the type of substituted hydrocarbon for each.

Plan   To identify the functional group, ignore the hydrocarbon chain. Usually, a functional group contains an atom other than carbon and hydrogen.

Solve   **Structure A** is a hydrocarbon chain joined to another hydrocarbon chain by a $-COO-$ group. It is an ester. **Structure B** is two hydrocarbon chains joined by a single O atom. It is an ether. **Structure C** has a hydroxyl group $(-OH)$ attached to a hydrocarbon chain. It is an alcohol. **Structure D** has a carboxyl group $(-COOH)$ at the end of a hydrocarbon chain. It is a carboxylic acid. **Structure E** has two chlorine atoms attached to a hydrocarbon chain. It is a halogenated hydrocarbon.

Reflect   An organic compound can contain more than one functional group. This is illustrated by two molecules in the practice problem.

Practice   Identify the functional group(s) in each organic molecule.

Structure A

Structure B

Structure C

Word Bank

ester

ether

alcohol

On a sheet of paper, write the word from the Word Bank that completes each sentence.

1. An _____ contains a hydroxyl group.

2. An _____ forms when an alcohol and a carboxylic acid bond at their functional groups.

3. An _____ consists of two hydrocarbon chains bonded to the same oxygen atom.

On a sheet of paper, write the answer to each question.

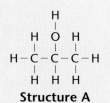

Structure A

4. Is structure A at the left a halogenated hydrocarbon, an alcohol, a carboxylic acid, or an ether?

5. Is structure B at the left an alcohol, carboxylic acid, ester, or ether?

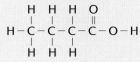

Structure B

6. Is structure C at the left a halogenated hydrocarbon, an alcohol, a carboxylic acid, or an ester?

Structure C

Critical Thinking

On a sheet of paper, write the answer to each question.

7. Compare the structures of a carboxylic acid and an ester.

8. Compare the structures of a halogenated hydrocarbon and an alcohol.

9. Ethylene glycol, used as antifreeze in car radiators, has the structure at the right. What can you infer about its melting point, boiling point, and solubility in water?

10. Copy each structure below. Circle the functional group and name the type of substituted hydrocarbon.

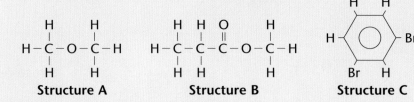

Structure A   **Structure B**   **Structure C**

INVESTIGATION 19

Materials

- safety goggles
- lab coat or apron
- gloves
- 250-mL beaker
- tap water
- distilled water
- hot plate
- test tube
- 10-mL graduated cylinder
- 3 mL of methanol
- 1.5 g of salicylic acid
- concentrated sulfuric acid in dropper bottle
- 100-mL beaker
- test-tube holder
- stirring rod

Making an Ester

Esters provide the flavors and scents of many fruits and flowers. How can you make an ester? In this investigation, you will prepare an ester by combining an alcohol and an acid. Will you be able to identify the scent of the product?

Procedure

1. Put on safety goggles, gloves, and a lab coat or apron.

2. Create a water bath by half-filling the large beaker with tap water. Put the beaker on a hot plate. Turn on the hot plate to medium. **Safety Alert: Do not touch the beaker with bare hands after it begins to warm. Do not leave the hot plate unattended while it is on.**

3. In the test tube, mix 3 mL of methanol, 1.5 g of salicylic acid, 3 mL of distilled water, and 5 drops of sulfuric acid, in that order. **Safety Alert: Sulfuric acid is corrosive. Handle it with care.**

4. Use the test-tube holder to place the test tube in the hot water bath on the hot plate. Leave it there for 5 minutes.

5. Add about 50 mL of distilled water to the small beaker.

6. Use the test-tube holder to remove the test tube from the hot water bath. Pour the contents into the small beaker of distilled water and stir. Turn off the hot plate.

Continued on next page

7. Allow the mixture to sit for a couple of minutes. Observe the smell of the liquid by wafting its vapors toward your nose, as shown.

Cleanup/Disposal
Dispose of the beaker contents in the proper waste container. Clean the glassware and return all equipment. Wash your hands.

Analysis
1. Describe the smell of the product of the reaction.

2. Sulfuric acid is not a reactant or a product of the reaction. What purpose does sulfuric acid have in this reaction?

Conclusions
1. The ester, methyl salicylate, is formed when methanol and salicylic acid react. What is the other product of the reaction?

2. Write a word equation for the reaction that produced the ester.

Explore Further
Use reference books to find the structural formulas for methanol, salicylic acid, and methyl salicylate. Using the structural formulas, write an equation for the reaction.

Objectives

After reading this lesson, you should be able to

◆ describe the general structure of four types of substituted hydrocarbons

◆ identify the functional group of a given organic molecule

In Lesson 2, you learned about halogenated hydrocarbons, alcohols, carboxylic acids, esters, and ethers. This lesson introduces four more substituted hydrocarbons.

Ketones and Aldehydes

Ketones and aldehydes have the same functional group, a **carbonyl group.** A carbonyl group is a carbon atom double-bonded to an oxygen atom: $\diagup C = O$. The difference between a ketone and an aldehyde is in the location of the functional group. **Ketones** have a carbonyl group in the middle of a hydrocarbon chain:

$$\begin{array}{c} O \\ \| \\ R-C-R' \end{array}$$

Aldehydes have a carbonyl group at the end of a chain:

$$\begin{array}{c} O \\ \| \\ R-C-H \end{array}$$

Because the carbonyl group is at the end of a chain in an aldehyde, its carbon atom is also bonded to a hydrogen atom. Because of the carbonyl group, aldehydes and ketones are polar compounds. However, as the length of the R chain increases, they become less polar. Their melting and boiling points are higher than ethers and hydrocarbons, but lower than alcohols and acids. A common ketone is propanone, also called acetone. Acetone is the main ingredient in nail polish remover and is an important solvent for organic compounds. Methanal, or formaldehyde, is an aldehyde used to preserve tissues.

Carbonyl group

A functional group consisting of a carbon atom double-bonded to an oxygen atom;

$$\begin{array}{c} O \\ \| \\ -C- \end{array}$$

Ketone

An organic compound that contains a carbonyl group within a hydrocarbon chain

Aldehyde

An organic compound that contains a carbonyl group at the end of a hydrocarbon chain

$$\begin{array}{ccccc} H & & O & & H \\ | & & \| & & | \\ H-C & - & C & - & C-H \\ | & & & & | \\ H & & & & H \end{array}$$

Acetone, C_3H_6O

$$\begin{array}{c} O \\ \| \\ H-C-H \end{array}$$

Methanal, CH_2O

Amines and Amides

Amines and amides contain a functional group called an **amino group.** This is a group of 3 atoms: $-NH_2$. It is similar to ammonia, hence its name. In **amines,** the amino group is bonded directly to the hydrocarbon chain:

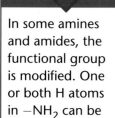

In **amides,** the amino group is bonded to a carbonyl group ($\rangle C = O$). Amides are produced when a carboxylic acid and an amine react.

In some amines and amides, the functional group is modified. One or both H atoms in $-NH_2$ can be replaced by a hydrocarbon chain.

Amines are proton acceptors. In aqueous solutions, they are almost as basic as ammonia. They have melting and boiling points well above those of alkanes of a similar mass. Small amines are polar enough to dissolve in water. Amphetamine (a stimulant) and ephedrine (a decongestant) are amines.

Amides have stronger intermolecular forces than amines. Thus, they are typically solids at room temperature. Small amides are very soluble in water. Amides are not basic or acidic. Urea (a biological waste product), acetaminophen (a pain reliever), and lidocaine (an anesthetic) are amides. Aspartame (a sweetener) contains both amine and amide functional groups.

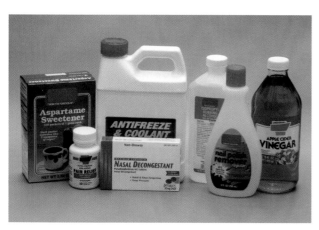

Amines and amides are found in many living organisms. They form the backbone of proteins, enzymes, and nucleic acids. You will read about these molecules in Lesson 6.

Figure 19.3.1 *Many familiar products contain organic compounds.*

Example 1 Identify the functional group in each organic molecule. Then identify the type of substituted hydrocarbon.

$$\begin{array}{ccccc} H & O & H & H & H \\ | & \| & | & | & | \\ H-C-C-C-C-C-H \\ | & & | & | & | \\ H & & H & H & H \end{array}$$

Structure A

$$\begin{array}{cccc} H & H & H & O \\ | & | & | & \| \\ H-C-C-C-C-H \\ | & | & | \\ H & H & H \end{array}$$

Structure B

$$\begin{array}{ccc} H & H & O \\ | & | & \| \\ H-C-C-C-N-H \\ | & | & | \\ H & H & H \end{array}$$

Structure C

$$\begin{array}{cc} H & H \\ | & | \\ H-C-C-N-H \\ | & | & | \\ H & H & H \end{array}$$

Structure D

Structure E

Read	You are asked to identify the functional group in each molecule. You are also asked to identify the type of substituted hydrocarbon for each.
Plan	To identify a functional group, ignore the hydrocarbon chain. Look for atoms other than carbon and hydrogen.
Solve	**Structure A** has a carbonyl group ($>C=O$) in the middle of the chain. It is a ketone. **Structure B** has a carbonyl group at the end of the chain. It is an aldehyde. **Structure C** has a carbonyl group and an amino group ($-NH_2$) at the end of the chain. It is an amide. **Structure D** has an amino group, but no oxygen atom. It is an amine. **Structure E** has a carbonyl group in the middle of a cyclic compound. It is a ketone.
Reflect	Cyclic compounds cannot be aldehydes unless a carbonyl group is on a branch off the main ring.
Practice	Identify the functional group(s) in each organic molecule.

Structure A

$$\begin{array}{cccc} H & Br & H & O \\ | & | & | & \| \\ H-C-C-C-C-H \\ | & | & | \\ H & H & H \end{array}$$

Structure B

$$\begin{array}{cccccccccc} H & H & H & H & O & H & H & H & H \\ | & | & | & | & \| & | & | & | & | \\ H-C-C-C-C-C-C-C-C-C-H \\ | & | & | & | & & | & | & | & | \\ H & H & H & H & & H & H & H & H \end{array}$$

Structure C

Table 19.3.1 lists the functional groups of the substituted hydrocarbons described in Lesson 2 and this lesson.

Table 19.3.1 Common Functional Groups		
Substituted Hydrocarbon	**Functional Group**	**Structure***
halogenated hydrocarbon	F, Cl, Br, or I atom	R$-$F, R$-$Cl, R$-$Br, or R$-$I
alcohol	hydroxyl group	R$-$O$-$H
carboxylic acid	carboxyl group	$$R-\overset{\overset{\displaystyle O}{\|\|}}{C}-O-H$$
ester	modified carboxyl group (H is replaced with R′)	$$R-\overset{\overset{\displaystyle O}{\|\|}}{C}-O-R'$$
ether	O atom	R$-$O$-$R′
ketone	carbonyl group	$$R-\overset{\overset{\displaystyle O}{\|\|}}{C}-R'$$
aldehyde	carbonyl group	$$R-\overset{\overset{\displaystyle O}{\|\|}}{C}-H$$
amine	amino group	$$R-\overset{\overset{\displaystyle H}{\|}}{N}-H$$
amide	carbonyl and amino groups	$$R-\overset{\overset{\displaystyle O}{\|\|}}{C}-\overset{\overset{\displaystyle H}{\|}}{N}-H$$

Each functional group is shown in red.

Link to >>>

Language Arts

The meaning of a science term is sometimes different from its meaning in everyday use. For example, in grocery stores, the word *organic* describes foods that are produced without the use of hormones, pesticides, and certain fertilizers. In chemistry, *organic* means something very different.

Word Bank
aldehyde
amine
ketone

On a sheet of paper, write the word from the Word Bank that completes each sentence.

1. A(n) _____ is a hydrocarbon chain with a carbonyl group in the middle.

2. Every amide and _____ contains an amino group.

3. A carbonyl group is located at the end of a(n) _____.

Structure A

On a sheet of paper, write the answer to each question. Refer to the structures in the left margin.

4. Is structure A a ketone, aldehyde, amine, or amide?

5. Is structure B a ketone, aldehyde, amine, or amide?

6. Is structure C a ketone, aldehyde, amine, or amide?

Structure B

Critical Thinking

On a sheet of paper, write the answer to each question.

7. Compare the structures of an aldehyde and a ketone.

8. Compare the structures of an amine and an amide.

Structure C

9. Vanillin is artificial vanilla flavoring. Its structure is at the right. What functional groups does it contain? What categories of substituted hydrocarbons could this structure belong in?

10. Copy each structure below. Circle the functional group and name the type of substituted hydrocarbon.

Structure A   **Structure B**   **Structure C**

What would happen if many small organic molecules bonded in a long chain? A **polymer** would form. Polymers are long organic molecules made of repeating structural units. The small molecules that bond to form polymers are called **monomers.** Monomers are often substituted hydrocarbons or hydrocarbons with double or triple bonds. One polymer molecule can be formed from tens of thousands of monomers.

Polymers are an essential part of your life. They are used to make many products, including plastic bottles, medical instruments, tires, shampoos, and artificial joints. Without polymers, there would be no artificial turf in sports arenas, no nonstick cookware, and no chewing gum. The polymers in these products are synthetic. However, there are many naturally occurring polymers. Cotton, wool, and silk are natural polymers used in fabrics. Rubber is found in nature and is also manufactured. Important polymers in living things include polysaccharides, proteins, and nucleic acids. These biological polymers are discussed in Lessons 5 and 6.

Many polymers are unreactive, which makes them an ideal material for containers to store foods or medicines. Many industrially important polymers are plastics. For example, polyethylene is a polymer of thousands of ethene (ethylene) molecules. This common plastic is used to make milk bottles, plastic toys, and household items. When ethene monomers bond, their double bonds become single bonds, as shown.

Ethene   **Ethene**   **Polyethylene**

The atoms in the left yellow box are the same ones in the right box. Many ethene monomers bonded together create polyethylene.

Polypropylene is another plastic. Its monomers are propene (propylene) molecules. Polypropylene is used in plastic toys, household items, packing materials, and artificial turf.

Propene   Propene   Polypropylene

Certain polymers have unique properties that make very useful products. For example, some polymers have a remarkable ability to repel water, trap heat, and resist burning. They are ideal for raincoats and other outerwear. They are also used to make clothing for firefighters and soldiers. Synthetic fleece is a relatively new material that also traps heat well. It is made from recycled plastic bottles. Figure 19.4.1 shows new polymer fibers made by recycling plastic. Other polymers are able to absorb large quantities of water. Disposable diapers contain polyacrylic acid. This polymer can absorb many times its own weight in liquid.

Figure 19.4.1 *The fibers on the rollers were made from recycled plastic bottles.*

Technology and Society

When polymer molecules that are dissolved in water become linked, they may form a gel. Gels have some properties of solids. Superabsorbent polymers are gels that can absorb water-based fluids. They are used as a fireproof coating in buildings. These gels can also be poured by hose directly on a fire to prevent it from spreading.

Lesson 4 REVIEW

Word Bank

double bonds

monomers

natural

plastic

polymers

unreactive

On a sheet of paper, write the word or phrase from the Word Bank that completes each sentence.

1. Many bonded _____ form a polymer.

2. Long chains of repeating structural units are called _____.

3. Ethene molecules contain _____, but a polyethylene molecule does not.

4. Cotton, wool, and silk are _____ polymers.

5. Many _____ household products are made from synthetic polymers.

6. Many polymers are ideal materials for containers because they are _____.

Critical Thinking

On a sheet of paper, write the answer to each question.

7. Name two ways you use polymers each day.

8. Give two examples of natural polymers.

9. Give two examples of synthetic polymers.

10. How are polymers different from the hydrocarbons you studied in Lessons 1, 2, and 3?

Materials

- safety goggles
- lab coat or apron
- gloves
- 50 mL of white glue
- 4 paper cups
- 5 g of borax
- 2 400-mL beakers
- 10-mL graduated cylinder
- 100-mL graduated cylinder
- 2 tongue depressors
- distilled water
- grease pencil
- stirring rod

Linking Polymers

When monomers bond, a polymer forms. What happens when polymers link together? White glue contains polymers. In this investigation, you will use borax to link the polymer strands in white glue to each other.

Procedure

1. Put on safety goggles, gloves, and a lab coat or apron.

2. Read through the entire procedure. Then design a data table you can use to record your observations.

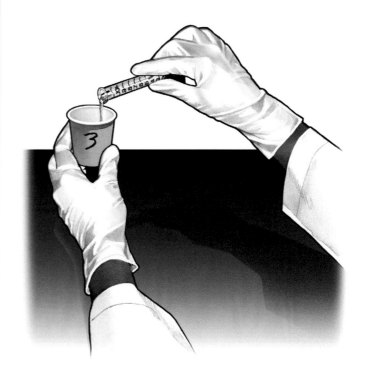

Continued on next page

3. Make a glue solution by mixing 50 mL of white glue and 50 mL of water in a beaker. Stir well. Using the large graduated cylinder, divide the solution evenly among the four cups. Label the cups 1, 2, 3, and 4.

4. Make a borax solution in the other beaker by dissolving about 5 g of borax in 100 mL of water.

5. Write a procedure for finding the best amount of borax solution to use to link the polymers in the white glue solution. You will judge which amount is the best by how long a strand you can form when you stretch the resulting linked polymers. In your procedure, include a hypothesis and any safety alerts.

6. After your teacher approves your procedure, perform the investigation. Test the four polymer samples.

Cleanup/Disposal

Dispose of your polymer samples in a proper waste container. Clean the glassware and return all materials. Wash your hands.

Analysis

1. Which sample produced the longest string?

2. What happened to the polymers in a sample if the sample did not pull into a string after adding borax?

Conclusions

1. Explain why the polymers pulled into a long string when a certain amount of borax was added.

2. Explain your answer to Analysis question 2.

Explore Further

Research the concept of cross-linking. Write a paragraph to explain how cross-linking relates to this investigation.

Organic chemistry is often called the chemistry of life. Organic compounds are found in every living organism. Cell walls are made of organic molecules. Inside cells, organic molecules are manufactured and used. Many of these biological molecules are polymers. Living organisms need these polymers to survive.

Carbohydrates

Carbohydrates are organic molecules that contain the elements carbon, hydrogen, and oxygen in a ratio of about 1:2:1. For every carbon atom, there are about 2 hydrogen atoms and 1 oxygen atom. The word *carbohydrate* came from the myth that carbohydrates are carbon molecules that are hydrated (that contain atoms from water).

Carbohydrates vary greatly in size and use. However, all carbohydrates are sugar molecules or larger molecules of bonded sugars. Sugar molecules are usually rings containing 5, 6, or 7 carbon atoms. The simplest carbohydrates are **monosaccharides.** Monosaccharides contain only one sugar unit. Fructose and glucose are monosaccharides. Fructose is the sugar in fruit, and glucose is the sugar used by the body to provide energy to cells and tissues.

Carbohydrate

An organic molecule that contains carbon, hydrogen, and oxygen in about a 1:2:1 ratio; a sugar molecule or a larger molecule of bonded sugars

Monosaccharide

A simple carbohydrate consisting of only one sugar unit

Disaccharide

A simple carbohydrate consisting of two sugar units bonded together

Fructose   **Glucose**

Disaccharides, such as lactose (milk sugar) and sucrose (table sugar), consist of two monosaccharides bonded together.

Lactose (galactose + glucose)

Some monosaccharides and disaccharides are easily digested by the human body and oxidized to release energy. However, large amounts of these simple sugars in the diet can cause tooth decay and obesity.

Polysaccharides are complex carbohydrates. They are polymers of monosaccharides. Starch is a polymer that consists of several hundred glucose monomers. Starch is found in rice, breads, cereals, and certain vegetables. When starch is digested by the body, it breaks down into glucose. Starch is a good source of energy, like simple sugars.

Starch

Cellulose is a similar polymer. It is made of hundreds to thousands of glucose monomers, depending on the source of the cellulose. Cellulose is a good source of dietary fiber because the human body does not digest it. Only a few animals, such as cows, termites, and goats, can digest cellulose. Cellulose is an abundant organic compound because it forms the cell walls of plants.

All carbohydrates are monosaccharides, disaccharides, or polysaccharides. Table 19.5.1 summarizes these carbohydrates and lists some examples.

Table 19.5.1 Types of Carbohydrates		
Carbohydrate Type	**Description**	**Examples**
monosaccharide	one sugar unit	glucose, fructose, galactose, altrose, ribose
disaccharide	two sugar units bonded together	lactose, sucrose, maltose, trehalose
polysaccharide	polymer of sugar units	starch, cellulose, glycogen, chitin

Carbohydrates serve three main purposes in the human body:

- Carbohydrates are a source of energy. They are easily digested and oxidized to release energy. This energy is quickly available to the brain, the nervous system, and many other tissues.

- The carbohydrate glycogen, a polymer of glucose, is used as a short-term storage of glucose. If glycogen is not broken down into glucose and used to release energy, it is converted into fats.

- Carbohydrates are a source of fiber. Some fiber is soluble in water and helps limit the absorption of fats from the intestines, thus reducing the risk of heart disease. Other fiber is insoluble. Both soluble and insoluble fiber are undigested and are not absorbed into the bloodstream.

Lipids

Lipids are organic molecules that contain long-chain carboxylic acids called **fatty acids.** Lipid molecules have fewer oxygen atoms than carbohydrate molecules. Fatty acids are important parts of biological membranes.

Oils, fats, and waxes are lipids. Lipids that come from plants are usually called oils. Examples are olive oil, peanut oil, and corn oil. Lipids that come from animals are usually called fats. Examples are lard (pork fat) and tallow (beef fat). Waxes, produced by plants, protect leaves and stems from water loss. In general, lipids are insoluble in water, but soluble in nonpolar solvents.

Science Myth

Myth: The terms *oil* and *fat* mean the same thing.

Fact: Fats usually come from animals, and oils usually come from plants. Also, oils are liquids at room temperature, while fats are solids. Both are types of lipids.

Many lipids in your diet are **triglycerides.** A triglyceride consists of three fatty acids bonded to a glycerol molecule. Glycerol is an alcohol with three carbon atoms and three hydroxyl groups. In a triglyceride, one fatty acid is bonded to each hydroxyl group.

$$H-\overset{\overset{\displaystyle H}{|}}{\underset{|}{C}}-O-\overset{\overset{\displaystyle O}{\|}}{C}-(CH_2)_{10}-\overset{\overset{\displaystyle H}{|}}{\underset{\underset{\displaystyle H}{|}}{C}}-H$$

$$H-\overset{|}{\underset{|}{C}}-O-\overset{\overset{\displaystyle O}{\|}}{C}-(CH_2)_{10}-\overset{\overset{\displaystyle H}{|}}{\underset{\underset{\displaystyle H}{|}}{C}}-H$$

$$H-\overset{\overset{\displaystyle H}{|}}{\underset{\underset{\displaystyle H}{|}}{C}}-O-H$$

$$H-\overset{|}{\underset{|}{C}}-O-H$$

$$H-\overset{|}{\underset{\underset{\displaystyle H}{|}}{C}}-O-H$$

Glycerol

$$H-O-\overset{\overset{\displaystyle O}{\|}}{C}-(CH_2)_{10}-\overset{\overset{\displaystyle H}{|}}{\underset{\underset{\displaystyle H}{|}}{C}}-H$$

Fatty acid

$$H-\overset{|}{\underset{\underset{\displaystyle H}{|}}{C}}-O-\overset{\overset{\displaystyle O}{\|}}{C}-(CH_2)_{10}-\overset{\overset{\displaystyle H}{|}}{\underset{\underset{\displaystyle H}{|}}{C}}-H$$

Triglyceride

The fatty acids in a lipid can vary. A saturated fatty acid, such as the one shown above, has only single bonds between its carbon atoms. A monounsaturated fatty acid contains one double bond among its carbon atoms. A polyunsaturated fatty acid contains two or more double bonds between its carbon atoms. Animal fats usually have more saturated fatty acids than plant oils.

Lipids serve many important functions in the human body:

• Lipids are a source of energy that can be stored. Like carbohydrates, many lipids are broken down to release energy. Gram for gram, lipids produce more than twice the energy produced by carbohydrates. The body can store triglycerides for future use.

• Certain lipids act as hormones, which regulate some of the functions of the body. Steroids, estrogen, and testosterone are examples of hormones.

Biochemistry is a branch of organic chemistry that focuses on biological molecules.

- Lipids aid vitamin absorption. Some vitamins, such as A, D, and E, are insoluble in water. When dissolved in nonpolar lipids, these vitamins can be transported.

- Many lipids are structural components of cells.

- Lipids protect vital organs from shock and help keep the body warm.

Chemistry in Your Life

Consumer Choices: Fake Fats

There are many opinions about what kinds of foods make the healthiest diet. But all experts agree that a diet high in fats is not healthy. Some lipids are necessary to carry out important functions in the body, such as producing hormones and providing energy. However, excess fats in the diet can result in obesity, heart disease, diabetes, cancer, and other health problems. For these reasons, scientists have developed fat substitutes:

- High-protein foods can be heated to form small molecules that taste creamy. These fat substitutes have fewer calories and health risks than fats.

- Gels formed from starch can replace the fats in some foods. A form of cellulose is also used to replace fats.

- Sucrose can replace glycerol in a fat molecule. The resulting compound is not absorbed by cells and passes through the body undigested.

The drawbacks to these fake fats include digestive problems. Also, some fat substitutes dissolve fat-soluble vitamins. Because the substitutes do not break down in the body, the vitamins are not released and used by the body.

1. Why is a no-fat diet not a good idea?

2. If you eat mostly fake fats, what might you do to be sure you receive enough vitamins?

On a sheet of paper, write the word or phrase from the Word Bank that completes each sentence.

1. A _____ is a long-chain carboxylic acid.

2. A _____ is a simple sugar.

3. When three fatty acids bond with a glycerol molecule, a _____ forms.

On a sheet of paper, write the letter of the answer to each question.

4. Which of the following is a polysaccharide?

   A sucrose   **C** cellulose

   B glucose   **D** triglyceride

5. Which of the following is a lipid?

   A starch   **C** glycerol

   B tallow   **D** lactose

6. Which of the following produces the most energy per gram in the body?

   A lipids   **C** cellulose

   B carbohydrates   **D** sucrose

Research and Write

Research types of cooking oils, such as canola oil, olive oil, corn oil, and safflower oil. For each oil, identify its source, its advantages and disadvantages in cooking, and any health benefits. Summarize your findings in a short report or poster project.

Critical Thinking

On a sheet of paper, write the answer to each question.

7. Compare fructose and glucose. How are they similar and different?

8. Compare cellulose and starch. How are they similar and different?

9. What are three functions of carbohydrates in the body?

10. What are three functions of lipids in the body?

Lesson 6 Proteins and Nucleic Acids

Objectives

After reading this lesson, you should be able to

- describe proteins and their functions in the body
- describe the composition of nucleic acids
- explain the role of DNA and RNA in the body

The word *protein* comes from a Greek word meaning "of first rank." Proteins are found in all cells and in almost all cell parts. They have a wide variety of functions in the human body. Nucleic acids are also found in every cell. Proteins and nucleic acids are large molecules that are essential to life. Both deserve the title "first rank."

Proteins

In the last lesson, you learned that polysaccharides are polymers of simple sugar units. **Proteins** are also polymers. Their monomers are organic molecules called **amino acids.** An amino acid is an organic molecule that contains an amino group and a carboxyl group. To form a protein, the amino group of one amino acid bonds with the carboxyl group of another amino acid. Figure 19.6.1 shows how amino acids bond to form proteins. The R and R′ represent the hydrocarbon part of the molecule. When two amino acids bond, one water molecule is also formed.

Protein

An organic polymer made from amino acids

Amino acid

An organic molecule with an amino group and a carboxyl group

All of the proteins in the human body are made from only 20 different amino acids. These amino acids differ only in their hydrocarbon side chain. Amino acids are classified as either essential or nonessential. Essential amino acids cannot be made by the body and must come from foods. Nonessential amino acids can be made by the body and do not need to be part of the diet.

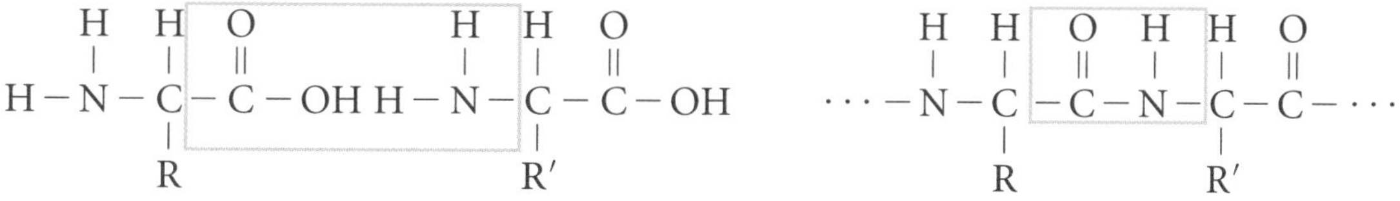

Amino acid **Amino acid** **Protein**

Figure 19.6.1 *Every amino acid has the same two functional groups. The carboxyl group of one amino acid bonds to the amino group of the next amino acid. For each bond formed, one water molecule is produced. The atoms that form water are shown in blue.*

Each protein is folded into a characteristic three-dimensional shape. Proteins can be round balls or long structures. Their shape is maintained by interparticle forces and bonds. The shape of a protein affects its chemical properties, allowing it to react with some substances and not with others.

Proteins have many vital functions in the human body:

- Certain proteins called enzymes are catalysts. Enzymes speed the reactions in the body. Enzymes speed the breakdown of foods into smaller, usable molecules. Enzymes also help cells break down these molecules, releasing energy.

- Proteins are structural parts of all body tissue. They form ligaments, tendons, and muscles, which allow the body to move.

- Proteins called collagen and keratin are structural parts of skin, hair, and cartilage.

- A protein called hemoglobin transports oxygen in the bloodstream.

- Proteins called antibodies protect the body from disease.

Achievements in Science

X-Ray Crystallography

Chemists use X-ray crystallography to determine the structure of molecules. X-rays are used because their wavelength is much shorter than that of visible light. The wavelength of X-rays is approximately the distance of the bond lengths between atoms. In X-ray crystallography, X-rays are diffused by crystals. Computers are used to produce a pattern that shows the shape of molecules in a sample.

X-ray crystallography has been especially useful in determining the three-dimensional structure of biological compounds. One pioneer in this field was Dorothy Crowfoot Hodgkin.

She determined the molecular structures of vitamin B12, pepsin, and penicillin. One of the most important structures she discovered was that of insulin, which is used to treat diabetes. Her work with vitamin B12 also led to developments in the treatment of pernicious anemia.

Other scientists have played important roles in developing and using X-ray crystallography. Rosalind Franklin's work on the dimensions and shape of DNA was critical in determining how traits are passed to an offspring. Kathleen Yardley Lonsdale confirmed the ring structure of benzene.

Nucleic acid

A large polymer of nucleotides that contains genetic information that cells need to reproduce

DNA

Deoxyribonucleic acid

RNA

Ribonucleic acid

Nucleotide

The monomer of a nucleic acid that consists of a phosphate group, a sugar, and a nitrogen base

Nitrogen base

A nitrogen-containing compound in a nucleic acid; thymine, guanine, cytosine, adenine, or uracil

Nucleic Acids

Nucleic acids are inside every living cell. They are large polymers that carry the genetic code that cells need to reproduce. Nucleic acids also control the production of proteins inside the cell. This production of proteins is how the genetic code is "read" by the cell. There are two kinds of nucleic acids: **DNA** (deoxyribonucleic acid) and **RNA** (ribonucleic acid). Both are made from complex monomers called **nucleotides.** One nucleic acid molecule contains thousands of nucleotides.

Each nucleotide has three parts: a phosphate group, a simple sugar, and a nitrogen compound called a **nitrogen base.** There are five possible nitrogen bases. Each has a letter abbreviation: adenine (A), thymine (T), guanine (G), cytosine (C), and uracil (U). The nucleotides in DNA and RNA differ in their sugar molecule and in the set of possible bases. An example of a nucleotide is shown in Figure 19.6.2. Table 19.6.1 compares the nucleotides in DNA and RNA.

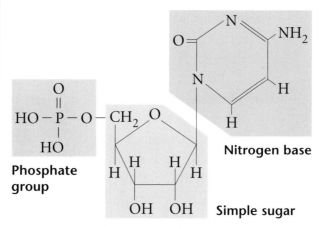

Figure 19.6.2 *This RNA nucleotide contains a phosphate group, the sugar ribose, and the base cytosine.*

Table 19.6.1 Nucleotides in DNA and RNA		
Nucleotide Component	**DNA**	**RNA**
sugar	deoxyribose	ribose
nitrogen base	A, C, G, or T	A, C, G, or U
phosphate	This functional group does not vary. It is the same in both DNA and RNA.	

Link to ⪢⪢⪢

Earth Science

Layers of energy-rich organic materials have been gradually turned into large coal beds and oil fields by the pressure of overlying rock. Because this process takes millions of years, fossil fuels are considered nonrenewable resources.

The backbone of a nucleic acid is made of alternating sugars and phosphates, as Figure 16.6.3 shows. A nitrogen base is bonded to each sugar molecule.

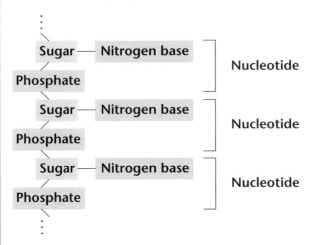

Figure 19.6.3 *A nucleic acid is a long chain of nucleotides.*

A DNA molecule consists of two long chains of nucleotides. These chains are called strands. The two strands spiral around each other. Each base on one strand lines up with a base on the other strand. Hydrogen bonding forms between these pairs of bases. This bonding acts like rungs in a ladder, holding the two strands together. The three-dimensional structure of DNA is called a double helix. It looks like a twisted ladder, as the model in Figure 19.6.4 shows.

An RNA molecule is a single strand of nucleotides.

Figure 19.6.4 *In DNA, the bases on each strand pair up, creating a double helix. Adenine always pairs up with thymine, and guanine always pairs up with cytosine.*

The genetic code for a cell is determined by the sequence of nitrogen bases in the cell's DNA. This base sequence is like a master key. It makes up the instructions for every protein made by that cell. A cell's genetic code is passed from one generation of cells to the next because the DNA tells how to make the next generation of cells. The genetic code in DNA is the basis for genetics and genetic engineering, two relatively new fields in science.

RNA has a different function in cells than DNA. While DNA stores a cell's genetic code, RNA carries copies of this code to make proteins.

Science at Work

Geneticist

One of the newer fields in science is genetics. Geneticists work to unlock the secrets of DNA and heredity. Geneticists often apply their work in the areas of medicine, agriculture, and forensics. Many geneticists work for pharmaceutical companies. They research the causes of diseases and birth defects. Then they look for ways to prevent or treat them. Some geneticists do agricultural research to develop improved crops. Others work in crime labs. They use DNA samples to make sure the right person is convicted of a crime.

Not all geneticists do research in labs. Some work as genetic counselors in clinics. They collect family histories and counsel people who are concerned about the possibility of genetic disorders.

Work in genetics requires much education and training. A master's degree in genetics

or a related field is often required. Some specific areas of genetics require special research training or a medical degree.

Lesson 6   R E V I E W

Match each description in the first column with a term in the second column. Write the letter of the answer on a sheet of paper.

1. Together with sugars, they form the backbone of DNA and RNA.

2. All 20 of these contain an amino group and a carboxyl group.

3. They form when amino acids bond in a long chain.

4. They contain ribose and exist as single strands.

5. They consist of a phosphate group, a simple sugar, and a nitrogen base.

6. They contain deoxyribose and exist as double strands.

A amino acids

B phosphates

C proteins

D DNA molecules

E nucleotides

F RNA molecules

Critical Thinking

On a sheet of paper, write the answer to each question.

7. How do proteins function as catalysts in the body?

8. Compare the structures of DNA and RNA.

9. What is the difference between essential and nonessential amino acids?

10. How do proteins contribute to the structure of tissues and cells?

Octane Ratings of Gasoline

When you pull up to a gasoline pump, you have a choice of fuels with different octane ratings. What do these values mean?

Gasoline is a mixture of several mid-sized hydrocarbons. An octane rating is a measure of how well the mixture keeps a car engine from "knocking." Knocking is caused by uneven burning of fuel in the engine. On the octane scale, a 0 value represents the large amount of knocking that occurs when unbranched heptane is burned. An octane rating of 100 represents the very small amount of knocking that occurs when 2,2,4-trimethylpentane is burned. This hydrocarbon is a chain of 5 carbon atoms with three 1-carbon branches. Two of these branches are on the second carbon atom in the chain. The other branch is on the fourth carbon atom in the chain.

Other octane ratings are based on how well a gasoline mixture burns compared to these standards. For example, an octane rating of 92 means that the fuel burns the way a mixture of 8 parts of heptane and 92 parts of 2,2,4-trimethylpentane would burn.

In general, branched hydrocarbons have a higher octane rating than hydrocarbons with few branches. Aromatic compounds have even higher octane ratings.

When gasoline is prepared at a refinery, straight-chain hydrocarbons can be changed to branched isomers by heating the vapors with aluminum chloride. Another refining process uses catalysts to change alkanes to aromatic compounds.

Usually, fuels with a higher octane rating provide better mileage—more miles per gallon. However, you should always check the owner's manual for the vehicle. Some engines are designed to operate most effectively on fuels with a low octane rating.

1. A certain gasoline has an octane rating of 89. What does this mean?

2. Explain how benzene can have an octane rating greater than 100.

Chapter 19 S U M M A R Y

- Organic chemistry is the study of organic compounds.

- Hydrocarbons contain only carbon and hydrogen atoms. There are four main types of hydrocarbons: alkanes, alkenes, alkynes, and aromatic compounds.

- A substituted hydrocarbon contains one or more functional groups.

- Halogenated hydrocarbons contain one or more halogen atoms. Alcohols contain a hydroxyl group, and carboxylic acids contain a carboxyl group.

- Esters are formed when an alcohol and a carboxylic acid react. Ethers are two hydrocarbon chains bonded to the same oxygen atom. Ketones have a carbonyl group in the middle of a chain. Aldehydes have a carbonyl group at the end of a chain.

- Amines contain an amino group. Amides have an amino group joined to a carbonyl group at the end of a chain.

- Polymers are long chains of repeating structural units. They form when monomers bond together.

- Monosaccharides and disaccharides are simple carbohydrates. Polysaccharides, such as starch and cellulose, are complex carbohydrates.

- Common lipids include oils and fats. They contain fatty acids, which are long-chain carboxylic acids.

- Proteins are long chains of amino acids.

- Nucleic acids are strands of nucleotides. Each nucleotide is made of a sugar, a phosphate, and a nitrogen base. DNA stores a cell's genetic code.

Vocabulary

alcohol, 754
aldehyde, 761
alkane, 745
alkene, 747
alkyne, 748
amide, 762
amine, 762
amino acid, 777
amino group, 762
aromatic compound, 749
carbohydrate, 771
carbonyl group, 761

carboxyl group, 755
carboxylic acid, 755
disaccharide, 771
DNA, 779
ester, 755
ether, 756
fatty acid, 773
flammable, 756
functional group, 753
halogenated hydrocarbon, 753
hydroxyl group, 754

inorganic compound, 744
isomer, 745
ketone, 761
lipid, 773
monomer, 766
monosaccharide, 771
nitrogen base, 779
nucleic acid, 779
nucleotide, 779
organic chemistry, 744
organic compound, 744

polymer, 766
polysaccharide, 772
protein, 777
RNA, 779
saturated, 746
structural formula, 744
substituted hydrocarbon, 753
triglyceride, 774
unsaturated, 746
volatile, 756

Word Bank

alkene

alkyne

amino group

aromatic
  compound

disaccharides

ester

ether

isomers

ketone

lipid

monomers

polysaccharides

protein

saturated

volatile

Vocabulary Review

On a sheet of paper, write the word or phrase from the Word Bank that completes each sentence.

1. A(n) _____ is a hydrocarbon that contains at least one double bond.

2. A(n)_____ is a hydrocarbon that contains a benzene ring.

3. Sucrose and lactose are examples of _____.

4. A(n) _____ is a long chain of amino acids.

5. A(n) _____ is a long-chain molecule that contains fatty acids.

6. A(n) _____ contains a carbonyl group within a hydrocarbon chain.

7. A polymer forms when many identical _____ bond in a long chain.

8. A(n)_____ contains at least one triple bond between carbon atoms.

9. Cellulose and starch are examples of _____.

10. When an alcohol reacts with a carboxylic acid, a(n) _____ forms.

11. A(n) _____ is two hydrocarbon chains joined by an oxygen atom.

12. Compounds with the same molecular formula, but different structural formulas, are _____.

13. A(n) _____ fatty acid or hydrocarbon has only single bonds between the carbon atoms.

14. The _____ is a functional group in both amines and amides.

15. A(n) _____ substance evaporates easily.

Continued on next page

Concept Review

On a sheet of paper, write the letter of the answer that completes each sentence. For questions 16–19, refer to the structures in the left margin.

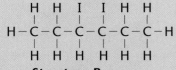

Structure A

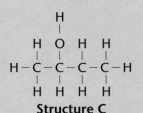

Structure B

Structure C

Structure D

16. Structure A is an example of a(n) _____.

A halogenated hydrocarbon
B aromatic compound
C carboxylic acid
D both B and C

17. Structure B is an example of a(n) _____.

A aromatic compound
B alkene
C halogenated hydrocarbon
D alkyne

18. Structure C is an example of a(n) _____.

A carboxylic acid
B alcohol
C ketone
D ester

19. Structure D is an example of a(n) _____.

A amine
B amide
C aromatic compound
D halogenated hydrocarbon

20. The backbone of a nucleic acid consists of alternating _____.

A phosphates and sugars
B nitrogen bases and amino acids
C sugars and nitrogen bases
D amino acids and phosphates

Critical Thinking

On a sheet of paper, write the answer to each question.

21. Describe how the boiling point of alkanes changes as the length of the chain increases.

22. List three natural polymers and three synthetic polymers.

23. Identify the type of substituted hydrocarbon each structure is. More than one answer may be possible.

Structure A

Structure B

Structure C

24. Identify the type of substituted hydrocarbon each structure is. More than one answer may be possible.

Structure A

Structure B

Structure C

25. Rank the following carbohydrates by size, from smallest to largest: cellulose, glucose, and lactose.

Test-Taking Tip After you have completed a test, compare each question to your answer. Ask yourself: Did I answer the question that was asked?

Appendix A: Reference Tables

Table A.1 Alphabetical Table of Elements

Element	Symbol	Atomic Number	Atomic Mass (amu)*	Element	Symbol	Atomic Number	Atomic Mass (amu)*
actinium	Ac	89	(227)	europium	Eu	63	152.0
aluminum	Al	13	27.0	fermium	Fm	100	(257)
americium	Am	95	(243)	fluorine	F	9	19.0
antimony	Sb	51	121.8	francium	Fr	87	(223)
argon	Ar	18	39.9	gadolinium	Gd	64	157.3
arsenic	As	33	74.9	gallium	Ga	31	69.7
astatine	At	85	(210)	germanium	Ge	32	72.6
barium	Ba	56	137.3	gold	Au	79	197.0
berkelium	Bk	97	(247)	hafnium	Hf	72	178.5
beryllium	B	4	9.0	hassium	Hs	108	(277)
bismuth	B	83	209.0	helium	He	2	4.0
bohrium	B	107	(264)	holmium	Ho	67	164.9
boron	B	5	10.8	hydrogen	H	1	1.0
bromine	Br	35	79.9	indium	In	49	114.8
cadmium	Cd	48	112.4	iodine	I	53	126.9
calcium	Ca	20	40.1	iridium	Ir	77	192.2
californium	Cf	98	(251)	iron	Fe	26	55.8
carbon	C	6	12.0	krypton	Kr	36	83.8
cerium	Ce	58	140.1	lanthanum	La	57	138.9
cesium	Cs	55	132.9	lawrencium	Lr	103	(262)
chlorine	Cl	17	35.5	lead	Pb	82	207.2
chromium	Cr	24	52.0	lithium	Li	3	6.9
cobalt	Co	27	58.9	lutetium	Lu	71	175.0
copper	Cu	29	63.5	magnesium	Mg	12	24.3
curium	Cm	96	(247)	manganese	Mn	25	54.9
darmstadtium	Ds	110	(281)	meitnerium	Mt	109	(268)
dubnium	Db	105	(262)	mendelevium	Md	101	(258)
dysprosium	Dy	66	162.5	mercury	Hg	80	200.6
einsteinium	Es	99	(252)	molybdenum	Mo	42	95.9
erbium	Er	68	167.3	neodymium	Nd	60	144.2

Table A.1 Alphabetical Table of Elements (continued)

Element	Symbol	Atomic Number	Atomic Mass (amu)*	Element	Symbol	Atomic Number	Atomic Mass (amu)*
neon	Ne	10	20.2	scandium	Sc	21	45.0
neptunium	Np	93	(237)	seaborgium	Sg	106	(266)
nickel	Ni	28	58.7	selenium	Se	34	79.0
niobium	Nb	41	92.9	silicon	Si	14	28.1
nitrogen	N	7	14.0	silver	Ag	47	107.9
nobelium	No	102	(259)	sodium	Na	11	23.0
osmium	Os	76	190.2	strontium	Sr	38	87.6
oxygen	O	8	16.0	sulfur	S	16	32.1
palladium	Pd	46	106.4	tantalum	Ta	73	181.0
phosphorus	P	15	31.0	technetium	Tc	43	(98)
platinum	Pt	78	295.1	tellurium	Te	52	127.6
plutonium	Pu	94	(244)	terbium	Tb	65	158.9
polonium	Po	84	(209)	thallium	Tl	81	204.4
potassium	K	19	39.1	thorium	Th	90	232.0
praseodymium	Pr	59	140.9	thulium	Tm	69	168.9
promethium	Pm	61	(145)	tin	Sn	50	118.7
protactinium	Pa	91	231.0	titanium	Ti	22	47.9
radium	Ra	88	(226)	tungsten	W	74	183.9
radon	Rn	86	(222)	uranium	U	92	238.0
rhenium	Re	75	186.2	vanadium	V	23	50.9
rhodium	Rh	45	102.9	xenon	Xe	54	131.3
roentgenium	Rg	111	(272)	ytterbium	Yb	70	173.0
rubidium	Rb	37	85.5	yttrium	Y	39	88.9
ruthenium	Ru	44	101.1	zinc	Zn	30	65.4
rutherfordium	Rf	104	(261)	zirconium	Zr	40	91.2
samarium	Sm	62	150.4				

*Most atomic masses are averages based on the element's isotopes.
They are rounded to the tenths place. An atomic mass in parentheses
is the mass of the element's most stable isotope.

Table A.2 Common Polyatomic Ions

1−	acetate, $C_2H_3O_2^{1-}$	cyanide, CN^{1-}	nitrate, NO_3^{1-}
	amide, NH_2^{1-}	formate, $HCOO^{1-}$	nitrite, NO_2^{1-}
	astatate, AtO_3^{1-}	hydrogen carbonate, HCO_3^{1-}	perbromate, BrO_4^{1-}
	azide, N_3^{1-}	hydrogen sulfate, HSO_4^{1-}	perchlorate, ClO_4^{1-}
	benzoate, $C_6H_5COO^{1-}$	hydroxide, OH^{1-}	periodate, IO_4^{1-}
	bismuthate, BiO_3^{1-}	hypobromite, BrO^{1-}	permanganate, MnO_4^{1-}
	bromate, BrO_3^{1-}	hypochlorite, ClO^{1-}	perrhenate, ReO_4^{1-}
	chlorate, ClO_3^{1-}	hypophosphate, $H_2PO_2^{1-}$	thiocyanate, SCN^{1-}
	chlorite, ClO_2^{1-}	iodate, IO_3^{1-}	vanadate, VO_3^{1-}
2−	carbonate, CO_3^{2-}	peroxydisulfate, $S_2O_8^{2-}$	sulfite, SO_3^{2-}
	chromate, CrO_4^{2-}	phosphite, HPO_3^{2-}	tartrate, $C_4H_4O_6^{2-}$
	dichromate, $Cr_2O_7^{2-}$	ruthenate, RuO_4^{2-}	tellurate, TeO_4^{2-}
	hexafluorosilicate, SiF_6^{2-}	selenate, SeO_4^{2-}	tellurite, TeO_3^{2-}
	molybdate, MoO_4^{2-}	selenite, SeO_3^{2-}	tetraborate, $B_4O_7^{2-}$
	oxalate, $C_2O_4^{2-}$	silicate, SiO_3^{2-}	thiosulfate, $S_2O_3^{2-}$
	peroxide, O_2^{2-}	sulfate, SO_4^{2-}	tungstate, WO_4^{2-}
3−	arsenate, AsO_4^{3-}	borate, BO_3^{3-}	hexacyanoferrate(III), $Fe(CN)_6^{3-}$
	arsenite, AsO_3^{3-}	citrate, $C_6H_5O_7^{3-}$	phosphate, PO_4^{3-}
4−	diphosphate, $P_2O_7^{4-}$	hexacyanoferrate(II), $Fe(CN)_6^{4-}$	orthosilicate, SiO_4^{4-}
1+	ammonium, NH_4^{1+}	plutonyl(V), PuO_2^{1+}	vanadyl(V), VO_2^{1+}
	neptunyl(V), PuO_2^{1+}	uranyl(V), UO_2^{1+}	
2+	mercury(I), Hg_2^{2+}	plutonyl(VI), PuO_2^{2+}	vanadyl(IV), VO^{2+}
	neptunyl(VI), NpO_2^{2+}	uranyl(VI), UO_2^{2+}	

Table A.3 Metric Measurement Prefixes

Prefix	Symbol	Multiplying Factor	Prefix	Symbol	Multiplying Factor
giga-	G	1,000,000,000 (or 10^9)	centi-	c	0.01
mega-	M	1,000,000 (or 10^6)	milli-	m	0.001 (or 10^{-3})
kilo-	k	1,000 (or 10^3)	micro-	μ	0.000001 (or 10^{-6})
hecto-	h	100	nano-	n	0.000000001 (or 10^{-9})
deka-	da	10	pico-	p	0.000000000001 (or 10^{-12})
deci-	d	0.1	fempto-	f	0.000000000000001 (or 10^{-15})

Table A.4 Symbols and Abbreviations*

α	alpha particle	K_f	freezing-point depression constant
β^-	beta particle	K_w	equilibrium constant for water
γ	gamma ray	k	rate constant
Δ	change in	L	liter (volume)
ν	frequency	(l)	liquid
ν	velocity	M, m	mass
amu	atomic mass unit (atomic mass)	M	molarity
(aq)	aqueous solution	m	meter (length)
atm	atmosphere (pressure)	m	molality
°C	degree Celsius (temperature)	mm Hg	millimeter of mercury (pressure)
c	speed of light	mol	mole (amount)
C_p	specific heat	n	number of moles
D	density	n	energy level
E	energy	n^0	neutron
E_a	activation energy	P	pressure
e^-, e^{1-}	electron	p^+	proton
°F	degree Fahrenheit (temperature)	Pa	pascal (pressure)
g	gram (mass)	pH	$-\log(H^{1+})$
(g)	gas	q	heat
H	enthalpy	R	gas constant
ΔH_c	heat of combustion	rem	Rem (radiation)
ΔH_f	standard heat of formation	s	second
ΔH_{fus}	heat of fusion	(s)	solid
ΔH_{rxn}	heat of reaction	SI	Système International d'Unités
ΔH_{vap}	heat of vaporization	STP	standard temperature and pressure
h	Planck's constant	T	temperature
Hz	hertz (frequency)	T_C	temperature in degrees Celsius
i	number of ions	T_K	temperature in kelvins
J	joule (energy)	ΔT_b	boiling-point elevation
K	kelvin (temperature)	ΔT_f	freezing-point depression
K	equilibrium constant	V	volt (electrical potential difference)
K_b	boiling-point elevation constant	V	volume

*For abbreviations of measurement units, the variable that the unit measures is in parentheses.

Table A.5 Equations

atomic mass

atomic mass =

$$(\text{mass of isotope A})\left(\frac{\text{percent abundance}}{100\%}\right) +$$

$$(\text{mass of isotope B})\left(\frac{\text{percent abundance}}{100\%}\right) + \cdots$$

boiling-point elevation $\Delta T_b = (K_b)(m)(i)$

Boyle's law $P_1 V_1 = P_2 V_2$

Charles's law $\dfrac{V_1}{T_1} = \dfrac{V_2}{T_2}$

combined gas law $\dfrac{P_1 V_1}{T_1} = \dfrac{P_2 V_2}{T_2}$

Dalton's law of partial pressure

$P_{\text{total}} = P_A + P_B + P_C + \cdots$

density $D = \dfrac{\text{mass}}{\text{volume}} = \dfrac{M}{V}$

dilution equation $M_1 V_1 = M_2 V_2$

Einstein's energy equation $E = mc^2$

enthalpy change for a liquid-gas change of state

$\Delta H = (m)(\Delta H_{\text{vap}})$

enthalpy change for a liquid-solid change of state

$\Delta H = (m)(\Delta H_{\text{fus}})$

enthalpy change when a substance changes temperature

$\Delta H = (m)(C_p)(\Delta T)$

equilibrium expression $K = \dfrac{[\text{C}]^c [\text{D}]^d}{[\text{A}]^a [\text{B}]^b}$

for $a\text{A} + b\text{B} + \cdots \rightleftarrows c\text{C} + d\text{D} + \cdots$

freezing-point depression

$\Delta T_f = (K_f)(m)(i)$

Gay-Lussac's law $\dfrac{P_1}{T_1} = \dfrac{P_2}{T_2}$

Graham's law $\dfrac{\nu_A}{\nu_B} = \sqrt{\dfrac{M_B}{M_A}}$

heat transfer $q = (m)(C_p)(\Delta T)$

heat of reaction

$\Delta H_{\text{rxn}} = (\text{sum of } \Delta H_f \text{ of products})$
$\qquad - (\text{sum of } \Delta H_f \text{ of reactants})$

ideal gas law $PV = nRT$

mass percent

mass percent $= \left(\dfrac{\text{grams of solute}}{\text{grams of solution}}\right) 100\%$

molality $m = \dfrac{\text{moles of solute}}{\text{kilograms of solvent}}$

molarity $M = \dfrac{\text{moles of solute}}{\text{liters of solution}}$

mole fraction

$X = \dfrac{\text{moles of one substance in mixture}}{\text{total moles of all substances in mixture}}$

percent composition

percent composition =

$\left(\dfrac{\text{total molar mass of element}}{\text{molar mass of compound}}\right) 100\%$

percent yield

percent yield $= \left(\dfrac{\text{actual yield}}{\text{theoretical yield}}\right) 100\%$

pH $\text{pH} = -\log[\text{H}^{1+}]$ or $[\text{H}^{1+}] = 10^{-\text{pH}}$

Planck's energy equation $E = h\nu$

rate law

rate $= k[\text{reactant A}]^m [\text{reactant B}]^n \cdots$

titration equation (for 1:1 acid:base ratio)

$M_a V_a = M_b V_b$

Ratios and Proportions

Ratios usually compare two numbers. They can be expressed in different forms. To compare 4 to 10, you could write 4:10 or $\frac{4}{10}$. The ratio $\frac{4}{10}$ is a fraction. In math equations, the fraction form of a ratio is used. For example, the equation, $B = \left(\frac{4}{10}\right)20$, contains the fraction $\frac{4}{10}$.

Simplified fractions make math operations easier. It is easier to calculate $\left(\frac{2}{5}\right)20$ than $\left(\frac{4}{10}\right)20$. Fractions can be simplified by dividing the numerator and denominator by a common factor.

$$\frac{12}{16} = \frac{12}{16} \div \frac{4}{4} = \frac{3}{4}$$

$$\frac{12N}{18} = \frac{12N}{18} \div \frac{6}{6} = \frac{2N}{3}$$

$$\frac{15}{5N} = \frac{15}{5N} \div \frac{5}{5} = \frac{3}{N}$$

When dividing terms that contain exponents with the same base, remember to subtract exponents.

$$\frac{18N^6}{20N^4} = \frac{18N^6}{20N^4} \div \frac{2N^4}{2N^4} = \frac{9N^2}{10}$$

A proportion is the expression of two equal ratios, such as $\frac{4}{8} = \frac{5}{10}$. Often, one number in a proportion is not known. For example, in the following proportion, N represents an unknown number.

$$\frac{9}{12} = \frac{N}{10}$$

Before solving for N, simplify the ratio $\frac{9}{12}$. Divide the 9 and the 12 by 3.

$$\frac{9}{12} \div \frac{3}{3} = \frac{3}{4} \qquad \text{so} \qquad \frac{3}{4} = \frac{N}{10}$$

The cross-product method is often used to solve for an unknown in a proportion.

$$\frac{3}{4} = \frac{N}{10} \qquad \begin{array}{l} \text{Multiply } 4 \times N. \\ \text{Multiply } 3 \times 10. \end{array}$$

Using this method, the above proportion can be written as

$$(4)(N) = (3)(10) \qquad \text{or} \qquad 4N = 30$$

In this equation, N has the coefficient 4. To get N by itself, multiply both sides of the equation by $\frac{1}{4}$ (the reciprocal of 4).

$$\left(\frac{1}{4}\right)4N = \left(\frac{1}{4}\right)30$$

$$N = \frac{30}{4}$$

The answer, $\frac{30}{4}$, can be simplified to $\frac{15}{2}$. Both are improper fractions. The answer can also be written as a proper fraction, $7\frac{1}{2}$, or as a decimal, 7.5.

The next two proportions are solved for A using the cross-product method. Neither proportion can be simplified before solving.

Problem 1	*Problem 2*
$\dfrac{4A}{9} = \dfrac{7}{12}$	$\dfrac{A}{B} = \dfrac{5}{C}$
$(9)(7) = (4A)(12)$	$5B = AC$
$63 = 48A$	

At this point in both problems, determine the coefficient of A. Then multiply each side by its reciprocal.

$\left(\dfrac{1}{48}\right)63 = 48A\left(\dfrac{1}{48}\right)$	$\left(\dfrac{1}{C}\right)5B = AC\left(\dfrac{1}{C}\right)$
$\dfrac{63}{48} = A$	$\dfrac{5B}{C} = A$

The answer to the first problem can be written as $\frac{63}{48}$, $\frac{21}{16}$, $1\frac{5}{16}$, or 1.3125.

Percents and Decimals

Percentages express a portion of a total. *Per cent* means "per hundred," so 25% means 25 out of 100 or $\frac{25}{100}$ (which is 25 times $\frac{1}{100}$). 25% can also be written in decimal form: 0.25. When performing math operations, the decimal form of a percentage is usually used.

To convert a percentage to a decimal, divide by 100 and drop the percent sign. This is the same as moving the decimal point two places to the left.

25% is the same as 0.25

For any percentage N%, $N\% = \frac{N}{100}$.

To convert a decimal to a percentage, multiply by 100%. This is the same as moving the decimal point two places to the right.

0.25 is the same as 25%

For any decimal number N, $N = N(100\%)$.

Sometimes one or two zeros need to be added to "mark" the two places that the decimal point moves. In the following examples, the added zeros are in blue.

1.6%   01.6% is 0.016

0.16%   000.16% is 0.0016

0.7   0.70 is 70%

1.3   1.30 is 130%

1   1.00 is 100%

There are three basic types of percent problems, shown below. In each one, the word *of* indicates multiplication. The word *is* can be replaced by an equal sign.

In a percent problem, *of* means $\times$ and *is* means $=$.

In a percent problem, the percentage must be converted to its decimal form.

Type 1
20% of 52 is N.
$(0.20)(52) = N$
$10.4 = N$

Type 2
3% of N is 18.
$(0.03)(N) = 18$
$\frac{0.03N}{0.03} = \frac{18}{0.03}$
$N = 600$

Type 3
N% of 30 is 90.
$\left(\frac{N}{100}\right)(30) = 90$
$0.30N = 90$
$\frac{0.30N}{0.30} = \frac{90}{0.30}$
$N = 300$

In the last two problems, dividing by a number is the same as multiplying by its reciprocal.

Solving Algebraic Equations

Solving equations using algebra is not hard if this basic rule is followed:

> A math operation performed on one side of an equation must be performed on the other side.

Think of an equation as being perfectly balanced at the equal sign. If you add a number to the left side, you must add the same number to the right side to keep it balanced. If you divide the left side by a number, you must divide the right side by the same number. Consider this simple equation:

$$N + 5 = 12$$

You know that $N = 7$ because $7 + 5 = 12$. But how would you solve for N by applying the above rule? Solving for N means performing math operations that result in an equation where "$N =$" is on one side. Subtracting 5 from both sides of the equation will accomplish this.

$$N + 5 = 12$$
$$N + 5 \, (-5) = 12 \, (-5)$$
$$N = 7$$

When 5 is subtracted from the left side, N is left by itself.

What operation would you perform to solve for N in $3N = 20$? To get N by itself, divide both sides by 3 or multiply both sides by $\frac{1}{3}$ (the reciprocal of 3).

$$3N = 20$$
$$\left(\frac{1}{3}\right)3N = 20\left(\frac{1}{3}\right)$$
$$N = \frac{20}{3}$$

An improper fraction, such as $\frac{20}{3}$, is an acceptable answer.

What operation would you perform to solve for N in the following equation?

$$\frac{3N}{5} = \frac{4}{7}$$

Multiply both sides by the reciprocal of $\frac{3}{5}$.

$$\left(\frac{5}{3}\right)\frac{3N}{5} = \frac{4}{7}\left(\frac{5}{3}\right)$$

$$N = \frac{20}{21}$$

The following equation is found on page 647 in Chapter 16. It is an equilibrium expression, where $K = 278$, and 3.53 and 0.575 are molarities. How would you solve for $[O_2]$?

$$\frac{278}{1} = \frac{(3.53)^2}{(0.575)^2[O_2]}$$

This has the form of a proportion, $\frac{A}{B} = \frac{C}{D}$. Use the cross-product method.

$$(1)(3.53)^2 = (278)(0.575)^2[O_2]$$

To isolate $[O_2]$, divide both sides by $(278)(0.575)^2$.

$$\frac{(3.53)^2}{(278)(0.575)^2} = \frac{(278)(0.575)^2[O_2]}{(278)(0.575)^2}$$

$$\frac{(3.53)^2}{(278)(0.575)^2} = [O_2]$$

Now use your calculator. Perform the two exponent operations first.

$$0.136 = [O_2]$$

The answer shows 3 significant figures. See pages 19–31 in Chapter 1 to review the use of significant figures when working with measurements.

Graphing

Scientists often use line graphs to show the relationship between two variables. The two variables are usually related by some mathematical rule. In many experiments, one variable is repeatedly changed by the experimenter. It is the independent variable. The other variable, called the dependent variable, responds to this change. The dependent variable is measured. The results are summarized in a data table, such as the one below.

Volume of a Gas Sample at Various Temperatures	
Temperature	Volume
298 K	101.3 mL
303 K	102.2 mL
308 K	103.4 mL
313 K	105.0 mL
318 K	106.7 mL
323 K	108.4 mL

With a set of data like this, a graph can be drawn. A line graph has a horizontal x axis and a vertical y axis. The point where the two axes cross is called the origin. The independent variable is plotted on the x axis. The dependent variable is plotted on the y axis. In this example, the independent variable is temperature.

To construct a graph, first draw the x and y axes on graph paper. Determine a scale for each axis that will fit the range of data. The two axes do not need to have the same scale. Then divide the axes into equal sections according to the scales you chose. Scales usually show whole-number values, but you do not need to write every whole-number value.

Each pair of values in the data table will represent one point on the graph. Plot each point on the graph. Then draw a line connecting the points. The line may be straight or curved to best fit the data.

To make a graph understandable, label each axis with the name of the variable it represents. Provide the measurement unit in parentheses. Then give your graph a title. Remember, a graph should be easy to read.

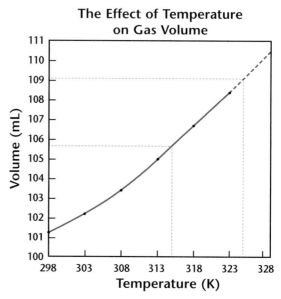

The Effect of Temperature on Gas Volume

Sometimes a scientist extrapolates to estimate a value that was not measured. To extrapolate means to read beyond the data given in a graph. By extending the graphed line, you can estimate the value of the dependent variable for a certain value of the independent variable. To do this, you may need to draw the graph on larger graph paper. Using the graph above, you can extrapolate the volume of the gas sample at 325 K. It is about 109.1 mL.

Sometimes a scientist interpolates. This means to read between two points on the graph. For example, find the value of 315 K on the x axis on the graph on page 796. Visualize a perpendicular line going from that point up to the graphed line. Then visualize a horizontal line going over to the y axis. Read the value for the dependent variable. At 315 K, the volume is about 105.7 mL.

Besides line graphs, scientists use circle graphs and bar graphs. A circle graph is suitable for showing how one quantity compares to the whole. For example, the circle graph below shows the percent composition of water. Water has a molar mass of 18.0 g/mol. It is 88.9% oxygen by mass.

Bar graphs are useful for comparing several quantities. The bar graph below compares the molar masses of some calcium compounds.

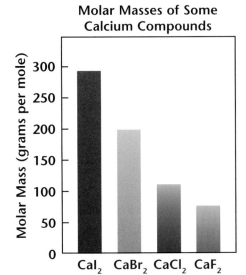

Percent Composition of Water

Oxygen
2.0 g/mol
88.9%

Hydrogen
16.0 g/mol
11%

Appendix C: Supplementary Problems

This appendix contains additional problems to supplement each chapter. On a sheet of paper, write the answer to each problem assigned by your teacher. For math problems, show your work.

Chapter 1

1. What are two qualitative properties of ground black pepper?

2. A student has three beakers containing equal volumes of room-temperature water. Each is placed 10 inches below a lightbulb. The bulbs are three different types. After 1 hour, the student measures the temperature of the water in each beaker. Which variable, bulb type or temperature, is the dependent variable? Explain your answer.

3. Write the following number in scientific notation: 8,750,000,000.

4. Write the following number in scientific notation: 0.000000000000135.

5. Change the following number to standard notation: 9.13×10^{-8}.

6. Change the following number to standard notation: 2.69×10^{11}.

7. Identify the significant figures in the following measurement: 80,210,000 mm.

8. Identify the significant figures in the following measurement: 0.00030700 km.

9. Solve: (2.750 cm)(3.3 cm). Express the answer in significant figures.

10. Solve: 193.18 miles + 4.6 miles. Express the answer in significant figures.

11. Which metric unit would be best for measuring the height of a chair?

12. Which metric unit would be best for measuring the volume of water in a glass?

13. Convert 3.206×10^{-2} km to millimeters.

14. Convert 0.0081 mL to microliters.

15. Convert 13.7 cg to decigrams.

16. Convert 83.5 kg to grams.

17. Calculate the density of an object with a mass of 27.2 g and a volume of 32 mL. Give the correct unit and number of significant figures in your answer.

18. Calculate the mass of a sample of mercury that has a density of 13.55 g/mL and a volume of 7.2 mL. Give the correct unit and number of significant figures in your answer.

19. Calculate the volume of a sample of chlorine with a density of 3.21 g/L and a mass of 4.5 g. Give the correct unit and number of significant figures in your answer.

20. Calculate the volume of a sample of iron with a density of 7.87 g/mL and a mass of 23.2 g. Give the correct unit and number of significant figures in your answer.

Chapter 2

1. Compare particles of ice with particles of water. Compare their movement, shape, and volume.

2. Give three physical properties of a hot cup of coffee.

3. "Gold is a yellow, shiny metal. It has a density of 19.3 g/mL. It is a solid at 20°C. Gold is a good conductor of heat and electricity. It does not react with many other elements or compounds." From this description, identify four physical properties of gold.

4. From the description in question 3, identify a chemical property of gold.

5. Butter melts in a hot frying pan. Is this a physical or chemical change?

6. Do chemical changes involve physical or chemical properties? Explain your answer.

7. A student mixes vegetable oil and vinegar to make a salad dressing. The mixture separates into two layers. Is the dressing a solution or a heterogeneous mixture? Explain your answer.

8. Identify the solute and solvent in an aqueous solution of sugar.

9. Is ground black and white pepper a homogeneous or heterogeneous mixture? Explain your answer.

10. From the periodic table, what do you know about mercury (Hg)?

11. From the periodic table, what do you know about hydrogen (H)?

12. Write the chemical symbols of the seven diatomic elements. Which are gases at 20°C?

13. Are most of the elements on the periodic table solids, liquids, or gases at 20°C?

14. Write the chemical symbols of the semimetals. Which element that touches the "staircase" is not a semimetal?

15. What is the chemical symbol of potassium? Is it a metal, semimetal, or nonmetal?

16. What is the chemical symbol of antimony? Is it a metal, semimetal, or nonmetal?

17. Give the name and number of each kind of atom in the chemical formula for iron(III) hydroxide, $Fe(OH)_3$.

18. Give the name and number of each kind of atom in the chemical formula for ammonium acetate, $NH_4C_2H_3O_2$.

19. Give the name and number of each kind of atom in the chemical formula for aspirin, $C_6H_4COOHC_2H_3O_2$.

20. Which of the following is not a compound: Na_2S, S_8, or SF_6? How do you know?

Chapter 3

1. What is the formula for each of the following molecular compounds?
A diphosphorous tetroxide
B nitrogen triiodide

2. What is the formula for each of the following molecular compounds?
A hexanitrogen octabromide
B silicon monocarbide

3. What is the formula for each of the following molecular compounds:
A oxygen difluoride
B sulfur dioxide

4. What is the symbol for a chromium(III) ion?

5. What is the symbol for a chloride ion?

6. What is the formula unit for the ionic compound formed by copper(I) and sulfur?

7. What is the formula unit for the ionic compound, lead (IV) oxide?

8. What is the formula unit for the ionic compound, barium sulfite?

9. What is the formula unit for the ionic compound, ammonium dichromate?

10. What is the formula unit for the ionic compound, calcium bicarbonate?

11. What is the formula unit for the ionic compound, manganese(III) phosphate?

12. What is the name of the molecular compound, B_4H_{10}?

13. What is the name of the molecular compound, Cl_2O_7?

14. What is the name of the molecular compound, N_2O_5?

15. What is the name of the ionic compound, Mn_2O_3?

16. What is the name of the ionic compound, $Ca(NO_2)_2$?

17. What is the name of the ionic compound, $Pb(CrO_4)_2$?

18. What is the name of the ionic compound, Cu_2CO_3?

19. How can you identify the formula of an acid?

20. What is the difference between the two compounds, H_2CO_3 and $NaHCO_3$?

Chapter 4

1. How many moles are in 7.23×10^{23} formula units of potassium chloride?

2. How many moles are in 2.35×10^{24} molecules of hydrogen?

3. How many atoms are in 8.25 mol of chromium?

4. How many formula units are in 0.035 mol of aluminum sulfate?

5. Calculate the molar mass of calcium hydroxide.

6. How many moles are in 73.2 g of N_2O_4?

7. What is the mass of 15.3 mol of chlorine gas?

8. How many moles are in 115 g of iron(II) nitrate?

9. What is the volume in liters of 0.53 mol of oxygen gas at STP?

10. How many moles of neon gas are in 225 L at STP?

11. What is the volume in milliliters of 2.75×10^{-3} mol of carbon monoxide at STP?

12. A solution is made by dissolving 75.2 g of $Ca(C_2H_3O_2)_2$ in enough water to make 925 mL of solution. What is the solution's molarity?

13. What mass of $(NH_4)_2CO_3$ is dissolved in 225 mL of a 0.139 M solution?

14. How many molecules of chlorine gas are in 103 L at STP?

15. What is the mass in grams of 8.05×10^{23} atoms of iron?

16. What mass of KOH is dissolved in 35.7 mL of a 0.96 M solution?

17. What is the percent composition of each element in ammonium nitrate?

18. What is the empirical formula of a molecular compound that contains 53.3% carbon, 11.1% hydrogen, and 35.6% oxygen by mass?

19. The molecular compound in question 18 has a molar mass of 135 g/mol. What is its molecular formula?

20. A hydrate of nickel(II) nitrate is heated, with the following results. What is the empirical formula of the hydrate?
mass of hydrate before heating $= 17.44$ g
mass of compound after heating $= 10.96$ g

Chapter 5

1. Write the following word equation as a chemical equation: Aqueous sodium hydroxide and aqueous hydrochloric acid react to produce liquid water and aqueous sodium chloride.

2. Write the following chemical equation as a word equation.
$NH_3(g) + O_2(g) \rightarrow NO_2(g) + H_2O(l)$

3. Write the products and their states in the following equation
$NaHCO_3(s) + HC_2H_3O_2(aq) \rightarrow$
$\quad H_2O(l) + CO_2(g) + NaC_2H_3O_2(aq)$

4. Balance the following equation.
$KOH(aq) + H_2SO_4(aq) \rightarrow$
$\quad\quad K_2SO_4(aq) + H_2O(l)$

5. Balance the following equation.
$C_3H_8(g) + O_2(g) \rightarrow CO_2(g) + H_2O(g)$

6. Balance the following equation.
$P_4O_{10}(s) + H_2O(l) \rightarrow H_3PO_4(aq)$

7. Balance the following equation.
$K(s) + N_2(g) \rightarrow K_3N(s)$

8. Balance the following equation.
$Fe_2(CO_3)_3(s) \rightarrow Fe_2O_3(s) + CO_2(g)$

9. Balance the following equation.
$Al(s) + CuCl_2(aq) \rightarrow AlCl_3(aq) + Cu(s)$

10. Identify the type of reaction shown in questions 4, 5, 6, 7, 8, and 9.

11. Which element can replace nickel in a single replacement: Cu, Sn, or Al?

12. Which element can replace chlorine in a single replacement: F, Br, or I?

For questions 13–20, identify the reaction type, predict the product(s), and balance the equation. If a reaction does not occur, write *no reaction*.

13. $C_6H_6 + O_2 \rightarrow$

14. $Al + S \rightarrow$

15. $K_2CO_3 \rightarrow$

16. $Zn + MgCl_2 \rightarrow$

17. $Sr(OH)_2 + HF \rightarrow$

18. $Ca + Cu(NO_3)_2 \rightarrow$

19. $H_2O \rightarrow$

20. $Mg + H_2O \rightarrow$

Chapter 6
For questions 1–3, use the following balanced equation.
$2C_6H_6 + 15O_2 \rightarrow 12CO_2 + 6H_2O$

1. If 25.0 mol of oxygen reacts, how many moles of water are produced?

2. If 8.40 mol of carbon dioxide forms, how many moles of C_6H_6 react?

3. If 14.2 mol of water forms, how many moles of carbon dioxide are made?

For questions 4–6, use the following balanced equation.

$$Fe_2(CO_3)_3 \rightarrow Fe_2O_3 + 3CO_2$$

4. If 75.2 g of $Fe_2(CO_3)_3$ reacts, how many moles of Fe_2O_3 form?

5. If 0.535 mol of CO_2 is made, how many grams of Fe_2O_3 form?

6. If 173 g of Fe_2O_3 forms, how many grams of $Fe_2(CO_3)_3$ react?

For questions 7–10, use the following balanced equation.

$$NaHCO_3(s) + HC_2H_3O_2(aq) \rightarrow$$
$$H_2O(l) + CO_2(g) + NaC_2H_3O_2(aq)$$

7. If 83.2 g of $HC_2H_3O_2$ reacts, how many molecules of water form?

8. If 5.62×10^{23} formula units of $NaC_2H_3O_2$ are produced, what mass of $NaHCO_3$ reacts?

9. If 35.7 g of water is produced at STP, what volume of carbon dioxide forms?

10. If 89.6 L of carbon dioxide is produced at STP, how many formula units of $HC_2H_3O_2$ react?

For questions 11–13, use the following balanced equation.

$$2KOH(aq) + H_2SO_4(aq) \rightarrow$$
$$K_2SO_4(aq) + 2H_2O(l)$$

11. If 0.0750 L of 1.31 M KOH reacts with excess sulfuric acid, what mass of water forms?

12. If 223 mL of 0.92 M H_2SO_4 reacts with excess KOH, how many formula units of K_2SO_4 are produced?

13. If 47.3 mL of 2.50 M KOH reacts with excess sulfuric acid, what mass of K_2SO_4 forms?

For questions 14–17, use the following balanced equation.

$$P_4O_{10} + 6H_2O \rightarrow 4H_3PO_4$$

14. A reaction is performed in which 32.5 g of P_4O_{10} reacts with excess water. What is the theoretical yield of H_3PO_4?

15. The reaction in question 14 has an actual yield of 40.2 g of H_3PO_4. What is the percent yield? (Hint: Use your answer from question 14.)

16. The same reaction is carried out, but this time 76.2 g of water reacts with excess P_4O_{10}. The percent yield of H_3PO_4 is 83.2%. What mass of H_3PO_4 was produced?

For questions 17–20, use the following balanced equation.

$$C_3H_8(g) + 5O_2(g) \rightarrow 3CO_2(g) + 4H_2O(g)$$

17. A reaction occurs when 35.3 g of C_3H_8 is combined with 115 g of oxygen. What is the limiting reactant? How do you know?

18. Based on the reactant amounts in question 17, what is the maximum mass of water that can form?

19. A reaction occurs when 53.5 g of C_3H_8 is combined with 217 g of oxygen. What is the maximum mass of carbon dioxide that can form?

20. A reaction occurs when 96.2 L of C_3H_8 is combined with 235 L of O_2 at STP. What is the maximum volume of carbon dioxide that can form at STP?

Chapter 7

1. How are gas pressure and gas volume related?

2. What are the three parts of the kinetic model?

3. Why is it dangerous to heat a sealed plastic container in a microwave oven?

4. A substance is at 173 K. What is this temperature in degrees Celsius?

5. Convert –44°C to kelvins.

6. A gas has a pressure of 212 kPa. What is this pressure in millimeters of mercury?

7. A gas has a pressure of 643 mm Hg. What is this pressure in atmospheres?

8. A gas mixture of argon, oxygen, and carbon monoxide has a total pressure of 3.53 atm. The partial pressure of argon is 27.5 kPa, and the partial pressure of oxygen is 1,153 mm Hg. What is the partial pressure of carbon monoxide? (Hint: Change all pressures to atmospheres first.)

9. A sample of oxygen gas is collected over water at 40°C. The total pressure of the mixture is 823 mm Hg. What is the partial pressure of the gas?

10. A gas sample has a pressure of 83.2 kPa and a volume of 15.2 L. What is its volume at 1.11 atm if temperature is constant?

11. A gas sample has a volume of 1,990 mL at –15°C. What is its volume at 32°C if its pressure does not change?

12. A gas sample has a volume of 2.15 L at 75°C and 75.9 kPa. At what temperature will its volume be 1.52 L if the pressure changes to 92.0 kPa?

13. A gas sample has a volume of 893 mL at –35°C and 855 mm Hg. What is its volume at STP?

14. What is the mass of 47.2 L of N_2 gas at –25°C and 735 mm Hg?

15. What is the volume of 83.2 g of argon at 37°C and 113 kPa?

16. What is the pressure of 22.5 g of NH_3 in a volume of 42.1 L at 82°C?

17. 72.1 g of fluorine gas has a volume of 63.6 L at 743 mm Hg. What is its temperature in degrees Celsius?

18. The gases N_2O, CCl_4, and HF are at the same temperature. Rank the speed of their particles from fastest to slowest.

19. Two gas samples, Xe and O_2, are at the same temperature. In which sample are the particles moving faster? How much faster?

20. Nitrogen molecules are 2.07 times faster than the particles of an unknown gas at the same temperature. Is the unknown gas $CHCl_3$ or HCl?

Chapter 8

1. Dalton's model of the atom differs from Thomson's model. Describe each one and explain how they are different.

2. Rutherford's gold foil experiment proved something that Thomson's atomic model did not show. What was it?

3. Which scientist is responsible for the discovery of the neutron?

4. Which scientist is responsible for the discovery of the electron?

5. Which scientist is responsible for determining the mass of an electron?

For questions 6–14, copy the chart below. Fill in the missing information in each row.

	Isotope	Symbol	Atomic Number	Mass Number	p^+	n^0	e^-	Charge
6.	strontium-88						36	
7.		$^{55}_{25}\text{Mn}^{3+}$						
8.						12	10	2+
9.		$^{128}_{52}\text{Te}^{2-}$						
10.				45	21		21	
11.					1	0	0	
12.						74	54	1−
13.			82	207				0
14.	selenium-79					45		2−

15. Which of the following is an isotope of $^{190}_{76}\text{Os}$: $^{190}_{77}\text{Ir}$, $^{190}_{75}\text{Re}$, $^{191}_{76}\text{Os}$, $^{192}_{77}\text{Ir}$, or $^{76}_{33}\text{As}$?

16. Based on the information in the table below, calculate the average atomic mass of neon.

Isotope	Atomic Mass (amu)	Percent Abundance
neon-20	19.992	90.51%
neon-21	20.994	0.21%
neon-22	21.991	9.28%

17. Based on the information in the table below, calculate the missing percent abundance.

Isotope	Atomic Mass (amu)	Percent Abundance
chromium-50	49.946	4.35%
chromium-52	51.941	83.79%
chromium-53	52.941	9.50%
chromium-54	53.939	?

18. Use the information in question 17 to find the average atomic mass of chromium.

19. An imaginary element, elementium, has an atomic number of 147. Based on the information in the table below, calculate the missing percent abundance.

Isotope	Atomic Mass (amu)	Percent Abundance
elementium-308	308.1	?
elementium-310	310.2	10.00%
elementium-314	314.2	60.00%

20. Use the information in question 19 to find the average atomic mass of elementium.

Chapter 9

1. What is the relationship between the frequency of a wave and its energy?

2. Is all radiant energy ionizing? Give some examples of ionizing radiation.

3. Make a chart showing the symbol and charge of each of these: a neutron, an alpha particle, a beta particle, and gamma rays.

4. What is the missing product in the following nuclear reaction?
$^{239}_{94}Np \rightarrow$ beta particle $+$?

5. What is the missing product in the following nuclear reaction?
$^{214}_{84}Po \rightarrow$ alpha particle $+$?

6. What is the missing product in the following nuclear reaction?
$^{230}_{90}Th \rightarrow$ alpha particle $+$?

7. What is the missing product in the following nuclear reaction?
$^{27}_{13}Al +$ alpha particle $\rightarrow$ neutron $+$?

8. What is the missing product in the following nuclear reaction?
$^{242}_{96}Cm +$ alpha particle $\rightarrow$ neutron $+$?

9. What is the missing product in the following nuclear reaction?
$^{239}_{92}U \rightarrow ^{239}_{93}Np +$?

10. What is the missing reactant in the following nuclear reaction?
$^{3}_{2}He +$? $\rightarrow ^{4}_{2}He + ^{1}_{1}H + ^{1}_{1}H$

11. Carbon-14 has a half-life of 5,730 years. About how old is a fossil that contains $\frac{1}{8}$ the amount of carbon-14 in living things?

12. A radioactive substance has an original mass of 88.0 g. After 6 half-lives, what mass is still radioactive?

13. A sample of a radioactive substance has a starting mass of 56.0 g. After 84.0 days, only 3.50 g is still radioactive. What is the half-life of this substance?

For questions 14–17, copy the chart below. Fill in the missing information for potassium-40, which has a half-life of 30 minutes.

	Time	Number of Half-Lives	Radioactive Mass Remaining
	0 minutes	0	200. g
14.	30 minutes		
15.	60 minutes		
16.	120 minutes		
17.	180 minutes		

18. What is the purpose of the steel and concrete surrounding the fuel chamber of a nuclear reactor?

19. What happens to the water surrounding the fuel rods in a nuclear reactor chamber? How is this used to generate electricity?

20. What would happen if the control rods in a nuclear reactor chamber were not able to drop down between the fuel rods?

Chapter 10

1. Bohr's model of the atom is called the planetary model. How is the electron cloud model different from Bohr's model?

2. Make a chart listing the orbitals in the first four energy levels of the atom.

3. How many *f* orbitals are there in energy level 3? In energy level 4?

4. What is the Aufbau principle, and how is it used?

5. What is wrong with the following electron configuration?
$1s^2 2s^2 2p^6 3s^2 3p^{10} 4s^2 3d^6$

For questions 6–14, write the electron configuration of each atom or ion. You may provide either the complete or abbreviated configuration.

6. oxygen (O)

7. phosphorus (P)

8. argon (Ar)

9. cadmium (Cd)

10. iridium (Ir)

11. Pb^{2+}

12. I^{1-}

13. Mo^{4+}

14. ruthenium (Ru)

15. Which ion has the electron configuration $1s^2 2s^2 2p^6 3s^2 3p^6 4s^2 3d^5$: Co^{2+}, V^{2+}, Ti^{3+}, or Ni^{3-}?

16. Draw the dot diagram for nitrogen.

17. Draw the dot diagram for argon.

18. Draw the dot diagram for ruthenium.

19. The dot diagram of a neutral atom shows 2 dots. Could it be Sc, Al, O, or C?

20. What are valence electrons? How are they used in dot diagrams?

Chapter 11

1. Zinc belongs to which family in the periodic table?

2. Barium belongs to which family in the periodic table?

3. Uranium belongs to which family in the periodic table?

4. Describe three different ways that scientists organized elements in early periodic tables.

5. How many valence electrons are in a potassium atom?

6. How many valence electrons are in a phosphorus atom?

7. Predict the most likely charge for gallium. Explain your choice using its electron configuration.

8. Predict the most likely charge for oxygen. Explain your choice using its electron configuration.

9. Rank the following from smallest to largest atomic radius: Ba, Mg, S, Ar.

10. Rank the following from smallest to largest ionic radius: Br^{1-}, Cl^{1-}, Na^{1+}.

11. Rank the following from smallest to largest radius: Mn, Mn^{2+}, Mn^{5+}.

12. Rank the following from smallest to largest radius: Cl, Cl^{1-}, Cl^{5+}.

13. Compare the shielding effect in neon and xenon atoms.

14. Which noble gas has the highest ionization energy?

15. Which alkali metal has the second lowest ionization energy?

16. Rank the following atoms from lowest to highest ionization energy: Ba, Mg, S, Ar.

17. Which element in period 4 has the second highest electron affinity?

18. Which element in group 13 has the lowest electron affinity?

19. Compare the properties of alkali metals and alkaline earth metals.

20. What is an allotrope? Give an example of an element with allotropes.

Chapter 12

1. Using electronegativity values, predict the type of bond between H and O in H_2O.

2. Using electronegativity values, predict the type of bond between Ca and F in CaF_2.

3. Using electronegativity values, predict the type of bond between chlorine atoms in Cl_2.

4. What is the total number of valence electrons in HF? Draw its dot diagram.

5. What is the total number of valence electrons in SO_3? Draw its dot diagram.

6. What is the total number of valence electrons in NBr_3? Draw its dot diagram.

7. What is the total number of valence electrons in OF_2? Draw its dot diagram.

8. What is the total number of valence electrons in SO_4^{2-}? Draw its dot diagram.

9. What is the molecular geometry of HF? Look at your dot diagram from question 4.

10. What is the molecular geometry of SO_3? Look at your dot diagram from question 5.

11. What is the molecular geometry of NBr_3? Look at your dot diagram from question 6.

12. What is the molecular geometry of OF_2? Look at your dot diagram from question 7.

13. What is the molecular geometry of SO_4^{2-}? Look at your dot diagram from question 8.

14. Which molecules in questions 4–7 are polar? Explain your reasoning for each.

15. What is the strongest interparticle force in HF?

16. What is the strongest interparticle force in SO_3?

17. What is the strongest interparticle force in NBr_3?

18. What is the strongest interparticle force in OF_2?

19. What is the strongest interparticle force in CaF_2?

20. What is the strongest interparticle force in elemental Ca?

Chapter 13

1. What amount of heat is needed to raise the temperature of 100. g of mercury from 17.3°C to 97.2°C? The specific heat of mercury is 0.139 J/g•°C.

2. What amount of heat is released when 252 g of tin at 112°C cools to 37.5°C? The specific heat of tin is 0.226 J/g•°C.

3. A 225-g sample of iron at 98.5°C is dropped into 72.4 g of water at 22.0°C. The final temperature of the mixture is 41.2°C. The specific heat of water is 4.18 J/g•°C. What is the specific heat of iron?

4. A 147-g sample of aluminum $(C_p = 0.902 \text{ J/g}\cdot°C)$ at 103°C is dropped into an unknown mass of water $(C_p = 4.18 \text{ J/g}\cdot°C)$ at 23.5°C. The final temperature of the mixture is 32.0°C. What is the mass of the water?

5. A 79.6-g sample of silver $(C_p = 0.235 \text{ J/g}\cdot°C)$ at a high temperature is dropped into 53.5 g of water $(C_p = 4.18 \text{ J/g}\cdot°C)$ at 25.5°C. The final temperature of the water is 28.9°C. What is the temperature change for the silver?

6. The reaction below is exothermic, and its $\Delta H_{rxn} = -2{,}712 \text{ kJ/mol } C_4H_9OH$. If 35.2 g of C_4H_9OH reacts, how much heat is released?
$$C_4H_9OH + 6O_2 \rightarrow 4CO_2 + 5H_2O$$

7. 21.2 g of CO_2 is produced by the reaction, $C + O_2 \rightarrow CO_2$. $\Delta H_{rxn} = -393.5 \text{ kJ/mol } CO_2$. How much heat is released by this reaction?

8. 823 kJ of heat is released by the reaction, $C_2H_4 + 3O_2 \rightarrow 2CO_2 + 2H_2O$. $\Delta H_{rxn} = -1{,}390 \text{ kJ/mol } C_2H_4$. What mass of C_2H_4 reacted to produce this heat?

9. 18.5 g of Al reacts with Fe_2O_3 according to the reaction below. $\Delta H_{rxn} = -853.9 \text{ kJ/mol } Fe_2O_3$. How much heat is produced?
$$Fe_2O_3 + 2Al \rightarrow Al_2O_3 + 2Fe$$

10. The reaction below is endothermic, and the $\Delta H_{rxn} = +26.9 \text{ kJ/mol } Fe_2O_3$. If 37.5 g of Fe reacts, how much heat is absorbed?
$$2Fe + 3CO_2 \rightarrow Fe_2O_3 + 3CO$$

For questions 11–15, use the standard heats of formation given in Table 13.3.1 on page 524.

11. What is the ΔH_{rxn} for the reaction, $CH_4(g) + 2O_2(g) \rightarrow CO_2(g) + 2H_2O(g)$?

12. What is the ΔH_{rxn} for the reaction, $P_4(s) + 6H_2O(l) \rightarrow 4H_3PO_4(l)$?

13. What is the ΔH_{rxn} for the reaction, $2HNO_3(aq) + Ba(OH)_2(s) \rightarrow$
$$2H_2O(l) + Ba(NO_3)_2(aq)?$$
$\Delta H_f = -228 \text{ kJ/mol for } Ba(NO_3)_2(aq)$.

14. $\Delta H_{rxn} = +398 \text{ kJ}$ for the reaction, $BaSO_4(s) \rightarrow BaO(s) + SO_3(g)$. What is the heat of formation of $BaO(s)$?

15. $\Delta H_{rxn} = -205.6 \text{ kJ}$ for the reaction, $H_2SO_4(aq) + 2NaOH(s) \rightarrow$
$$Na_2SO_4(aq) + 2H_2O(l).$$
If ΔH_f for $Na_2SO_4(aq)$ is $-1{,}387 \text{ kJ/mol}$, what is the ΔH_f for $NaOH(s)$?

16. Does entropy increase or decrease in the following reaction? Explain your answer.
$$Ba(OH)_2 \cdot 8H_2O(s) + 2NH_4NO_3(aq) \rightarrow$$
$$2NH_3(g) + Ba(NO_3)_2(aq) + 10H_2O(l)$$

17. The reaction in question 16 is very endothermic. Is this reaction spontaneous always, sometimes, or never? Explain your answer.

18. Does entropy increase or decrease in the following reaction? Explain your answer.
$$2N_2(g) + 5O_2(g) \rightarrow 2N_2O_5(g)$$

19. For the reaction in question 18, $\Delta H_{rxn} = +28.4 \text{ kJ/mol}$. Is the reaction spontaneous always, sometimes, or never? Explain your answer.

20. For the reaction below, $\Delta H_{rxn} =$ −4,594 kJ/mol. Is this reaction exothermic or endothermic? Does entropy increase or decrease? Is this reaction spontaneous always, sometimes, or never? Explain your answers.

$$5N_2O_4(l) + 4N_2H_3CH_3(l) \rightarrow$$
$$12H_2O(g) + 9N_2(g) + 4CO_2(g)$$

Chapter 14

1. What is the difference between sublimation and deposition?

2. What is the difference between boiling and evaporation?

3. Describe how liquid particles freeze in terms of interparticle forces.

For questions 4–9, refer to Figure 14.2.2 on page 553.

4. What is the approximate boiling point of ethanol at a pressure of 100 mm Hg?

5. At about what pressure does water boil at 90°C?

6. What is the approximate boiling point of water at a pressure of 400 mm Hg?

7. At about what pressure does ethanol boil at 70°C?

8. What is the approximate boiling point of water at a pressure of 600 mm Hg?

9. At about what pressure does ethanol boil at 50°C?

For questions 10–15, refer to the constants in Figure 14.3.1 on page 559.

10. How much heat is required to change 35.0 g of liquid benzene at 60.0°C to gaseous benzene at 101°C?

11. How much heat is released when 86.1 g of gaseous benzene cools from 115°C to liquid benzene at 41.3°C?

12. How much heat is needed to change 47.3 g of ice at −17.1°C to liquid water at 43.2°C?

13. How much heat is released when 25.0 g of gaseous water at 100.0°C is cooled to liquid water at 15.0°C?

14. How much heat is needed to change 37.5 g of liquid water at 45.1°C to gaseous water at 115°C?

15. How much heat is needed to increase the temperature of 75.2 g of ice at −23.1°C to gaseous water at 107.0°C?

For questions 16–18, refer to Figure 14.4.3 on page 567.

16. Water is a liquid at 1 atm and 75°C. If the pressure drops to 0.0060 atm at the same temperature, what happens to the state of water?

17. Water is a solid at 0.0060 atm and 0°C. If the pressure increases to 218 atm at the same temperature, what happens to the state of water?

18. Water is a gas at 1 atm and 200°C. If the temperature drops to 70°C at the same pressure, what happens to the state of water?

19. List four unique properties of water. Explain how each is important.

20. Why is water called a "universal solvent"?

Chapter 15

1. What is the difference between a solution, a colloid, and a suspension?

2. What are two ways to keep gas solutes dissolved in water?

For questions 3–9, refer to Figure 15.2.2 on page 588.

3. How much solute is needed to saturate a solution of KCl at 60°C?

4. How much solute is needed to saturate a solution of NH_3 at 30°C?

5. A solution of NaCl contains 40. g of solute in 100. g of water at 50°C. Is the solution saturated, unsaturated, or supersaturated?

6. A solution contains 40. g of NH_4Cl in 100. g of water at 70°C. How many more grams of solute are needed to saturate this solution?

7. Which substance is the least soluble at 40°C?

8. At what temperature will 10.0 g of NH_3 form a saturated solution in 100. g of water?

9. What mass of HCl is needed to saturate 200. g of water at 70°C?

For questions 10–12, write the net ionic equation for each set of reactants. Use the solubility rules on page 594.

10. $Al(NO_3)_3(aq) + NaOH(aq) \rightarrow$

11. $K_3PO_4(aq) + Mg(NO_3)_2(aq) \rightarrow$

12. $HNO_3(aq) + KOH(aq) \rightarrow$

13. A 10.0 M solution of HCl is diluted with water. The original volume is 52.1 mL. The final volume is 2.00 L. What is the molarity of the new solution?

14. A chemist has 8.00 M HNO_3, but needs 1.00 M HNO_3. What volume of the concentrated solution should be used to make 250. mL of the dilute solution?

15. 25.2 g of KOH dissolves in 175 g of water to make 200.2 g of solution. Calculate the molality, mass percent, and mole fraction of KOH for this solution.

16. 72.3 g of $C_{12}H_{22}O_{11}$ dissolves in 225 g of water to make 297.3 g of solution. Calculate the molality, mass percent, and mole fraction of $C_{12}H_{22}O_{11}$ for this solution.

17. A solution contains 150. g of water and has a molality of 0.750 m KNO_3. What mass of KNO_3 is in this solution?

18. 35.1 g of Na_2SO_4 dissolves in 225 g of water. $K_b = 0.51°C/m$ for water. Water boils at 100°C. What is the boiling point of this solution?

19. 25.7 g of $Al(NO_3)_3$ dissolves in 350. g of water. $K_f = 1.86°C/m$ for water. Water freezes at 0°C. What is the freezing point of this solution?

20. 57.2 g of $C_6H_{12}O_6$ dissolves in 163 g of water. What is the freezing point of this solution? Use the constants given in question 19.

Chapter 16

1. Why does powdered zinc and 1.0 M HCl react faster than chunks of zinc and 0.5 M HCl?

2. Why does powdered zinc and 1.0 M HCl react faster at 50°C than at 25°C?

For questions 3–9, refer to the following diagram.

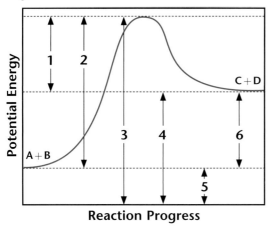

Reaction Progress

3. Which arrow represents the heat of reaction?

4. Which arrow represents the potential energy of the activated complex?

5. Which arrow represents the activation energy for the reverse reaction?

6. Which arrow represents the activation energy for the forward reaction?

7. Which arrow represents the potential energy of the products?

8. Is this reaction exothermic or endothermic? How do you know?

9. Which arrows would be affected by the addition of a catalyst?

10. What is the overall balanced equation for the following reaction mechanism?

Step 1	$A+B \rightarrow X+Y$	*slow*
Step 2	$A+Y \rightarrow Z$	*fast*
Step 3	$A+Z \rightarrow X$	*fast*

11. What is the rate law for the mechanism in question 10?

For questions 12–15, refer to this equilibrium:
$2Cl_2(g) + 2H_2O(g) \rightleftharpoons 4HCl(g) + O_2(g)$

12. Write the equilibrium expression.

13. Calculate the value of K if $[Cl_2] = 0.520\ M$, $[H_2O] = 0.486\ M$, $[HCl] = 2.56\ M$, and $[O_2] = 1.35\ M$.

14. At a different temperature, $K = 0.0035$, $[Cl_2] = 1.65\ M$, $[H_2O] = 1.23\ M$, and $[HCl] = 0.221\ M$. Calculate $[O_2]$ at this temperature.

15. Compare the equilibrium systems described in questions 13 and 14. In which system are the products favored? How do you know?

For questions 16–20, refer to the following system at equilibrium.
$2NOCl(g) + energy \rightleftharpoons 2NO(g) + Cl_2(g)$

16. In which direction will the equilibrium shift if the temperature increases? Why?

17. In which direction will the equilibrium shift if $[Cl_2]$ increases? Why?

18. In which direction will the equilibrium shift if $[NO]$ decreases? Why?

19. In which direction will the equilibrium shift if the pressure increases? Why?

20. In which direction will the equilibrium shift if the temperature decreases? Why?

Chapter 17

For questions 1–3, identify the acid, base, conjugate acid, and conjugate base.

1. $HC_2H_3O_2 + CH_3NH_2 \rightleftharpoons$
$\qquad CH_3NH_3^{1+} + C_2H_3C_2^{1-}$

2. $H_2PO_4^{1-} + OH^{1-} \rightarrow H_2O + HPO_4^{2-}$

3. $H_2PO_4^{1-} + H_2O \rightleftharpoons OH^{1-} + H_3PO_4$

4. In a titration, a 35.0-mL sample of an HNO_3 solution is neutralized by 72.1 mL of 0.115 M NaOH. The reaction is $HNO_3 + NaOH \rightarrow NaNO_3 + H_2O$. What is the molarity of the acid?

5. In a titration, a 0.735 M HBr solution is neutralized by 27.3 mL of 0.525 M KOH. The reaction is $KOH + HBr \rightarrow H_2O + KBr$. What is the volume of the acid solution?

6. In a titration, a 51.2-mL sample of 0.375 M HF is neutralized by 63.5 mL of an NaOH solution. The reaction is $HF + NaOH \rightarrow NaF + H_2O$. What is the molarity of the base?

7. In a titration, a 42.5-mL sample of 1.13 M $HC_2H_3O_2$ is neutralized by 0.575 M NaOH. The reaction is $NaOH + HC_2H_3O_2 \rightarrow H_2O + NaC_2H_3O_2$. What is the volume of the base?

For questions 8–16, copy the table below. Fill in the missing information in each row.

	Solution pH	$[H^{1+}]$	$[OH^{1-}]$	Acidic or Basic?
8.	3			
9.	10			
10.		3.0×10^{-9}		
11.		8.5×10^{-4}		
12.			6.2×10^{-11}	
13.			1.5×10^{-3}	
14.	12.5			
15.		7.5×10^{-10}		
16.			4.6×10^{-9}	

17. A 0.1 M KOH solution is made. Is its pH closest to 1, 4, 9, or 13? Explain your answer.

18. A 0.1 M HNO_2 solution is made. Is its pH closest to 1, 4, 9, or 13? Explain your answer.

19. What kind of salt is produced when HBr and NH_3 react?

20. What kind of salt is produced when HF and KOH react?

Chapter 18

For questions 1–5, give the oxidation number of each element in the compound or ion.

1. $KMnO_4$

2. $XeOF_4$

3. $C_2O_4^{2-}$

4. $Mg_2P_2O_7$

5. IF_4

For questions 6–10, identify the reactant that is oxidized and the reactant that is reduced.

6. $Cr_2O_7^{2-} + Cl^{1-} \rightarrow Cr^{3+} + Cl_2$

7. $NO_2^{1-} + Al \rightarrow NH_3 + AlO_2^{1-}$

8. $BiO_3^{1-} + Mn^{2+} \rightarrow MnO_4^{1-} + Bi^{3+}$

9. $MnO_4^{1-} + Al \rightarrow MnO_2 + Al(OH)_4^{1-}$

10. $Cu + Ag^{1+} \rightarrow Ag + Cu^{2+}$

For questions 11–14, balance each redox reaction.

11. $NO_2^{1-} + Al \rightarrow NH_3 + AlO_2^{1-}$

12. $Mn^{2+} + BiO_3^{1-} \rightarrow MnO_4^{1-} + Bi^{3+}$

13. $Al + MnO_4^{1-} \rightarrow MnO_2 + Al(OH)_4^{1-}$

14. $Cr_2O_7^{2-} + Cl^{1-} \rightarrow Cr^{3+} + Cl_2$

15. A voltaic cell is made with lead, iron, and solutions containing their cations. What is the half-reaction in the anode? What is the half-reaction in the cathode? To which electrode will the cations in the salt bridge move?

16. A voltaic cell is made with zinc, aluminum, and solutions containing their cations. What is the half-reaction in the anode? What is the half-reaction in the cathode? To which electrode will the anions in the salt bridge move?

17. A voltaic cell is made with tin, copper, and solutions containing their cations. What is the half-reaction in the anode? What is the half-reaction in the cathode? To which electrode will the electrons move?

18. A voltaic cell is made with nickel, manganese, and solutions containing their cations. What is the half-reaction in the anode? What is the half-reaction in the cathode? To which electrode will the electrons move?

19. What is the purpose of putting a thin layer of zinc on the exterior of steel car parts?

20. What is the main difference between an electrolytic cell and a voltaic cell?

Chapter 19

For questions 1–4, identify each structure as an alkane, alkene, alkyne, or aromatic compound.

1.

2.

3.

4.

For questions 5–17, identify the type of substituted hydrocarbon each structure is. If there is more than one functional group on a structure, identify all types.

5.

6.

7.

8.

```
     H  H  H   H  H  H  O
     |  |  |   |  |  |  ||
 H - C- C- C - C- C- C- C - O - H
     |  |  |   |  |  |
     H  H  |   H  H  H
          H - C - H
              |
              CH₃
```

9.

```
     H  Br        H  H
     |  |         |  |
 H - C- C- C ≡ C- C- C - H
     |  |         |  |
     H  Br        H  H
```

10.

11.

```
     H  OH H  H
     |  |  |  |
 H - C- C- C- C - H
     |  |  |  |
     H  H  OH H
```

12.

```
     H  NH₂ H  H  H  H
     |  |   |  |  |  |
 H - C- C —  C- C- C- C - H
     |  |   |  |  |  |
     H  H   Cl H  H  H
```

13.

```
     H  H  H  O  H  H  H  H
     |  |  |  ||  |  |  |  |
 H - C- C- C- C- C- C- C- C - H
     |  |  |     |  |  |  |
     H  H  H     H  OH H  H
```

14.

```
     H            H  O  H
     |            |  ||  |
 H - C- C ≡ C - C- C- N - H
     |            |
     H            H
```

15.

```
     H  NH₂ H
     |  |   |
 H - C- C — C - O - H
     |  |   |
     H  H   H
```

16.

```
     H  Cl H  O
     |  |  |  ||
 H - C- C- C- C - O - H
     |  |  |
     H  I  H
```

17.

18. What are two important biological polymers? Describe how each is used by the body.

19. Why are proteins and nucleic acids considered to be "of first rank"?

20. What are two differences between RNA and DNA?

Glossary

Absolute temperature (ab´ sə lüt tem´ pər ə chər) Temperature measured on the Kelvin scale (p. 271)

Absolute zero (ab´ sə lüt zir´ ō) The temperature at which particles in matter stop moving and have no kinetic energy; 0 K (p. 271)

Accuracy (ak´ yər ə sē) How close a measurement is to the correct or accepted value (p. 17)

Acid (as´ id) A compound that produces H^{1+} ions when dissolved in water; *also* a compound that is a proton (H^{1+}) donor (pp. 115, 664)

Acid-base reaction (as´ id bās rē ak´ shən) A reaction in which an acid reacts with a base to produce water and a salt (p. 203)

Acidic (ə sid´ ik) Having a pH below 7 (p. 677)

Acidic salt (ə sid´ ik sȯlt) The salt produced from a strong acid and a weak base (p. 688)

Actinide (ak´ tə nīd) Any of the elements with atomic numbers 90 to 103; the actinides follow actinium (89) in the periodic table (p. 424)

Activated complex (ak´ tə vā tid kəm pleks´) A group of atoms that temporarily forms when two or more reactant particles collide (p. 627)

Activation energy (E_a) (ak´ tə vā shən en´ ər jē) The minimum amount of energy needed to break bonds in reactants and cause a reaction to occur (p. 622)

Activity series (ak tiv´ ə tē sir´ ēz) A list of elements that is organized from the most reactive element to the least reactive element (p. 196)

Actual yield (ak´ chü əl yēld) The amount of product measured in a lab (p. 244)

Alcohol (al´ kə hȯl) A hydrocarbon chain that contains a hydroxyl group (p. 754)

Aldehyde (al´ də hīd) An organic compound that contains a carbonyl group at the end of a hydrocarbon chain (p. 761)

Alkali metal (al´ kə lī met´ l) An element other than hydrogen in column 1 of the periodic table (p. 424)

Alkaline earth metal (al´ kə lin ėrth met´ l) An element in column 2 of the periodic table (p. 424)

Alkane (al´ kān) A hydrocarbon that has only single bonds between carbon atoms (p. 745)

Alkene (al´ kēn) A hydrocarbon that has at least one double bond between carbon atoms (p. 747)

Alkyne (al´ kīn) A hydrocarbon that has at least one triple bond between carbon atoms (p. 748)

Allotrope (al´ ə trōp) A form of an element that has a different bonding arrangement than another form of the same element (p. 449)

Alloy (al´ oi) A solid solution containing metals (p. 58)

Alpha particle (al´ fə pär´ tə kəl) A helium nucleus, which consists of 2 protons and 2 neutrons, but no electrons (p. 311)

Amide (am´ īd) An organic compound that contains an amino group bonded to a carbonyl group (p. 762)

Amine (ə mēn´) An organic compound that contains an amino group bonded directly to the hydrocarbon chain (p. 762)

Amino acid (ə mē´ nō as´ id) An organic molecule with an amino group and a carboxyl group (p. 777)

Amino group (ə mē´ nō grüp) A functional group consisting of a nitrogen atom bonded to 2 hydrogen atoms (p. 762)

Amorphous (ə môr´ fəs) Having no orderly, repeating pattern of particles (p. 549)

Anion (an´ ī ən) An atom or group of atoms with a negative charge; a negative ion (p. 91)

Anode (an´ ōd) The positively charged electrode in a cathode-ray tube; the electrode toward which electrons move; *also* the half-cell of a voltaic cell in which oxidation takes place; the electrode from which electrons move (pp. 307, 724)

Antioxidant (an tē ok´ sə dənt) A stable molecule that reacts with a free radical, reducing its effect (p. 719)

Aqueous solution (ā´ kwē əs sə lü´ shən) A solution in which the solvent is water (p. 58)

Aromatic compound (är ə mat´ ik kom´ pound) A hydrocarbon that contains at least one benzene ring (p. 749)

Asymmetric (ā sə met´ rik) Having an unbalanced arrangement (p. 487)

Atmosphere (atm) (at´ mə sfir) A unit for measuring pressure (p. 137)

Atmospheric pressure (at mə sfir´ ik presh´ ər) The pressure exerted by the weight of the atmosphere (p. 265)

a	hat	e	let	ī	ice	ȯ	order	u̇	put	sh	she	ə	a	in about
ā	age	ē	equal	o	hot	oi	oil	ü	rule	th	thin		e	in taken
ä	far	ėr	term	ō	open	ou	out	ch	child	ŦH	then		i	in pencil
â	care	i	it	ȯ	saw	u	cup	ng	long	zh	measure		o	in lemon
													u	in circus

Atom (at´ əm) The smallest particle of an element that has the properties of that element (p. 65)

Atomic mass (ə tom´ ik mas) The average mass of an atom of an element (p. 131)

Atomic mass unit (amu) (ə tom´ ik mas yü´ nit) A unit of mass that equals $\frac{1}{12}$ the mass of a carbon atom with 6 protons and 6 neutrons; 1 amu is approximately the mass of a proton or neutron (p. 325)

Atomic number (ə tom´ ik num´ bər) The number of protons in an atom (p. 65)

Atomic radius (ə tom´ ik rā´ dē əs) The distance from the nucleus of an atom to its outermost electron orbitals; a measure of the size of an atom (p. 432)

Aufbau principle (ouf´ bou prin´ sə pəl) A rule stating that electrons fill orbitals that have the lowest energy first (p. 392)

Avogadro's number (a və gä´ drōz num´ bər) 6.02×10^{23}; the number of particles in 1 mol (p. 127)

B

Barometer (bə rom´ ə tər) An instrument that measures atmospheric pressure (p. 269)

Base (bās) A compound that produces OH^{1-} ions when dissolved in water; *also* a compound that is a proton (H^{1+}) acceptor (pp. 203, 664)

Basic (bā´ sik) Having a pH above 7; alkaline (p. 677)

Basic salt (bā´ sik sòlt) The salt produced from a weak acid and a strong base (p. 689)

Bent (bent) Having a tetrahedral geometry that is affected by two lone pairs (p. 482)

Beta particle (bā´ tə pär´ tə kəl) A high-energy electron that is emitted when a neutron in the nucleus of an atom breaks down (p. 346)

Binary (bī´ nər ē) Containing two elements (p. 86)

Boil (boil) To change from a liquid to a gas (p. 547)

Boiling point (boil´ ing point) The temperature at which the vapor pressure of a liquid equals the atmospheric pressure (p. 552)

Boiling-point elevation (ΔT_b) (boil´ ing point el ə vā´ shən) The temperature difference between the boiling point of a solution and the boiling point of the pure solvent (p. 607)

Boyle's law (boilz lò) The law that says that gas pressure and gas volume are inversely proportional at constant temperature (p. 278)

Brittle (brit´ l) Having the property of shattering when hit with force (p. 496)

Buffer (buf´ ər) A solution that resists a change in pH when a small amount of an acid or base is added (p. 690)

C

Calorimetry (kal ə rim´ ə trē) The measurement of heat transfer (p. 509)

Cancer (kan´ sər) A disease in which cells grow without control and divide rapidly (p. 340)

Carbohydrate (kär bō hī´ drāt) An organic molecule that contains carbon, hydrogen, and oxygen in about a 1:2:1 ratio; a sugar molecule or a larger molecule of bonded sugars (p. 771)

Carbonate (kär´ bə nāt) A compound that contains the CO_3^{2-} ion; it can decompose to produce carbon dioxide (p. 190)

Carbonyl group (kär´ bə nil grüp) A functional group consisting of a carbon atom double-bonded to an oxygen atom (p. 761)

Carboxyl group (kär bok´ səl grüp) A functional group consisting of a carbon atom double-bonded to an oxygen atom and single-bonded to a hydroxyl group (p. 755)

Carboxylic acid (kär bok sil´ ik as´ id) An organic compound that contains a carboxyl group at the end of a hydrocarbon chain (p. 755)

Catalyst (kat´ l ist) A substance that increases the rate of a reaction without taking part in the reaction (p. 623)

Cathode-ray tube (kath´ ōd rā tüb) A glass tube with an electrode at each end (p. 307)

Cathode (kath´ ōd) The negatively charged electrode in a cathode-ray tube; the electrode from which electrons move; *also* the half-cell of a voltaic cell in which reduction takes place; the electrode toward which electrons move (pp. 307, 724)

Cation (kat´ ī´ ən) An atom or group of atoms with a positive charge; a positive ion (p. 91)

Charge (chärj) A certain amount of electricity (p. 64)

Charles's law (chärl´ ziz lò) The law that says that gas volume and gas temperature are directly proportional at constant pressure (p. 280)

Chemical bond (kem´ ə kəl bond) A bond formed when two atoms share or transfer electrons (p. 65)

Chemical change (kem´ ə kəl chānj) A change in a substance that results in one or more different substances being formed (p. 52)

Chemical equation (kem´ ə kəl i kwā´ zhən) An equation that uses symbols to represent a chemical reaction (p. 176)

Chemical equilibrium (kem´ ə kəl ē kwə lib´ rē əm) The state of a reversible reaction when the rate of the forward reaction equals the rate of the reverse reaction (p. 641)

Chemical formula (kem´ ə kəl fôr´ myə lə) A group of symbols that shows the number and kinds of atoms in a compound (p. 72)

Chemical property (kem´ ə kəl prop´ ər tē) A characteristic that describes how a substance changes into one or more different substances (p. 51)

Chemical reaction (kem´ ə kəl rē ak´ shən) The chemical changes involved when one or more substances react, forming one or more different substances (p. 52)

Chemical symbol (kem´ ə kəl sim´ bəl) A one- or two-letter symbol that represents an element (p. 65)

Chemist (kem´ist) A scientist who studies matter and how it changes (p. 2)

Chemistry (kem´ ə strē) The study of matter and how it changes (p. 2)

Coefficient (kō ə fish´ ənt) A number to the left of the symbol or formula of a substance in a chemical equation (p. 181)

Colligative property (kə li´ gə tiv prop´ ər tē) A physical property of a solution that depends on the number of dissolved solute particles (p. 606)

Collision theory (kə lizh´ ən thē´ ər ē) The idea that a reaction occurs when particles of matter collide with enough energy to break bonds and form new bonds (p. 622)

Colloid (kol´ oid) A mixture of particles that are evenly dispersed in another substance; colloid particles are too small to settle out, but are not dissolved (p.583)

Combination reaction (kom bə nā´ shən rē ak´ shən) A chemical reaction in which two or more small reactants form one larger product (p. 189)

Combined gas law (kəm bind´ gas lȯ) The law that shows how gas pressure, volume, and temperature are related; a combination of the laws of Boyle, Charles, and Gay-Lussac (p. 282)

Combustion reaction (kəm bus´ chən rē ak´ shən) A chemical reaction in which a compound or element burns by reacting with oxygen (p. 190)

Compound (kom´ pound) A substance that consists of two or more kinds of atoms that are bonded (p. 72)

Concentrated (kon´ sən trā tid) Having a large amount of solute compared to another solution; strong (p. 140)

Concentration (kon sən trā´ shən) The amount of solute in a certain volume of solution (p. 140)

Condense (kən dens´) To change from a gas to a liquid (p. 546)

Condensed state (kən densd´ stāt) A liquid or solid state (p. 547)

Conjugate acid (kon´ ja gāt as´ id) The molecule or ion formed when a base accepts a proton (p. 665)

Conjugate base (kon´ ja gāt bās) The molecule or ion formed when an acid donates a proton (p. 665)

Constant (kon´ stənt) A fixed number in an equation, often represented by a letter or symbol (p. 287)

Conversion factor (kən ver´ zhən fak´ tər) A ratio that shows how two units are related (p. 34)

Corrosion (kə rō´ zhən) The weakening of a metal by oxidation (p. 720)

Covalent bond (kō vā´ lənt bond) A chemical bond in which electrons are shared between two atoms (p. 462)

Critical point (krit´ ə kəl point) The critical pressure and critical temperature of a substance (p. 568)

Critical pressure (krit´ ə kəl presh´ ər) The pressure required to condense a gas at the critical temperature (p. 568)

Critical temperature (krit´ ə kəl tem´ pər ə chər) The temperature above which a gas cannot be condensed to a liquid (p. 568)

Crystal (kris´ tl) A solid that has particles arranged in an orderly, repeating pattern (p. 548)

Crystal lattice (kris´ tl lat´ is) The three-dimensional pattern of particles in a crystal (p. 548)

D

Dalton's law of partial pressure (dält´ nz lȯ ov pär´ shəl presh´ ər) The law that states that the total pressure of a gas mixture is the sum of the pressures of each gas in the mixture (p. 274)

Decomposition reaction (dē kom pə zish´ ən rē ak´ shən) A chemical reaction in which one large reactant breaks down into two or more smaller products (p. 190)

a	hat	e	let	ī	ice	ȯ	order	u̇	put	sh	she		ə	a	in about
ā	age	ē	equal	o	hot	oi	oil	ü	rule	th	thin		e	in taken
ä	far	ėr	term	ō	open	ou	out	ch	child	ᴛʜ	then		i	in pencil
à	care	i	it	ȯ	saw	u	cup	ng	long	zh	measure		o	in lemon
													u	in circus

Degree Celsius (°C) (di grē′ sel′ sē əs) A unit for measuring temperature (p. 32)

Density (D) (den′ sə tē) The mass of a sample of matter divided by its volume (p. 39)

Dependent variable (di pen′ dənt vâr′ ē ə bəl) A variable that responds to an independent variable (p. 5)

Deposition (dep ə zish′ ən) The process of changing from a gas directly to a solid (p. 547)

Derived unit (di rīvd′ yü′ nit) A measurement unit created by multiplying or dividing other units (p. 39)

Diatomic (dī ə tom′ ik) Existing as pairs of bonded atoms (p. 67)

Diffusion (di fyü′ zhən) The movement of particles from an area of high concentration to an area of low concentration (p. 295)

Dilute (də lüt′) Having a small amount of solute compared to another solution; weak (p. 140)

Dipole-dipole force (dī′ pōl dī′ pōl fôrs) A permanent attractive force between oppositely charged ends of two polar molecules (p. 494)

Direct proportion (də rekt′ prə pôr′ shən) A relationship between two quantities in which one increases as the other increases (p. 280)

Disaccharide (dī sak′ ə rīd) A simple carbohydrate consisting of two sugar units bonded together (p. 771)

Dispersion force (dis per′ shən fôrs) A weak, temporary force of attraction between two particles that results from a temporary closeness of electrons within each particle (p. 492)

Dissociation (di sō sē ā′ shən) The process that occurs when an ionic compound breaks apart and separates into individual ions in water (p. 581)

DNA (dē en ā) Deoxyribonucleic acid (p. 779)

Dot diagram (dot dī′ ə gram) A simple diagram that uses dots to represent the valence electrons of an atom or ion (p. 411)

Double bond (dub′ əl bond) A covalent bond in which two atoms share two pairs of electrons (p. 469)

Double-replacement reaction (dub′ əl ri plās′ mənt rē ak′ shən) A reaction in which the ions in two compounds trade places, forming two new compounds (p. 202)

Dry cell (drī sel) A voltaic cell in which the half-cells contain an electrolyte that is a paste instead of a solution (p. 727)

Ductile (duk′ təl) Having the ability to be pulled into a wire (p. 452)

E

Electrical potential difference (i lek′ trə kəl pə ten′ shəl dif′ ər əns) The difference in electron pressure between the anode and cathode in a voltaic cell (p. 729)

Electric current (i lek′ trik kėr′ ənt) The flow of electrons (p. 723)

Electrochemical process (i lek trō kem′ ə kəl pros′ es) A process that converts electrical energy into chemical energy, or chemical energy into electrical energy (p. 731)

Electrochemistry (i lek′ trō kem′ ə strē) The study of the relationship between electrical energy and chemical reactions (p. 723)

Electrode (i lek′ trōd) A metal piece that conducts electricity; *also* a metal object used for the purpose of conducting electric current into or out of an electrochemical cell (pp. 307, 724)

Electrolysis (i lek trol′ ə sis) The use of electrical energy to cause a chemical change (p. 731)

Electrolyte (i lek′ trə līt) A substance that can conduct electricity when melted or in aqueous solutions (p. 581)

Electrolytic cell (i lek′ trə lit′ ik sel) A cell in which electrons are forced to move from the anode to the cathode by an external source of electricity (p. 731)

Electromagnetic radiation (i lek′ trō mag net′ ik rā dē ā′ shən) Energy that can travel through space; also called radiant energy (p. 338)

Electromagnetic spectrum (i lek′ trō mag net′ ik spek′ trəm) The whole range of electromagnetic radiation (p. 339)

Electron (i lek′ tron) A particle with a negative charge in an atom (p. 64)

Electron affinity (i lek′ tron ə fin′ ə tē) The amount of energy released when an electron is added to an atom (p. 442)

Electron cloud (i lek′ tron kloud) An indistinct region of space around the nucleus that describes the probable location of electrons (p. 385)

Electron configuration (i lek′ tron kən fig yə rā′ shən) The arrangement of electrons in an atom's orbitals and energy levels (p. 392)

Electronegativity (i lek′ trō neg′ ə tiv′ ə tē) The ability of an atom to attract electrons in a chemical bond (p. 463)

Electroplating (i lek′ trə plāt′ ing) The process of depositing a thin layer of metal on an object in an electrolytic cell (p. 733)

Element (el′ ə mənt) A substance that is made of only one kind of atom (p. 65)

Emission spectrum (i mish´ ən spek´ trəm) The arrangement of separate colors in light that is emitted when the atoms of a substance are energized and viewed through a prism; plural is emission spectra (p. 383)

Empirical formula (em pir´ ə kəl fôr´ myə la) A formula that shows the smallest whole-number ratio of atoms in a compound (p. 154)

Endothermic (en dō thėr´ mik) Absorbing heat (p. 508)

End point (end point) The point in a titration when the indicator shows that the equivalence point has been reached (p. 670)

Energy (en´ ər jē) The ability to do work or produce heat (p. 53)

Energy level (en´ ər jē lev´ əl) An area of space where electrons can move (p. 384)

Enthalpy (*H*) (en´ thəl pē) The amount of heat a sample has at a certain pressure and temperature; heat content (p. 519)

Entropy (en´ trə pē) A measure of the disorder or randomness of a system (p. 527)

Enzyme (en´ zīm) A biological catalyst (p. 624)

Equilibrium constant (*K*) (ē kwa lib´ rē əm kon´ stənt) A unique constant that describes the equilibrium of a specific reaction at a certain temperature (p. 645)

Equilibrium expression (ē kwa lib´ rē əm ex presh´ ən) A mathematical equation relating product concentrations to reactant concentrations at chemical equilibrium (p. 642)

Equilibrium system (ē kwa lib´ rē əm sis´ təm) A reaction that is in a state of chemical equilibrium (p. 641)

Equivalence point (i kwev´ ə ləns point) The point in a neutralization reaction at which all of the acid has reacted with all of the base (p. 669)

Ester (es´ tər) An organic compound formed by the bonding of an alcohol chain to a carboxylic acid chain at the oxygen atoms of each functional group (p. 755)

Ether (ē´ thər) An organic compound in which two hydrocarbon chains are bonded to the same oxygen atom (p. 756)

Evaporation (i vap ə rā´ shən) The process that occurs when particles at the surface of a liquid gain enough energy to leave the liquid and become a gas (p. 547)

Excess reactant (ek´ ses rē ak´ tənt) The reactant in a chemical reaction that is not completely used up; more than enough of this reactant is present (p. 250)

Exothermic (ek´ sō thėr´ mik) Producing heat (p. 508)

F

Family (fam´ ə lē) A column of elements in the periodic table; also called a group (p. 424)

Fatty acid (fat´ tē as´ id) A long-chained carboxylic acid; a component of a lipid (p. 773)

First law of thermodynamics (fėrst lȯ ov thėr mō dī nam´ iks) A law that states that the energy of the universe is constant (p. 511)

Fission reaction (fish´ ən rē ak´ shən) The splitting of a large nucleus into two or more smaller pieces (p. 365)

Flammable (flam´ ə bəl) Having the property of burning easily (p. 756)

Formula unit (fôr´ myə lə yü´ nit) A chemical formula for an ionic compound (p. 98)

Free radical (frē rad´ ə kəl) An extremely reactive particle containing an atom with an unpaired electron (p. 719)

Freeze (frēz) To change from a liquid to a solid (p. 547)

Freezing-point depression (ΔT_f) (frēz´ ing point di presh´ ən) The temperature difference between the freezing point of a solution and the freezing point of the pure solvent (p. 610)

Frequency (ν) (frē´ kwən sē) The number of wave peaks that pass a given point in a certain amount of time (p. 338)

Functional group (fungk´ shə nəl grüp) An atom or group of atoms that replaces a hydrogen atom in a hydrocarbon (p. 753)

Fusion reaction (fyü´ zhən rē ak´ shən) The joining of two small atoms to form a larger one (p. 369)

G

Gamma rays (gam´ ə rāz) Ionizing radiation with a very high energy (p. 340)

a	hat	e	let	ī	ice	ȯ	order	u̇	put	sh	she	ə	a in about
ā	age	ē	equal	o	hot	oi	oil	ü	rule	th	thin		e in taken
ä	far	ėr	term	ō	open	ou	out	ch	child	ŦH	then		i in pencil
â	care	i	it	ȯ	saw	u	cup	ng	long	zh	measure		o in lemon
													u in circus

Gas (gas) A state of matter with no definite shape or volume; it takes the shape and volume of its container (p. 51)

Gas constant (R) (gas kon′ stənt) The fixed value of R in the ideal gas law; $R = 0.0821$ L·atm/mol·K or 8.31 L·kPa/mol·K (p. 287)

Gay-Lussac's law (gā′ lə sakz′ lȯ) The law that states that gas pressure and gas temperature are directly proportional at constant volume (p. 281)

Graham's law (grā′ əmz lȯ) A law that states that the greater the molar mass of a gas, the slower its particles move at constant temperature (p. 295)

Gram (g) (gram) A unit for measuring mass (p. 32)

H

Half-cell (haf′ sel) A single electrode immersed in a solution of its ions (p. 724)

Half-life (haf′ līf) The time is takes for half of a radioactive sample to decay (p. 356)

Half-reaction (haf rē ak′ shən) One of two reactions that together make up a complete redox equation (p. 711)

Halogen (hal′ ə jən) An element in column 17 of the periodic table (p. 424)

Halogenated hydrocarbon (hal′ ə jen ā tid hī′ drō kär′ bən) An organic compound that contains one or more halogen atoms (p. 753)

Heat (hēt) The energy that is transferred between objects that have different temperatures (p. 508)

Heat of combustion (ΔH_c) (hēt ov kəm bus′ chən) The amount of heat released in a combustion reaction per 1 mol of a reactant or product (p. 520)

Heat of fusion (ΔH_{fus}) (hēt ov fyü′ zhən) The amount of heat transferred when 1 g of a substance melts or freezes (p. 559)

Heat of reaction (ΔH_{rxn}) (hēt ov rē ak′ shən) The amount of heat released or absorbed in a chemical reaction per 1 mol of a reactant or product (p. 519)

Heat of vaporization (ΔH_{vap}) (hēt ov vā pər i zā′ shən) The amount of heat transferred when 1 g of a substance boils or condenses (p. 559)

Hertz (Hz) (hėrts) A unit for measuring wave frequency that equals 1 cycle per second (p. 338)

Heterogeneous mixture (het ər ə jē′ nē əs miks′ chər) A mixture in which one or more substances are unevenly mixed throughout (p. 57)

Homogeneous mixture (hō mə jē′ nē əs miks′ chər) A mixture in which all of the individual substances are evenly mixed throughout; a solution (p. 57)

Hydrate (hī′ drāt) An ionic compound that is chemically combined with water in a specific ratio (p. 163)

Hydrocarbon (hī′ drō kär′ bən) A compound that contains only carbon and hydrogen; when burned, it produces carbon dioxide and water (p. 191)

Hydrogen bonding (hī′ drə jən bond′ ing) A strong attractive force between the hydrogen atom of one polar molecule and an oxygen, nitrogen, or fluorine atom of another polar molecule (p. 494)

Hydroxyl group (hī drok′ səl grüp) A functional group that consists of an oxygen atom bonded to a hydrogen atom (p. 754)

Hypothesis (hī poth′ ə sis) A possible explanation based on facts and reason (p. 4)

I

Ideal gas (ī dē′ əl gas) A gas that is described by the kinetic model (p. 266)

Ideal gas law (ī dē′ əl gas lȯ) The law that shows the relationship between the pressure, volume, number of moles, and temperature of a gas (p. 287)

Immiscible (i mis′ ə bəl) A description of two liquids that do not dissolve in each other (p. 581)

Independent variable (in di pen′ dənt vâr′ ē ə bəl) A variable that is changed by the experimenter (p. 5)

Indicator (in′ də kā tər) A substance that is one color in an acid and another color in a base (p. 670)

Infrared rays (in′ frə red′ rāz) Nonionizing radiation with wavelengths longer than visible light (p. 340)

Inner transition metal (in′ ər tran zish′ ən met′ l) Any of the elements in the lanthanide or actinide series (p. 424)

Inorganic compound (in ôr gan′ ik kom′ pound) Any compound that is not organic (p. 744)

Insoluble (in sol′ yə bəl) A description of a solid that does not dissolve in a liquid (p. 580)

Intermediate (in tər mē′ dē it) A particle in a reaction mechanism that is not an initial reactant or a final product (p. 635)

Interparticle force (in tər pär′ tə kəl fôrs) An attractive force between particles in a substance (p. 492)

Inverse proportion (in vėrs′ prə pôr′ shən) A relationship between two quantities in which one increases as the other decreases (p. 278)

Ion (ī′ on) An atom or group of atoms with a positive or negative electrical charge (p. 91)

Ionic bond (ī on′ ik bond) A chemical bond that results when electrons are transferred from one atom to another (p. 462)

Ionic compound (ī on´ ik kom´ pound) A compound consisting of one kind of cation and one kind of anion (p. 91)

Ionic radius (ī on´ ik rā´ dē əs) The distance from the nucleus of an ion to its outermost electron orbitals; a measure of the size of an ion (p. 435)

Ionization energy (ī ən i zā´ shən en´ ər jē) The amount of energy needed to remove a valence electron from an atom (p. 440)

Ionizing radiation (ī´ ə nīz´ ing rā dē ā´ shən) High-energy radiation that can remove an electron from a substance (p. 340)

Isoelectronic (ī sō i lek tron´ ik) Having the same number of electrons (the same electron configuration) an ion of one element is isoelectronic with a neutral atom of another element (p. 408)

Isomer (ī´ sə mər) A compound that has the same chemical formula as another compound, but has a different structure (p. 745)

Isotope (ī´ sə tōp) An atom that has the same number of protons as another atom, but a different number of neutrons (p. 318)

J

Joule (J) (jül) The SI unit for energy (p. 440)

K

Kelvin (K) (kel´ vən) The SI unit for measuring temperature (p. 32)

Ketone (kē´ tōn) An organic compound that contains a carbonyl group within a hydrocarbon chain (p. 761)

Kinetic energy (ki net´ ik en´ ər jē) The energy of motion (p. 180)

Kinetic model (ki net´ ik mod´ l) A set of assumptions about how particles act; used to explain the physical properties of gases (p. 266)

L

Lanthanide (lan´ thə nīd) Any of the elements with atomic numbers 58 to 71; the lanthanides follow lanthanum (57) in the periodic table (p. 424)

Law of conservation of energy (lȯ ov kon sər vā´ shən ov en´ ər jē) A law that states that energy cannot be created or destroyed (p. 181)

Law of conservation of matter (lȯ ov kon sər vā´ shən ov mat´ ər) A law that states that matter cannot be created or destroyed (p. 180)

Le Chatelier's principle (lə shot´ əl āz´ prin´ sə pəl) A principle that states that a reversible reaction at equilibrium will shift to relieve a stress (p. 649)

Limiting reactant (lim´ ə ting rē ak´ tənt) The reactant in a chemical reaction that is used up first; it limits the amount of product (p. 249)

Linear (lin´ ē ər) Having a flat, straight geometry (p. 478)

Lipid (lip´ id) An organic molecule that contains fatty acids (p. 773)

Liquid (lik´ wid) A state of matter that has a definite volume, but takes the shape of its container (p. 50)

Liter (L) (lē´ tər) A unit for measuring volume (p. 32)

M

Malleable (mal´ ē ə bəl) Having the ability to be rolled into sheets or hammered into shapes without breaking (p. 452)

Mass (_M_, _m_) (mas) How much matter an object contains (p. 2)

Mass defect (mas dē´ fekt) The difference between the mass of a nucleus and the sum of the masses of its particles (p. 365)

Mass number (mas num´ bər) The total number of particles in the nucleus of an atom (p. 319)

Mass percent (mas pər sent´) The mass of a solute divided by the mass of the solution, expressed as a percentage (p. 603)

Matter (mat´ ər) Anything that has mass and takes up space (p. 2)

Melt (melt) To change from a solid to a liquid (p. 547)

Meltdown (melt´ doun) An uncontrolled chain reaction in a nuclear reactor that produces enough heat to melt the radiation shielding (p. 368)

Metal (met´ l) An element found on the left side of the periodic table; often a shiny solid that can conduct heat and electricity (p. 66)

Metallic bonding (mə tal´ ik bond´ ing) A strong attractive force among metal atoms that occurs because valence electrons are shared, creating a sea of electrons (p. 495)

Meter (m) (mē´ tər) The SI unit for measuring length (p. 32)

Miscible (mis´ ə bəl) A description of two liquids that dissolve in each other (p. 581)

a	hat	e	let	ī	ice	ȯ	order	u̇	put	sh	she	ə	a	in about
ā	age	ē	equal	o	hot	oi	oil	ü	rule	th	thin		e	in taken
ä	far	ėr	term	ō	open	ou	out	ch	child	ᴛʜ	then		i	in pencil
à	care	i	it	ȯ	saw	u	cup	ng	long	zh	measure		o	in lemon
													u	in circus

Mixture (miks´ chər) Two or more substances mixed together; the properties of each substance are not affected by mixing (p. 56)

Molality (***m***) (mō lal´ ə tē) The number of moles of solute per kilogram of solvent (p. 602)

Molarity (***M***) (mō lâr´ ə tē) The number of moles of solute per liter of solution (p. 140)

Molar mass (mō´lər mas) The mass in grams of 1 mol of a substance; molar mass has the unit grams per mole (g/mol) (p. 131)

Mole (**mol**) (mōl) A unit for measuring the amount of a substance; 1 mol contains 6.02×10^{23} atoms, molecules, or formula units (p. 126)

Molecular compound (mə lek´ yə lər kom´ pound) A compound containing atoms of two or more elements that are bonded together by sharing electrons (p. 86)

Molecular formula (mə lek´ yə lər fôr´ myə lə) A formula that gives the actual number of each kind of atom in a molecule (p. 154)

Molecular geometry (mə lek´ yə lər jē om´ ə trē) The particular shape of a molecule (p. 478)

Molecule (mol´ ə kyül) A neutral group of two or more atoms that are bonded together by sharing electrons; the smallest unit of a molecular compound (p. 89)

Mole fraction (***X***) (mōl frak´ shən) The moles of one substance in a mixture divided by the total moles of all substances in the mixture (p. 604)

Mole ratio (mōl rā´ shē ō) A ratio or fraction that compares the moles of two or more substances (p. 155)

Monatomic (mon ə tom´ ik) Existing as single atoms (p. 67)

Monomer (mon´ ə mər) One of several identical molecules that bond together to form a polymer; after bonding, the monomer becomes one structural unit of the polymer (p. 766)

Monosaccharide (mon ə sak´ ə rīd) A simple carbohydrate consisting of only one sugar unit (p. 771)

N

Net ionic equation (net ī on´ ik i kwā´ zhən) A chemical equation that shows only the ions that are part of the reaction; the spectator ions are removed (p. 596)

Neutralization reaction (nü trə li zā´ shən rē ak´ shən) An acid-base reaction (p. 669)

Neutral salt (nü´ trəl sȯlt) The salt produced from a strong acid and a strong base (p. 688)

Neutron (nü´ tron) A particle with no charge in the nucleus of an atom (p. 64)

Nitrogen base (nī´ trə jən bās) A nitrogen-containing compound in a nucleic acid; thymine, guanine, cytosine, adenine, or uracil (p. 779)

Noble gas (nō´ bəl gas) An element in column 18 of the periodic table (p. 404)

Nonelectrolyte (non i lek´ trə līt) A substance that does not conduct electricity when melted or in aqueous solutions (p. 581)

Nonionizing radiation (non ī´ ə nīz ing rā dē ā´ shən) Low-energy radiation that cannot remove an electron from a substance (p. 340)

Nonmetal (non met´ l) An element found on the right side of the periodic table; often a gas or dull solid that does not conduct heat or electricity (p. 66)

Nonpolar covalent bond (non pō´ lər kō vā´ lənt bond) A chemical bond in which electrons are equally shared (p. 465)

Nonpolar molecule (non pō´ lər mol´ ə kyül) A molecule in which the positive charges and the negative charges are both balanced in the middle of the molecule (p. 486)

Nonspontaneous (non spon tā´ nē əs) Not occurring without the addition of energy (p. 534)

Normal boiling point (nôr´ məl boil´ ing point) The temperature at which the vapor pressure of a liquid equals 1 atm (p. 552)

Normal melting point (nôr´ məl melt´ ing point) The temperature at which a solid changes to a liquid at a pressure of 1 atm (p. 568)

Nuclear reaction (nü´ klē ər rē ak´ shən) A change within the nucleus of an atom (p. 338)

Nuclear reactor (nü´ klē ər rē ak´ tər) The device in which fission chain reactions occur inside a nuclear power plant (p. 368)

Nucleic acid (nü klē´ ik as´ id) A large polymer of nucleotides that contains genetic information that cells need to reproduce (p. 779)

Nucleotide (nü´ klē ə tīd) The monomer of a nucleic acid that consists of a phosphate, a sugar, and a nitrogen base (p. 779)

Nucleus (nü´ klē əs) The center of an atom; consists of neutrons and protons (p. 64)

O

Octet rule (ok tet´ rül) A rule that says atoms tend to transfer or share electrons to obtain 8 electrons in their outer energy level (p. 469)

Orbital (ôr´ bi tl) A region of space described by a shape that shows the probable location of an electron in an atom (p. 386)

Organic chemistry (ôr gan´ ik kem´ ə strē) The study of the structures, properties, and reactions of organic compounds (p. 744)

Organic compound (ôr gan´ ik kom´ pound) Any compound that contains carbon, except for carbon oxides, carbides, cyanides, and carbonates (p. 744)

Oxidation (ok´ sə dā´ shən) A chemical reaction in which an atom or ion loses electrons (p. 700)

Oxidation number (ok´ sə dā´ shən num´ bər) The charge that an atom in a compound would have if its bonds were ionic; the oxidation number of a neutral, unbonded atom equals 0, and the oxidation number of a charged atom is its charge (p. 701)

Oxidizing agent (ok´ sə dī zing ā´ jənt) The reactant that causes another reactant to be oxidized; the reduced reactant (p. 708)

P

Partial pressure (pär´ shəl presh´ ər) The pressure of one particular gas in a mixture of gases (p. 274)

Pascal (Pa) (pa skəl´) The SI unit for measuring pressure (p. 269)

Percent composition (pər sent´ kom pə zish´ ən) A set of values that tells the percentage by mass of each element in a compound (p. 150)

Percent yield (pər sent´ yēld) A percentage that compares the actual product yield with the theoretical product yield (p. 244)

Period (pir´ ē əd) A row of elements in the periodic table (p. 425)

Periodic table (pir ē od´ ik tā´ bəl) A table that shows the names and symbols of elements and is organized by atomic number and electron arrangement (p. 66)

pH (pē āch) A way of describing the H^{1+} concentration of a solution; the pH scale ranges from 0 to 14 (p. 676)

Photoelectric effect (fō tō i lek´ trik e fekt´) An effect that occurs when electrons are emitted from the surface of a metal as light strikes the metal (p. 382)

Photon (fō´ ton) A bundle or package of energy (p. 382)

Physical change (fiz´ ə kəl chānj) A change in a substance that affects its physical properties, but not its chemical properties (p. 52)

Physical property (fiz´ ə kəl prop´ ər tē) A characteristic of a substance that can be observed without changing the substance (p. 50)

Polar covalent bond (pō´ lər kō vā´ lənt bond) A chemical bond in which electrons are not equally shared (p. 465)

Polarity (pō lâr´ ə tē) The presence of separate areas of positive and negative charge (p. 492)

Polar molecule (pō´ lər mol´ ə kyül) A molecule with a slight positive charge on one end and a slight negative charge on the other end; also called a dipole (p. 486)

Polyatomic (pol´ ē ə tom´ ik) Existing as groups of three or more bonded atoms (p. 67)

Polyatomic ion (pol´ ē ə tom´ ik ī´ on) A group of two or more atoms that acts as one ion and has one charge (p. 101)

Polymer (pol´ ə mər) A long organic molecule made of repeating structural units (p. 766)

Polysaccharide (pol ē sak´ ə rīd) A complex carbohydrate consisting of many sugar units bonded together to form a polymer (p. 772)

Potential energy (pə ten´ shəl en´ ər jē) The energy of position or composition (p. 180)

Precipitate (pri sip´ ə tāt) A solid that forms out of a solution (p. 593)

Precision (pri sizh´ ən) How close a measurement is to other measurements of the same thing (p. 17)

Pressure (P) (presh´ ər) The force acting on a certain area (p. 265)

Product (prod´ əkt) A substance that is produced by a chemical reaction (p. 176)

Protein (prō´ tēn) An organic polymer made of amino acids (p. 777)

Proton (prō´ ton) A particle with a positive charge in the nucleus of an atom (p. 64)

Q

Qualitative (kwol´ ə tā tiv) Describing something without using numbers (p. 2)

Quantitative (kwon´ tə tā tiv) Describing something using measurement and numbers (p. 2)

a	hat	e	let	ī	ice	ô	order	u̇	put	sh	she	ə	a	in about
ā	age	ē	equal	o	hot	oi	oil	ü	rule	th	thin		e	in taken
ä	far	ėr	term	ō	open	ou	out	ch	child	ᴛʜ	then		i	in pencil
â	care	i	it	ȯ	saw	u	cup	ng	long	zh	measure		o	in lemon
													u	in circus

Radiant energy (rā´ dē ənt en´ ər jē) Energy that can travel through space; also called electromagnetic radiation (p. 338)

Radiation (rā dē ā´ shən) Energy or particles that can travel through space (p. 338)

Radioactive (rā´ dē ō ak´ tiv) Giving off radiation due to a nuclear change (p. 343)

Radioactive decay (rā´ dē ō ak´ tiv di kā´) The breakdown of an unstable nucleus, resulting in radioactivity (p. 343)

Radioactivity (rā´ dē ō ak tiv´ ə tē) The release of radiation caused by radioactive decay (p. 343)

Radioisotope (rā´ dē ō ī´ sə tōp) An isotope that has an unstable nucleus and is therefore radioactive (p. 343)

Radiotherapy (rā´ dē ō ther´ ə pē) The treatment of cancer by directing a beam of radiation at a specific area in the body or placing a radioactive substance inside the body (p. 361)

Radiotracer (rā´ dē ō trā´ sər) A tiny amount of a radioactive compound that is swallowed or injected so its path through the body can be traced (p. 361)

Rate constant (k) (rāt kon´ stənt) A unique constant that is part of the rate law for a specific reaction (p. 638)

Rate-determining step (rāt di ter´ mən ing step) The step in a reaction mechanism with the highest activation energy; it is the slowest step and determines the reaction rate (p. 635)

Rate law (rāt lȯ) A mathematical equation that shows how the rate of a reaction depends on the concentration of the reactants (p. 638)

Reactant (rē ak´ tənt) A substance that is used up in a chemical reaction (p. 176)

Reaction mechanism (rē ak´ shən mek´ ə niz əm) A series of small reaction steps that describes how a chemical reaction occurs (p. 635)

Reaction rate (rē ak´ shən rāt) The speed of a reaction; the rate at which a product forms or a reactant is used up (p. 622)

Redox reaction (rē´ doks rē ak´ shən) An oxidation-reduction reaction (p. 700)

Reducing agent (ri dūs´ ing ā´ jənt) The reactant that causes another reactant to be reduced; the reactant that is oxidized in a redox reaction (p. 708)

Reduction (ri duk´ shən) A chemical reaction in which an atom or ion gains electrons (p. 700)

Rem (rem) (rem) A unit used to measure radiation that affects organisms (p. 341)

Representative element (rep ri zen´ tə tiv el´ ə mənt) Any of the elements in columns 1, 2, and 13–18 of the periodic table (p. 407)

Reversible reaction (ri ver´ sə bəl rē ak´ shən) A reaction in which the products can react to form the reactants (p. 641)

RNA (är en ā) Ribonucleic acid (p. 779)

Salt (sȯlt) An ionic compound made of a cation from a base and an anion from an acid (p. 203)

Salt bridge (sȯlt brij) A tube containing spectator ions that connects the half-cells in a voltaic cell and maintains the charge balance between them (p. 725)

Saturated (sach´ ə rāt id) Having the maximum amount of solute dissolved in a given amount of solvent at a specific temperature; *also* having only single bonds between carbon atoms (pp. 586, 746)

Scientific method (sī ən tif´ ik meth´ əd) A method of study used by scientists (p. 4)

Scientific notation (sī ən tif´ ik nō tā´ shən) A shortcut method for writing very large and very small numbers; for example, 9.88×10^{12} or 1.3×10^{-7} (p. 11)

Second law of thermodynamics (sek´ ənd lȯ ov ther mō dī nam´ iks) A law that states that the entropy of the universe is always increasing (p. 528)

Semimetal (sem i met´ l) An element that has properties of both a metal and a nonmetal; located between metals and nonmetals on the periodic table (p. 66)

Shielding effect (shēld´ ing ə fekt´) The blocking of valence electrons from the attractive force of the nucleus by inner electrons (p. 442)

Significant figure (sig nif´ ə kənt fig´ yər) A meaningful digit in a measured value; the significant figures in a given value are all of the certain digits plus one estimated digit (p. 19)

Single bond (sing´ gəl bond) A covalent bond in which two atoms share one pair of electrons (p. 469)

Single-replacement reaction (sing´ gəl ri plās´ mənt rē ak´ shən) A reaction in which an element and a compound react to form a different element and a different compound (p. 196)

Solid (sol´ id) A state of matter that has a definite shape and volume (p. 50)

Solubility (sol yə bil´ ə tē) The amount of solute that dissolves in a certain amount of solvent to create a saturated solution at a given temperature and pressure (p. 588)

Soluble (sol´ yə bəl) A description of a solid that dissolves in a liquid (p. 580)

Solute (sol´ yüt) A substance that is dissolved in a solvent to create a solution (p. 58)

Solution (sə lü´ shən) A homogeneous mixture of one or more solutes dissolved in a solvent (p. 58)

Solvation (sol vā´ shən) The process in which solvent particles attract and surround solute particles, causing them to dissolve (p. 580)

Solvent (sol´ vənt) The substance that a solute is dissolved in; usually the substance in a solution that is present in the greatest amount (p. 58)

Specific heat (C_p) (spi sif´ ik hēt) The amount of heat needed to raise the temperature of 1 g of a substance by 1°C (p. 508)

Spectator ion (spek´ tā tər ī´ on) An ion that remains aqueous and does not take part in a reaction (p. 595)

Spontaneous (spon tā´ nē əs) Occurring naturally as predicted (p. 534)

Standard heat of formation (ΔH_f) (stan´ dərd hēt ov fôr mā´ shən) The enthalpy change when 1 mol of a compound is formed from its elements in their standard states (p. 524)

Standard molar volume (stan´ dərd mō´ lər vol´ yəm) 22.4 L/mol, the volume of 1 mol of any gas at STP (p. 137)

Standard solution (stan´ dərd sə lü´ shən) The solution of known concentration in a titration (p. 670)

Standard state (stan´ dərd stāt) The state of an element at 1 atm and 25°C (p. 524)

Standard temperature and pressure (STP) (stan´ dərd tem´ pər ə chər and presh´ ər) A temperature of 0°C and a pressure of 1 atm (p. 137)

State (stāt) The physical form of a substance; solid, liquid, or gas (p. 50)

Stoichiometry (stoi´ kē om´ ə trē) The study of amounts in chemical reactions (p. 220)

Stress (stres) A change in the conditions of a system at equilibrium (p. 649)

Strong acid (strȯng as´ id) An acid that completely ionizes in water (p. 682)

Strong base (strȯng bās) A base that completely dissociates in water (p. 682)

Structural formula (struk´ chər əl fôr´ myə lə) A model that uses element symbols and bond lines to represent a molecule (p. 744)

Sublevel (sub lev´ əl) A small level within an energy level where electrons can move (p. 385)

Sublimation (sub lə mā´ shən) The process of changing from a solid directly to a gas (p. 547)

Subscript (sub´ skript) A number written just below the writing line; in chemical formulas, it tells the number of atoms of a certain element (p. 67)

Substance (sub´ stəns) A kind of matter with a definite makeup and definite chemical and physical properties; an element or a compound (p. 56)

Substituted hydrocarbon (sub´ stə tüt id hī´ drō kär´ bən) An organic compound in which one or more hydrogen atoms are replaced by a functional group (p. 753)

Supersaturated (sü pər sach´ ə rāt id) Having more than the maximum amount of solute dissolved in a given amount of solvent at a given temperature (p. 586)

Superscript (sü´ pər skript) A number that is written just above the writing line (p. 11)

Surface tension (sėr´ fis ten´ shən) The inward pull from hydrogen bonding that prevents a liquid from spreading out (p. 566)

Suspension (sə spen´ shən) A mixture of particles that are evenly dispersed only when the mixture is shaken; suspension particles eventually settle out (p. 583)

System (sis´ təm) All of the substances involved in a change (p. 511)

T

Technology (tek nol´ ə jē) The application of science to help people or improve their lives (p. 7)

Tetrahedral (tet´ rə hē´ drəl) Having a pyramid-shaped geometry (p. 480)

Theoretical yield (thē ə ret´ ə kəl yēld) The ideal amount of product predicted by stoichiometry (p. 244)

Theory (thē´ ər ē) A widely accepted hypothesis that has been tested many times (p. 5)

a	hat	e	let	ī	ice	ô	order	ủ	put	sh	she	ə	a	in about
ā	age	ē	equal	o	hot	oi	oil	ü	rule	th	thin		e	in taken
ä	far	ėr	term	ō	open	ou	out	ch	child	∓H	then		i	in pencil
â	care	i	it	ȯ	saw	u	cup	ng	long	zh	measure		o	in lemon
													u	in circus

Thermodynamics (thėr mō dī nam´ iks) The study of energy changes that accompany chemical and physical changes (p. 508)

Third law of thermodynamics (thėrd lȯ ov thėr mō dī nam´ iks) A law that states that the entropy of an ideal solid at 0 K is zero (p. 528)

Titration (tī trā´ shən) The process of determining the molarity of an acid or base solution by using a neutralization reaction (p. 670)

Transition metal (tran zish´ ən met´ l) Any of the elements in columns 3–12 of the periodic table (p. 407)

Transmutation (tran smyə tā´ shən) The process that occurs when an isotope of one element changes into an isotope of a different element (p. 344)

Transuranium element (tran syü rā´ nē əm el´ ə mənt) Any of the elements with atomic numbers greater than 92 (p. 351)

Triglyceride (trī glis´ ə rīd) A lipid consisting of three fatty acids bonded at each of the three hydroxyl groups in a glycerol molecule (p. 774)

Trigonal planar (trī´ gō nl plā´ nər) Having a flat, triangle-shaped geometry (p. 479)

Trigonal pyramidal (trī´ gō nl pə ram´ ə dəl) Having a tetrahedral geometry that is affected by a lone pair (p. 481)

Triple bond (trip´ əl bond) A covalent bond in which two atoms share three pairs of electrons (p. 469)

Triple point (trip´ əl point) The temperature and pressure at which all three states of a substance exist together (p. 568)

Tyndall effect (tin´ dl ə fekt) The scattering of light in all directions (p. 583)

U

Ultraviolet rays (ul´ trä vī´ ə lit rāz) Ionizing radiation with wavelengths shorter than visible light (p. 340)

Unit (yü´ nit) A standard amount used for measuring (p. 32)

Unit conversion (yü´ nit kən vėr´ shən) The process of changing a measurement from one unit to another (p. 34)

Unsaturated (un sach´ ə rā tid) Having less than the maximum amount of solute dissolved in a given amount of solvent at a given temperature; *also* having one or more double or triple bonds between carbon atoms (pp. 586, 746)

V

Valence electron (vā´ ləns i lek´ tron) An electron in an *s* or *p* orbital in the highest energy level of an atom (p. 394)

Valence-shell electron-pair repulsion (VSEPR) theory (vā´ ləns shel i lek´ tron pâr ri pul´ shən thē´ ər ē) The idea that molecular geometry is determined by minimizing the repulsion between valence electron pairs (p. 478)

Vapor pressure (vā´ pər presh´ ər) The pressure created by an evaporated liquid (p. 552)

Variable (vâr´ ē ə bəl) A condition or a characteristic of matter that is measured or controlled in an experiment (p. 5)

Velocity (*ν*) (və los´ ə tē) The speed of an object in a certain direction (p. 295)

Volatile (vol´ ə təl) Having the property of evaporating easily (p. 756)

Volt (V) (vōlt) A unit of electrical potential difference (p. 729)

Voltaic cell (vol tā´ ik sel) A device that converts chemical energy into electrical energy (p. 723)

Volume (V) (vol´ yəm) The amount of space an object takes up (p. 2)

W

Water vapor (wot´ ər vā´ pər) Gaseous water (p. 275)

Wavelength (wāv´ lengkth) The distance from one wave peak to the next (p. 338)

Weak acid (wēk as´ id) An acid that partially ionizes in water (p. 683)

Weak base (wēk bās) A base that partially dissociates in water (p. 683)

X

X-rays (eks´ rāz) Ionizing radiation that can pass through soft body tissue, but not bone (p. 340)

Index

Noble gases defined, 404, 411, 417, 424, 440, 443, 451, 457, 458
Nomenclature. *See* Names
Nonelectrolyte defined, 581
Nonionizing radiation defined, 340, 342, 376
Nonmetals
    activity series for, 197
    bonding in, 465, 467
    defined, 66, 71, 81
    dispersion forces in, 493
    valence electrons in, 429, 456
Nonpolar covalent bond defined, 465–67, 468, 502
Nonpolar molecules
    defined, 486–89
    solvents for, 566, 580, 581
Nonspontaneous defined, 534, 538
Normal boiling point defined, 552, 556
Normal melting point defined, 568, 576
Nuclear bombardment, 351–55
Nuclear chemistry. *See* Nuclear reactions
Nuclear energy, 366–69, 371
Nuclear equations. *See* Nuclear reactions
Nuclear medicine, 360–61, 376, 377
Nuclear power plants, 366–69, 376, 412
Nuclear reactions. *See also* Half-life
    alpha decay, 343–45, 348, 350
    beta decay, 346–48, 350
    balancing equations, 344–45, 352–55, 376
    bombardment, 351–55
    decay, modeling of, 363–64
    defined, 338, 342
    fission, 365–69, 372–74, 376, 377
    fusion, 369–72, 376, 377
Nuclear reactors defined, 368
Nucleic acids defined, 779–80, 784, 786
Nucleotides defined, 779, 784
Nucleus defined, 64, 311–12, 315, 332, 372
Numbers. *See* Math review; Scientific notation; Significant figures
Nutritionist, 513

Obsidian, 549
Octane ratings, 783

Octet rule defined, 469, 475, 477, 502
Oils, 773
Oncologist, 467
Orbitals defined, 386–89, 399, 403, 417, 432. *See also* Valence electrons
Ore, 732
Organic chemistry defined, 744, 745, 784
Organic compound defined, 744, 747, 751
Osteryoung, Janet, 726
Osteryoung, Robert, 726
Oxidation defined, 700, 705, 721, 738, 739
Oxidation numbers defined, 701–03, 705, 707, 739, 740
Oxidation-reduction reactions. *See* Redox reactions
Oxidation states. *See* Oxidation numbers
Oxidizing agents defined, 708, 709, 713, 738–40
Oxygen, 65, 67, 76, 185, 297, 319, 393, 396, 450–51, 454, 700, 701, 746
Ozone, 297, 450, 640

Paper chromatography. *See* Chromatography
Paraffin, 573, 746
Partial pressure defined, 274–77, 301, 302
Particle accelerators, 351, 354, 356
Particles
    alpha (*See* Alpha particles)
    beta (*See* Beta particles)
    motion in gases, 266, 268, 292–93
    speed and kinetic energy of, 294–96, 298, 508
    stoichiometry with, 127–30, 144, 232–38, 242, 258
    subatomic, 325, 346
Pascal defined, 269, 273, 301
Patterns. *See* Periodic table patterns
Pauling, Linus, 472
Percent abundances, 326, 327, 328, 332
Percentages, 151, 794
Percent yield defined, 243–48, 258–61
Percent composition defined, 150–53, 156–58, 170, 171
Perfluorocarbons, 615
Periodic table of elements
    defined, 66, 68–69, 80
    ionic charges in, 92–93

labeled for electron configurations, 405–6, 416
    organization of, 422–24, 456
Periodic table patterns
    atomic radius, 432–37, 443, 456
    electron affinity, 442–44, 456
    electron configurations, 392–96
    electronegativity, 463–68, 496, 502, 503
    ionization energy, 440–44, 456
    valence electrons, 428–31, 456
Periods defined, 425, 427, 434, 440, 442, 444, 445, 456
Petroleum, 501, 539
Phase-change materials, 573
Phase changes. *See* State changes
Phase diagrams, 567–69, 571–72
Phenolphthalein, 672
Phosphates, 780, 782
Phosphorus, 484
Photoelectric effect defined, 382, 388, 389, 417
Photons defined, 382, 417
Photosynthesis, 709, 773
Photovoltaic cells, 388
pH defined, 676–81
pH scale, 676–81, 685, 694, 695
Physical changes
    defined, 52, 53, 55, 59, 75, 80, 81
    endothermic (*See* Endothermic changes)
    entropy and, 528, 531
    exothermic (*See* Exothermic changes)
Physical properties
    defined, 50, 55, 67, 81
    of water, 565–70, 574
Planck, Max, 382
Planck's constant, 382
Plasmas, 51, 313
Plastics, 192, 213
Polar covalent bonds defined, 465–67, 468, 502
Polarity
    in bonds, 465–68
    chromatography and, 490–91
    defined, 492, 503
    of ionic compounds, 492
    of molecules, 486–91, 499–500, 502, 566
    solvation and, 580
Polar molecules
    defined, 486–89
    solvents for, 566, 580, 581
Polarography, 726

limiting and excess reactants, 249–54, 255–56, 258–61

mass and, 226–31, 241, 258–61

number of particles and, 233–34, 238, 241

percent yield, 243–46, 247–48, 258–61

solutions and, 239–42, 258–61

Stoney, George J., 307

STP. *See* Standard temperature and pressure

Strassman, Fritz, 366

Stress defined, 649, 652, 655, 659, 660

Strong acids defined, 682, 686–87, 694

Strong bases defined, 682–83, 685, 694, 695

Strontium, 412

Structural formulas defined, 744

Subatomic particles, 325, 346. *See also* Electrons; Neutrons; Protons

Sublevels defined, 385–87, 416, 417, 429

Sublimation defined, 547, 551, 567, 575

Subscripts defined, 70, 73, 90, 97, 104

Substances defined, 2, 56, 59, 61, 62–63, 80, 732

Substituted hydrocarbons defined, 753, 784, 787

Sucrose, 73–74, 106, 581, 771

Sulfur, 70, 410, 451

Sulfur dioxide, 119, 474

Supersaturated defined, 586, 587, 590, 616–18

Superscripts defined, 11, 121, 401, 429

Surface area, 582, 616, 623, 629, 658

Surface tension defined, 566, 570

Suspensions defined, 583

Symbols, 791

Symbols of elements, 70, 73

Synthesis reactions. *See* Combination reactions

Systems

defined, 511, 541

entropy in, 528

equilibrium, 641–44, 652, 654

energy changes in, 508–16, 527, 540

T

Table salt. *See* Sodium chloride

Table sugar. *See* Sucrose

Tacke, Ida, 366

Technetium, 352

Technology, 6, 7, 44

Technology and Society

alloys, 59

alum in paper, 669

ammonia, production, 245

automatic doors, 388

ceramics, 536

chromatography, 60

crop rotation, 14

CRT monitors, 310

diamonds and graphite, 652

fireworks, 384

flameless ration heaters, 197

food preservation, 474

fullerenes, 449

gasoline additives, 754

Geiger counters, 347

heating oil, 13

helium, liquid, 551

hot packs, 586

ion implantation, 429

liquid crystals, 555

luminescence, 719

mass spectroscopy, 158

metals and ores, 230

methane production, 207

packaging materials, 296

plasmas, 313

polymers and gels, 583

production costs, 650

radioactive dating, 361

scuba tank regulators, 275

sunglasses, 101

superinsulated windows, 511

table salt, 93

tap water, 141

voltammetry, 728

Temperature

absolute, 271, 301

critical, 568, 570

entropy and, 528

equilibrium and, 645, 649–52, 654

heat transfer and, 508, 509, 516

interparticle forces and, 493

kinetic energy and, 264, 268, 279, 298, 300, 508

measurement of, 5, 32, 44, 271–72, 300

molality and, 608, 612

particle speed and, 294–96, 298, 508

pressure and, 281, 292–93

reaction rate and, 623, 626, 658

regulation of, 555, 573

solubility and, 588, 589, 591–92

solvation and, 582, 585, 616

specific heat and, 510

spontaneity and, 534, 535, 537, 538, 540

state changes and, 547, 557, 558, 562, 574, 576, 610

unit conversions, 271–73

vapor pressure and, 552, 553, 554, 558

volume and, 280, 285–86

Tertiary ionic compounds. *See* Polyatomic ions

Tetrahedral defined, 480, 481, 484, 485, 503

Theoretical yield defined, 244, 246, 259

Theory defined, 5, 45, 312

Thermodynamics defined, 508, 511, 522, 528, 537, 541

Thin films, 550

Third law of thermodynamics defined, 528

Thomson, J.J., 307, 308, 310, 332, 436

Time, 32

Tin, 67

Titrations defined, 669–73, 674–755, 694–97

Transition metals defined, 407, 409, 424, 425, 452, 457, 472, 721

Transmutations defined, 344, 346, 350, 353, 376, 377

Transuranium elements defined, 351, 352, 355, 377

Triglycerides defined, 774, 776

Trigonal planar defined, 479, 484, 485, 503

Trigonal pyramidal defined, 480–81, 484, 485, 487

Triple bond defined, 469

Triple point defined, 568, 570, 576

Tyndall effect defined, 583

U

Ultraviolet rays defined, 340

Uncertain digits, 18

Unit conversions defined, 34–37, 131, 134–35, 144, 145, 172, 226–31, 258

Units

abbreviations for, 33, 791

base (*See* Base units)

cancellation of, 36

conversions (*See* Unit conversions)

defined, 32

derived (*See* Derived units)

formula (*See* Formula units)

metric prefixes for, 33, 790

Unsaturated defined, 586, 590, 616, 746
Uranium, 344, 345, 354, 366, 367, 373

Photo and Illustration Credits

Cover photos: background, © Royalty-free/PhotoDisc; inset, © Royalty-free/PhotoDisc; p. ix, © Royalty-free/PhotoDisc; p. xxiv, © Royalty-free/PhotoDisc; p. 3, © Royalty-free/Shutterstock; p. 7, © Eurelios/Phototake; p. 12, © Don Jacobs; p. 22, © RDF/Visuals Unlimited; p. 36, © Royalty-free/PhotoDisc; p. 43, © Phil Degginger/Color-Pic Inc.; p. 48, © Royalty-free/Shutterstock; p. 50, © Corbis; p. 53 (left), © Royalty-free/Shutterstock, p. 53 (right), © Corbis; p. 57 (left), © Royalty-free/Shutterstock, p. 57 (center), © Royalty-free/Shutterstock, p. 57 (right), © Royalty-free/Shutterstock; p. 60, © Tom Pantages; p. 70, © Medical-on-Line/Alamy Images; p. 79, © Benelux Press BV/Photo Researchers, Inc.; p. 84, © Peter Arnold, Inc./Alamy Images; p. 86 (left), © Gary Dyson/Alamy Images; p. 86 (center), © Royalty-free/Shutterstock; p. 86 (right), © Corbis; p. 87, Copyright 2005, American Chemical Society. All rights reserved; p. 92(left), © Kevin Schafer/Peter Arnold, Inc.; p. 92 (right), © Richard Megna/Fundamental Photographs, NYC; p. 94, Courtesy of NASA Jet Propulsion Laboratory; p. 111, © Matthew Richardson/Alamy Images; p. 119, © Corbis; p. 124, © Royalty-free/Shutterstock, p. 127, © Richard Megna/Fundamental Photographs, NYC; p. 152, © Mauro Fermariello/Photo Researchers, Inc.; p. 163, © Paul Silverman/Fundamental Photographs, NYC; p. 164, © Tom Pantages; p. 169, © Jeff J. Daly/Fundamental Photographs, NYC; p. 174, © Royalty-free/Shutterstock; p. 180, © Paul Katz/Index Stock Imagery; p. 191, © Donald Miralle/Getty Images; p. 192, © Javier Larrea/PIXTAL/Age Fotostock; p. 198, © Peticolas/Megna/Fundamental Photographs, NYC; p. 202, © Richard Megna/Fundamental Photographs, NYC; p. 211, © Rosenfeld/zefa/Corbis; p. 213, © Maximilian Stock Ltd/Photo Researchers, Inc.; p. 218, © Scott Tysick/Masterfile; p. 226, © Painet Stock Photos; p. 232, © Roger Ball/Corbis; p. 253, © Rudi Von Briel/PhotoEdit; p. 257, © Spencer Grant/PhotoEdit; p. 262, © Royalty-free/Shutterstock; p. 272, © Joe Raedle/Getty Images; p. 287, © Myrleen Ferguson Cate/PhotoEdit; p. 290, © David Young-Wolff/PhotoEdit; p. 299, © Cordelia Molloy/Photo Researchers, Inc.; p. 304, © Royalty-free/Shutterstock; p. 314, © Tom Tracy Photography/Alamy Images; p. 321, © Jeff Daly/Visuals Unlimited; p. 326, © David Young-Wolff/PhotoEdit; p. 331, © Stephen Derr/Getty Images; p. 336, © Corbis; p. 348, © Custom Medical Stock Photo; p. 351, © David Parker/Photo Researchers, Inc.; p. 359, © James King-Holmes/Photo Researchers, Inc.; p. 366, © Royalty-free/PhotoDisc; p. 371, © William Rivelli/Getty Images; p. 375, © Science Source/Photo Researchers, Inc.; p. 380, © Royalty-free/Shutterstock; p. 388, © Robert & Linda Mostyn/Eye Ubiquitous/Corbis; p. 405, © AP Images; p. 415, © Phototake Inc./Alamy Images; p. 420, © Royalty-free/Shutterstock; p. 423, © Science Museum/SSPL/The Image Works, Inc.; p. 426, © Rob James/Alamy Images; p. 448, © Bettmann/Corbis; p. 449 (top), © Lester V. Bergman/Corbis; p. 449 (bottom), © Lawrence Lawry/Getty Images; p. 453, © Steve Dunwell/Index Stock Imagery; p. 455, © Lonnie Duka/Index Stock Imagery; p. 460, © Royalty-free/Shutterstock; p. 467, © Brad Wilson/Getty Images; p. 497, © David Young-Wolff/PhotoEdit; p. 501, © Alex Mares-Manton/Getty Images; p. 506, © Royalty-free/Shutterstock; p. 513, © Will & Deni McIntyre/Photo Researchers, Inc.; p. 515 (top), © Michael Newman/PhotoEdit; p. 515 (bottom), © Elwin Williamson/Index Stock Imagery; p. 520, © Getty Images; p. 527 (left and right), © David Young-Wolff/PhotoEdit; p. 539, © Michael Ventura/PhotoEdit; p. 544, © Royalty-free/Shutterstock; p. 546, © Andrew Lambert Photography/Photo Researchers, Inc.; p. 549 (top), © Doug Martin/Photo Researchers, Inc.; p. 549 (bottom), © Janine Wiedel Photolibrary/Alamy Images; p. 555, © Jonathan Nourok/PhotoEdit; p. 566, © George Bernard/Animals Animals; p. 573, © Martyn F. Chillmaid/Photo Researchers, Inc.; p. 578, © Royalty-free/Shutterstock; p. 583, © Tom Pantages; p. 584, © Tom Pantages; p. 587 (left and right), © Richard Megna/Fundamental Photographs, NYC; p. 600, © Brand X/ImageState; p. 615, © Spencer Grant/PhotoEdit; p. 620, © Stephen Frink/Corbis; p. 624, © Charles D. Winters/Science Photo Library/Photo Researchers, Inc.; p. 631, © Geoff Tompkinson/Photo Researchers, Inc.; p. 636, © Michael Newman/PhotoEdit; p. 657, © Lester Lefkowitz/Corbis; p. 662, © Royalty-free/Shutterstock; p. 670, © Andrew Lambert Photography/Photo Researchers, Inc.; p. 672, © Tony Freeman/PhotoEdit; p. 680, © Philippe Psaila/Photo Researchers, Inc.; p. 684, © Photo Resource Hawaii/Alamy Images; p. 693, © Mira/Alamy Images; p. 698, © Cary Wolinsky/Aurora Photos; p. 700 (left), © PhotoLink/Getty Images; p. 700 (right), © Francis Dean/Dean Pictures/The Image Works, Inc.; p. 720, © Royalty-free/Brand X Pictures; p. 727, © Kim Fennema/Visuals Unlimited; p. 729, © Greg Cosgrove/Grant Heilman Photography; p. 733, © Sam Ogden/Photo Researchers, Inc.; p. 737, © Paul S. Howell/Getty Images; p. 742, © Royalty-free/Shutterstock; p. 762, © Tom Pantages; p. 767, © Robin Nelson/PhotoEdit; p. 775, © FoodCollection/Index Stock Imagery; p. 780, © Alfred Pasieka/Photo Researchers, Inc.; p. 781, © Roger Tully/Getty Images; p. 783, © Myrleen Ferguson Cate/PhotoEdit; investigation illustrations: John Edwards Illustration

The Periodic Table of Elements

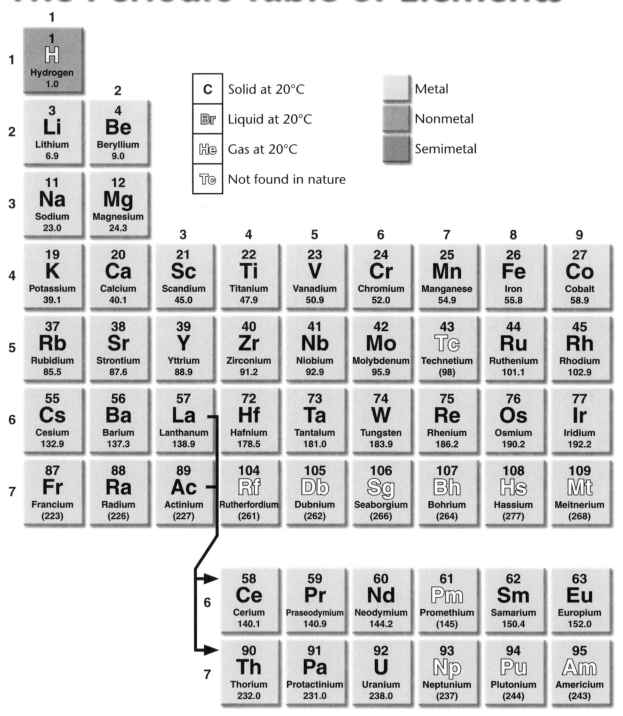